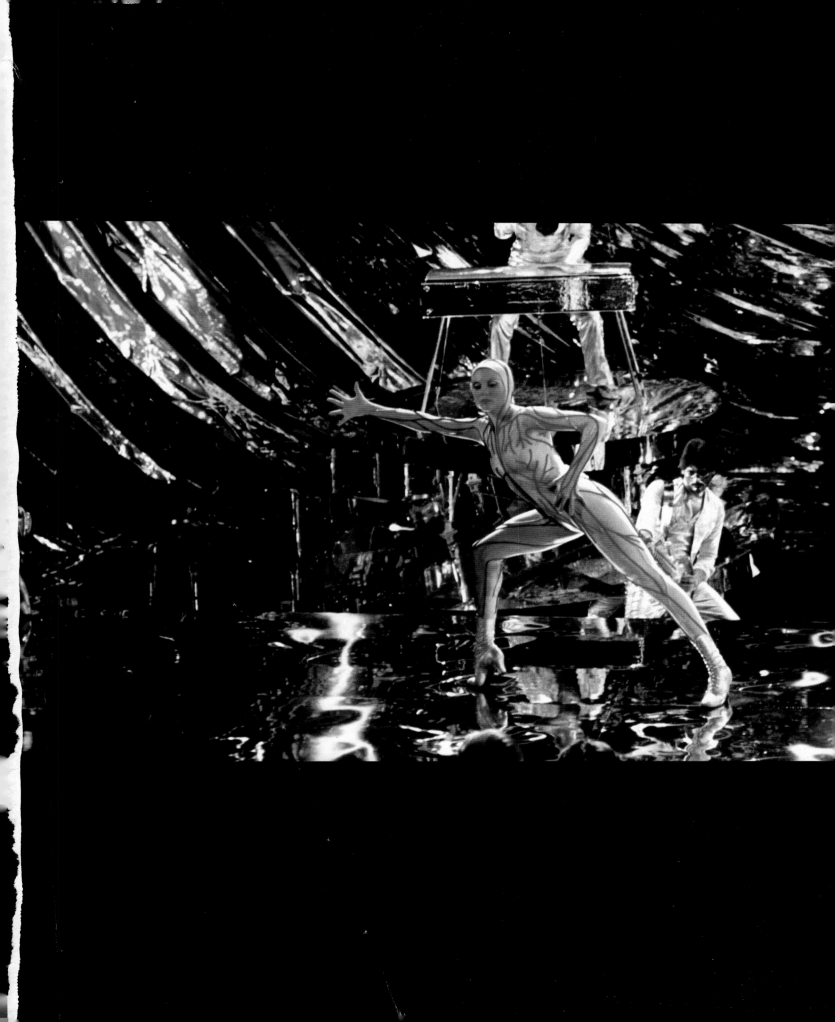

TED SENNETT

GREAT MOVIE DIRECTORS

HARRY N. ABRAMS, INC.

Publishers, NEW YORK

AFI PRESS

In loving memory
of
my mother-in-law
HILDA LUSTER

PROJECT DIRECTOR: Margaret L. Kaplan
EDITOR: Lory Frankel
DESIGNER: Dirk Luykx
PHOTO EDITOR: John K. Crowley

Library of Congress Cataloging-in-Publication Data
Sennett, Ted.
  Great movie directors.
  Bibliography: p. 290
  Filmography: p. 291
  Includes index.
  1. Moving-picture producers and directors.
I. Title.
PN1998.A2S43   791.43'0233'0922   86-1238
ISBN 0-8109-0718-6

Times Mirror Books

Printed and bound in Japan

CONTENTS

Acknowledgments

I am deeply grateful to the many people who helped me carry out this prodigious project. Their efforts on my behalf have meant a great deal to me during the long months.

Once again I want to thank all the good people of Abrams for their patience, understanding, and assistance. They include my editor, Lory Frankel, creative and diligent as always; the book's talented designer, Dirk Luykx; and John Crowley, whose enthusiastic and tireless search for photographs was not only welcome but also indispensable. Much thanks as well to Margaret Kaplan, Leta Bostelman, and Barbara Lyons. As always, I am everlastingly grateful to Susan Grode for her efforts in arranging permissions and for her warm support.

I am grateful to the Directors Guild of America for its support and cooperation, with special thanks to David Shepard, Selise Eiseman, Robert Wise, Joseph Youngerman, and George Sidney, who was kind enough to permit me to use some of his own magnificent photographs. I would like to note here that the opinions expressed in the book are mine and are not endorsed by the Directors Guild.

I should like to thank the people who helped me obtain such beautiful visual material: the ever-valuable Jerry Vermilye; Robert Cushman of the Margaret Herrick Library of the Academy of Motion Picture Arts and Sciences; Steve Newman and Alan Gavoni of Metro-Goldwyn-Mayer; Jess Garcia and Ron Chan of Warner Bros.; Bette Einbinder of 20th Century-Fox; Ivy Orta, Helen La Varre, and Alan Press of Columbia Pictures; Nancy Cushing-Jones and Corinne DeLuca of Universal Pictures; Audree Malkin of the Theatre Collection at UCLA's Research Library; and Leith Adams, archivist at the University of Southern California. I also want to acknowledge the valuable research assistance of the staff of the Billy Rose Collection of the New York Public Library at Lincoln Center.

There are several people whom I would like to single out for special mention. One is Curtis F. Brown, whose perceptive and sharp-eyed reading of my manuscript is, as always, greatly appreciated. Another is Lisa Rosenberg, who prepared the Filmographies and who provided me with many of the quotations from the directors. In this respect, "Dialogues on Film" from *American Film* Magazine proved to be extremely helpful.

Finally, no book I ever write would be complete without an expression of my love and gratitude to my wife, Roxane, and to my children, Bob, David, and Karen. They sustain me, warm me, keep me on my toes, and make the entire enterprise worthwhile.

PAGE *1* All That Jazz: BOB FOSSE *(Fox, 1979).*
PAGES *2–3* A Child Is Waiting: JOHN CASSAVETES *(United Artists, 1963). John Cassavetes (left) watches as the cameraman films Judy Garland and Burt Lancaster.*
PAGES *4–5* Camille: GEORGE CUKOR *(MGM, 1937). George Cukor (standing at left) directs Greta Garbo and Robert Taylor.*
PAGES *6–7* Exodus: OTTO PREMINGER *(United Artists, 1960). On location in Israel, director Otto Preminger enjoys a laugh as a propman tries to cope with a newborn donkey.*
PAGES *8–9* Singin' in the Rain: GENE KELLY *and* STANLEY DONEN *(MGM, 1952). Cyd Charisse and Gene Kelly dance the "Broadway" ballet.*
PAGE *12* Moby Dick: JOHN HUSTON *(Warner Bros., 1956). Director Huston (bottom right) works with his crew aboard the* Pequod.

FOREWORD

Let's begin with the mystique of the film director. Some folks think of the director as a snake charmer who mesmerizes wily serpents until they perform beautifully. Others, to continue the circus analogy, think of the director as a lion tamer.

Through the ninety-year history of cinema, a few directors have indeed been hypnotists, and a few others sadists. In general, however, directors are hard-working professionals who take their recipe from the movies' founding father, Thomas A. Edison, who was once said to have explained genius as 10 percent inspiration and 90 percent perspiration.

What we do as directors varies substantially according to our individual projects, dispositions, and skills. Most directors are great persuaders. Certainly each of us listens to, mediates among, and tries to inspire the best from each craftsperson who collaborates in movie-making. We are concerned with the psychology of our characters and our audiences. Even under pressure, the best directors have a keen sense of structure and proportion. We integrate controllable visual, dramatic, and musical arts at the same time that we seize opportunities in real-world weather, landscape, and light. Although we do not create the elements that go into a film, our point of view determines their acceptance, modification, and placement. For this reason, those directors who conscientiously guide their works from script to screen are often designated the *authors* of their films.

Protecting the authorial or "creative" rights of the director was a major incentive for those who founded the Directors Guild of America in 1936: King Vidor, Rouben Mamoulian, Lewis Milestone, John Ford, Frank Borzage, William A. Wellman, Howard Hawks, Henry King, Richard Wallace, Rowland V. Lee, Frank Tuttle, A. Edward Sutherland, and Herbert J. Biberman. To this day, enhancing opportunities for higher-quality work remains paramount among the Guild's principles, as does its efforts to tirelessly police and protect the benefits, economic and otherwise, due its members.

Assistant Directors and Unit Production Managers, key members of the film director's team, are also represented by the Directors Guild. They are concerned with the logistical and economic management of the production process. They run the set, they keep the records, and they schedule the shots. Critics cannot possibly isolate their many contributions, but directors depend upon them. Some directors have employed the same assistants on many successive films; in earlier years, Charlie Dorian worked with Clarence Brown, Wingate Smith with John Ford, "Hezzi" Tate with Cecil B. DeMille, Billy Kaplan with Victor Fleming, Joseph C. Youngerman with William Wellman, Art Black with Frank Capra, Nate Watt with Lewis Milestone, and Tom Shaw with John Huston. I hope that a future book will illuminate the work of these extremely important yet little-known contributors to the process of making movies.

For the present, we are honored that the Golden Jubilee of the Directors Guild of America should be marked by the publication of the most sumptuous volume ever dedicated to our craft. While Mr. Sennett's opinions are, of course, his own and not those of the Guild, his historical perspective, his enthusiasm for the many periods and genres of film, his decency, and his genuine respect for cinema, its makers, and its audiences serve us all well.

Gilbert Cates
PRESIDENT
DIRECTORS GUILD OF AMERICA

INTRODUCTION

Directing Movies

How would one define "film director"?

Like the blind men trying to describe an elephant, one can come up with many possible explanations, many ways of pinpointing what a film director actually does during the long, arduous days of preproduction and filming. Any movie reference book will tell you, in brief, that the director is the person who is directly in charge of all creative aspects, both interpretive and technical, of a film production, the one who mixes all the ingredients—from the acting to the lighting—that contribute to the final look of a motion picture. Of course, this formal definition does not cover the many roles the film director may be called on to play before the wrap-up: tyrant, father- (or mother-) confessor, psychiatrist, bosom pal, teacher, baby sitter, and arbiter of stormy battles. Every director at some time has had to cajole, wheedle, rebuke, bully, or soothe the people he needs to help him get through the making of a movie.

Ask a movie buff what a director does, and he may summon up memories of, say, Roscoe Dexter (Douglas Fowley) in the classic Gene Kelly–Stanley Donen musical *Singin' in the Rain*. Driven to near-madness by the baffling, brand-new complications of sound, this director in cap and riding breeches rushes around the set in a permanent state of hysteria as everything unravels around him. Ask a film director what his job is like, and you may be regaled with descriptions of physical distress not so far removed from Roscoe Dexter's distraught condition. William Wellman found that directing assaulted the nerves in a variety of ways: "nervous tension, strain, stress, the jitters, the willies, the heebie-jeebies, all wrapped up in that thing called 'a director's stomach' " (Wellman, *A Short Time for Insanity*). After ten days of shooting, Arthur Hiller claims to go into a manic-depressive state. George Lucas has admitted that he gets "physically sick. I get a very bad cough and a

cold when I direct. . . . It's like climbing mountains, cut and bruised and freezing cold, and you lose your toes and everything and then you get it done and it's all worth it" (*Action*, January–February 1974).

Of course, when film directors talk about their craft, or, on a loftier level, their art, the physical ailments disappear. Despite the tribulations, despite the alarmingly bulging budgets, the missed cues, and the temperamental stars, their love for films and filmmaking remains pervasive, enduring, and sustaining. George Cukor asserted that making a film was "a joyous experience" (*Film Culture*, Fall 1964). Orson Welles affirmed that he was "besotted with love for the medium" (*The New York Times Magazine*, 14 July 1985). Without discounting the toll that it takes, Robert Altman thinks of filmmaking as "a natural high and the only life in the world for me"; it marks "a time of beginning, a time of struggle, a time of doubt and fear, a time when you feel your power, a time when you grow old" (*Action*, January–February 1972). Time and again directors will talk of their elation and their deep satisfaction when the vision they have brought to a film has been fully realized.

Interestingly, when film directors discuss their work, many resort to musical references or compare their job to that of an orchestra conductor. Both are required to blend many disparate elements into a unified and seamless whole, the conductor realizing his interpretation of a piece of music out of a combination of instruments, the director creating a film out of the efforts of writers, actors, and technicians. Peter Bogdanovich has written, "Pure cinema is complementary pieces of film put together. Like notes of music to make a melody" (*The Cinema of Peter Bogdanovich*). Directors as diverse as William Wyler, John Cromwell, and François Truffaut have described themselves as orchestra conductors. Fred Zinnemann enlarged on the idea: "There is a good deal of similarity between a conductor and a director, in the sense that you work with a large number of people. What you have to do is persuade them of your own vision so that they form one body working together for one purpose: to get the ideal result" (*American Film*, January–February 1986).

Film directors may share an overall perception of their intentions and goals, but when it comes to dealing with the elements that go into the making of a film they will often reveal different attitudes. For example, while most directors recognize the importance of the writers and many choose to have them close at hand during shooting, other directors regard the screenplay as a launching pad for their own visionary flights, or, on a more down-to-earth basis, as the blueprint on which they or the actors can make changes or embellishments. Arthur Hiller prefers to have the writer with him on the set "because it's his baby and he can help me with special problems, and also because a film takes on a life of its own. It grows and it changes as you move along with the filming, and you have to adjust to it" (*American Film*, October 1979). Martin Ritt agrees with Hiller, claiming to keep writers on the set "because I recognize the importance of the job and I don't want to be suddenly left by myself" (*American Film*, November 1983). Many directors collaborate actively with the writers, feeling that the writer and director together can best shape the material to be filmed. Joseph Losey was one such director, working closely with such writers as Harold Pinter to ensure that the script remained in line with his overall concept. (The special rewards and problems of the director who is also the writer are too complex to be discussed here.)

On the other hand, while acknowledging the crucial need for a polished shooting script, many directors believe that a film necessarily exists beyond the printed word as a living entity that takes different shapes and directions as it forms. Frank Capra, one of the most durable of film directors, never looked upon the script as gospel of any kind. "You have to tell a story visually," he has written, "and a script is not visual. The visual sometimes just takes over. Don't forget you're making a film, not photographing a script" (*American Film*, October 1978). John Schlesinger affirmed that "it's ridiculous to regard the script as the final absolute blueprint. I believe that a film has to grow as you're making it, and you should be able to alter things accordingly" (*Films and Filming*, November 1969). For screenwriters who, over the years, have seen their work drastically revised, often without consultation, such attitudes can be painful indeed. Yet as Lawrence Kasdan, himself a writer-direc-

tor, has pointed out, there is no real battle between the writer and the director: "The director has won it. He will do with the script as he wishes. . . . It's the director's movie. I resisted that fact for years, but it's a fact" (*American Film*, April 1982).

Many directors express a similar affirmative-yet-cautious attitude toward the cinematographer. On the whole, they work in close and cordial harmony with their cameramen, expecting them, like the set and costume designers or the actors, to help carry out the directorial vision of the film. Although few directors balk at receiving suggestions or contributions from the cameramen, the great majority insist on assuming total control of the film's visual style. John Huston maintains a strong rapport with his cameraman, yet at the end of each shot he will look to see if the cameraman has brought off the intended effect. Elia Kazan will leave no decisions, including camera angles or the composition of a close-up, to anyone but himself. And Sydney Pollack believes that "the way in which the film is photographed is part of the directorial concept." He adds, "I'm not saying I'm a cameraman, but I would never go to a cameraman and say, 'I don't know what to do here. I want a kind of soft look, kind of fuzzy. What do you think?' Then I would get *his* vision of the scene" (*American Film*, April 1978).

The director's wariness of the cinematographer usually stems from the latter's affinity for putting too much of himself into a scene; he will occasionally intrude into the smooth flow of a scene with odd or striking camera angles that bear no relation to the story. George Cukor believed that "cameramen get into all kinds of habits and one has to watch over them very carefully. It's best to have someone with an open mind who won't put in all sorts of boring shadows and things like that" (*Film Culture*, Fall 1964). John Schlesinger recognized the same tendency: "So often the cameraman is more interested in what the scene looks like than in what you're trying to say with it. What I tend to do is to try and bring a cameraman into what the scene is really about rather than just what it looks like" (*American Film*, December 1979).

Over the years, successful directors have repeatedly stressed the importance of keeping the camerawork unobtrusive. William Wyler aimed for camera movements that are "smooth, unnoticed if possible, and that help to make the scene more interesting." He objected to directors who use the camera as a toy: "They think it's something to play around with. You see a lamp or post sailing across the foreground for no damn reason. It doesn't help the scene. It means nothing. The movement of camera and the use of camera should be such as to enhance the scene and to give good composition and clarity" (*American Film*, July 1976). Richard Brooks has echoed this feeling about the camera: "If anybody at any time says, 'Wow, what a shot,' you've lost the audience.... They should never see the camera move" (*American Film*, October 1977). In his forthright way, John Ford may have had the most practical approach to working with the cinematographer: "You tell the cameraman to place the camera here and get in so-and-so and so-and-so, so he does it. That's all there is to it.... I don't like to move the camera much. It throws the audience off. It says, 'This is a motion picture. This ain't real'" (McBride and Wilmington, *John Ford*).

Each element the director must handle in creating a film plays a significant role, and none is more significant than the actor. The actor is the director's conduit to the audience, the tool with which he can express whatever vision, or meaning, or images of joy or horror he is striving to put on film. As Frank Capra said, "It isn't the director to the audience or the cameraman to the audience. It's actors to audience, people to people" (*American Film*, October 1978). Therein lies the challenge to the film director: to make that invisible connection palpable in every scene. William Wyler understood its primary importance: "People who separate directing from acting make a great mistake, because I consider the first function of a director to be the acting. There's no such thing as a bad performance and a good actor. They don't go together" (Masden, *William Wyler*).

Granted that the actor is the most crucial element for the director, how have directors treated their casts of players over the many decades of filmmaking? Clearly, film history tells us that more than one director looked upon his actors as marionettes, or chess pieces, or cattle, or, in general, as irritating, obstructionist means to an end. A few apparently continue to use bullying tactics. Most directors, however, deal sensitively and knowingly with their actors. Robert Wise has always prided himself on maintaining a reasonably calm atmosphere on the set ("I'm not one of those directors who feel they have to keep everybody stirred up to get the best out of them," *Action*, January–February 1976). Elia Kazan insists on getting to know his actors very well ("I take them to dinner. I talk to them. I meet their wives. I find out what the hell the human material is that I'm dealing with," *American Film*, March 1976). Irvin Kershner establishes a mood of mutual need and trust ("I want to feel close to the actors, and I want them to feel close to me," *American Film*, January 1981). Most directors perceive the vulnerability and insecurity of their actors and find a

way, whether with steel or with velvet gloves, to transmute these feelings into performance.

On the set, working with the actors for long and wearying stretches, the director may choose to—or may be required to—draw the reins in tightly, depending on a variety of circumstances. Yet most directors have enormous respect for their actors and willingly give them the space and the opportunity to uncover new layers of the characters they are portraying. Many directors find that especially skilled actors can often contribute nuances and shadings beyond the printed words of the screenplay. Edward Dmytryk watched in astonishment as Spencer Tracy, perhaps the finest of screen actors, made a speech that on paper looked too long and literary sound entirely extemporaneous through his adroit delivery. Early in his direction of Judy Garland, Vincente Minnelli would lead her to the emotional center of a scene and then allow her to add her own distinctive heartbeat. Directing *A Star Is Born*, George Cukor recalled keeping the camera on James Mason for "an eternity" throughout the climactic scene in which he decides to kill himself. The result was possibly Mason's finest moment on film.

Many directors spend part of the critical period before the cameras turn in close contact with the actors, thinking through their roles together. Frank Perry, for example, works with his actors to construct a full history for each character, down to his or her early psychic trauma, in a process resembling psychoanalysis. However, the moment of truth occurs on the first day of shooting, a moment George Cukor described with characteristic clarity:

You can do all sorts of preparation but nothing can be planned out perfectly ahead of time. The proof of the pudding is in the eating. You know, you can talk and you establish a sort of friendly relationship. But when you're before the cameras with your actress, you're sort of alone with your god. There you are. When the cameras start to purr it really happens. Up to then it was very polite and hopeful and cordial. You establish a relationship before but the real "working relationship" doesn't happen until you're working. (*Film Culture*, Fall 1964)

As in his view of cameramen, John Ford enjoyed cutting through speculation with a blunt note of practicality. On working with actors, he remarked, "They read the script, they know what you want, they get out in front of the camera and say, 'What do we do?,' and I tell 'em, and they do it, usually in the first take" (McBride and Wilmington, *John Ford*).

Finally, how much control can—or should—the director exercise over his film? Most leading directors have contended that they are the governing force behind the film, the equivalent of the orchestra conductor through whom all the music flows. (This contention, of course, has been the spur to many a studio battle.) The concept of the director as the person in supreme charge of every facet and decision turns up regularly in interviews and writings on film:

The films that have expressed the greatest unity, and given the most satisfaction to the viewer, have been those in which the guiding hand has been imposed on every section of the film's many divisions. Story, casting, settings, photography, acting should all bespeak *one* mind.   KING VIDOR, in Richard Bare, *The Film Director*

I think a director should do absolutely everything. I think the sets are his. The costumes are his. The editing is his. I'm a believer in the dominance of one person who has a vision.   ELIA KAZAN, *American Film*, March 1976

I was the enemy of the major studios. I believed in one man, one film. I believed that one man should make the film. I just couldn't accept art as a committee. I could only accept art as an extension of the individual. One man's ideas should prevail.   FRANK CAPRA, *American Film*, October 1978

I'm a megalomaniac. You have to be one to make a good film. You have to believe that whatever decision you make, you're right, even if you're wrong. Because it's *my* film.   ROMAN POLANSKI, *Action*, January–February 1972

Inevitably, the one man, one film theory leads us to the realm of *auteur* criticism, a topic that can hardly be avoided altogether in any book on film directing. The origins of the *auteur* theory—the belief that the director is the "author" and primary voice of any film and that the style and *mise en scène* of a film (the *how*) is more important than its subject (the *what*)—need not be traced here in any detail. First advanced in the mid-fifties by François Truffaut when he was still a critic with the influential French periodical *Cahiers du Cinéma*, the *auteur* theory enshrined such directors as Alfred Hitchcock and Vincente Minnelli while sparking new interest in previously neglected directors such as Nicholas Ray and Douglas Sirk. After Truffaut and many of his fellow critics, including Jean-Luc Godard and Claude Chabrol, turned to filmmaking themselves, the concept was picked up by the English film magazine *Movie*; it was then launched in America by Andrew Sarris in his landmark article "Notes on the Auteur Theory in 1962," which appeared in the Winter 1962–63 issue of *Film Culture*. The debate over its validity and relevance has raged, or at least simmered, ever since.

From the start, a principal criticism leveled against the *auteur* theory has been that it tended to elevate minor directors of modest achievement into the front ranks by dint of their recurring style and motifs. By the same token, it has led to the cursory and unwarranted dismissal of many directors of proven professional quality whose craftsmanship is undeniable but who lack an all-pervasive style by *auteur* standards. One of these directors, William Wyler, took the time to respond many years after his retirement:

. . . I've been accused by critics of being a director without a signature. Well, I rather enjoy being that sort of director. I enjoy doing different things. Filmmaking is my business, or was my business, and they didn't say to me, make melodramas or comedies, or musicals, they just said make films.   (*Films and Filming*, October 1981)

Although subject to misinterpretation and exaggeration—Andrew Sarris himself has pointed out that the *auteur* theory is only one way, not the only way, to explain cinema, and that the *what* of any film deserves as much consideration as the *how*—the *auteur* theory has had a lasting impact on film criticism. Its influence remains evident to the present day, as witness a January 1986 article on Woody Allen in *The New York Times Magazine* entitled "*Auteur! Auteur!*"

Auteur or not, the director clearly needs diverse qualities to cope with the formidable task of creating a film. Frank Borzage, one of the best directors, summarized these qualities in a forthright way:

A director should have some of the qualities of a leader, the ability to make decisions that are right most of the time, and the quality which inspires confidence in those about him. He must have a world of patience and resourcefulness to overcome obstacles without too much deliberation. He must have a lot of cooperation and some luck.

As an afterthought, Borzage added, "There probably aren't many such persons this side of heaven" (cited in Richard Koszarski, *Hollywood Directors, 1914–1940*).

★

A few words about this book:

Written at a time when the Directors Guild of America was celebrating the fiftieth anniversary of its founding, this book pays tribute to over two hundred directors, largely but not exclusively American, who have contrib-

OPPOSITE   Mata Hari: GEORGE FITZMAURICE (*MGM, 1932*). *George Fitzmaurice (center) directs Greta Garbo as alluring spy Mata Hari and Ramon Novarro as the Russian lieutenant who becomes her victim and her lover.* OVERLEAF   *Alfred Hitchcock, the master of suspense, directs a scene.*

uted indelibly or substantially to the development of film. Among the directors covered are those who have received the prestigious award given annually by the Directors Guild for excellence in theatrical direction, as well as the periodic winners of the D. W. Griffith Award.

My intent has been to convey the style and essence of these men and women, from the earliest silent days to the present, who worked long and diligently to turn flickering images into memorable motion pictures. Together with many other talented directors who could not be covered in this book because of space limitations, they helped to create an industry, a popular art, and a perennially joyful source of entertainment.

This book is for all the film directors, with gratitude for the pleasure and enlightenment they brought us, and continue to bring us, across the years.

THE DIRECTORS

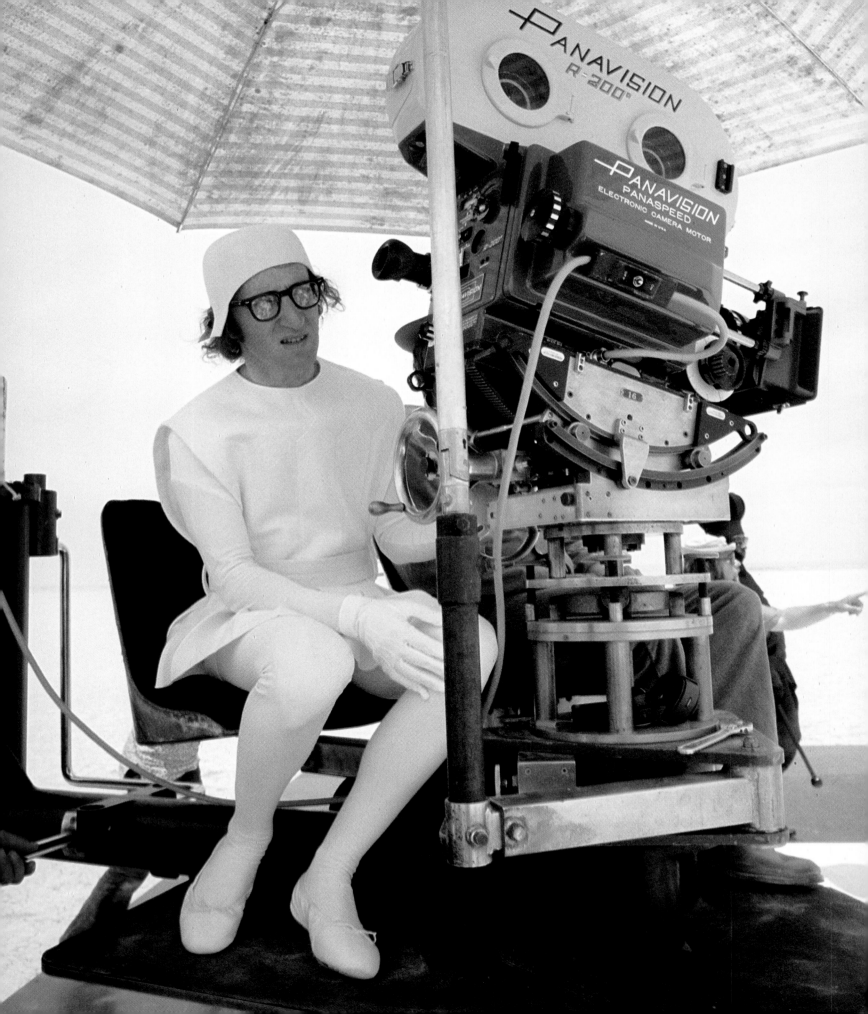

ROBERT ALDRICH (1918–1983)   Robert Aldrich's characters frequently teeter on the knife-edge of hysteria, which gives overwrought actors like Jack Palance, Kirk Douglas, and Gene Wilder the opportunity to throw restraint to the winds in his films: Palance as the tormented movie star in *The Big Knife* (1955), Kirk Douglas as an outlaw innocently committing incest in *The Last Sunset* (1961), and Wilder as a rabbi out West in *The Frisco Kid* (1979). (But then, Wilder's stock-in-trade *is* hysteria.) Aldrich enjoys tossing people who are none too stable to begin with into a dark maelstrom of violence and disorder, and it doesn't matter whether they are victimizer (Bette Davis in the camp classic *What Ever Happened to Baby Jane*, 1962) or victim (Bette Davis in *Hush . . . Hush, Sweet Charlotte*, 1965). Like Howard Hawks, Aldrich is interested in groups of men under special pressure (*Attack!*, 1956; *The Dirty Dozen*, 1967); unlike Hawks, he seldom chooses to ease the pressure with sentiment, although he dispenses much hearty humor. Aldrich has been criticized for his excessive violence and his misogyny (his women are usually grotesques or nonentities), but at his best, he can create scenes that bristle with tense action, as in the widely admired Mickey Spillane mystery thriller *Kiss Me Deadly* (1955).

★

I don't rehearse a film. I never know where I'm going to put the camera. Funniness is organic, like sitting around with a lot of people when something loopy happens. What you write is not what you shoot at all. I've shot the middle of a movie again and again and eventually put it somewhere else.   WOODY ALLEN, interview in *The New Yorker,* 4 February 1974, cited in Jay Leyda, ed., *Voices of Film Experience* (New York: Macmillan, 1977), p. 5.

WOODY ALLEN (born 1935)   The face and the demeanor do not change: over the years, through all the different styles and trends, Woody Allen has remained Allen Stewart Konigsberg, the short, thin, unprepossessing Jewish New Yorker with a shock of thinning, flyaway hair, an apologetic voice, and the worried look of a yeshiva student who has wandered into the wrong neighborhood. He is the fellow you may remember from your high school days, the brainy kid who could barely conceal his obsession with girls and who covered every slight, every insult with a barbed joke. Konigsberg-turned-Allen has parlayed this persona first into a clever and original stand-up comedian, then into an immoderately funny stage and screen actor-writer, and ultimately into an actor-writer-director who is the foremost creator

of comedy films. By this time there is no doubt that he has become a mature filmmaker who has learned to fuse cinematic material into a seamless entity. That being said, it should be added that Woody Allen, whether writing, acting, or directing, can still make us laugh with his definitive portrait of the contemporary urban, neurotic, put-upon male.

The Brooklyn-born Allen began as a gag writer, progressed to writing comedy material for stage revues and television shows, and ultimately—at the urging of his agents—turned to performing stand-up comedy in the early sixties. He soon developed the familiar image of the wily nebbish who could make fun of his (and, incidentally, everyone else's) many hang-ups about the perils of adulthood. By the late sixties, his forlorn and owlish countenance was well known to everyone. He had appeared in several movies (*What's New Pussycat?*, 1965, which he also wrote; *Casino Royale*, 1967), and he had written two hit plays (*Don't Drink the Water*, 1966; *Play It Again, Sam*, 1969). He had also created *What's Up,*

ABOVE   What Ever Happened to Baby Jane: ROBERT ALDRICH (*Warner Bros.*, 1962). *Vicious and deranged Jane Hudson (Bette Davis) tells her wheelchair-bound sister, Blanche (Joan Crawford), about her missing parakeet, as the housekeeper, Elvira Stitt (Maidie Norman), looks on suspiciously.*
Aldrich's exercise in ghoulish melodrama brought the two golden-age stars together for the first time.
OPPOSITE   Sleeper: WOODY ALLEN (*United Artists, 1973*). *On the set, Allen considers his next shot, wearing the garb of the best-dressed man of the year 2073. This uproarious futuristic comedy sustained an antic mood from first to last.*

Hannah and Her Sisters: WOODY ALLEN *(Orion, 1986). Hannah (Mia Farrow) and her husband, Elliot (Michael Caine), two of the characters in Allen's finest film to date. In this comedy, Allen exchanged his usual bitter flavor for a becoming warmth, generosity, and romantic feeling.*

Tiger Lily? (1966), in which he dubbed a cheap Japanese thriller with his own hilarious selection of wisecracks, puns, and non sequiturs.

Allen began directing in 1969, with *Take the Money and Run*. A spoof of the gangster film, complete with portentous narrator and "documentary" footage, it had its share of funny scenes (notably a bungled bank robbery), which did not entirely conceal the movie's makeshift quality. This improved in the second film, *Bananas* (1971), a Marxian (Brothers, not Karl) satire on the explosive, temporary nature of South American politics. Many of the gags found their targets, and Allen provoked howls of laughter as a New York products tester who accidentally becomes dictator of a banana republic. He faltered with *Everything You Ever Wanted to Know about Sex** *(*But Were Afraid to Ask)* (1972), a series of coarse, sex-oriented sketches suggested by Dr. David Reuben's popular book. After starring in, but not directing, a film version of his play *Play It Again, Sam* (1972), he presented one of his best films, an imaginative and ingenious futuristic spoof entitled *Sleeper* (1973). Apart from displaying Allen's increasing skill as a filmmaker, the movie offered slyly satirical dialogue, clever sight gags, and well-executed special effects. Playing the owner of a health food store who awakens in the year

2073 after a minor operation, Allen was the very picture of bafflement and confusion, and Diane Keaton followed him every step of the way as a scatterbrained establishment girl of the future who turns into a revolutionary.

After making *Love and Death* (1975), an uneven but handsomely produced and often uproarious excursion into the *angst*-filled world of the Russian novelists, and playing the leading role in Martin Ritt's comedy-drama *The Front* (1976), Allen scored a major triumph with *Annie Hall* (1977). It was not only his most personal film to date—with collaborator Marshall Brickman, he drew on his own relationship with ex-girlfriend and costar Diane Keaton—it also marked an advance in his filmmaking ability. Beautifully photographed by Gordon Willis (his first for Allen), it subordinated the usual assortment of Allenesque gags (although there were many funny lines) to a winning and observant love story of two hopeless neurotics, a comedian named Alvy Singer (Allen) and a dithering, insecure would-be singer named Annie Hall (Diane Keaton). The movie was cited the year's best picture, and awards also went to Allen (as director and cowriter) and Keaton.

Always willing to experiment, Allen turned next, to everyone's surprise, to an entirely serious drama, *Interiors* (1978). Clearly influenced by the stark, introspective films of Ingmar Bergman, it dealt with tortured family relationships that culminate in the suicide of the mother, brilliantly played by Geraldine Page. Both Page and Allen (as director) received Oscar nominations. In his next film, *Manhattan* (1979), Allen returned to the milieu he knew best. It turned out to be one of his finest films to date: a dark-hued comedy that mixed laughter and poignancy with rare dexterity. Once again the story focused on the love affair of two urban neurotics, but around this central situation Allen constructed a mosaic of Manhattanites and their hedonistic, selfish, and essentially unrewarding lives. *Manhattan* was also one of Allen's most fully accomplished movies, stunningly photographed in black-and-white by Gordon Willis (Manhattan never looked so good) and enhanced by a soundtrack of lush, symphonically arranged Gershwin music.

While no Allen film of the eighties until *Hannah and Her Sisters* matched *Manhattan* in excellence, many of them have had their rewards. Allen continued to emulate the master directors he admired with such films as *Stardust Memories* (1980), a fascinating, often brilliant, but also self-indulgent and sour-flavored homage to Federico Fellini, and *A Midsummer Night's Sex Comedy* (1982), a visually enchanting tribute to Ingmar Berg-

man's *Smiles of a Summer Night* that turned out to be disappointingly thin and attenuated. *Zelig* (1983), an intriguing cinematic experiment, spoofed solemn film documentaries by recounting the history of one Leonard Zelig (Allen), a self-effacing nonentity who is so anxious to blend into the background that he actually takes on the appearance of anyone around him. Zelig's journey through twentieth-century history was ingeniously spliced into actual historical footage, with risible results. There was also much laughter to be had from *Broadway Danny Rose* (1984), a genial, engaging story of a small-time Broadway agent, which happily dispensed with much of the acerbic tone that permeated Allen's later films. Mia Farrow, in a role vastly different from the soulful waifs she usually played, was delightful as the squeaky-voiced, trampish girl who becomes involved in Danny Rose's adventures. However, in *The Purple Rose of Cairo* (1985), she reverted to type as a wispy, daydreaming housewife whose movie idol comes off the screen to woo her. Notwithstanding the admiring critics who spoke about the movie's juxtaposition of dreams and reality, it was a surprisingly wan and insubstantial one-joke affair.

With *Hannah and Her Sisters* (1986), Allen again dipped into the deepest well of his talent (as he had with *Manhattan*) to create his finest film to date. A richly textured romantic comedy, the movie covers two years in the lives of three New York sisters (Mia Farrow, Barbara Hershey, and Dianne Wiest) and the men in their mutually entangled lives. The ravishing New York photogra-

phy and the lush, varied background score inevitably recalled *Manhattan*, and the characters were Allen's familiar urban neurotics, whose passions and hang-ups he examined with his usual satirical humor and more than a touch of rue. There the resemblance ends, however, for *Manhattan*'s chill of unfulfilled hopes and dreams has given way to a generosity and an affirmative spirit that make *Hannah* glow. Once more, *Hannah and Her Sisters* made us grateful for Woody Allen's gifts, and for the pleasure of his witty, inventive, and extravagantly entertaining movies.

★

It's the only life in the world for me. I don't know what else I would do. Film making, really, is a chance to live many lifetimes—every project having a full circle of its own. A time of beginning, a time of struggle, a time of doubt and fear, a time when you feel your power, a time when you grow old, it's all there. Every film demands different things from you. It's wonderfully painful and tremendously exciting. ROBERT ALTMAN, interview with John Cutts, *Films and Filming*, January–February 1972, p. 36.

ROBERT ALTMAN (born 1925)   One of the most free-spirited, inventive, as well as erratic directors to achieve recognition in the early seventies, Robert Altman has won praise for his innovative approach to filmmaking and provoked censure (particularly in the eighties) for making far too many cold, remote, obfuscating movies. Whatever the critical reaction to his work, Altman has firmly retained his individuality and his ability to surprise and intimidate. Back in 1975 he remarked, "I try to get a little over my head, try to get in trouble, try to keep myself frightened, do things that are impossible. It helps me keep fairly straight" (*Midwest* Magazine, 27 July 1975). He has been keeping at it ever since.

Altman's films apparently have had one overriding purpose: to take the long-established, long-accepted tenets of American folklore as expressed in the movies and to treat them with bitter, ironic, and irreverent humor. No director in recent years has worked so assiduously at skewering the traditional film genres, including the war movie (*M*A*S*H*), the Western (*McCabe and Mrs. Miller, Buffalo Bill and the Indians*), and the private-eye melodrama (*The Long Goodbye*). In *Nashville*, his master-

---

Manhattan: WOODY ALLEN (*United Artists, 1979*). *Isaac Davis (Woody Allen) plays the harmonica as his young girlfriend, Tracy (Mariel Hemingway), sips a soda. One of Allen's best films,* **Manhattan** *is an observant, sardonic comedy concerning neurotic Manhattanites who grope for but seldom find happiness and fulfillment.*

LEFT   Nashville: ROBERT ALTMAN (*Paramount, 1975*). *Director Altman on the set. This ambitious film, Altman's finest to date, combined scathing satire and political commentary to create an unflattering view of America in the seventies.*
BELOW   McCabe and Mrs. Miller: ROBERT ALTMAN (*Warner Bros., 1971*). *John McCabe (Warren Beatty, center) indulges in a game of cards. Altman's gritty Western deliberately avoided the usual horse-opera conventions in its story of a gambler-turned-entrepreneur (Beatty) who comes to a sad end in the ramshackle town of Presbyterian Church.*

LEFT   Nashville: ROBERT ALTMAN (*Paramount, 1975*). *Director Altman on the set. This ambitious film, Altman's finest to date, combined scathing satire and political commentary to create an unflattering view of America in the seventies.*
BELOW   McCabe and Mrs. Miller: ROBERT ALTMAN (*Warner Bros., 1971*). *John McCabe (Warren Beatty, center) indulges in a game of cards. Altman's gritty Western deliberately avoided the usual horse-opera conventions in its story of a gambler-turned-entrepreneur (Beatty) who comes to a sad end in the ramshackle town of Presbyterian Church.*

ABOVE   Coal Miner's Daughter: MICHAEL APTED (*Universal, 1980*). *Loretta Lynn (Sissy Spacek) strums a guitar on her porch while her daughter listens. Apted's movie offered an uncondescending, unsentimental look at the world of country music, and Spacek's Oscar-winning performance gave substance to this basically familiar show business biography.*
RIGHT   Coming Home: HAL ASHBY (*United Artists, 1978*). *Jane Fonda as Sally Hyde, married to an officer serving in Vietnam, with her lover, paraplegic veteran Luke Martin (Jon Voight). The film was moving, yet it never seemed entirely sure whether it meant to be a triangular love story or a treatise on the searing personal impact of the Vietnam War.*

piece, he took on America itself, satirizing, among other things, the nation's political naiveté, easy corruption, and blatant vulgarity. On the whole, Altman's world is a sometimes comic and sometimes dangerous lunatic asylum where, in order to survive, one must be as crazy or as venal as everyone else, or at least cheerfully and unrestrainedly eccentric.

Early in his film career, Altman revealed a determination to create a sense of real life in his movies. To this end he used techniques that, while not original with him, gave his films a startling new coloration. In the manner of Orson Welles in *The Magnificent Ambersons*, he filmed many scenes with overlapping dialogue that conveyed the sense of events taking place in the moment, and he was not averse to having accidental noises on the soundtrack that obscured what was being said. He would often have the actors improvise their dialogue, or he would film a rehearsal as the final take. He achieved the intended result: baffling, irritating, or intriguing critics and viewers alike.

Born in Kansas City, Altman worked there making industrial films, acquiring valuable experience as a producer, director, writer, and editor. His attempts to break into the Hollywood film industry finally led to two low-budget features, *The Delinquents* (1957) and *The James Dean Story* (1957), a documentary, which, in turn, led to his long and busy employment as a television director. In 1968 he was given the chance to return to feature film-making with *Countdown*, a fictionalized drama about America's space program. He followed this small but well-done film with *That Cold Day in the Park* (1969), a bizarre drama made in Canada concerning a frustrated and dangerously deranged spinster (Sandy Dennis), the first portrait in Altman's gallery of sex-hungry, unhinged women.

Altman scored his first major critical and popular success in 1970 with *M*A*S*H*. A jet-black and wildly irreverent comedy, the movie used the setting of a mobile army surgical hospital during the Korean War to mock the futility and idiocy of *all* war, while not failing to depict its attendant horrors. As two zany, disrespectful surgeons, Elliott Gould and Donald Sutherland achieved stardom, and the film itself won an Oscar nomination and critical admiration. Few seemed to point out—or care—that many of the pranks instituted by the medical Rover Boys were cruel rather than funny, as well as flagrantly misogynistic.

Inevitably, Altman did not allow the commercial success of *M*A*S*H* to sidetrack him from his personal approach to filmmaking. Over the next five years he directed movies that, for all their virtues and their fresh approach to old forms, could never hope to win a wide audience. In *Brewster McCloud* (1970), he created a strange fantasy about an eccentric young man (Bud Cort) who encounters all sorts of comic and nasty interruptions while attempting to realize his dream of flying around Houston's Astrodome with his man-made wings. *McCabe and Mrs. Miller* (1971) won either enthusiastic praise or angry dismissal for its sardonic, unvarnished view of the winning of the West. Greed, corruption, and hopelessness banished all traces of pioneer courage or resilience as an entrepreneurial cowboy and madam (Warren Beatty and Julie Christie) form a partnership to build a combined gambling casino and whorehouse. While *McCabe and Mrs. Miller* pulled the rug out from under Western movie myths, *The Long Goodbye* (1973) inverted the detective genre to show that the concept of the morally superior private eye was an anachronism in a corrupt age. Altman next made a pair of somewhat more accessible films: *Thieves Like Us* (1974), a moody remake of the doomed-young-lovers story previously filmed in 1948 as *They Live By Night*, and *California Split* (1974), a hectic, amiable comedy about gambling. In the latter film, Altman used the device of overlapping dialogue to a greater extent than ever before, to sometimes bewildering but not displeasing effect. He also used the constantly moving camera that had been an effective but little-noted feature of *The Long Goodbye*.

With *Nashville* (1975), Altman achieved his finest work to date. An original, complex, and ambitious film, it used Nashville's world of country music as a central metaphor of American life in the seventies, exposing its hypocrisy, cynicism, vulgarity, and propensity for violence. Altman assembled a huge cast of players, including Keith Carradine, Lily Tomlin, Ronee Blakley, and Henry Gibson, allowing them not only to improvise their dialogue but also to write their own songs for the movie. (Carradine's "I'm Easy" won an Oscar.) Joan Tewkesbury's brilliant screenplay intertwined the stories of twenty-four principal characters as they maneuver for position at a monster rally of music and politics; underlying their funny or poignant stories was an unmistakable layer of bitter satire.

Altman's later attempts to duplicate *Nashville*'s pattern of many interlocking stories fell short. Both *A Wedding* (1978), a dark comedy about various crises at a nouveau riche wedding, and *Health* (1980), a satire on the health industry (with strong political overtones), hit their targets only intermittently. Despite the lure of star names, neither received wide general release. Nor did *Buffalo Bill and the Indians or Sitting Bull's History Lesson* (1976) find an audience willing to sit through its wicked, ironic debunking of the myth of the Western hero. While far from being a hit, *3 Women* (1977) fascinated many by its experimental approach and its psychological portrait of three unstable women. Altman began the eighties with *Popeye* (1980), a distressingly ugly and joyless musical version of the venerable comic-strip character, and he has spent the past few years directing film adaptations of what he felt were deserving, serious plays, such as *Come Back to the Five and Dime, Jimmy Dean, Jimmy Dean* (1982), *Streamers* (1983), and *Fool for Love* (1985).

Whether he will continue in this vein remains to be seen, but we can be certain that Robert Altman will always exercise his right to independent thinking and filmmaking. No doubt he will make other films that provoke us to reflect on the dark shadows that lurk in the bright promise of the American dream, and no doubt he will add to his retinue of fools, charlatans, and strivers. Whatever he chooses to do, it will be worth watching.

★

MICHAEL APTED (born 1941)   British director Michael Apted has had an interesting career since attracting attention in the seventies with several films, including *The Triple Echo* (1973) and *Stardust* (1975). His 1979 film *Agatha*, about the mysterious eleven-day disappearance of novelist Agatha Christie (Vanessa Redgrave) in 1926, won good reviews if not wide attendance, and then Apted scored a success with his first American movie, *Coal Miner's Daughter* (1980). A long, often effective, but basically unexceptional movie about country singer Loretta Lynn, it earned an Oscar for Sissy Spacek, who excelled as the doggedly ambitious Lynn. Apted's subsequent films, which include *Continental Divide* (1981), *Gorky Park* (1983), and *Firstborn* (1984), have been competent enough. Apted has demonstrated greater success with documentaries, particularly with *28 Up* (1985), about a number of young British people from diverse social and economic backgrounds who were interviewed at seven-year intervals. Most recently, Apted turned to comedy with *Critical Condition* (1986), starring Richard Pryor.

★

DOROTHY ARZNER (1900–1979)   Hollywood's only woman director in the thirties, Dorothy Arzner has finally come into her own in recent years. Now recognized as a consummate craftsman, with admirable attention to carefully worked out details and a clean, direct visual

style, she also offered a gallery of women who learned to make their way in a man's world. Arzner herself worked her way up from the ranks, starting as a stenographer in 1919 and moving to script clerk, cutter, and editor. Her editing of the bullfight scenes in Rudolph Valentino's *Blood and Sand* (1922) impressed director James Cruze, who allowed her to edit his landmark Western, *The Covered Wagon* (1923).

Many of the leading actresses of the thirties appeared under Arzner's direction: Sylvia Sidney in *Merrily We Go to Hell* (1932), Katharine Hepburn in *Christopher Strong* (1933), Rosalind Russell in *Craig's Wife* (1936), and Joan Crawford in *The Bride Wore Red* (1937). For these, as for all her films, Arzner prepared extensively before shooting began, yet she was known for her flexibility during shooting. Producers admired her professionalism— Samuel Goldwyn, for example, entrusted her with *Nana* (1934), his launching vehicle for his new European star Anna Sten, but the result was not encouraging. In recent years her 1940 film *Dance, Girl, Dance*, in which a chorus girl (Maureen O'Hara, badly miscast) becomes a dance star on her own terms, has won some attention because of its feminist attitude.

★

HAL ASHBY (born 1936)   Well known as an editor for a number of years—he won an Academy Award for *In the Heat of the Night* in 1967—Hal Ashby began directing in 1970, using a light, loose touch that has appealed to many actors. His second film, *Harold and Maude* (1971),

---

Manhattan Cocktail: DOROTHY ARZNER *(Paramount, 1928). Cameraman Harry Fischbeck, director Dorothy Arzner, and star Richard Arlen on the set of the film.*

an off-the-wall black comedy about the improbable love affair of a suicidal teen-ager (Bud Cort) and a life-affirming old woman (Ruth Gordon), developed into a cult favorite over the years, although much of the material induces more winces than laughs. He scored his greatest commercial and critical success in 1978 with *Coming Home,* a strong, believable drama about the romance of a disabled Vietnam soldier (Jon Voight) and an officer's wife (Jane Fonda). Both actors won Academy Awards for that year, and Ashby was nominated.

Ashby's seventies comedies were variable: Jack Nicholson and Randy Quaid gave exceptional performances in *The Last Detail* (1973), a bawdy yet touching film about sailors transporting a colleague to the brig; *Shampoo* (1975) was an overrated, self-indulgent dissection of upper-strata Californians; and *Being There* (1979) was a clever but essentially one-joke satire about a childlike gardener (Peter Sellers, in an Oscar-winning performance) who becomes a national celebrity. In a more dramatic vein, *Bound for Glory* (1976) told the story of composer–folk singer Woody Guthrie (David Carradine) with strong period detail and Oscar-winning photography by Haskell Wexler. In the eighties, however, Ashby's *Second Hand Hearts* (1981), *Lookin' to Get Out* (1982), and *The Slugger's Wife* (1985) arrived and vanished with little notice, and *Let's Spend the Night Together* (1983), a concert film based on three separate performances from the Rolling Stones' 1981 tour, attracted only cursory interest. Ashby's latest film is *8 Million Ways to Die* (1986), with Jeff Bridges and Rosanna Arquette.

★

RICHARD ATTENBOROUGH (born 1923)   After more than twenty-five years as a solidly dependable British actor, Sir Richard Attenborough made his debut as a director with *Oh! What a Lovely War!* (1969), which demonstrated the qualities that appeared in his later films: an ability to orchestrate sequences of enormous scope and great skill in keeping his actors from being overwhelmed by that scope. *Oh! What a Lovely War!* dealt with the lunacy of war in a scathingly funny and often moving satire that combined sketches, vignettes, and songs. After directing *Young Winston* (1972), a rather stodgy film on the early years of Winston Churchill, Attenborough returned to the military scene with a different kind of war movie: an

impressively staged story of a bungled campaign during World War II, *A Bridge Too Far* (1977) merited far greater critical approval. (Many critics seem to react with knee-jerk disapproval of any film with a star-filled cast.) Attenborough's 1982 *Gandhi* received widespread critical and popular praise and an Academy Award for its striking production values, his masterly staging of epic-sized highlights, and an astonishingly lifelike performance by Ben Kingsley as the Indian leader.

Attenborough's film version of the classic Broadway musical *A Chorus Line* (1985) was as good as one could expect considering the built-in difficulties that had confounded many well-known filmmakers, especially the lack of a central plot, or, for that matter, any plot in the usual sense. Attenborough concentrated on the experiences—poignant, funny, or bitter—of the chorus dancers, and allowed their dazzling footwork to make the point about talent and dedication in the theater. The result was a superior musical.

★

JOHN G. AVILDSEN (born 1937)   After working at various jobs, mainly as an assistant director, John Avildsen attracted attention with one of the early films he directed, a grim, rather overheated drama about a hard-hat bigot named *Joe* (1970). He also directed Jack Lemmon in an Oscar-winning performance as an anguished businessman in *Save the Tiger* (1973). Then came rousing success with his production of *Rocky* (1976), a boxing film that craftily gave a new sheen to the old familiar clichés.

Craig's Wife: DOROTHY ARZNER *(Columbia, 1936). Alma Kruger (left) gets a chilly reception from Rosalind Russell. Russell gave a surprisingly believable performance in Arzner's adaptation of George Kelly's play about an icy perfectionist who wrecks her marriage.*

Audiences cheered as underdog Sylvester Stallone, a limited actor who had written the screenplay as his own starring vehicle, knocked his opponent into insensibility in the ring. Rocky Balboa, of course, has since become an industry in himself as he keeps rising, phoenix-like, to repeated victories.

Avildsen's later films have been uneven, reaching a true low point with a painfully unfunny screen version of Thomas Berger's novel *Neighbors* (1982), with John Belushi sadly miscast in his last role as a meek suburbanite set upon by weird neighbors. However, Avildsen had a hit with *The Karate Kid* (1984), another entry in the "underdog" series pioneered by *Rocky*.

ABOVE   Rocky: JOHN G. AVILDSEN *(United Artists, 1976). Battling his way to the top, fighter Rocky Balboa (Sylvester Stallone) gets support from his manager, Mickey (Burgess Meredith). The movie cleverly reshaped the old boxing film subgenre for contemporary audiences, winning an Academy Award in the process. Avildsen also won an Oscar and a Directors Guild of America Award for his direction.*

OPPOSITE, ABOVE   Gandhi: RICHARD ATTENBOROUGH *(Columbia, 1982). Gandhi (Ben Kingsley, center) moves serenely among his adoring admirers. Attenborough managed the staggering logistics of the production with admirable skill.*

OPPOSITE, BELOW   Reds: WARREN BEATTY *(Paramount, 1981). Diane Keaton and Warren Beatty played Louise Bryant and John Reed, radical-minded lovers who are swept up in the Russian Revolution. Beatty received an Oscar and a Directors Guild Award for his direction.*

★

LLOYD BACON (1890–1955)   Lloyd Bacon might well qualify for the role of the Forgotten Director. At Warners he was the director of record on *42nd Street* (1933), *Footlight Parade* (1933), *Wonder Bar* (1934), and *Gold Diggers of 1937* (1936), but most people associate these movies with the eye-popping kaleidoscopic visions of their dance director, Busby Berkeley. Yet Bacon handled the tough, slangy dialogue with the ease of a veteran and a skill that Berkeley seemed unable to muster in his solo films as director. Bacon was extraordinarily prolific: over a period of fifteen years, he turned out well over fifty films for the studio, most of them brisk, solidly entertaining movies that reflected his years of learning comedy techniques as an indefatigable foil to Charlie Chaplin and a director of comedy shorts for Mack Sennett.

In addition to the musical extravaganzas, his movies included *The Singing Fool* (1928), Warners's first all-dialogue production, a cluster of films starring James Cagney at his feisty, rambunctious best, the amusing gangster comedy *A Slight Case of Murder* (1938), and that sentimental paean to football's great coach, *Knute Rockne—All American* (1940). One of Bacon's best thirties films was *Marked Woman* (1937), a hard-as-nails melodrama about dance-hall "hostesses."

In the forties Bacon moved to Fox, where he turned

out light musicals and comedies of no special distinction (*I Wonder Who's Kissing Her Now*, 1947; *Mother Is a Freshman*, 1949). Comedy remained his special forte, and he demonstrated his knack at handling broad slapstick with two Lucille Ball comedies for Columbia, *Miss Grant Takes Richmond* (1949) and *The Fuller Brush Girl* (1950). Bacon's films made up in pace and vigor what they lacked in style.

★

JOHN BADHAM (born 1939)　Born in England and raised in Alabama, John Badham gradually worked his way up to become associate producer to Steven Spielberg. He directed for television, then turned to feature films with the comedy *The Bingo Long Traveling All-Star and Motor Kings* (1976), about a black baseball team in 1939. His second film, *Saturday Night Fever* (1977), was a huge success, owing more to John Travolta's charismatic performance as a high-stepping teen-ager and to the music and dancing than to Badham's direction. His other movies have been a mixed bag—*Dracula* (1979) was a highfalutin remake of the Bram Stoker novel, with a lounge-lizard vampire in Frank Langella, but *Blue Thunder* (1983) and

WarGames (1983) were enjoyable films, most likely to please bright teen-agers who would appreciate the far-fetched plots and elaborate gadgetry. He contributed *American Flyer* (1985) to the victory-against-all-odds sub-genre (sports division). Most recently, Badham directed *Short Circuit* (1986), with Steve Guttenberg and Ally Sheedy.

★

WARREN BEATTY (born 1937)　A leading film actor since 1961, Warren Beatty turned director in 1978 with *Heaven Can Wait*, a likable remake of Alexander Hall's *Here Comes Mr. Jordan* (1941). He won an Oscar nomination for his direction (shared with Buck Henry) and for his performance as a football player prematurely sent to heaven. Three years later, Beatty directed a vastly more ambitious movie, *Reds* (1981). A lavish and expertly staged epic, the film focused on John Reed (Beatty) and his deeply committed involvement with Communism, the Russian Revolution, and a free-spirited woman named Louise Bryant (Diane Keaton). The screenplay (by Beatty and Trevor Griffiths) delineated the turbulent historical events that shaped the lives of Reed and Bryant, as well as the smaller, more intimate events that also determined their fates. As an interesting linking device, the film used the testimony of actual witnesses to the events, including such eminent persons as Henry Miller, Rebecca West, and Will Durant, as well as many others less well known. On the whole, the production was impressive and fascinating, although also somewhat unwieldy and surprisingly uninvolving. *Reds* won Oscars for Beatty (for his direction), for Maureen Stapleton (as Emma Goldman), and for Vittorio Storaro for his superb cinematography.

ABOVE, RIGHT　Kramer vs. Kramer: ROBERT BENTON *(Columbia, 1979). Dustin Hoffman impresses his young son (Justin Henry) with his office. The film offered a perceptive look at the subject of child custody and divorce.* ABOVE, LEFT　*Star Dustin Hoffman (left), director-writer Robert Benton (right), and producer Stanley Jaffe converse on the set during the filming. Hoffman and Benton both received Oscars for their work, as did the film itself; Benton also won the Directors Guild Award.*
OPPOSITE　Footlight Parade: LLOYD BACON *(Warner Bros., 1933). This eye-popping production number to "By a Waterfall," staged by Busby Berkeley, climaxed a lively backstage musical. Bacon kept James Cagney and the Warners team of players moving briskly through their paces.*

★

ROBERT BENTON (born 1932) In 1972, Robert Benton added directing to his writing credits *(Bonnie and Clyde, What's Up, Doc?)* with the Western *Bad Company;* to date, the results have revealed an ability to re-create a particular milieu and a smoothly professional visual style that seldom calls undue attention to itself. In the seventies, he went from *The Late Show* (1977), a clever and surprisingly violent crime thriller saturated with offbeat comedy (the stars were Art Carney and Lily Tomlin, who pointedly updated the thirties convention of the private eye and his too-helpful helpmate), to the hugely successful *Kramer vs. Kramer* (1979), an honestly affecting drama about the problems of divorce and child custody, for which Dustin Hoffman received an Oscar as a father desperately trying to cope with his new status as a single parent. The film itself also won, as did Benton, for his direction and his screenplay, and Meryl Streep, for her performance as Hoffman's ex-wife. After making a minor Hitchcockian thriller entitled *Still of the Night* (1982), Benton received a second Oscar (as did his star, Sally Field) for *Places in the Heart* (1984), a deeply felt movie about a struggling, tenacious farm woman in Depression Texas. Benton's direction and screenplay vividly evoked a sense of time and place (perhaps a bit too prettified), and Field received unusually fine support from Danny Glover and John Malkovich.

★

BRUCE BERESFORD (born 1940) Australian director Bruce Beresford established his reputation in America with *Breaker Morant* (1980), a searing drama involving the trumped-up trial of three Australian officers during the Boer War. The movie resembled Stanley Kubrick's

ABOVE Places in the Heart: ROBERT BENTON *(Tri-Star, 1984). Sally Field starred as Edna Garvey, a woman struggling to keep her farm and family together during the Depression years. Benton's sturdy Academy Award–winning direction bolstered this affecting view of a bleak period in America's past.*
BELOW The Emerald Forest: JOHN BOORMAN *(Embassy, 1985). Charley Boorman (left), the director's son, played a boy who is kidnapped by natives in the Amazon jungle and grows up to become a loyal member of the tribe. The film's stunning photography partly compensated for its rambling story.*
OPPOSITE, ABOVE Tender Mercies: BRUCE BERESFORD *(Universal/AFD, 1983). Troubled, down-on-his-luck country singer Robert Duvall plays his guitar for young Allan Hubbard. Australian director Beresford succeeded admirably in capturing the film's strictly American ambiance.*
OPPOSITE, BELOW Gold Diggers of 1935: BUSBY BERKELEY *(First National, 1935). Berkeley's extravagant musical number "The Words Are in My Heart" involved fifty-six chorus girls in white evening gowns seated at fifty-six white baby-grand pianos. Berkeley moved the pianos in rhythm to the music by placing a small man dressed in black under each piano and having him follow black tape markings on the shiny black floor.*

Paths of Glory (1957) in its subject matter and theme but was actually more incisive and controlled. Earlier, Beresford had won mostly local attention with his ribald comedy *The Adventures of Barry McKenzie* (1972) after years of producing, and in many cases directing, photographing, and editing, numerous shorts for the British Film Institute. Other of his Australian films include *Don's Party* (1976), *The Getting of Wisdom* (1977), and *Puberty Blues*

(1981). In 1983, Beresford directed his first American film, *Tender Mercies*, a small but moving Oscar-winning story (by Horton Foote) about a has-been country singer (Robert Duvall) who puts his life back together after falling in love with a young Texas widow (Tess Harper). Duvall won an Academy Award for his performance as the introspective singer, effectively using silences and facial expressions to convey his submerged feelings. Hopefully, the disaster of Beresford's elaborate production of *King David* (1985) will be offset by his film adaptation of Beth Henley's play *Crimes of the Heart* (1986), with stellar actresses Jessica Lange, Diane Keaton, and Sissy Spacek.

★

BUSBY BERKELEY (1895–1976)   Busby Berkeley's legendary status as the dance director who revolutionized the film musical with his dazzling, kaleidoscopic numbers has been fully recorded elsewhere. His audacious, inventive use of the camera to create startling effects has never been duplicated. As a director fully in charge of a

film, Berkeley was less successful. His musical movies during his last years at Warners seemed tired and skimpy. Although *Gold Diggers of 1935* (1935) contained his greatest number, "The Lullaby of Broadway," the story element lagged even more than usual under his direction. His last movie before leaving Warners, *They Made Me a Criminal* (1939), was a routine remake of *The Life of Jimmy Dolan* (1933), with John Garfield as a boxer who believes he has killed his opponent in the ring.

When Berkeley went to MGM, he directed three of the studio's popular, breezy musicals costarring Judy Garland and Mickey Rooney (*Babes in Arms*, 1939; *Strike Up the Band*, 1940; *Babes on Broadway*, 1941), and he launched Gene Kelly's career with *For Me and My Gal* (1942). The following year, for Fox, he directed *The Gang's All Here* (1943), a gaudy musical and Berkeley's first color film, in which he indulged every whim with an explosion of photographic effects and gimmicks. After a long and anguished period, which included a nervous breakdown, Berkeley returned to Warners in 1948 to supervise the musical numbers in Doris Day's first film, *Romance on the High Seas*. His last movie was a lightweight, agreeable musical for MGM, *Take Me Out to the Ball Game* (1949), although he later directed musical numbers for such films as *Small Town Girl* and *Easy to Love* (both 1953). Interest in his career revived in the late sixties, climaxed by his association with a 1970 stage revival of *No, No, Nanette*, which put his former star Ruby Keeler back into her tap shoes.

★

CURTIS (KURT) BERNHARDT (1899–1981) Busily engaged in German theater and films in the late twenties and early thirties (he directed UFA's first sound film), Curtis Bernhardt immigrated to France when the Nazis rose to power. After directing films there for six years, he came to Hollywood in 1940, where he made his home at Warner Bros. for most of the decade. His films for the studio included a number of hard-breathing "weepers" for female stars (*My Reputation*, 1946, with Barbara Stanwyck; *A Stolen Life*, 1946, with Bette Davis; *Possessed*, 1947, with Joan Crawford). No other studio managed to endow this subgenre with the high degree of polish and professionalism that Warners attained in the forties, helped by directors like Bernhardt, writers like Casey Robinson and Catherine Turney, and composers like Max Steiner, who enveloped the sudsy stories in his highly emphatic music.

At MGM in the late forties and fifties, Bernhardt occasionally continued to dramatize the emotional upheavals of women (*Interrupted Melody*, 1955, with Eleanor Parker; *Gaby*, 1956, a remake of *Waterloo Bridge*, with Leslie Caron). He also handled more lighthearted material, such as an ornate but lifeless new version of *The Merry Widow* (1952), with Lana Turner, and a swashbuckling adventure film, *Beau Brummell* (1954), with Stewart Granger and Elizabeth Taylor. For RKO he directed, among several films, a sentimental, over-the-years drama called *The Blue Veil* (1951), starring Jane Wyman as one of those sacrificial women—here a beloved nursemaid—Hollywood loves to extol.

★

BUDD BOETTICHER (born 1916) Budd Boetticher's reputation rests on the series of modestly budgeted, tightly structured, pictorially striking Westerns he made between 1956 and 1960. Usually produced by Harry Joe Brown, written by Boetticher and Burt Kennedy, and starring Randolph Scott, whose craggy visage and taciturn manner were in the tradition of William S. Hart, these films won an enthusiastic following even among critics not especially favorable to the genre. The titles often set the mood of isolation in a hostile land: *The Tall T* (1957), *Buchanan Rides Alone* (1958), *Ride Lonesome* (1959), and so on. At a time when "adult" Westerns were flooding the screens, these films stood out by virtue of restoring the traditional concept of a clear moral order—good versus evil, honor versus disgrace.

Boetticher's life before and after this Western cycle

was as eventful as any of his films. In his early years he had been a professional matador in Mexico, which ultimately led to his directing two films about bullfighting, *The Bullfighter and the Lady* (1951) and *The Magnificent Matador* (1955). In 1960, Boetticher left for Mexico to film a documentary about his friend, the matador Carlos Arruza. He filmed over many years, finally completing it in 1967, after Arruza was killed in an automobile accident. During this period, Boetticher suffered a severe mental and physical collapse. When *Arruza* was released in 1972, the *New York Times* critic called it "a magnificent documentary" that "may belong among the last great examples of classical filmmaking." Boetticher's last Western, *A Time for Dying*, was completed in 1969 but released in 1971 after the death of its producer and star, Audie Murphy.

★

PETER BOGDANOVICH (born 1939) The question, of course, has been asked many times: Why did Peter Bogdanovich, one of the "hottest" young directors of the early seventies, lose his way only a few years later in the treacherous maze of movie-making? *The Last Picture Show* (1971), his most successful film, clearly showed that he had a basic grasp of cinematic techniques and, more important, that he could handle a large cast of familiar and unfamiliar players with admirable skill. Then along came such films as *At Long Last Love* (1975) and *Nickelodeon* (1976), and critics shook their heads in bewilderment, while audiences stayed away in droves. Only now, in the eighties, has Bogdanovich begun to regain his former footing.

A dedicated film and theater buff who had worked as an actor, director, and writer, Bogdanovich was given his first chance by producer-director Roger Corman, who had helped such other aspiring directors as Martin Scorsese and Francis Coppola. Under Corman's auspices, Bogdanovich was assigned to direct a low-budget thriller called *Targets* (1968), but under unusual terms: he had to complete the film in two weeks, using Boris Karloff for only two days, and incorporating footage from Karloff's 1963 movie *The Terror*. *Targets* proved to be an effective little melodrama concerning a clean-cut young husband and father (Tim O'Kelly) who suddenly goes berserk with a rifle and is ultimately dispatched by a horror film star (Karloff, playing himself) at a drive-in movie theater showing *The Terror*. The film had a good Hitchcockian sense of the evil that can lurk in everyday surroundings, and although few people saw it, it attracted some strong reviews.

Then came *The Last Picture Show*. Filmed in black-and-white, it offered an evocative view of life in a small Texas town in the early fifties, when boredom, restlessness, and economic decline were conspiring to bring about the town's inevitable demise, symbolized by the closing of the town's tiny movie theater. Set against a background of gray landscapes, shabby stores, and desolate prairie streets, the movie, written by Bogdanovich and Larry McMurtry (from McMurtry's novel) focused mainly on the misadventures (mainly sexual) of two aimless high school seniors, finding a second theme in the frustrations of the town's older citizens. Bogdanovich assembled a cast of promising young actors (Jeff Bridges, Timothy Bottoms, Cybill Shepherd), and he drew exceptionally fine performances from the more seasoned performers, Ben Johnson, Cloris Leachman (both Oscar winners), and Ellen Burstyn. *The Last Picture Show* received enthusiastic reviews and numerous other Oscar nominations, including one for Best Picture.

Bogdanovich continued his winning streak with *What's Up, Doc?* (1972), a frenetic, often funny, and immensely popular screwball comedy loosely modeled after Howard Hawks's *Bringing Up Baby*, and *Paper Moon* (1973), an engaging comedy set in the Depression thirties. The film's story (the adventures of a wily con man and his even wilier little companion), its rambling, episodic style, and its black-and-white photography were

The Last Picture Show: PETER BOGDANOVICH (*Columbia, 1971*). *In a rage, Duane Jackson (Jeff Bridges) has just struck his best friend, Sonny Crawford (Timothy Bottoms). Bogdanovich's compassionate, finely wrought film centered on life in a dying Texas town in the fifties.*

all intended to evoke the sort of homespun entertainment that moviegoers favored in the thirties. Ryan O'Neal and his daughter Tatum costarred, with young Tatum winning an Academy Award as Best Supporting Actress for her performance as the resourceful little schemer.

Bogdanovich's next film, *Daisy Miller* (1974), was an attractively staged, perfectly respectable, but rather dry adaptation of Henry James's novel, marred by Cybill Shepherd's flat performance in the title role. His next two films, however, were dismal failures with both critics and audiences. *At Long Last Love* (1975), an attempt to recapture the charm and insouciance of thirties musicals, offered little aside from its witty Cole Porter score and amusing Art Deco sets. *Nickelodeon* (1976), a long and affectionate tribute to the early days of movie-making, was only sporadically entertaining. In recent years, Bogdanovich has returned intermittently with such films as *Saint Jack* (1979) and *They All Laughed* (1981), which received scant attention. *Mask* (1985), his latest film to date, won largely favorable notices for its touching true story of a facially disfigured teen-ager (Eric Stoltz) and his mother (Cher). Even so, Bogdanovich appears to have a long way to go before he recaptures the heady days of the early seventies. It is a distance he may yet travel in the years ahead.

★

JOHN BOORMAN (born 1933)   After establishing a reputation as a maker of television documentaries, English

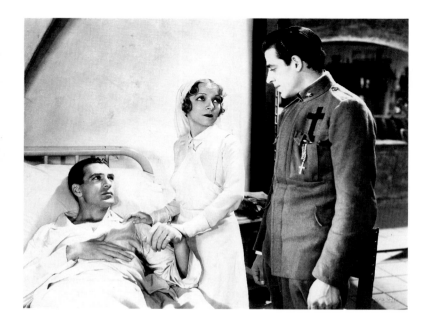

director John Boorman made his film debut with *Having a Wild Weekend* (1965), a pale imitation of the Beatles' *A Hard Day's Night* that substituted the Dave Clark Five for the Fabulous Four. He then came to the United States to direct two films starring Lee Marvin, *Point Blank* (1967) and *Hell in the Pacific* (1968). *Point Blank,* a grim, violent gangster melodrama, drew many admiring notices for its driving pace and spectacular camerawork. Boorman's greatest success came in 1972 with *Deliverance,* an unrelenting film version of James Dickey's harrowing cautionary novel about a group of civilized men who are forced to confront primitive evil during a weekend canoe trip.

After the harsh realism of *Deliverance,* Boorman suddenly veered to the realm of fantasy and science fiction, directing Sean Connery in a futuristic melodrama called *Zardoz* (1974) and Richard Burton in *Exorcist II: The Heretic* (1977), a bewildering sequel to William Friedkin's popular 1973 movie. He fared much better in 1981 with *Excalibur,* a lavishly staged and surprisingly mature rendition of the King Arthur legend. His most recent film to date, *The Emerald Forest* (1985), won praise for its visual beauty but, like other Boorman films, it was criticized for its muddled and unsustained narrative, about a man's search for his kidnapped son deep in the Amazon jungle.

★

A director should have some of the qualities of a leader, the ability to make decisions that are right most of the time, and the quality which inspires confidence in those about him. He must have a world of patience and resourcefulness to overcome obstacles without too much deliberation. He must have a lot of cooperation and some luck. There probably aren't many such persons this side of heaven. FRANK BORZAGE, in Joe Bonica, ed., *How Talkies Are Made,* cited in Richard Koszarski, *Hollywood Directors, 1914–1940* (New York: Oxford University Press, 1976), p. 237.

FRANK BORZAGE (1893–1962)   The operative word for Frank Borzage is romance. Of all the major directors who worked at their peak in the thirties, Borzage was the most genuinely romantic, infusing his films with a lyrical glow that set his lovers apart from the harsh world around them. An innovator in the use of soft-focus and gauzy photography, Borzage gave his heroines a gentleness and a vulnerability that eminently suited the screen personalities of such actresses as Janet Gaynor and Margaret Sullavan.

Borzage arrived in Hollywood in 1912 as an aspiring

actor. Within four years he had appeared in a great many movies, first as a villain and then as a leading man. When he began directing, in 1916 or earlier, he tried his hand at routine Westerns and melodramas. With his first major film, *Humoresque* (1920), it became clear that his strength lay in imbuing a sentimental story with genuine warmth and sincerity. Fannie Hurst's tale of a young Jewish violin virtuoso who strays too far from his New York ghetto roots (later remade by Jean Negulesco) was filmed by Borzage with a restraint and finesse that characterized many of his later efforts. Borzage also had a great success with *Secrets* (1924), starring Norma Talmadge as a noble wife and mother. The following year he joined Fox to share major directing credits with John Ford and Raoul Walsh.

With the release of *Seventh Heaven* in 1927, Borzage established his reputation as the screen's foremost romanticist. Audiences were enchanted with the love story of Chico (Charles Farrell), the Parisian sewer worker, and Diane (Janet Gaynor), the abused street waif with whom he shares a ''heavenly'' room. As usual, these Borzage lovers also share adversity, here in the form of World War I, which separates the lovers. Ultimately, a blinded Chico returns to his beloved Diane to renew their near-mystical romance. Without spoken dialogue (there are sound effects and a musical score), the film succeeded in generating a romantic aura that is almost palpable. *Seventh Heaven* won Academy Awards for Borzage and Janet Gaynor and launched Gaynor and Charles Farrell as a popular movie team. (Borzage reunited them the following year in *Street Angel*, to less effect.)

Borzage's penchant for depicting the vicissitudes of young, often married lovers continued throughout the thirties in films that are still fondly remembered. In virtually every instance, the lovers are required to surrender their private dream world to a grim, and sometimes tragic, reality. Borzage's adaptation of Ernest Hemingway's *A Farewell to Arms* (1932), involving the romance of a British nurse (Helen Hayes) and an American (Gary Cooper) serving in the Italian army during World War I, ended with the death of the heroine. *Man's Castle* (1933), one of Borzage's lesser-known but most interesting films, pitted Loretta Young and her shantytown lover (Spencer Tracy) against the bleakness of the Depression. Occasionally, Borzage would permit himself a lighter touch with romance. On one occasion, in *Desire* (1936), he even ventured into the territory usually reserved by Ernst Lubitsch (Lubitsch only produced), offering a sophisticated, smooth-as-cream tale of the affair between an alluring jewel thief (Marlene Dietrich) and an Ameri-

can engineer (Gary Cooper). And in *History Is Made at Night* (1937), he directed one of his oddest movies of the period: an amalgam of romantic comedy and melodrama that starred Jean Arthur as a wife fleeing from a jealous husband into the arms of a Parisian headwaiter (Charles Boyer). Both films benefited from the glistening visual style that usually permeated Borzage's efforts.

Borzage's idealism—lovers conquering adversity against heavy odds, and sometimes even beyond death itself—sometimes spilled over into a kind of woozy mysticism, a belief that a vague otherworldliness often guided men's actions. When overstressed, this strain in his films resulted in his least satisfactory work. In *Green Light* (1937), involving the tribulations of an idealistic doctor (Errol Flynn), he tried to translate Lloyd C. Douglas's philosophy about man's ultimate destiny into film, with scant success. In *Strange Cargo* (1940), he hinted strongly that the guiding spirit among a group of desperate escaped convicts was none other than Jesus Christ reincarnated. The combination of melodrama and religiosity did not work in the film's favor.

Two of Borzage's best films of the period starred Mar-

ABOVE   The Mortal Storm: FRANK BORZAGE (MGM, 1940). *A victim of Nazi persecution, Freya (Margaret Sullavan) expires in the arms of her beloved Martin (James Stewart). Although Borzage's drama about the early rise of fascism suffered from naiveté and evasiveness, many of the scenes were moving and effective.*
OPPOSITE   A Farewell to Arms: FRANK BORZAGE (Paramount, 1932). *The priest (Jack La Rue) visits Lt. Frederic Henry (Gary Cooper) in the army hospital, with nurse Catherine Barkley (Helen Hayes) in attendance. Borzage infused his version of Ernest Hemingway's novel with a romantic glow, focusing more on the tragic affair of Cooper and Hayes than on the war action surrounding them.*

garet Sullavan, whose inimitably throaty voice and poignant air made her the ideal Borzage heroine. In *Three Comrades* (1938), Erich Maria Remarque's story of the bitter aftermath of World War I in Germany was somewhat diluted to accommodate the ill-fated romance of Pat (Sullavan) and Erich (Robert Taylor). Scenes of violence and upheaval were overshadowed by the tender liaisons of the couple, ending with Pat's death from tuberculosis (movingly played by Sullavan) in Erich's arms. The actress also came to a sad end in Borzage's adaptation of Phyllis Bottome's novel *The Mortal Storm* (1940). Here she played Freya, the daughter of a Jewish family destroyed by fascism in the early years of Hitler's rise to power. The film is overstated and simplistic in the style of the period, and its evasiveness (using "non-Aryan" instead of "Jew") is not to its credit, but Borzage managed scenes of power and beauty, such as the mock wedding of Freya and Martin (James Stewart), the young man she loves, before they flee the country. Freya's demise, just after they cross the border to safety, closes an affecting film.

For whatever reasons, the quality of Borzage's films fell off markedly in the forties. His sentimental romances (*Smilin' Through*, 1941; *Till We Meet Again*, 1944) seemed faded, dispirited, anachronistic. Nor could Borzage bring much vitality to *Stage Door Canteen* (1943), another of the all-star, self-congratulatory tributes the people of show business felt compelled to make to themselves in wartime. Only *Moonrise* (1949), a somber drama about a young Southerner (Dane Clark) fleeing from a murder he was goaded into committing, came close to matching

the quality of his earlier work, although it was ultimately submerged in murkiness. For his last film, *The Big Fisherman* (1959), Borzage returned to the work of one of his favorite authors, Lloyd C. Douglas, for a wide-screen Biblical drama.

Borzage's romantic spirit informed and pervaded his best films. If this spirit, on occasion, teetered dangerously close to the edge of blatant sentimentality, it rarely toppled over. The reason is clear; Borzage believed in his star-crossed lovers, and this belief, carried over in the performances he drew from his stars, made audience surrender not only probable but inevitable.

★

JOHN BRAHM (1893–1982)   Born in Hamburg, the son of a well-known stage actor, John Brahm was a stage director in Europe and then an editor, screenwriter, and production supervisor in London before directing his first film, a remake of *Broken Blossoms* (1936), which starred Emlyn Williams and Brahm's wife, Dolly Haas. In Hollywood from 1937, Brahm directed many films for nearly twenty years, his best being two suspenseful thrillers with Laird Cregar, *The Lodger* (1944) and *Hangover Square* (1945). In both films, under Brahm's firm direction, Cregar played stalking killers with the sort of panache that made him a popular villain of the forties. During the same period Brahm, to give equal time to the ladies, directed two movies about dangerously destructive women, *Guest in the House* (1944) and *The Locket* (1946). In 1956, he moved to television.

★

HERBERT BRENON (1880–1958)   This Dublin-born director made his debut in 1912 and was soon acclaimed as a major figure. He directed Australian swimming star Annette Kellerman in her well-regarded debut film, *Neptune's Daughter* (1914), and throughout the twenties, he worked on scores of films with sizable budgets and leading players. Brenon was adept at many kinds of films; his movies range from airborne fantasy (*Peter Pan*, 1924, with Betty Bronson) to down-to-earth drama (*Sorrell and Son*, 1927), from rousing adventure (the first *Beau Geste*, 1926) to tragic romance (*Laugh, Clown, Laugh*, 1928, with Lon Chaney as a lovelorn, self-sacrificing clown). One of his favorite films, *War Brides* (1916), introduced the distinguished actress Alla Nazimova to films in an adaptation and extension of the playlet with which she had toured vaudeville. Apparently a testy and argumentative man, Brenon voiced great skepticism about the potential of sound, and his talking films were not well

★

JAMES L. BROOKS (born 1940)   James Brooks scored a major and impressive success with his first effort as a director, *Terms of Endearment* (1983). The movie was a bit too long, but its over-the-years story of the scratchy, complex relationship between a mother (Shirley MacLaine) and daughter (Debra Winger) managed to combine comedy and tragedy in felicitous proportions without losing its footing. Shirley MacLaine won an Oscar for her sterling performance as the impossible mother, and so did the film, Brooks (as director and author of the screenplay), and Jack Nicholson (Best Supporting Actor for his performance as MacLaine's neighbor). Brooks's previous credits were as a successful television writer ("The Mary Tyler Moore Show," "Taxi") and as the author of the diverting screenplay (from Dan Wakefield's novel) of the Burt Reynolds–Jill Clayburgh comedy, *Starting Over* (1979).

★

MEL BROOKS (born 1926)   A leading comedy writer for television, especially for the legendary "Your Show of Shows" with Sid Caesar, Mel Brooks brought his special brand of undisciplined and lunatic humor to films in 1968 with *The Producers*. A frantic farce about a conniving theatrical producer (Zero Mostel, at full throttle), it was an indefinable mixture of satire, burlesque, and "Borscht Belt" humor, climaxed by a riotous stage musical called *Springtime for Hitler*. Brooks repeated the pattern throughout the seventies, with diminishing returns. *Blazing Saddles* (1973) and *Young Frankenstein* (1974), the best of the lot, spoofed familiar movie genres (Westerns and horror films) with a nonstop barrage of

received. In 1934 he went to England, where he continued to direct until 1940.

★

JAMES BRIDGES (born 1936)   An actor and writer in all the performing media, James Bridges directed his first feature, *The Baby Maker*, in 1970. His film about law students, *The Paper Chase* (1973), won strong reviews and an Academy Award for John Houseman, who played the overbearing Professor Kingsfield (and has continued to play him, with variations, ever since). Bridges was even more successful with the topical thriller *The China Syndrome* (1979), which involved Jane Fonda, Jack Lemmon, and Michael Douglas in a suspenseful story about a nuclear accident. (The combined nervous energy generated by the three leads probably could have fueled its own nuclear plant.) *Urban Cowboy* (1980), a tangy story about a young "macho" man and his life in blue-collar Texas, gave John Travolta one of his better roles. Four years later, although the elements seemed right, Travolta was unable to rescue *Perfect* (1985), Bridges's romantic comedy about the fitness industry.

ABOVE   Terms of Endearment: JAMES L. BROOKS (*Paramount, 1983*). *Shirley MacLaine and Jack Nicholson enjoy a quirky romance in this perceptive, affecting comedy-drama that won Brooks both the Oscar and the Directors Guild Award.*

OPPOSITE   Hangover Square: JOHN BRAHM (*Fox, 1945*). *Laird Cregar, a homicidal musician, is fascinated by music hall singer Linda Darnell. Brahm's atmospheric thriller contained Cregar's last performance.*

RIGHT   Young Frankenstein: MEL BROOKS (*Fox, 1974*). *Young Dr. Frankenstein (Gene Wilder) worships at the feet of his haughty fiancée, Elizabeth (Madeline Kahn). Brooks's lunatic farce parodied the popular horror films of the thirties and forties.*

jokes that were funny, tasteless, and both funny *and* tasteless. The material was broader than two barn doors, but Brooks used actors (Gene Wilder, Madeline Kahn, Marty Feldman, Cloris Leachman) who knew how to play it.

In 1976, Brooks tried his hand at turning out a silent movie, appropriately called *Silent Movie*, that worked only intermittently. He was more successful, at least commercially, with *High Anxiety* (1977), a sendup of Alfred Hitchcock that succeeded only in demonstrating that Brooks had a superficial knowledge of Hitchcock's

style and that he recognized the key scenes in the master director's body of work. His 1981 film, *History of the World, Part I*, brought together a cluster of comedians in a quick survey of historical events that earned very few laughs. Its scattershot humor, combining ethnic gags, bathroom gags, snips of parody, and gobs of burlesque, made for an unsavory stew. Brooks has since acted in but not directed a remake of Ernst Lubitsch's *To Be or Not to Be* (1983).

★

RICHARD BROOKS (born 1912)   Richard Brooks wrote and directed his first feature film (a middling melodrama called *Crisis*) in 1950 after working for years in radio and then in films as a writer. (He also wrote several novels, including *The Brick Foxhole*, which was the basis for Edward Dmytryk's *Crossfire*.) Five years later, after some routine movies, he finally displayed a hectic, muscular style in *The Blackboard Jungle* (1955), a forceful drama based on Evan Hunter's novel about violence in New York City's schools. As a writer-director, Brooks turned

---

ABOVE   Cat on a Hot Tin Roof: RICHARD BROOKS *(MGM, 1958). A frustrated Maggie (Elizabeth Taylor) finds herself scorned by her husband, Brick (Paul Newman). Brooks's film version of Tennessee Williams's play obscured Brick's homosexual attachment to his late friend, leaving his rejection of the ravishing Maggie all the more unfathomable.*
OPPOSITE   The Yearling: CLARENCE BROWN *(MGM, 1946). The Baxter family, Ma (Jane Wyman), Penny (Gregory Peck), and son Jody (Claude Jarman, Jr.), work together on the family harvest. Brown's adaptation of Marjorie Kinnan Rawlings's classic novel was saturated with his deep affection for American rural life.*

out some supercharged films laced with vigorous action (*The Professionals*, 1966, a rousing Western version of Homer's *Iliad*, is the best example); unfortunately, he often reduced more complex material to the same melodramatic level. Thus, his versions of classic novels (*The Brothers Karamazov*, 1958; *Elmer Gantry*, 1960; *Lord Jim*, 1965) are superficial and unsatisfying despite the strenuous effort and expensive production values.

Brooks's two excursions into Tennessee Williams country had mixed results. His glossy production of *Cat on a Hot Tin Roof* (1958) diluted the play's stronger content by barely referring to the central character's homosexuality and giving the movie an unconvincing hopeful ending. But he did get an excellent performance from Elizabeth Taylor as Maggie the Cat. On the other hand, *Sweet Bird of Youth* (1962) was a Southern fried turkey that Brooks could not make more palatable. Brooks's 1967 version of Truman Capote's *In Cold Blood* had flaws, mainly a disconcerting mixture of styles, but its chilling true story of the murder of a Kansas farm family and the pursuit and conviction of the killers still packed a considerable wallop. Most recently Brooks directed *Fever Pitch*

(1985), an overwrought drama about compulsive gambling.

★

CLARENCE BROWN (born 1890)   One of MGM's leading directors for many years, Clarence Brown was known as the man who could handle the changing moods and vagaries of the luminous Greta Garbo. He directed her at her most alluring in seven movies, including *Flesh and the Devil* (1927), *Inspiration* (1931), *Anna Karenina* (1935), and *Conquest* (1937). He also contributed a footnote to film history by directing her first sound film, *Anna Christie* (1930); ("Give me a whiskey, ginger ale on the side. And don't be stingy, baby," were her first spoken words). Many years later he said, "I had a special way with her. I never gave her direction in anything louder than a whisper. We stood around discussing a scene and no one ever knew what we were saying. She liked that" (*Los Angeles Times*, 5 July 1977).

During his busy MGM years, Brown directed other of the studio's leading players in many of their glossiest vehicles, giving the films a pace and a sheen that made the

movie-hungry audiences of the thirties ignore the pulp-ish plots. Clark Gable starred in many of them (*Possessed*, 1931; *Wife vs. Secretary*, 1936; *Idiot's Delight*, 1939), as did Joan Crawford, with whom Brown also had a special rapport. Directing her in such films as *Sadie McKee* (1934) and *The Gorgeous Hussy* (1936), he recalls the "terrific vulnerability" that made him give her the extra security she required on each day's shooting, even to the extent of placing black flats around the set as a screen.

Many of Brown's films affectingly evoked the warmth and sentiment of rural American life, as in *Ah, Wilderness!* (1935), *Of Human Hearts* (1938), *The Human Comedy* (1943), and *The Yearling* (1946). One decidedly offbeat film of Brown's, *Intruder in the Dust* (1949), presented a much darker vision of small-town America with its story of an attempted lynching in a Southern town. But Brown worked more successfully with sentiment, which was pervasive in such popular films as *The White Cliffs of Dover* (1944) and *National Velvet* (1944), the film that established Elizabeth Taylor as a teen-age star. Brown's romanticism and his subtle visual style probably stemmed from his early years as an assistant to director Maurice Tourneur, whose films have a lush, almost dreamlike quality. Brown also directed some notable silent films, including *The Eagle* (1925), with Rudolph Valentino, *The Goose Woman* (1925), and *Kiki* (1926). He retired in 1953.

★

TOD BROWNING (1882–1962)   Tod Browning is best remembered as a master of the macabre, a reputation based on his films with the astonishing Lon Chaney and his two horror classics *Dracula* (1931) and *Freaks* (1932). Browning had worked as one of D. W. Griffith's assistants, as well as an actor, on *Intolerance* before he began directing in 1917. After turning out many ordinary movies, he established his reputation with *The Unholy Three* (1925), a melodrama about a trio of bizarre crooks that starred Chaney as a ventriloquist in drag, a kind of Ms. Edgar Bergen. He continued his fruitful association with Chaney in such films as *The Black Bird* (1926), *The Road to Mandalay* (1926), *The Unknown* (1927), *London after Midnight* (1927), and others. Most of the films gave Chaney the opportunity to indulge his penchant for grotesque makeup, and also allowed Browning to indulge his obsessive fascination with deformed humans and their co-

Dracula: TOD BROWNING *(Universal, 1931). The sinister Count Dracula (Bela Lugosi) leads his latest victim (Helen Chandler) through his cobwebbed castle. Although much of Browning's classic horror film is actually stagebound and static, it has several sequences of chilling power.*

vert sexuality, a fascination that sets him apart from other creators of horror films.

In 1931 Browning created a sensation with his adaptation of Bram Stoker's novel *Dracula*, which had been a successful Broadway play. Its expressionistic sets, its crudely drawn but still chilling atmosphere of lurking evil, and Bela Lugosi's flamboyant performance as the vampire had audiences enthralled. It was *Freaks*, however, that made Browning notorious. One of the most bizarre melodramas ever filmed, it aroused anger and disgust with its tale of a group of revenge-minded circus freaks, played, incidentally, by real freaks, and it was withdrawn from circulation for many years. None of Browning's later films measured up to these two, although *The Devil Doll* (1936) had moments of disturbing power.

★

DAVID BUTLER (1894–1979)   After years of acting in silent films, David Butler began directing in 1927. Over a forty-year career he worked for Fox, Paramount, and Warner Bros., churning out scores of likable, unpretentious, efficiently made comedies and musicals. (He often collaborated on the stories and screenplays.) At Fox he directed demure Janet Gaynor in three of her early sound musicals, the best being *Sunny Side Up* (1929), and he was the favorite director of the immensely talented little Shirley Temple, guiding her through such popular confections as *Bright Eyes* (1934), *The Littlest Rebel* (1935), and *Captain January* (1936). At Warners in the forties and fifties, his forte was the musical, typically a gaudy, entertaining, unremarkable film starring Dennis Morgan

It Happened One Night:
FRANK CAPRA *(Columbia, 1934). Stars Claudette Colbert and Clark Gable on the set with director Capra. Unexpectedly, this delightful movie proved to be a nationwide success, winning many Oscars and starting a trend for comedies about ordinary folk.*

(*Shine On, Harvest Moon*, 1944) or Doris Day (*Lullaby of Broadway*, 1951; *Calamity Jane*, 1953).

★

I lean towards the comedy approach. My whole career has been making films laughing at ourselves (and myself); which is perhaps the reason that all my pictures with one exception (Lost Horizon) *have been about American people. I know Americans better than people of any other country and by knowing them better I think I know what they laugh at and what should be laughed at.* FRANK CAPRA, in *The Book of Hollywood Quotes*, compiled by Gary Herman (London: Omnibus Press, 1979).

FRANK CAPRA (born 1897) Frank Capra extols the common man. Or, more precisely, he extols the uncommon common man, the fundamentally decent and honorable person who, beaten and nearly destroyed by the forces of evil and corruption, can rally his forces (headed by his loyal family and friends) and restore order and serenity to his immediate world. Capra himself has stated the Capra theme, prevalent in all but two of his films: "A simple honest man, driven into a corner by predatory sophisticates can, if he will, reach down into his God-given resources and come up with necessary handfuls of courage, wit, and love to triumph over his environment" (*The Name above the Title*, p. 186). If today this sounds naive and simplistic, we should remember that the sentiment was heartily endorsed by movie audiences of the bleak Depression thirties. We should also remember that it was not only optimism that made Capra the foremost populist director of the time, it was also the warmth and bubbling humor of his stories and screenplays (often contributed by Robert Riskin), the energy and brisk pace of his direction, and the sturdy professionalism of his players, who became a kind of informal stock company. Many years later, when his style was no longer in favor, Capra was wise enough to leave the movie scene. But he left an indelible legacy of memorable and well-loved films in a long career that was justly honored with the AFI Life Achievement Award in 1982.

If Capra's films often clamor with patriotic fervor or reveal an unshakable belief in the American dream, it is unquestionably due, in part, to the director's personal history. Only six when his poor Italian family immigrated to California, Capra managed to get an education (at the California Institute of Technology) before working at various jobs around the country. An early interest in filmmaking led him to menial jobs in the field, and ulti-

mately to working as a gag writer for Mack Sennett's comedy two-reelers. Here he developed the sense of comic pacing that he would later apply to his own films. At Sennett's studio he also helped to develop the elfin, childlike persona of Harry Langdon, directing him in short films and also in his two best feature films, *The Strong Man* (1926) and *Long Pants* (1927). Ironically, it was Langdon's decision to fire Capra that brought him to Columbia, where he not only directed his most durable films but also succeeded in raising the studio from its Poverty Row status.

At Columbia, Capra sharpened his skills by directing a number of serviceable, second-level feature films in various genres, including several that helped to launch the careers of future star actresses such as Jean Harlow (*Platinum Blonde*, 1931) and Barbara Stanwyck (*The Miracle Woman*, 1931). One of his most unusual movies of this early period (and one unlike any he ever made again) was an exotic melodrama with surprising sexual overtones, *The Bitter Tea of General Yen* (1932), concerning a Chinese warlord (Nils Asther) and his beautiful captive (Barbara Stanwyck). However, Capra was much more interested in expressing his sentiments about the social order of the day, and, especially, in reassuring America's beleaguered "little people" about their rightful place in the scheme of things. In *American Madness* (1932) he offered as his protagonist an idealistic bank president (Walter Huston) who loans money on the basis of character rather than assets and nearly lives to regret it. (This film was the first in which Capra deliberately shot scenes at a faster speed than usual to keep viewers engrossed.) The following year Capra had his first (and unexpected) success in some time: a sentimental Damon Runyon comedy called *Lady for a Day* (1933) pleased audiences with its story of an elderly derelict (May Robson) who is transformed into a *grande dame* in order to meet the daughter she has not seen for years.

With his next film, *It Happened One Night* (1934), Capra entered the permanent annals of film history. The story of how this small, unwanted, indifferently received movie (even its stars, Clark Gable and Claudette Colbert, appeared in it reluctantly) became a nationwide triumph and won five Oscars has been often told as a classic case of premature rejection. The fact that it was charmingly written (by Robert Riskin, Capra's favorite scenarist) and played, and that it recognized and appreciated the lives of ordinary Americans who rode in buses and lived in auto courts did not go unnoticed by the ticket-buying public. *It Happened One Night* propelled both Columbia and Frank Capra into the big time. It was also

the first full expression of Capra's extraordinary ability to extract relaxed and unaffected performances from his actors.

Capra now moved into the most triumphant period of his career, making films that dramatized his deeply held faith in the fundamental goodness of the ordinary man and winning vast audiences in the process. The heroes carried different names—Longfellow Deeds, Jeff Smith, or John Doe—but they fit the same basic, eventually predictable pattern: naive, eccentric, and idealistic, they are nearly crushed by greedy lawyers, corrupt politicians, or native fascists, but rise to fight again. Fortunately, Capra diluted the implied sanctimonious preaching with an infusion of good-natured humor, handled with ease and skill by such actors as Gary Cooper, James Stewart, and Jean Arthur. His "Misters" were irresistible: *Mr. Deeds Goes to Town* (1936) was a wry and genial comedy about a "pixilated" greeting-card poet who inherits a fortune, and *Mr. Smith Goes to Washington* (1939), one of Capra's most overtly flag-waving films, starred James Stewart as a starry-eyed young senator who satisfies every viewer's wish-fulfillment fantasy by routing the corrupt and greedy politicians. Both men suffer the slings and arrows of derision and condemnation, but, happily, they end up triumphant and safe in the waiting arms of the enchanting Jean Arthur. (What more could a populist hero want?)

Capra faltered only when he insisted on adapting previously successful material to his patented style; although it won him another Oscar, *You Can't Take It with You* (1938) sacrificed some of the play's inspired nuttiness to sentiment (the movie itself won the Best Picture award). *Meet John Doe* (1941) also marked a slight notch down for Capra; a cautionary tale about the dangers of American fascism, it suffered from too heavy, too insistent a touch as well as a patently unconvincing climax.

Apart from *Lost Horizon* (1937), a lavishly made fantasy based on James Hilton's novel, Capra stayed with contemporary Americana, comfortably and successfully, until World War II. After the war, to which he contributed a series of well-regarded documentaries entitled *Why We Fight*, he returned to this niche with *It's a Wonderful Life* (1946). A perennial holiday favorite, this film had uncharacteristically dark undertones as it related how small-town family man George Bailey (James Stewart) is saved from suicidal despair by his guardian angel (Henry Travers). Undeniably warmhearted and well intentioned, the movie tends to use sentiment like a weapon, beating us not into insensibility but into a mechanical and not truly earned emotional response.

While not among his best, Capra's remaining films until his retirement delivered some pleasures. *State of the Union* (1948) retained much of the verbal dexterity of the Howard Lindsay–Russel Crouse political play; it starred Spencer Tracy and a miscast Katharine Hepburn (in the role intended for Claudette Colbert). Two Bing Crosby features—*Riding High* (1950, a remake of Capra's 1934 *Broadway Bill*) and *Here Comes the Groom* (1951)—were amiable enough diversions. After an eight-year lapse, Capra directed his last two films, both in a more familiar vein. *A Hole in the Head* (1959) starred Frank Sinatra as another free-spirited Capraesque society misfit, while

Pocketful of Miracles (1961) tried unsuccessfully to match his original version, *Lady for a Day*. The times no longer favored Capra's brand of sentiment, and he decided to close out his career.

Frank Capra unquestionably deserves a high place in the pantheon of film directors. Under his careful and loving guidance, his gallery of stumbling but persevering idealists, dreamers, and eccentrics carried on the humanistic tradition, which Capra considered "the one permanent victory of our queer race over cruelty and chaos." There is no doubt that they also marched to a distinctly American beat, but the beat could be invigorating. (Was there ever a more shamelessly heart-stirring climax than that of *Mr. Smith Goes to Washington*?) Capra's pride in his adopted country and his faith in the ordinary man may have an old-fashioned, even anachronistic ring in the cynical eighties, but that ring continues to resonate unmistakably down through the years.

★

JOHN CARPENTER (born 1948)   Like George Lucas, John Carpenter made his first feature, *Dark Star* (1974), by expanding a student short made at the University of Southern California. After assembling some credits as a television and film writer (*Eyes of Laura Mars*, 1978), he enjoyed a huge, unexpected success with his third feature film, *Halloween* (1978), coauthored with Debra Hill. An unnerving horror melodrama with a nice Hitchcockian instinct for jolting the audience with sudden spurts of violence, *Halloween* became the highest-grossing independent film ever made in the United States. Unfortunately, Carpenter's subsequent films were disappointing. *The Fog* (1980), *Escape from New York* (1981), *The Thing* (1982), and *Christine* (1983) had moments of shock and some well-executed special effects, but their relentless attack on the viewer's nerves and sensibility grew monotonous after a while. Happily, Carpenter changed pace in 1984 with *Starman*, a charming and even romantic fantasy about an alien (ingratiatingly played by Jeff Bridges) who takes the form of Karen Allen's late husband.

★

JOHN CASSAVETES (born 1929)   The reactions to John Cassavetes's improvisational style are seldom indifferent. One either admires his attempt to depict the truth about human relationships through a constantly probing camera and unstructured, off-the-cuff dialogue by his actors or one tends to find his films tedious and self-indulgent. Inevitably, there are points to be made on

both sides: on the one hand, working especially with a gifted actress like his wife, Gena Rowlands, Cassavetes's approach can result in stunning insights into his troubled, vulnerable characters; on the other hand, as in *Husbands* (1970), one longs for a swift end to the boisterous carryings-on of his boy-man heroes. Yet Cassavetes remains one of our most original directors.

Cassavetes was a fairly prominent actor in television and films (*Edge of the City*, 1957; *Saddle the Wind*, 1958) when he decided to direct his first feature film, *Shadows*, in 1961. Filmed on 16-millimeter stock at a cost of only forty thousand dollars, this crude, partially improvised drama about an interracial romance was striking enough to command interest from the major studios. When his two studio-made films, *Too Late Blues* (1962) and *A Child*

Gloria: JOHN CASSAVETES *(Columbia, 1980). John Cassavetes on the set. Although more structured and less improvisational than other of his films,* Gloria *still rambled aimlessly, and it never found a consistent tone.*

Is Waiting (1963), failed to take off, he returned to independent filmmaking. With *Faces* (1968) and *Husbands*, Cassavetes developed his improvisational style, which called for his actors to flesh out their characters from their own psyches and improvisational skill rather than from scripted dialogue, which was only used as a springboard to convey emotions. He often used a hand-held camera to bolster the feeling of immediacy. A small group of friends and collaborators, including Peter Falk and Ben Gazzara, joined with Cassavetes to carry out the concept. *Faces* investigated the marriage of a middle-aged suburban couple (Lynn Carlin and John Marley) who separate for a night and sleep with others (Fred Draper and Gena Rowlands), while *Husbands* traced the sometimes painful, sometimes uproarious four-day binge of three married friends (Peter Falk, Ben Gazzara, and John Cassavetes) after the death of a crony.

Cassavetes had a commercial success with *A Woman under the Influence* (1974), which used a fully prepared screenplay. Once again some scenes overstayed their welcome, but Cassavetes managed to carry out several wrenching scenes of a family's disintegration under the burden of the mother and wife's mental illness. Using Cassavetes's freewheeling style to create a many-faceted portrait, Rowlands was extraordinary as this pitiable character (she won an Oscar nomination). Six years later, she won a second nomination for her starring role as a tough, resourceful ex-gun moll in *Gloria* (1980). Even though Cassavetes kept to a straighter narrative line than usual, he could not make the story convincing (Gloria defends a Puerto Rican boy from the gangsters who murdered his family). *Love Streams* (1984) won some strong reviews for its story revolving around an alcoholic, womanizing Hollywood writer (Cassavetes) and his sister (Gena Rowlands). Most recently, Cassavetes directed his first all-out comedy, *Big Trouble* (1985), starring Alan Arkin as an insurance salesman who accidentally becomes involved in criminal activities.

★

GILBERT CATES (born 1934)   Gilbert Cates was a leading television producer and director, as well as a stage director, before he turned to films. His first film, *Rings Around the World* (1967), merely strung together a number of circus acts. His second, a film version of Robert Anderson's play *I Never Sang for My Father* (1970), which Cates had produced for the stage, had considerable merit. Its strong and moving story of a father-son relationship rarely slipped into pretentiousness, and Melvyn Douglas was magnificent—crotchety, exasperating, and vul-

nerable—as the father. It was not a commercial success. Cates's next film was even better, although again it fared only moderately well at the box office. Under Cates's skillful direction, Joanne Woodward gave one of her best performances in *Summer Wishes, Winter Dreams* (1973), playing a troubled wife and mother at midlife crisis. Cates's subsequent films (*One Summer Love*, originally released as *Dragonfly*, 1976; *The Promise*, 1979) continued to deal with personal relationships on a small, intimate scale, but he veered into more commercial areas with the sex comedy *The Last Married Couple in America* (1980) and *Oh, God! Book II* (1980), a sequel to the popular *Oh, God!* (1977).

★

I remain just one thing and one thing only, and that thing is a clown. It places me on a far higher plane than any politician.   CHARLES CHAPLIN, in *The Book of Hollywood Quotes*, compiled by Gary Herman (London: Omnibus Press, 1979), p. 84.

CHARLES CHAPLIN (1889–1977)   At the height of his extraordinary fame, roughly between the years 1915 and 1925, Charles Spencer Chaplin was probably the most

---

ABOVE   I Never Sang for My Father: GILBERT CATES (*Columbia, 1970*). *This often moving drama focused on the tangled love-hate relationship between Gene Hackman and his difficult old father, Melvyn Douglas. Douglas's performance, unclouded by old-age sentiment, won him an Oscar nomination.*
OPPOSITE   Husbands: JOHN CASSAVETES (*Columbia, 1970*). *During their four-day spree, friends Peter Falk, John Cassavetes, and Ben Gazzara come to understand some home truths about their lives. Although far too long and diffuse, the film contained scenes that were funny and revealing.*

familiar and most beloved figure in the world. Whether known as Charlie, Charlot, Carlitos, or the Little Fellow, in America, France, or any other country, his indomitable, resourceful, and compassionate Tramp sparked laughter and affection. On the one hand, the common folk adored his irrepressible vulgarity, his unabashed slapstick, and his comic defiance of authority. His baggy pants and outsize shoes indicated an impoverished state that many people identified with all too well. On the other hand, Charlie also wore a derby and carried a cane; he aspired wistfully to refinement. Intellectuals responded with enthusiasm to the artistic side of Chaplin: the expressive pantomime, the little balletic dances, the delicate balance of sadness and laughter. For many years, at least until the early sound era, Chaplin was regarded as the funniest man alive and the premier comic artist of motion pictures.

Time and the changing winds of opinion have not done much to erode this estimate. There are, and probably always have been, severe criticism of his shortcomings. Critics and biographers have written at length about his excessive sentimentality, his simplistic political and social ideas, the shabbiness of even his later productions, when he could afford to spend more on sets and costumes. The probably futile argument over the relative merits of Chaplin and Buster Keaton continues, with neither side ever scoring a clear victory. Yet one can be certain that films such as *The Gold Rush* and *City Lights* will survive as long as there are people left to laugh at the antics of the dauntless Little Tramp.

Chaplin's rise from a wretched London slum child to international star has often been traced—even by Chaplin himself, in an autobiography that is more discreet than revealing. Step by step, with a resilience and determination as strong as the Tramp's, he evolved from an inconspicuous music hall entertainer into a beloved icon. Starting in 1914 and moving from studio to studio, Chaplin honed his skills behind and in front of the camera, so that by 1917, such films as *Easy Street*, *The Cure*, and *The Immigrant* engendered wide enthusiasm for their beautifully timed gags and sequences. In this group of films, he learned how to break up the improvised comic action into a series of cumulative shots. Only a year later, his first three-reeler, *A Dog's Life* (1918), and his satirical war comedy *Shoulder Arms* (1918) displayed a structural unity, an attention to realistic detail, and a virtually seamless narrative, while *The Kid* (1921), despite its occasional mawkishness, represented Chaplin's finest effort to that date at blending sentiment and comedy.

With *The Gold Rush* (1925), Chaplin reached the apogee of his work in the silent era. Both poignant and riotously funny in its account of the Alaskan adventures of the Lone Prospector, the movie peaked in its least fre-

netic moments, such as the celebrated sequence in which the starving hero must resort to eating his shoe and he consumes it, piece by piece, as if it were the most exquisite delicacy. Clearly, Chaplin needed no spoken words to be eloquent, and when sound arrived, he was in no hurry to join the parade. (He regarded sound "as an addition, not a substitute.") In *City Lights* (1931), his first film to appear after the new technology had replaced the old, he decided to eschew all talk in his tale of the Tramp and the blind girl (Virginia Cherrill) he befriends. The movie worked beautifully as the last pure expression of Chaplin's silent art, mixing his usual exuberant slapstick with such sublime moments as the final lingering close-up on Charlie when, after the girl has regained her sight, she sees her benefactor for the first time.

Although they contain superbly funny sequences, Chaplin's sound films have often been denigrated for their lapses into cloying sentimentality (*The Great Dictator*, 1940), unrelieved misanthropy (*Monsieur Verdoux*, 1947), or shrill political naiveté (*A King in New York*, 1957). One, however, qualifies as a masterpiece, although it is really a silent film with synchronized noises and a gibberish song by Chaplin at the end. For all its occasional misfired gags and heavy touches, *Modern Times* (1936) succeeds in satirizing the dehumanization of man in an industrialized society with inventiveness and visual wit. Few of Chaplin's films offer as many memorable scenes: Charlie nearly destroyed by his factory's bizarre "eating machine," or caught up in the intricate machinery, or, unforgettably, gliding around an empty department store on roller skates.

Many books have analyzed Chaplin's films in close

OPPOSITE, ABOVE The Gold Rush: CHARLES CHAPLIN (*United Artists, 1925*). *Villainous Black Larsen (Tom Murray) orders the Lone Prospector (Charlie Chaplin) into the freezing Klondike night. Looking on is burly Big Jim McKay (Mack Swain). Many critics consider this film to be the summit of Chaplin's achievements in the twenties.*

OPPOSITE, BELOW City Lights: CHARLES CHAPLIN (*Charlie Chaplin/United Artists, 1931*). *The Tramp (Charlie Chaplin) enjoys his position in the home of tippling millionaire Harry Myers (tippling again at the left). Butler Allan Garcia serves him. Chaplin halted production when sound took over, then decided to complete the film as a silent, using only a few moments of gibberish speech and his original musical score.*

RIGHT Modern Times: CHARLES CHAPLIN (*United Artists, 1936*). *Driven to a nervous collapse by the monotony and mechanization of his job, Charlie creates pandemonium in the factory. His comic crackup provided one of the film's many highlights.*

garded as his moral turpitude, Charlie Chaplin finally received the honors long due him. In 1972, at an emotional ceremony, he was presented with a special Academy Award for "the incalculable effect he has had on making motion pictures the art form of this century." And in 1975 he was knighted by Queen Elizabeth. These were gratifying gestures, and yet it is the Little Tramp who endures, forever helpful and hopeful despite all the tribulations, forever ready to confront a bully or comfort a waif. The immortal Tramp continues to banish misery with laughter as he waddles down the weary road of life.

★

MICHAEL CIMINO (born 1943) The vagaries of Hollywood and filmmaking have seldom been dramatized as vividly as with the career to date of Michael Cimino. Starting in 1971 as a writer—he collaborated on the screenplays for *Silent Running* (1972) and *Magnum Force* (1973)—Cimino was given his first major opportunity by his mentor, Clint Eastwood, who assigned him to write and direct a quirky thriller called *Thunderbolt and Lightfoot* (1974). In 1978, he won plaudits with his first major production, *The Deer Hunter*, a searing and provocative film about the impact of the Vietnam War on a group of closely knit Pennsylvania steelworkers. It won five Academy Awards, including one for Cimino. Two years later, he directed *Heaven's Gate* (1980)—a disaster of monumental proportions. A sprawling epic Western focusing on the bitter war between immigrant farmers and ruthless cattlemen in nineteenth-century Wyoming, the movie had some extraordinarily vivid battle scenes and meticulously handled period details, but the chaos surrounding the production (recounted in the book *Final Cut*) resulted in an incoherent narrative with many inexplicable characters. Cimino was singled out as the prime example of the self-indulgent director who, while undeniably talented, was losing untold millions for the beleaguered film industry. Cimino returned in 1985 with *Year of the Dragon*, whose violent story of crime in New York's Chinatown sparked some controversy.

detail, yet much less has been written about his working techniques as a director. Until the sound era, Chaplin worked without a scenario most of the time, improvising ideas with his players and letting them take their course. He would shoot a scene repeatedly, hoping that a long succession of trial runs, alterations, and retakes would produce the effect—and the laughs—he hoped for. Apparently, he was indifferent to the amount of film he expended or the number of times he reshot a scene. He remained in total command, never allowing anyone to come on the set when he was directing. (Part of this secrecy may have been due to his exasperation with the comedians who were imitating him and trying to duplicate his techniques.)

His total absorption in the content of his films seems to have been at the expense of a visual style. Early in his career, once he had decided what the camera could do for him and came to believe that the placing of the camera was the sole basis for cinematic style, he appeared to have had no further interest in changing his techniques or enhancing the *mise en scène* of his movies. Even in his later films, he paid scant attention to the backgrounds; most of his sets are disconcertingly flat and skimpy. *A Woman of Paris* (1923), the one serious drama he directed and in which he played no role, was an exception: its realistic scenes of Paris life indicate that Chaplin could convey a sense of time and place when he was not involved with his own performance before the camera.

In the years before his death, after all the vilification in the press for his political leanings and for what was re-

★

JACK CONWAY (1887–1952) Andrew Sarris dismisses Jack Conway with the remark, "Few of his films are worth mentioning, even in passing" (*The American Cinema*, p. 254). Well, now. Conway may have been swallowed up by the studio system, but a number of his MGM movies have the entertainment value and technical skill to merit much more than a glance. He succeeded in restraining at least some of Wallace Beery's hamminess in *Viva Villa!* (1934), a fictional but vigorous account of the Mexican revolutionary; his comedy *Libeled Lady* (1936)—a merry affair in which Jean Harlow excelled as a girl left too many times at the altar—was one of the best-remembered of the thirties; and, despite all the critical carping over the years, *A Tale of Two Cities* (1935) remains a respectable and often stirring version of the Dickens novel. True, his credits include such clinkers as *Lady of the Tropics* (1939) and *Dragon Seed* (1944, codirected with Harold S. Bucquet), but many other of his numerous MGM movies are expertly made and enjoyable (*A Yank at Oxford*, 1938; *Love Crazy*, 1941), and some of them made good use of the virile presence of Clark Gable (*Too Hot to Handle*, 1938; *Boom Town*, 1940; *Honky Tonk*, 1941). Conway started his career as an actor in 1909, then learned the director's craft as an assistant to D. W. Griffith. His films as a director date from the early teens.

★

You know what it's like to be a director? It's like running in front of a locomotive. If you stop, if you trip, if you make a mistake, you get killed. How can you be creative with that thing behind you? Every day I know it's $8,000 an hour. It forces me to decisions I know will work. I can't afford to take a chance. FRANCIS COPPOLA, interview in *Newsweek*, cited in *Action*, March–April 1975, p. 23.

FRANCIS COPPOLA (born 1939)   Francis Coppola does it all, which is not to say that he always does it well, or economically, or even sensibly. An enormously talented and driven director who also produces and often coauthors his films, Coppola has occasionally succeeded in working within the studio system, as with the two enthusiastically reviewed and widely attended *Godfather* movies. More often, he lavishes time and money on deeply personal projects that have slim commercial prospects. For every gamble that pays off creatively, such as the prodigiously expensive, trouble-plagued war film *Apocalypse Now*, there has been a box-office and critical disaster like *One from the Heart*, or a film like *The Conversation*, which won (and deserved) critical approval but failed to sell tickets. In recent years, with the exception of the bloated enterprise called *The Cotton Club*, he has confined himself to small, intense, and somewhat self-conscious film versions of S. E. Hinton's popular youth novels, *The Outsiders* and *Rumble Fish*.

Born in Detroit, the son of flutist and composer Carmine Coppola, he spent his apprentice years with Roger Corman, working at various jobs until he was given the chance to direct his own film, a gory, low-budget horror movie called *Dementia 13* (1963). After writing several screenplays, Coppola convinced Seven Arts to let him direct *You're a Big Boy Now* (1967), a manic, irreverent, and often disjointed comedy about an innocent young man's determination to experience the joys of sex. (Coppola had already purchased the film rights to the novel and had also written the screenplay.) The movie's generally good reception won him the plum assignment of directing the film version of the long-popular Broadway musical *Finian's Rainbow* (1968). The result, however, was disheartening. The musical's badly dated material, a surprisingly ugly physical production, and some poorly selected leading players overwhelmed the still-charming score. Coppola fared better with *The Rain People* (1969), concerning an unhappy, pregnant housewife (Shirley Knight) who goes "on the road." That same year he founded his own San Francisco–based company, American Zoetrope, with George Lucas as his vice-president.

ABOVE   Libeled Lady: JACK CONWAY (MGM, 1936). *Jean Harlow toys with William Powell, to Spencer Tracy's obvious annoyance. A merry comedy with many bright quips, this movie also boasted MGM's glistening production values and star power (Myrna Loy was the fourth member of the romantic quadrangle).*
OPPOSITE   The Great Dictator: CHARLES CHAPLIN (United Artists, 1940). *The rivalry between Benzini Napaloni (Jack Oakie), dictator of Bacteria, and Adenoid Hynkel (Chaplin), dictator of Tomania, was the springboard for much of the hilarity in this film. Here, Hynkel registers supreme annoyance with his bombastic "friend."*

Coppola stunned critics and audiences with his next film: an elaborately produced and richly textured adaptation of Mario Puzo's best-selling novel *The Godfather* (1972). Coppola's multifaceted portrait of the Corleone crime family, headed by the formidable Vito Corleone (Marlon Brando), brought the gangster film to a new level of intensity and excitement. Scene after scene of explicit violence was skillfully carried out by Coppola, and an exceptional cast that included James Caan, Al Pacino, and Diane Keaton played with conviction. *The Godfather: Part II* (1974) improved on the original: vast in scope and awesomely impressive in execution, it swept both backward and forward in time as it expanded and deepened the story of the Corleone family. The question has persisted as to whether the films romanticize or gloss over the viciousness of crime in America or whether they graphically expose what Hannah Arendt called "the banality of evil." Intention aside, both films received high praise, and both received Academy Awards as Best Picture in their respective years of release.

Between the two *Godfather* films, Coppola managed to complete one of his personal projects, an incisive study of the paranoia induced by wiretapping and surveillance entitled *The Conversation* (1974). Gene Hackman played an amoral wiretapper who finds himself ensnared in his own technological nightmare; the final image of this man, alone in the apartment that he himself has wrecked in search of "bugs," was shattering in its implications.

Coppola next launched his most ambitious undertaking to date, a vast, complex drama that would capture the horror, brutality, and senselessness of the Vietnam War. The many obstacles (by both man and nature) that managed to disrupt and delay the production of *Apocalypse Now* (1979) have been duly recorded, but the film ultimately vindicated Coppola's exhausting efforts, if not its staggering cost of $31 million. Few films have ever conveyed as vividly the terror and disorientation of combat or offered a more demonic vision of war. If there were serious flaws (particularly in the final section involving the monstrous, demented Kurtz, played by Marlon Brando), these were offset by Coppola's magnificent staging of the battle sequences and even his handling of the few quieter moments, such as the water burial of one of the men who has been killed in a skirmish.

Unfortunately, Coppola's films in the eighties have failed to match his achievements in the seventies. His attempt to restore some of the romance, lyricism, and glamour of the film musical as exemplified by Vincente

TOP Apocalypse Now: FRANCIS COPPOLA *(United Artists, 1979). Francis Coppola runs through a scene with Marlon Brando. Brando's appearance toward the end of the film, as the bloated monster Kurtz, came as a distracting coda to Coppola's brilliant and harrowing war drama.*
ABOVE The Conversation: FRANCIS COPPOLA *(Paramount, 1974). In Coppola's critically acclaimed thriller, Gene Hackman gave a devastating performance as a master of surveillance and wire-tapping who becomes the victim of his own expertise.*

Minnelli (with several bows to Federico Fellini) with *One from the Heart* (1982) fell flat; the movie lacked charm and lightness, and the cast was largely uncharismatic. Nor could Coppola find much comfort in the reception of *The Cotton Club* (1984), a musical drama that tried (and failed) to re-create the special ambiance of the era in which the famed black nightclub flourished in Harlem. Coppola's S. E. Hinton youth films of 1983 won some admirers, but *The Outsiders* worked too strenuously at matching the style of Nicholas Ray's *Rebel Without a Cause*, and *Rumble Fish*, reaching for a kind of grandiose lyricism, was covered with arty barnacles.

Coppola's recent track record may have slowed him down, but it has certainly not put him out of the race. (His latest film, *Peggy Sue Got Married*, 1986, stars Kathleen Turner and Nicholas Cage.) He has always been his own man, seeking to make films on his own terms. His stamina, persistence, and, of course, very real gifts in pursuing his craft have carried him through to success in the past. No doubt they will do so again.

★

ROGER CORMAN (born 1926)   A busy, prolific producer-director since the fifties, Roger Corman is best known for the cycle of stylish horror films he created in the sixties. Based largely on the tales of Edgar Allan Poe, these tightly budgeted films made vivid use of color, decor, and special effects to frighten the audience, as opposed to Tod Browning's emphasis on the grotesque nature and implicit evil of his characters. *The Pit and the Pendulum* (1961), *The Masque of the Red Death* (1964), and *The Tomb of Ligeia* (1965) were especially effective examples of Corman's style. Most often he worked with the same people: screenplay by Richard Matheson, photography by Floyd Crosby, and design by Daniel Haller. Many of them starred Vincent Price, whose saturnine manner and mellifluous voice became indelibly identified with this highly popular horror series. Before and after this period, Corman produced and/or directed films in other genres, especially the gangster film (*Machine Gun Kelly*, 1958; *I, Mobster*, 1959; *The St. Valentine's Day Massacre*, 1967). On a more serious note, as a producer he was a valuable mentor to rising young directors such as Francis Coppola and Peter Bogdanovich, whose first films he

The House of Usher: ROGER CORMAN *(American-International, 1960). Mark Damon (right), a visitor to the mysterious house of Usher, receives a personal tour from his brother-in-law-to-be, Vincent Price. The film marked Price's first appearance in a horror film by Corman; he would soon become a mainstay of Corman's Technicolor exercises in terror.*

produced. Later he went into film distribution, importing such films as Ingmar Bergman's *Cries and Whispers* and *Autumn Sonata*.

★

COSTA-GAVRAS (born 1933)   Greek director Costa-Gavras is one of the few directors who has been able to combine strong political commentary with melodramatic action and achieve a degree of commercial acceptance. Although his debut film, *The Sleeping Car Murders* (1966), was a conventional suspense thriller, in 1969 he won international recognition with *Z*, which indicted the Greek junta regime with sledgehammer force and an inventive use of the camera. His subsequent films, including *The Confession* (1970), *State of Siege* (1973), and *Special Section* (1975), had limited appeal, but in 1982, Costa-Gavras scored his greatest success to date with *Missing*, a harrowing political drama about a man's search for his son, who is missing after a violent South American coup d'état. Jack Lemmon gave one of his best performances—edgy, feverish, and totally convincing—as the anguished father.

★

JOHN CROMWELL (1888–1979)   From the swashbuckling adventure of *The Prisoner of Zenda* (1937) to the gritty women's prison drama of *Caged* (1950) is a long movie distance, but John Cromwell traveled it with relative ease. His work as a film director, after a successful stage career as an actor, director, and producer, took him into virtually every kind of film, from emotional family dra-

ma (*The Silver Cord*, 1933; *Since You Went Away*, 1944) to exotic romance (*Algiers*, 1938; *Anna and the King of Siam*, 1946). Romance was probably his long suit—viewers recall Charles Boyer as Pepe Le Moko in *Algiers*, catching his breath at his first vision of Hedy Lamarr (and who could blame him?), or Carole Lombard weathering the tribulations of married life (*Made for Each Other*, 1939, with James Stewart) or an affair with a married man (*In Name Only*, 1939, with Cary Grant). There are moviegoers who still sigh at the memory of *The Enchanted Cottage* (1945), probably recalling Dorothy McGuire's radiance rather than the story's puerility.

Like George Cukor, Cromwell resented being called "a woman's director," but he did very good work with actresses. He permitted Bette Davis to pull out all emotional stops as the vicious Mildred in *Of Human Bondage* (1934) when he might have counseled restraint, and the gamble paid off; she was startling in her intensity. He extracted solid performances not only from good actresses like Davis, Lombard, and Margaret Sullavan (*So*

ABOVE Missing: COSTA-GAVRAS (*Universal*, 1982). *Anguished father Ed Horman (Jack Lemmon) registers fear and despair as he searches for his missing son in a South American country racked by civil war. No specific country was named, but Chile was clearly intended as the locale for this riveting political melodrama.*

OPPOSITE, ABOVE LEFT Heaven's Gate: MICHAEL CIMINO (*United Artists*, 1980). *Couples waltz on the grounds of Harvard University (the scene was actually filmed at Oxford University) during the graduation ceremonies of 1870. This opening sequence, although too long, was beautifully staged; well over three hours later, however, most viewers could discern why this gargantuan Western constituted one of the screen's classic disasters.*

OPPOSITE, ABOVE RIGHT Year of the Dragon: MICHAEL CIMINO (*MGM/ UA*, 1985). *During a massacre in a restaurant, policeman Mickey Rourke tries to keep television reporter Ariane from being hit. Cimino's viscerally exciting melodrama about corruption in New York's Chinatown aroused the ire of many Chinese-Americans.*

OPPOSITE, BELOW Apocalypse Now: FRANCIS COPPOLA (*United Artists*, 1979). *The entourage of the demented Colonel Kurtz awaits the patrol boat that is bringing Captain Willard, whose mission is to "terminate Kurtz's command with extreme prejudice," i.e., assassinate him. Coppola's magnificent war film was a journey into the hell-on-earth of the Vietnam War.* ABOVE *Francis Coppola (bottom center, with beard) directs a scene for this ambitious drama.*

Ends Our Night, 1941) but also from more problematical performers like Jennifer Jones, charming and not too mannered, despite her dislike of her role, in *Since You Went Away*, and Kim Stanley, striking if not very believable as a tormented movie queen in *The Goddess* (1958). On the other hand, he was unable to curb the absurd excesses of Katharine Hepburn as the world's unlikeliest hillbilly in *Spitfire* (1934). After a long retirement from films, Cromwell returned to acting in a few films during the seventies, most notably in Robert Altman's *3 Women* (1977).

★

ALAN CROSLAND (1894–1936)   Alan Crosland was a studio director at Warners with almost a decade's worth of minor credits when he stepped (or rather, stumbled) into the pages of film history by directing two landmark films: *Don Juan* (1926), starring John Barrymore, was the first feature with synchronized music, and *The Jazz Singer* (1927) was the first feature-length talkie (although most of the film was actually silent). A lachrymose drama punctuated with songs and sobs, it at least gave au-

diences the chance to see and, especially, hear Al Jolson perform in his inimitably florid style. The balance of Crosland's career was, to put it mildly, undistinguished—he directed one more film with Jolson, *Big Boy* (1930), and three more with Barrymore, *When a Man Loves* (1927), *The Beloved Rogue* (1927), and *General Crack* (1929). He also directed *On with the Show* (1929), one of the early backstage musicals. Crosland died in a car crash in 1936.

★

JAMES CRUZE (1884–1942)   A former stage and film actor, James Cruze is best remembered for his direction of *The Covered Wagon* (1923), the first epic-sized Western. Although crudely plotted, the film presented the rituals that were to become familiar features of the genre: a dangerous river crossing, a buffalo hunt, a simple funeral, and wagons struggling to move through a blizzard. Cruze was a prolific and reliable, if not very imaginative, director, with a wide range of subjects that carried him through the twenties and thirties. His *Beggar on Horseback* (1925) was an offbeat, surrealistic version of the George S. Kaufman–Marc Connelly play, but most of Cruze's other twenties films were in a conventional vein. An exception was *The Great Gabbo* (1929), a strange variation of the possessed-ventriloquist theme (*Dead of Night, Magic*), with Erich von Stroheim as the egomaniacal Gabbo who can only express his feelings through his dummy.

Cruze's movies of the thirties had either a racy toughness (*Washington Merry-Go-Round*, 1932; *I Cover the*

Waterfront, 1933) or a folksy if somewhat musty charm (his two movies with Will Rogers: *Mr. Skitch*, 1933, and *David Harum*, 1934). *Sutter's Gold* (1936), a fictionalized biography of frontiersman John Sutter, was neither racy nor folksy, merely dull and almost fatally expensive; it nearly sent Universal Studios into bankruptcy. Like other directors of much greater renown, Cruze died virtually penniless.

★

I try to make every picture the best. It's the only way to work. There must be a climate of amiability and fun and excitement. Every picture I do is the first one I've ever done and the last. Making a picture is enormously important to me and the experience is a joyous one. GEORGE CUKOR, in Richard Overstreet, "Interview with George Cukor," *Film Culture*, April 1964.

GEORGE CUKOR (1899–1983) One of the most adroit, most civilized, and most consistently entertaining of film directors, George Cukor enjoyed a long career that took him from the beginning of the sound era, through the studio-controlled thirties and forties (he was one of MGM's mainstays in those years), into the unstable fifties and sixties, when the studio system finally weakened and collapsed, and ultimately to his last film, *Rich and Famous* (1981), directed at age eighty-one. With a style that seldom failed to be discreet and tasteful, yet was always open to cinematic possibilities, Cukor guided his players smoothly through virtually every genre from screwball comedy to large-scale musical. In the case of two of his most gifted actresses, Katharine Hepburn and Judy Holliday, he shaped and embellished

their screen personalities, softening some of Hepburn's abrasiveness and eccentricities, and (especially in *The Marrying Kind*) nurturing the poignant and vulnerable aspects of Holliday's essentially comic personality. And Cukor directed Garbo in her most extraordinary performance, helping her to turn the hackneyed, tried-and-true material of *Camille* into durable gold.

Over the years, certain misconceptions have persisted about George Cukor. Even in his last years, he was regarded primarily as a director who worked best with actresses—and, indeed, he did draw many excellent performances from such varied ladies as Hepburn, Garbo, Joan Crawford, Audrey Hepburn, and Maggie Smith. But the appellation of women's director (which irritated him enormously) was actually an unfair cliché; his films contain any number of splendid performances by actors (Charles Boyer in *Gaslight*, Ronald Colman in *A Double Life*, James Mason in *A Star Is Born*, to cite only a few). Cukor is also regarded as among the most refined and sophisticated of directors (offscreen he was known as a cultivated gentleman), but this would ignore the boisterous vulgarity he clearly enjoyed depicting in such movies as *Dinner at Eight*, *The Women*, and *Heller in Pink Tights* (1960).

Cukor came to films as a dialogue director after establishing himself as an outstanding stage director in the middle and late twenties. (Through all his years in films,

---

The Covered Wagon: JAMES CRUZE (*Famous Players-Lasky, 1923*). *This view of the wagon train moving across the uncharted plains indicates the scope of Cruze's outsize Western. His direction was fairly sluggish and the plot trite, but central scenes depicting the Western rituals were well handled, and Karl Brown's photography conveyed the majesty of the setting.*

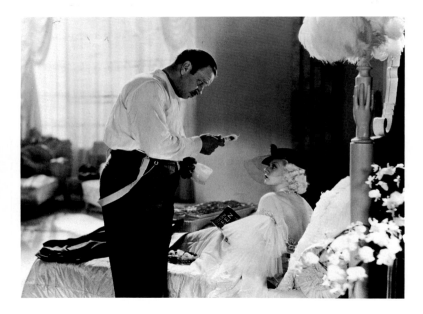

Cukor remained true to the theater in spirit—many of his movies were either stage adaptations or, like *The Royal Family of Broadway* and *A Double Life*, dealt with theater people.) His first films for Paramount were negligible, although *The Royal Family of Broadway* (1930) retained much of the charm of the Kaufman-Ferber play *The Royal Family*, and *Tarnished Lady* (1931) introduced the mercurial Tallulah Bankhead to the movies. Cukor left Paramount in a dispute with Ernst Lubitsch over *One Hour with You* (1932), for which he received codirector credit after arbitration.

Joining RKO and producer David Selznick, whom he had known earlier, Cukor moved into one of the richest periods of his career. Here, in the early thirties, he directed Constance Bennett in several films that took advantage of her brittle, glamorous personality, the best being *What Price Hollywood* (1932), a drama (suggested by the life of director Marshall Neilan) that presaged the later *A Star Is Born* in its rising star-marries-falling star Hollywood story. But the most significant event of the period was Cukor's direction of a thin, angular, exceedingly odd young actress named Katharine Hepburn, who was introduced as costar to John Barrymore in a film version of Clemence Dane's play *A Bill of Divorce-*

ment (1932). Awkward and unformed as she was, something fresh and startling about her performance kept audiences alert and interested. Before he left RKO for MGM, Cukor directed her in one of her most luminous films, a tender, exquisitely photographed (by Henry Gerrard) adaptation of Louisa May Alcott's classic novel *Little Women* (1933). Cukor's direction of this film is a prime example of his ability to deal intelligently and delicately with the most sentimental, dust-laden material.

That same year Cukor (together with Selznick) moved to Metro-Goldwyn-Mayer, where his elegant style and sensibility found a compatible home. His first two MGM films were among his best-remembered: a multistar version of the hit play *Dinner at Eight* (1933), which contained dollops of witty, acerbic dialogue and matchless performances by Marie Dressler as an aging actress and Jean Harlow as a vulgar nouveau riche wife, and *David Copperfield* (1934), a lovingly detailed adaptation of Dickens's novel, with a memorable performance by W. C. Fields as the bombastic and hopelessly insolvent Mr. Micawber.

Inevitably, every major MGM actress was given the chance to work under Cukor's firm but gentle tutelage. For several, the benefit of Cukor's direction could not

ABOVE   Dinner at Eight: GEORGE CUKOR (MGM, 1933). *In one of the most glorious marital mismatches in Hollywood history, burly businessman Wallace Beery battles with his vulgar, cheating wife Jean Harlow. This adaptation of the George S. Kaufman–Edna Ferber play glittered with MGM stars at the top of their form, skillfully put through their paces by George Cukor.*
RIGHT   David Copperfield: GEORGE CUKOR (MGM, 1934). *Freddie Bartholomew as David and W. C. Fields as the immortal Mr. Micawber, in George Cukor's version of the Dickens novel. Fields embodied Micawber so completely that it is surprising to note that the role was originally intended for Charles Laughton.*

appreciably increase their limited talent: the studio's resident "lady," Norma Shearer, tried gamely but vainly to simulate an ardent teen-age girl in Cukor's elaborate rendition of Shakespeare's *Romeo and Juliet* (1936), nor was Joan Crawford more than mildly persuasive playing Gertrude Lawrence's stage role in *Susan and God* (1940). Both actresses fared much better as costars in Cukor's brashly entertaining adaptation of Clare Boothe's *The Women* (1939), playing, respectively, a betrayed wife and her vulgar nemesis. Crawford was especially good as the grasping salesgirl-turned-Park Avenue matron, and even better in one of Cukor's few dramas, *A Woman's Face* (1941), as a bitter, horribly scarred woman who finds redemption in love. Garbo also veered wildly in her two films with Cukor, touching immortality and the hearts of audiences as *Camille* (1937) and covering herself with embarrassment in a woeful attempt at romantic comedy called *Two-Faced Woman* (1941). To round off Cukor's list of stellar actresses, Ingrid Bergman gave an Oscar-winning, bravura performance as a tormented wife in one of the director's sleekest and most popular films, *Gaslight* (1944), based on Patrick Hamilton's stage thriller.

Cukor's techniques in working with actresses were as varied as their temperaments, but he followed several rules of thumb. He learned when it would be expedient to speak, and when to be quiet, and how to develop the actress's trust in—and respect for—the director, while also instilling confidence in the actress. "She should know," he remarked, "that you're a very sympathetic and intelligent audience.... The director should be interested in acting, in actors, and not in himself.... It's all a collaboration. I think you've got to anticipate: What can *they* do, what can I give *them*, what can *they* get out of me?" (*American Film*, February 1978, pp. 34–35).

During the thirties and forties, Cukor continued to develop his special relationship with Katharine Hepburn. By the late thirties, especially as a madcap heiress in Howard Hawks's *Bringing Up Baby* (1938), the actress had managed to shed some of the affectations that plagued her RKO films. Even so, exhibitors still considered her "box-office poison." Under Cukor's guidance, she blossomed into an enchanting comedienne, first with *Holiday* (1938), which Cukor directed from Philip Barry's play—she was an independent-minded rich girl who wins her stuffy sister's fiancé—and then with another Barry comedy, *The Philadelphia Story* (1940), which she had performed on Broadway. Cukor's stylish handling of sophisticated material was never so palpable as in this silken story of a snobbish, upper-crust woman who learns humility and humanity. It remained for Cukor to bring to its fullest fruition Hepburn's teaming with Spencer Tracy. In *Adam's Rib* (1949), with the advantage of a clever Ruth Gordon–Garson Kanin screenplay, Cukor made the best use of their inimitable meshed styles, and their scenes together as married attorneys crackled with wit and mutual rapport. Their loving but scratchy relationship—her crisp intelligence confronting his down-to-earth bluntness—was even more evident in the diverting comedy *Pat and Mike* (1952).

The bright lights of Cukor, Hepburn, Tracy and the writing team of Gordon and Kanin in *Adam's Rib*, their most successful collaboration, were almost eclipsed by a marvelous Broadway actress in her first major film role. As a comically desperate wife who shoots her straying husband, Judy Holliday revealed a refreshingly original and ingratiating style that dominated every scene in

---

The Philadelphia Story: GEORGE CUKOR (MGM, 1940). *George Cukor on the set with his favorite actress, Katharine Hepburn. Cukor had directed Hepburn in her first film,* A Bill of Divorcement, *in 1932. Here, eight years later, he guided her through the role she had played triumphantly on the stage and which reestablished her in films as a major star after years of being labeled "box-office poison."*

which she appeared. Her performance finally convinced Columbia's reluctant studio head, Harry Cohn, to cast her in her star-making Broadway role of Billie Dawn in the film version of Garson Kanin's play *Born Yesterday* (1950). Although she won an Oscar as the dumb but crafty Billie under Cukor's direction, the movie itself was surprisingly static and lifeless. Two years later, Cukor finally presented her to best advantage in *The Marrying Kind* (1952), again with the able assistance of Ruth Gordon and Garson Kanin. Their screenplay about the up-and-down marriage of a young couple (Judy Holliday and Aldo Ray) and Cukor's astute direction created a memorable film, funny and poignant. The creative team (sans Gordon) repeated in 1954 with a lighter but no less enjoyable movie, *It Should Happen to You*, about a girl (Holliday) who finds "instant" celebrity by putting her name on a billboard.

With the decline of the major studios in the fifties, Cu-

ABOVE Adam's Rib: GEORGE CUKOR (*MGM, 1949*). *Katharine Hepburn tearfully resents her mistreatment at the hands of husband Spencer Tracy. This comedy of married attorneys who find themselves on opposite sides of a highly publicized case was written adroitly by Garson Kanin and Ruth Gordon, played by the stars at their peak, and given smooth-as-silk direction by George Cukor.*

OPPOSITE *In the process of directing, George Cukor tries to explain the emotion he wants from one of his actors. A witty and erudite man, Cukor imbued his best work with the joy of filmmaking; he took delight in eliciting vibrant performances from the larger-than-life players who starred in his films.*

kor worked where the projects would take him. Although his films diminished perceptibly in quality, they were still good enough to make use of his well-honed director's skills. His 1954 remake of *A Star Is Born* was troubled by many production problems, not the least of them being the unstable behavior of the star, Judy Garland, but Cukor managed to rise above its tribulations. The performances he drew from Garland and James Mason rendered the often-told story of a Hollywood marriage buffeted by changing fortunes genuinely affecting. The gifted, neurasthenic star also contributed tour-de-force musical interludes. Although not in a class with the best MGM musical films, *Les Girls* (1957) contained several attractive musical numbers, a clever story idea, and a glorious performance by Kay Kendall, a beautiful actress with an elegantly comic style. Cukor's sumptuous reconstruction of the landmark stage musical *My Fair Lady* (1964) was actually less inventive than *Les Girls,* but it won Cukor his first Academy Award after five nominations.

A number of other Cukor films in the last few decades of his career fared poorly, for various reasons. He seemed the wrong choice to direct the flamboyant soap-operatic behavior of Anna Magnani and Anthony Quinn in *Wild Is the Wind* (1957), and he could do nothing to relieve the foolishness of the lightheaded *Let's Make Love* (1960), with Marilyn Monroe and Yves Montand. Other projects, such as *Justine* (1969) and *Travels with My Aunt* (1972), had merit, but they were too "special," too eccentric to win favor with audiences or conventional-minded critics, and *The Blue Bird* (1976) was an ill-conceived venture. Sadly, his last film, *Rich and Famous* (1981), a loose remake of *Old Acquaintance* (1943), was a coarse, unappealing film that made one long for Vincent Sherman's frankly emotional, entertaining original.

Still, George Cukor has left much to remember and cherish. His best films will continue to engage us with their buoyancy, elegance, and grace. For over half a century, he worked diligently at his craft with humor and professional aplomb. In his *American Film* interview in 1978, he summed up his career with characteristic modesty and unpretentiousness:

You do whatever you can. It's all filtered through one's sensibilities, what you think is funny, what you think is touching, these things. All of you, when you work, you'll find that out. I just try to tell the story as best I can (p. 48).

On the whole, it worked for him. And out of what he thought was funny, what he thought was touching, he created some of the greatest American films.

ABOVE My Fair Lady: GEORGE CUKOR (Warner Bros., 1964). Flanked by Colonel Pickering (Wilfrid Hyde-White) and Mrs. Higgins (Gladys Cooper), the transformed Eliza (Audrey Hepburn) attends the Embassy ball. Cukor received his only Oscar for directing this opulent film version of the Alan Jay Lerner–Frederick Loewe stage musical.

OPPOSITE Four Daughters: MICHAEL CURTIZ (Warner Bros., 1938). As Priscilla Lane's chip-on-the-shoulder husband, John Garfield made an auspicious debut in Curtiz's family drama (Garfield's only previous film work was as an extra five years earlier in Footlight Parade). His intense performance in this film made him an instant star.

★

Moving pictures is the cruelest business in the world. You must be like a boxer all the time, with your left hand out.... In Europe, if an actor or director establishes himself, he lives forever. Here, if he doesn't make dough, they kick him out. Hollywood is money, money, money, and the nuts with everything else. How can any man be conceited when he sees the climb and then the awful nosedive? MICHAEL CURTIZ, in *The Book of Hollywood Quotes*, compiled by Gary Herman (London: Omnibus Press, 1979), p. 16.

MICHAEL CURTIZ (1888–1962) Among the great directors, Michael Curtiz is a leading paradox. On the one hand, there was the public Michael Curtiz—the ferocious, arrogant, and volatile Hungarian who stomped across sets in his fur-trimmed overcoat, hurling abuse at his actors in broken English and making enemies every step of the way. (Errol Flynn particularly detested him.) On the other hand, there was the director Michael Curtiz—the skilled craftsman who directed well over one hundred films at Warner Bros. over a quarter of a century, many of them among the most popular and profitable ever made. At the heart of the paradox is the fact that this abrasive man somehow contrived to subordinate his personality to the needs and demands of the studio system. In fact, it could be said that the Warners style—the driving pace, the energetic acting, the emphatic musical score, and the uncluttered camerawork—was synonymous with the Curtiz style in most of his films in the thirties and forties, although Curtiz usually added clever visual touches of his own.

Curtiz had been directing films all over Europe when Jack Warner saw one of his films and brought him to America in 1926. Within a few years, he had become one of the studio's most active and hard-working directors. By the thirties, there was hardly a genre that had not benefited from his crisp, expressive, no-nonsense style. (Amazingly, Curtiz would sometimes start shooting a film before reading the script.) Many of his early films, such as *The Strange Love of Molly Louvain* and *Doctor X* (both 1932), showed evidence of a Germanic influence in the dark, moody lighting and the expressionistic touches in the sets, but Curtiz quickly adapted to the straightforward, sharp-edged Warners approach.

With no loss of pace, Curtiz could turn out a rapid-fire comedy for the brash talents of James Cagney (*Jimmy the Gent*, 1934), a horror thriller filmed in early two-color Technicolor (*The Mystery of the Wax Museum*, 1933), or an exotic romance (*Mandalay*, 1934). Curtiz worked in all genres; he was even assigned to several of Warners's patented social dramas. One of his better thirties films was *Black Fury* (1935), a bleak and sometimes powerful tale starring Paul Muni as a foreign-born coal miner who becomes the central figure in a strike. Curtiz's *Angels with Dirty Faces* (1938), with James Cagney and the Dead End Kids, was one of the period's most popular expressions of the prevailing ''society-is-against-us'' theme.

With *Captain Blood* (1935), Curtiz established his reputation as a master of the costume adventure film. Although crude in some aspects, with exclamatory or scene-setting titles that seemed lifted out of the silent era, *Captain Blood* had a crackerjack story of high-seas piracy, revenge, and romance, and it starred the dashing Errol Flynn in his first major role. Through the rest of the decade and into the forties, Curtiz, often with the aid of second-unit directors such as B. Reeves Eason, directed lavish swashbucklers replete with energetic action scenes. *The Charge of the Light Brigade* (1936), *The Adventures of Robin Hood* (1938, in which he replaced William Keighley), and *The Sea Hawk* (1940) proved irresistible fare for fantasizing moviegoers. Apparently, they were also the battlegrounds for the stormy relationship—a curious combination of mutual need and loathing—between Curtiz and his star Errol Flynn.

By the close of the thirties, Curtiz had amply demonstrated his versatility—he moved with ease from the rugged boxing background of *Kid Galahad* (1937) to the warm family atmosphere of *Four Daughters* (1938), a smoothly textured, enormously popular drama about a close-knit family that introduced John Garfield to movie

audiences. Through the forties, this versatility continued to be astonishing. If Warners at wartime sought to inject audiences with patriotic fervor, Curtiz offered *Yankee Doodle Dandy* (1942), brimming with George M. Cohan's forthright American music, or *This Is the Army* (1943), Irving Berlin's rousing tribute to the nation's fighting soldiers, or the controversial *Mission to Moscow* (1943), glowing with praise for our allies in the Soviet Union. If escapist entertainment were required, he contributed such musicals as *Night and Day* (1946), a tuneful but largely fanciful and flatly played biography of Cole Porter, or *Romance on the High Seas* (1948), which introduced a pert blonde singer named Doris Day. Even nostalgic Americana, an area one would not have thought ideally suited to Curtiz's fiercely Hungarian nature, was beautifully represented in his 1947 film adaptation of the long-running stage play *Life with Father*.

Two of Curtiz's forties films stand out from the rest. One was *Casablanca* (1942), that legendary and uncanny

mixture of romance and wartime intrigue. Reams, of course, have been written trying to explain the reasons for this movie's durability as a popular favorite for more than four decades. Some of the reasons are evident: it is a crackling good adventure story of scheming and skulduggery in an exotic locale as well as a tale of love kindled, lost, and then found again. Its dialogue, always teetering on—but never toppling over—the edge of absurdity, is as widely quoted and remembered as that in any sound film ever made. Its cast could not be improved upon—each character is perfectly realized, from the complex hero, Rick Blaine (Humphrey Bogart), who is turned from bitter cynicism to commitment, to the ambivalent Captain Renault (Claude Rains), happy to play both sides against the middle. What gives *Casablanca* its permanent resonance, however, is the romantic relationship between Rick and Ilsa Lund (Ingrid Bergman), the beautiful woman who reappears in Rick's life. To say that Curtiz's smooth direction is only one factor in the movie's fame is not to diminish his contribution.

Curtiz also enjoyed an enormous success with *Mildred Pierce* in 1945. Apart from revitalizing Joan Crawford's declining career after years as an MGM star, the film allowed Curtiz to work in the then-popular *film noir* style, which, after all, had its roots in the Germanic tradition from which Curtiz emerged. True, the story, derived from James M. Cain's novel, contained heavy doses of soap opera—a mother obsessed with her vicious, ungrateful daughter tries to protect the girl from the consequences of her nefarious deeds—but the elements were distinctly in the *noir* mode: an opening murder with the victim crying "Mildred!," night scenes heavy with rain, fog, or shadow, a pervasive air of foreboding. Curtiz's skilled direction brought a welcome forcefulness to many of the melodramatic scenes.

In the fifties, Curtiz could still turn out a good movie. *The Breaking Point* (1950), a loose adaptation of Ernest Hemingway's *To Have and Have Not*, was superior to, although not as well known as Howard Hawks's 1944 version. However, after he left the Warners fold in the early

LEFT Casablanca: MICHAEL CURTIZ (*Warner Bros.*, 1942). *Michael Curtiz strolls on the set of the film with his leading lady, Ingrid Bergman. When Bergman replaced Ann Sheridan and Humphrey Bogart took over from Ronald Reagan, a magical melding occurred that has helped to make this romantic melodrama perhaps the most frequently watched movie of all. And Michael Curtiz deserves no small credit for keeping us dazzled and alert at the umpteenth viewing.*
OPPOSITE Mildred Pierce: MICHAEL CURTIZ (*Warner Bros.*, 1945). *Her life at its lowest ebb, Mildred Pierce (Joan Crawford) contemplates suicide. Curtiz's study of sacrificial mother love, based on James M. Cain's novel, eminently suited Crawford's style, and she won an Oscar for her performance.*

fifties, his career suffered. Elements that Curtiz could ordinarily count on to be professionally sound conspired to defeat him. An atrocious screenplay worked against the lilting Irving Berlin score for *White Christmas* (1954). The weight of its scenery and inept acting crushed *The Egyptian* (1954). An uncharismatic leading man—a single-named Danish singer, Oreste—undermined *The Vagabond King* (1956). Only *The Proud Rebel* (1958), a sentimental post–Civil War drama about a Southern widower (Alan Ladd) and his mute son (David Ladd), showed some merit. Curtiz's days of glory as a director had clearly passed.

If Curtiz's last decade as a filmmaker was unrewarding, it could not detract from his very real achievements in the thirties and forties. He had shown that even under the thumb of a very powerful studio like Warner Bros., it was possible to create some gold along with the inevitable pounds of dross. As a human being, he would not seem to qualify for the Jean Hersholt Humanitarian Award. But as a director, he was the centerpiece of a golden period of filmmaking at Warners. Michael Curtiz made many good films, and as long as Bogart can say to Bergman, "Here's looking at you, kid," he will be remembered.

★

JULES DASSIN (born 1911)   An actor and radio writer before coming to Hollywood in 1940, Connecticut-born Jules Dassin began directing feature films in the early forties. He did not make his mark until the late forties, with a series of hard-hitting and realistic *films noirs*. *Brute Force* (1947) and *Thieves' Highway* (1949) generated sparks

er on Sunday (1960), a ribald comedy about a good-hearted prostitute that gained immense popularity in America. He also had a hit with *Topkapi* (1964), a zestful comedy-melodrama revolving around an elaborate jewel heist, which featured an Oscar-winning supporting performance by Peter Ustinov. More recently, Dassin directed *A Dream of Passion* (1978), a grim and rather pretentious drama about a fiery Greek actress (Melina Mercouri) who, while playing Medea on the stage, becomes obsessed with an American woman (Ellen Burstyn) in prison for murdering her children.

★

DELMER DAVES (1904–1977) A dependable director with a good, strong, visual style and solid craftsmanship, Daves worked at many studios in many genres for over twenty years. He started out as a prop boy (*The Covered Wagon* was one of his assignments), then moved to acting and scriptwriting before finally turning to directing at Warners in 1943. (He continued to write many of his own scripts.) Many of his films deal with men who achieve some degree of self-discovery through an ordeal: John Garfield as the blinded veteran in *Pride of the Marines* (1945) and Humphrey Bogart as a desperate escaped convict in *Dark Passage* (1947) are among Daves's many severely tested heroes. This theme carried through to Daves's superior Westerns, such as *Broken Arrow* (1950), a landmark film in the depiction of sympathetic Indians, *The Last Wagon* (1956), and *3:10 to Yuma* (1957), a small but taut and classically structured film that was by far the best of the *High Noon* imitations.

with their gritty dialogue and tough, uncompromising situations, and *The Naked City* (1948) offered stunning on-location photography of New York City. Unfortunately, at this promising juncture, Dassin was forced into exile by the hearings of the House Un-American Activities Committee. He went to England, where he directed the excellent *Night and the City* (1950), a *film noir* that turned the London underworld into a sinister, expressionistic trap for a desperate hustler (Richard Widmark).

In France Dassin began the second major phase of his career, which, on the whole, was not as successful as the first. He had a commercial success with *Rififi* (*Du Rififi Chez les Hommes*, 1955), a suspenseful caper movie, and an artistic success with *He Who Must Die* (*Celui Qui Doit Mourir*, 1958), a stark allegory of Christianity in the modern world. In the sixties, Dassin began his Greek period with his wife, Melina Mercouri, which peaked with *Nev-*

ABOVE The Naked City: JULES DASSIN (*Universal, 1948*). *Policemen Don Taylor (right) and Barry Fitzgerald (seated in the car) pursue a fleeing hood through New York City streets. The movie's routine plot benefited enormously from the vivid on-location photography.*
RIGHT Dark Passage: DELMER DAVES (*Warner Bros., 1947*). *Humphrey Bogart, as an escaped convict fleeing from wrongful imprisonment, is menaced at gunpoint in Daves's churning melodrama. Set in San Francisco, a favorite location for films noirs, the movie took several twisty but not always believable turns.*
OPPOSITE On the Avenue: ROY DEL RUTH (*Fox, 1937*). *Rich girl Madeleine Carroll (on the telephone) has aunt Cora Witherspoon's clear disapproval. Under Del Ruth's expert direction, the movie combined a bright script that could have passed muster as a screwball comedy with a generous batch of lively Irving Berlin songs.*

Daves's Westerns are also noteworthy for the unusual complexity and ambiguity of their characters.

When Daves returned to Warners toward the end of his career, his work faltered—a number of movies (*A Summer Place*, 1959; *Parrish*, 1961; *Susan Slade*, 1961; *Rome Adventure*, 1962) were florid soap operas that had blond Troy Donahue for their leading man. His vapid performances at the center of each film created a vacuum that could not be filled or offset. Daves retired in the mid-sixties.

★

ROY DEL RUTH (1895–1961)   Roy Del Ruth is another director too easily dismissed in critical concentration on the major figures. By no means a major director, he still churned out a goodly number of pleasing entertainments during a career that spanned thirty-five years. He began directing feature films in the mid-twenties after an apprenticeship with Mack Sennett (as writer and gag man). His thirties films at Warners, including the first version of *The Maltese Falcon* (1931), *Taxi* (1932), *Blessed Event* (1932), and *Lady Killer* (1933), are typical of the studio's output of rapid-fire, breezy programmers. He also directed a number of lively musicals at Fox and MGM, and two of them—*Thanks a Million* (1935) and *On the Avenue* (1937)—number among the best of the decade, sassy and satirical in the best Fox thirties style. His later musicals—both at MGM (*Du Barry Was a Lady*, 1943; *Broadway Rhythm*, 1944) and at Warners (*The West Point Story*, 1950; *On Moonlight Bay*, 1951)—were larger in scale but not as good; they lacked the pace and vitality of his earlier efforts. In the long run Del Ruth may be best remembered for those slangy, spirited little Warners comedies and melodramas of the thirties that were unpretentious showcases for the considerable talents of the studio's stock company.

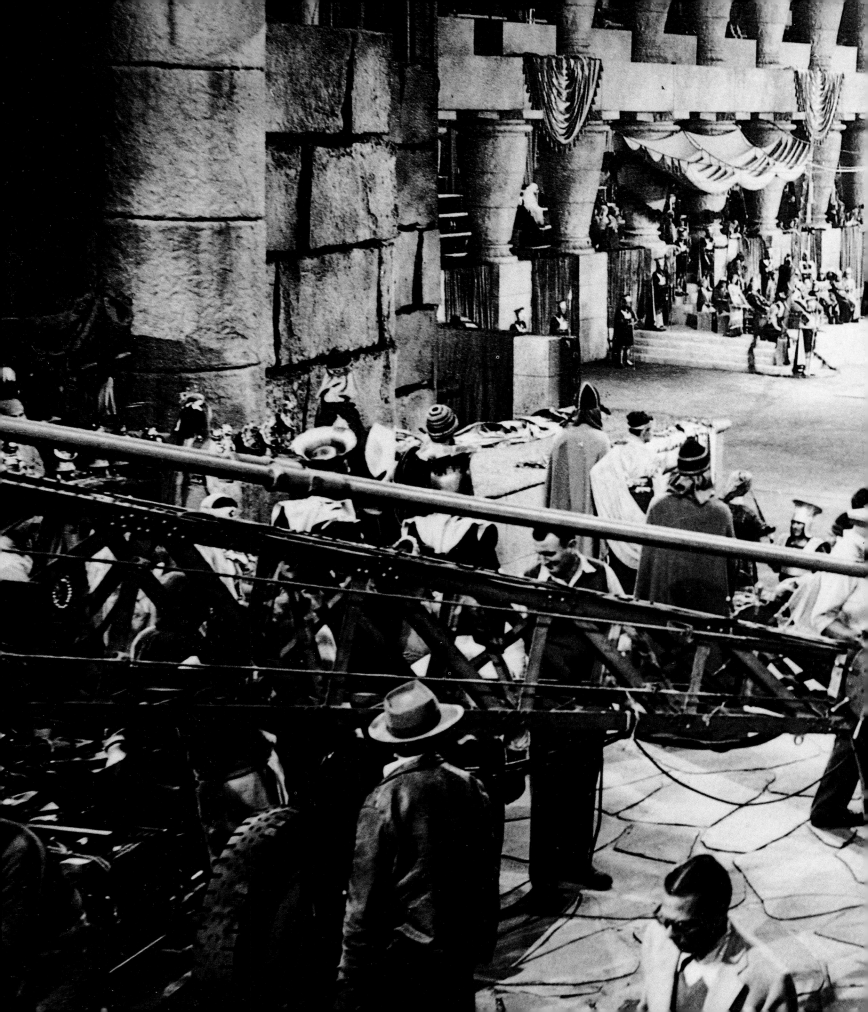

★

Imagine, the horizon is your stage limit and the sky your gridiron. No height limit, no close-fitting exits, no conserving of stage space, just the whole world open to you as a stage; 1,000 people in a scene do not crowd your accommodations. It was a new feeling, a new experience. . . . I felt inspired. I felt that I could do things which the confines of a theatre would not permit. CECIL B. DE-MILLE, interview in *New York Dramatic Mirror,* 1913, cited in Jay Leyda, ed., *Voices of Film Experience* (New York: Macmillan, 1977), p. 105.

CECIL B. DEMILLE (1881–1959)   Over the years, the critical pendulum on Cecil Blount DeMille has swung both ways. Although he is generally regarded as the screen's master of the historical epic and religious spectacle, the many flaws and shortcomings of his films have often been enumerated: the grade-school dialogue, the simplistic characterizations, the uneasy combination of humble piety and leering sex, and, above all, DeMille's stubborn refusal to acknowledge changing film trends. On the other hand, he has been hailed as a born showman and consummate storyteller whose movies are well-paced and seldom boring. By avoiding cinematic gimmicks he allowed viewers to concentrate on the straightforward narrative and simple action, which they frequently found entertaining. It could be said that DeMille never cheated his audience.

DeMille's early years were spent in the theater, mostly as an actor and writer and as general manager of his mother's theatrical company. In 1913, with partners Jesse L. Lasky and Samuel Goldfish (later Goldwyn), he formed a motion picture company to produce a sensational six-reel film entitled *The Squaw Man* (1914). Its huge success helped the young company to grow into the prestigious Paramount Pictures and also established DeMille as a driving force in the industry whose elaborate films set new standards. During this burgeoning period, DeMille not only personally produced and directed

many films but also took part in writing the screenplays and supervising the work of other directors. He developed many new stars, including Gloria Swanson, Bebe Daniels, and Wallace Reid.

DeMille's silent films resembled his later outsize epics in their penchant for titillating audiences with suggestions of illicit or extramarital sex and then neutralizing the naughty implications with a layer of finger-pointing Victorian morality. (The wicked may enjoy themselves, but they pay for their sins in the long run.) Movies such as *Male and Female* (1919) reflected the changing postwar attitude toward sexual activity, but lest it be said that DeMille condoned these goings-on, he added such cautionary titles as *Don't Change Your Husband* (1919) and *Why Change Your Wife?* (1920). DeMille also made certain to inject a liberal amount of sex into his silent Biblical spectacles such as *The Ten Commandments* (1923) and *The King of Kings* (1927).

He moved confidently into the sound era, continuing to stress size over sense and action over talk. Although his sonorous readings of the prologues may imply that he took his screenplays seriously, he actually treated them merely as springboards to large, tumultuous events that he could stage with aplomb. As before, he drew on history and the Bible for inspiration, relating the story of early Christianity and its tribulations in ancient Rome in *The Sign of the Cross* (1932) or recounting the story of *Cleopatra* (1934) and her liaisons with Antony and Caesar. Amusingly, in both films he cast the very modern, wryly sophisticated Claudette Colbert as wicked women in opulent garb. During the thirties, DeMille

PRECEDING PAGES   Samson and Delilah: CECIL B. DEMILLE *(Paramount, 1949). Cecil B. DeMille, on the camera boom, directs a scene for his lavish Biblical spectacle. DeMille insisted on complete control of his productions, and his ability to balance a staggering number of elements was truly impressive.* RIGHT   The Greatest Show on Earth: CECIL B. DEMILLE *(Paramount, 1952). Henry Wilcoxon, James Stewart, and Betty Hutton comfort each other after a fire has destroyed the circus. DeMille's colorful tribute to the Ringling Brothers and Barnum & Bailey Circus edged out such films as* The Quiet Man *and* High Noon *for the Oscar; its unabashed mixture of corn, glitter, and circus thrills won DeMille the approval of his peers that had eluded him for most of his long career.*

also turned to the Western past for several thumping, elaborate horse operas, including *The Plainsman* (1937) and *Union Pacific* (1939).

In the forties and beyond, DeMille continued to offer audiences the same kind of grandiose film, showing little interest in the new directions reshaping the film industry. His favorite actor of this period was virile, taciturn Gary Cooper, who battled Indians in *North West Mounted Police* (1940), led a group of wounded Marines to safety in *The Story of Dr. Wassell* (1944), and braved the American frontier with Paulette Goddard in *Unconquered* (1947). The latter joined John Wayne and Ray Milland in DeMille's seafaring adventure *Reap the Wild Wind* (1942), but the film's real star was the giant squid that grapples with Wayne in the rousing climax. Not unexpectedly, DeMille found time to tap the Bible for more stories of faith-versus-sin, including *Samson and Delilah* (1949) and his final film, a remake of *The Ten Commandments* (1956), in which Anne Baxter spoke this deathless line to Charlton Heston: "Oh, Moses, you adorable fool!"

In 1952, his lavish circus film *The Greatest Show on Earth* was named Best Picture by the Motion Picture Academy. Although DeMille himself was deprived of the director's award—it went to John Ford for *The Quiet Man*—the Oscar signaled the film industry's recognition of one of its true pioneers, who had served it well for four decades. He also served his audiences well, giving them the sort of eye-popping entertainment they had come to expect from the screen's bravura Barnum.

★

WILLIAM DE MILLE (1878–1955) Far less known than his younger brother Cecil (who spelled his name differently), William de Mille was also far less ambitious in his filmmaking. Originally brought to California by his brother to help establish a script department, de Mille was actually more interested in the theater and had already established credentials as a playwright. In 1915, he finally began to direct and produce films, many of which received favorable attention from the critics. Not unexpectedly, a number of them were adaptations of successful plays, such as *What Every Woman Knows* (1921), *Miss Lulu Bett* (1921), *Clarence* (1922), *Grumpy* (1923), and *Icebound* (1924). Although few of these films have survived, it was clear that William was more intellectually inclined than Cecil and certainly a more subtle filmmaker. De Mille also wrote many original screenplays, and he adapted some of his own plays for other directors, including brother Cecil. His last film, *His Double Life* (1933), codirected with Arthur Hopkins, was

adapted from Arnold Bennett's novel *Buried Alive* and starred Roland Young and Lillian Gish.

★

JONATHAN DEMME (born 1944) After a few minor films (*Caged Heat*, 1974; *Crazy Mama*, 1975) that revealed an original point of view lurking somewhere behind the sensational subject matter, Jonathan Demme attracted critical if not audience interest with *Handle with Care* (1977, originally called *Citizens Band*), a loosely constructed and very amiable comedy about the CB radio craze. Two years later he had an even greater critical success with *Melvin and Howard* (1980), a small, odd, entertaining, and observant comedy based on the true story of one Melvin Dummar (Paul LeMat), the Utah gas station owner who claimed that Howard Hughes had left him a sizable portion of his fortune after he gave the eccentric old man a ride in his truck. Mary Steenburgen won an Oscar for her funny, touching performance as Melvin's wife. The film promised a bright future for Demme, but his next film, *Swing Shift* (1983), was only moderately interesting. A comedy-drama nicely steeped in forties wartime ambiance, it starred Goldie Hawn as a young wife who enjoys a brief fling with a fellow factory worker (Kurt Russell) while her husband is in service. Most recently, Demme directed *Stop Making Sense* (1984), a concert film starring the new-wave rock band Talking Heads, which won some highly favorable notices.

★

BRIAN DE PALMA (born 1940) Born in Newark, New Jersey, Brian De Palma first attracted critical attention with *Greetings* (1968) and *Hi, Mom!* (1970), two wickedly satirical comedies about the counterculture of the late sixties, both starring young Robert De Niro. But it was his lurid melodramas over the past dozen years—from *Sisters* (1973) to *Body Double* (1984)—that have caused some critics to drape him with the sizable mantle of Alfred Hitchcock. On the whole, it is not a very good fit. De Palma's movies, especially *Carrie* (1976) and *Dressed to Kill* (1980), have some of Hitchcock's adroit visual style (note the museum scene in the latter film), and he occasionally approximates the master's sudden jolts, the sense of lurking menace in ordinary surroundings. Like Hitchcock, he enjoys confusing audiences about a character's identity (see Hitchcock's *Vertigo* and De Palma's *Obsession*, 1976), and he too is partial to sometimes indigestible gobs of black humor. In his film *Blow Out* (1981), De Palma echoed Hitchcock's tendency to ride over gaps in logic with riveting scenes of lurid melodrama.

Unlike Hitchcock, however, De Palma is unable to conceal the gaping holes in the plots, and his many moments of explicit gore and violence, which seem to be required in our permissive age, only detract from rather than add to the movies' impact. (In *Psycho*, Hitchcock's most overtly violent film, we imagine much more than we see.) De Palma's 1983 remake of *Scarface* was his most ambitious movie to date and also the most flagrant example of his excessive style: three hours of relentless unpleasantness. His 1984 film *Body Double* was vintage De Palma: a tricky, suspenseful tale saddled with one of the nastiest murder scenes ever filmed and replete with echoes of Hitchcock films. It proved once again that De Palma has learned some of the master magician's tricks but has not yet mastered the magic. Most recently, he turned to comedy with *Wise Guys* (1986), starring Joe Piscopo and Danny De Vito.

★

ANDRE DE TOTH (born 1910)   Born in Hungary, Andre de Toth first worked in Hungarian films in various capacities, including director, then went to England, where he joined producer-director Alexander Korda as a second-unit director. In Hollywood from 1943, de Toth directed many Western films, most of them expertly made and beautifully photographed. His films with Randolph Scott (*Carson City*, 1952; *The Stranger Wore a Gun*, 1953; and others) may have lacked the crisp, clean style and the nuances of Budd Boetticher's Westerns with Scott of around the same time, but they had their share of vigorous action. His occasional non-Western films (*Dark Waters*, 1944; *Monkey on My Back*, 1957) were mostly routine. De Toth has only one good eye, but it did not deter him from directing one of the most successful of the 3-D features of the fifties, *House of Wax* (1953). In later years he worked in Europe as a director and producer.

★

WILLIAM DIETERLE (1893–1972)   Nobody would ever accuse William Dieterle of being an especially exciting or innovative director, but he was conscientious, methodical, and highly dependable, and quite often these qualities resulted in a solid and admirable movie. German-born Dieterle started as an actor in silent films, then began directing in 1923 while continuing to act. He immigrated to Hollywood in 1930, spending the entire decade of the thirties at Warners, where at first he directed *The Last Flight* (1931), an interesting drama about alienated postwar pilots, followed by many of the studio's crisp, breezy programmers (*Lawyer Man*, 1932; *Grand Slam*, 1933; and others). At Jack Warner's insistence, he was made codirector of famed German director Max Reinhardt's trouble-plagued production of *A Midsummer Night's Dream* (1935), and it is difficult to determine who was responsible for the movie's virtues or for its excesses. As one of the most reliable directors on the lot, Dieterle was assigned to a series of elaborate, meticulously detailed, and somewhat musty biographical dramas starring Paul Muni (or *Mr.* Paul Muni, as he was often billed). *The Story of Louis Pasteur* (1936), *The Life of Emile Zola* (1937), and *Juarez* (1939) were widely admired in their day for their conscientious attempts to re-create historical events.

In 1939, before the release of his best biographical film for Warners, *Dr. Ehrlich's Magic Bullet* (1940), Dieterle moved to RKO, where he directed a good if cluttered version of *The Hunchback of Notre Dame* (1939), with Charles Laughton as a convincingly grotesque Quasimodo, and the film for which he is best remembered, a fine adaptation of Stephen Vincent Benét's story "The Devil and Daniel Webster," released in 1941 as *All That Money Can Buy*. Produced and directed by Dieterle under an obviously stringent budget, the film was a moody, expressive piece of Americana with several haunting and powerful scenes, such as the ghostly ball at Jabez Stone's mansion and the climactic trial in the barn. (Bernard Herrmann's evocative score won an Oscar.)

Dieterle's films in the forties, mostly for Paramount, were less successful, but they revealed a romantic streak in his nature not apparent in his earlier work. Such films as *I'll Be Seeing You* (1944), *Love Letters* (1945), *Portrait of Jennie* (1949), and *September Affair* (1951) involved Jennifer Jones, Joseph Cotten, and other players in brief, ill-fated, tender encounters, often to the strains of lush string music. The conventional melodramas he directed (*The Accused*, 1949; *Dark City*, 1950) at least restored him to the kind of fast-paced material he had turned out regularly at Warners. He also directed Rita Hayworth in a gaudy and foolish *Salome* (1953) and Elizabeth Taylor in *Elephant Walk* (1954), a florid romantic drama set on a tea plantation in Ceylon. In 1958, he returned to Europe, directed four movies, and then retired.

with social overtones, concerned the murder of a Jew by a vicious bigot. (In the source material, a novel by Richard Brooks, the victim was a homosexual.) Dmytryk drew fine performances from the cast, especially Robert Ryan, who excelled as the murderer seething with hatred and resentment. Dmytryk had no opportunity to make other films before he was sent to prison for a year.

After his release, Dmytryk went into self-imposed exile in England, then returned to testify against several of his former colleagues. He resumed filmmaking in the early fifties, concentrating on large-budget films that, while worthwhile in many ways, lacked the forcefulness and originality of his earlier work. His film version of Herman Wouk's *The Caine Mutiny* (1954) never caught fire, despite the mostly able efforts of a cast headed by Humphrey Bogart. He turned out two solidly made Westerns, *Broken Lance* (1954) and *Warlock* (1959), then veered off the tracks with rambling attempts at epic stories, *Raintree County* (1957) and *The Young Lions* (1958). In the sixties, Dmytryk's films shifted to the lurid: *Walk on the Wild Side* (1962), *The Carpetbaggers* (1964), and *Where Love Has Gone* (1964) all shared in the kind of "let's-be-wicked-now-that-restraints-have-eased" fever prevalent in filmmaking during that decade.

★

EDWARD DMYTRYK (born 1908) Until he was found guilty of Communist affiliation by the House Un-American Activities Committee in 1947, Edward Dmytryk was a prolific director noted for his work at RKO after years of editing at Paramount (including *Ruggles of Red Gap*) and directing bread-and-butter films for Columbia. His best RKO movies, vivid crime melodramas in the *film noir* style, included *Murder My Sweet* and *Cornered* (both 1945), which changed the screen image of Dick Powell from piping tenor to tough guy. His most successful film, *Crossfire* (1947), a suspenseful, well-crafted thriller

ABOVE   Crossfire: EDWARD DMYTRYK (RKO, 1947). *Detective Robert Young (at right) questions suspect Robert Ryan in this tense thriller. The film created a stir by using rabid anti-Semitism as the killer's motive; apart from its social overtones, it was a skillfully made melodrama, moodily photographed in the* film noir *style.*

RIGHT   Singin' in the Rain: STANLEY DONEN *and* GENE KELLY *(MGM, 1952). Gene Kelly and Stanley Donen confer on the set. Three years earlier, as codirectors of* On the Town, *they had advanced the musical film by shooting some of the scenes on actual New York City locations. Their exuberant direction of* Singin' in the Rain *contributed greatly to the nonstop merriment.*

Grant, Ingrid Bergman, Deborah Kerr, and the match-less Kay Kendall). However, he broke the mold with *Two for the Road* (1967), a biting, funny, inordinately clever discourse on modern marriage, viewed through a complex kaleidoscope of past and present. Audrey Hepburn and Albert Finney excelled as the alternately bickering and loving couple. Hepburn also starred for Donen in *Charade* (1963), an extremely diverting Hitchcockian thriller. In recent years, Donen has had more than his share of mistakes (*The Little Prince*, 1974; *Lucky Lady*, 1975; *Saturn 3*, 1979; and the truly execrable *Blame It on Rio*, 1983), but he can still stand alone as a director with a high degree of grace and imagination.

★

GORDON DOUGLAS (born 1909)   After directing some of the ''Our Gang'' comedies for several years, Gordon Douglas graduated to feature films in 1939, and for over three decades he directed many movies in virtually every genre for virtually every major studio. While competently made in the main, several compared unfavorably with earlier versions of the same stories. *Young at Heart* (1954), a glossy musical remake of *Four Daughters* (1938), lacked the warmth and charm of the original. *The Fiend Who Walked the West* (1958) reduced Henry Hathaway's taut *Kiss of Death* (1947) to the ludicrous. Douglas's 1966 remake of John Ford's classic *Stagecoach* (1939) was disastrous, flatly handled and cast against all reason with such unsuitable actors as Bing Crosby and Red Buttons.

But there were plus signs as well. Douglas's 1954 science-fiction movie *Them*, about giant ants on a rampage, was one of the better fifties movies in that overworked

★

STANLEY DONEN (born 1924)   It may be time to move beyond the constantly reiterated point that Stanley Donen worked best as a hyphenated director. True, his films with Gene Kelly (*On the Town*, 1949; *Singin' in the Rain*, 1952; *It's Always Fair Weather*, 1955) are top-flight achievements, and *The Pajama Game* (1957), codirected with George Abbott, is exuberant fun. But Donen's best musical films have more than their share of class, visual beauty, joy, and whatever else a musical needs, including great performers. *Seven Brides for Seven Brothers* (1954) is still one of the greatest dance musicals, due not only to its cast of professional dancers but also to Donen's own expertise as a dancer and choreographer. And *Funny Face* (1957) overrides its dated aspects with the virtues of Fred Astaire's still-faultless dancing, Audrey Hepburn's beguiling presence, and, above all, stylish musical numbers.

With his occasional comedies (*Indiscreet*, 1958; *Once More, with Feeling*, 1960; *The Grass Is Greener*, 1960), Donen showed a penchant for verbose, tepid drawing-room formats with attractive leading players (Cary

ABOVE   Charade: STANLEY DONEN (*Universal, 1963*). *Audrey Hepburn attempts to flee from an ambiguously motivated Cary Grant. This enjoyable thriller mixed suspense, romance, and comedy in the style of Alfred Hitchcock, even sprinkling a few Hitchcock-like surprises along the way.*
RIGHT   Kiss Tomorrow Goodbye: GORDON DOUGLAS (*Warner Bros.*, 1950). *Underworld kingpin James Cagney is roughed up by conniving cop Ward Bond while Barton MacLane and Barbara Payton look on. Douglas's tough melodrama followed hard on the heels of Cagney's triumph in* White Heat, *without duplicating that success.*

with many leading players of the period, including Lon Chaney, Mary Pickford, the Gish sisters, Gloria Swanson (eight films), and, especially, Douglas Fairbanks, with whom he enjoyed a long and happy association (*Robin Hood*, 1922, one of his most extravagant films; *The Iron Mask*, 1929; plus nine other movies). Most of these films were briskly paced and technically proficient, and they displayed their stars to full advantage.

Dwan moved easily into the sound era (*While Paris Sleeps*, released in 1932, is considered his best early talkie), but after a while he was relegated mostly to "B" movies. At Fox for a while, he directed several of Shirley Temple's films, including one of her most charming and best-loved vehicles, *Heidi* (1937). His most elaborate production was *Suez* (1938), a largely fanciful account of how the Suez Canal was built by a Ferdinand de Lesseps who looked a lot like Tyrone Power. He continued to direct a great many minor films in the forties, including several raucous, fast-paced comedies based on familiar antique stage farces (*Up in Mabel's Room*, 1944; *Getting Gertie's Garter*, 1946) and a batch of films starring the not conspicuously talented Queen of Republic Pictures, Vera Ralston (*Surrender*, 1950; *Belle Le Grand*, 1951; and others). His best film of the period was *Sands of Iwo Jima* (1949), a well-made war film with an excellent Oscar-nominated performance by John Wayne. Toward the end of his career, Dwan directed a number of small-scale but tightly made Westerns such as *Cattle Queen of Montana* (1954) and *Tennessee's Partner* (1955).

★

genre. *Kiss Tomorrow Goodbye* (1950) and *Come Fill the Cup* (1951) gave James Cagney fairly good follow-ups after the high of *White Heat* (1949). And Douglas did a reasonable job of guiding Frank Sinatra through his hardboiled phase in *Tony Rome* (1967) and *The Detective* (1968). We should also grant at least one cheer for any director who could wade through the treacle of Liberace's *Sincerely Yours* (1955) without gagging.

★

ALLAN DWAN (1885–1981)   A true film pioneer and a versatile, astonishingly prolific director, Allan Dwan had a career that encompassed half a century and hundreds of movies. In the silent era, deeply influenced by D. W. Griffith, he was virtually a one-man filmmaker, turning out scores of movies for which he not only acted as director but also as producer, writer, editor, and cutter. A trained engineer, he was also responsible for many important technical innovations, including the dolly shot, which he invented for *David Harum* in 1915. During this prodigiously active period, he directed films

ABOVE   Heidi: ALLAN DWAN (*Fox, 1937*). *Little Heidi (Shirley Temple) confronts her crusty but loving grandfather (Jean Hersholt). Dwan's adaptation of Johanna Spyri's novel captured most of its storybook charm, and Shirley was at her adorable best.*
PRECEDING PAGES   The Great Race: BLAKE EDWARDS (*Warner Bros., 1965*). *On the set of his extravagant comedy, director Edwards tosses a custard pie at hapless Natalie Wood, while a pie-splattered Jack Lemmon (left) looks on. The scene revived the pie-in-the-face tradition that had been a mainstay of movie slapstick for many years.*

BLAKE EDWARDS (born 1922)   A true child of Hollywood—his father and grandfather were both in the film business—Blake Edwards was an actor and writer before turning to directing in the mid-fifties. Highlights of his first decade include an adaptation of Truman Capote's novella *Breakfast at Tiffany's* (1961), in which Audrey Hepburn gave one of her most captivating performances as that lightheaded, quicksilver waif, Holly Golightly, and the first two films in the hugely popular "Pink Panther" series, *The Pink Panther* and *A Shot in the Dark* (both 1964), which introduced the character of the monumentally inept Inspector Clouseau (Peter Sellers). *A Shot in the Dark*, generously studded with uproarious sight gags, was especially funny. Edwards also directed several serious films: a suspenseful thriller entitled *Experiment in Terror* (1962), with a truly chilling opening sequence, and *Days of Wine and Roses* (1962), in which Jack Lemmon and Lee Remick gave exemplary performances as an alcoholic couple.

By the mid-sixties, Edwards's work began to falter—*The Great Race* (1965) and *Darling Lili* (1970) were expensive failures, lavish and occasionally amusing but out of tune with the times. A very good Western, *Wild Rovers* (1971), could not find an audience for its offbeat view of the old West. Through most of the seventies, he concentrated on producing, directing, and coscripting sure-fire sequels to *The Pink Panther* (*The Return of the Pink Panther*, 1975; *The Pink Panther Strikes Again*, 1976), which inevitably diminished in quality and interest. Late in the decade he began directing a series of comedies starring his wife, Julie Andrews, that stretched his hectic, energetic style to the limit. *10* (1979) and *Victor/Victoria* (1982) were

clever but essentially one-joke films that lost their comic momentum before the end. *10* traced the erotic obsession of Dudley Moore with the ravishing Bo Derek, and *Victor/Victoria* involved a thirties nightclub singer (An-

LEFT   S.O.B.: BLAKE EDWARDS (*Paramount, 1981*). *Blake Edwards directs a scene on the beach. Reaction to his blistering satire on Hollywood mores ranged from admiring to hostile.*
RIGHT   Blow Out: BRIAN DE PALMA (*Filmways, 1981*). *Brian De Palma and star John Travolta rehearse a scene for this high-powered thriller. Travolta played a sound technician who becomes embroiled in a murder and cover-up scheme. The film contains echoes from many sources, including Hitchcock, Antonioni, and Coppola.*

drews) who becomes a star attraction by assuming the disguise of a man who impersonates a woman. The androgynous humor paled quickly despite a valiant effort by Robert Preston as a flamboyant homosexual performer. Preston also failed to save *S.O.B.* (1981), a mean-spirited diatribe against the excesses of Hollywood. While the "Pink Panther" series limped to a close with *Curse of the Pink Panther* (1983), Edwards featured his wife yet another time in *The Man Who Loved Women* (1983), a meretricious comedy with serious overtones about a woman-chaser (Burt Reynolds) with psychiatric problems. In 1984 he directed Dudley Moore in *Micki and Maude*, as a man who just happens to have two pregnant wives.

★

GEORGE FITZMAURICE (1885–1940)   One of the lesser-known directors of the silent and early sound eras, Paris-born George Fitzmaurice nevertheless enjoyed a rather enviable track record as the director of a number of visually striking, commercially successful films. A meticulous craftsman, he prepared everything in careful detail before shooting, and many of his films reveal signs of his early training as an artist. Among his most notable movies are *The Cheat* (1923), with Pola Negri, *The Son of the Sheik* (1926), with Rudolph Valentino, and *The Night of Love* (1927), with Ronald Colman and Vilma Banky, all romantic dramas. He also directed Garbo in two of her vehicles of the early thirties: as the seductive, ill-fated spy *Mata Hari* (1932) and as the nightclub singer Zara, who may or may not be the long-lost wife of an Italian officer (Melvyn Douglas), in *As You Desire Me* (1932). His last films for MGM were mostly lightweight comedies such as *Petticoat Fever* (1936) and *Live, Love and Learn* (1937).

★

ROBERT J. FLAHERTY (1884–1951)   Unquestionably one of the screen's most creative and most innovative figures in the field of the documentary film, Robert Flaherty invested true everyday events with beauty and a sort of poetic grandeur. As both the cinematographer and di-

rector of his movies, he displayed a visual sense unequaled by many more ambitious filmmakers. Sadly, he was unable to begin or complete many projects of exceptional promise.

After his extraordinary first film, *Nanook of the North* (1922), which detailed the primitive existence and daily tribulations of an Eskimo family, Flaherty devoted himself to the life of the Samoans in the South Seas. The result was *Moana* (1926), a lovely portrait of a Samoan boy and his family that failed to find its audience. Due to many setbacks, Flaherty completed only three films over the next quarter of a century. *Man of Aran* (1934), made in the Aran Islands off the coast of Ireland, dealt with the endless battle of the island fishermen to wrest a living from the pitiless sea. *The Land* (1942) concerned poor migrant farm workers in the American South and West. The leisurely, expressive *Louisiana Story* (1948) depicted the life of a young Cajun boy in the bayou country,

RIGHT   Mata Hari: GEORGE FITZMAURICE *(MGM, 1932). Ravishing spy Mata Hari (Greta Garbo) lures her Russian lieutenant (Ramon Novarro) into revealing military secrets. Unfortunately, the spider falls for the fly, leading to her ultimate demise in front of a firing squad.*
OPPOSITE   Man of Aran: ROBERT J. FLAHERTY *(Gaumont-British, 1934). Robert Flaherty (at left) directs a scene for his stark, poetic film about life in the rugged Aran Islands off the coast of Ireland. Flaherty used Aranite natives to depict the bitter, precarious existence constantly threatened by the raging sea.*

whose life is suddenly changed when a derrick is brought in to sink an oil well beneath the swamps.

Flaherty codirected several feature films that won some acclaim; unfortunately, he never received screen credit for some of these, having walked off the set before their completion when he found he could not agree with his collaborators. This occurred with *White Shadows of the South Seas* (1928, codirector W. S. Van Dyke), an exotic romance with Monte Blue, and also with *Tabu* (1931, codirector F. W. Murnau), a South Seas story using native actors. He managed to collaborate satisfactorily with Zoltan Korda on *Elephant Boy* (1937), directing the exterior scenes for this adventure tale starring Indian actor Sabu. He had planned several other productions before his death.

★

VICTOR FLEMING (1883–1949) Victor Fleming would warrant a place in film history if only because he was the credited director on two of the most popular (if not the two *most* popular) movies ever made: *Gone with the Wind* and *The Wizard of Oz* (both 1939). His actual involvement with these films has been amply recorded elsewhere, but it can be said with some justification that neither of them is considered "a Victor Fleming movie." Fleming's career as a feature director began in 1919 after years of working as a cinematographer with Allan Dwan and D. W. Griffith. It peaked in the thirties at MGM where, as a contract director, he handled some of the studio's best-attended movies, especially lively adaptations of the classic novels *Treasure Island* (1934) and *Captains Courageous* (1937).

Although Fleming was regarded at MGM as a man's director—and, indeed, a fondness for lusty or rowdy male behavior is evident in many of his films—he was also able to bring out Jean Harlow's special mixture of carnality and comedy in two of her best movies, *Red Dust* (1932) and *Bombshell* (1933). He declined in the for-

ties with such weak films as *Dr. Jekyll and Mr. Hyde* (1941), with Spencer Tracy—wrong in both roles—*Adventure* (1945), starring a mismatched Clark Gable and Greer Garson ("Gable's Back and Garson's Got Him!"), and *Joan of Arc* (1948)—his last film—an elaborate, tedious costume drama. Although his work overall was uneven, Fleming, especially in the thirties, infused MGM's slick professionalism with his own energetic and muscular style.

★

I suppose everybody pursues one idea in many guises. In any event, everybody tends to emphasize those aspects of life he finds the most interesting. Movie directors certainly do. What interests me are the consequences of a tragic moment—how the individual acts before a crucial fact, or in an exceptional circumstance. That is everything. JOHN FORD, interview with Jean Mitry, *Cahiers du Cinéma*, March 1955, cited in Andrew Sarris, ed., *Interviews with Film Directors* (New York: The Bobbs-Merrill Company, 1967), p. 160.

JOHN FORD (1895–1973) Is John Ford the preeminent American sound director? Certainly Orson Welles, for all the lapses and disappointments of his later years, was more innovative. There are many other directors (Woody Allen, Steven Spielberg) whose names are much more familiar to the moviegoing public. And even Howard Hawks, whose career parallels Ford's in so many ways, had a more eclectic output, working in genres and subgenres that Ford never approached or touched on only occasionally.

Yet John Ford transcends all the others in many important ways. Many directors began their careers in the silent era, but very few can claim Ford's amazing durability. He directed his first verified feature film, *Straight Shooting*, in 1917, and his last, *Seven Women*, in 1966: nearly a half-century of superior filmmaking. Other directors have permeated their films with a personal vision of life or an identifiable visual style, but very few have offered a vision as strong, as compelling, or as inherently American as Ford's, or a visual style that encompassed such a remarkable combination of sweeping images and economy of expression. Other directors—Preston Sturges, for example—have assembled their own "stock

company" of players and their own supporting staff. But is there any group of actors more tightly knit than Ford's? The faces of Ward Bond, Harry Carey, Victor McLaglen, and, of course, John Wayne are etched in every filmgoer's memory. Behind the camera, Ford continually relied on such photographers as Winton C. Hoch, Bert Glennon, Gregg Toland, and Archie Stout, and such screenwriters as Dudley Nichols, Frank S. Nugent, and Lamar Trotti. Together, they created a physical and moral universe characterized by a sense of order and discipline, a reverence for the ties of family and community, and an abiding love for the land and its traditions. In cinematic terms, it is a universe that is uniquely Ford's.

Above all, John Ford has earned the unstinting praise of his peers. Asked by a *Playboy* interviewer to identify the American director he admired most, Orson Welles replied, "The old masters, by which I mean John Ford, John Ford, and John Ford." Interviewed in *Films and Filming* (October 1964), Sidney Lumet remarked, "Almost anything that any of us has done you can find in a John Ford film." And after Ford's death, Frank Capra wrote, "He was pure Ford—which means pure great. John was half-tyrant, half-revolutionary; half-saint, half-satan; half-possible, half-impossible, half-genius, half-Irish, but all director and for all time" (*Action*, November–December 1973, p. 10). During his lifetime, Ford received the Academy Award four times (for *The Informer, The Grapes of Wrath, How Green Was My Valley,* and *The Quiet Man*), and he was presented with the AFI Life Achievement Award in 1972.

Ford can truly be numbered among the Hollywood pioneers. Born in Maine, the thirteenth child of Irish immigrants, he arrived in the film capital in 1913, a teenager anxious to join his brother Francis, who was working at Universal Studios as an actor, director, and writer. Only a few years later, John (or Jack, as he was called then) was an assistant director, and by 1917, at age twenty-two, he had directed his first feature film. By the end of the silent era, he had turned out many films, mostly straightforward Westerns starring Harry Carey. Of these, the most important was *The Iron Horse* (1924), a large-scale frontier drama about the building of the transcontinental railroad, with George O'Brien as the rugged hero. Crude in some ways, the film contained many of the elements that would appear later in Ford's films: the feeling for outdoor spectacle, the idealization of the pioneer West, and the rowdy Irish humor. He also directed *Four Sons* (1928), a lachrymose drama of wartime sacrifice that demonstrated his feeling for close family relationships.

Gone with the Wind: VICTOR FLEMING (MGM, 1939). The ongoing relationship between Rhett Butler (Clark Gable) and Scarlett O'Hara (Vivien Leigh) formed the emotional and romantic center of this perennially popular movie. Fleming, a good friend of Gable's, was taken off the completion of The Wizard of Oz *and signed to direct this film.*

new, Dudley Nichols's screenplay infused the characters with fresh vitality. Above all, John Ford's direction gave the film pace and excitement, and the few scenes photographed in Monument Valley—an imposing area of about two thousand square miles on the Arizona-Utah border—brought a new, open-air expansiveness to the Western. Monument Valley, Ford's most familiar physical landscape, came to signify his moral landscape as well, expressing in its majesty his feelings about the order of existence and the permanence of nature. It also represented the battleground on which men, usually Ford's hard-riding cavalrymen, fought to preserve what he regarded as unassailable principles of justice and right. (Only late in his career, when his vision darkened, did Ford question the moral ambiguity of the Indian battles fought in his beloved Monument Valley and elsewhere.)

Ford's most successful Westerns in the forties and fifties, for all their bristling action scenes and violent encounters, were essentially hymns to pioneer America. *My Darling Clementine* (1946) related the often-told story of Marshal Wyatt Earp's conflict with the murderous Clanton clan, but what one recalls best are scenes of ritual that bind the characters to each other, such as the community dance celebrating the opening of the town church. *Wagonmaster* (1950) was perhaps Ford's purest expression of pioneer tenacity; its story of a Mormon trek westward was epitomized by repeated shots of wagons snaking through the valley. *Fort Apache* (1948),

Inevitably, Ford's forty-year sound career is dominated by his Western films. These films distilled the essence of his belief in America and its people. They embodied his conviction that the sturdy American values that had settled the wilderness—courage, perseverance, strong family bonds—were not only worth cherishing but also worth fighting for. For Ford, such words as "duty" and "honor" were not vague abstractions but living realities. His was an essentially conservative point of view, and, coupled with his conservative politics, it caused him to lose points with some members of the critical fraternity. But none could dispute the power or the beauty of the Western images in such films as *Stagecoach, She Wore a Yellow Ribbon,* or *The Searchers.*

Stagecoach set the mark in 1939, not only revitalizing the Western genre, which had fallen into disrepute for many years, but also solidifying the elements that became part of the classic Western mold. While its story of a group of stagecoach passengers who share a dangerous adventure on the way to Lordsberg was not exactly

ABOVE   The Grapes of Wrath: JOHN FORD *(Fox, 1940). On their journey to California, the Joad family is stopped along the road. In the car: Rosasharn (Dorris Bowdon), Ma (Jane Darwell), and Tom (Henry Fonda). Nunnally Johnson's adaptation of the John Steinbeck novel diluted the social content to emphasize one family's enduring strength in the face of adversity.*
RIGHT   Tobacco Road: JOHN FORD *(Fox, 1941). John Ford (second from left) directs Gene Tierney and Ward Bond (on the ground) in this adaptation of the long-running play. The movie substituted uninhibited farce and sentiment for the play's ribaldry and trenchant view of human depravity. At right: Charley Grapewin as Jeeter Lester.*

She Wore a Yellow Ribbon (1949), and *Rio Grande* (1950) made up a trilogy of films in praise of the military and its staunch heroes. The screenplays of these films usually closed with a ringing salute to America's soldiers. At the end of *Fort Apache,* John Wayne pays tribute to the men of the regular army: "They'll keep on living as long as the regiment lives. . . . They're better men than they used to be."

Ironically, Wayne's speech honors Colonel Owen Thursday (Henry Fonda), his martinet commander, who perversely led his troops into a suicide mission. Ford clearly believed that society needed its heroes to admire and imitate, even if their heroism was unfounded. He never appeared to doubt the dubious consequences of offering up a deliberate falsehood (or, if you will, "legend") as the truth. In fact, Ford's Western films largely omitted shadings and complexities until *The Searchers* (1956), regarded by many as his greatest in the genre. A richly textured, beautifully mounted Western (screenplay by Frank S. Nugent, photography by Winton Hoch), the movie related the odyssey, inward as well as outward, of Ethan Edwards, a man driven to find the niece captured by Indians years before. In one of his best roles, John Wayne fully expressed the bitter hostility, the loneliness, and the ultimate salvation of this obsessed character. (Civilization has no place for him; at the end he returns to the lonely life.) John Ford's steadying hand, faltering only in allowing an excessive running time and some dry, dull stretches, gave *The Searchers* a stature rare in Westerns.

Some parts of *The Searchers* presaged Ford's increasingly somber vision of humanity that surfaced in his sixties Westerns. Instead of a soothing view of bigotry turning to tolerance—Ethan Edwards sweeping up his Indianized niece and saying, "Let's go home, Debbie"—*Two Rode Together* (1961) showed a hostile town lynching a terrified young boy—also a former Indian captive—when he kills the crazed old woman who had claimed him as her "son." A yet bleaker film—even its sets were dark and constricted—*The Man Who Shot Liberty Valance* (1962) represented Ford's dirge for the death of the Old West he had depicted so often in his movies. And in *Cheyenne Autumn* (1964), Ford attempted to apologize for and correct the image of the American Indian that he and virtually every other director of Westerns had presented in their films. Centering on the mournful and disastrous trek of three hundred Cheyenne Indians from an Oklahoma reservation to their ancestral home in Wyoming, the film was never quite as moving as Ford had intended. Still, it reflected a view of humanity far re-

moved from the unquestioning heroics of his Westerns two decades earlier.

Ford's non-Western films have not fared as well over the years. Movies once revered by the critics (*The Informer,* 1935; *The Grapes of Wrath,* 1940) have been downgraded, while others, once considered minor films, have been given the cachet of critical analysis and approval (*The Prisoner of Shark Island,* 1936; *The Sun Shines Bright,* 1953). However, the pendulum may yet swing back in the opposite direction. For all of what Andrew Sarris calls its "calculated expressionism and maudlin sentimentality," *The Informer* retains moments of singular power (especially Gypo Nolan's inquisition) and a remarkable performance by Victor McLaglen, which Ford wrung from the limited actor by continually badgering, cajoling, and threatening him. For all of its dated New Deal proselytizing, *The Grapes of Wrath* remains one of the screen's great social dramas; under Ford's direction, Nunnally Johnson's well-crafted screenplay out of John Steinbeck's novel, Gregg Toland's somber, low-key photography, and deeply felt performances by Henry Fonda, Jane Darwell, and the rest of an impeccable cast come together to form a stark but memorable portrait of Dust Bowl America.

Several of Ford's non-Western films triumph over their faults and continue to linger in the minds of movie-

How Green Was My Valley: JOHN FORD *(Fox, 1941). Dai Bando (Rhys Williams) teaches young Huw (Roddy McDowall) to defend himself from school bullies as Huw's family looks on. Ford's lovely adaptation of the bestselling novel embodied his reverence for family values.*

goers. After more than four decades, *How Green Was My Valley* (1941) is still a cherished film, a sentimental but loving adaptation of Richard Llewellyn's novel about a Welsh family's tribulations in an impoverished mining town. Few films contain scenes of such piercing beauty and tenderness (the singing miners returning to their homes; young Huw walking through the valley with his father) or performances of such absolute rightness, especially Donald Crisp as the elder Morgan and Sara Allgood as his tenacious wife. Ford's warm regard for the family unit, as well as his mastery of the evocative detail

ABOVE Cheyenne Autumn: JOHN FORD *(Warner Bros., 1964). Ford's powerful film depicted the plight of the Cheyenne Indians who, angered by the white man's deceit and evasions, decided in 1878 to make the painful trek back to their homeland, 1500 miles away.*
OPPOSITE, BELOW Amadeus: MILOS FORMAN *(Orion, 1984). The inexpressibly vulgar, audacious young Mozart (Tom Hulce) leads the orchestra in one of his own compositions. Emperor Joseph II (Jeffrey Jones, in white) can be seen seated behind Mozart.* OPPOSITE, ABOVE *Milos Forman directs a scene for this adaptation of Peter Shaffer's play.*

and his skill with actors are evident throughout the film. *The Quiet Man* (1952) is memorable in an entirely different vein. In his gloriously photographed tribute to all things Irish, Ford had the good sense to surround the central story of John Wayne's hectic courting of Maureen O'Hara with players (Barry Fitzgerald, Mildred Natwick, and many actors of Ireland's Abbey Theatre) who were wonderfully adept at handling the rowdy, boisterous Gaelic humor.

Ford's flaws are clear even in the best of his films. His all-stops-out sentimentality and his clamorous Irish slapstick can make the teeth ache. Some of his films, particularly of the thirties, are overlaid with arty barnacles. But at his best, which was often, he was one of the screen's master storytellers and instinctive artists. One can hear tough, irascible "Pappy" Ford laughing at being called an artist, but there is no doubt that he was able to create poetic images on film, images that have become a permanent part of our consciousness.

★

MILOS FORMAN (born 1932) Czechoslovakian director Milos Forman enjoyed his first major triumph when his film *One Flew over the Cuckoo's Nest* won all five top Academy Awards (best film, director, actress, actor, screenplay) in 1975, a feat achieved only once before, by *It Happened One Night* in 1934. Incisively directed by Forman, *Cuckoo's Nest* was a powerful drama, set in a vaguely defined mental hospital, concerning the repression of nonconformity in a conformist society. As the defiant, life-embracing patient Randle McMurphy, Jack Nicholson, heading an impeccable cast, gave a bravura performance. Apparently, he also helped Forman to reinforce the kind of flexible and spontaneous acting style the director favored in his films.

Forman had come to America in the late sixties after scoring successes with several films—including *Loves of a Blonde* (1965) and *The Fireman's Ball* (1968)—in his native country. The broadly comic, satirical tone of these films carried over into Forman's first American film, *Taking Off* (1971). Since *Cuckoo's Nest*, Forman has directed *Hair* (1979), an adaptation of the long-running sixties rock

musical that already seemed anachronistic in the seventies, and *Ragtime* (1981), an elaborate, sprawling, ultimately disappointing adaptation of E. L. Doctorow's novel about life in the America of 1906. Forman's visually stunning version of Peter Shaffer's play *Amadeus* (1984) returned him to the heady days of *Cuckoo's Nest;* the movie won a total of eight Academy Awards.

★

BOB FOSSE (born 1927)   A renowned and active stage choreographer and director, Bob Fosse transposed his dynamic, athletic, and sometimes frenetic style to the screen with his first movie, an overbusy adaptation of the Broadway musical *Sweet Charity* (1969). His second film, a stunning, imaginative film version of the stage success *Cabaret* (1972), was a total triumph and arguably the greatest musical film of the seventies. Out of Christopher Isherwood's ''Berlin Stories'' and John Van Druten's play *I Am a Camera,* Fosse fashioned a complex mosaic of Berlin in the early thirties, when the seeds of fascism were sprouting everywhere. His direction here, unlike in *Sweet Charity,* was controlled, incisive, and on the mark. Liza Minnelli contributed a bravura performance as the hedonistic Sally Bowles, and Joel Grey was

mesmerizing as the cabaret's leering Master of Ceremonies. The film won a total of eight Academy Awards.

Fosse's subsequent films have been controversial and invariably fascinating: *Lenny* (1974), a stark drama on the life of comedian Lenny Bruce, brilliantly played by Dustin Hoffman; *All That Jazz* (1979), an autobiographical account of one man's hectic experiences in the theater that is a dazzling, bittersweet hymn to the musical stage; and *Star 80* (1983), a harrowing, compelling, and greatly undervalued drama based on the short life and brutal murder of *Playboy* centerfold and actress Dorothy Stratten. They have all shown skill in handling film techniques, although none has measured up to *Cabaret.*

★

JOHN FRANKENHEIMER (born 1930)   The film career of John Frankenheimer yields a puzzling picture. By the mid-sixties, after a long and very busy career as a director of television dramas, Frankenheimer had built up an almost equally strong reputation as a film director. His most successful movies, including *Birdman of Alcatraz*

LEFT   *With an abundance of talent, Bob Fosse has been able to balance his career as a director and choreographer on both stage and screen. At its best his vibrant, inventive style succeeds in igniting the material.*
OPPOSITE   Cabaret: BOB FOSSE *(Allied Artists, 1972). Liza Minnelli electrified the screen as Sally Bowles in Fosse's adaptation of the Broadway musical. Fosse improved on the original, fusing the trenchant drama of early fascism in Germany with brilliantly staged musical numbers that often commented sardonically on the action.* ABOVE   *Bob Fosse (left) directs Joel Grey as the Master of Ceremonies.*

(1962), *The Manchurian Candidate* (1962), and *Seven Days in May* (1964), were vigorous, absorbing dramas with social and political overtones. In the Winter 1966–67 issue of *Film Heritage*, Alan Casty wrote that Frankenheimer's film *Seconds* (1966) established him (along with Stanley Kubrick) as "the most important and distinctive of the new independent Hollywood directors." Then Frankenheimer moved to Europe, and during this period the public ignored his films while the critics savaged them. His adaptation of Bernard Malamud's novel *The Fixer* (1968), for example, was nearly bludgeoned to death—Pauline Kael called his staging and handling of the actors "almost incomprehensibly solemn and inept." Lost in the general condemnation was a fine performance by Alan Bates as a Jew accused of a crime in pre-Revolutionary Russia.

ABOVE   The Manchurian Candidate: JOHN FRANKENHEIMER *(United Artists, 1962). In a drug-induced hallucination, soldiers Frank Sinatra and Laurence Harvey imagine they are attending a ladies' gardening lecture. Frankenheimer's thriller injected overtones of political and social satire into its story of a soldier (Harvey) brainwashed to become an assassin.*

OPPOSITE   The Fixer: JOHN FRANKENHEIMER *(MGM, 1968). Director Frankenheimer (seated at center) waits to shoot a pogrom scene in a courtyard of Budapest that served as a Jewish ghetto until World War II. The movie received harsh notices, yet it contained some compelling scenes in its story of a Jew (Alan Bates) accused of a crime in pre-Revolutionary Russia.*

RIGHT   The Barretts of Wimpole Street: SIDNEY FRANKLIN *(MGM, 1934). Elizabeth Barrett (Norma Shearer) confronts her tyrannical father (Charles Laughton) in Franklin's reverential version of Rudolf Besier's play. Twenty-three years later, Franklin remade the story with Jennifer Jones and John Gielgud; it was his last film.*

Where to go but up? Frankenheimer returned to form (and to the United States) in the seventies, directing a creditable version of Eugene O'Neill's *The Iceman Cometh* (1973), with Lee Marvin and Robert Ryan (in one of his last and best performances). Later in the decade he directed a highly charged melodrama entitled *Black Sunday* (1976), which was one of the best of the "what-if" series of films about cataclysmic public disasters. (In this one, international terrorists try to blow up the Super Bowl.) While he has surfaced occasionally in recent years, his films (*The Challenge*, 1982; *The Holcroft Covenant*, 1985) have again dropped into obscurity.

★

SIDNEY FRANKLIN (1893–1972)   Over the years Sidney Franklin earned a reputation as the director of smooth, stylish, often expensive productions designed to showcase the screen's most glamorous actresses, including Greta Garbo, Norma Shearer, and Marion Davies. He found a congenial home at MGM, where he was a personal favorite of producer Irving Thalberg. Not surprisingly, many of his films for the studio starred Shearer, who was married to Thalberg (*Private Lives*, 1931; *The Barretts of Wimpole Street*, 1934). Franklin has been accused of being dull, and it is true that many of his movies lack sparkle, but under his direction Garbo exuded an exotic sultriness in *Wild Orchids* (1929), the Lunts had

was a harrowing, repellent drama about a horribly possessed child and the desperate effort to exorcise her demons. His later films (*Sorcerer*, 1977; *The Brink's Job*, 1978; *Deal of the Century*, 1983) have been disappointing, no better than routine in style or execution, the low point being *Cruising* (1980), a grim, exploitative melodrama about the homosexual underworld. Friedkin's most recent movie, *To Live and Die in L.A.* (1985), returned him to the crime thriller, but the *New York Times* reviewer characterized it as "so relentlessly, nastily trendy that it comes close to self-parody."

★

SAMUEL FULLER (born 1911) Samuel Fuller has always been his own man. Tough, independent-minded, and uncompromising, he fashioned a group of films in the fifties and sixties that won him wide admiration, especially in Europe, for their crisp, forthright style and also attracted criticism for their brutality and their conservative and chauvinistic (some say jingoistic) point of view. Whatever one's perception of Fuller's films, some of them remain watchable today, with strong if simplistic characterizations and many well-handled action scenes.

A scriptwriter in the mid-thirties, Fuller began directing in the late forties, after achieving a distinguished record with the infantry in World War II. From the first, his films were noted for their hard edge and their direct, uncluttered approach to basic situations. Perhaps his best film of the fifties, *Pickup on South Street* (1953), was a gritty, violent thriller set in the underworld of crooks, detectives, and Communist spies (Thelma Ritter was superb

a merry time in *The Guardsman* (1931), and John Barrymore seemed to relish his *Reunion in Vienna* (1933). Franklin took over the direction of *The Good Earth* (1937) from George Hill and did a worthy job of adapting Pearl Buck's novel about China. After Irving Thalberg's death, Franklin turned to producing, with credits that included *Mrs. Miniver* (1942), *Madame Curie* (1943), and *The Yearling* (1946). He retired from films after directing a remake of *The Barretts of Wimpole Street* (1957).

★

WILLIAM FRIEDKIN (born 1939) A busy television director for many years, William Friedkin has had two major hits since turning to films in the late sixties. The Oscar-winning *The French Connection* (1971) was a vivid, explosive crime melodrama highlighted by one of the most breathlessly exciting car chases ever filmed, and *The Exorcist* (1973), adapted from William Peter Blatty's novel,

---

ABOVE The French Connection: WILLIAM FRIEDKIN *(Fox, 1971). Gene Hackman won an Academy Award for his performance as the hard-nosed, unyielding detective Popeye Doyle, who uncovers a narcotics ring in New York City. Friedkin and the film also received Oscars.*
RIGHT The Naked Kiss: SAMUEL FULLER *(Allied Artists, 1964). Constance Towers starred as a reformed prostitute seeking to build a new life in Fuller's lurid but well-directed melodrama.*

as an ill-fated stool pigeon). Some critics also admired Fuller's small-scale films on the Korean War (*Fixed Bayonets, The Steel Helmet*, both 1951) for their realistic milieus and uncompromising views of combat.

In the late fifties and early sixties, starting with *The Crimson Kimono* (1959), Fuller produced, wrote, and directed a series of low-budget crime films that had their expected share of defenders and detractors. *Underworld U.S.A.* (1961), centering on Cliff Robertson's efforts to avenge his father's murder, covered familiar ground, but Fuller managed some exceptionally powerful moments. (Robertson promises forgiveness to a dying witness, then mutters "Sucker!" as the witness dies.) Other films, such as *Shock Corridor* (1963), concerning a reporter (Peter Breck) who feigns insanity to expose a killer in a mental hospital, and *The Naked Kiss* (1964), about a reformed prostitute, while undeniably lurid, drew compelling force from their very raw vitality. In recent years, Fuller returned to filmmaking with a well-received war film entitled *The Big Red One* (1980) and with *White Dog* (1982), which focused on a dog that is trained to attack black people on sight. Although it was patently antiracist, controversy over its point of view has kept the movie from being theatrically released by Paramount. Most recently, Fuller directed a French film called *Thieves after Dark* (1983).

★

TAY GARNETT (1894–1977) Tay Garnett began directing films in 1928 after working as a writer for Mack Sennett, Hal Roach, and others. His films in the thirties (*China Seas*, 1935; *Love Is News*, 1937; and others), while not exactly polished, kept up a lively, entertaining pace. One of his few dramas of the period, *One Way Passage* (1932), provoked tears with its story about two doomed lovers (Kay Francis and William Powell). By the forties, moving from studio to studio, he had dabbled in almost every kind of film, from the bawdy (Marlene Dietrich ogling John Wayne in *Seven Sinners*, 1940) to the bathetic (Martha Scott as a beloved schoolmarm in *Cheers for Miss Bishop*, 1941). Working for a stretch at MGM, he directed films of larger scope and ambition, including the strong war drama *Bataan* (1943), and elaborate costume dramas designed for the rather arch, decorous style of Greer Garson (*Mrs. Parkington*, 1944; *The Valley of Decision*, 1945). His best film is probably *The Postman Always Rings Twice* (1946), a tough, steamy melodrama based on James Cain's novel. As scheming, adulterous lovers, John Garfield and Lana Turner exuded more sexuality than Jack Nicholson and Jessica Lange generated in Bob

Rafelson's raunchy 1981 remake, with all its explicitness. Garnett's films in the fifties and sixties were infrequent and not very good.

★

MICHAEL GORDON (born 1909) A stage actor and director, Michael Gordon entered films in 1940, starting out with such low-budget films as *Boston Blackie Goes Hollywood* (1942) and *Crime Doctor* (1943). In the late forties and early fifties, he directed more prestigious movies, which vary in quality. *Another Part of the Forest* (1948) and *Cyrano de Bergerac* (1950) presented earnest but rather plodding versions of stage plays (the latter seemed to have omitted most of the color and flamboyance of the Rostand original). On the other hand, *I Can Get It for You Wholesale* (1951), based on the Jerome Weidman novel, was a brisk, sassy comedy-drama about the garment industry. During the harrowing McCarthy years, Gordon was blacklisted. He returned to films in the late fifties with an entirely different style. His greatest success was the 1959 *Pillow Talk*, which launched the series of popular romantic comedies starring Doris Day and Rock Hudson. *Move Over, Darling* (1963), his remake of the Irene Dunne–Cary Grant film *My Favorite Wife* (1940), co-starred Day with James Garner. Unfortunately, it demonstrated the crucial difference between the lighthearted sophistication of the "screwball" era and the glossier but forced, vacuous comedy style of the sixties.

The Valley of Decision: TAY GARNETT (*MGM, 1945*). *Greer Garson, Jessica Tandy, and Gregory Peck appeared in Garnett's elaborate but superficial adaptation of Marcia Davenport's novel. Garson played a resourceful housemaid who later marries Peck, scion of a wealthy Pittsburgh steel family.*

Fontaine's archness for the romantic drama *The Constant Nymph* (1943). And certainly Tyrone Power gave his finest performance as the scheming carnival roustabout in the bleak melodrama *Nightmare Alley* (1947).

Aside from the last film and a fatuous, windy adaptation of W. Somerset Maugham's *The Razor's Edge* (1946), Goulding's films during his tenure at Fox in the forties and fifties tended to the sleek and lightweight (*Claudia*, 1943; *We're Not Married*, 1952; among others). No matter what the material, his skill with actors seldom faltered. Under his direction, Mary Astor and Anne Baxter won Oscars as Best Supporting Actress for their roles in, respectively, *The Great Lie* (1941) and *The Razor's Edge*. There were limits, however: Goulding could not coax a credible performance out of Eleanor Parker as the nasty waitress Mildred in his drab 1946 remake of *Of Human Bondage*. It should be noted that Goulding began his career as a writer in the silent years (*Tol'able David*, 1921; *Dante's Inferno*, 1924) and later wrote many of the screenplays for the films he directed.

★

EDMUND GOULDING (1891–1959)   Edmund Goulding has been accused of lacking a distinctive personal style, a charge that can and has been leveled against many directors who labored diligently and professionally in the Hollywood groves. In this case it means that Goulding, a British-born man of refinement, chose to remain discreetly in the background while the actors in his films gave memorable performances under his confident direction. Was Joan Crawford ever better than as the ambitious secretary Flaemschen in Goulding's *Grand Hotel* (1932)? The essence of Bette Davis's peak period—her strongest and most poignant emoting—can be found in *Dark Victory* (1939) and *The Old Maid* (1939), both Goulding films. He even managed to subdue some of Joan

★

ALFRED E. GREEN (1889–1960)   The amazingly prolific Alfred E. Green directed feature films from 1917 to 1954, turning out crisp, unpretentious entertainments in every genre. His greatest success came late in his career with *The Jolson Story* (1946), a tribute to the singer that mixed a schmaltzy story with Jolson's schmaltzy style in a way that audiences found palatable. Much earlier, Green had directed many popular silent films starring Mary Pickford, Wallace Reid, Thomas Meighan, and other luminaries of that period. For most of the thirties,

ABOVE   Dark Victory: EDMUND GOULDING *(Warner Bros., 1939). A superior director of actresses, Goulding guided Bette Davis through one of her finest performances in this moving drama. As a dying heiress who falls in love with and marries her doctor (George Brent), she played with intensity and conviction.*

RIGHT   The Jolson Story: ALFRED E. GREEN *(Columbia, 1946). Top entertainer Al Jolson (Larry Parks) talks with his old friend Steve Martin (William Demarest) while his wife Julie (Evelyn Keyes) looks on. Green topped his long career with this entertaining but shamelessly bogus biography of the singer.*

he was one of Warners's busiest resident directors, grinding out his share of the studio's quick-paced programmers, such as *Union Depot* (1932), *The Narrow Corner* (1933), and *Dark Hazard* (1934), and occasionally more prestigious films, such as *Disraeli* (1929) and *The Green Goddess* (1930), both with *Mr.* George Arliss. He directed Bette Davis in her Oscar-winning performance as an alcoholic actress in *Dangerous* (1935), and although Davis went through her paces with appropriate intensity (what aspiring actress doesn't relish playing a drunkard?), the movie was feeble. Few of his forties entries contain much of interest, and his later attempt to repeat the Jolson success with *The Eddie Cantor Story* (1953) fell afoul of its tired screenplay and an inept performance in the title role. He later turned to television.

★

In the year 2024 the most important single thing which the cinema will have helped in a large way to accomplish will be that of eliminating from the face of the civilized world all armed conflict. Pictures will be the most powerful factor in bringing about this condition. With the use of the universal language of moving pictures the true meaning of the brotherhood of man will have been established throughout the earth. D. W. GRIFFITH, in *The Book of Hollywood Quotes*, compiled by Gary Herman (London: Omnibus Press, 1979), p. 11.

D. W. GRIFFITH (1875–1948) At what point in time did the movies turn in the direction of art? It could be argued persuasively that the moment arrived at the premiere of D. W. Griffith's *The Birth of a Nation* on 8 February 1915 at Clune's Auditorium in Los Angeles (and again a month later at the Liberty Theater in New York City), when the stunned audience realized that it was watching a film unlike any other until that time: a massive, sweeping, three-hour epic that took the medium of film into an exciting and significant new dimension. With this one film, Griffith refuted those who thought of movies as a clever toy, designed for idle amusement, showing how film could be used as a powerful vehicle for expressing ideas, stirring the emotions, and stimulating the imagination. With *The Birth of a Nation* and especially with *Intolerance*, released the following year, Griffith influenced an entire generation of filmmakers and left his indelible imprint on the work of many directors.

Griffith did not invent cinematic techniques; he took such techniques as crosscutting, parallel action, the close-up, dramatic lighting, and rhythmic editing, which already existed in crude forms, and used them creatively for maximum effect. With an instinctive understanding of film, he shaped these techniques into a unique cinematic language that became a basic primer for future filmmakers. Drawing on the skilled aid of a staff that remained with him for many years, especially cameramen Billy (G. W.) Bitzer and Karl Brown, Griffith forged the first and strongest link in the evolution of motion pictures. He also developed a new and subtler style of acting for the screen that replaced the usual bombastic emoting derived from the stage and brought to the fore a group of performers (Lillian Gish, Mae Marsh, Henry B. Walthall, and many more) who contributed importantly to film history.

The Kentucky-born son of a lieutenant colonel who had fought heroically for the South in the Civil War, David Wark Griffith was a struggling stage actor and aspiring writer who, disappointed by his lack of success, turned to the infant film industry for a new career. He finally won a leading role in *Rescued from an Eagle's Nest* (1907), directed by pioneer filmmaker Edwin S. Porter, and he also began selling stories to the Biograph Studios. Biograph gave him the chance to direct his first feature, *The Adventures of Dollie* (1908), and by the following year, he was directing scores of films in many genres for the studio. Many of these films, for all their crudeness, showed a basic awareness of dramatic and visual composition. Before he left Biograph in the fall of 1913, he had directed a number of two-reelers and one lavish four-reel film (actually, the first ever) called *Judith of Bethulia* (1914).

Ambitious and seeking more creative challenges, Griffith joined Reliance-Majestic as head of production. At first he turned out a number of unsuccessful films, but all the while he was preparing to film his large-scale and prodigiously expensive adaptation of the Reverend Thomas Dixon's virulently racist novel *The Klansman*, which Griffith ultimately called *The Birth of a Nation*. A fanciful, highly romanticized view of the South in the years of the Civil War and Reconstruction, it related the story of two families, the Northern Stonemans and the Southern Camerons, as their lives change and intertwine during those years. It was an astonishing achievement in which scenes of enormous scope (Civil War battles, the siege of Atlanta) alternated with small, intimate moments that gave the film its unique power.

Inevitably, *The Birth of a Nation*, with its view of shiftless, corrupt, and power-hungry blacks and a noble Ku Klux Klan riding to the rescue of besieged whites, stirred up a storm of controversy that has never really subsided. Black groups urged the banning of the film, and many of

size and splendor in which Griffith weaves together four separate stories (the fall of Babylon, the betrayal and crucifixion of Christ, the massacre of the Huguenots in 1572, and a modern story of injustice) into a cinematic fugue. Griffith never again used cinematic techniques with such skill and assurance: imaginative intercutting, mood-enhancing lighting, and brilliant camerawork (by Billy Bitzer) combined to create spectacular sequences that would be impressive in any decade.

Although *Intolerance* deeply influenced filmmakers around the world, it was a severe box-office disappointment that drained Griffith, both financially and emotionally. After ending his association with the Triangle Corporation, the company he had started with Mack Sennett and Thomas Ince, Griffith joined Adolph Zukor's company, Famous Players-Lasky (later Paramount), where he made a number of films—some of them lost—with Lillian Gish (*The Greatest Thing in Life*, 1918; *True Heart Susie*, 1919; and others). Small-scaled and unpretentious, these films depended in large part on the star's wistful charm and her well-honed acting skills. She was rarely better than in Griffith's *Broken Blossoms* (1919), a bleak and poignant melodrama about the pure love of a Chinaman (Richard Barthelmess) for an abused waif (Gish). The film was the first released by Griffith through United Artists Corporation, which he had founded that year with Mary Pickford, Douglas Fairbanks, and Charlie Chaplin.

In the years that followed, Griffith found a level of commercial and critical success, but it never matched his earlier exalted position, and he never again made films with quite the same virtuosity. He enjoyed a hit with *Way Down East* (1920), a tear-jerking drama that featured a suspenseful climax with Lillian Gish trapped on an ice floe. He also directed Lillian and Dorothy Gish in a lavishly staged historical drama, *Orphans of the Storm* (1922), in which the sisters keep losing and finding each other during the turbulent days of the French Revolution. There were other films, including a panoramic tale of the Revolutionary War, appropriately called *America* (1924), and, in contrast, *Isn't Life Wonderful* (1924), an ironic title for a small but touching drama of life in postwar Germany, largely filmed on location. Griffith's last independent production, it clearly signaled a career on the decline.

During the balance of the twenties, Griffith was required to work at the studios with neither the creative independence he valued so highly nor the technical crew or stock company players he had nurtured during earlier years. Without the power to select his stories or

the reviews attacked it angrily. Others came to Griffith's defense, claiming that he had merely fallen heir to the naive attitude of a born Southerner who expected blacks to be docile. Arguments over the film's racism continue to this day—and, by this time, few doubt that Griffith sincerely believed that he was presenting an impartial account of events. The fact remains that this undisputed masterpiece is open to charges of bigotry; however, such charges cannot alter the film's importance or its achievement. With *The Birth of a Nation*, Griffith single-handedly moved film out of the nickelodeon and into the realm of art.

Hurt and bewildered by the accusation of racism, yet in no way apologetic for his point of view, Griffith decided to expand *The Mother and the Law*, a film he had already completed, into an awesome four-part epic that would trace man's inhumanity to man over the centuries. The result was *Intolerance* (1916), not only his greatest film but certainly one of the greatest of all films. Discounting its clear faults, it is a work of unparalleled

ABOVE   The Birth of a Nation: D. W. GRIFFITH (*Epoch Producing Co., 1915*). *Southern maiden Flora Cameron (Mae Marsh) shares a reflective moment with her adoring brother Ben (Henry B. Walthall), affectionately known as "The Little Colonel." Griffith looked upon Marsh, who was a favorite of his, as the essence of feminine purity.*

OPPOSITE   Way Down East: D. W. GRIFFITH (*United Artists, 1920*). *D. W. Griffith directs Richard Barthelmess and Lillian Gish (at right) in a scene from this tear-jerking drama. The film contains an extraordinary sequence in which Gish wanders through a blizzard onto a frozen river; trapped on a floe when the ice breaks up, she finds herself in a life-threatening situation as she is carried perilously close to a waterfall.*

ing, Hathaway directed a group of well-paced, engrossing movies based on true-life stories, including *The House on 92nd Street* (1945), *13 Rue Madeleine* (1947), and *Call Northside 777* (1948). He also guided Richard Widmark in his sensational film debut as a psychotic killer in the blistering melodrama *Kiss of Death* (1947). In many of Hathaway's films, the heroes find themselves in situations that call on them to prove their manhood or integrity or to justify their actions, often in violent confrontations. "Nuggin" Taylor (Gary Cooper) in *Souls at Sea* (1937) and Nick Bianco (Victor Mature) in *Kiss of Death* are only two of the many Hathaway characters who find themselves facing and then resolving moral dilemmas.

In the fifties at Fox, Hathaway continued to work in virtually every genre. However, these more expensive, large-screen efforts had less going for them than his earlier, smaller-scale films. Westerns such as *Garden of Evil* (1954), *From Hell to Texas* (1958), and *The Sons of Katie Elder* (1965) had their share of action sequences but lacked some of the conviction of the earlier movies. Hathaway failed to surmount such inappropriate assignments as the lavish knights-in-armor saga *Prince Valiant* (1954) or the basically soap-operatic *Woman Obsessed* (1959). Even the hugely popular, entertaining *True Grit* (1969) drew most of its attraction from John Wayne's Oscar-winning performance as the fat, ornery, one-eyed Rooster Cogburn. Altogether, though, the sum total of Hathaway's work warrants a respectable place among film directors.

★

I don't analyze things. I found that people like the same girls I like, that people laugh at the same things that amuse me, and that people like the same scenes that I do. So I just go blindly ahead and do them. I only hope the day doesn't come when they don't like it, because then I'll be very confused. But right now I don't have any doubts or hesitancy. HOWARD HAWKS, interview with David Austin, *Films and Filming,* October 1968.

HOWARD HAWKS (1896–1977) Howard Hawks did it all, and he did it his way. Screwball comedies, crime films, private-eye thrillers, Westerns—Hawks excelled at these and other genres, and he carried them off in a style that can truly be called uniquely Hawksian. It is a direct, uncluttered, unpretentious style that believes in

the virtues of a good old-fashioned story, well told. Hawks's best films, and there are many, are carefully structured and efficient. Hawks knew his craft and didn't have to prove that he did. He didn't believe in camera trickery or razzle-dazzle; he not only kept the camera at eye level, he also avoided close-ups and montages. Like other great directors, he knew how to make the best use of the creative people who worked regularly in his films, such actors as John Wayne and Walter Brennan, such writers as Jules Furthman, Ben Hecht, and Leigh Brackett.

Hawks's films are so spare and lean and so devoid of intellectual content that they do not lend themselves to heavy critical analysis, which is probably why film scholars neglected them for so long. Now it is common to write about his distinct overriding theme: a concern with men in groups, confronted with stress or life-threatening danger. Proudly professional, the Hawksian hero frequently finds himself in a risky situation to which he must willingly respond with courage and resilience and, above all, without self-pity or sentimentality. The worst sin, the unforgivable sin, is loss of self-control. (Of

---

Kiss of Death: HENRY HATHAWAY (Fox, 1947). On his way to prison, Nick Bianco (Victor Mature, left) makes friends with hood Tommy Udo (Richard Widmark). This gritty melodrama marked the film debut of Widmark, who created a memorable characterization in the maniacal Udo.

course, in Hawks's comedies, the reverse if true—the comic impetus often comes exactly from the hero's loss of self-control. Hawks's favorite comic actor, Cary Grant, repeatedly suffers humiliation or is forced to behave idiotically, in such films as *Bringing Up Baby*, *I Was a Male War Bride*, and *Monkey Business*.)

If Hawks's world is dominated by men, that is not to say that his women are given short shrift. It may take a while for some of Hawks's women to understand the male code of behavior—Jean Arthur in *Only Angels Have Wings* must learn about stoicism in the face of death—but they frequently display the same feisty, defiant, don't-mess-with-me attitude as the men. Ann Dvorak in *Scarface* chooses to die in a hail of gunfire with her brother (Paul Muni). And who would want to tangle with Hildy Johnson (Rosalind Russell) in *His Girl Friday* or Sugarpuss O'Shea (Barbara Stanwyck) in *Ball of Fire*? In Hawks's classic Western *Red River*, it is Joanne Dru who finally resolves the dangerous feud between John Wayne and his adopted son (Montgomery Clift). Although he excludes women from the circle of male camaraderie, Hawks clearly admires, respects, and loves them.

Hawks's rugged attitude toward life and his feeling for dangerous action and adventure reflect his early years as a racing driver and as a pilot with the Army Air Corps in World War I. His interest in aviation waned, however, when he discovered the film business. From the early twenties on, he worked at various jobs, including cutter, screenwriter, and assistant director, until Fox finally assigned him to direct one of his own scripts, *The Road to Glory* (1926), a drama (unrelated to Hawks's 1936

movie of the same title) about a blind girl (May McAvoy) who regains her faith and her sight.

From the first, Hawks worked within the established genres, giving his movies a swiftness and pace that revealed a forthright approach to storytelling. The dialogue in his first sound films is spare and functional. *The Dawn Patrol* (1930), a World War I aviation story, later remade by Edmund Goulding, sounds familiar Hawksian themes—the burden of wartime command, the close bonds of men in groups—with a crispness marred only by early sound excesses. *The Criminal Code* (1931), a taut drama on similar themes, substitutes a prison warden for an air force officer. Only a year later, Hawks directed his first masterwork, a blistering gangster film entitled *Scarface* (1932). Loosely based on the ignominious career of "Scarface" Al Capone, it used harsh, uncompromising, and sometimes stylized images to trace the career of Tony Camonte (Paul Muni) from his rise in the criminal ranks to his brutal death in a shoot-out.

Throughout the thirties, moving from studio to studio, Hawks directed films in a variety of genres, including swift action films that drew on his interest in flying (*Ceiling Zero*, 1935; *Only Angels Have Wings*, 1939) or rac-

ABOVE Scarface: HOWARD HAWKS (*United Artists, 1932*). *In this still-powerful crime melodrama, Paul Muni (left) starred as vicious gang lord Tony Camonte. At right is Vince Barnett as Tony's loyal, dim-witted aide Angelo.*
LEFT Bringing Up Baby: HOWARD HAWKS (*RKO, 1938*). *Constable Slocum (Walter Catlett) is inclined to throw the book at paleontologist David Huxley (Cary Grant) and madcap Susan Vance (Katharine Hepburn). Hawks kept the plot of this screwball comedy spinning merrily, if a bit frenetically.*

ing (*The Crowd Roars*, 1932) and lusty period dramas such as *Barbary Coast* (1935) and *Come and Get It* (1936, with William Wyler). Comedy, however, proved to be his special forte; the pacing, high energy, and slightly sardonic air he brought to melodrama appeared to work doubly well in screwball farce. By the end of the decade, Hawks had contributed three sublime entries to the

OPPOSITE   El Dorado: HOWARD HAWKS (*Paramount, 1967*). *In his next-to-last film, Howard Hawks (at right) directs (left to right) Charlene Holt, Edward Asner, Robert Mitchum, and James Caan. The movie was the middle entry in a triumvirate of Westerns (Rio Bravo and Rio Lobo were the others) in which Hawks played variations on the same plot line.*

RIGHT   Butch Cassidy and the Sundance Kid: GEORGE ROY HILL (*Fox, 1969*). *Robert Redford, Katharine Ross, and Paul Newman pose for a tintype in this immensely entertaining Western adventure. The movie took a cheerful revisionist view of the Old West, bringing a contemporary attitude to the familiar situations.*

BELOW   The Long Riders: WALTER HILL (*United Artists, 1980*). *Stacy and James Keach as the James brothers ride furiously at the head of their gang during a violent shoot-out. Hill filled the roles of several outlaw brothers with real-life brothers (the Keaches, Carradines, Quaids, and Guests).*

genre: *Twentieth Century* (1934), *Bringing Up Baby* (1938), and, especially, *His Girl Friday* (1940) crackled with inventive humor and gave full rein to the comedic talents of such players as Carole Lombard, Cary Grant, Katharine Hepburn, and Rosalind Russell. Grant, in particular, with his exuberant, debonair, tongue-in-cheek style, meshed perfectly with Hawks.

In the forties, Hawks continued to follow the patterns of previous years. Once again his comedies focused on the discomfited male (Gary Cooper as a prim professor overwhelmed by a stripper in *Ball of Fire*, 1941, Cary Grant as an army officer forced to wear drag in order to see his new wife in *I Was a Male War Bride*, 1949). There was also his continuing interest in accounts of World War I, which surfaced in his reverential biography of the popular hero *Sergeant York* (1941). Nor had Hawks lost his ability to showcase promising new actresses who displayed a tough-minded, independent attitude toward men and life; in 1944 he introduced a willowy, husky-voiced twenty-year-old named Lauren Bacall in an adaptation of Ernest Hemingway's novel *To Have and Have Not*. Humphrey Bogart costarred in a pairing that generated electricity, audience approval, and a marriage, roughly in that order. The two were teamed again in *The Big Sleep* (1946), a complex mystery thriller based on Raymond Chandler's novel. Hawks handled his first excursion into the murky waters of *film noir* with his usual skill, scoring well on racy dialogue, sinister atmosphere, and sexually charged performances.

In 1948 Hawks tried his hand at his first Western, with spectacular results. Widely regarded as one of the great films in the genre, *Red River* fused the story of a complex man whose pride and arrogance nearly result in his destruction with the historically based account of the opening of the Chisholm Trail in the 1860s. In one of his best performances, John Wayne starred as a rancher obsessed with building a cattle empire who clashes bitterly with his adopted son (Montgomery Clift) over the ways to achieve that goal. Any weaknesses in the screenplay paled beside the sweep and grandeur with which Hawks invested his central sequences, especially the rousing start of the cattle drive, a cattle stampede, and a dangerous river crossing. For all the spectacle, this Western is exceptionally rich in characterization as well, and it points up a favorite Hawks theme: man's strength lies in his unity with others in a common cause, and an isolated man cannot survive in a hostile world.

The fifties and sixties marked a falling off for Hawks. He tried to extend his franchise on screwball comedy with such films as *Monkey Business* (1952) and *Man's Fa-*

vorite Sport? (1964), yet another embarrassed-male story, but the results were mostly strained. He dabbled unsuccessfully in costume adventure with *Land of the Pharaohs* (1955). And, most interestingly, he not only directed a second Western, *Rio Bravo* (1959), but offered loose variations on the same story in two others, *El Dorado* (1967) and his last film, *Rio Lobo* (1970). *Rio Bravo* was by far the most accomplished. Although it hardly deserves its exalted reputation, its story of a group of oddly assorted misfits who come together to rout the villains is laced with humor, well-paced action scenes, and boisterous performances.

Hawks was awarded a special Oscar in 1974, four years after his final movie, but he probably refused to take it too seriously. He had done his job well for many years, stamping his uncomplicated point of view on a long series of films that, unintentionally but ineluctably, qualified as art. Like many of his heroes, Hawks would be pleased to be called a professional at his craft. And, although he might deny it, he would be glad to know that many of his films manage to stay as durable as anything can in this impermanent world.

★

GEORGE ROY HILL (born 1922)   George Roy Hill's output of films may have been uneven since his debut in 1962, but it includes two of the most popular movies of the past few decades (*Butch Cassidy and the Sundance Kid* and *The Sting*), a captivating musical (*Thoroughly Modern*

Millie), and quite a few oddball entries that deserve re-evaluation *(Slaughterhouse Five, Slap Shot)*. Add to this a narrative skill and the ability to bring out the best not only in charismatic stars but also in young performers (the teen-age girls in *The World of Henry Orient* and the teen-age lovers of *A Little Romance)*, and you have a director of commendable achievement.

Hill began as an actor and, after serving in World War II and the Korean War, he turned to directing and writing for the stage and television in the fifties. He made his film debut with an adaptation of Tennessee Williams's wafer-thin comedy *Period of Adjustment* (1962), which gave Jane Fonda one of her early roles, and followed this with *Toys in the Attic* (1963), a rather dreary version of Lillian Hellman's none-too-compelling play. With *The World of Henry Orient* (1964), he offered a cheerful and inordinately funny comedy about an eccentric pianist (Peter Sellers) who is pursued by two adoring teenagers. His large-budget filming of James Michener's novel *Hawaii* (1966), however, turned out to be a mammoth bore. Hill's only musical, *Thoroughly Modern Millie* (1967), was, on the whole, a success: a sprightly and well-mounted (if overlong) spoof of the giddy twenties, it starred Julie Andrews as a resourceful flapper and featured a batch of enjoyable musical numbers.

Hill finally achieved a truly rousing commercial hit with the Western *Butch Cassidy and the Sundance Kid* (1969), which teamed Paul Newman and Robert Redford as a pair of genial, devil-may-care, turn-of-the-century outlaws. A lively mixture of slapstick and traditional Western adventure, the movie viewed the familiar rituals of the genre (chases, shoot-outs, and so on) through a sixties sensibility. Four years later, the actors were teamed again in an even more successful film, *The Sting* (1973), an enjoyable, cleverly constructed comedy-melodrama concerning two con men who outwit a crime czar in an elaborate scheme. It was lightweight material, but it won an Oscar as Best Picture and gave Hill his only Academy Award. In between *Butch Cassidy* and *The Sting*, Hill directed *Slaughterhouse Five* (1972), which adapted Kurt Vonnegut's novel into a bewildering but intermittently inspired satirical fantasy about a New York optometrist (Michael Sacks) who becomes a time-traveler. Hill's 1977 comedy about hockey, *Slap Shot*,

both amused and alienated audiences with its virtually nonstop profanity.

Since *Slap Shot*, Hill has directed only a few films: the charming *A Little Romance* (1979), with Laurence Olivier doing one of his lovable-old-codger turns as an elderly Cupid who chaperones and advises two youngsters in love; *The World According to Garp* (1982), an adaptation of John Irving's popular novel that was either acclaimed as an imaginative rendition of the book or dismissed as a muddled, misguided combination of absurdist black comedy, grim tragedy, and satire; and *The Little Drummer Girl* (1984), a dispirited filming of John Le Carré's novel. Most recently, Hill has been teaching drama at Yale.

★

WALTER HILL (born 1942) Walter Hill's long suit as a director appears to be his effective staging of scenes of violent action. His characters, whether chasing or being chased, move as if propelled by an inner motor that never stops. To date his most popular film has been *48 Hrs.* (1982), a tough, brutal comedy-melodrama that benefited from Eddie Murphy's ingratiating performance as a streetwise convict temporarily released from prison. However, two of Hill's earlier films were much more interesting. In *The Warriors* (1979), about a street gang's desperate flight through the city, Hill's inventive direction, achieving a nightmarish quality with the striking use of color, turned New York into a bizarre fantasy world. *The Long Riders* (1980), also imaginatively photographed, offered an original, extremely violent view of the Wild West's best-known outlaws, including the James and Younger brothers. Hill's most recent movies have been disappointing: *Streets of Fire* (1984) combined visual pyrotechnics, rock music, and melodrama into a glittering but pointless film, and *Brewster's Millions* (1985) starred Richard Pryor in a lame remake of the antique farce.

★

ARTHUR HILLER (born 1923) Canadian-born Arthur Hiller had chalked up some impressive television credits on major dramatic shows when he entered films in the late fifties. While he has worked assiduously in most genres, his movies add up to a decidedly mixed bag. On the credit side, *The Americanization of Emily* (1964) took a well-aimed swipe at the madness of warfare; *The Hospital* (1971) confined its satirical attack on man's lunacy to a city hospital. Both films owed their success more to the iconoclastic wit of Paddy Chayefsky's screenplays than

---

Sergeant York: HOWARD HAWKS *(Warner Bros., 1941). Gary Cooper (left), shown here with Joe Sawyer, won an Oscar for his performance as conscientious objector-turned-World War I hero Alvin York. Made at a time when America's entrance into World War II was imminent, the movie vibrated with patriotic fervor.*

they did to Hiller. On the debit side, Hiller was unable to cope with the inanity of Neil Simon's script for *The Out-of-Towners* (1970), and he fared only marginally better with Simon's *Plaza Suite* (1971). He also brought a heavy touch to the film version of the Broadway musical *Man of La Mancha* (1972). Hiller's most popular film to date has been *Love Story* (1970), or "How to Die Tastefully and Quietly from the Movie Disease." Millions sobbed as Ali McGraw expired; notwithstanding, the movie probably merited Carol Burnett's hilarious spoof on television.

Although he works best with comic material, Hiller tends to make the common mistake of confusing frantic activity with humor. In such films as *Silver Streak* (1976) and *The In-Laws* (1979), born victims Gene Wilder and Alan Arkin work themselves into a frenzy as they get deeper in trouble, with diminishing returns. In recent years, Hiller has been prolific, with credits that include tepid comedies about theater people (*Author! Author!*, 1982; *Romantic Comedy*, 1983), a safe, tame drama about a homosexual relationship (*Making Love*, 1981), and a frenetic satirical comedy on the teaching profession (*Teachers*, 1984).

★

I don't want to film a "slice of life" because people can get that at home, in the street, or even in front of the movie theater. They don't have to pay money to see a slice of life. And I avoid out-and-out fantasy because people should be able to identify with the characters. Making a film means, first of all, to tell a story. That story can be an improbable one, but it should never be banal. It must be dramatic and human. What is drama, after all, but life with the dull bits cut out. ALFRED HITCHCOCK, in François Truffaut, with Helen G. Scott, *Hitchcock* (New York: Simon and Schuster, 1966), p. 71.

ALFRED HITCHCOCK (1899–1980)   In the moral universe of Alfred Hitchcock, nobody is safe, and nobody is blameless. In the climactic scene of *Strangers on a Train*, Guy Haines grapples on a runaway carousel with Bruno Anthony, the silkily insidious psychopath who has murdered Guy's wife, yet Guy himself has harbored dark impulses toward her. We share the viewpoint of L. B.

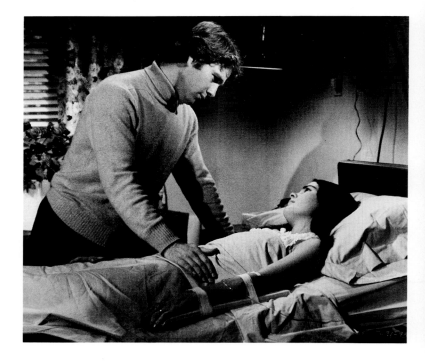

ABOVE   *Love Story*: ARTHUR HILLER (*Paramount, 1970*). *Ryan O'Neal comforts a dying Ali McGraw. Hiller's adaptation of the best-selling novel was responsible for many drenched handkerchiefs.*
OPPOSITE   *Alfred Hitchcock permits himself a faint smile, a change from the solemn demeanor that concealed a wicked, even diabolical sense of humor. Even the most harrowing of Hitchcock's films contains glints of black humor.*

Jeffries, trapped in a wheelchair throughout *Rear Window*, as he witnesses a panorama of life (including a possible homicide)—but, seen from a different perspective, he is a voyeur with pressing romantic problems of his own. In *Psycho*, one of the screen's most horrific moments occurs when Marion Crane, a thief who has absconded with a large sum of money intended for her employer, finds brutal death at the hands of the demented, mother-fixated Norman Bates. These people have discovered what Alfred Hitchcock always knew, that behind the lace curtain (or the shower curtain), the Beast crouches, waiting to spring upon us all. In city streets and motel rooms, in concert halls and cornfields, the seeds of evil are beginning to sprout, and some of them may be in our own minds. For over half a century, Hitchcock delighted in visualizing everyone's private demons, including his own.

Hitchcock's exalted status in the hierarchy of film directors has never been questioned. He has been called—and rightly so—"the supreme technician of the American cinema," "one of the greatest masters of pure cinema," and the screen's peerless purveyor of terror and suspense. For a time, particularly in the sixties, some critics viewed him not only as a brilliant filmmaker but also as one of the cosmically great artists of the century, with universal themes and concerns. French critics of the New Wave were especially adept at rooting out profundities. More recently, however, as Hitchcock's pri-

vate and public lives have been placed under intense scrutiny, the tide of adulation has turned. Hitchcock the artist has been replaced by Hitchcock the dirty old man whose films expose his ugliest, most fearful hang-ups and obsessions. We have learned about his lifelong fear of authority, especially the police, his taste for sadomasochism, his ambiguous, contradictory attitude toward women, and, most sadly, his late-in-life senility and alcoholism. We have read, perhaps far too much, about his fondness for brutal practical jokes.

Inevitably, somewhere between the genius and the ogre lies the truth. The best of Hitchcock's films never fail to dazzle us with their technical virtuosity, their deft and sometimes audacious handling of plot and character, and their mesmerizing suspense, all mixed with a generous amount of astringent wit and gallows humor. Yet the master sometimes faltered, with movies that are seriously flawed or no better than routine. There is also no doubt that Hitchcock's principal themes—the evil in ordinary life, the loss of identity, shared guilt, and reality versus the appearance of reality—can be traced throughout his life and work. Yet knowledge of Hitchcock's personal proclivities has no particular relevance to our understanding or appreciation of his work. It adds little to our judgment of his films.

Hitchcock entered films in 1920 as a designer of title cards for the London branch of Famous Players-Lasky (later Paramount). Several years later he was hired as scriptwriter and assistant director by the company that had taken over the Famous Players studios, and ultimately, on location in Munich, he directed his first complete feature film, *The Pleasure Garden* (1925). An ordinary story that ended with a burst of melodramatic action, the film contained glimmers of the director-to-come (it opens with a bit of voyeurism—music hall patrons ogle chorus girls through their binoculars as the girls rush down a spiral staircase). It was Hitchcock's third feature, *The Lodger* (1926), that marked his true debut as a filmmaker. A thriller concerning a lodger (matinee idol Ivor Novello) suspected of being Jack the Ripper, it introduced Hitchcock's recurring theme of an innocent man trapped in a web of incriminating circumstances, and it also revealed his innate ability to achieve maximum impact by the swiftest, most economical means. (The movie begins with a blonde girl screaming, and within minutes we know that a murder has been committed.)

Although Hitchcock's first sound film, *Blackmail* (1929), had its inevitable crudities—he made most of it as a silent and then reshot many scenes with sound—it also indicated that he knew how to make expert use of the new medium. A melodramatic tale of a hapless girl (Anny Ondra) who kills a would-be rapist in self-defense and is blackmailed for the crime, the movie included a well-remembered scene in which the girl, at breakfast with her family, picks out the word "knife" in the babble of voices and is impelled to pick up a knife similar to the one she had used for the killing. In a climactic scene in and around the British Museum, Hitchcock used the Shuftan process, which made it possible to combine miniature representations of scenery in the background and actual action in the foreground. *Blackmail* won admiring reviews from the critics, but Hitchcock's next few films, with the exception of *Murder* (1930), another technically innovative thriller, with the bold theme of homosexuality, were minor efforts.

During this formative period in England, Hitchcock did not hit his stride until 1934, when he directed *The Man Who Knew Too Much,* his first popular success. A tight, suspenseful tale of an innocent family's involvement in international skulduggery, it contained many of the elements of style and technique that Hitchcock would hone in the years ahead: the touches of visual and verbal wit, the sudden shock effects, the climactic set piece (here, an attempted assassination in Albert Hall), and the headlong pace that seldom paused for logic or probability. Hitchcock followed this film with an even greater success, *The Thirty-Nine Steps* (1935), a dexterous blend of intrigue, romance, and comedy in which Robert Donat and Madeleine Carroll scrambled across Scotland, pursued by spies and police. Hitchcock directed other notable if uneven films during these years (*The Secret Agent, Sabotage,* both 1936), peaking in 1938 with *The Lady Vanishes.* A train filled with devious, dangerous, or comic passengers (among them Margaret Lockwood, Michael Redgrave, and Dame May Whitty) became the setting for Hitchcock's clever, diverting mystery. By now Hitchcock was England's foremost film director.

Intrigued by Hollywood's technical superiority, Hitchcock decided, in 1939, to accept an offer by David O. Selznick to make his first American film. An adaptation of Daphne du Maurier's pulpish best-selling novel *Rebecca* (1940), it was actually more of a Gothic romance—a young bride encounters menace and dark secrets from the past—than a Hitchcockian thriller. Hitch-

Foreign Correspondent: ALFRED HITCHCOCK (*United Artists, 1940*). *Passengers (left to right) Joel McCrea, George Sanders, Laraine Day, and Herbert Marshall struggle to escape from a downed plane. This cleverly staged climactic sequence was only one of many in Hitchcock's diverting thriller.*

cock gave Robert E. Sherwood and Joan Harrison's screenplay a smooth and sinister veneer, and his skill turned the de Winter mansion Manderley into an important character in the movie. *Rebecca* won an Academy Award as Best Picture and assured Hitchcock of major assignments in Hollywood. His next film, *Foreign Correspondent* (1940), returned him to the milieu of international intrigue, with reporter Joel McCrea hurtling across Europe to uncover dastardly plots. Hitchcock infused the cluttered and not always credible story line with a combination of dark comedy (Edmund Gwenn as a jolly little hired killer) and enormous technical skill. Reviewers and audiences marveled at the key scenes, especially an assassination amid hundreds of umbrellas and the climactic plane crash at sea, in which Hitchcock created the astonishing illusion of the Atlantic Ocean rushing through the windows of the doomed plane.

Hitchcock's productive period in the forties is studded with films in which he not only refined and deepened his art with variations on "pure cinema" but in which he rewove his familiar themes into new patterns. Some of his films were straightforward exercises in suspense, placing innocent people in jeopardy (*Suspicion*, 1941, and *Saboteur*, 1943, notable for its harrowing final sequence atop the Statue of Liberty). Others were experiments that challenged Hitchcock's ingenuity: in *Lifeboat* (1944), he used no music and confined the entire action to the boat of shipwreck survivors, and in *Rope* (1948), he filmed the tale of perverse murder and its detection in one room, using a succession of continuous ten-minute takes. For his silken thriller *Notorious* (1946), he stirred a new ingredient into his usual fare of an endangered woman trapped in a nest of vipers: a passionate romance between the two principals (Ingrid Bergman and Cary Grant) that not only gave off much more sexual heat than any previous Hitchcock film but also grew more

complex as it progressed—he loves her but also reviles her for what he falsely perceives as her sins. Hitchcock in no way neglected his technical virtuosity; the movie's justly famous sequences, highlighted by the reception at which Bergman gives Grant a crucial key, are small miracles of directorial expertise. Hitchcock's most interesting film of this period is *Shadow of a Doubt* (1943), his purest embodiment of the theme of lurking evil in everyday surroundings. In the sunlit streets and ordered houses of a California town, sweet young Charlie (Teresa Wright) finds herself linked with her beloved but homicidal uncle (Joseph Cotten) in disturbing ways. Her shattered serenity can only be mended when, in their last desperate struggle on the platform of a moving train, he topples into the path of an oncoming train.

In the late forties, Hitchcock's credits included films that failed to excite either critics or ticket-buyers. *The Paradine Case* (1947), involving courtroom theatrics, seemed dry and static; *Under Capricorn* (1949) relentlessly churning out its lady-in-distress melodrama, was heavy and unsatisfying. With *Strangers on a Train* (1951), however, Hitchcock returned to top form, beginning the richest and most rewarding period of his career. During this time, Hitchcock combined his basic themes and concerns with dazzling cinematic expertise. His films of the fifties exude confidence, none more so than *Strangers on a Train* which, despite Hitchcock's dissatisfaction, remains one of his most fascinating movies. Here, the recurring concept that we are all capable of black deeds is embedded in a suspenseful tale of a man (Farley Granger) trapped in a diabolical plot with a smooth-talking psychopath (Robert Walker). In scene after scene, Hitchcock provokes the viewer's anxiety by cleverly making ordinary objects (glasses, a cigarette lighter) the focus of sinister situations; a tennis match takes on fearful urgency; a life-and-death struggle takes place on an out-of-control carousel.

In several of the movies that followed *Strangers on a Train*, Hitchcock continued to combine the theme of shared guilt with his favorite plot line of the ordinary man caught up in an unfathomable nightmare. The protagonists of *I Confess* (1952) and *Rear Window* (1954) become deeply entangled in events that threaten their lives, yet each of them has a hidden secret or a flawed character that binds him to the source of his predicament, and, indeed, to all humanity. *Rear Window*, in particular, plays out a cautionary tale of the dire consequences of voyeurism, of prying too deeply into the lives of others. Most viewers, of course, blithely ignored this subtext to enjoy *Rear Window* as a crackling thriller with a

terrifying climax, as well as an intriguing cinematic experiment in which Hitchcock, using one large set, photographed the entire film from the viewpoint of one man.

Throughout the fifties, at the peak of his form, Hitchcock offered diverting entertainments that, whatever their inner meaning, kept audiences in a blissful state of suspense. Although he missed his mark with *The Trouble with Harry* (1956), an only fitfully amusing black comedy, he scored with *The Man Who Knew Too Much* (1956), an expansive and exciting remake of his 1934 film, and *North by Northwest* (1959, a breathtaking comedy-adventure in which a bewildered Cary Grant is pursued cross-country by both enemy agents and counterintelligence men. Perhaps no other Hitchcock film contains as many sequences that have become a permanent part of movie lore: Grant's perilous car ride down a winding mountain road; the crop-dusting sequence (without crops but with a deadly plane); and, of course, the desperate flight of hero and heroine across the chiseled faces of Mount Rushmore. *North by Northwest* deals with a frequent Hitchcock subject: the loss of (or confusion over) one's identity, which figures prominently as well in *The Wrong Man* (1957), *Vertigo* (1958), and other films.

Vertigo warrants special mention as one of Hitchcock's strangest, most argued-over films. It has been called a seminal work of art, as well as the film that most reveals Hitchcock's private predilections. A somber and disturbing tale of sexual obsession, it certainly qualifies as Hitchcock's darkest movie. He permits nothing to relieve the pall: we watch acrophobiac James Stewart move to despair and near-madness as he twice (once in actuality) precipitates the death of the woman he loves (Kim Novak). There is no doubt of the film's morbid fascination, yet a viewer not inclined to play amateur psychoanalyst with Hitchcock's personal inclinations may be surprised to discover that *Vertigo* is at heart a contrived and clumsily executed thriller, with long periods of tedium, especially in the first half.

Hitchcock's interest in aberrant behavior (man's and nature's) surfaced again in his first two sixties films, *Psy-*

OPPOSITE   North by Northwest: ALFRED HITCHCOCK (*MGM, 1959*). *In this famous sequence, Roger Thornhill (Cary Grant) flees from the plane that is dusting crops where there are no crops. The movie both amused and excited audiences with its twisty plot turns and cleverly staged sequences.*
OVERLEAF   The Trouble with Harry: ALFRED HITCHCOCK (*Paramount, 1956*). *Hitchcock (seated at center) directs Edmund Gwenn and Mildred Natwick in a scene from this whimsical mystery-comedy. Hitchcock used the beautiful New England setting and nonchalant attitude of the principal characters as a deliberate contrast to the central story revolving around a disappearing corpse.*

cho (1960) and *The Birds* (1963). Both films rate high in the Hitchcock canon as reflections of the irrationality that can come upon us unaware. A movie that has been subject to the closest scrutiny and analysis, *Psycho* projects us into the disordered mind of young Norman Bates (Anthony Perkins), where the combined forces of a mother fixation and sexual frustration smolder, ready to explode into violence. The brutal shocks engendered by the movie disturb us because they not only upset our expectations (an apparent heroine and an inquisitive detective are both horribly murdered) but also force us to identify with the murderer. *The Birds* jolts us by depicting another disordered world (much vaster than the Bates Motel), in which man's feathered friends run rampant in a grim, unreasoning barrage of violence. In Hitchcock's perverse fantasy, the universe has been tipped off balance and human law no longer applies.

For the rest of his career, Hitchcock failed to match the artistry—or the wizardry—of his earlier films. Inadequate casting, a muddled screenplay that lacked sufficient suspense, or perhaps a suggestion of weariness and lassitude in Hitchcock's direction overode the strong virtues of such movies as *Marnie* (1964), *Torn Curtain* (1966), and *Topaz* (1969). The best of his later films was probably *Frenzy* (1972), a thriller that combined surprisingly explicit violence and not-so-surprising black humor in its story of a strangler of women at large in London. Hitchcock's seamless style and perfectly honed technique once again came to the fore in this film—his last substantial hit. His final film, *Family Plot* (1976), a return to the black comedy thriller, again proved disappointing.

Over the years, other directors have tried to match the wit, dexterity, and assurance of Alfred Hitchcock. Some have applied too heavy a hand; others have made the mistake of believing that technical ingenuity alone—sudden cuts, a restless or swooping camera—can compensate somehow for a dull or nonexistent story or feeble acting. Many have probed the outer layer of Hitchcock's movies without getting one inch below the surface. But the image of Hitchcock continues to loom the largest, and not only in physical bulk. We may never

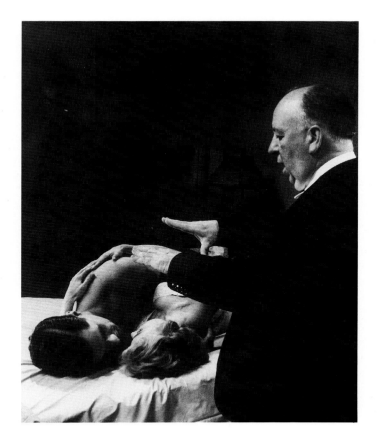

know what truly lurked behind that inexpressive, implacable countenance, but we can always return to the images on the screen and the fearful, troublesome, deliciously chilling shadows they have cast across our minds forever.

★

RON HOWARD (born 1954) After years as an actor on television and in films, young Ron Howard moved to directing and soon learned how to hit a popular nerve. *Night Shift* (1982), his first major film, amiably if not especially tastefully brought comedy into the morgue; Henry Winkler played a morgue attendant who goes into the prostitution business. Happily, his next film, *Splash* (1984), traded morbidness for fantasy. A disarming, sweet-natured romantic comedy-fantasy, it related the story of a man and a mermaid. Both films revealed Howard's skill with young comic actors—*Night Shift* featured a sensational performance by Michael Keaton as Winkler's flaky, enterprising friend, and *Splash* extracted most of its comic juices from Tom Hanks and John Candy as unlikely brothers. The rotund Candy, in particular, was extremely funny as a ribald, happy-go-lucky fellow who revels in his oafishness. Howard had an-

---

ABOVE Psycho: ALFRED HITCHCOCK *(Paramount, 1960). Hitchcock directs John Gavin and Janet Leigh in the opening scene of his grisly thriller. Leigh appeared to be the film's heroine, until Hitchcock characteristically—and shockingly—reversed our expectations in the upcoming shower scene.*
OPPOSITE The Power and the Glory: WILLIAM K. HOWARD *(Fox, 1933). Colleen Moore encourages her ambitious husband Spencer Tracy in his goals for the future. Howard's study of the rise and fall of a tycoon made use of techniques later reflected in Orson Welles's* Citizen Kane.

other success with *Cocoon* (1985), a wish-fulfillment fantasy that, for all its good intentions and wonderful cast of veteran actors (Don Ameche, Hume Cronyn, Jessica Tandy, and others), exhibited a narrow, insulting view of old age. His most recent comedy, *Gung Ho* (1986), involved the clash of cultures that occurs when a Japanese firm takes over an auto plant in a small town.

★

WILLIAM K. HOWARD (1899–1954) William K. Howard's films in the thirties merit more attention than Howard's reputation would indicate. At the least, they were more individualistic than the films of many others who worked within the studio system, as Howard had since the silent era. His most notable movie, *The Power and the Glory* (1933), related the somber but engrossing story of a ruthless tycoon (Spencer Tracy) whose personal life is a tragic failure. Preston Sturges's screenplay combined nonchronological flashbacks and offscreen commentary (the studio called it "narratage") in a way that clearly presages *Citizen Kane*. Other interesting films include *Transatlantic* (1931), a seaborne Grand Hotel story that juggled its many plots with surprising aplomb; *Sherlock Holmes* (1932), which brought the great detective into the thirties, with amusing results; and *Mary Burns, Fugitive* (1935), a good example of the innocent-trapped-into-crime subgenre prevalent in the thirties, with Sylvia Sidney as the resident lady in distress. *The Princess Comes Across* (1936) served up an entertaining combination of comedy and mystery that derived most of its fun from Carole Lombard's impersonation of a fake Garbo-like movie queen. Howard faltered in the forties with low-grade productions, then retired from films.

★

HUGH HUDSON (born 1936) British director Hugh Hudson turned out documentaries and television commercials before directing his first feature film, *Chariots of Fire* (1981). The movie, an absorbing drama based on the true story of two men—a Scottish missionary (Ian Charleson) and a Jewish student at Cambridge (Ben Cross)—who compete in the 1924 Olympics, was an international success. A handsome production, intelligent screenplay (an Oscar went to Colin Welland), and first-rate performances fleshed out a familiar, glossy, inspirational drama done in the style of, say, a "Masterpiece Theater" television miniseries. The movie won the year's Best Picture award, and Vangelis's score, with its omnipresent theme, also received an Oscar.

Hudson's second film, *Greystoke: The Legend of Tarzan,*

Lord of the Apes (1984), probably shocked the Johnny Weissmuller Fan Club with its unusual recasting of the Tarzan legend. Certainly, it left audiences bemused. Still, it was sumptuously mounted (the early jungle scenes fairly glistened), and the climax, with young Greystoke-Tarzan (Christopher Lampert) tearfully embracing his dying ape-father in a London park, moved many viewers. Hudson's latest film to date, *Revolution* (1985), the first film in many years to deal with the American Revolutionary War, concerned a farmer (Al Pacino) who is drawn reluctantly into the conflict.

★

There is so much talk of style and technique, of my "unifying technique," of "a Huston scene," and I've always been fascinated to hear what it was. I myself haven't the vaguest idea. Critics are so fond of talking about "a personal film" or "a personal style." I don't really know what they mean. I don't think they've really thought about it. JOHN HUSTON, in Gerald Pratley, *The Cinema of John Huston* (South Brunswick, N.J., and New York: A. S. Barnes, 1977), p. 210.

JOHN HUSTON (born 1906) A lusty and life-embracing man, John Huston has taken on a variety of roles and pursued a number of interests in his long and fruitful lifetime. At one time or another a boxer, a horse breeder, a painter, a writer, an actor, and, of course, a director, Huston has been so prodigiously busy over the years that it seems something of a miracle that he managed to turn out so many brilliantly crafted, thoroughly profes-

sional, and entertaining films. If his movies have proved uneven in quality, if he sometimes exhibits bad judgment in his choice of projects, he has also shown that he can rise above his failures and come sailing in with a brand-new triumph. How exhilarating to see him follow the heavy-footed *Annie* and the murky *Under the Volcano* with the dexterous *Prizzi's Honor*! Although Huston has been dropped as a darling of the more serious critics for some time now, his position among the master directors remains secure; few would have questioned the conferral of the AFI Life Achievement Award on him in 1983.

Over the years, Huston has tended to downplay his role as a filmmaker. (In his autobiography *An Open Book*, p. 361, he wrote, "I don't think of myself as simply, uniquely, and forever a director of motion pictures.") He has also denied repeatedly that he is an *auteur* with recurrent themes and attitudes. Yet many of his films feature a recognizable Huston protagonist: a man outside the mainstream of society, an offbeat loner or rebel who refuses to be swallowed up by the system and who, despite the terrible odds, attempts to reach some impossible goal. He often—but not always—goes down to defeat, yet there is a kind of triumph in the striving, and

he is sometimes ennobled by the effort. Fred C. Dobbs in *The Treasure of the Sierra Madre* and Charlie Allnut in *The African Queen* represent the two sides of the coin. A snarling, suspicious misfit who pursues a dream of gold in the inhospitable mountains, Dobbs wins the gold and then loses it and his life at the hands of Mexican rene-

ABOVE   The Bible: JOHN HUSTON *(Fox, 1966). George C. Scott as Moses and director Huston pose together against a background of ancient ruins. Huston also played the role of Noah and spoke as the offscreen voice of God.*
OPPOSITE, ABOVE   Cocoon: RON HOWARD *(Fox, 1985). Wilford Brimley, Hume Cronyn, and Don Ameche try to convince a reluctant Jack Gilford to join them in the mysteriously revitalizing pool. Ron Howard's popular fantasy offered veteran actors a chance to shine in leading roles.*
OPPOSITE, BELOW   Chariots of Fire: HUGH HUDSON *(The Ladd Co./ Warner Bros., 1981). Ian Charleson played Eric Liddell, a Scottish missionary who believes he can best honor the Lord by winning the race in the 1924 Olympics. "God made me devout," he says, "and God made me fast."*

gades. Charlie is an unkempt boat captain who, to his own astonishment, finds himself launched on a desperate adventure with a high-minded spinster named Rose (Katharine Hepburn), whom he comes to love and admire. The fact that both these characters are played masterfully by Humphrey Bogart is, in part, a testament to Huston's ability with actors. Dobbs and Allnut are figures in a Huston gallery that includes the doomed criminals of *The Asphalt Jungle*, the comically inept criminals of *Beat the Devil* (1954), the lost souls of *The Misfits*, and many others.

The son of splendid actor Walter Huston, John Huston was an ailing, bookish child who spent his early years traveling with his parents. Following a full recovery, however, he developed a wide range of interests that led to his becoming, among other things, a boxer, an officer in the Mexican cavalry, and an actor. Ultimately, he turned to writing as a livelihood; in the early thirties he wrote several screenplays for films starring his father. He ran out of assignments by 1932, and spent the next few lean years studying painting in Paris, editing a magazine, and acting.

In 1937 Huston joined the Warners writing staff, where he turned out a number of well-received screenplays, either alone or in collaboration (*Jezebel, Juarez, Sergeant York,* and others). By 1941 he was eager to try his hand at directing—he had always felt that directing was an extension of writing—and his first assignment was yet another version of a Dashiell Hammett mystery that had been filmed twice before. By adhering closely to the book, adding artful touches of his own, and casting the movie with performers who were miraculously right for their roles, Huston created a classic mystery in *The Maltese Falcon* (1941). After directing Bette Davis in an overheated drama, *In This Our Life* (1942), and bringing together the *Falcon* trio, Humphrey Bogart, Mary Astor, and Sydney Greenstreet, for *Across the Pacific* (1942), a fair pre–Pearl Harbor espionage melodrama, Huston joined the Signal Corps, where he directed several superb documentaries, including *The Battle of San Pietro* and *Let There Be Light.*

Returning to Warners after the war, Huston directed one of his best films, *The Treasure of the Sierra Madre* (1948), which adapted B. Traven's novel about three drifters in Mexico whose search for gold ends in disillusion and death. A powerful and corrosive drama of greed (in fact, it resembled Erich von Stroheim's *Greed* in some scenes), the movie gave Huston's father Walter one of his best screen roles, as a sly, toothless old prospector, for which he received a well-deserved Oscar. (John received Oscars for direction and for the acrid screenplay.) In this film, Huston developed his visual technique of placing the actors in a frame so that their size and position reflected their actions. In the next few years, he reached the summit of his success with popular, well-wrought films, among them *The Asphalt Jungle* (1950), an incisive and influential crime drama and a key film in Huston's recurring theme of striving losers, and *The African Queen* (1952), an enormously enjoyable Afri-

can adventure that made a virtue of the odd pairing of Humphrey Bogart and Katharine Hepburn.

Enraged by the McCarthy "witch hunt," Huston left America to take up residence in Ireland. At the same time, he entered a long period of decline. He thrashed through various themes and styles, apparently unable to pull any of them together; all of his films exhibited a slackness in execution or misjudgments in casting. Some of the more ambitious films were *Moby Dick* (1956), a worthy adaptation of Melville's novel, weakened by the casting of Gregory Peck as Ahab, and *The Unforgiven* (1960), a sprawling Western. While it has several well-staged action scenes, the latter tried to absorb too many themes and plot lines, and Audrey Hepburn was strangely cast as an Indian girl protected by her white "family" from the tribe that wants to reclaim her. *The Misfits* (1961), a flawed and diffuse but also curiously affecting film about aimless modern-day cowboys and the troubled divorcée who comes into their lives, offered Arthur Miller's first screenplay and the last film perform-

The Maltese Falcon: JOHN HUSTON (*Warner Bros., 1941*). *Detective Sam Spade (Humphrey Bogart) gets the "helpless woman" treatment from duplicitous Brigid O'Shaughnessy (Mary Astor). Huston's first film as director turned out to be a model of its kind: a tense, steely, miraculously well-cast detective thriller revolving around an endlessly fascinating group of characters.*

ances of both Clark Gable and Marilyn Monroe. In the sixties, Huston tried his hand at solemn biographical drama (*Freud*, 1962), Tennessee Williams soul searching (*The Night of the Iguana*, 1964), and Carson McCullers psychodrama (*Reflections in a Golden Eye*, 1967) without great success, although each of these films had its merits. In the last film, Huston continued his occasional experiments with muted color that had begun in 1953 with *Moulin Rouge*.

Happily, the seventies saw Huston regaining much of his earlier stature, with a series of interesting, well-received films, notably *Fat City* (1972), *The Man Who Would Be King* (1975), and, especially, *Wise Blood* (1979), an odd, fascinating adaptation of Flannery O'Connor's novel about a self-styled preacher (Brad Dourif) who forms the Church Without Christ. Tightly edited (Huston insists on doing all his own editing in the camera), these films displayed his confident style with suitable material. More recently, though, Huston made the serious mistake of directing his first large-scale musical, *Annie* (1982), a cumbersome and joyless version of the stage

hit, a property ill-suited to his talents. His film of Malcolm Lowry's *Under the Volcano* (1984) had its champions, but many found it tedious viewing.

As before, Huston on a downswing was soon followed by Huston back at the peak of his powers. He triumphed with his latest film to date, *Prizzi's Honor* (1985), an exceedingly black—and funny—comedy-melodrama about Mafia "family" activities. It worked on several levels: as a sly satire on the traditional gangster film, as an offbeat romance with several nasty shocks along the way, and as a demonstration of Huston's undimmed skill with actors. (He has said repeatedly that, unlike other directors, he gives his actors very little room, expecting them to make no creative contributions to the screenplay.) *Prizzi's Honor* was a commentary on the way the world has changed since *The Maltese Falcon* premiered over forty years earlier. In *The Maltese Falcon*, a man who lives in the shadowed world between law and lawlessness and who adheres to his own private code of behavior finally makes what may be his one honorable decision: to turn the treacherous woman he loves over to

ABOVE The Misfits: JOHN HUSTON (*United Artists, 1961*). *On the set with director Huston, star Marilyn Monroe, and Monroe's husband Arthur Miller, who wrote the screenplay. Quirky and uneven, the film still managed to elicit compassion for its motley collection of lost and groping souls.*

LEFT The Treasure of the Sierra Madre: JOHN HUSTON (*Warner Bros., 1948*). *Walter Huston, Humphrey Bogart, and Tim Holt excelled as three drifters seeking gold in the Mexican mountains. John Huston's brilliant direction offered many stark images of the greed that can lead men insidiously to distrust, hatred, and murder.*

the police. In *Prizzi's Honor,* a man who lives totally outside the law, adhering only to the "family" code, opts to kill the treacherous woman he loves. The end result may be the same (death for the woman), but the codes are worlds apart.

Prizzi's Honor has brought John Huston new acclaim and focused new awareness on his major contribution to filmmaking. He has been denigrated in the past and probably will be again, but nobody is more amused than Huston himself by the changing winds of critical favor. He can be sure that whatever the shifting perception of his work, he created a number of films that will unquestionably endure. Like many of the loners and losers in his films, he keeps springing back to tell us that he isn't ready to give up yet on the comic-tragic game of life.

★

REX INGRAM (1892–1950) Dublin-born Rex Ingram—not to be confused with the black actor of the same name—entered films in 1913 after a meeting with Edison's son Charles. He finally achieved success as a director with *The Four Horsemen of the Apocalypse* (1921), an

elaborate drama concerning the fortunes of a South American family, with young Rudolph Valentino in the leading role. Many of his subsequent films were similarly lavish, romantic, and rich in imagery, including such beautifully staged swashbucklers as *The Prisoner of Zenda* (1922) and *Scaramouche* (1923), both starring Lewis Stone (long before the days of Judge Hardy), as well as Ingram's wife, Alice Terry. Ingram's favorite photographer on many of these films was John F. Seitz, who invented the matte shot. Ingram also contributed to film

history when he cut Erich von Stroheim's *Greed* from twenty-four to eighteen reels after the studio objected to the movie's gargantuan length. (Writer June Mathis, under Irving Thalberg's supervision, then cut it down to ten reels.) In the mid-twenties, Ingram set up his own studio in Nice with his wife, but it was too small to convert to sound, and he retired in the early thirties.

★

NORMAN JEWISON (born 1926) Norman Jewison's two principal virtues are his ability to fill a frame with sharply observed visual detail and a nervous drive and energy that can make the screen pulsate with excitement. Sometimes, however, an excess of these virtues turns them into vices, and Jewison has been accused of reaching too strenuously for cinematic effects. While a film like . . . *And Justice for All* (1979) rivets the attention, its story of a young lawyer (Al Pacino) engulfed in chaos and corruption is so supercharged, so galvanized by Jewison's direction that the movie itself, like the hero, seems on the verge of a nervous collapse. At his best,

---

ABOVE The Four Horsemen of the Apocalypse: REX INGRAM (*Metro, 1921*). *Rudolph Valentino dances a torrid tango with Beatrice Dominguez. Ingram worked at directing for eight years before scoring a triumph with this lavish adaptation of Vicente Blasco Ibañez's novel.*

OPPOSITE, ABOVE Fiddler on the Roof: NORMAN JEWISON (*United Artists, 1971*). *Motel the tailor (Leonard Frye) confesses his love for Tzeitel (Rosalind Harris). Jewison's adaptation of the long-running stage musical enriched and deepened the original material, resulting in one of the best musicals of the seventies.*

OPPOSITE, BELOW Prizzi's Honor: JOHN HUSTON (*Fox, 1985*). *Huston directed this very black comedy with all of his long-established skill, giving wry and surprising twists to the gangster genre.*

however, as in *Fiddler on the Roof,* Jewison can dazzle the eyes with rich and glowing images (and the actual outdoor setting seems to give him room to breathe and expand his resources).

One of the most successful directors to emerge from television in the sixties, Jewison began his film career on a light note that gave no indication of his later intensity. At Universal, he directed a group of airy comedies, two of which (*The Thrill of It All,* 1963, and *Send Me No Flowers,* 1964) starred the pert and underappreciated Doris Day. With *The Cincinnati Kid* (1965), on which he replaced Sam Peckinpah as director, he moved into a different kind of film, bringing some force to a story that attempted but failed to do for poker what Robert Rossen's *The Hustler* had done for pool. He then had an unexpected success with *The Russians Are Coming the Russians Are Coming* (1966), a farce about an imagined invasion of a New England coastal town that was more frantic than funny; it showed early signs of Jewison's occasional inability to control his material.

Jewison finally achieved a major hit with *In the Heat of the Night* (1967), a tense and well-crafted if conventional murder melodrama, set in Mississippi, that drew its strength from the relationship between Rod Steiger as a redneck police chief and Sidney Poitier as a wily, intelligent black detective from Philadelphia. Steiger won an Academy Award, as did the film, and Jewison received his first Oscar nomination. Jewison had only moderate success with *The Thomas Crown Affair* (1968), a bank robbery melodrama that added some amusingly bold sexual byplay to the usual mix, and *Gaily, Gaily* (1969), an atmospheric comedy loosely based on Ben Hecht's account of his rowdy life in the Chicago of 1910. He enjoyed his greatest success with the film adaptation of the Broadway stage musical *Fiddler on the Roof* (1971), a beautifully staged and deeply moving account of Jewish life in a poor Russian village at the start of the pogroms.

Jewison's films did not fare well in the balance of the seventies. Often the ambition did not quite match the achievement, and such movies as *Jesus Christ, Superstar* (1973), *Rollerball* (1975), and *F.I.S.T.* (1978) suffered from the director's hectic style (*F.I.S.T.* allegedly suffered from some postproduction tampering as well). As usual, however, Jewison came up with some visually effective scenes in each. In recent years his work has ranged from a mildly amusing romantic comedy, *Best Friends* (1982),

Rollerball: NORMAN JEWISON (*United Artists, 1975*). *Norman Jewison (at center, on the boom camera) prepares to shoot an elaborate scene for this futuristic melodrama.*

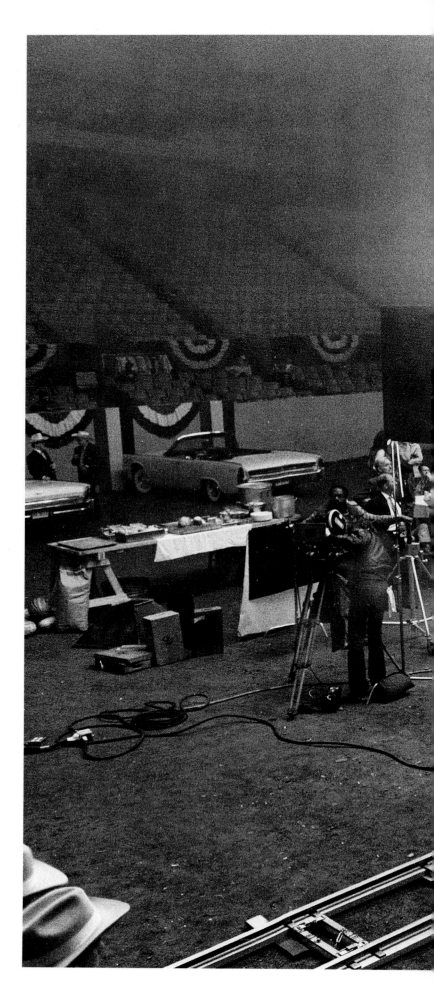

his best roles, as an alcoholic ex-teacher who rises to a moment of glory. Although Kanin captured Ginger Rogers's perky charm in the comedy *Bachelor Mother* (1939), he allowed her to lapse into coyness in *Tom, Dick and Harry* (1941). His 1940 screwball comedy *My Favorite Wife* with Irene Dunne and Cary Grant, although missing the finesse of their earlier pairing in Leo McCarey's *The Awful Truth* (1937), had its share of hilarious moments. Kanin returned briefly to direction in the late sixties.

★

PHIL KARLSON (1908–1985) Phil Karlson began directing in the mid-forties and made his reputation with the series of crisp, taut, and unusually violent crime melodramas he directed with skill in the fifties, including *99 River Street* (1953), *Tight Spot* (1955), and *The Brothers Rico* (1957). The best of the group is probably *The Phenix City Story* (1955), based on the true story of the corruption and terrorism that afflicted the town of Phenix City, Alabama, and the events surrounding the murder of the town's leading antivice crusader. Karlson's forceful direction and an authoritative performance by John McIntyre as the crusader set the film a few cuts above the standard crime exposé.

From this point on, Karlson's films fell several notches. Two of his better efforts were *Gunman's Walk* (1958), a Western centering on a bitter father-son conflict, and *Hell to Eternity* (1960), an effective war film about a true-life Marine hero who single-handedly caused the surrender of one thousand Japanese soldiers. Karlson also directed two of the Matt Helm (Dean Martin) James Bond imitations (*The Silencers*, 1966; *The Wrecking Crew*, 1969); neither matched the original in polish or entertainment. In 1973, he had his first commercial success with *Walking Tall*, based on the true exploits of Southern sheriff Buford Pusser.

★

to *A Soldier's Story* (1984), derived from the prize-winning play about a murder investigation at a Southern army post. Many of the reviewers of Jewison's latest film, *Agnes of God* (1985, based on John Pielmeier's play), seemed to focus on Jane Fonda's chain-smoking rather than the story of yet another investigation, this one into the alleged murder of a newborn baby by a young nun.

★

GARSON KANIN (born 1912) Garson Kanin has enjoyed many careers in the theater and in films: as an actor, playwright, and stage director, as the author of a number of witty, polished screenplays, usually with his wife, Ruth Gordon (*A Double Life*, 1948; *Adam's Rib*, 1949; among others), and as the director of some pleasing films, mainly in the late thirties and early forties. His first films (*A Man to Remember*, 1938; *The Great Man Votes*, 1939), while small in scope, had an appealing honesty and warmth. The latter film gave John Barrymore one of

---

ABOVE   My Favorite Wife: GARSON KANIN (RKO, 1940). *Kanin's sprightly comedy starred Cary Grant as a man bewildered to learn that his first wife (Irene Dunne), presumed dead in a shipwreck, has returned to the land of the living. As in* The Awful Truth, *the two made a charming team, bouncing off each other with seemingly effortless skill.*
OPPOSITE, ABOVE   The Right Stuff: PHILIP KAUFMAN (The Ladd Co./ Warner Bros., 1983). *Astronaut Alan Shepard (Scott Glenn) is cheered after returning from a space mission. This long film never seemed clear as to whether it wanted to glorify or deflate the Mercury space programs and its astronauts.*
OPPOSITE, BELOW   The Big Chill: LAWRENCE KASDAN (Columbia, 1983). *This perceptive comedy of sixties activists almost twenty years later boasted fine ensemble acting from a cast that included (left to right) William Hurt, JoBeth Williams, Jeff Goldblum, Meg Tilly, Tom Berenger, and Kevin Kline.*

LAWRENCE KASDAN (born 1949) Before turning to direction, Lawrence Kasdan had established himself as a writer who clearly understood the unalloyed pleasures of moviegoing in a vanished time—he coauthored the screenplays for two of the "Star Wars" trilogy, *The Empire Strikes Back* (1980) and *Return of the Jedi* (1983), and, alone, he wrote the diverting, slightly tongue-in-cheek screenplay for *Raiders of the Lost Ark* (1981). His first film as a director, *Body Heat* (1981), was an on-target but overly calculated pastiche of forties *film noir*—dumb lawyer is entrapped by sexy socialite—complete with sweaty close-ups involving dark and deadly events. For his sec-

ond film, *The Big Chill* (1983), he traded movie nostalgia for personal nostalgia, to superior effect. Kasdan directed this funny, rueful look at the way activists of the sixties have more or less adjusted to society in the eighties from an incisive and intelligent script he coauthored with Barbara Benedek, drawing a splendid ensemble performance from a talented cast. The movie won three Oscar nominations, including one for Best Picture. With *Silverado* (1985), a rip-roaring anthology of Western movie clichés given a contemporary patina, Kasdan returned to old movies as a subject.

★

PHILIP KAUFMAN (born 1936)   Philip Kaufman's major credit to date is undoubtedly *The Right Stuff,* the 1983 film based on Tom Wolfe's book about America's astronauts. Although a box-office disappointment, the movie had many moments of startling, even awesome beauty, especially in the sections on space flight. Unfortunately, much of the film contained indigestible gobs of inexplicable lowbrow comedy masquerading as satire. (For example, press reporters, all wearing hats in the style of the thirties' Lee Tracy, scampered about acting like insensitive buffoons.) Kaufman's best previous film was his effective 1978 remake of Don Siegel's *Invasion of the Body Snatchers,* which boasted stronger production values than the 1956 original but perhaps a few less thrills. Kaufman's 1979 film *The Wanderers* resembled Walter Hill's *The Warriors* (also 1979) in its near-expressionistic view of a violent street gang, this one made up of Italian-American teen-agers in the Bronx in 1963. However, it lacked the unified style and technical wizardry of Hill's movie. Kaufman's earlier Western, *The Great Northfield, Minnesota Raid* (1972), offered a fresh, unusually realistic interpretation of the familiar legend surrounding the James and Younger brothers.

★

I don't think any of my films are completely successful. But taking them all together, I'm proud of them. I think I've done something that is myself.   ELIA KAZAN, "Dialogue on Film," *American Film,* March 1976, p. 35.

ELIA KAZAN (born 1909)   If a film director can be compared to a music conductor who must coordinate all the instruments of the orchestra into a single sound, then it can truly be said that Elia Kazan created a number of memorable cinematic symphonies during a long and distinguished career. His career in the theater has been equally, if not more, illustrious, but "Gadge" Kazan

brought to films the same emotional intensity, vivid theatrical sense, and, above all, remarkable ability with actors that he had brought to his stagings of *Death of a Salesman* and *A Streetcar Named Desire.* If some of the notes have become shrill and strident in the past few decades, he remains a master director whose "music" continues to reverberate in the annals of film.

Born in Constantinople (now Istanbul), Kazan immigrated to America with his Greek parents at the age of four. Early on he recognized his absorbing interest in the theater and attended Yale's Drama School. In 1932 he joined the Group Theatre as an actor and assistant stage manager, appearing in a number of plays before turning to directing. Years of hard work at developing his talents finally culminated in resounding success in the forties, when he became one of Broadway's most outstanding directors. An abiding interest in films—he had made several documentaries in the thirties and early forties—finally led to his first feature movie, an adaptation of Betty Smith's best-selling novel *A Tree Grows in Brooklyn*

ABOVE   A Tree Grows in Brooklyn: ELIA KAZAN *(Fox, 1945). Young Francie Nolan (Peggy Ann Garner) shares a moment with her irresponsible, alcoholic father (James Dunn). In his feature-film debut, Kazan demonstrated his ability to elicit strong performances from his actors. Garner shone in one of the loveliest performances ever given by a child actress, and Dunn won an Oscar as Best Supporting Actor.*
OPPOSITE   A Streetcar Named Desire: ELIA KAZAN *(Warner Bros., 1951). The coy, kittenish attitude of Blanche Dubois (Vivien Leigh) gets short shrift from her brother-in-law, Stanley (Marlon Brando). Kazan revealed a dazzling artistry in re-creating Tennessee Williams's play for the screen, drawing bravura performances from his leading players.*

(1945). Although its rambling, episodic narrative betrayed Kazan's inexperience, the film was a moving and evocative view of a poor family's tribulations in Brooklyn's Williamsburg district "a few decades ago." James Dunn and Peggy Ann Garner won Oscars for their sensitive performances.

Kazan's subsequent films in the forties brought him added recognition and acclaim, largely because of his willingness to deal with social issues usually ignored or carefully muted in motion pictures. His film version of Laura Z. Hobson's novel *Gentleman's Agreement* (1947) centered on a forthright approach to anti-Semitism. Although it won three Academy Awards (including one for Kazan), it now seems tame and ingenuous rather than hard-hitting. Similarly, *Pinky* (1949), which focused on a light-skinned black girl (Jeanne Crain) passing for white, has lost its sheen of boldness over the years. Kazan was on much sturdier ground with *Boomerang!*

(1947), a riveting melodrama about the upheavals surrounding a priest's murder. Using the semidocumentary style pioneered by the film's producer, Louis de Rochemont, Kazan revealed an increasing cinematic skill in his adroit staging of key scenes, such as the interrogation of the chief suspect and his explosive trial.

While working in films, Kazan had continued to direct for the stage, scoring one of his greatest successes in 1947 with Tennessee Williams's *A Streetcar Named Desire*. When the play was finally brought to the screen in 1951, Kazan was able to cast all but one of the principal actors in his stage version—Jessica Tandy was replaced by Vivien Leigh to provide "star" power—and he brought to the film all his cumulative ability as a director. Although he could not shake off the film's theatrical origins, Kazan created a superlative film that drew its greatest tension from the inevitable clashes of faded, mentally deteriorating Southern belle Blanche DuBois (Vivien Leigh) and

her brutish brother-in-law, Stanley Kowalski (Marlon Brando). Their scenes together, particularly the climactic encounter, epitomized Kazan's skill at extracting the best work from his players. The movie won many Oscars, including a second for Kazan.

During this richly productive period of his career, Kazan directed Marlon Brando in two other films that established the actor as a major star and bolstered Kazan's reputation as an important director. In *Viva Zapata!* (1952), which cast Brando as the legendary Mexican revolutionary, Kazan used the film's broad canvas and handled the huge company of players with assurance and expansiveness. The other film, *On the Waterfront* (1954), a seething, trenchant drama set in the desolate reality of New York City's docks, was perhaps his greatest achievement. In his now-legendary performance, Marlon Brando played a slightly punch-drunk ex-boxer who decides to blow the whistle on the vicious dock boss (Lee J. Cobb) and his lackeys. The film is the best example of Kazan's ability to "orchestrate" a movie: all components, including Budd Schulberg's screenplay, Boris Kaufman's photography, Leonard Bernstein's music, and sterling performances by mainly New York–trained actors, combined to give *On the Waterfront* its honored status (it won many Oscars, including a third for Kazan). In some quarters, however, the movie was viewed as an apology for—or explanation of—Kazan's damaging testimony before the House Un-American Activities Committee.

Surprisingly, Kazan's slow descent from the pinnacle of his film career began with one of his most admired

movies. His adaptation of John Steinbeck's novel *East of Eden* (1955), a story of cataclysmic family relationships, had undeniable power. It also established James Dean in a stardom that was confirmed and virtually sanctified with his second film, *Rebel Without a Cause*. However, it waxed intensely overwrought in so many scenes that the movie appeared to be suffering from a nervous breakdown. This failing became more pronounced in such later films as *Splendor in the Grass* (1961), based on William Inge's original screenplay about the devastation wrought by teen-age sexual frustration, and *The Arrangement* (1969), Kazan's nearly incoherent version of his novel, which failed to mesh several visual styles. During the fifties, Kazan also directed several films that, while they had their vociferous champions, now seem crude and unfocused. *Baby Doll* (1956), another journey on the Tennessee Williams streetcar, boiled down to a lusty but pointless comedy-drama centering on the vengeful seduction of a childlike young wife, played to sizzling perfection by Carroll Baker. *A Face in the Crowd* (1957), a bitter cautionary tale about the corruptive powers of

ABOVE   America America: ELIA KAZAN (*Warner Bros., 1963*). *Writer-producer-director Elia Kazan rehearses a scene with his star, Stathis Gaillelis. Kazan drew on his own family's past for this deeply personal film about the adventures of a young Greek immigrant (Gaillelis) as he makes his way to the United States.*

LEFT   On the Waterfront: ELIA KAZAN (*Columbia, 1954*). *At a government hearing, an enraged Johnny Friendly (Lee J. Cobb) tries to get at Terry Malloy (Marlon Brando) for testifying against him. Kazan's hard-hitting drama of racketeering on New York City's docks offered a first-rate example of ensemble acting, yet the film was dominated by Brando's stunning, fully realized performance as Terry.*

television, was written (by Budd Schulberg, from his story) and directed with sledgehammer force but little finesse.

In the sixties, Kazan moved in a different direction: he broke his longstanding ties with the theater and directed several films that reflected his increasing interest in American themes and values. In the most personal of these, *America America* (1963), he returned to his own family's past to depict the immigrant life experienced by his Greek uncle as he traveled from Turkey to the United States. The film sprawled and meandered, but some scenes displayed Kazan at his vigorous best. His sparse output during the next decade alternated between *The Visitors* (1972), about an ex-GI who is threatened by his returning buddies for testifying about their crimes during the Vietnam War, and an elaborate adaptation of F. Scott Fitzgerald's *The Last Tycoon* (1975). In recent years, he has turned to writing novels.

On the whole, Elia Kazan has made an indelible contribution to films (and, of course, to the theater as well) that cannot be measured by individual failures or triumphs. In promoting "the Method," he strongly influenced an entire generation of actors, not only Marlon Brando but also actors both new and established (Rod Steiger, James Dean, Karl Malden, Eva Marie Saint), to whom he brought an exciting new perspective that was, and in many cases still is, mirrored in their best work. And during his best period, from the late forties to the early fifties, he directed a group of remarkable films that continue to glow as beacons on the long road of motion picture history.

★

BUSTER KEATON (1895–1966) There is a sublime moment in Buster Keaton's masterpiece *The General* in which Buster and his girl, aboard the train that is madly pursuing his beloved train *The General*, must refuel the boiler with firewood. The girl, none too bright, picks up a tiny piece and drops it delicately into the boiler. Buster retains his famous deadpan expression but his eyes speak volumes. He picks up a splinter of wood and drops it into the boiler after hers. Suddenly his arms leap forward and he shakes her vigorously for a few seconds. And then he kisses her.

It is all there: the repose in the middle of a crisis that can suddenly flicker into action, the stoic acceptance of life's tribulations, the devotion to a nincompoop (and Buster's girls are often nincompoops) that always propels him into trouble. And there at the center, as always, is Buster, the little man with the unsmiling face who,

confronted with a hostile environment, reacts dexterously, resourcefully, and with miraculously perfect comic timing, to save the day, or the heroine, or the train. Buster Keaton was, beyond question, one of the supreme comic artists—perhaps *the* supreme comic artist—of the silent screen.

Keaton's rise from the ranks has often been traced: his early work with his friend Fatty Arbuckle, his series of two-reelers in the early twenties that already showed his instinctive knowledge of how to use film, his peak period from 1923 to 1928 when he starred in and directed (or codirected) a goodly number of the best silent comedies ever made, including *The Navigator* (1924), *Sherlock Jr.* (1924), and *Go West* (1925). Somewhat less has been written about Keaton as a director, however. Unlike Chaplin, who appeared to be indifferent to the components other than his own persona, Keaton as director was intimately concerned with the visual look of his films, with the intricate details of setting and costume.

Keaton understood that filmmaking is a collaborative art, and early on he assembled a team that worked for him for many years, helping him carry out his comedic vision. The team included Clyde Bruckman, a writer and gag man credited as codirector of *The General*; technical

---

The Navigator: BUSTER KEATON *and* DONALD CRISP (*Metro, 1924*). *Millionaire Rollo Treadway (Buster Keaton) finds himself stranded aboard an ocean liner with only one other passenger, girlfriend Kathryn McGuire. Their funny and harrowing adventures made up one of Keaton's best silent films.*

wizard Fred Gabouri, who helped Keaton create many of the massive props about which he constructed his brilliant sight gags, such as the house frame in *Steamboat Bill, Jr.* (1928) that collapses on the imperturbable Buster and just barely misses crushing him to death; and cameraman Elgin Lessley, who worked with Keaton in extending the possibilities of film. Together, they created the multiple exposure in *The Playhouse* (1921) in which nine Busters in blackface appear on screen and sing and dance in unison, and the first combination of live and cartoon action, which occurs in *The Three Ages* (1923). In *Sherlock Jr.*, Keaton himself used the techniques of film—montage, jump cuts, and so on—to demonstrate the hero's shifts between illusion and reality.

No film of Keaton's better reveals his gifts both before and behind the camera than *The General* (1927). Lavishly made and uproariously funny, *The General* has been aptly described by William Bayer as "a comedy, an historical reconstruction, a chase movie, a war movie, and a film that exhibits the major theme of Buster Keaton's work: Man versus the Machine" (*The Great Films*, p. 73). As Southern engineer Johnnie Gray struggles to reclaim his train from the Northern troops, scene after scene is orchestrated in a spiraling crescendo that leads to the film's climax and its most spectacular and beautifully photographed moment: a Northern train tumbling off a collapsing bridge. Along the way, Keaton the actor and Keaton the director carry out sequences that are both precarious and hilarious, such as Buster's encounter with a recalcitrant cannon.

With the end of the silent era, Keaton's fortunes declined. Ill-used by MGM in the early sound years, he found that his style of physical comedy had dropped out of favor (talk and more talk were the requirements), and a deteriorating personal life (heavy drinking and a bitter divorce) did not help to make him more employable. For a number of years, sadly forgotten, he worked as a bit actor, assistant director, or uncredited gag writer. Ultimately, however, a series of public appearances, plus a part in Charlie Chaplin's *Limelight* (1952), helped to remind critics and audiences of Keaton's comic genius. He was the subject of a bland biographical film, *The Buster Keaton Story* (1957) with Donald O'Connor, and continued to play small or medium roles in many films.

If the last few decades of his life were not worthy of his genius, they fail to obscure the filmmaker whose dedication and skill wrought durable treasures on film and gave us the stone-faced little man pensively enduring life's whirlwind.

★

WILLIAM KEIGHLEY (1889–1984) Working mostly at Warner Bros. after many years in the theater, William Keighley directed scores of films in almost every genre. He was most successful with the studio's gangster and adventure films (*Bullets or Ballots*, 1936; *The Prince and the Pauper*, 1937), where he could keep the pace fast and furious. ("Motion pictures means 'move,'" he once said. "And if you don't move, the audience moves out on you.") He also liked to throw in occasional splashes of humor. He codirected two of his best films, the religious fable *The Green Pastures* (1936, with Marc Connelly) and that sublime swashbuckler *The Adventures of Robin Hood* (1938, with Michael Curtiz, who replaced him behind the camera). Alone, he put James Cagney through his vigorous paces in *G Men* (1935), *Each Dawn I Die* (1939), *The Fighting 69th* (1940), and *Torrid Zone* (1940).

Warners's touch with comedy tended toward the unsubtle. Unfortunately, Keighley applied this heavy Warners touch to shrill, hard-breathing versions of such stage comedies as *The Man Who Came to Dinner* (1941) and *George Washington Slept Here* (1942). (Frank Capra, who should have known better, nearly demolished *Arsenic and Old Lace* with the same approach.) Forcing James Cagney and Bette Davis into a farcical mold did not augur well either, and Keighley's *The Bride Came C.O.D.* (1941), a comedy about a runaway heiress and an aviator, amused only sporadically. For all the colorful background and swordplay, his last film, *The Master of Ballantrae* (1953) with Errol Flynn, was only a pale reminder of Flynn's earlier adventure films.

★

GENE KELLY (born 1912)   Gene Kelly's long and glorious career as one of the great musical stars has been fully documented elsewhere. It is sufficient to say that his mastery of dance on film has been topped only by Fred Astaire, and at moments his ebullient spirits, smiling countenance, and talented feet have given as much pleasure as Astaire's smooth ballroom sophistication. Together with Stanley Donen, Kelly directed three of the best musicals of the Arthur Freed era at MGM—none better than that eternally fresh, irresistible classic *Singin' in the Rain* (1952), in which Kelly as star leaped and splashed his way into film immortality. In *On the Town* (1949), based on the stage show about three sailors on leave in New York City, Kelly and Donen broke new ground for the musical by filming some scenes on location in Manhattan. *It's Always Fair Weather* (1955) was a sort of loose follow-up to *On the Town*—the sailors have a none-too-happy postwar reunion; its rather sour tone and dated television aspects kept it from the upper echelon. Alone, Kelly also directed the deeply personal *Invitation to the Dance* (1956), a four-part dance musical that disappointed at the box office.

As a solo director, Kelly has fared less well. Several of his comedies strike a mildly leering note that is somewhat off-putting. (*A Guide for the Married Man*, 1967, had Walter Matthau learning the art of adultery, and *The Cheyenne Social Club*, 1970, had cowpokes James Stewart

and Henry Fonda inheriting a bawdyhouse.) Kelly's one big musical, *Hello, Dolly!* (1969), drew largely hostile notices from the critics, but it is better than its reputation. Some of the more modest musical numbers sparkle with an easygoing, old-fashioned charm, and a miscast Barbra Streisand manages to rise above it all with the force of her personality.

★

IRVIN KERSHNER (born 1923)   Years before directing the second and best film in the "Star Wars" trilogy, *The Empire Strikes Back* (1980), Irvin Kershner had attracted attention as the director of some original offbeat films dealing with daft or eccentric individuals at odds with the world. Most notable were *The Luck of Ginger Coffey* (1964), concerning an Irish misfit on the loose in Montreal; *A Fine Madness* (1966), which related the wild adventures of a seedy poet (Sean Connery) in New York City; and *The Flim Flam Man* (1967), starring George C.

ABOVE   The Fighting 69th: WILLIAM KEIGHLEY *(Warner Bros., 1940). Cocky James Cagney (at right) exchanges words with fellow soldier Alan Hale. Keighley's tribute to the battalion that distinguished itself in World War I thumped the patriotic drums very loudly, stirring in some doughboy humor and a corny plot about Cagney's metamorphosis from coward to hero.*
OPPOSITE, BELOW   The General: BUSTER KEATON *and* CLYDE BRUCKMAN *(Buster Keaton/United Artists, 1927). Southerner Johnnie Gray (Keaton) dispenses a badly needed shot of oil to his beloved train,* The General. OPPOSITE, ABOVE   *In the film's most spectacular sequence, a Northern army train crashes as the bridge collapses. This epic comedy, a lavish and well-constructed film studded with uproariously funny moments, is generally regarded as Keaton's greatest.*

Scott as a W. C. Fieldsian Southern con man. Kershner's female characters were also slightly over the edge; Barbra Streisand played a fantasizing housewife in *Up the Sandbox* (1972), and Faye Dunaway in *Eyes of Laura Mars* (1978) had a bizarre "gift" that permitted her to see murders being committed before they happened. One of Kershner's best films is *Loving* (1970), a rueful comedy starring George Segal in one of his best performances as an unhappy suburbanite. In 1983, he directed Sean Connery in his return appearance (after twelve years) as James Bond in *Never Say Never Again;* unfortunately, despite the presence of Connery, the movie had much less to offer than the others in the series.

★

I've had more fun directing pictures than most people have playing games.   HENRY KING, article in the *New York Times*, 30 June 1978.

HENRY KING (1886–1982)   Henry King's exceptionally long career as a director has much in common with John Ford's. Like Ford, his years as a director span the silent era and continue into the sixties. Like Ford, King drew his inspiration from the American scene, especially from the traditional, tranquil ways of the nation's small-town life. Like Ford, he was strongly influenced by D. W. Griffith: Ford even played an extra in *The Birth of a Nation*, and King's *Tol'able David* clearly owes a debt to Griffith. Unlike Ford, however, King has never earned the

approbation of film scholars. At best, they will praise his craftsmanship, his durability, and his track record at turning out commercial successes. More often, he is criticized for his "plodding intensity" and for being "turgid and rhetorical in his storytelling style" (Sarris, *The American Cinema*, p. 234). Yet the evidence of his many films remains to tell us that King deserves reevaluation, and that he may well be, as Frank Capra called him, "the most underpublicized filmmaker in Hollywood."

Born in Virginia, Henry King entered films as an actor and occasional writer in 1912 and began directing only three years later, while continuing to act. Most of his early films are lost to us. He scored his first success in 1919 with an army comedy called *23½ Hours Leave*. Two years later, he directed *Tol'able David* (1921), a lovely film of rural America in which Richard Barthelmess starred as the wronged but intrepid young farm hero. Other of his notable silent films include that perennially popular drama of sacrificial mother love, *Stella Dallas* (1925), with Belle Bennett and a young Ronald Colman, and *The Winning of Barbara Worth* (1926), in which a gauche actor named Gary Cooper played his first important role.

The qualities that pervaded *Tol'able David*—the deep feeling for small-town and rural atmosphere, the details that revealed character quietly and unobtrusively—could be seen in a number of King's thirties films for Fox (later 20th Century-Fox), especially in the charming *State Fair* (1933), with Will Rogers and Janet Gaynor. Too often, however, these qualities faded next to the hoary plot and bland leading lady (Rochelle Hudson in *Way Down East*, 1935; Loretta Young in *Ramona*, 1936, the studio's first Technicolor film). By the end of the decade, with larger budgets, King had directed three of Fox's most popular entertainments of the period: the Irving Berlin musical *Alexander's Ragtime Band* (1938), which owed more to Berlin's lively score than to the placid narrative sections; *In Old Chicago* (1938), highlighted by a well-staged re-creation of the Great Chicago Fire of 1871; and *Jesse James* (1939), a vigorous, if totally fanciful, first-rate Western filmed in the gaudy yet somehow pleasing Technicolor of the period (it was buoyed by some of the fine character actors often found in John Ford's films). All three films starred King's favorite actor, Tyrone Power.

OPPOSITE The Empire Strikes Back: IRVIN KERSHNER *(Fox, 1980). This second entry in the "Star Wars" series continued the adventures of Luke Skywalker (Mark Hamill), Princess Leia (Carrie Fisher), their friends, and their enemies.*

LEFT Jesse James: HENRY KING *(Fox, 1939). Star Tyrone Power enjoys a slice of watermelon on the set with director King.*

In the forties, King continued his nostalgic evocation of the American past with such films as *Maryland* (1940), *Chad Hanna* (1940), and *Remember the Day* (1941). A warm glow, as well as an unusually graceful visual style, also permeated his engaging period comedy *Margie* (1946), with Jeanne Crain as a teen-ager in the twenties. He offered his most ambitious view of the nation's history in *Wilson* (1944), an impressively mounted but not especially compelling biography of President Woodrow Wilson. Although it won five Academy Awards, the movie was unsuccessful at the box office. He went beyond Americana in many other films: lavish adventure films (*Captain from Castile*, 1947; *Prince of Foxes*, 1949); a flawed but reverent and touching religious drama, *The Song of Bernadette* (1943); and *Twelve O'Clock High* (1949), an intelligent study of the intolerable pressures of command in wartime.

At the end of the decade, King directed a trend-setting film characteristic of his work only in the deliberate pace and close attention to detail. One of the first films to depict the dark side of the Western gunslinger, *The Gunfighter* (1950) presented him as a tired, lonely man unable to escape his notorious past. Gregory Peck played the legendary Johnny Ringo, who rides into town to visit his estranged wife, finds the usual mixture of hero worship, envy, and disapproval, and finally meets his end at the hands of a swaggering young bully. Substituting quiet character development for action, the movie was talky yet spare and moving, a worthy departure for King.

In the fifties, King continued his pursuit of American themes with such examples of affectionate nostalgia as *I'd Climb the Highest Mountain* (1951), *Wait Till the Sun Shines, Nellie* (1952), and, especially, *Carousel* (1956), a lavish and appealing adaptation of the Rodgers and Hammerstein musical drama, which was marred only by a jarring juxtaposition of fantasy and reality. Early in the decade, King joined the vogue for Biblical spectacle with *David and Bathsheba* (1951), which traced their steamy romance at ponderous length. Most ambitiously, he directed film versions of two Ernest Hemingway stories, *The Snows of Kilimanjaro* (1952) and *The Sun Also Rises* (1957). The star casts and expensive production values did not camouflage King's failure to create the visual equivalent of Hemingway's oblique, understated style and dialogue. As his last film, King directed an adaptation of F. Scott Fitzgerald's *Tender Is the Night* (1962). Not the least of its shortcomings was Jennifer Jones's mannered performance as the mercurial Nicole Diver.

The balance of criticism on Henry King has never been particularly favorable. He has been accused of having an indifferent technique, tortoise-like pacing, and (horrors!) no overriding theme or point of view. Yet he warrants an honorable place in film history for the well-honed skill he brought to his films and for the clarity of his vision, however rose-colored, of what America was like in other times. It may be that his best work is epitomized by the star of three of his major films, Gregory Peck: not especially exciting but thoroughly dependable, deeply American in feeling and spirit, and capable, on occasion, of rising to the heights.

★

HENRY KOSTER (born 1905) Prolific, German-born Henry Koster was a busy writer of German films for a number of years when he fled his country in 1933 as the Nazis rose to power. In Hollywood from 1936, at Univer-

ABOVE   100 Men and a Girl: HENRY KOSTER *(Universal, 1937). Musician Adolphe Menjou leads daughter Deanna Durbin in a song. At the piano: Mischa Auer. Under Koster's direction, Durbin had made a sensational feature-film debut a year earlier in* Three Smart Girls *(1936).*
OPPOSITE, ABOVE   In Old Chicago: HENRY KING *(Fox, 1938). Among the exhausted survivors of the Great Chicago Fire of 1871 are (left to right) Mrs. O'Leary (Alice Brady), her son Dion (Tyrone Power), and singer Belle Fawcett (Alice Faye). This spectacular sequence—one of the best of the thirties—roused the reviewer for the* New York Times *to enthusiasm: "At the first cry of 'Fire' the screen suddenly flowers into beauty, violence, and terror."*
OPPOSITE, BELOW   Alexander's Ragtime Band: HENRY KING *(Fox, 1938). Alice Faye sings an Irving Berlin tune accompanied by the band led by Tyrone Power. At the piano: Don Ameche. The generous number of infectious Berlin songs offset the humdrum plot to make this over-the-years chronicle one of the most popular musical films of the period.*

★

STANLEY KRAMER (born 1913) For more than three decades, since he began directing as well as producing, Stanley Kramer has been roundly chastised and even condemned for the pious didacticism that permeates many of his films. He has been accused of settling on "safe" issues, of indicting ideas (racial prejudice and genocide) that no longer need indicting. David Denby in *The Atlantic Monthly* (January 1970) asserted that "Kramer's ambitions and his failures have often been linked to a kind of muddled and opportunistic liberalism." And in *The American Cinema,* Andrew Sarris wrote that Kramer "has been such an easy and willing target for so long that his very ineptness has become encrusted with tradition."

Granted that Kramer frequently reaches all too simplistically for the large social statement at the expense of other aspects of filmmaking, it is still possible to record some real achievements. At a time when independent film production scarcely seemed viable, Kramer formed a company, Screen Plays, Inc., to produce a series of films that dealt modestly but commendably with social issues (*Home of the Brave,* 1949, on racial prejudice; *The Men,* 1950, on paraplegic veterans). He later joined with Columbia to produce a number of more prestigious films, including *Death of a Salesman* (1951) and *The Caine Mutiny* (1954), and in 1952, he produced the classic Western *High Noon,* releasing it through United Artists. These films and others established him as a producer with a sense of responsibility and the desire to mix a little roughage into the familiar Hollywood pablum.

As a director—his first credit was *Not as a Stranger* in 1955—Kramer seemed to operate on the assumption that combining a Large Theme, however obvious, with an All-Star Cast would guarantee success, even if his own contributions tended to the bland and ineffectual. Thus he took on the subject of world annihilation in *On the Beach* (1959), numbering Gregory Peck, Ava Gardner, and Fred Astaire among the victims. (That year he received the Irving G. Thalberg Memorial Award.) He confronted the Nazi atrocities in *Judgment at Nuremberg* (1961), giving dramatic star turns to such luminaries as Spencer Tracy, Marlene Dietrich, Burt Lancaster, and Judy Garland. And he dealt with the early rise of Nazism in his adaptation of Katherine Anne Porter's *Ship of Fools* (1965), whose passenger list included Vivien Leigh, Simone Signoret, and Jose Ferrer. The concerns of these films were not exactly fresh or controversial, and in most instances Kramer's sincerity failed to overcome his

sal, MGM, and Fox, Koster directed a great many movies in all genres, many of which movie buffs recall with pleasure. In the thirties, he established his reputation as the director of a series of charming musicals starring girlish singer Deanna Durbin (*Three Smart Girls,* 1936; *100 Men and a Girl,* 1937; *First Love,* 1939; and so on). His skill at handling the young star undoubtedly led to his assignment as director of MGM's winsome little Margaret O'Brien in *Music for Millions* (1944) and *The Unfinished Dance* (1947).

Koster's credits over thirty years include musicals (*Wabash Avenue,* 1950; *Flower Drum Song,* 1961), whimsical fantasy (*The Bishop's Wife,* 1947; *The Luck of the Irish,* 1948), historical costume dramas (*Desiree,* 1954; *The Virgin Queen,* 1955), and Mary Chase's amiable burst of whimsy, *Harvey* (1950), starring James Stewart and that delightful butterball, Josephine Hull. Stewart became Koster's favorite star in the sixties, appearing in three of his family-oriented comedies. Koster gained the perhaps dubious distinction of directing the first CinemaScope epic, *The Robe* (1953).

shortcomings as a director. A certain patness and smugness prevailed, never more so than in Kramer's 1967 film *Guess Who's Coming to Dinner.* Here the subject of racial intermarriage was handled decorously and even pointlessly—what parents could possibly object to their daughter, white or black, marrying the supremely talented, handsome, and intelligent Sidney Poitier? The movie's only pleasure came from watching the interplay between the inimitable Spencer Tracy and Katharine Hepburn in their last teaming.

Despite his repeated efforts, Kramer has never fared well with the large-scale, all-star film. Actually, his best films have been modest in scale. *The Defiant Ones* (1958), with Tony Curtis and Sidney Poitier as escaping convicts who are chained together and who ultimately exchange mutual hatred for a modicum of brotherhood, blared forth its message, but it was presented effectively under Kramer's astute direction. And *Bless the Beasts & Children* (1971), despite clumsy staging and a shrilly delivered diatribe against the abuse of the innocent, hardly de-

served the abrupt dismissal by critics and audiences. This story of a group of boys, themselves the victims of neglect and cruelty, who try to prevent the casual slaughter of buffaloes scored some affecting moments.

After the dire failure of *The Runner Stumbles* in 1979, Kramer suspended filmmaking, resuming only recently. Whatever his limitations (and Kramer is apparently aware of them), his presence and his input are welcome if only to remind us that the subject matter of film should not—and must not—be forever divorced from the needs and problems of society.

ABOVE Judgment at Nuremberg: STANLEY KRAMER (*United Artists, 1961*). *Stanley Kramer (right) shoots a scene for this star-heavy drama about the Nazi war-criminal trials. In the dock (left to right): Burt Lancaster, Torben Meyer, Martin Brandt, and Werner Klemperer.*
OPPOSITE The Defiant Ones: STANLEY KRAMER (*United Artists, 1958*). *Fleeing from the law, escaped convicts Tony Curtis and Sidney Poitier pause to catch their breath. Although their being chained together was a blatantly symbolic gesture, the film gained momentum and excitement as the men overcame their mutual hatred in a desperate bid for survival.*

★

STANLEY KUBRICK (born 1928) The world of Stanley Kubrick's films is not a place to go for certainty or consolation. It is a grim, cynical, and absurd world inhabited by either acquiescent victims or corrupt, passionately committed men of power. The humor stings, the images often startle in their disturbing force. It is a nightmare world—not one of fire-breathing demons and devils but of faceless cogs devoid of feelings or aspirations, trapped in a desolate utopia. In *2001: A Space Odyssey*, people grow bored and weary in their technological paradise. In *A Clockwork Orange*, men function as ice-cold, destructive machines, living in antiseptic apartments. The only hope, and it is a slim one, is that man may some day fight to regain his lost humanity.

Inevitably, this vision has made Kubrick one of the most original as well as controversial of film directors. On the one hand, he has been acclaimed as a unique artist with a brilliant visual style, and on the other he has been criticized as pretentious, cold, and brazenly self-indulgent. Against Kubrick's assertions that he intends his

films to give the emotional impact of music—that a movie should be "a progression of moods and feelings"—his detractors point to the chilly perfection of his work, the emphasis on form and structure that leaves too many viewers not only impressed but also baffled and restless. Yet it is uniquely Kubrick's vision, which he has achieved by maintaining full control of his productions (with the exception of *Spartacus*).

Born in the Bronx, New York, Kubrick was a movie addict from his teen years, viewing a countless number of films. He began, however, with photography, working as a photographer for *Look* Magazine before turning to filmmaking. Within a few years he had created several short documentary films and made his feature debut with *Fear and Desire* (1953), a low-budget thriller for which he performed almost every function. He repeated this one-man act with *Killer's Kiss* (1955), an offbeat *film noir*, then attracted wide critical attention with *The Killing* (1956), a taut crime drama about a race-track robbery, and *Paths of Glory* (1957), a blistering attack on the duplicity and corruption of military leadership in wartime. While neither film was especially polished, both re-

vealed Kubrick's cinematic flair and darkly cynical point of view.

After an only intermittently effective attempt at a sword-and-toga saga in *Spartacus* (1960) and an abrasively funny but basically unsuccessful adaptation of Vladimir Nabokov's novel *Lolita* (1962), Kubrick directed his most trenchant film, the nightmare comedy *Dr. Strangelove*, subtitled *How I Learned to Stop Worrying and Love the Bomb* (1964). A corrosive satire on the folly of man when faced with nuclear disaster, *Dr. Strangelove* aimed its fire at many targets, especially the nation's military and political leaders and their lunatic obsession with fail-safe points, hot lines, Communist plots, and such. Peter Sellers starred in three roles: as Lt. Mandrake, an English officer desperately trying to avert a world catastrophe; as America's well-meaning but ineffectual President Muffley; and, most brilliantly, as the arrogant German scientist Dr. Strangelove, vainly trying to control his Nazi impulses.

Kubrick's films have always required long and conscientious preparation—he conceives and designs each film as if it were a chess game—and so his output has been relatively sparse. He followed *Dr. Strangelove* four years later with one of his most controversial movies, the epic *2001: A Space Odyssey* (1968). The central situation of the movie was familiar from many more modest films—a spaceship carrying five astronauts investigates a mysterious slab on the moon. But it soon became clear that Kubrick had profound issues in mind: he was attempting no less than a psychedelic voyage into the future of mankind. With the help of a team of production designers and special-effects people, he made a bold attempt to lift the science-fiction genre into new realms of theology, philosophy, and abstract science. Some found the result thrilling; others thought it numbing and tedious.

Kubrick's subsequent films have continued to receive this double edge of approval and dismissal. The visually stunning *A Clockwork Orange* (1971) adapted Anthony Burgess's novel into a frightening portrait of a future

world steeped in mindless violence—anarchic, repressive, and utterly without hope. Critics either applauded the dazzling production or disapproved of the unrelieved cynicism. *Barry Lyndon* (1975) impressed with its breathtaking photography and opulent scenery, but its measured pace induced sleep rather than excitement. Although some critics were taken with *The Shining* (1980), many others believed that its striking imagery, and some terrifying scenes, could not conceal the essential triteness of the story, which dealt with the demonic and violent events at a deserted hotel. Recently, Kubrick returned to filmmaking with a war drama entitled *Full Metal Jacket* (1986).

To his credit, Kubrick has defied pigeonholing and has dared to expand the horizon of film. He has sought to make each of his movies, rather than a passing time-killer, an indelible experience that involves its viewers emotionally and philosophically, and he has often succeeded.

★

GREGORY LA CAVA (1892–1952) Gregory La Cava's light, frolicsome, improvisational touch with comedy may have come from his early years as cartoonist and animator. Whatever the source, it resulted in some de-

---

ABOVE Stage Door: GREGORY LA CAVA *(RKO, 1937). Aspiring actress Katharine Hepburn, pretending that she has a romantic assignation with producer Adolphe Menjou, greets her disgruntled roommate Ginger Rogers. La Cava's version of the George S. Kaufman–Edna Ferber play retained the basic story but wisely altered the play's tone and approach to create a warmer, funnier, and more accessible tribute to the theater's ever-hopeful actresses.*
OPPOSITE Dr. Strangelove or: How I Learned to Stop Worrying and Love the Bomb: STANLEY KUBRICK *(Columbia, 1964). Kubrick's blackest of black comedies skewered the military mentality as represented here by a meeting in the War Room. President Muffley (Peter Sellers), presiding at the right, announces, ''You can't fight in here! This is the War Room!''*

lightfully airy films that gave suitable roles to such come-diennes as Claudette Colbert, Carole Lombard, Irene Dunne, Ginger Rogers, and Katharine Hepburn. Described by Frank Capra as a man "with a brilliant, fertile mind and a flashing wit," he began directing in the silent era and reached his stride in the thirties with two memorable movies: the definitive screwball comedy *My Man Godfrey* (1936), in which madcap Carole Lombard pursued all-wise butler William Powell, and *Stage Door* (1937), which improved on the stage play about aspiring actresses.

La Cava's comedies contained gleams of bitter-flavored social commentary; he evidently enjoyed mocking the rich, as he did in *Godfrey* and, especially, in the Ginger Rogers comedy *Fifth Avenue Girl* (1939). (Rogers calls rich folks "cadavers" and "wax dummies who've had an overdose of dill pickles.") His straight dramas were much less successful. One of them, *Gabriel over the White House* (1933), was an offbeat, interesting drama about a weak, self-indulgent American president (Walter Huston) who undergoes a mystical experience that transforms him into a world leader for peace and justice. Refusing to adhere to scripts or shooting schedules, La Cava kept losing film assignments until there were none at all. He stopped making movies five years before his death.

★

The secret of making good pictures, in my opinion, is to create situations that will cause a clash between characters whom filmgoers will like and those who will evoke hatred. Once established as a sympathetic character, a screen player may commit any evil on the calendar without losing the audience's respect. FRITZ LANG, interview in *Film Pictorial*, 5 June 1937, cited in Jay Leyda, ed., *Voices of Film Experience* (New York: Macmillan, 1977).

FRITZ LANG (1890–1976) Trapped in a hostile world, pursued by dark and sinister forces bent on his annihilation, the Langian hero is consumed by a fate he cannot escape. Often the agent of his doom is a beautiful woman, her destructive power concealed in a lovely face and figure. Not even the pure and selfless love of another woman can save him. Alienated, alone, and guilty of some nameless crime, he may hate his persecutors and seek revenge, but he can find no solace in it. His destiny has been sealed.

If this typical protagonist of Fritz Lang's cinematic universe suggests the grim milieu of *M*, *Fury*, and *You Only Live Once* rather than the formula entertainment of *Cloak*

and Dagger (1946), *Rancho Notorious* (1952), and *Moonfleet* (1955), it is because Lang's somber and remorseless vision harmonized more deeply with the pessimism of Germany in the twenties and America in the Depression thirties, both with their political and social upheavals, than with the relatively hopeful postwar forties and fifties. Lang never really deserted that vision; his later work includes such desolate exercises in hopelessness as *Human Desire*, *Beyond a Reasonable Doubt*, and his fifties masterpiece, *The Big Heat*. But the films that have helped him retain his reputation as one of the towering figures in American and German cinema largely appear in the early rather than the late period of his career.

Born in Vienna, Fritz Lang was working aimlessly at a career in art when he discovered the magic of films by way of the young and burgeoning German motion picture industry. (His art background is evident in the sets and pictorial composition of his films.) By 1919 he had written and directed his first movie, *Halbblut (The Half-Breed)*, a drama that already took up his persistent theme of a man ruined by his love for a woman. Within a few years, in collaboration with Thea Von Harbou, who later

ABOVE Fury: FRITZ LANG (*MGM, 1936*). *A terrifying mob gathers, bent on lynching Spencer Tracy for a crime he did not commit. A relentless social drama, this film contained Lang's strongest American statement concerning man as a creature trapped and hounded by fate.*

OPPOSITE The Big Heat: FRITZ LANG (*Columbia, 1953*). *Glenn Ford draws a bead on the beaten Lee Marvin in Lang's top-notch crime drama. Ford's cop was a typical Langian protagonist, a revenge-minded man caught up in (and almost destroyed by) a trap of his own making.*

became his wife, Lang had made his name known internationally with a series of well-crafted, dark-toned thrillers that reflected the decaying conditions in Germany at the time. His most famous and ambitious silent film, *Metropolis,* was released in 1927. A futuristic melodrama depicting a tyrannical society ruled by robots, the movie was notable for its brilliantly imaginative sets and impressive special effects.

After several more films, Lang directed his masterwork of the early sound period, *M* (1931). A riveting psychological thriller based on the true case of a child murderer, the movie merged a realistic documentary approach with creative, expressionistic touches that emphasized the terror of the situation. With enormous skill, Lang used the camera and the soundtrack to depict a city gripped with fear and a desperate killer unable to control his murderous impulses. Peter Lorre was unforgettable as this pitiable creature, rising to dramatic heights in his long, anguished monologue to those who have finally trapped him.

When *Das Testament des Dr. Mabuse* (*The Last Will of Dr. Mabuse,* 1931) was banned by the government because of its anti-Nazi sentiments, Lang fled the country, first to France, where he directed *Liliom* (1935), and then to the United States. (He was also afraid that the Germans would discover his half-Jewish background, especially after Goebbels, to his amazement, had offered him the job of making Nazi films.) His first American film, *Fury* (1936), indicated his pervading interest in man as a helpless fly caught up in a complex spider's web made up of the many social, political, and psychological strands of

his time. Spencer Tracy starred as an ordinary man accused of a heinous crime he did not commit and forced to confront a vicious lynch mob. Lang's next two films mined a similar vein. *You Only Live Once* (1937) pitted an innocent, framed Henry Fonda against an insensitive, implacable system of justice; unable to escape, Fonda and wife Sylvia Sidney are mowed down in a hail of police bullets. *You and Me* (1938) also starred Sidney, the ubiquitous Depression heroine, this time married to ex-con George Raft and forced to conceal her own prison past. As a surprising extra feature, the movie included original songs by German composer Kurt Weill.

Although the balance of Lang's career never quite measured up to his earlier work, a number of his films warrant an honorable place among his credits. Considering his European background and profoundly pessimistic point of view, one would hardly consider him a candidate as a director of Westerns, yet he made two creditable films in that genre, *The Return of Frank James* (1940) and *Western Union* (1941). Still, he was clearly more comfortable with the thriller format, and during the war years he contributed several taut melodramas, including the anti-Nazi *Hangmen Also Die* (1942) and an adaptation of Graham Greene's novel *Ministry of Fear* (1944). He also directed *The Woman in the Window* (1944) and *Scarlet Street* (1945), two superior *films noirs* starring Edward G. Robinson.

Lang's best movie of the fifties was *The Big Heat* (1953), a grim and extremely violent crime drama with a different Langian twist: here the victim—a cop (Glenn Ford) whose wife is murdered by a car bomb intended for him—embarks on a one-man crusade of bitter vengeance against the mob, only to learn (almost too late) that revenge leaves a sour taste and that his vendetta has made him as vile as the men he is pursuing. Bluntly and objectively, Lang creates a cold, remorseless world devoid of compassion and moral order. As the moll who gets a cup of scalding coffee hurled in her face, Gloria Grahame portrayed one of the few sympathetic women in Lang's films.

After directing *Beyond a Reasonable Doubt* (1956), concerning a man (Dana Andrews) who finds himself trapped in his own scheme—he pretends to be guilty of murder to get a firsthand view of the criminal justice system—Lang decided to make no more films in America. His last few projects were either abandoned or heavily mutilated, and he made only two more films in Germany. His final years were spent in retirement in Beverly Hills.

One never approaches Fritz Lang's films for comfort

or reassurance. With a unique camera eye that knew how to find the most revealing detail in any scene, he probed the deepest and darkest recesses of human violence and corruption. His people—the criminals, the wicked schemers, the pathetic victims—can cling to very little as they move relentlessly toward the abyss. But the films they inhabit will continue to fascinate us, even as they chill us, for many years to come.

★

WALTER LANG (1898–1972)   For a quarter of a century, from the mid-thirties to 1960, Walter Lang was one of Fox's mainstays, a director who could be counted on to turn out sprightly, colorful entertainments guaranteed to please audiences without taxing their minds. Many were musicals like *Week-End in Havana* (1941), *Coney Island* (1943), and *Mother Wore Tights* (1947), all gussied up in Fox's gaudiest Technicolor and often starring the studio's resident blondes, Alice Faye and Betty Grable. In the fifties, Lang directed musicals that ranged from the sublime (*The King and I*, 1956, boasting sumptuous decor and a soaring Rodgers and Hammerstein score) to the ridiculous (*There's No Business Like Show Business*, 1954, an inexpressibly vulgar tribute to a show business family). He also ran the gamut with little Shirley Temple, directing her last two films for the studio: *The Little Princess* (1939, one of her best) and *The Blue Bird* (1940, one of her worst, a ten-ton fantasy). His comedy films (*Second Honeymoon*, 1937; *Sitting Pretty*, 1948; *Cheaper by the Dozen*, 1950; and others) were generally pleasant and inoffensive. The last two actually owed their success more to Clifton Webb's amusing, supercilious style than to Lang.

★

It's distressing when a film is over. You work for months with a group of people, it's a circus and you're the ringmaster, then suddenly it's over and you are on your own—you feel a terrible sense of having been deserted, and lonely. It takes me two or three months to recoup.
DAVID LEAN, interview with Roderick Mann, *Los Angeles Times*, Sunday Calendar, 10 April 1983, p. 21.

DAVID LEAN (born 1908)   One of England's most distinguished film directors, David Lean won renewed admiration—and a third Academy Award—in 1984 for his absorbing and thoroughly satisfying film version of *A Passage to India*. After an absence of fourteen years and two previous films (*Doctor Zhivago*, 1965, and *Ryan's Daughter*, 1970) that received many carping reviews,

Lean demonstrated his qualities once again: a high degree of professionalism, a meticulous attention to detail, and enormous skill with actors. Occasionally, his screenplays have let him down—where his direction was precise, they were rambling, discursive, and imprecise—but at his best, Lean has given audiences the sense of being in the hands of a superb technician who knows the exact effect he wants to achieve.

Lean entered films as a teen-ager in 1927 and eventually worked his way up to editing feature films by 1934 (*Pygmalion*, 1938; *One of Our Aircraft Is Missing*, 1942). In 1942 he began his director's career with a prestigious film, Noel Coward's stirring war drama *In Which We Serve* (Coward served as codirector as well as leading player, author of the screenplay, and composer of the musical score), which saluted the heroism of men aboard a British fighting ship. Lean continued his associ-

ABOVE   The King and I: WALTER LANG (*Fox, 1956*). *Anna (Deborah Kerr) and her son (Rex Thompson) meet the King of Siam (Yul Brynner), while Kralahome (Martin Benson) waits in attendance. Lang's lavish adaptation of the long-running Rodgers and Hammerstein musical preserved Brynner's memorable performance as the autocratic yet puzzled king.*
OPPOSITE, ABOVE   2001: A Space Odyssey: STANLEY KUBRICK (*MGM, 1968*). *Astronaut Bowman (Keir Dullea) embarks on a staggering voyage into space and into his own psyche. Kubrick's ambitious film sought to portray the cosmic evolution of mankind over the centuries and into the future.*
OPPOSITE, BELOW   A Passage to India: DAVID LEAN (*Columbia, 1984*). *Mrs. Moore (Peggy Ashcroft) and Dr. Aziz (Victor Banerjee) begin their fateful journey to the mysterious Marabar caves. Lean's virtues as a director—his painstaking care with the background, his professional polish, and his skill with actors—were evident throughout this film.*

ation with Coward in his next three films: *This Happy Breed* (1944), a tribute to British pluck and resilience; *Blithe Spirit* (1945), a buoyant adaptation of Coward's play about a ghostly wife's return to home and hearth; and *Brief Encounter* (1946), an adult romance that featured outstanding performances by Celia Johnson and Trevor Howard as two middle-aged people, married to others, who fall helplessly in love.

Lean turned next to the novels of Charles Dickens. His versions of *Great Expectations* (1947) and *Oliver Twist* (1948) were notable for their authentic Dickensian atmosphere, superlative performances, and briskly paced narratives, which managed to keep the novelist's dense plots from becoming cluttered on film. He followed these with a series of movies that demonstrated his ability to extract commendable performances from eccentric actors who were often eager to give more to a role than was necessary. Ralph Richardson was effective and even restrained as a dedicated builder of experimental airplanes in Lean's *Breaking Through the Sound Barrier* (1952), and although Charles Laughton played in his usual ripe (and sometimes overripe) fashion as a bombastic father in *Hobson's Choice* (1954), Lean kept him from overpowering the story or overshadowing the oth-

er performances. Best of all, Lean guided Katharine Hepburn through one of her finest performances, as a spinster discovering Venice and love in *Summertime* (1955).

In 1957 Lean embarked on an entirely new phase in his career, directing the first of a series of large-scale, expensive productions that appeared every few years. *The Bridge on the River Kwai* (1957), adapted from Pierre Boulle's novel, was simultaneously a powerful statement of war's folly, focusing on the dangers of the obsessed military mind, and a crackling adventure story set in the Burmese jungle. Under Lean's assured direction, the screenplay balanced two main strands of plot: the bitter conflict between the Japanese commander of a prison camp (Sessue Hayakawa) and a strong-willed British colonel (Alec Guinness), and the adventures of a group of commandos sent to blow up the bridge built by the colonel's men. Lean won an Academy Award for his direction, a feat he repeated five years later with *Lawrence of Arabia*.

Lean's highly touted production of *Lawrence of Arabia* (1962) turned out to be a flawed but often impressive spectacle based on the "Arabian" period in the life of soldier-adventurer T. E. Lawrence. The Robert Bolt screenplay traced Lawrence (played in bravura style by Peter O'Toole, another actor in need of Lean's disciplined direction) as he changed from minor government official to obsessed Arab leader. However, the character emerged as enigmatic and unmoving, and only Lean's magnificent staging of the battle scenes relieved the film's generally turgid tone.

Lean directed two widely spaced films before his long hiatus, but neither fully justified the wait or the vast expenditure of time and money. His adaptation of Boris Pasternak's sprawling novel *Doctor Zhivago* (1965) surely required a small fortune to create its vivid canvas of Russian life in the early years of the century, but the personal drama, principally an over-the-years love affair between Zhivago (Omar Sharif) and his beloved Lara (Julie Christie), was oddly remote and unaffecting. *Ryan's Daughter* (1970) satisfied even less; it overinflated a simple story of the adulterous romance between an Irish girl (Sarah Miles) and a battle-weary British officer (Christopher Jones). Despite a valiant effort, Robert Mitchum seemed out of place as the girl's dull, sober-

Ryan's Daughter: DAVID LEAN *(MGM, 1970). High on a cliff, swept by hurricane-force winds, David Lean (at the right of the camera, wearing a trenchcoat) works with his camera crew to film a climactic scene. Lean waited nearly a year on Ireland's west coast for a storm of awesome size.*

minded husband. However, John Mills won the Best Supporting Actor Oscar for his portrayal of the village half-wit.

With *A Passage to India*, Lean returned to prominence, inheriting the kind of reverent attention given to a major director who has been away too long. It was fully deserved—his adaptation of E. M. Forster's novel of India had the scope expected by now of a Lean film, but it also had the narrative pace, the scrupulous attention to background, and the confident acting of Lean's best work. Dame Peggy Ashcroft, in particular, gave a memorable performance as the gentle, troubled old Mrs. Moore. (She justly received the year's award as Best Supporting Actress.)

Like many other directors whose particular imprint remains elusive, Lean has been called impersonal, one whose sparse body of work is technically proficient and admirable, without the touch of eccentricity or daring that signifies greatness. To say this, however, is to demean the very real achievements of someone who uses the vast resources of film to the fullest. David Lean needs no dissection of his inner life or recurring idiosyncrasies to take his place among the finest film directors.

★

MITCHELL LEISEN (1898–1972)   Mitchell Leisen was often accused of emphasizing the decor of his films—the sheen and shimmer of the settings and costumes—above the story content. Indeed, the physical production occasionally submerged everything else, as in *Death Takes a Holiday* (1934), a somber fantasy with an air of otherworldliness, and, especially, *Lady in the Dark* (1944), an overblown fantasy that drowned the story in a sea of sequins and other glitter. This tendency may well have carried over from Leisen's years as a prominent costume designer and art director, especially for Cecil B. DeMille. Despite this tendency, Leisen directed some of the most sparkling romantic comedies and dramas of the thirties, films like *Easy Living* (1937) and the delightful *Midnight* (1939). If these movies derive much of their charm from the screenplays of Preston Sturges, Billy Wilder, and Charles Brackett and from the witty presence and grace of such actresses as Jean Arthur and Claudette Colbert, Leisen wielded the baton to their music. Nor were his best films all foam and froth. *Arise My Love* (1940) and *Hold Back the Dawn* (1941) display a genuine compassion and regard for the plight of war-torn lovers and displaced refugees in an uncertain world.

Most of Leisen's forties films (*Frenchman's Creek*, 1944; *Golden Earrings*, 1947) fell below the level of his earlier work. With the remaining flashes of his visual elegance, he tried to conceal the fact that his brand of chic glamour was becoming anachronistic. By the fifties, however, his career had declined for a variety of reasons to the point that he retired to open a popular tailor shop in Beverly Hills.

★

ROBERT Z. LEONARD (1889–1968)   Of the many directors who labored in the MGM vineyards during the thirties and forties, perhaps none suited the studio's gloss-and-glitter style better than Robert Zigler Leonard. After having directed many films for many studios starting in 1914, Leonard found his most compatible home in Leo's Lair. He turned out many enjoyable and lushly mounted films there, tangling with high drama (*Strange Interlude*, 1932) and high camp (*Ziegfeld Girl*, 1941). Should we be inclined to denigrate Leonard's films, we might remember that he directed the best of the Jeanette MacDonald–Nelson Eddy operettas (*Maytime*, 1937) and a superlative adaptation of Jane Austen's *Pride and Prejudice* (1940), in which Greer Garson and Laurence Olivier exchanged witty quips with aplomb. His musical films were mainly routine, although *In the Good Old Summertime* (1949) inherited at least a modicum of the charm of its predecessor, Ernst Lubitsch's *The Shop Around the Corner* (1940). Leonard worked well and often with such glamorous actresses at MGM as Joan Crawford, Norma Shearer, Myrna Loy, and Lana Turner; presumably, he had some experience dealing with them, having been married to two silent film stars, Mae Murray and Gertrude Olmstead.

★

Any director who tries to pander to public taste while he ignores his own is riding for a fall. Similarly, a director who sets out to make a movie to please only himself is also asking for trouble. A director must believe in the property he is doing, but must also consider what the public wants and needs. The two go hand in hand....
MERVYN LEROY, *Mervyn LeRoy: Take One,* as told to Dick Kleiner (New York: Hawthorn Books, 1974), p. 129.

MERVYN LEROY (born 1900)   With a remarkable career as director and producer that spans nearly four decades, Mervyn LeRoy can claim distinction as one of Hollywood's most adroit and solid professionals. He has worked in every genre, making films that range from grittily realistic to lushly romantic. His best films have been marked by a strong narrative pace, vigorous performances, and, often, a palpable pleasure in the power and magic of movie-making. There may not be a certifiable LeRoy style, but his movies bear the unmistakable stamp of someone who knows his craft.

LeRoy turned director in 1927, after years as an actor and vaudeville performer. (As a teen-ager he billed himself as "The Boy Tenor of the Generation.") He had appeared in a number of silent films before becoming a gag writer and comedy specialist, and then finally director. At Warners from the start, LeRoy was quick to master

ABOVE   Pride and Prejudice: ROBERT Z. LEONARD (MGM, 1940). *Proud Elizabeth Bennet (Greer Garson) engages in conversation with the haughty Mr. Darcy (Laurence Olivier) and Sir William Lucas (E. E. Clive). Looking on is Edward Ashley as Mr. Wickham. Under Leonard's direction, the film captured the spirit of Jane Austen's novel, particularly in the sly parry and thrust of Elizabeth and Darcy.*
OPPOSITE   Easy Living: MITCHELL LEISEN (Paramount, 1937). *Director Leisen adjusts Jean Arthur's hair on the set. This lighthearted romantic comedy boasted a screenplay by Preston Sturges about a working-class Cinderella (Arthur) who becomes involved with a tycoon and his son.*

the studio's patented style of rapid-fire action and dialogue, giving a brisk touch to movies with such racy titles as *Naughty Baby* (1929), *Hot Stuff* (1929), and *Playing Around* (1930).

When Warners launched a new musical cycle with *42nd Street* (1933), LeRoy was swiftly assigned to another mammoth musical featuring the eye-popping kaleidoscopic musical numbers of Busby Berkeley. *Gold Diggers of 1933* (1933) proved to be one of the best of the cycle, with a bright, wisecracking screenplay, a cast of studio players at the top of their form, and musical sequences that surpassed those of *42nd Street* in size and audacity. LeRoy's penchant for dramatizing social issues emerged in the film's last number, a fervent plea for discarded war veterans entitled "Remember My Forgotten Man." His concern with national problems, coupled with Warners's propensity for taking stories from the headlines, resulted in his most memorable films of the decade.

In 1930 the studio released LeRoy's *Little Caesar,* a crude but powerful melodrama that, along with *The Public Enemy* in 1931, marked the peak of the gangster cycle that intrigued Depression audiences. As the vain, vicious kingpin mobster Caesar Enrico Bandello ("Shoot first and argue afterwards"), Edward G. Robinson gave an electrifying performance that propelled him into stardom. LeRoy's driving pace rode roughshod over the primitive sound techniques to give the movie an exciting momentum. In *I Am a Fugitive from a Chain Gang* (1932), he directed an even more forceful social document, a searing indictment of America's penal system in which an innocent man (Paul Muni) is turned into a bitter hunted animal after his experience in a corrupt Georgia prison. Although unpolished and sometimes overemphatic in its staging, LeRoy's *They Won't Forget* (1937) unflinchingly exposed the brutality of the lynch mob and the corruption of political expediency.

In 1938 LeRoy moved to MGM, where he acted as producer only for a few films, notably *The Wizard of Oz* (1939), before returning to directing. Freed from the restrictions of Warners's tight budgets, his style changed drastically as he made use of MGM's expansive resources. The grim realism of his Depression melodramas in the thirties gave way to the sleek and elaborate romances of the forties, particularly the tragic love story of *Waterloo Bridge* (1940), with Vivien Leigh as an ill-fated ballerina-turned-prostitute, and the hugely popular *Random Harvest* (1942), starring Ronald Colman and Greer Garson in James Hilton's tale of a love that triumphs over amnesia. LeRoy also directed MGM films in different veins: a romanticized, handsomely produced biography of *Madame Curie* (1943), a sturdy war drama, *Thirty Seconds over Tokyo* (1944), and the gigantic costume spectacle *Quo Vadis* (1951).

In the late forties, LeRoy's unobtrusive style became a drawback when applied to remakes of well-known earlier films. His versions of *Little Women* (1949), *Roberta* (titled *Lovely to Look At*, 1952), and *Rose Marie* (1954), for all the lavish MGM trappings, were flat and unexciting. Nor could star power completely conceal the pulpish nature of *Any Number Can Play* (1949), with Clark Gable, and *East Side, West Side* (1949), with a name-studded cast. LeRoy fared much better when he returned to Warner Bros. in the mid-fifties to direct a number of screen versions of Broadway plays and musicals. *Mister Roberts* (1955), inherited by LeRoy when John Ford fell ill, was a sure-fire audience winner, a rowdy and poignant comedy about a becalmed cargo ship during World War II. *No Time for Sergeants* (1958) also could hardly miss; it rested on the time-honored concept of a country bumpkin outwitting the U.S. Army. However, *A Majority of One* (1962) and *Gypsy* (1962) both suffered from a heavy touch and from the miscasting of Rosalind Russell as, respectively, a Jewish mother at large in Japan and Gypsy Rose Lee's ambitious mother.

Over the years, Mervyn LeRoy has served movie audi-

ABOVE   I Am a Fugitive from a Chain Gang: MERVYN LEROY *(Warner Bros., 1932). Jim Allen (Paul Muni, center) begins his hopeless life as a shackled chain-gang prisoner. This crude but powerful social drama had an impact on America's penal system.*

LEFT   Madame Curie: MERVYN LEROY *(MGM, 1943). Greer Garson and Walter Pidgeon, one of America's most popular screen teams in the forties, impressed as Marie and Pierre Curie, the scientists who discovered radium. Reverent and a little ponderous, the film nevertheless dramatized some of the frustration, exhaustion, and elation of scientific experimentation.*

ences well. For all the lapses, he has proved, on balance, a high-ranking director. Apart from his technical skill, which he honed and polished from his early days at Warners, he offered an unabashed and appealing enthusiasm for the trade he followed for so many years. (His sets were known to be light and cheerful places where he often indulged a fondness for practical jokes.) In his autobiography he wrote:

Has there ever been such a challenging, exciting, daring career as that of a movie director? You take some words on paper, a camera loaded with strips of celluloid, a group of actors, some lights and props and sets and costumes, and from all that you create—what? Just some shadows that dance on a screen and hold millions of people enthralled. (*Mervyn LeRoy: Take One,* p. 222)

Not as an afterthought, he added, "I love motion pictures, and I always will." Whether in setting Little Caesar on his path to doom or reuniting Ronald Colman and Greer Garson in a warm embrace, the love shows.

★

RICHARD LESTER (born 1932)   Richard Lester's hyperactive, dizzying style of directing first achieved recognition in 1964 with *A Hard Day's Night,* a frantic, madcap musical farce starring the Beatles as a kind of latter-day Marx Brothers. The Philadelphia-born Lester, who began his career as a television director with CBS, had settled in England some time earlier after spending a few years roaming around Europe. Subsequent to the success of *A Hard Day's Night,* he applied the same approach to an amusing, fast-paced romantic comedy (*The Knack . . . and How to Get It,* 1965); another inventive excursion into Beatles lunacy (*Help!,* 1965); and a wild musical farce (*A Funny Thing Happened on the Way to the Forum,* 1966). All had moments of hilarity, as well as stretches of overexertion. Lester had a larger budget for *How I Won the War* (1967), an extremely black comedy that mocked war-film clichés in feverish, surrealistic style.

In the seventies, Lester brought his perspective to familiar heroic figures, offering a tongue-in-cheek version of *The Three Musketeers* (1974) that combined swashbuckling and slapstick, and taking a more serious view of Robin Hood and his beloved Maid Marian in *Robin and Marian* (1976). The latter film, which portrayed the couple in their autumnal years, was not well received, but its lushly beautiful production, commendable performances by Sean Connery and Audrey Hepburn, and poignant final scene made it well worth watching. Lester's

films with American settings (*Petulia,* 1968; *The Ritz,* 1976; *Butch and Sundance: The Early Days,* 1979; *Finders Keepers,* 1984) did not fare well either, but he scored a success with *Superman II* (1981), a lively sequel to Richard Donner's original *Superman* (1978). The inevitable law of diminishing returns, however, applied to *Superman III* (1983), which Lester directed in his old frenetic style, with labored results.

★

ALBERT LEWIN (1894–1968)   Albert Lewin strove to bring "culture" to films; unfortunately, his idea of culture was something exotic, rarefied, and clogged with murky symbolism. For his first film as writer-director, he adapted Somerset Maugham's novel *The Moon and Sixpence* (1942) into a solemn, rather plodding drama of a tortured artist (George Sanders) patterned after Paul Gauguin. Between 1945 and 1957, Lewin wrote and produced five films that resembled hothouse flowers, too "special" to survive in the movie world of garden-variety plants. They included *The Picture of Dorian Gray* (1945), which combined Oscar Wilde and MGM with curious but intriguing results; the unique and bizarre *Pandora and the Flying Dutchman* (1951), which cast Ava Gardner and James Mason in an exquisitely photographed, modern-dress version of the legend; and *The*

Robin and Marian: RICHARD LESTER *(Columbia, 1976). Sean Connery and Audrey Hepburn as a no-longer-young Robin Hood and his once-beloved Maid Marian, now a nun. Audiences were not eager to accept this sober, revisionist view of the legendary couple, but the film dealt movingly with their final time together.*

Living Idol (1957), a high-toned recycling of the standard old theme beloved by makers of low-budget horror films: the pretty young heroine whose soul is taken over by a predatory beast, in this case a jaguar. In his early career, Lewin worked as head of MGM's script department in the twenties, ultimately becoming Irving Thalberg's closest associate. In the thirties he was a producer at MGM and at Paramount.

OPPOSITE, ABOVE Gypsy: MERVYN LEROY *(Warner Bros., 1962). Karl Malden, Rosalind Russell, and Natalie Wood express in song their pleasure at being "Together." The number was ultimately deleted from the release print of the film.*

OPPOSITE, BELOW South Pacific: JOSHUA LOGAN *(Fox, 1958). Nurse Nellie Forbush (Mitzi Gaynor) and planter Emile de Becque (Rossano Brazzi) share an enchanted evening. Rodgers and Hammerstein's lilting score continued to caress the ears, but a stagy, heavy-handed production kept this film version of the long-running Broadway musical from staying afloat.*

★

ANATOLE LITVAK (1902–1974) One of the more interesting, if uneven, Hollywood directors, Anatole ("Tola") Litvak returned, time and again, to the theme of the woman as victim. In many of his films from the thirties to the sixties, his female characters either find themselves trapped in a dire situation not of their own making (*Sorry, Wrong Number*, 1948; *The Snake Pit*, 1948, his only Oscar nomination; *Anastasia*, 1956) or are willing and even eager to sacrifice themselves for love (*The*

ABOVE The Snake Pit: ANATOLE LITVAK *(Fox, 1948). In a clear reflection of the title, Olivia de Havilland stands helplessly at the center of a roomful of mental hospital inmates. Although much of the psychiatric content now seems naive and simplistic, Anatole Litvak's adaptation of Mary Jane Ward's novel included some vivid, harrowing sequences.*

Sisters, 1938; *All This and Heaven Too*, 1940; *The Deep Blue Sea*, 1955). James Cagney also offered himself up for sacrifice in *City for Conquest* (1940), entering the boxing ring and eventually losing his eyesight to help his musically gifted brother (Arthur Kennedy). At their best, these films were smoothly and professionally crafted, although seldom consistent in style.

Litvak's early career is worth noting. Russian-born, he worked at various theatrical jobs in Western Europe for a number of years, ultimately fleeing Germany, where he had settled, after the rise of the Nazis. (He was Jewish.) In France, he scored a great international success with *Mayerling* (1937), starring Charles Boyer and Danielle Darrieux as Austrian Crown Prince Rudolph and his Maria—doomed lovers out of history. Although the film was lushly romantic, and a number of his subsequent films betrayed a strong romantic streak, Litvak also had an interest in the documentary style; there is much documentary footage in *Confessions of a Nazi Spy* (1939), *Decision Before Dawn* (1951), and other of his films, and during World War II he collaborated with Frank Capra on the excellent *Why We Fight* series. One of Litvak's last films, *The Night of the Generals* (1967), a compelling story of a psychotic and homicidal German general (Peter O'Toole) in the final days of the war, deserved more consideration than the critics gave it. In the early sixties, Litvak settled in Paris.

★

FRANK LLOYD (1888–1960)   Although he directed scores of films over four decades, Frank Lloyd qualifies as yet another Forgotten Director. He worked skillfully within the studio system, and his movies include two Academy Award winners (*Cavalcade* and *Mutiny on the Bounty*), but he seldom received critical coverage. He was content to entertain in an unpretentious style, and apparently this has given him a ticket to anonymity.

Born in Scotland, Lloyd came to the United States in 1913 and worked briefly as an actor before turning to direction. His silent films included a production of *A Tale of Two Cities* (1917), with William Farnum, and a loose adaptation of *Oliver Twist* (1922), with Jackie Coogan as Oliver and Lon Chaney as Fagin. By the start of the sound era, he had achieved a solid reputation as a craftsmanlike, reliable director. His last silent film, *The Divine Lady* (1929), earned him an Oscar for Best Director. Many of his early sound films suffered from routine stories and indifferent acting; in 1933, however, he attracted wide attention with *Cavalcade*, an adaptation of Noel Coward's over-the-years chronicle of a tenacious British

family. It won high praise (and three Academy Awards, including one for Lloyd) for its unabashed patriotic fervor and lavish production, although today its air of self-congratulation is rather irksome.

Although he shuttled from studio to studio in the thirties, Lloyd's most successful and best-remembered film was made at MGM. *Mutiny on the Bounty* (1935) remains the definitive version of the adventure tale, a rousing, flavorsome story of rebellion at sea featuring one of Charles Laughton's most extravagant performances as the ruthless Captain Bligh. Lloyd's films for Paramount had something of the same narrative pace, even if they lacked MGM's lavish production values. They included *Wells Fargo* (1937), a brisk if overlong Western, and *If I Were King* (1938), a fanciful tale of swashbuckling poet François Villon (Ronald Colman) with a script by Preston Sturges.

During the war years, Lloyd joined six other directors in guiding *Forever and a Day* (1943), Hollywood's effusive, multistar tribute to the British, and he directed James Cagney and Sylvia Sidney in *Blood on the Sun*

ABOVE   Mutiny on the Bounty: FRANK LLOYD (*MGM, 1935*). *A tense confrontation between Fletcher Christian (Clark Cable) and Captain Bligh (Charles Laughton). Lloyd's lusty seafaring adventure was highlighted by Laughton's marvelously hammy performance.*
OPPOSITE   Camelot: JOSHUA LOGAN (*Warner Bros.-Seven Arts, 1967*). *King Arthur (Richard Harris) and his Guenevere (Vanessa Redgrave) exchange vows. Although this sumptuous adaptation of the stage musical contained some of Lerner and Loewe's most bewitching songs, the gargantuan sets, ponderous pace, and oppressive close-ups overpowered a basically fragile story.*

(1945), a fairly good melodrama set in Japan during the thirties. After this film, he retired to his ranch, returning nearly a decade later to direct *The Shanghai Story* (1954). His last movie, *The Last Command* (1955), was an expensive, mediocre Western centering on the Battle of the Alamo.

★

JOSHUA LOGAN (born 1908)   One of the theater's outstanding directors and playwrights, Joshua Logan planted his stage roots in the late twenties when he founded the University Players, a stock group of actors that included such promising talents as Henry Fonda, James Stewart, and Margaret Sullavan. In the thirties, after acting in and directing many plays, Logan had a brief sojourn in Hollywood, where he codirected (with Arthur Ripley) the romantic drama *I Met My Love Again* (1938). He soon returned to the theater, where by the fifties he had gained a reputation as a tireless creator of hit plays. (His book *Josh: My Up and Down, In and Out Life* recorded the true cost of his fame in mental anguish and breakdown.)

In the mid-fifties, Logan returned to film directing with two successful movies: *Picnic* (1955), an effective if overproduced adaptation of William Inge's play about sexual stirrings in a small Kansas town, and *Bus Stop* (1956), another Inge play. The latter, more modestly scaled, was highlighted by Marilyn Monroe's luminous performance as a wistful "chantoosie" pursued by amorous cowboy Don Murray. He also had a popular suc-

cess with *Sayonara* (1957), a handsomely mounted East-West romance based on James Michener's novel and starring Marlon Brando in one of his more convincing performances. (Red Buttons and Miyoshi Umeki won Oscars in their supporting roles.)

Logan's subsequent films have been mostly screen versions of the Broadway musicals he directed, including *South Pacific* (1958), *Fanny* (1961, but with the music used only in the background), *Camelot* (1967), and *Paint Your Wagon* (1969). On the whole, they were elephantine and overblown, displaying little of the cinematic style that had characterized much of his earlier work. *South Pacific*, in particular, was seriously marred by experimental lighting with colored filters, while *Camelot* and *Paint Your Wagon* suffered from a curious turgidity and joylessness and from the casting of inappropriate or nonsinging players in leading roles.

★

JOSEPH LOSEY (1909–1984)   One of the most personal and independent-minded of contemporary filmmakers, Joseph Losey received his full share of bouquets and brickbats in a career that spanned more than four decades. Many have admired his intense cinematic style, his original approach to the delineation of character, and his abiding concern with the lost, vulnerable, often desolate souls in a corrupt world. Others have criticized him as pretentious, self-indulgent, and deliberately obscure.

Losey's background is at least as interesting as his films. While still in his early twenties, he was the stage manager of the first live show ever produced at New York City's Radio City Music Hall, and a few years later he created *The Living Newspaper*, an innovative stage production influenced by the work of German author Bertolt Brecht. Brecht continued to influence him, and in 1947, Losey directed a well-received production of the playwright's *Galileo Galilei*, starring Charles Laughton. On the strength of this production, he was signed by RKO to direct his first feature film, *The Boy with Green Hair* (1948), a fairly obvious fable about discrimination against those who are "different." His next films, especially *M* (1951) and *The Big Night* (1951), revealed his sympathy for society's outcasts as well as his revulsion for those who would brutalize them.

Ironically, that same year (1951), Losey himself became an outcast when he was summoned before the House Un-American Activities Committee and identified as a former Communist. Blacklisted by the film industry, he decided to settle in England. His first films there were released under a pseudonym.

Losey's twenty-odd-year period in England was the most fruitful and rewarding of his career. In a series of complex, stylishly produced films, Losey offered a darkly pessimistic view of his new country: the corruption and decay of its ruling class (*The Servant*, 1963), the brutality of its system of military justice (*King and Country*, 1964), and the spiritual and sexual malaise of its intellectuals (*Accident*, 1967). Writer Harold Pinter provided the cryptic, multilayered screenplays for *The Servant* and *Accident*, as he did for one of Losey's finest films, *The Go-Between* (1971), which subtly examined the innocent—and not-so-innocent—cruelties that can wreck lives.

Occasionally, Losey's eccentric style failed to mesh with a suitable script, and the resulting films could attract no viewers but cultists, despite the star presence of Elizabeth Taylor and Richard Burton (*Boom!*, 1968), or Burton *sans* Taylor (*The Assassination of Trotsky*, 1972). One of Losey's later films, *Mr. Klein* (1977), focused sensitively on an arts dealer (Alain Delon) mistaken as a Jew during World War II. His last film, *Steaming* (1984), was adapted from Nell Dunn's play about a group of women who bare their souls as well as their bodies in a shabby public bathhouse.

★

For myself, I do not believe in this present craze for covering a set with directors of dialogue, directors of dancing, directors of music, and all the other would-be directors who are interfering with the Director's work. I would not make a picture that way, for it could not be a satisfactory picture with so many minds trying to govern it. ERNST LUBITSCH, interview in *American Cinematographer*, cited in Jay Leyda, ed., *Voices of Film Experience* (New York: Macmillan, 1977).

ERNST LUBITSCH (1892–1947) How would one define "the Lubitsch touch"? Many critics have tried to pinpoint the elusive "touch" that lent his films their distinctively wry, sardonic flavor and their visual elegance, and, time after time, confirmed his status as the master of screen sophistication. It might appear in a few fleeting moments of film: in *The Merry Widow*, when everything in Sonia's room (including her dog) suddenly turns from black to white as she decides to end her mourning; in the opening of *Trouble in Paradise*, when the fruity romantic tenor of a gondolier in Venice is abruptly undercut by garbage flung from a window into the canal; in *Ninotchka*, when a tipsy Garbo, succumbing to the amorous advances of Melvyn Douglas, pretends to be "shot" by a firing squad for her sins. (The "shot" is the pop of a cork from a bottle of champagne.) The Lubitsch "touch"

is evident in entire sequences: for example, in *Monte Carlo*, in which Jeanette MacDonald sings "Beyond the Blue Horizon" from a train window, and peasants in the field join in a reprise as they watch the train pass; or in the café scene in *The Shop Around the Corner*, in which Lubitsch manages to blend humor and heartbreak in delicate proportions.

Whatever ingredients Lubitsch managed to stir into his movies—both sweet and tart—the delicious results were primarily his own. This is not to slight the very real achievements of his scenarists, including Samson Raphaelson, Ernest Vadja, Billy Wilder, and Charles Brackett, who provided the solid framework for his films. But around this framework Lubitsch constructed a durable edifice in which his knowing characters could carry out their romantic and sexual games. He was known, in fact, to be the total architect of his films, who provided detailed blueprints of every scene, complete with all the necessary specifications.

The Berlin-born Lubitsch had already achieved an international reputation when he came to America in 1921. At first an actor with Max Reinhardt's theater company and then a slapstick comedian in German silent films,

ABOVE The Go-Between: JOSEPH LOSEY (Columbia, 1971). *Young Dominic Guard becomes the secret letter carrier for Alan Bates and Julie Christie in Losey's subtle, beautifully designed film.*
OPPOSITE One Hour with You: ERNST LUBITSCH *and* GEORGE CUKOR (Paramount, 1932). *Lubitsch (with cigar) and Cukor (to his right) codirect a scene with Jeanette MacDonald and Maurice Chevalier. The seeming amity between the two directors ended when Cukor insisted on codirectorial credit for directing over a few weeks while Lubitsch was away.*

Lubitsch gradually abandoned acting and began writing and directing his own films, finally achieving success with *The Eyes of the Mummy* (1918), with Pola Negri. His satirical comedy *The Oyster Princess* (1919), an even greater hit, revealed for the first time the sly humor and precise attention to detail that would characterize his later films. Audiences began to pay attention to movies by this young German director, and *Madame Du Barry* (1919, called *Passion* in the United States) earned more money than any other foreign silent film ever released in the United States.

In Hollywood during the twenties, Lubitsch adapted himself with remarkable felicity to American manners and mores, while retaining a good measure of his European attitude toward such basic topics as sex and money. In 1924, a year after being deeply impressed by Chaplin's *A Woman of Paris*, Lubitsch directed *The Marriage Circle*, a roundelay of marital escapades. It became the first in a series of triumphant comedies that crystallized his style. Perfectly timed, mildly risqué, and played by performers who knew how to express emotion with a lifted eyebrow or a cryptic smile, such films as *Kiss Me Again* and *Lady Windermere's Fan* (both 1925) amused and titillated movie audiences with their casual approach to marital discord.

With the arrival of sound, Lubitsch had no trouble adding witty spoken dialogue and songs to his tales of dalliance and misalliance, creating a perfect blend of fluid camera work, clever editing, bright screenplays, and deft performances. In his first sound film, *The Love Parade* (1929), he teamed Jeanette MacDonald (her first film) with French singer Maurice Chevalier in a story,

ripe with sexual innuendo, of an imperious queen tamed by the dashing prince consort she marries. The director managed some mischievous Lubitschean moments, including a swipe at money-mad Americans. On screen, the stars seemed ideally matched, belying their mutual antipathy. They went their separate ways in Lubitsch's next two musicals, *Monte Carlo* (1930) and *The Smiling Lieutenant* (1931), only to be reunited in *One Hour with You* (1932). A musical remake of *The Marriage Circle*, it was a charming trifle about a flirtatious married couple, with some amusing songs. The film was also the center of a heated controversy over the director's credit (George Cukor demanded cocredit for directing for a few weeks while Lubitsch was away). Fortunately, the team reached a glorious peak in their final film together: *The Merry Widow* (1934) was a totally enchanting rendition of the Franz Lehár operetta for which Lubitsch staged the lavish musical numbers with dazzling skill.

With the conspicuous exception of a bitter antiwar drama entitled *The Man I Killed* (1932, also called *Broken Lullaby*), Lubitsch's nonmusical films of the thirties managed, in some instances, to retain the champagne sparkle of his musicals. In *Trouble in Paradise* (1932), he directed one of the finest comedies of the thirties, a witty and stylish bauble of two romantically inclined jewel thieves (Herbert Marshall and Miriam Hopkins) and their attractive prey (Kay Francis). The high level diminished somewhat with *Design for Living* (1933), another triangular diversion, very loosely derived from the Noel Coward play; the principal players lacked the ultrachic, brittle approach required for Coward. It declined even further with *Angel* (1937) and *Bluebeard's Eighth Wife* (1938), although the former film, centering on Marlene

Dietrich's extramarital affair with Melvyn Douglas, has its admirers. With *Ninotchka* (1939), Lubitsch was fully back on course, directing a comedy that mixed captivating romance with a malicious spoof of the glum, austere Soviets. The story of a beautiful but humorless Russian emissary (Greta Garbo) who discovers love and laughter in Paris, it was graced with a glowing performance by Garbo in her first comedic role.

Lubitsch provided other joys to savor after *Ninotchka*. *The Shop Around the Corner* (1940) displayed the director in a warmer, less acerbic mood than usual, although his lightly mocking awareness of the human comedy (and underlying tragedy) still comes through. Its gentle story concerning two pen pals who are unaware that they work in the same shop showed an unexpectedly tender regard for life's small pleasures and sorrows. *Heaven Can Wait* (1943), Lubitsch's first film in color, also had its sentimental side, but the plot—a newly deceased roué reviews his life—gave Lubitsch the chance to insert many wickedly funny satirical "touches." (He received his third Oscar nomination and lost to Michael Curtiz for *Casablanca*, only to receive a special Academy Award three years later.) His more sardonic nature, however, reemerged in *To Be or Not to Be* (1942), a controversial black comedy about a theater troupe during the Nazi occupation of Poland. Plagued by illness, Lubitsch managed to complete only one more film, *Cluny Brown* (1946), a moderately amusing comedy about British class distinctions. Against his doctor's wishes, Lubitsch began directing *That Lady in Ermine* (1948); he died in mid-production. (Otto Preminger completed the film.)

What would Lubitsch himself make of the very high regard in which his best films are held? With his ubiquitous cigar firmly clamped between his teeth, he probably would deflate the honor with some witty, boisterous remark. But he probably would also be pleased to know that his peers rightly looked upon him as "a giant" whose "talent and originality were stupefying" (Orson Welles), "the most elegant of screen magicians" (Billy Wilder), and a man "whose films bore the recognizable and indelible stamp of the gay, clever, witty, mischievous master" (William Wyler).

With a touch of malice and an abundance of charm, Ernst Lubitsch laughed at human foibles and desires, ours and his own. And his laughter has echoed merrily down the years.

★

GEORGE LUCAS (born 1944)   Like his friend and colleague Steven Spielberg, George Lucas apparently has had a direct line to his audiences, offering them a vision that coincides perfectly with their innermost needs and dreams. Like Spielberg, his is a vision of youthful adventure where heroes triumph not only by physical strength and stamina but also by honesty, decency, and intrinsic rightness. Clearly, it all works: although he has not directed a film for many years, Lucas was responsible for creating—or has been deeply involved in the creation of—some of the most popular films ever made.

Lucas met with success early in his career when, at the suggestion of his mentor Francis Coppola, he was asked by Warners to direct his first feature film, *THX 1138* (1971), an expansion of the prize-winning film he had made some years earlier at the University of Southern California. This visually striking film won only modest attention. Only two years later, Lucas had his first major hit with *American Graffiti* (1973), a nostalgic, bittersweet evocation of life in a small California town in the early sixties. Made on a tiny budget in only twenty-eight nights, the funny and rueful movie captured the teenage mores and attitudes of the period. Four years later,

Lucas had his most sizable hit in *Star Wars* (1977), an imaginative and immensely diverting science-fiction fantasy that won ten Academy Award nominations and virtually became an industry in itself.

After *Star Wars*, Lucas relinquished his director's chair to others. He produced and wrote the story for *The Empire Strikes Back* (1980), the sequel to *Star Wars* that was directed by Irvin Kershner, and he produced and coauthored the screenplay for *Return of the Jedi* (1983), the third film in the trilogy, directed by Richard Marquand. Through his company, Lucasfilm, Ltd., he produced Steven Spielberg's extraordinarily successful *Raiders of the Lost Ark* (1981), also joining with Spielberg to create the story for this adroit, tongue-in-cheek adventure.

★

I think it's important that work not be that important. That's why I don't work out here [Hollywood]. I don't want that life and death feeling about work. I don't take a trade paper, not even in my office. I don't give a damn who got an indie prod contract.... What I don't know is how all the guys out here resist the pressure. I just want to be able to do my own work, including things that you know aren't going to make two cents.   SIDNEY LUMET, *Los Angeles Times*, Sunday Calendar, 4 September 1983, p. 22.

SIDNEY LUMET (born 1924)   Although Sidney Lumet has directed films in an array of styles and genres, he has always worked best in the milieu that contains his deepest roots: the urban East, or, more specifically, the bustling, dog-eat-dog world of New York City. The characters one remembers most keenly from Lumet films are

OPPOSITE, LEFT   Trouble in Paradise: ERNST LUBITSCH (*Paramount, 1932*). *Herbert Marshall and Miriam Hopkins excelled as amorous jewel thieves in this wonderfully witty comedy. The film epitomized Lubitsch's style of sophisticated romance.*

OPPOSITE, RIGHT   Ninotchka: ERNST LUBITSCH (*MGM, 1939*). *Greta Garbo and Melvyn Douglas share an intimate moment in Lubitsch's effervescent romantic comedy. The ads proclaimed "Garbo Laughs!"—and so did audiences, which enjoyed this witty, lighthearted spoof of the somber Soviets.*
ABOVE   American Graffiti: GEORGE LUCAS (*Universal, 1973*). *Bob Falfa (Harrison Ford) and his girl (Linda Christensen) wait anxiously for any takers for a drag race. George Lucas's film focused on the aspirations, dreams, and disappointments of teen-agers living in a small California town in the early sixties.*

the tough-skinned, combative, eccentric men and women who struggle to stay in the fight even when the odds are against them: the embattled policemen of *Serpico* and *Prince of the City* (1981), the desperate bank robber of *Dog Day Afternoon*, the sharp-tongued television crowd of *Network*, or the dying activist mother of *Garbo Talks*. Many of Lumet's people are angry at a society they perceive as cruel or uncaring. On the whole, they are stubborn, resilient, and not always likable.

Aside from his predilection for urban combat, Lumet has been noted for his skill in drawing the best performances from his actors. His films teem with Academy Award nominees and winners who have professed in print their admiration for Lumet's ability to extract their finest work. Was Rod Steiger ever better than as the anguished Sol Nazerman in *The Pawnbroker*, or did Katharine Hepburn ever give a greater dramatic performance than as the drug-ridden mother of *Long Day's Journey into Night*? We can recall with pleasure Al Pacino in *Serpico* and *Dog Day Afternoon*, Peter Finch and Faye Dunaway in *Network*, Ingrid Bergman in *Murder on the Orient Express*, and Paul Newman in *The Verdict*. Even his unsuccessful films—and Lumet has had his share of flops—contain performances that stay in the mind, such as Vanessa Redgrave in *The Sea Gull* (1968), James Mason in *Child's Play* (1972), and Anne Bancroft in *Garbo Talks* (1984).

The son of a famous player in the Yiddish theater, Lumet spent his early years as a stage and radio actor. In the fifties, he became one of the most successful and sought-after directors of the so-called golden era of television drama. His next step inevitably took him to the movies. He made his feature debut with *12 Angry Men* (1957), adapted from Reginald Rose's television play. Well regarded in its day (it was nominated for an Academy Award), the film now seems patly contrived and obvious, despite earnest acting by Henry Fonda and Lee J. Cobb as opposing jurors in a murder trial. His next two films, *Stage Struck* (1958) and *That Kind of Woman* (1959), went virtually unnoticed.

Lumet then turned to directing adaptations of plays by leading dramatists, with uneven results. While played with feverish intensity by such high-voltage actors as Anna Magnani, Marlon Brando, Raf Vallone, Katharine Hepburn, and Ralph Richardson, the theatrical origins of *The Fugitive Kind* (1960, based on Tennessee Williams's *Orpheus Descending*), *A View from the Bridge* (1962, by Arthur Miller), and *Long Day's Journey into Night* (1962, by Eugene O'Neill) were too apparent. Only *Long Day's Journey*, virtually a literal transcription of the play, succeeded in evoking an intended pity and terror as it took a troubled New England family through one harrowing day and evening.

Lumet's films in the sixties were a mixed bag, causing many critics to decry his lack of a consistent style or quality. For every *Fail Safe* (1964), an expert, suspenseful entry in the "doomsday" cycle of films, or *The Pawnbroker* (1965), a searing study of a ravaged man who is painfully recalled to life, there were such failed projects as a discursive, hollow adaptation of Mary McCarthy's novel *The Group* (1966), or *The Deadly Affair* (1967), a confusing version of John Le Carré's novel *Call for the Dead*. Nor did Lumet improve his reputation with such films as *The Appointment* (1969), an attempt to imitate the popular romantic French movies of the period (epitomized by *A Man and a Woman*), or *Last of the Mobile Hot-Shots* (1970), a feeble version of Tennessee Williams's play *The Seven Descents of Myrtle*. Lumet even faltered in familiar territory, such as the arch but sporadically amusing comedy *Bye Bye Braverman* (1968), revolving around a group of New York intellectuals attending a friend's funeral.

LEFT   Long Day's Journey into Night: SIDNEY LUMET (*Embassy Pictures, 1962*). *Katharine Hepburn gave one of her most eloquent dramatic performances as Mary Tyrone, the anguished wife of ex-matinee idol James Tyrone, magnificently played by Ralph Richardson. This somewhat stagebound adaptation of Eugene O'Neill's autobiographical play contained scenes of volcanic power.*

OPPOSITE   The Verdict: SIDNEY LUMET (*Fox, 1982*). *Sidney Lumet directs Paul Newman and Charlotte Rampling in a scene from this drama centering on a hard-drinking, burned-out lawyer (Newman) who tenaciously fights his way to a courtroom triumph. Newman received an Oscar nomination for his performance.*

Happily, with the early seventies came a marked improvement in his films. Lumet made good use of New York locations and Al Pacino's intense, street-smart persona in two excellent films, *Serpico* (1973) and *Dog Day Afternoon* (1975), and with the enormous help of a dazzling screenplay by Paddy Chayefsky, he made *Network* (1976) into a scathing satire on the lunacy and self-serving corruption that are an inevitable part of the television industry. He also turned out a diverting, attractively wrapped entertainment package based on Agatha Christie's novel *Murder on the Orient Express* (1974). Usually, Lumet kept his eye on more serious matters than mere murder, particularly the nature of justice in a corrupt world. *The Verdict* (1982) managed an absorbing variation on the courtroom drama, focusing on an alcoholic Boston lawyer (Paul Newman) who finds redemption in a medical negligence case, while *Daniel* (1983), patterned on the Rosenberg case, was a flawed but powerful, underrated film about the haunted children of a New York couple executed as spies. Lumet directed this adaptation of the E. L. Doctorow novel *The Book of Daniel* with intelligence and feeling. His most recent film, *Power* (1986), scrutinized the world of the "media consultants" who sell political candidates to the public.

If Lumet's films are variable and sometimes misguided (his extravagant 1978 version of the stage musical *The Wiz* was a disaster), he can nevertheless claim to have tackled central issues of our time with forceful conviction and unbounded energy. In his best films, he has created a gallery of memorably embattled characters.

And, indisputably, he has given us his own repository of unforgettable screen performances.

★

At that time comics had, for the most part, a tendency to "do too much." With Laurel and Hardy we introduced a nearly opposite comic conception. I tried—we tried—to direct them in such a way that they showed nothing, expressed nothing, which had the consequence of making the public, which was waiting for the opposite, laugh. We restrained ourselves so much in showing the actors' feelings that the public couldn't hold back its laughter, and laughed because we remained serious. LEO MCCAREY, interview in *Cahiers du Cinéma*, January 1967, cited in Jay Leyda, ed., *Voices of Film Experience* (New York: Macmillan, 1977), p. 105.

LEO MCCAREY (1898–1969) At his best a master of comedy and sentiment, Leo McCarey enjoyed more than forty years as a distinctive director, writer, and producer. He unquestionably hit his peak in the thirties, when his rowdy sense of humor and taste for slapstick could accommodate both the Marx Brothers and W. C. Fields, while his deeply rooted sentimentality could also find expression in a poignant drama like *Make Way for Tomorrow*. Occasionally, humor and sentiment merged beautifully in a film like *Love Affair*. If he faltered in the forties and fifties, it was because the sentiment began to curdle around the edges—*The Bells of St. Mary's* has an even higher sugar content than *Going My Way*—and because the wide screen and color seemed somehow inappropriate and too grandiose for the straightforward and rather nondescript McCarey style, which was seldom concerned with the visual effects that the new technology could muster. *An Affair to Remember* (1957), his remake of *Love Affair* (1939), is an object lesson in the wrong way to re-create a minor classic. The story is the same—lovers meet, separate, and are reunited—but whereas *Love Affair* relied on the inherent charm, grace, and razor-sharp timing of its leading players, Irene Dunne and Charles Boyer, and on the delicate balance of laughter and sorrow in McCarey's screenplay, *An Affair to Remember* submerges its no less charming and attractive stars, Deborah Kerr and Cary Grant, and the screenplay (mostly unchanged) in miles of glistening CinemaScopic scenery.

McCarey entered films in 1916, working at various jobs until he joined Hal Roach in 1923 as a gag writer and director of Charlie Chase's comedy shorts. Within a few years he was writing most of Laurel and Hardy's short comic films as well as directing some of them. By 1929,

which Charles Laughton excelled as a very proper British butler who finds himself in the wild American West. Laughton's expressive reading of the Gettysburg Address to a group of grizzled, awed Westerners is one of the highlights of thirties movies, beautifully handled by McCarey with the right balance of humor and sentiment. McCarey also directed *The Awful Truth* (1937), a prime example of "screwball" comedy—in fact, a virtual definition of the subgenre, with its amusing screenplay (by Viña Delmar), its air of sophisticated lunacy, and its deft performances by actors (Irene Dunne and Cary Grant) who knew their way around a comedy line. McCarey's direction won that year's Academy Award. A drastic change of pace from all the hilarity came with McCarey's poignant *Make Way for Tomorrow* (1937), an ironic (or inexplicable) title for one of the screen's few dramas about the desperate problems of old age. As the elderly couple who must part, presumably forever, Beulah Bondi and Victor Moore were exemplary under McCarey's sympathetic direction. (The movie was made with Paramount's reluctant consent, and subsequently the studio fired McCarey.)

For the most part, McCarey's credits in the forties and fifties were disappointing. Although audiences greatly approved of his two Bing Crosby Father O'Malley films, *Going My Way* (1944) and *The Bells of St. Mary's* (1945)—McCarey received a second Oscar for writing and directing the former—they were a little too thick with the blarney, a little too heavy with the sentiment to equal his best work. However, they had the virtues of being enter-

he began to direct feature films that starred some of the most popular comic entertainers of the period. Eddie Cantor in *The Kid from Spain* (1932), Mae West in *Belle of the Nineties* (1934), and W. C. Fields in *Six of a Kind* (1934) worked at close to their freewheeling best under McCarey's direction. However, he scaled the heights with the Marx Brothers in *Duck Soup* (1933), regarded by many as their greatest film. In this nonstop barrage of outrageous gags, slapstick situations, and non sequiturs, the Marxes blithely skewered the idiocies of war. It has been said that nobody really directed the brothers, but McCarey appears to have kept their anarchy under reasonable control and in good working order. (He is said to have suggested the film's celebrated highlight, the mirror scene.)

McCarey's thirties films were by no means all raucous pie-in-the-face comedies. Humor of a gentler kind warmed up his 1935 version of *Ruggles of Red Gap*, in

ABOVE   Ruggles of Red Gap: LEO MCCAREY (*Paramount, 1935*). *Charles Ruggles (left) and Mary Boland enjoy the services of proper British butler Ruggles (Charles Laughton), whom they won in a poker game. McCarey directed this amiable comedy at a leisurely pace, extracting an impeccable and even restrained performance from Laughton.*
RIGHT   Make Way for Tomorrow: LEO MCCAREY (*Paramount, 1937*). *In one of many lovely moments, Lucy and Barkley Cooper (Beulah Bondi and Victor Moore, center) share the dance floor at the hotel where they spent their honeymoon many years earlier. McCarey's first attempt at drama, this film presented a sensible, honestly moving portrait of old age.*
OPPOSITE   Network: SIDNEY LUMET (*MGM/UA, 1976*). *Peter Finch won a posthumous Academy Award as Howard Beale, the television newscaster who becomes a mad prophet exhorting viewers to take action against an oppressive society. Lumet's blistering view of the television industry benefited from strong performances and Paddy Chayefsky's dazzling dialogue.*

taining and inoffensive, which could not be claimed for two later films. *Once upon a Honeymoon* (1942) tried vainly to combine romantic comedy (Ginger Rogers and Cary Grant exchanging quips and kisses as they flee across wartorn Europe) with the tragedy of the Holocaust and its concentration camp victims. *My Son John* (1952), a crude cautionary tale on the dangers of Communist infiltration, struck a heavy note.

Clearly, Leo McCarey's heart and talent belonged in the thirties, where his temperament could induce laughter without inhibition and tears without apology. It is true that he continued to flourish past the thirties, but our deepest gratitude must go to the director who placed those unlikely warriors Groucho, Chico, and Harpo in a besieged shack with Margaret Dumont, who helped Irene Dunne and Cary Grant prove that married love (and even ex-married love) could be romantic and sexy, and who parted Beulah Bondi from Victor Moore in a scene that still reverberates with tenderness and sorrow. Jean Renoir remarked that "Leo McCarey is one of the few directors in Hollywood who understand human beings." Disputable or not, the remark reminds us of how much we treasure McCarey's crazy, impudent, and loving people.

★

NORMAN Z. McLEOD (1898–1964)   Brisk, lively, knockabout comedy was Norman Zenos McLeod's forte throughout a directorial career that flourished in the thirties and continued into the late fifties. His style,

however, was seldom evident; he lacked the idiosyncrasies and touches of individuality that made the work of some of his contemporaries (McCarey, La Cava, and others) so rewarding. He made his feature film debut in 1928 after working with such directors as William Wellman and Howard Hawks. McLeod enjoyed the distinct advantage of having some of Hollywood's most gifted comic performers as the stars of his best films—the Marx Brothers romped through two of their early screen efforts, *Monkey Business* (1931) and *Horse Feathers* (1932), under his direction, and Cary Grant, Constance Bennett, and Roland Young cavorted in the lighthearted fantasy *Topper* (1937). Danny Kaye was directed by McLeod in two of his better Goldwyn movies, *The Kid from Brooklyn* (1946) and *The Secret Life of Walter Mitty* (1947). His musicals, however, did not have much flair or style; the only entertainment value in *Lady Be Good* (1941), *Panama Hattie* (1942), or *Let's Dance* (1950) came from an occasional song-and-dance number. McLeod also directed such expert farceurs as Mary Boland, Gracie Allen, W. C. Fields, Red Skelton, and Bob Hope—a formidable array of talent.

★

The screen is the most powerful, exciting, and contemporary medium. One of these days we will learn to do it justice.   ROUBEN MAMOULIAN, in Andrew Sarris, ed., *Interviews with Film Directors* (New York: The Bobbs-Merrill Company, 1967), p. 292.

ROUBEN MAMOULIAN (born 1898)   After more than five decades, the status of Rouben Mamoulian as one of the screen's great innovators—as a director who used sound, color, and the camera in new and exciting ways—remains undimmed. He has long risen above the attacks of movie moguls who dismissed him as a gadfly unable to fall in line with studio practice. And he has survived the harsh judgment of contemporary critics; in 1933, for example, Dwight Macdonald wrote that his productions were "glib, imitative, chic, with a fake elegance, a pseudo-wit, and a suggestion of Oriental greasiness" (*Dwight Macdonald on Movies*, p. 81). In truth, Mamoulian's films, from his first, *Applause* (1929), to his last, *Silk Stockings* (1957), can now be seen as the work of a master stylist whose wit, elegance, and grace are unmistakable. Mamoulian had a lifelong interest in movement and rhythm in film, and, at his best, as in the enchanting *Love Me Tonight*, he made the screen shimmer and glow with a matchless kinetic energy.

Born in Russia of Armenian descent, Mamoulian enjoyed a busy life in the theater in Moscow and London

before coming to America in 1923 to direct operas and operettas at the George Eastman Theatre in Rochester, New York. In 1927 he had his first major success as the director of the Theatre Guild's acclaimed production of Du Bose Heyward's *Porgy*, the play that was the basis for Gershwin's folk opera *Porgy and Bess* (which Mamoulian also directed in 1935). Aware of his reputation as an imaginative director, Paramount offered him the direction of an early sound film, *Applause*, at its studios in Astoria, New York. Although he had to fight for every innovation, Mamoulian was determined that the movie—the lachrymose tale of an aging, broken-down burlesque queen (Helen Morgan)—would ignore the restrictions imposed by primitive sound techniques. He insisted on making the cumbersome sound camera flexible, actually moving it into the action and permitting it to comment on the heroine's shabby burlesque world. His fluid direction turned a trite story into a moving one.

Mamoulian continued to experiment in the films that followed *Applause*. In *City Streets* (1931), a gangster tale more concerned with the romantic tribulations of Sylvia Sidney and Gary Cooper than with violent shootouts, Mamoulian used sound in original ways that are now familiar—for example, at one point he superimposed Cooper's voice shouting "Beer!" over Sidney's anguished face to emphasize her disillusion with the racket that has trapped them both. In *Dr. Jekyll and Mr. Hyde* (1932), certainly the best version of Robert Louis Stevenson's novella, he made daring use of the subjective camera, especially in the famous opening sequence in which

we see everything from Jekyll's point of view, with the camera showing him for the first time as he begins his medical lecture. The transformation scene is another marvel—a combination of clever trick photography and a cacophonous soundtrack—that continues to dazzle audiences. Mamoulian is also quite bold for his time in emphasizing Jekyll's strong sexual feelings as a source of his change into the repulsive Hyde.

Repressed sexuality also figured in Mamoulian's *Queen Christina* (1933), one of the few films to succeed in capturing Greta Garbo's mystique. In the film's most celebrated sequence, he suggests Christina's exultant new awareness of physical passion as she moves about the room she has shared with her lover (John Gilbert), touching the furniture. The closing moments of *Queen Christina* are also famous, consisting of a long, lingering close-up of Garbo as her ship moves out to sea after the death of her lover. Mamoulian instructed Garbo to make

LEFT Applause: ROUBEN MAMOULIAN *(Paramount, 1929). Blowsy burlesque queen Kitty Darling (Helen Morgan) tries to hold her no-good boyfriend (Fuller Mellish, Jr.). Mamoulian's landmark film used the new technology of sound in innovative ways, often coordinating the dialogue and the photography for maximum effect.*

RIGHT Love Me Tonight: ROUBEN MAMOULIAN *(Paramount, 1932). No longer bored or frustrated, princess Jeanette MacDonald enjoys the amorous attention of tailor Maurice Chevalier. Mamoulian's delectable musical sparkled with melody, wit, and a romantic aura.*

OPPOSITE Topper: NORMAN Z. MCLEOD *(MGM, 1937). Bewildered Cosmo Topper (Roland Young) confronts the ghosts of his friends George and Marion Kerby (Cary Grant and Constance Bennett). This blithely amusing comedy-fantasy generated several less amusing sequels.*

her face a mask, "a blank sheet of paper" on which each member of the audience could write his or her own interpretation.

In 1932, all of Mamoulian's feeling for cinematic art and innovation converged in his masterpiece, *Love Me Tonight*. A tall and bracing glass of bubbling champagne, this romantic musical has the slightest of plots—an amorous tailor (Maurice Chevalier) pretends to be a baron as he awakens the slumbering sexuality of a bored princess (Jeanette MacDonald)—but the wittiest and most sophisticated of screenplays. Circling around this wisp of a story, studded with charming songs ("Mimi," "Isn't It Romantic"), are some delightful characters,

deftly guided by Mamoulian: the princess's old uncle (C. Aubrey Smith), her silly-ass suitor (Charles Butterworth), and a man-hungry countess (Myrna Loy). The movie abounds in sequences attesting to Mamoulian's ingenuity, none more so than the justly famous opening in which Chevalier's chorus of "Isn't It Romantic" is repeated by others in quick succession until it arrives at Princess Jeanette, who sings it fervently as she sits alone in her castle. (The future lovers are thereby linked before they meet.) A hunt scene becomes a kind of ballet as the music follows the movement of the horses and hounds as they race through the woods.

Although Mamoulian's inventiveness hardly ceased

after this film, many critics have contended that he never again reached this peak. It is true that his subsequent films are uneven in quality and sometimes uncertain in tone, but in many instances the virtues outweigh the faults. *We Live Again* (1934), a romantic drama based on Tolstoy's novel about a dashing prince (Fredric March) who finds regeneration in his ill-fated love for a peasant girl, had some luminous scenes. Unfortunately, Samuel Goldwyn's protégée Anna Sten lacked star quality, and Mamoulian's staging weighed heavily on an already ponderous plot. *Becky Sharp* (1935) rates a place in motion picture history by virtue of being the first film in the new three-color Technicolor process; otherwise, it was dramatically sluggish, and Miriam Hopkins's artful, scheming Becky failed to convince. Mamoulian's 1937 musical *High, Wide and Handsome* was another case in point: a hybrid mixture of rugged Western melodrama and idealized musical comedy, it never quite jelled despite the pleasurable scenes and some lilting Jerome Kern songs.

If Mamoulian's later films were less than they might have been, they continued to display his feeling for choreographed movement and rhythm and his imaginative use of color. In *Golden Boy* (1939), burdened with Clifford Odets's already dated play (sprinkled with self-conscious flights of "little people" poetry), he managed one fight scene of brutal intensity. *The Mark of Zorro* (1940) told its swashbuckling story with surprising pace and vitality and featured a splendid climactic duel between hero Tyrone Power and villainous Basil Rathbone. Power also starred in Mamoulian's remake of *Blood and Sand* (1941), which submerged an overripe story of a bullfighter in vibrant and often stunning Technicolor.

Throughout the latter part of his career, Mamoulian battled with the studio hierarchy, which cost him several plum assignments, and much of his activity in the forties was in the theater rather than in films. Even when he managed to complete a film, quarrels and upheavals compromised the result. His musical adaptation of Eugene O'Neill's *Ah, Wilderness!*, entitled *Summer Holiday*, was completed in 1946 but released without fanfare in 1948. Although it failed ignominiously with critics and the public, it remains one of his liveliest films. A joyful slice of Americana, it is notable for Mamoulian's brilliant use of color in key sections, especially in an artfully staged Fourth of July picnic sequence, and the bar scene in which a blonde bar girl (Marilyn Maxwell) metamorphoses into a goddess under the gaze of the sodden young hero (Mickey Rooney). Stage assignments kept Mamoulian out of films for nearly a decade, when he returned to direct his final film, *Silk Stockings* (1957), a musicalized version of the 1939 Lubitsch movie *Ninotchka* that had been on Broadway in 1955. Although it lacked some of the panache of the best MGM musicals, *Silk Stockings* had one inescapable virtue in Fred Astaire. At its best, it exuberantly celebrated the art of dance, as Astaire and Cyd Charisse whirled through some remarkable routines to Cole Porter music.

Rouben Mamoulian's legacy of film is small but singu-

OPPOSITE   Queen Christina: ROUBEN MAMOULIAN (*MGM, 1933*). *Rouben Mamoulian directs Greta Garbo in a scene from this historical drama. Mamoulian recalls that Garbo at first refused to rehearse, claiming that rehearsals made her stale. Mamoulian insisted on showing her two takes, one made with rehearsal and one without. Garbo chose the take made after rehearsal. "From then on," he remembers, "it was wonderful" ("Dialogue on Film," American Film, January–February 1983).*

RIGHT   Silk Stockings: ROUBEN MAMOULIAN (*MGM, 1957*). *Having discovered love and Paris, Ninotchka (Cyd Charisse) dances rhapsodically with Steve Canfield (Fred Astaire). Their splendid dancing gave impetus to an otherwise unexceptional musical version of the film* Ninotchka, *based on the stage musical adaptation.*

larly precious. There is a quality of lyricism and unforced charm that emerges in his best films at unexpected moments. In *Applause*, blowsy Kitty Darling, her worn face softened by love, sings a lullaby while her daughter simultaneously whispers a prayer. In *Love Me Tonight*, the venerable C. Aubrey Smith bursts into a chorus of ''Mimi'' that lifts our spirits. In *Summer Holiday*, young Richard and his adored Muriel cannot contain their joy any longer and suddenly begin to perform a polka across the greenest of green grass. Despite the severest of disappointments over the years, Mamoulian has always remained spiritedly optimistic. In an interview in the January–February 1983 issue of *American Film*, he noted, ''We must all strive to elevate the quality of motion pictures. We must affirm and insist that the ultimate goal of a film, no matter what the subject matter it deals with, is to add to the beauty and goodness of life, to the dignity of human beings, and to our faith in a better future.''

★

I can remember vividly how tough it was on actors and actresses when the silent pictures gave way to talkies. That microphone was a nemesis—if you didn't record well, you were finished. There was a fire one day at Paramount, and Clara Bow ran out screaming, ''I hope to Christ it was the sound stages.'' JOSEPH L. MANKIEWICZ, in *The Book of Hollywood Quotes*, compiled by Gary Herman (London: Omnibus Press, 1979), p. 11.

JOSEPH L. MANKIEWICZ (born 1909)   If verbal dexterity were all, if a polished wit counted more than a well-developed visual style and sense of pacing, then Joseph Mankiewicz would have earned an even higher place in the pantheon of writer-directors. Over the long years of his career, Mankiewicz at his best has offered some of the most intelligent, most urbane, most brightly amusing screenplays ever committed to film. Although he too often indulged his tendency to pause while one of his characters inveighs against farm subsidies, oil-depletion allowances, or the neglect of teachers, in such films as *A Letter to Three Wives* and *All about Eve* he created a rough American equivalent of the comedy of manners. Even his more unconventional, less successful films, like *The Barefoot Contessa* and *The Honey Pot* (1967), boast characters marvelously articulate (sometimes too articulate) on matters of life, love, and everything else. Unfortunately, Mankiewicz's writing skills usually surpassed his skill as a director. Too often, his movies are static and visually uninteresting, winning greater accolades for their dazzling screenplays and/or accomplished performances

(Mankiewicz often extracted wondrously fine performances from his leading players) than for their direction.

The younger brother of Herman J. Mankiewicz, the brilliant, scathingly witty writer who collaborated with Orson Welles on *Citizen Kane*, Mankiewicz came to Hollywood in the late twenties, mainly writing original screenplays for Paramount and MGM before becoming a producer at MGM in the thirties. (Although he was nominated for an Oscar for cowriting *Skippy*, 1931, his best writing credit was a hilarious, ramshackle, almost surrealistic farce entitled *Million Dollar Legs*, 1932.) He did not get a chance to direct until he joined 20th Century-Fox in the forties, when the studio assigned him to replace an ailing Ernst Lubitsch on a brooding Gothic melodrama called *Dragonwyck* (1946). His forties films as a director, including such efforts as *The Late George Apley* and *The Ghost and Mrs. Muir* (both 1947), made up in charm what they lacked in polish.

It was when he returned to writing that Mankiewicz succeeded in raising his films to a new level. A longtime devout lover of the theater, Mankiewicz succeeded, in *A Letter to Three Wives* (1949) and, especially, *All about Eve* (1950, a movie *about* the theater), in creating characters who spoke articulately, intelligently, and often sarcastically on a variety of subjects, but mostly about themselves and each other. *All about Eve* bristles with badinage as sharply pointed and as observant of human idiosyncrasies and foibles as any that ever found its way to the screen. *A Letter to Three Wives*, an acerbic tale of three marriages on the brink of collapse, won Best Direction and Best Screenplay Oscars for Mankiewicz, while *All about Eve* was named Best Picture (Bette Davis deserved the Oscar for her performance as the mercurial Margo Channing, but it went to Judy Holliday for *Born Yesterday*). Around this time Mankiewicz also directed a blistering melodrama called *No Way Out* (1950), with young Sidney Poitier as a doctor caught up in the racial disorder sparked by a vicious bigot (Richard Widmark).

In the fifties and sixties, Mankiewicz moved into new areas and genres, with mixed results. He retained his gift for dialogue as well as the need to speak out on mat-

OPPOSITE, ABOVE   Sleuth: JOSEPH L. MANKIEWICZ *(Fox, 1972). Mystery writer Andrew Wyke (Laurence Olivier) plays a series of elaborate and ultimately deadly games with his wife's lover, Milo Tindle (Michael Caine). Mankiewicz's highly enjoyable film version of Anthony Shaffer's play kept audiences on their toes with its clever twists and ingenious gadgetry.*
OPPOSITE, BELOW   An Unmarried Woman: PAUL MAZURSKY *(Fox, 1978). Divorced and lonely, Erica (Jill Clayburgh) finds new romance with artist Saul (Alan Bates). Clayburgh's sure, multifaceted performance sparked Mazursky's intelligent, incisive film.*

All about Eve: JOSEPH L. MANKIEWICZ *(Fox, 1950). Mankiewicz's brittle comedy-drama about the theater, which he wrote as well as directed, starred Bette Davis in a bravura performance as temperamental actress Margo Channing. Celeste Holm (right) played her friend Karen, and Thelma Ritter (center) gave a scene-stealing performance as Margo's sardonic, plain-speaking maid Birdie.*

ters that concerned him, and he could bring out the best in actresses whose thespian ability was limited. But something quirky entered into his films, some seemingly perverse desire to draw on or inject material that was guaranteed to baffle or irritate the audience. *People Will Talk* (1951), an entertaining, verbose comedy-drama about an unorthodox physician (Cary Grant) who marries his pregnant young patient (Jeanne Crain), occasionally stopped in its tracks to discuss medical ethics and introduced an odd subplot involving the doctor's mysterious patient (Finlay Currie). In *The Barefoot Contessa* (1954), concerning an ill-fated Spanish dancer (Ava Gardner) who becomes a movie star and the men who are entranced and obsessed by her, Mankiewicz studded his screenplay with speeches that either dazzled or bored viewers, depending on their frame of mind. This brilliant, self-indulgent drama commented sardonically on Hollywood and international high society. And Mankiewicz's film version of Tennessee Williams's *Suddenly, Last Summer* (1959) was a calculated risk that didn't pay off. Williams's bizarre tale involving madness, homosexuality, and cannibalism received an honest production that didn't entirely shirk the ugly aspects of the story (mercifully, the devouring of the young homosexual poet Sebastian by the boys he used occurs offscreen), and Elizabeth Taylor as the tormented girl facing a lobotomy worked hard to create a character. But the film was more of a clanking, overbaked melodrama than a serious study of aberration and destructive mother love.

Although Mankiewicz worked best with sharp-witted or sharp-tongued contemporary characters, he ventured twice into the ancient world of togas. In 1953 he directed (surprisingly, under MGM's auspices) a production of *Julius Caesar* that worked admirably in most ways, with a forthright, uncluttered black-and-white production and a star-heavy cast that spoke the verse reasonably well. (James Mason made an exceptional Brutus, and Marlon

170

Brando played a distinctly odd but always interesting Mark Antony.) On the other hand, Mankiewicz's opulent, trouble-plagued production of *Cleopatra* (1963), which he inherited from Rouben Mamoulian, was a costly mistake, with Elizabeth Taylor starring as the petulant queen.

Mankiewicz's last two contributions to films were a sardonic offbeat Western of sorts, entitled *There Was a Crooked Man* ... (1970), and an entertaining adaptation of Anthony Shaffer's tricky two-character play *Sleuth* (1972). Despite his long absence from the screen, the achievements of his best films remain vital. The gifts he had as a writer—bringing to films a whiplash wit that reflected an amused concern with the foolish ways of people—and to some extent as a director are uncommon enough to stand out in the history of film.

★

ANTHONY MANN (1906–1967) A reliable director for nearly thirty years, Anthony Mann made his strongest bid in the fifties with a series of intelligent, well-made Westerns that gave a more complex dimension to the familiar easy-going persona of James Stewart. A New York stage actor and director before coming to Hollywood in 1938, Mann worked for David O. Selznick and Preston Sturges (as assistant director on *Sullivan's Travels*) before launching his own first feature, *Dr. Broadway*, in 1942. A series of low-budget films followed for various studios, the best being the neatly constructed, atmospheric *films noirs* he directed in the late forties (*T-Men, Raw Deal,* both 1948). In 1950, Mann launched his Western cycle with three films that offered interesting variations on the genre. *Devil's Doorway* took up the plight of the American Indians, a topic that had not been handled sympathetically for some time. *The Furies* used its Western locale for a harsh psychological study of a father-daughter relationship that might have intrigued Freud. The best and most conventional Western of the trio was *Winchester 73*. A lively, episodic tale that followed "the gun that won the West" as it passes from hand to hand, it focused on James Stewart's grim desire for revenge against his treacherous brother. Mann used the Western landscape to great advantage, and he gave his actors the room to flesh out their characters.

Mann's subsequent Westerns enjoyed the added benefit of color, but the focus remained on the principal

characters played by Stewart and their multifaceted relationships with other figures in the story. In *Bend of the River* (1952), Stewart starred as a tough, laconic cowboy trying to live down a sordid past who finds his salvation in leading a group of pioneer farmers to Oregon. In one of Mann's best films, *The Naked Spur* (1953), he gave a fine, intense performance as a bitter, lonely, and anguished man who has turned bounty hunter for private reasons. Notable for its rounded characterizations and believable dialogue, the movie was, in fact, a record of one man's futile obsession with reclaiming his lost innocence. *The Far Country* (1955), a lesser work, starred Stewart as a misanthropic cattleman attempting to move his herd into Alaskan territory. In the excellent *The Man from Laramie* (1955), Stewart again focused on revenge as he finds himself caught up in the machinations and private warfare of a powerful ranch family. For all their bright color, these films reflected dark shadows and intimations.

Mann used Stewart in a more traditional role in a tuneful, appealing musical biography, *The Glenn Miller Story* (1954). He continued to direct superior Westerns for the rest of the decade, using other stalwart figures of the genre, such as Henry Fonda (*The Tin Star*, 1957) and Gary Cooper (*Man of the West*, 1958). The latter film was especially good, involving another complex father-son relationship (a favorite Western theme of the period), in which the son (Cooper) must ultimately kill his evil father (Lee J. Cobb) in order to establish his own identity. The movie presented a bleaker vision than any of

The Man from Laramie: ANTHONY MANN (Columbia, 1955). Falsely accused of stealing, Will Lockhart (James Stewart) is dragged by a horse. Mann's powerful Western involved such familiar Western themes as revenge and a father-son conflict, set against ruggedly beautiful vistas.

Mann's Westerns with Stewart, offering no final release for its beleaguered hero.

In the sixties, Mann went to Europe for the balance of his career, concentrating on lavish historical spectacles in the nature of *Spartacus*, which he had begun to direct before being replaced. *El Cid* (1961), with Charlton Heston in one of his granite-like portrayals as Spain's national hero, contained magnificent sets and costumes that easily overshadowed the tedious narrative. A box-office success, it was followed by a costly failure; despite a star-filled cast that included Sophia Loren, James Mason, Alec Guinness, and Stephen Boyd, *The Fall of the Roman Empire* (1964) collapsed under its own weight. Mann returned to less awesome projects in 1965 with *The Heroes of Telemark*, a scenic war drama of the Norwegian underground in World War II. In 1967, he died during the filming of *A Dandy in Aspic*, ending a creditable if not distinguished career.

★

DANIEL MANN (born 1912)   For the first decade of his film career, which began in the early fifties, Daniel Mann was noted for drawing prize-winning performances from his leading ladies, if not for his cinematic skill. His first movie, *Come Back, Little Sheba* (1952), won an Oscar for the wonderful Shirley Booth, repeating her stage role as the frumpy wife of an alcoholic (a game but miscast Burt Lancaster). Under his direction, Italian actress Anna Magnani won an Academy Award as the passionate Serafina in Tennessee Williams's *The Rose Tattoo* (1955), edging out Susan Hayward, in another Mann-di-

rected performance, as singer-actress Lillian Roth in *I'll Cry Tomorrow*. And Elizabeth Taylor received an Oscar for her performance as a high-priced call girl in Mann's version of John O'Hara's *Butterfield 8* (1960).

In the last few decades, Mann inexplicably has opted to film threadbare or imitative material, including *Our Man Flint* (1966), a pyrotechnic melodrama in the James Bond tradition; *Willard* (1971), a ghoulish entry in the demonic-animal horror cycle, in which an army of rats is the agent of destruction; and *The Revengers* (1972), a violent Western with echoes of *The Wild Bunch*. His best work in recent years was the television drama *Playing for Time* (1980), a moving and powerful true story (scripted by Arthur Miller) about Auschwitz survivor Fania Fenelon.

ABOVE   Separate Tables: DELBERT MANN *(United Artists, 1958). Major Pollock (David Niven) and Sybil Railton-Bell (Deborah Kerr) share their sad and shabby lives at a genteel British seaside resort in this adaptation of Terence Rattigan's play. Niven won an Oscar for his performance as the breezy but fraudulent major who harbors a dark secret in his past.*
LEFT   Come Back, Little Sheba: DANIEL MANN *(Paramount, 1952). Mann made his director's debut with this film adaptation of William Inge's play about a frowsy housewife (Shirley Booth) and her alcoholic husband (Burt Lancaster). Booth excelled in her Academy Award–winning role of Lola.*

★

DELBERT MANN (born 1920) During his thirty-odd-year career as a television and film director, Delbert Mann has switched styles several times, with variable results. After accumulating impressive credits as a director of television dramas, Mann made his theatrical debut in 1955 with *Marty*, based on Paddy Chayefsky's television play. Its sensitive, compassionate attention to the concerns of ordinary people endeared it to critics and audiences, and it won four Academy Awards (Best Film, Best Actor, Best Director, and Best Screenplay). Through the balance of the fifties, Mann continued to favor stories that dealt with striving, unexceptional men and women. He returned to Paddy Chayefsky's "little people" for two more films, *The Bachelor Party* (1957) and *Middle of the Night* (1959). Two plays in a similar vein were turned into notable Mann movies: Terence Rattigan's *Separate Tables* (1958) examined the emotional problems of people stopping out of season at a British seaside hotel, and William Inge's *The Dark at the Top of the Stairs* (1960) probed the tensions and the heartaches of an average Oklahoma family in the twenties.

In the sixties, Mann turned to lighter, more commercial ventures, including a number of frothy comedies. Two of them, *Lover Come Back* (1962) and *That Touch of Mink* (1962), starred Doris Day in her familiar naughty-but-nice mix-ups. In 1970, he began to direct again for television, turning out adaptations of literary works, glossy but pulpish romantic dramas, and an occasional family film. In 1980, he directed an impressive new television production of *All Quiet on the Western Front* that made the familiar antiwar story seem freshly minted. *Night Crossing* (1982), his last theatrical film to date, concerned two families who escape from East Berlin in a hot-air balloon.

★

GEORGE MARSHALL (1891–1975) A director who can comfortably accommodate the contrasting comedic styles of such performers as Laurel and Hardy, W. C. Fields, Bob Hope, and Martin and Lewis deserves our admiration for versatility and endurance. Extraordinarily prolific and admirably resilient over more than fifty years, Marshall specialized during the silent era in comedy and action shorts, then graduated to feature films exclusively, working in many genres for many studios. Comedy was his bailiwick, however, and he brought a cheerful, unpretentious style to W. C. Fields's larcenous activities (*You Can't Cheat an Honest Man*, 1939), Bob

Hope's gag-laden brashness (*The Ghost Breakers*, 1940; *Fancy Pants*, 1950), and the slapstick antics of Martin and Lewis (*My Friend Irma*, 1949). Marshall's *Destry Rides Again* (1939) mixed comedy and Western action in agreeable proportions and revitalized the sagging career of Marlene Dietrich by changing the remote Teutonic vamp into a tough, bawdy saloon singer.

Marshall's lengthy credits include two curiosities: the truly bizarre mystery-comedy *Murder, He Says* (1945) and an experimental Western musical called *Red Garters* (1954), which used deliberately stylized, unrealistic settings. Occasionally he was assigned a melodrama or action film, the best of which was *The Blue Dahlia* (1946), a neatly turned Raymond Chandler *film noir*, with Alan Ladd and Veronica Lake. He also worked frequently with the overexuberant Betty Hutton. The last years of his career were not as felicitous—he directed a number of bland comedies, including several with Bob Hope and Jerry Lewis that were painfully inferior to his earlier efforts with these comedians.

★

ARCHIE MAYO (1891–1968) Starting in the mid-twenties, Archie Mayo spent his most rewarding period at Warners in the thirties, turning out brisk, no-nonsense

---

Destry Rides Again: GEORGE MARSHALL (Universal, 1939). *Everyone in the saloon except James Stewart ducks when Frenchy (Marlene Dietrich) prepares to fire. Dietrich revitalized her career by drastically altering her image from the exotic woman of mystery to the bawdy, befeathered dance hall queen of Marshall's comedy Western.*

more than comfortable) existence until circumstances propel them into a bewildering and wildly different way of life. And so we have, among others, Peter Sellers discovering the world of the hippie in *I Love You, Alice B. Toklas,* the "swinging" couples of *Bob & Carol & Ted & Alice* confronting the turned-on world of modern-day California, or Lenny Baker in *Next Stop, Greenwich Village* discovering life itself. And in the truest sense, both Art Carney in *Harry and Tonto* and Robin Williams in *Moscow on the Hudson* discover America. The culture shock is apparent, and the pitfalls are many, but Mazursky's people manage to survive with humor and resilience. The result is a body of immensely likable movies, and, not so incidentally, a gallery of immensely likable performances, true to Mazursky's low-key vision.

An actor at first (he appeared in *The Blackboard Jungle* and other films), the Brooklyn-born Mazursky turned to writing in the sixties, finally winning a four-year stint as one of the writers on Danny Kaye's television show.

programmers like *The Mayor of Hell* (1933), *Convention City* (1933), and *Bordertown* (1935). Occasionally he was given a more prestigious movie, such as *The Petrified Forest* (1936), a wall-bound version of Robert E. Sherwood's stage play that pitted Leslie Howard's aestheticism against Humphrey Bogart's barbarism and found both obsolete. Mayo's *Black Legion* (1937), one of Warners's social dramas of the period, dealt with the routing of a hate-mongering secret organization very much like the Ku Klux Klan. His films in the mid-forties, after he left Warners, were mainly routine efforts such as *The Great American Broadcast* and *Charley's Aunt* (both 1941). His musical *Orchestra Wives* (1942) had little to recommend it besides the pure, sweet sounds of Glenn Miller's band.

★

PAUL MAZURSKY (born 1930)   Paul Mazursky's loosely structured, charmingly eccentric movies will always have a special appeal for those who know and understand the milieu he created and the people who inhabit it. His characters usually have a sane, comfortable (or

ABOVE   The Petrified Forest: ARCHIE MAYO *(Warner Bros., 1936). In a desert diner, sensitive writer Leslie Howard (left) shares a moment of understanding with waitress Bette Davis. Looking on are Genevieve Tobin and Paul Harvey. The film version of Robert E. Sherwood's play concentrated more on the melodrama than on the intended symbolism.*
RIGHT   Harry and Tonto: PAUL MAZURSKY *(Fox, 1974). Septuagenarian Harry (Art Carney) sets out on his cross-country travels with his friend and confidant Tonto. Mazursky's abiding affection for eccentrics and oddballs was evident throughout this rambling, likable movie.*

Eventually, he succeeded in selling a screenplay, *I Love You, Alice B. Toklas* (1968, written with Larry Tucker), and the resulting film (directed by Hy Averback), a satirical comedy about a "square" Jewish lawyer turned on by some marijuana brownies, earned some laughs. Mazursky decided to direct his next project himself, scoring a popular hit with the marital comedy *Bob & Carol & Ted & Alice* (1969). Its view of two married couples who desperately try to adopt the California life style of wifeswapping and group therapy received some harsh appraisal, but the movie now rates as one of the key comedies of the period, signaling a more relaxed, amused approach to marital problems. The script (by Mazursky and Larry Tucker) generated many laughs, especially in the scenes involving the less "hip" of the couples, played with comic finesse by Elliott Gould and Dyan Cannon.

Mazursky's next two films (*Alex in Wonderland*, 1970; *Blume in Love*, 1973) failed to make a stir, but he bounced back with *Harry and Tonto* (1974), an amiable comedy about a septuagenarian (Art Carney, in an Oscar-winning performance) who sets out across America with his pet cat Tonto, and with *Next Stop, Greenwich Village* (1976), a partly autobiographical, moderately successful account of an aspiring actor in the fifties. Two years later, Mazursky had his greatest hit of the seventies with *An Unmarried Woman* (1978), a wry, funny, and touching study of a woman (Jill Clayburgh) suddenly facing divorce, loneliness, and the single life. Clayburgh gave an extraordinarily fine performance, capturing every nuance as the woman moved from despair to affirmation, and Mazursky's screenplay deserved plaudits for coming to the core truth of an unhappy situation rather than creating villains or victims. (Both the film and Clayburgh received Oscar nominations.) His next film, *Willie and Phil* (1980), went virtually unnoticed—unfortunately for those who would have enjoyed this affectionate tribute to François Truffaut's *Jules and Jim*.

In his most recent films, Mazursky has continued to place his resilient characters in unfamiliar surroundings. *Tempest* (1982) was a whimsical comedy, loosely based on Shakespeare's play, about a New York architect (John Cassavetes) who reacts to his midlife crisis by moving to an isolated Greek island with his teen-age daughter (Molly Ringwald). It was hardly calculated to please audiences—and it didn't—but its odd sense of humor,

picturesque scenery, and capable cast made it very watchable. Mazursky was on much safer ground with *Moscow on the Hudson* (1984), directing comedian Robin Williams in his best performance to date as a defecting Russian musician in Manhattan. Mazursky's nimble direction kept viewers from noticing that many of the situations taxed credulity. Most recently he directed *Down and Out in Beverly Hills* (1986), a noisy, uproarious comedy about a California bum (Nick Nolte) who disrupts the unhappy household of Richard Dreyfuss and Bette Midler.

★

LEWIS MILESTONE (1895–1980)   Several years after winning an Oscar as Best Comedy Director (the first and last ever awarded in that category) for *Two Arabian Knights* (1927), Russian-born Lewis Milestone reached the pinnacle of his career with *All Quiet on the Western Front* (1930), his adaptation of Erich Maria Remarque's novel. For all its crudities, the film was a powerful and eloquent view of war as a harrowing charnel house, and its impact was enormous. (Both the movie and Milestone received Academy Awards.) Over the next three decades, Milestone proved to be a capable director with (inevitably) a special affinity for the war film, although he often failed to rise above inferior material or do justice to proven properties. His remakes of such sure-fire stories as *Les Miserables* (1952) and *Mutiny on the Bounty* (1962, his last completed film) were mostly uninspired.

All Quiet on the Western Front: LEWIS MILESTONE *(Universal, 1930). Anguished young German soldier Paul Baumer (Lew Ayres) huddles in a trench with a dying French soldier (Raymond Griffith). Milestone's still-powerful film depicted war as a horrifying charnel house.*

Milestone's approach to the war film is an interesting study in contrasts. Whereas *All Quiet on the Western Front* strives to convey the horror and ferocity of battle, his war films during World War II strenuously emphasize the nobility and sacrifice not only of the men in combat but of the civilians caught up in the conflict. Such films as *The Purple Heart* (1944) and *A Walk in the Sun* (1945) were awash in high-flown sentiment; the latter film even had its combat soldiers waxing self-consciously "poetic" during the pauses between battles. While made with the best of intentions, Milestone's films about resistance to Nazi tyranny bordered on hysteria. Lillian Hellman's florid screenplay didn't help *The North Star* (1943), and *Edge of Darkness* (1943) fought against the casting of such unlikely Norwegians as Errol Flynn and Ann Sheridan. Perhaps times of war call for feverishly patriotic, aggressive films; *All Quiet on the Western Front*, after all, dealt with war recollected in tranquillity. Even so, the dispar-

ity in tone and attitude between the two decades is striking.

Milestone also turned out some commendable non-war films, notably *The General Died at Dawn* (1936), a colorful melodrama (with a screenplay by Clifford Odets) set in a China torn by civil strife, and *Of Mice and Men* (1940), a generally effective film version of John Steinbeck's novel and play about two drifters (Burgess Meredith and Lon Chaney, Jr.) who meet their tragic destiny on a California ranch. Milestone contributed a lurid, hard-breathing, yet undeniably absorbing melodrama ("wicked woman" variety) entitled *The Strange Love of Martha Ivers* (1946) to the *film noir* cycle of the forties. While Milestone succeeded in making a vigorous and funny version of the Hecht-MacArthur play *The Front Page* (1931) in the early sound years, his forties comedies (*Lucky Partners*, 1940, and *My Life with Caroline*, 1941) suffered from his uncertain touch with comedy and lackluster material. When he found himself facing far too many aborted projects in the fifties and sixties, Milestone moved to television.

★

JOHN MILIUS (born 1944)   If Rambo were asked to name his favorite movie director, he might well answer, "John Milius"—that is, if he could identify Milius at all. With his unabashedly right-wing political credo, his attraction to violence, and his belief in taking brutal action against an implacable enemy, no matter the consequences, Milius would be sure to please Sylvester Stallone's muscular hero. Inevitably, he has his vociferous defenders and equally vociferous detractors; like many of his characters, he remains fiercely independent in his filmmaking.

A successful writer before turning to direction—he coauthored the Oscar-nominated screenplay for *Apocalypse Now* with Francis Coppola— Milius worked on the scripts for *Magnum Force* (1973, coauthored with Michael Cimino), *Jeremiah Johnson* (1972, with Edward Anhalt), and *The Life and Times of Judge Roy Bean* (1972), which he had hoped to direct as well. He finally made his director's debut in 1973 with *Dillinger*, yet another version of the notorious career of the arch-criminal. Milius handled the *mise en scène* expertly, particularly the very violent gun battles, but his screenplay was awkward and the cast tended to overplay. His next film, *The Wind and the Lion* (1975), was an elaborately produced adventure story with strong jingoistic overtones. It starred Sean Connery as a Berber chieftain who kidnaps an American woman (Candice Bergen) and her two children. Milius tried to analyze the cult of the California surfer in *Big Wednesday* (1978); despite some original concepts, the movie failed to attract much attention.

In the eighties, Milius turned to simple-minded adventure with *Conan the Barbarian* (1982), a long, expensive, and exceedingly gory film starring body-builder Arnold Schwarzenegger as the invincible medieval warrior. With *Red Dawn* (1984) he moved into the future, offering an apocalyptic view of an America invaded by armed Russian and Cuban forces. The movie was widely condemned for its simplistic and irresponsible approach to global relations, but many found the action viscerally exciting.

★

In this age, when mankind's frailties and foibles give way to the impersonal efficiency of the computer, I cling to the human comedy with all its cockeyed hopes. A man doesn't marry three times if he isn't an incurable roman- *tic. But my romanticism has never precluded me from my work which, in the final analysis, is the story of my life.*   VINCENTE MINNELLI, *I Remember It Well* (Garden City, N.Y.: Doubleday 1974), p. 379.

VINCENTE MINNELLI (1910–1986)   One of the supreme stylists in American films, and the preeminent director of musicals, Vincente Minnelli repeatedly dazzled our eyes with visions of beauty, spun out of a magical combination of components: settings, costumes, performances, words, and music, all in the service of his art. No director, musical or otherwise, used color with such precision and dexterity, creating shimmering images that have remained indelibly in the minds of filmgoers. If there was one overall flaw in his work, it was that he tended to place style over substance; in some of his films, notably *Yolanda and the Thief*, the decorative artifice overwhelms the material, leaving a sensation of discomfort and dissatisfaction, much as if one had eaten too many cream-filled chocolates.

Whereas Minnelli's best musical films are national treasures, his nonmusical films tend to be ignored. Admittedly, some of them come across as overstated and feverish (*Home from the Hill*, 1960, is a good example), but when the style meshes with the subject matter, as in *The Bad and the Beautiful* and *Lust for Life*, the result can be invigorating and fascinating to watch. In other instances, the Minnelli style is ideally suited to a particular sequence: Emma Bovary's incurable romanticism is fully expressed in the famous ballroom sequence of *Madame Bovary*. Minnelli also had a flair for comedy, as evidenced particularly in the charming and lighthearted *Father of the Bride*.

Minnelli was actually born into show business; at the age of three he toured with his family's tent show in the last days of vaudeville. Eventually, he worked as an assistant stage manager and then as a stage designer in New York. In 1933, at the age of twenty-three, he became art director of Radio City Music Hall. Clearly, Minnelli had found an ideal niche, where he could develop and apply his skill at creating romantic or glamorous illusion in the Music Hall's lavish stage revues. Inevitably, he was spotted and brought to Hollywood, by MGM producer Arthur Freed, who believed that Minnelli could bring fresh talent to the musical film.

OPPOSITE   The Wind and the Lion: JOHN MILIUS (*MGM/UA, 1975*). *In this romantic adventure, Sean Connery (center) starred as a Berber chieftain whose kidnapping of an American woman (Candice Bergen) and her two children sparks an international incident.*

son. *Cabin in the Sky* also demonstrated some of the characteristics Minnelli would later develop in his more elaborate musical films, notably a penchant for stylized decor.

Minnelli's first major musical after *Cabin in the Sky* was also his first acknowledged masterpiece. *Meet Me in St. Louis* (1944), an enchanting if idealized view of America at the turn of the century, represented a breakthrough in the musical genre. Minnelli conceived the film as a fully integrated entity, involving believable people in believable situations, and he wove the musical numbers naturally and seamlessly into the overall fabric rather than isolating them, the invariable practice in almost all previous musicals. The result was memorable, as a luminous Judy Garland led an exemplary cast through the not-very-earthshaking incidents in the lives of the Smith family of St. Louis. *Meet Me in St. Louis* marked the true beginning of Minnelli's fruitful association with Arthur Freed's brilliant musical unit at MGM.

Minnelli's forties musicals that followed *Meet Me in St. Louis*, for all their merits and their talented casts, fell down a notch. A bit overripe and cluttered, such films as *Yolanda and the Thief* (1945) and *The Pirate* (1948) got by on the strength of their respective dancing stars, Fred Astaire and Gene Kelly, who needed to use all their charm to keep the films from collapsing under the weight of all the ornate but heavy sets. Sometimes, however, the Minnelli style worked beautifully, as in the stunning "Limehouse Blues" sequence in the lavish, uneven

At first, however, Minnelli was used only to create isolated musical numbers. (One of his most original appeared in *Strike Up the Band*, 1940, in which pieces of fruit become musicians in an animated symphony orchestra.) Having earned his spurs, he won his first feature assignment, an adaptation of *Cabin in the Sky* (1943), an all-black Broadway musical fantasy. Although its modest budget was evident and its attitude toward blacks often patronizing, the musical had its joys, not the least being Ethel Waters re-creating her stage role of Petunia Jack-

ABOVE   An American in Paris: VINCENTE MINNELLI (MGM, 1951). *Gene Kelly dances in the closing ballet that evoked various art styles to George Gershwin's music. The musical's weaknesses faded in the bright glow of its many virtues, not the least of which was Kelly's dancing.*
RIGHT   Father of the Bride: VINCENTE MINNELLI (MGM, 1950). *Exhausted after their daughter's wedding, Spencer Tracy and wife Joan Bennett contemplate the ruins of their home. Minnelli carried off this thoroughly enjoyable comedy with a light and expert touch, drawing solid humor from small but recognizable situations.*

Jack Buchanan. In this case, the closing ballet, a spoof of Mickey Spillane's lusty detective novels, was cleverly and stylishly presented.

Minnelli's (and MGM's) last great musical of the fifties was *Gigi* (1958), an exquisitely mounted production derived from Colette's novel. The film evoked the enchanting Lubitsch and Mamoulian operettas of the thirties in its slightly tongue-in-cheek insouciance and high-gloss wit—not to mention the bracing presence of an older but still debonair Maurice Chevalier. Cecil Beaton's splendid settings and costumes, Joseph Ruttenberg's lovely color photography, and a witty and melodious score by Alan Jay Lerner and Frederick Lowe contributed to the film's triumph. All of Minnelli's romanticism, elegant style, and visual finesse converged in the staging and rendition (by Louis Jourdan) of the title song. *Gigi* walked away with an unprecedented nine Academy Awards, including one for Minnelli.

musical revue *Ziegfeld Follies* (1946). With the help of designer Irene Sharaff and choreographer Robert Alton, Minnelli created a stunning number set in a London slum, in which Fred Astaire, as a Chinese coolie, is fatally attracted to Lucille Bremer.

With *An American in Paris* (1951), Minnelli launched the first of a trio of fifties musicals that would guarantee him an honored place in the annals of musical films. *An American in Paris*, despite its studio-built City of Lights, a less than sparkling book, and a long closing ballet that is both imaginative and pretentious, glowed with its own romantic spirit and with magical musical numbers set to rhapsodic Gershwin music. Gene Kelly and enchanting newcomer Leslie Caron excelled in the leading roles. The film won six Oscars, including one for Best Picture. Two years later, Minnelli returned to the milieu he loved best, the musical theater, with *The Band Wagon* (1953), a witty and brightly tuneful musical comedy about the travails of an incoming Broadway show. Here the elements were perfectly blended: a knowing screenplay by Betty Comden and Adolph Green, lilting songs by Howard Dietz and Arthur Schwartz, and a matchless cast headed by Fred Astaire, Cyd Charisse, and England's elegant

ABOVE   Gigi: VINCENTE MINNELLI *(MGM, 1958). Gaston (Louis Jourdan) and young Gigi (Leslie Caron) romp happily on the beach at Trouville. Minnelli's enchanting musical made the most of Lerner and Loewe's beautiful score, Cecil Beaton's stunning sets and costumes, and a first-rate cast that included Maurice Chevalier.*

RIGHT   Brigadoon: VINCENTE MINNELLI *(MGM, 1954). Director Minnelli (left) works with his star, Gene Kelly, during the filming of this adaptation of the Lerner and Loewe musical. Despite a capable cast and many lovely songs, the musical failed to match the charm and sparkle of the original play.*

Minnelli actually made more nonmusical films than musicals and, as noted, a number of these are worth citing. Often they dealt with people who tended to mix or confuse fantasy with reality: the fatally romantic heroine of *Madame Bovary* (1949); the self-absorbed movie folk of *The Bad and the Beautiful* (1952) and *Two Weeks in Another Town* (1962); the mental patients and, in a sense, their emotion-racked guardians in *The Cobweb* (1955); and the tormented genius Vincent van Gogh in *Lust for Life* (1956). Although Minnelli managed an affecting version of *Tea and Sympathy* (1956), the stage play about teen-age *angst*, many of his dramatic films also share a tendency to overstatement, an inclination to edge a scene into flamboyance or melodrama. Nowhere is this excessiveness more apparent than in the florid Elizabeth Taylor–Richard Burton romantic drama *The Sandpiper* (1965). Nowhere is it less apparent than in *The Clock* (1945), one of Minnelli's early films, a small, engaging story of the wartime romance that quickly springs up between Judy Garland and Robert Walker. The unforced charm of this film also prevailed in *Father of the Bride* (1950) and its sequel, *Father's Little Dividend* (1951), leading to the supposition that Minnelli may have been more suited to comedy than to hard-breathing drama.

It is sad that his last film to date, *A Matter of Time* (1976)—a romantic drama concerning a young chambermaid (Liza Minnelli) in pre–World War I Europe who learns about life and love from an eccentric old countess (Ingrid Bergman)—was virtually incoherent. Minnelli has repudiated this film, which was taken away from him and badly mutilated by others. This was not the first time he had to endure concessions and unwanted changes in his work. Yet, like Honoré Lachaille in *Gigi*, Vincente Minnelli can reflect on his past with pride and pleasure, and remember that he brought us the priceless gift of his magical, enduring musical films and, best of all, the generous outpourings of his own romantic heart.

★

ROBERT MULLIGAN (born 1925) Robert Mulligan's best films demonstrate a special regard for the inarticulate longings and frustrations of children and young people; he has also coaxed expert performances from the relatively inexperienced actors who play these characters. In his initial feature after years as a leading television director, Mulligan directed Anthony Perkins in his first starring role as mentally ill ballplayer Jimmy Piersall in *Fear Strikes Out* (1957). Subsequently, in *To Kill a Mockingbird* (1962), he extracted lovely performances from Mary Badham and Philip Alford as the children of Southern law-

yer Gregory Peck, caught up in grim events during one long-ago summer, and he guided young Ellen O'Mara through a heartbreaking performance in *Up the Down Staircase* (1967) as an overweight, desperately unhappy student.

Summer of '42 (1971) had its share of sentimental twaddle, but it also had scenes that astutely expressed the sad-comic condition of teen-age sexuality. Once again the young actors—Gary Grimes, Jerry Houser, and others—came through with fine performances. Mulligan captured the easy charm of Steve McQueen in two films, *Love with the Proper Stranger* (1963) and *Baby, the Rain Must Fall* (1965). His recent credits, however, have not been outstanding. After *Same Time, Next Year* (1979), a serviceable version of the Broadway comedy, came *Kiss Me Goodbye* (1982), a feeble comedy-fantasy very loosely based on the Brazilian film *Doña Flor and Her Two Husbands*.

★

F. W. MURNAU (1888–1931) German director F. W. Murnau made his reputation in the twenties with two

ABOVE   To Kill a Mockingbird: ROBERT MULLIGAN (*Universal, 1962*). *Stalwart lawyer Atticus Finch (Gregory Peck) becomes deeply involved in defending a black man at a trial for rape. On hand are his son Jem (Philip Alford), daughter Scout (Mary Badham), and their friend Gill (John Megna). Mulligan's adaptation of Harper Lee's novel succeeded in evoking the unseen terrors of childhood.*

OPPOSITE   Sunrise: F. W. MURNAU (*Fox, 1927*). *Farmer George O'Brien steals away from his sleeping wife (Janet Gaynor) to keep a secret tryst with the wicked city woman. Murnau's luminous style turned a simple story of betrayal and redemption into a powerfully moving classic silent drama.*

masterly films: *Nosferatu the Vampire* (1922), a horror film based on Bram Stoker's *Dracula* that broke new ground by using real locations for its macabre story rather than stylized studio sets, and *The Last Laugh* (1924), a brilliant drama that dispensed entirely with the usual titles. Karl Freund's imaginative use of a freely moving camera in the latter film was an important—and influential—advance in motion pictures.

Invited to Hollywood on the strength of *The Last Laugh*, Murnau directed *Sunrise* (1927), one of the greatest of silent films. Murnau turned a simple story of a straying farmer (George O'Brien) and his devoted wife (Janet Gaynor) into a drama of exceptional power and lyricism. He blended the expressionistic techniques developed in the German cinema with the more naturalistic demands of Hollywood, and the result was a timeless film. After directing two more films for Fox, Murnau joined with documentary filmmaker Robert Flaherty to make a film called *Tabu* (1931). When they disagreed about the approach, Murnau bought out Flaherty's share and completed the film himself. Although *Tabu*

had a timeworn plot, it also had remarkable photography, and Murnau gave the film an otherworldly aura that sets it apart from other exotic melodramas. With what looked like a brilliant career ahead of him, Murnau tragically was killed in a car crash at the age of forty-two, days before the premiere of *Tabu*.

★

JEAN NEGULESCO (1900–1984) Romanian-born Jean Negulesco was a noted Parisian painter and stage designer who came to the United States in 1927 and remained. After some years as a second-unit or associate director, he began directing films at Warners in the forties. These years saw his best films: either brooding, shadow-laden melodramas such as *The Mask of Dimitrios* (1944) and *Three Strangers* (1946) or lushly emotional dramas such as *Humoresque* (1947) and *Johnny Belinda* (1948). *Johnny Belinda* was probably Negulesco's best film (and his personal favorite), a touching drama, steeped in the atmosphere of a small Nova Scotia town, of a deaf-mute girl's plight. Jack Warner disliked the film intensely and

fired Negulesco, then tried to rehire him after the movie won twelve Oscar nominations (Jane Wyman received the award for Best Actress), but he had already moved to Fox.

Unfortunately, something happened to Negulesco's work from this point on. Some of his early Fox films had merit, including *Road House*, 1948, his first for the studio, and *Three Came Home*, 1950. Then, assigned largely to the studio's big-budget, CinemaScope efforts, he turned out movies that, while visually stunning, were empty and juiceless, depending for their success on star power and glitzy production values. *How to Marry a Millionaire* (1953), *Three Coins in the Fountain* (1954), and *Woman's World* (1954) all focused, lightly and superficially, on the

emotional or romantic entanglements of women. Negulesco's musical *Daddy Long Legs* (1955) had some bright moments but suffered from the basic mismatching of Fred Astaire and Leslie Caron.

★

MARSHALL (MICKEY) NEILAN (1891–1958)   Mickey Neilan's personal life, much more colorful than any of his films, might itself make a movie called *Boy Wonder*. When barely twenty, he was chauffeur to D. W. Griffith, who suggested that he try his hand at film acting. He did so, successfully, and until he began directing in 1914, Neilan was a matinee idol of silent films, a handsome, romantic figure who eventually starred opposite Mary

Pickford, Ruth Roland, and Blanche Sweet. While still in his twenties, he became one of Hollywood's highest-paid, most sought-after directors, turning out one lavish, popular movie after another, many of them notable for their skillful lighting and emotionally involving stories. He directed Mary Pickford in some of her greatest successes, including *Rebecca of Sunnybrook Farm* (1917), *The Little Princess* (1917), and *Daddy Long Legs* (1919). When his wild playboy life—heavy drinking and carousing—caught up with him, his assignments dwindled in number and importance. Ultimately, his alcoholism rendered him unemployable.

At his peak, Neilan directed silent versions of such perennial properties as *In Old Kentucky* (1920), *Penrod* (1922), and *Tess of the D'Urbervilles* (1924). His few sound credits include the original versions of the marital comedy *The Awful Truth* (1929) and Damon Runyon's *The Lemon Drop Kid* (1934). His last few films, including *Sing While You're Able* and *Swing It, Professor* (both 1937), were wretched indications of how far he had fallen since his glory days. A year before his death, Neilan returned briefly to acting, playing a senator in Elia Kazan's *A Face in the Crowd*.

★

RALPH NELSON (born 1916)   For years a television director with impressive credits, Ralph Nelson made his feature film debut with the film version of *Requiem for a Heavyweight* (1962), which he had directed for TV. While the film was certainly smoother and less primitive than the video original, it somehow lacked the same impact, despite a stellar cast headed by Anthony Quinn, Jackie Gleason, Julie Harris, and Mickey Rooney. On two occasions, Nelson extracted Academy Award–winning performances from his actors: Sidney Poitier won for his role as the resourceful drifter who helps a group of nuns in *Lilies of the Field* (1963), and Cliff Robertson received an Oscar for his creative performance as a retarded man in *Charly* (1968). Since some of his films are so benign

(*Father Goose*, 1964; *Flight of the Doves*, 1971), it comes as something of a surprise to learn that Nelson directed two of the most brutal and explicitly violent Westerns of recent years: *Duel at Diablo* (1966) and *Soldier Blue* (1970).

OPPOSITE   Johnny Belinda: JEAN NEGULESCO (*Warner Bros., 1948*). *In an idyllic farm setting, hapless young deaf-mute Belinda (Jane Wyman) proudly shows her baby, born after she was raped by the town bully, to her father (Charles Bickford). Wyman won an Oscar for her sensitive performance under Negulesco's capable direction.*

ABOVE   Her Wild Oat: MARSHALL NEILAN (*First National, 1927*). *Colleen Moore (left) starred as the owner of a lunch wagon who decides to sweep into high society. Her customer at the right is friend Lila Lee.*

RIGHT   Charly: RALPH NELSON (*Cinerama, 1968*). *Retarded Charly Gordon (Cliff Robertson), destined to be turned into a temporary genius by medical science, visits the experimental mouse Algernon in the laboratory. The movie was manipulative and none too credible, but Robertson worked diligently at conveying Charly's changing mental status.*

★

FRED NIBLO (1874–1948)   Fred Niblo is best remembered for his direction of lavish, lively costume epics in the silent years, including *The Mark of Zorro* (1920) and *The Three Musketeers* (1921), both with Douglas Fairbanks, and *Blood and Sand* (1922), with Rudolph Valentino. Niblo had come to Hollywood in 1917 after working in the theater as a producer and director and was assigned to direct a group of movies starring his second wife, Enid Bennett. He also directed the mammoth 1926 spectacle *Ben-Hur,* although second-unit director B. Reeves Eason staged the famous chariot race. (Niblo rescued the newly formed Metro-Goldwyn-Mayer, on the verge of sinking under the movie's expense, by taking over on location in Italy for a while and then completing

it in Hollywood.) Later in the twenties, he directed Garbo in *The Temptress* (1926) and *The Mysterious Lady* (1928). A few years after the coming of sound, his career ended. Curiously for someone who had directed Garbo, Vilma Banky, and Norma Talmadge in soulful dramas, one of his better sound efforts was a slapstick Western comedy called *Way Out West* (1930). He later acted in several films.

★

MIKE NICHOLS (born 1931)   In the late fifties, two performers named Mike Nichols and Elaine May worked a special magic all by themselves. On a bare stage without scenery or props, they skewered modern hang-ups and pretensions with brilliant satirical wit, to the delight of their audiences. The team split up in 1961, and Nichols

turned to play directing with spectacular success, beginning in 1963 with Neil Simon's *Barefoot in the Park* and continuing with such hits as *Luv* and *The Odd Couple*.

In 1966 he made his first film, *Who's Afraid of Virginia Woolf?*, with equally spectacular results. Adapted from Edward Albee's lacerating play about a marriage made in hell, the movie featured a startling bravura performance by Elizabeth Taylor as the frowsy, shrewish wife and a perhaps even better performance by Richard Burton as her defeated husband. If the film betrayed a novice's lack of cinematic skill (attempts to "open up" the play were very awkward), Nichols more than compensated for it in his second film. A landmark movie, *The Graduate* (1967) crystallized an entire generation with its ruefully comic portrait of Benjamin Braddock (Dustin Hoffman, in a star-making performance), alienated from life around him, afloat and drifting in a sea of despond. His sexual adventure with Mrs. Robinson (Anne Bancroft) and his eccentric courting of her daughter (Katharine Ross) were marvelously delineated in the Calder Willingham–Buck Henry screenplay and brilliantly enacted under Nichols's astute direction. He received that year's Oscar as Best Director; surprisingly, the Best Picture award went to *In the Heat of the Night*.

To date, none of Nichols's subsequent films has matched *The Graduate*, although several deserve serious reevaluation. His adaptation of Joseph Heller's novel *Catch-22* (1970), an uneasy mixture of bitterly satirical comedy and somber tragedy, had many stunning scenes that captured the book's jaundiced view of a world gone mad in wartime. *Carnal Knowledge* (1971) dissected the perennially adolescent sexual hang-ups of two men (Jack Nicholson and Art Garfunkel) in a blistering and merciless comedy conceived in the style of a series of Jules Feiffer cartoons. (Feiffer, in fact, wrote the wickedly funny screenplay.) After two box-office and critical failures—*The Day of the Dolphin* (1973) and *The Fortune* (1975)—Nichols confined himself to stage direction until *Silkwood* (1983), a long but absorbing drama based on the true story of Karen Silkwood (Meryl Streep), who died under mysterious circumstances after she blew the whistle on foul play in the nuclear materials factory she worked in. Nichols returned to the subject of modern marriage with his latest film, *Heartburn* (1986), based on Nora Ephron's novel.

In a way, Mike Nichols on screen has never really left Elaine May on stage. Most of his films reveal the same cheerfully mocking, lightly acerbic approach to human foibles as his classic confrontations with May. He may not be consistent in his director's style, and he may nev-

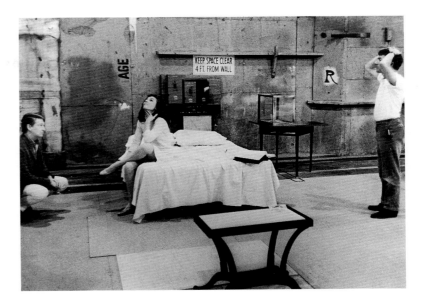

ABOVE   The Graduate: MIKE NICHOLS (*Avco Embassy, 1967*). Nichols (left) rehearses a scene with Anne Bancroft and Dustin Hoffman. He received an Oscar for directing this wise, funny comedy about alienation in the sixties.
BELOW   Who's Afraid of Virginia Woolf?: MIKE NICHOLS (*Warner Bros., 1966*). Nichols made an auspicious directorial debut with this blistering film version of Edward Albee's play. Elizabeth Taylor won an Oscar as shrewish, vulgar Martha, and Richard Burton excelled as George, her opponent in the marital war.

OPPOSITE   Ben-Hur: FRED NIBLO (*MGM, 1926*). Ramon Novarro as Ben-Hur grapples with Roman soldiers in Niblo's gargantuan production. Pointing at left: Francis X. Bushman as Messala. The film was rereleased in 1931 with added music and sound effects.

er prove to be a major film director, but what does that matter when we can respond to his foolish mortals with sardonic laughter?

★

MAX OPHULS (OPULS) (1902–1957) Like Josef von Sternberg, Max Ophuls (Opuls in the United States) emphasized form over content, bathing his films in shimmering images and using the camera to re-create romantic, long-vanished times and places. This is most evident in his last four films, made in France (*La Ronde, Le Plaisir, The Earrings of Madame de . . . ,* and *Lola Montés*), and also in his most famous American film, *Letter from an Unknown Woman* (1948). A tragic story of unrequited love, starring Joan Fontaine in one of her best performances, *Letter from an Unknown Woman* evoked turn-of-the-century Vienna in dazzling detail; it was unquestionably the most European of Ophuls's American films.

Born in Germany, where he was a noted stage director in the twenties, Ophuls fled the country after the Reichstag fire, becoming a naturalized French citizen in 1938. He came to Hollywood in 1941, assigned to direct Howard Hughes's new star Faith Domergue in *Vendetta.*

ABOVE   Catch-22: MIKE NICHOLS (*Paramount, 1970*). *Nichols (left) relaxes on the set with Orson Welles, who played General Dreedle in this adaptation of Joseph Heller's novel. The often brilliant film used a variety of comic devices to make noncomic points about the insanity of war.*
RIGHT   Letter from an Unknown Woman: MAX OPHULS (*Universal, 1948*). *Ophuls gave a smooth and glistening texture to this moist romantic drama concerning Joan Fontaine's unrequited, lifelong passion for Louis Jourdan.*

After six weeks of filming without interference, he was fired by Hughes, who returned from a stay in the hospital and apparently took an immediate dislike to Ophuls. (Ophuls may have enjoyed a bit of a vendetta himself with his film *Caught*, 1949, which focused on a sadistic, half-mad millionaire probably modeled after Howard Hughes.) His three other American films, made later in the decade, were more interesting for their use of settings and their camerawork than for their story lines, although the last, *The Reckless Moment* (1949), was a well-written suspense tale with a special feeling for the California locale.

★

ALAN J. PAKULA (born 1928)   After producing films for twelve years, Alan Pakula fulfilled a lifelong dream of directing, beginning with the modest hit *The Sterile Cuckoo* (1969), a touching, oddball comedy-drama with a star-making performance by Liza Minnelli in her second movie role as the eccentric Pookie Adams—a kind of trial run for her triumphant Sally Bowles in *Cabaret* (1971). Pakula veered in an entirely different direction with his second film, *Klute* (1971), a taut thriller centering on a tough, intelligent call girl (Jane Fonda, in a brilliant, Oscar-winning performance) who is stalked by a homicidal sadist. The girl's odd relationship with the detective assigned to the case (Donald Sutherland) actually aroused more interest than the stalking-killer aspect of the story. Pakula directed Fonda in two later films (*Comes a Horseman*, 1978; *Rollover*, 1981) without duplicating the success of *Klute*. His 1979 romantic comedy, *Starting Over*, blended a funny, pointed screenplay about life after divorce with expert performances by Burt Reynolds, Jill Clayburgh, and Candice Bergen.

Pakula's two most exceptional films to date have been *All the President's Men* (1976), an incisive, totally absorbing political melodrama based on *Washington Post* reporters Bob Woodward and Carl Bernstein's sensational investigation of the Watergate break-in, and *Sophie's*

Choice (1982), a flawed but haunting and powerful drama (from William Styron's novel) about a Holocaust survivor and the tormented relationship between her and her mad Brooklyn lover (Kevin Kline). Meryl Streep gave a multifaceted, Academy Award–winning performance as Sophie. Pakula's most recent film is *Dream Lover* (1985), a psychological thriller with Kristy McNichol.

★

ALAN PARKER (born 1944)   Since 1976 British director Alan Parker has made films with so much drive and energy, so many qualities in script and production, that one wishes they were better as a whole. Despite their merits, they all share an overall lack of cohesion and discipline. After working as a writer and director of television commercials, Parker directed *Bugsy Malone* (1976), a cute but ultimately wearying gimmick film in which child actors performed a musical spoof of the gangster film. (Young Jodie Foster stood out as a pint-sized vixen.) *Fame* (1980), a sort of junior-division *Chorus Line*, had several galvanizing musical numbers (its score by Michael Gore won an Oscar) that seemed oddly detached from the story of aspiring performers at New York's High School for Performing Arts, and *Shoot the Moon* (1982) compromised Bo Goldman's searing, intelligent screenplay about a disintegrating family with over-indulgent direction. Parker's best film to date is probably *Midnight Express* (1978), a grim, violent drama ostensibly about—but actually only suggested by—the story of one Billy Hayes (Brad Davis) and his harrowing imprisonment in a Turkish jail for the crime of drug smuggling.

OPPOSITE, ABOVE   Sophie's Choice: ALAN J. PAKULA (*Universal, 1982*). *Sophie (Meryl Streep) and her dangerously unstable lover, Nathan (Kevin Kline), embrace in their Brooklyn apartment. Under Pakula's direction, Streep gave a stunning performance as the Polish Auschwitz survivor who harbors a shattering secret in her past.*
OPPOSITE, BELOW   All the President's Men: ALAN J. PAKULA (*Warner Bros., 1976*). *Robert Redford, playing investigative reporter Bob Woodward, receives direction from Alan J. Pakula. Pakula used few cinematic flourishes to tell the compelling story of what lay behind the Watergate break-in.*
ABOVE   Midnight Express: ALAN PARKER (*Columbia, 1978*). *Brad Davis comforts fellow prisoner John Hurt in a scene from this powerful yet somewhat manipulative drama of life in the hell of a Turkish prison. Parker never permits the viewer a moment's respite from the terrifying events.*

As melodrama, the movie was compelling and harshly effective, with Academy Awards going to Oliver Stone for his screenplay and to Giorgio Moroder for his pulsating musical score. Parker's 1985 film *Birdy* is perhaps his most interesting. A visually striking, often touching adaptation of William Wharton's novel, it covered many (maybe too many) themes and ideas in its story of a disturbed and suffering young man who identifies with birds. Apart from an ending that unaccountably seemed to trash everything that had gone before, the movie worked quite well, and Parker demonstrated firmer control over his material than usual.

★

SAM PECKINPAH (1925–1984) At the start of Sam Peckinpah's most famous film, *The Wild Bunch* (1969), soldiers ride into a dusty Western town as a group of children gleefully watch red ants devouring scorpions. At the film's end, the Bunch's surviving members are massacred in one of the bloodiest battles ever filmed. From first to last, Peckinpah offered his very own vision of a cruel, uncaring, and overwhelmingly violent world. It was not a vision calculated to delight many critics and large sections of the paying public, and, coupled with his rough, explosive personality and hard-living ways, it cost him a great deal in personal fulfillment. Many of his films were taken away from him and ineptly recut and reedited, and after a relatively successful period in the early seventies, his career diminished with a series of weak or sadly neglected films. Yet, throughout his lifetime, he refused to compromise with the producers and studios seeking to tame his unfettered spirit.

Although some of Peckinpah's best films *(Ride the High Country, Junior Bonner)* contain little violence—in fact, next to *The Wild Bunch* or *Straw Dogs* they seem almost gently idyllic—his work has always been overshadowed by the controversial question of the efficacy and the intention of all that incessant bloodletting. Many critics have taken at face value the director's insistence that his purpose is to make us all aware of the danger that comes with desensitizing violence, or making it seem easy or glamorous, as has happened in the media. Instead, he wanted us to feel the horror and the pain that comes with violence so that we could lessen or even eliminate its presence in a hate-filled world. Others have remarked that the violent images are sometimes softened by a kind of perverse beauty that makes them oddly acceptable rather than truly terrifying.

A true man of the West, the grandson of Western pioneers, Peckinpah came to films in the mid-fifties after acting and directing in the theater. He played occasional small roles, then turned to writing and directing for television. Not surprisingly, he was most successful with Westerns, bringing an air of verisimilitude to such series as "The Rifleman" and "The Westerner." The star of "The Westerner," Brian Keith, suggested Peckinpah as director of a modest feature film, *The Deadly Companions* (1961). Peckinpah's second film, *Ride the High Country* (1962), attracted critical if not public attention. Beautifully photographed by Lucien Ballard, who worked on many Peckinpah films and helped to give them their smooth visual style, this elegiac, autumnal film about two aging cowhands (Randolph Scott and Joel McCrea) and their last days of glory contained one of the most poignant scenes in the long history of the genre: the final parting of the cowhands, with McCrea slowly sinking out of the frame as he dies. Peckinpah's next film presaged his future problems—the studio badly cut *Major Dundee* (1965), an expensive Western concerning a motley group of men who join together to fight Apaches, and Peckinpah disowned the film.

It was not until 1969 that Peckinpah scored even a moderate success, with *The Wild Bunch*. Influential and widely imitated, the film was a bitter, blood-splattered tale about a group of misfit outlaws led by Pike Bishop (William Holden) and their last days in a changing West that no longer valued friendship, honor, or courage. Ironically, the Bunch still retains a vestige of the creed that guided the lives of the old Westerners, and they even have their professional pride. That same creed surfaced in Peckinpah's next—and vastly different—Western, *The Ballad of Cable Hogue* (1970), a kind of latter-day fable about an old codger (Jason Robards) who learns to profit from—but is ultimately killed by—the coming of progress to the West. This immensely likable and inventive film deserved a wider audience.

In the seventies, Peckinpah continued to alternate between starkly violent and gentler projects. *Straw Dogs* (1971), filmed in England, drew considerable fire for its explicitly gory depiction of an isolated American (Dustin Hoffman) trying to defend his home from vicious thugs. The media attention lavished on this film should have gone to Peckinpah's *Junior Bonner* (1972), a genial, low-key comedy about a rodeo rider (Steve McQueen) and his relationship with his family. Peckinpah returned to a more familiar style with his last two Westerns, *Pat Garrett and Billy the Kid* (1973) and *Bring Me the Head of Alfredo Garcia* (1974), which offered the expected mix of violence, black humor, and a sardonic revisionist view of Western American history. There was little audience or

critical interest in *The Killer Elite* (1975), with James Caan, or in Peckinpah's sole war film, *Cross of Iron* (1977). Only *Convoy* (1978), an action film about a crusading trucker, was reasonably successful.

Maverick directors have always found it difficult to tread the well-worn Hollywood path, and the rebellious, outspoken Peckinpah was no exception. Some of the blood he shed on the screen may also have been shed by him metaphorically as he saw so many of his films mutilated by the studios. But he left behind one film, *The Wild Bunch*, that reshaped the Western genre, and other films that paid tribute, without compromise or sentimentality, to the proud, strong, melancholy men who forged a nation.

ABOVE   Junior Bonner: SAM PECKINPAH *(Cinerama, 1972). Rodeo rider Junior Bonner (Steve McQueen, right) talks with his boisterous father, Ace (Robert Preston), who was once a rodeo star. One of Peckinpah's warmest, most accessible films, this comedy-drama was drenched in the atmosphere of the rodeo circuit.*
OVERLEAF   The Wild Bunch: SAM PECKINPAH *(Warner Bros.-Seven Arts, 1969). One of the many moments of explosive action in Peckinpah's brilliant, extremely violent Western.*

★

There is a certain attempt on my part to unsettle the audience, really. To catch them as unaware as the characters in the film are being caught unaware.... Very early on, as I watch a film, I feel that I know just what it is going to be about—I know where it's going to get to eventually. And I'd rather that should not be so in my films.   ARTHUR PENN, in *The Book of Hollywood Quotes*, compiled by Gary Herman (London: Omnibus Press, 1979), p. 57.

ARTHUR PENN (born 1922)   One of the most interesting and successful of the many directors who emerged from television and the theater in the sixties, Arthur Penn may also be the most representative film director of that turbulent decade. In those years of upheaval and rebellion, with many of the nation's people, especially the young, at fierce odds with America's involvement in an unpopular war, voices were needed to express the surging emotions of the alienated. At his peak in the late sixties, Penn was one of those voices, reshaping the old

familiar film genres to show us that society's outcasts will often turn to violence out of their despair and helplessness. Curiously, he combined this deep and intense interest in a changing America with a film style derived from Europe, particularly from the early New Wave films of François Truffaut and Jean-Luc Godard.

Penn came to films after a long and distinguished career as a director of many prestigious television dramas and as a leading Broadway director whose hits included *Two for the Seesaw* and *The Miracle Worker*. At the height of his stage and television career, he had directed one film that already expressed many of the themes and concerns he would develop in later movies. *The Left-Handed Gun* (1958), derived from a television play by Gore Vidal, was ostensibly a Western about Billy the Kid (played in intense Actors Studio fashion by Paul Newman), but this Billy, portentously and self-consciously photographed, seemed more like a contemporary juvenile delinquent, angry and confused by a world he never made.

Penn's film career actually got under way five years later with his direction of *The Miracle Worker* (1962), based on the William Gibson play he had staged on Broadway. The story of the young deaf-mute Helen Keller and her dedicated teacher Annie Sullivan did not work as well on film as it had in the theater—the play's

flaws seemed magnified—but Penn managed to retain the deeply emotional center, helped by two extraordinary performances by young Patty Duke as Helen and Anne Bancroft as Annie. Both actresses won Oscars for the roles they had played so triumphantly on stage. After returning to the theater for several years, he came back to film with two interesting failures. A bold but misguided attempt at an experimental European-style art film, *Mickey One* (1965), about a nightclub comedian (Warren Beatty) fleeing from the mob for committing some nameless crime, may be described as a cryptic, Kafka-like *film noir*. *The Chase* (1966) had remarkable credits—a screenplay by Lillian Hellman and a cast headed by Marlon Brando, Jane Fonda, and Robert Redford—but it lost credibility with its cluttered and feverish story of violence and corruption in a Texas town. True to Penn's style, both films, in addition to touching on his favorite theme of outcasts in a hostile society, contained implied comments on the contemporary scene: *Mickey One* on the evil of the McCarthyist mentality and its penchant for faceless accusations, *The Chase* on the violence that comes with an indiscriminate use of guns.

In 1967, Penn finally achieved an international reputation with his landmark film, *Bonnie and Clyde*. On the surface an account of Clyde Barrow and Bonnie Parker, a pair of small-time bank robbers and killers who briefly became cult figures in the Depression thirties, the film actually reformulated the crime genre, mixing very black comedy, spurts of graphic violence, and several pinches of social commentary to draw a parallel between the thirties and the sixties. An able cast, headed by Warren Beatty as Clyde, Faye Dunaway as Bonnie, and Gene Hackman as Clyde's brother, combined with Penn's astute direction and a strong screenplay by Robert Benton and David Newman, made the film a compelling experience. Since the movie deliberately invited ambiguous attitudes toward the murderous protagonists, audiences and critics were either fascinated or repelled by the sudden switches from boisterous farce to unflinching brutality. Oscars went to Estelle Parsons for her supporting performance as Clyde's shrill sister-in-law and to Burnett Guffey for his brilliant, burnished photography.

After directing *Alice's Restaurant* (1969), a rueful elegy

ABOVE   The Miracle Worker: ARTHUR PENN (*United Artists, 1962*). *Patty Duke as the young, uncontrollable deaf-mute Hellen Keller and Anne Bancroft as her teacher Annie Sullivan both won Oscars for repeating their superlative stage performances in this film adaptation of the William Gibson play.*
OPPOSITE   The Swimmer: FRANK PERRY (*Columbia, 1968*). *Burt Lancaster enjoys a brief, tender liaison with young Janet Landgard in this adaptation of John Cheever's short story. Despite its flaws, the movie lingered in the mind as a perceptive, often on-target examination of a troubled suburbanite.*

on the decline of the once-vigorous hippie movement of the sixties, based in part on Arlo Guthrie's ballad, Penn took on his most ambitious project, a film version of Thomas Berger's novel *Little Big Man* (1970). Once again he reconstructed a film genre, this time satirizing and demolishing the longstanding myths about the Old West that Western movies had perpetuated for decades. The picaresque adventures of 121-year-old Jack Crabb (Dustin Hoffman, in a splendid performance) as he experiences a series of historical events (Custer's Last Stand and others) were used to comment on the unconscionable abuse of minority groups, the sometimes dangerous idiocy of military command, and the American reverence for undeserving heroes, all topics of some obvious relevance to the American involvement in Vietnam. Penn used a mixture of styles that ranged from slapstick comedy to near-documentary realism.

Since *Little Big Man*, Penn has directed only four films, none of which has measured up to his earlier work. In *Night Moves* (1975), Penn reshaped the *film noir* of the forties, as he had the crime and Western genres, giving some extra depth to the usual tangle of complications and adding an expected amount of explicit violence, including an unusually gory climax. He cast his revisionist eye on the Western once more in *The Missouri Breaks* (1976), but this unrelievedly brutal and pretentious movie, with an outrageous performance by Marlon Brando as a bizarre "regulator," itself seemed in dire need of revision. *Four Friends* (1981) was an odd, interesting, only

intermittently successful film that traced the lives of four adolescents (especially a Yugoslavian boy) through the sixties. Most recently, Penn directed *Target* (1985), a spy thriller about a retired CIA operative (Gene Hackman), now a respectable businessman, who is drawn back into the vortex of espionage when his wife is kidnapped by foreign agents.

Over many years, Arthur Penn has established himself as an intelligent and creative director whose films have taken the established genres in new directions. On the whole, he has revealed a dark vision—an America where violence can explode in a moment's notice and in the unlikeliest places: on a placid, small-town street *(Bonnie and Clyde)*, on a majestic Western plain *(Little Big Man)*, or at a lavish outdoor wedding *(Four Friends)*. Whatever his lapses in the last fifteen years, Arthur Penn is a skilled director of unusually strong convictions who is committed to making us see what we, as Americans, have been and what we have become—and perhaps moving us in the direction of what we can be.

★

FRANK PERRY (born 1930) After working in film, theater, and television in various capacities, Frank Perry made his directorial debut with *David and Lisa* (1962), a perceptive, moving story of troubled teen-agers. His subsequent films, often filmed in New York and environs, continued to deal with people in emotional turmoil. *The Swimmer* (1968), an underrated, trouble-plagued film based on a John Cheever story, concerned an unhappy suburbanite (Burt Lancaster) who reviews his failed life as he swims through his neighbors' swimming pools on a summer day, while *Diary of a Mad Housewife* (1970) offered some sharp, rueful observations on the plight of a long-suffering young wife and mother (Carrie Snodgress). Tuesday Weld played another neglected wife, this one going to pieces amid the glitziness of Los Angeles, in *Play It as It Lays* (1972), based on Joan Didion's novel.

In 1975, Perry took a break from gloom with one of his best films, the amiable, oddball comedy *Rancho Deluxe*, concerning two present-day cattle rustlers, then re-

OVERLEAF LEFT Bonnie and Clyde: ARTHUR PENN (*Warner Bros., 1967*). *Bonnie (Faye Dunaway) and Clyde (Warren Beatty) humiliate the police officer (Denver Pyle) who will ultimately kill them in the blood-splattered finale. Penn's film originally drew fire for its startling blend of rowdy farce and explicitly gory violence; today it stands as a landmark film of its period.*
OVERLEAF RIGHT Tess: ROMAN POLANSKI (*Columbia, 1980*). *Tess (Nastassia Kinski), Thomas Hardy's ill-fated heroine, gazes pensively through a window. Polanski's beautiful film won Oscars for its photography, costume design, and art direction.*

turned to *Sturm und Drang* with *Mommie Dearest* (1981), which related how Joan Crawford lost the Mother-of-the-Year Award. Most recently, Perry returned to the lighter touch with *Compromising Positions* (1985), an enjoyable, brightly written comedy-mystery that went astray in the second half. Until 1970, Perry worked with his wife Eleanor, who wrote the screenplays for his films.

★

SIDNEY POITIER (born 1924)   Sidney Poitier reached the peak of his popularity as a movie star in the sixties. In the process, he became the first black to win the Best Actor Oscar. His intense acting style, stressing personal conviction, firmness of purpose, and an innate decency, brought strength to such films as *Lilies of the Field* (1963), his Oscar role, *In the Heat of the Night* (1967), and *Guess Who's Coming to Dinner* (1967).

Poitier began directing in the early seventies, choosing to work in comedy, a vein far different from the sober projects in which he had appeared previously. *Uptown Saturday Night* (1974), *Let's Do It Again* (1975), and *A Piece of the Action* (1977), three raucous farces starring Poitier and Bill Cosby as fast-stepping lodge brothers who are constantly in trouble, won the biggest

ABOVE   Stir Crazy: SIDNEY POITIER *(Columbia, 1980). Richard Pryor and Gene Wilder find themselves behind bars in a case of mistaken identity. Poitier's direction kept the stars spinning from one outrageous situation to another.*

OPPOSITE   Chinatown: ROMAN POLANSKI *(Paramount, 1974). Jack Nicholson and Faye Dunaway played a detective and his client caught in a web of treachery, corruption, and murder in Polanski's artful thriller. Polanski filtered the longstanding tradition of the detective film through a seventies sensibility.*

audiences. *A Warm December* (1973) took the familiar "fatally-ill-heroine-finds-love" story that brought women to tears in the thirties and updated it with black characters. Lately, Poitier has returned to his frenetic style with *Stir Crazy* (1980), a popular comedy starring Gene Wilder and Richard Pryor, and *Hanky Panky* (1982), a comedy thriller that gave Gene Wilder one more chance to wax hysterical. His 1985 film *Fast Forward* played yet another variation on the venerable but ever-popular theme of talented kids seeking fame in the Big Apple.

★

ROMAN POLANSKI (born 1933)   The work of many directors has been affected by the events of their lives, but seldom have personal experiences so strongly affected professional achievements as in the case of Roman Polanski. A child of the Holocaust, he saw his parents taken to a concentration camp, where his mother died. A small, frail Jewish boy, he endured many harrowing experiences before World War II ended. Many years later, his wife, actress Sharon Tate, and three of her friends were horribly murdered by Charles Manson and his followers in one of the most widely discussed crimes in recent American history. It is hardly surprising, therefore, that most of his films over the years are surfeited with images of violence, alienation, and obsession, reflecting aberrations of the human mind. The breathtaking color photography of Polanski's acclaimed 1980 production of *Tess* may have muted his sense of the grimly implacable forces at large in the universe, but the fate of Thomas Hardy's heroine remained uncompromisingly harsh. Most of Polanski's movies, even those laced with humor (of the blackest variety), deal with man's most sinister impulses.

A stage actor throughout his teen years after the war, Polanski had also nurtured a love of film from an early age. Consequently, he was elated at being accepted by the famous Polish Film School at Lodz, where he studied film techniques, especially directing, for five years. While at the school, he created several short films, including one, *Two Men and a Wardrobe* (1959), that won five international awards. After graduating from the school, he moved to Paris for several years, then returned to Poland to direct his first feature film, *Knife in the Water* (1963). An odd, cryptic drama about the potentially dangerous relationship that springs up between an edgy sportswriter, his cool wife, and the surly hitchhiker they pick up on the way to their boat, the film won international acclaim for its strong visual style and subtle exploration of sexual tensions.

Following a three-year sojourn in Paris, Polanski went to London, where he directed *Repulsion* (1965), a psychological horror film starring Catherine Deneuve as a young Belgian girl whose disorientation and deep sexual frustration lead her to commit several murders. Polanski depicted her hallucinations and homocidal attacks in brutal and unsettling detail that fascinated some viewers and repelled others. The film embodied Polanski's recurring themes: the disorder in the universe, the deadly confusion of fantasy and reality, and the dangers of thwarted sexuality. *Repulsion* resembled Hitchcock (*Psycho,* in particular) crossed with Grand Guignol.

After *Cul de Sac* (1966), a bizarre black comedy on the theme of sexual humiliation, and a horror spoof entitled *The Fearless Vampire Killers or Pardon Me But Your Teeth Are In My Neck* (1967), Polanski directed his first Hollywood movie, the sensationally successful *Rosemary's Baby* (1968). A chilling adaptation of Ira Levin's novel about diabolism in modern-day New York, it struck a deep note of terror in audiences by combining the sinister images of ancient devil-worship with the bright daylight images of a bustling metropolis. Polanski drew an expert performance from Mia Farrow as the young wife who is impregnated by Satan, and he took a lesson from the master, Alfred Hitchcock, by imbuing everyday places—an empty closet, a deserted hallway—with frightening vibrations.

The murder of his wife in 1969—and the attendant publicity that placed lurid emphasis on his life style rather than on the crime—caused Polanski to return to Eu-

rope, where he eventually secured French citizenship. His blood-splattered adaptation of *Macbeth* (1971) inevitably suggested to many critics that he was attempting to exorcise the demons of the Manson case, but its strikingly original approach to the play found its partisans. When he finally came back to the United States, it was to direct one of his most impressive films, *Chinatown* (1974). A brilliant and atmospheric homage to the private-eye melodramas of the thirties and forties, it managed to stir several dollops of explicit sex and violence into its tangled nest-of-vipers plot. Robert Towne's screenplay, an intricate web of double crosses and deceptions, won an Oscar, and nominations went to the film itself, Polanski, and stars Jack Nicholson and Faye Dunaway. However, Polanski's 1976 French production of *The Tenant,* a bizarre drama of murder and mayhem in a Paris apartment building, attracted little but cult attention.

In 1977, under complex and ambiguous circumstances, Polanski was charged with raping a thirteen-year-old model and aspiring actress. He pleaded guilty to the least severe of six counts, and when threatened with deportation after spending forty-two days in prison, he fled to Europe, a fugitive from American justice. His work, however, continued: he managed to find the backing for his production of *Tess,* which received enthusiastic notices for its stately and exquisite rendition of Hardy's novel. Although some critics asserted that Polanski had not captured Hardy's concept that Tess was as much a victim of her own passionate nature as of men and society, the film deserved its acclaim. Since *Tess,* Polanski has completed *Pirates,* a swashbuckling comedy.

★

SYDNEY POLLACK (born 1934)   After more than two decades as a dependable director of mostly entertaining genre films, Sydney Pollack has emerged in the eighties as an outstanding figure with important credits. An increasingly subtle visual style and a greater assurance and ease in working with the star actors he favors have made such movies as *Tootsie* (1982) and *Out of Africa* (1985) not only commercially successful but also first-rate examples of filmmaking.

An actor, a drama instructor, and then a leading television director for a number of years, Indiana-born Pollack made his debut as a film director in 1965 with *The Slender Thread,* a fairly taut drama with Anne Bancroft and Sidney Poitier. Several moderate successes with points of offbeat interest, especially *The Scalphunters* (1968) and *Castle Keep* (1969), were followed by his first

major success, *They Shoot Horses, Don't They?* (1969). A riveting, uncompromising drama, it used the marathon dancers of the Depression years as a metaphor for human despair and resilience. Jane Fonda exuded weariness and cynicism as a burned-out dancer, and Gig Young won a Best Supporting Oscar for his bravura performance as the marathon's sleazy master of ceremonies.

With *Jeremiah Johnson* (1972), a beautifully photographed film about a mountain man alone in the wilderness, Pollack continued his association with Robert Redford that had begun with *This Property Is Condemned* in 1966 and has extended through four other films. Redford costarred with Barbra Streisand in one of the most popular films of the seventies, *The Way We Were* (1973), an over-the-years romantic drama that succeeded in overriding a fairly muddled screenplay, particularly the sections involving the political upheavals of the fifties,

with the unmistakable charisma of its stars. Redford's star presence also helped Pollack's competent, Hitchcockian spy thriller, *Three Days of the Condor* (1975), with Faye Dunaway, and *The Electric Horseman* (1979), a prefabricated but enjoyable comedy with Jane Fonda that was a throwback to the cowboy-meets-a-lady romances

ABOVE   Three Days of the Condor: SYDNEY POLLACK (*Paramount, 1975*). *Pollack (center) directs a scene in the midst of New York City's bustle. His suspenseful melodrama starred Robert Redford as a man caught up in murderous international intrigue.*

OPPOSITE, ABOVE   Tootsie: SYDNEY POLLACK (*Columbia, 1982*). *In his convincing disguise as a television actress, Dustin Hoffman has a woman-to-woman talk with Jessica Lange. Pollack's hugely successful comedy kept the premise amusing and believable almost until the end, helped by Hoffman's funny, inventive performance.*

OPPOSITE, BELOW   Out of Africa: SYDNEY POLLACK (*Universal, 1985*). *Meryl Streep as Karen Blixen mingles with the African natives. Pollack's Academy Award–winning film brilliantly captured the beauty and mystique of Africa, but it was less successful in delineating Blixen's romance with hunter Denys Finch Hatton (Robert Redford).*

of the thirties and forties. Pollack also tackled journalistic morality (or lack of it) in his modestly successful *Absence of Malice* (1981).

In 1982 Pollack had his greatest commercial hit with *Tootsie,* a delightful and observant comedy about an out-of-work actor (Dustin Hoffman, amazingly good) who, disguised as a woman, becomes a soap-opera sensation. Except for a rather messy and unconvincing climax in a television studio, the film scored in all ways, even making an understated pitch for better understanding between the sexes. *Tootsie* received Oscar nominations for Pollack, Hoffman, and the film itself, among others, with an award going to Jessica Lange for her performance as the television actress who enchants Hoffman. In 1985, Pollack switched gears with his most ambitious film to date, an adaptation of Isak Dinesen's (real name Karen Blixen) memoirs, *Out of Africa*. The story of the Danish author's coming to terms with the African continent and people, and her romance with hunter-adventurer Denys Finch Hatton (Robert Redford), made for a rather rambling and episodic narrative, but the visual magnificence of the production and Meryl Streep's towering performance as Karen offset the liabilities.

★

OTTO PREMINGER (1906–1986)   Over the years, there was little ambiguity about the public Otto Preminger. For nearly half a century, he was perceived as an outspoken, opinionated producer-director who was known to treat his actors with hearty contempt. However, the consensus on Preminger as a film director remains unmistakably two-sided. On the one hand, he has been regarded as a competent craftsman with no discernible style whose battles for greater frankness and openness in films and whose choice of controversial subject matter were well publicized for their box-office impact. On the other hand, his best films have been subjected to critical reappraisal and not found wanting. Some have written about the nuances in his work, especially his concern with the hidden aspects of personality, with characters who conceal part of their true identity (Waldo Lydecker in *Laura*, Brigham Anderson in *Advise and Consent,* and

others). His objective camera has been defended as an attempt to force audiences to *see,* to take a position on critical issues.

Born in Vienna, Preminger worked for several years as actor, director, and ultimately theater manager for famed German director Max Reinhardt. In 1935, Preminger came to America to direct a play. In Hollywood the following year, he directed a few minor films for Fox. Before long, he quarreled with Darryl F. Zanuck, who fired him. When he returned to the studio some years later, it was as an actor, playing a stiff-necked Nazi officer in *The Pied Piper* (1942). When he was asked to play another Nazi in *Margin for Error* (1943), which he had also staged on Broadway, Preminger insisted on being allowed to direct as well. His career as a film director was finally under way.

Although he was to direct many ambitious films in the next few decades, it may well be that Preminger's more modest efforts at Fox in the forties, particularly his *films noirs,* contain his best work. Certainly *Laura* (1944) remains his masterpiece. Inherited from Rouben Mamoulian, this most silken of mystery dramas was Preminger's first major critical and popular success. Artfully, he wove together many first-rate components, especially a witty screenplay lightly scented with the odor

RIGHT   Laura: OTTO PREMINGER *(Fox, 1944). Detective Dana Andrews informs an astonished Gene Tierney that until this moment she has been regarded as a murder victim. Preminger's peerless mystery drama involved a fascinating group of characters in a tale of obsessive love.*
OPPOSITE   Five Easy Pieces: BOB RAFELSON *(Columbia, 1970). Jack Nicholson starred as Robert Eronica Dupea, a rootless young oil worker and ex-pianist struggling to come to grips with his life. The movie received the New York Film Critics Award as best picture.*

the hard-breathing Southern drama *Hurry Sundown* (1967) or the hectic comedy *Skidoo* (1968). A modestly scaled *Tell Me That You Love Me, Junie Moon* (1970), a poignant story of three social misfits, deserved wider attention. Preminger's few other films in recent years, *Rosebud* (1975) and *The Human Factor* (1979), were summarily dismissed by both critics and audiences.

In the long run, Preminger may be remembered more for his contributions to the film industry—the fight to liberalize the production code, the championing of independent producers, the insistence on using black and blacklisted performers—than for the artistry of his films. But that would not in any way diminish the many excellences of his best work or his overall achievement in extending the limits of American film.

★

BOB RAFELSON (born 1934)   Bob Rafelson traveled the familiar route of writing, producing, and directing for television before turning to movies in 1968, with a rock film entitled *Head*. (Rafelson was a cocreator of the Monkees, a prefabricated pop group of the late sixties, which starred in *Head*.) The movie went largely unnoticed, but his second film, *Five Easy Pieces* (1970), was a surprising success. Audiences responded to its offbeat but fascinating story of an alienated man, skillfully played by Jack Nicholson. Rafelson followed this film, clearly influenced by European filmmakers in its attitude and ambiance, with *The King of Marvin Gardens* (1972), again starring Nicholson; this time, the deliberately murky and rather pretentious tone alienated critics and audiences. *Stay Hungry* (1976), an interesting comedy-drama about a rich young Southerner (Jeff Bridges) who champions the colorful residents of a rickety health spa for body-builders, was better, or at least more accessible. (It was basically Frank Capra material recycled for a new generation.) Rafelson's 1981 remake of *The Postman Always Rings Twice*, starring Jack Nicholson, had good thirties atmosphere and excellent photography (by Sven Nykvist) but fewer erotic sparks, for all the sexually explicit scenes, than the glossy 1946 version with Lana Turner and John Garfield.

of decadence and perversity, into a near-perfect entity. There was also solid merit in other of Preminger's excursions into the dark side of human nature, such as *Fallen Angel* (1945) and *Where the Sidewalk Ends* (1950), both replete with such classic *film noir* characters as the wicked woman and the brutal cop. He was much less successful with the tepid musical *Centennial Summer* (1946), or with the expensive but leaden film version of Kathleen Winsor's "scandalous" best-seller *Forever Amber* (1947).

With *The Moon Is Blue* in 1953, Preminger entered his most controversial period. His first independent production, the movie, a basically innocuous comedy from the Broadway play, created a furor by daring to use such forbidden words as "pregnant" and "virgin." It was released without a Production Code Seal of Approval. Several years later, his film of Nelson Algren's novel *The Man with the Golden Arm* (1955) also created a storm of controversy by boldly depicting the tortured life of a drug addict. Later Preminger films followed the pattern of challenging Hollywood taboos—*Anatomy of a Murder* (1959) with its explicitly frank language and *Advise and Consent* (1962) with its use of homosexuality as a plot device. During these busy years, Preminger, to his credit, saw fit to employ many underused black actors by directing two major all-black productions, *Carmen Jones* (1954) and *Porgy and Bess* (1959).

The sixties were Preminger's weakest period. Such films as *Exodus* (1960), *The Cardinal* (1963), and *In Harm's Way* (1965), for all their vast scope, star casts, and significant subject matter, remained stubbornly commonplace and shallow, nor was there much entertainment value in

---

OVERLEAF LEFT   Exodus: OTTO PREMINGER (*United Artists, 1960*). *Paul Newman and Otto Preminger discuss a scene for this sprawling adaptation of Leon Uris's best-selling novel about the early travails of Israel.*
OVERLEAF RIGHT   The French Lieutenant's Woman: KAREL REISZ (*United Artists, 1981*). *Ernestina (Lynsey Baxter), the daughter of a wealthy Dorset businessman, hangs on the arm of her fiancé, Charles (Jeremy Irons). Harold Pinter's clever, literate screenplay (from John Fowles's novel) juxtaposed two unrelated periods of time with a minimum of confusion.*

★

IRVING RAPPER (born 1898)   Irving Rapper would warrant mention if only for *Now, Voyager* (1942), that classic example of movie kitsch. Although he reputedly balked at inheriting the assignment from Michael Curtiz, he managed to orchestrate Bette Davis's transformation from ugly duckling to swan with finesse and surprising emotional impact. (Paul Henreid's two-cigarette *shtick* is a permanent part of movie lore.) Rapper's many other films, directed mostly for Warners, show a certain slackness. His biographical film *The Adventures of Mark Twain* (1944), for example, moved sluggishly, relieved only by its pleasing period atmosphere, which was also a saving grace of Rapper's film about a small-town minister, *One Foot in Heaven* (1941). The deficiencies of his stage adaptations were not entirely his fault; they suffered from fatally odious comparisons. Eleanor Parker couldn't begin to duplicate Margaret Sullavan's stage glow in *The Voice of the Turtle* (1947), nor could Gertrude Lawrence come within hailing distance of Laurette Taylor's legendary stage performance in *The Glass Menagerie* (1950). Bette Davis, on the other hand, was an entirely respectable substitute for Ethel Barrymore in Rapper's *The Corn Is Green* (1945). His later movies included a weak imitation of *All about Eve,* entitled *Forever Female* (1954), and a bland adaptation of Herman Wouk's none-too-profound novel *Marjorie Morningstar* (1958).

★

NICHOLAS RAY (1911–1979)   One of the more original directors who flourished in the fifties, Nicholas Ray has achieved cult status with many *auteur* critics. He is noted mainly for his sharply developed visual sense and his concern with society's misfits, whom he often portrays as bitter, troubled, and dangerous. His best film is probably *Rebel Without a Cause* (1955), a drama about alienated youth that made a star and cult hero of sulking, anguished James Dean. Other interesting movies about lost souls include Ray's first feature, *They Live By Night* (1948), a Bonnie-and-Clyde variation concerning doomed young lovers fleeing from the law; *In a Lonely Place* (1950), about a borderline psychotic screenwriter (Humphrey Bogart) involved in a murder; and *The Lusty Men* (1952), possibly the best movie ever made about rodeo life, with Robert Mitchum as a worn, aging rodeo rider. Even Jesse James became a juvenile delinquent betrayed by a hostile society in Ray's *The True Story of Jesse James* (1957). Although it attracted much critical attention and approval, Ray's Western *Johnny Guitar* (1954) is

an odd and ugly little film, in which the frankly sensual *grande dame* of saloonkeepers (Joan Crawford) squares off against the sexually repressed spinster ranch owner (Mercedes McCambridge). The only true amusement comes from watching the contrasting acting styles of Crawford (Old Hollywood) and McCambridge (Actors Studio).

★

ROBERT REDFORD (born 1937) After nearly twenty years as a major movie star noted for his many strong performances and virile good looks, Robert Redford made his debut as a film director with a winner, *Ordinary People* (1980). A moving and carefully wrought drama of a family's deterioration after the accidental death of an older son, the film won many Academy Awards: for Redford's skillful direction, for Alvin Sargent's beautifully crafted screenplay from Judith Guest's novel, for Timothy Hutton's sensitive performance as the son shattered by the tragedy, and for the film itself.

ABOVE Johnny Guitar: NICHOLAS RAY *(Republic, 1954). Sterling Hayden as Johnny Guitar and Joan Crawford as saloonkeeper Vienna in Ray's baroque Western. The movie's reputation as a classic surely depends on perverse reasoning: any film with so much bizarre dialogue, mannered acting, and undisciplined direction must surely rank as a masterpiece of the genre.*
OPPOSITE Now, Voyager: IRVING RAPPER *(Warner Bros., 1942). Nostalgic moviegoers still recall the love affair of unhappily married Jerry Durrence (Paul Henreid) and reconstructed spinster Charlotte Vale (Bette Davis). Among the well-remembered lines in this well-seasoned corn is the last: as they part, Davis tells Henreid, "Don't ask for the moon—we have the stars."*
RIGHT Ordinary People: ROBERT REDFORD *(Paramount, 1980). Robert Redford guides Mary Tyler Moore through a scene for this honest, searching view of a troubled family. Redford's first try at directing won him an Academy Award and the Directors Guild Award.*

★

KAREL REISZ (born 1926) Born in Czechoslovakia, Karel Reisz immigrated to England in 1938, where he eventually became involved with Tony Richardson, Lindsay Anderson, and other aspiring young directors in what came to be known as the Free Cinema Movement. His career in British films was interesting but erratic. After several short or medium-length documentary films, including the acclaimed *We Are the Lambeth Boys* (1959), he scored his first feature-length hit with *Saturday Night and Sunday Morning* (1961), a grittily realistic drama that caused a stir with its uncompromising view of the British working class. It also made a star of Albert Finney, who appeared in Reisz's next film, a pallid remake of Emlyn Williams's mystery-thriller *Night Must Fall* (1964). Reisz then attracted renewed critical attention with *Morgan!* (1966), an irreverent black comedy about a seriously maladjusted nonconformist (David Warner) who is obsessed with gorillas. This was followed in 1969 by *Isadora* (*The Loves of Isadora* in the United States), a lavish, wildly uneven drama in which Vanessa Redgrave gave an adroit performance as the famed, scandalous dancer. The movie was badly mutilated by its American distributors and never found its audience.

Reisz's several American-made films in the seventies were grim, offbeat enterprises not calculated to please the general run of moviegoers. *The Gambler* (1974) was a harsh study of a compulsive gambler (James Caan), and *Who'll Stop the Rain?* (1978) adapted Robert Stone's novel *Dog Soldiers* into a violent melodrama about a Vietnam veteran (Nick Nolte) involved in drug smuggling in Cali-

fornia. But Reisz had a major hit with the British-made *The French Lieutenant's Woman* (1981), an exquisitely produced and fascinating version (by Harold Pinter) of John Fowles's complex, best-selling novel. Most recently, Reisz directed *Sweet Dreams* (1985), starring Jessica Lange in an Oscar-nominated performance as ill-fated country singer Patsy Cline.

★

TONY RICHARDSON (born 1928) When Henry Fielding's bawdy hero Tom Jones came roaring onto the screen in 1963, Tony Richardson's reputation as a film director reached its highest peak. An unrestrainedly ribald and giddily entertaining version of the novel, *Tom Jones* gave plum roles to many of England's finest character actors and bolstered the career of Albert Finney as goodhearted, lascivious Tom. The movie won four Oscars (including for Best Picture and Best Director) and

confirmed Richardson's status as a leading stage and film director. Previously, he had enjoyed a string of successes in the theater, topped by his landmark production of John Osborne's "kitchen-sink" play *Look Back in Anger*, which he filmed in 1959. His other films before *Tom Jones* mined a similar vein of gritty realism: *The Entertainer* (1960), *A Taste of Honey* (1962), and *The Loneliness of the Long Distance Runner* (1962) focused effectively on the gray, shabby lives and frustrated dreams of England's lower class.

Unfortunately, none of Richardson's subsequent films has measured up to this heady period in his film career.

ABOVE   Tom Jones: TONY RICHARDSON (*Lopert, 1963*). *George A. Cooper is not a little peeved at discovering Albert Finney in bed with his wife Joyce Redman.* OPPOSITE   *Tony Richardson directs Susannah York in a scene for this Oscar-winning film. A bawdy delight, the movie charted the amorous career of its hero with a winning audacity.*

For his first Hollywood film, he brought an inept version of William Faulkner's *Sanctuary* (1961) to the screen. For his second, he raided Evelyn Waugh's novel *The Loved One* (1965), with no discernible improvement. In broadly satirizing Hollywood's thriving funeral business, it fulfilled its advertised promise to be offensive but missed the hoped-for humor. Richardson was more successful with *The Charge of the Light Brigade* (1968), a handsomely produced, bitterly satirical view of British military history, worlds removed from Michael Curtiz's rousing 1936 version. He foundered again, however, with *Joseph Andrews* (1977), another Fielding novel that he obviously hoped to parlay into a cinematic romp. In his 1984 film *The Hotel New Hampshire*, he tried gamely but futilely to dramatize John Irving's best-selling novel.

★

MICHAEL RITCHIE (born 1938)   A veteran television director, Michael Ritchie turned to film directing in 1969 and has since turned out some commendable movies that do not always get the attention they deserve. His two vehicles for Robert Redford were solid efforts: *Downhill Racer* (1969) offered an incisive look at the little-known world of skiing competition, and *The Candidate* (1972) expertly penetrated the smooth veneer of a fighting liberal who becomes defused by his political campaign. In his best work, *Smile* (1975), he presented a razor-sharp, sardonic, and funny view of a beauty pageant. Ritchie's other films to date have run to highs and lows. He had his greatest popular success with *The Bad News Bears* (1976), a rambunctious comedy about a kids' baseball team, and he had some rowdy fun with the football comedy *Semi-Tough* (1978). *The Island* (1980), on the other hand, was nasty stuff: a wretched thriller about a reporter trapped on a Caribbean island with a strange tribe. Ritchie's comedy *The Survivors* (1983) depicted two oddly matched men (Walter Matthau and Robin Williams) who resort to desperate survival tactics

in order to escape a revenge-minded thug. Most recently, Ritchie directed *The Golden Child* (1986), a comedy with Eddie Murphy.

★

MARTIN RITT (born 1920)   For nearly thirty years, Martin Ritt has directed a number of compelling, dramatically sound films that express his deep and personal commitment to human rights and his concern with social and political issues. At his best, with the considerable help of actors like Paul Newman, cameramen like James Wong Howe, and writers like Irving Ravetch and Harriet Frank, he has been able to translate his liberal beliefs into vigorous and commercially viable entertainment. Across the years, he has also sustained a reputation as a first-rate director of actors.

Starting as an actor himself, Ritt turned to directing for the stage after the war, then moved to directing and producing for television. In 1951 he was blacklisted for his early left-wing activities—as a teen-ager he had joined the Communist Party—and it became impossible for him to find employment. For a while he returned to the theater (his staging of Arthur Miller's *A View from the Bridge* was well received); he worked with Paul Newman and Joanne Woodward at the Actors Studio. Finally, he was offered his first feature film, *Edge of the City* (1957), adapted by Robert Alan Aurthur from his television play *A Man Is Ten Feet Tall*. An earnest, patly conceived echo of *On the Waterfront*, it submerged its message of racial brotherhood in a melodramatic plot about two freight-yard workers, a life-embracing black (Sidney Poitier) and a troubled white (John Cassavetes).

ABOVE   Semi-Tough: MICHAEL RITCHIE *(United Artists, 1978). Raucous action on the football field with Miami players (left to right) Brian Dennehy, Burt Reynolds, and Kris Kristofferson. Jill Clayburgh costarred as the girl in contention in this adaptation of Dan Jenkins's novel.*
OPPOSITE, ABOVE   The Long, Hot Summer: MARTIN RITT *(Fox, 1958). On the set of the film, Paul Newman (center) discusses a scene with director Martin Ritt (left), as Orson Welles looks on. Many scenes in Ritt's version of William Faulkner's stories crackled with tension and excitement.*
OPPOSITE, BELOW   Sounder: MARTIN RITT *(Fox, 1972). Nathan Lee (Paul Winfield) and his son David Lee (Kevin Hooks) stand in a field with their dog, Sounder. Ritt's sensitive, intensely moving story of a black family in the Deep South of the thirties featured an extraordinary performance by Cicely Tyson as the proud, resourceful mother of the family.*

Ritt's subsequent assignments had him dealing with adaptations of literary works by leading American writers, but what may be called the Fox treatment—widescreen CinemaScope, dazzling color, and star-heavy casts—diminished the impact of the material, making the films seem turbid and unconvincing. Of his two William Faulkner adaptations, *The Long, Hot Summer* (1958) and *The Sound and the Fury* (1959), only the former had real merit (plus relentless scenery-chewing by Orson Welles), while *Hemingway's Adventures of a Young Man* (1962) unsuccessfully dramatized some of the author's stories about Nick Adams. The following year, Ritt had his first major success with *Hud* (1963), derived from Larry McMurtry's novel about the new West. Paul Newman starred as the amoral, avaricious Hud, who clashes with his cantankerous old father (Melvyn Douglas) in what was clearly intended as a conflict of present-day and latter-day values. Douglas and Patricia Neal (as an earthy housekeeper) won Oscars, and Newman received a nomination (as did Ritt) for this harsh, stinging movie.

Ritt's compassion for the underdog—poor, struggling blacks, innocent political victims, and workers without rights—surfaced in many of his films in the seventies. He had his largest commercial hit with *Sounder* (1972), a

Hud: MARTIN RITT *(Paramount, 1963). The alienation of three generations of Bannons is reflected in this scene from Martin Ritt's contemporary Western drama. Paul Newman (left) starred as the amoral Hud, contemptuous of the traditional ways of his father (Melvyn Douglas, center). Brandon de Wilde (right) played Hud's young nephew, who comes to understand his uncle's avaricious nature.*

sensitive and deeply moving film about poverty-stricken black sharecroppers in the Depression South. However, other films on racial themes were less successful. *The Great White Hope* (1970), based on the play about black heavyweight fighter Jack Johnson, had Oscar-nominated performances by James Earl Jones and Jane Alexander, but it was disappointingly shrill and heavy-handed. The well-intentioned *Conrack* (1974), about teacher Jon Voight's attempts to break through to his poor Southern black students, came across as bland. Many admired Ritt's *The Front* (1976), which attempted to come to grips with the shameful blacklisting era in the fifties (and which employed a number of blacklisted people on both sides of the camera), but the movie was glum and sanctimonious, with only a few golden moments from Woody Allen as a cashier who becomes a "front" for blacklisted writers. At this point, Ritt seemed to fare better with films that emphasized strong characters over strong issues. *Pete 'n' Tillie* (1972), for example, a comedy-drama about an oddly matched married couple (Carol Burnett and Walter Matthau) who survive a tragedy, often scored effectively.

Except for *Norma Rae* (1979), which won an Oscar for Sally Field as a Southern textile worker who becomes a dedicated union organizer, Martin Ritt's most recent films have eschewed social comment. *Back Roads* (1981) took up the romance of a prostitute (Sally Field) and a drifter (Tommy Lee Jones) and tried, unsuccessfully, to make light of it. *Cross Creek* (1983), adapted from Marjorie Kinnan Rawlings's semiautobiographical book, portrayed a writer (Mary Steenburgen, exuding her usual offbeat charm) with warmth. However, audiences didn't take to its languid, low-key style or undramatic subject. Ritt's most recent movie, *Murphy's Romance* (1985), brought back the ubiquitous Sally Field, this time as a divorcée who comes to Arizona to raise horses and finds a badly needed friend in druggist James Garner.

★

JEROME ROBBINS (born 1918)   One of ballet's and the theater's outstanding choreographers, Jerome Robbins re-created many of his electrifying dances for the film version of the Leonard Bernstein–Stephen Sondheim musical *West Side Story* (1961). He also shared the director's credit, and the Academy Award for Best Direction, with Robert Wise. According to Wise, Robbins originally wanted to be more deeply involved in the film's production but finally agreed to an arrangement in which he would direct the music and dance numbers and Wise

would direct the story aspects. Although Robbins left after working on over 50 percent of the filming, his vibrant dances, crackling with energy and excitement, were integral to the film's great success.

★

MARK ROBSON (1913–1978)   Mark Robson was a director who knew his craft well but was not necessarily inspired by it. At RKO in the early forties, he and Robert Wise brilliantly coedited Orson Welles's *Citizen Kane* (1941) and *The Magnificent Ambersons* (1942), Robson without screen credit. After Welles left the studio, Robson was assigned to Val Lewton's low-budget horror unit, where he directed such films as *The Seventh Victim* (1943) and *Bedlam* (1946). While they were tightly made

and atmospheric—*Bedlam*, with settings modeled on Hogarth, conveyed a feeling of claustrophobic terror in scenes set in London's notorious asylum—none measured up to Jacques Tourneur's *Cat People* (1942), which Robson had edited for Lewton.

Many of Robson's films seem to play second fiddle to similar films made by others. The big-budget *Champion* (1949) and *The Harder They Fall* (1956) are less effective boxing dramas than Robert Wise's low-budget *The Set-Up* (1949). *Bright Victory* (1951), about a blinded soldier, lacks the impact of Delmer Daves's *Pride of the Marines*

West Side Story: ROBERT WISE *and* JEROME ROBBINS *(United Artists, 1961). Bernardo (George Chakiris), leader of the Sharks, dances down a New York street with his gang members. Robbins repeated his staging of the dazzling dances, and Wise kept a firm hand on the dramatic portions.*

(1945). And *The Prize* (1963) is ersatz Hitchcock. In the fifties and sixties, at Fox, Robson directed some glossy, large-budget films, including *Peyton Place* (1957) and *Valley of the Dolls* (1967). His best film during that period came from MGM: *Trial* (1955) told a gripping story involving racial prejudice, politics, and murder. Robson's few films in the seventies, including *Happy Birthday, Wanda June* (1971) and *Earthquake* (1974), were negligible.

★

HERBERT ROSS (born 1927)   An outstanding choreographer in films *(Doctor Dolittle, Funny Girl)* and a noted director of many Broadway plays and musicals, Herbert Ross directed his first movie in 1969, a leaden musical version of James Hilton's *Goodbye, Mr. Chips*, in which Peter O'Toole, despite all odds, gave an admirable performance as the beloved teacher. Ross's skill with actors was also evident in *The Goodbye Girl* (1977), with a charismatic portrayal by Richard Dreyfuss of an intense aspiring actor; in *The Seven-Per-Cent Solution* (1976), or "Sherlock Holmes Meets Sigmund Freud," with an inventive performance by Nicol Williamson as Holmes; and in the ballet drama *The Turning Point* (1977), with the virtuosic *pas de deux* of Shirley MacLaine and Anne Bancroft as battling longtime friends.

Ross has also directed a number of film versions of Neil Simon's plays (*The Sunshine Boys*, 1975; *California Suite*, 1978; *I Ought to Be in Pictures*, 1982), usually unsurprising and fairly enjoyable mixtures of one-liners, sentiment, and reassuring middle-class values. Ross's adaptations of plays by other writers (Bill Manhoff's *The Owl and the Pussycat*, 1970; Woody Allen's *Play It Again, Sam*, 1972) could have used a lighter touch. His best film to date may well be *Pennies from Heaven* (1981), an undervalued, frequently dazzling film that contrasted the grim reality of the story and background (unhappy sheet-music salesman in Depression America) with the fantasy evoked by the popular songs of the period. In 1984 Ross had a surprising success with *Footloose*, a semimusical that brought an eighties style and ambiance to the old forties plot of a "square" town galvanized by "with-it" kids. His 1985 comedy *Protocol* was a mildly amusing vehicle for Goldie Hawn.

★

ROBERT ROSSEN (1908–1966)   On and off the screen, Robert Rossen was deeply concerned with man as a social and political animal. On the screen, this concern was reflected in many of his screenplays for Warner Bros. as well as in the films he directed. Off the screen, it cost him years of pain and despair, for others as well as himself. Like the principal characters in *All the King's Men*, *Body and Soul*, and other of his films, he was brought down not only by society but also by his own character flaws.

Born in the poverty and violence of New York City slums, Rossen came to Hollywood in 1936 as a Warners contract screenwriter. Caught up in radical politics and a belief in social idealism, he injected some of his feelings into his scripts, which included *They Won't Forget* (1937, on the horrors of lynching), *Dust Be My Destiny* (1939, on injustice in a Depression society), and *Out of the Fog* (1941, on the need to oppose fascism). Although he joined the Hollywood contingent of the Communist Party, he had renounced the Party by 1945.

In the late forties, Rossen turned to directing, with

LEFT   Champion: MARK ROBSON *(United Artists, 1949). Kirk Douglas gave one of his best early performances as Midge Kelly, a boxer who claws his way to the top and comes to regret it. Robson's version of the Ring Lardner story softened some of the harsher details, giving the hero redeeming qualities scarcely evident in the original.*
OPPOSITE, ABOVE   The Goodbye Girl: HERBERT ROSS *(Warner Bros., 1977). The initial antagonism of Elliot Garfield (Richard Dreyfuss) and Paula McFadden (Marsha Mason) eventually blossoms into romance. Neil Simon's diverting original screenplay was in good hands; Herbert Ross directed briskly, and Dreyfuss gave an engaging, Oscar-winning performance.*
OPPOSITE, BELOW   Pennies from Heaven: HERBERT ROSS *(MGM/UA, 1981). Steve Martin and Bernadette Peters dance, Ginger-and-Fred style, in Ross's original if not totally successful musical. The film's highlights include several elaborate, imaginatively staged musical numbers.*

marked success. While his first film, *Johnny O'Clock* (1947), was a routine underworld melodrama, his next two films established his reputation. The strong drama *Body and Soul* (1947) portrayed a boxer (John Garfield) who comes close to destroying himself through recklessness and greed. Rossen's incisive direction and power-driven performances by Garfield and Canada Lee helped to offset Abraham Polonsky's rather self-conscious and overfancy screenplay. *All the King's Men* (1949), a slashing adaptation of Robert Penn Warren's novel, focused on a conniving hayseed named Willie Stark (Broderick Crawford) who rises to become his state's demagogic governor until he is brought down by an assassin's bullet. Obviously modeled on the notorious Huey Long, the character was vividly presented under Rossen's forceful direction from his own screenplay. Despite some flaws—the movie's middle section sags with vague plotting about Willie's adopted son, and some scenes called for smoother handling—*All the King's Men* deserved its awards, which included Best Picture, Best Actor (Crawford), and Best Supporting Actress (Mercedes McCambridge, as Willie's feisty troubleshooter).

In 1951 Rossen directed *The Brave Bulls,* one of the best films ever made about bullfighting. However, that year he found himself in serious trouble when the House Un-American Activities Committee identified him as a Communist. Refusing to testify about his membership or to identify others as past members, he was blacklisted by the film industry. Two years later, he changed his mind and testified openly before the Committee, acknowledging his past association with the Party and naming over fifty colleagues. Apparently, this testimony cost him years of deep personal anguish, and he never returned to Hollywood.

When he did return to directing, it was only intermittently and without conspicuous success. Although he won respectful notices for his somber, stately *Alexander*

the Great (1956), which he also produced and wrote, his other movies (*Island in the Sun,* 1957; *They Came to Cordura,* 1959) hardly belonged in the same class as his earlier efforts. (The latter film was more interesting for what it implied than for its story—an Army officer branded as a coward finds redemption through his ordeal in the desert.) Then came *The Hustler* (1961), Rossen's best film since *All the King's Men.* A dark, pungent drama set in the world of pool sharks, it returned to Rossen's familiar theme of the professional—here a pool hustler (Paul Newman)—who is nearly destroyed by his obsession to achieve greatness, in this case by winning a match against the country's top billiard player (Jackie Gleason). Brilliant acting by Newman, Gleason, and Piper Laurie (as a crippled, ill-fated derelict) combined with Rossen's film direction and Eugene Shuftan's Academy Award–winning photography to create the director's most fully realized film.

Lilith (1964), Rossen's final movie, was a critical and popular failure, but it still has its champions. A strange, mesmerizing drama set in a Maryland asylum, it centered on a young therapist trainee (Warren Beatty) who becomes obsessed with the mad inmate Lilith (Jean Seberg). Filled with murky symbolism and high-toned dialogue thickly applied in Rossen's own screenplay, the film is worlds removed from the straightforward, naturalistic style of Rossen's earlier movies. Yet it offers an-

OPPOSITE, ABOVE   All the King's Men: ROBERT ROSSEN *(Columbia, 1949). Demagogue-on-the-rise Willie Stark (Broderick Crawford) tries to shake hands with Raymond Greenleaf while John Ireland and Mercedes McCambridge look on. Rossen's strong but flawed adaptation of Robert Penn Warren's novel scathingly exposed how the American democratic process could be perverted.*

OPPOSITE, BELOW   The Hustler: ROBERT ROSSEN *(Fox, 1961). Pool hustler Eddie Felson (Paul Newman, left) prepares for a match with champion Minnesota Fats (Jackie Gleason) in this scene from Rossen's taut, expressive drama on the world of billiards.*

RIGHT   Lilith: ROBERT ROSSEN *(Columbia, 1964). Robert Rossen discusses a scene with Warren Beatty. Rossen's last film received largely unfavorable notices for its cryptic, fuzzy tale of a young occupational therapist (Beatty) who falls in love with a patient (Jean Seberg) at a private mental hospital.*

other—and final—portrait of someone brought to the brink of the abyss through forces both within and outside of his own psyche.

We should not read too much into the tortured images of Rossen's last work. Whatever private demons may have haunted him from the past, whatever personal ideas about obsession or betrayal may have filtered into his films, he was a director whose best work warrants our respect and attention. Back in 1964, Richard Schickel called him "an underrated movie-maker." Over two decades later, he may still be right.

★

WESLEY RUGGLES (1889–1972) The brother of inimitable character actor Charlie Ruggles, Wesley Ruggles started as a Keystone Kop and comedy player in the silent era. He began directing in 1917 and continued to

turn out movies in almost every genre until 1946. After directing a large-scale version of Edna Ferber's *Cimarron* (1931) for RKO, he reached a peak at Paramount in the thirties, where he collaborated with writer Claude Binyon on a series of comedies that made good use of his experience with Mack Sennett. He directed Mae West in one of her best and most popular comedies, *I'm No Angel*, 1933 ("Beulah, peel me a grape")—but did one actually *direct* Mae West or did one simply let nature take its course? On three occasions, Ruggles reinforced Clau-

OPPOSITE   I'm No Angel: WESLEY RUGGLES *(Paramount, 1933). As Tira, the circus queen, Mae West was certainly no angel, but her legion of fans wanted it that way. Ruggles gave her all the leeway she needed for her racy wisecracks and hip-swinging antics.*
BELOW   Accent on Youth: WESLEY RUGGLES *(Paramount, 1935). Wesley Ruggles on the set with star Sylvia Sidney. Samson Raphaelson's play about a middle-aged playwright's infatuation with his secretary became a mildly pleasant romantic comedy on the screen.*

dette Colbert's special brand of slightly tongue-in-cheek sophistication (*The Gilded Lily*, 1935; *The Bride Comes Home*, 1935; *I Met Him in Paris*, 1937), giving these films a romantic sheen that set them apart from the more slapstick efforts of the period. Later, at Columbia and MGM, Ruggles directed some less-than-memorable movies, including the Clark Gable–Lana Turner wartime romance *Somewhere I'll Find You* (1942) and the military comedy *See Here, Private Hargrove* (1944).

★

Mark Rydell (born 1933)   After years as an actor and television director, Mark Rydell made his debut as a film director with *The Fox* (1968), a fascinating and, for the time, quite bold film based on a D. H. Lawrence novella about a lesbian relationship. His subsequent movies include an immensely entertaining, underappreciated adaptation of William Faulkner's novel *The Reivers* (1969); *Cinderella Liberty* (1974), a quirky, likable comedy-drama about a sailor's relationship with a good-hearted whore and her mulatto son; and Bette Midler's debut film, *The Rose* (1979), an ear-shattering musical drama about a doomed rock star modeled on Janis Joplin. His most successful film to date has been *On Golden Pond* (1981), a

drama about old age in which the expert acting of Henry Fonda (in his last role) and Katharine Hepburn, both Oscar winners, did much to neutralize the shamelessly tear-jerking effects. (One glorious, unaffected moment: Hepburn singing and dancing by herself in the woods.) In 1984, Rydell directed *The River*, in which superior performances by Sissy Spacek and Mel Gibson as a beleaguered farm couple helped to strengthen a cliché-ridden story.

★

Mark Sandrich (1900–1945)   Mark Sandrich is one of those directors whose near-anonymity is not due to a lack of talent but to the fact that his best-known films are invariably identified with their stars rather than their di-

ABOVE   On Golden Pond: MARK RYDELL *(Universal/AFD, 1981). Feisty Norman Thayer (Henry Fonda) celebrates his eightieth birthday with family and friends (left to right, Dabney Coleman, Jane Fonda, Katharine Hepburn, and Doug McKeon). Rydell squeezed every ounce of emotion out of the maudlin screenplay, ultimately relying heavily on the personal charisma of his stars.*
OPPOSITE   Top Hat: MARK SANDRICH *(RKO, 1935). In an Art Deco nightclub, the chorus dances the "Piccolino." One of the best of the Fred Astaire–Ginger Rogers musicals,* Top Hat *breezed through its silly plot, leaving ample room for the delightful musical numbers.*

rector. In the mid-thirties, after some years as a director of short films—his *So This Is Harris* won an Oscar in 1933—he worked on no less than five of the delightful musicals with Fred Astaire and Ginger Rogers, highlighted by *Top Hat* (1935) and *Follow the Fleet* (1936). Since Astaire himself worked assiduously at creating the memorable song-and-dance numbers with Rogers, the handling of the rather foolish story lines was left to Sandrich, who got through them reasonably well, although without any demonstration of style. At Paramount in the forties, he directed (and also produced) several negligible Jack Benny comedies, but he also managed to chalk up some serviceable credits, including the Irving Berlin musical *Holiday Inn* (1942), teaming Bing Crosby and Fred Astaire for the first time; *Skylark* (1941), a frothy comedy with Claudette Colbert; and *So Proudly We Hail* (1943), an intense drama about nurses in war-

time. He died during the filming of Irving Berlin's *Blue Skies* (1946).

★

FRANKLIN J. SCHAFFNER (born 1920)   Franklin J. Schaffner was established as one of television's most outstanding directors when he turned to feature films in 1963 with *The Stripper*, derived from William Inge's play *A Loss of Roses*. This fairly turgid, unrewarding movie about a thirtyish stripper who has a romance with a teen-ager made a strong contrast with Schaffner's next movie, *The Best Man* (1964), a lively political drama adapted by Gore Vidal from his own successful play about a presidential battle. Although Schaffner usually blooms into craftsmanship and efficiency with good material, these qualities disappear under the influence of inferior material, and his subsequent films have been

variable in quality, ranging from the well-made, popular science-fiction fantasy *Planet of the Apes* (1968) to the ill-advised musical *Yes, Giorgio* (1982), with opera star Luciano Pavarotti in his first (and possibly last) movie role. The lavish but tedious *Nicholas and Alexandra* (1971), on the demise of Czarist Russia, and *Papillon* (1973), a long, long drama about an escape from Devil's Island, also belong to the latter category. To date, Schaffner's finest film has been *Patton* (1970), which succeeded as both a sweeping war drama and a full-bodied portrait of the controversial general George S. Patton, Jr., played with fire and eloquence by George C. Scott. *Patton* won seven Academy Awards, including one for Schaffner, Scott, and the film itself.

★

FRED SCHEPISI (born 1939) Fred Schepisi directed several films in his native Australia before turning out his first American movie, *Barbarosa* (1982), an offbeat, pleasing Western about a legendary outlaw (Willie Nelson)

who reluctantly teams up with a country boy (Gary Busey) as both flee from enemies bent on revenge. This was followed by *Iceman* (1984), a fascinating, well-executed piece of science fiction about a Neanderthal man (John Lone) discovered frozen in ice and brought back to life by scientists, who, in the time-honored tradition of movie scientists, argue over what to do with him. *Plenty* (1985), Schepisi's most ambitious film to date, starred Meryl Streep in an adaptation of David Hare's play about a fierce, neurotic Englishwoman moving toward madness in the years after World War II.

★

JOHN SCHLESINGER (born 1926) One of the most capable directors working today, London-born John Schlesinger reached a career peak in the sixties with two films that demonstrated his ability to deal with vastly different milieus. With ease and perceptiveness, he moved from the international playgrounds of Europe in the harshly satirical *Darling* to the lower depths of New York City in the affecting *Midnight Cowboy*. In both films, he also revealed his enormous skill in working with actors—he had been an actor years before—making a star (and Oscar winner) of Julie Christie as the ambitious, fickle heroine of *Darling* and confirming Dustin Hoffman's astonishing verstility in his role as the scruffy Ratso Rizzo in *Midnight Cowboy*.

An active television director since 1957, Schlesinger attracted the attention of filmmakers by winning first prize at the 1961 Venice Film Festival for his forty-five-minute documentary *Terminus*. The following year he made his movie debut with *A Kind of Loving* (1962), a slice-of-English-life drama with Alan Bates. His second film, *Billy Liar* (1963), received good notices and brought stardom to Tom Courtenay, who played a daydreaming layabout. *Darling* (1965), about a model named Diana Scott who sleeps and claws her way into high society, brought Schlesinger international recognition. Schlesinger's direction—and Julie Christie's performance—perfectly realized Frederic Raphael's lacerating, Oscar-winning screenplay. Incisive acting, by Glenda Jackson and Peter Finch, and a strong script (by Penelope Gilliatt) also figured in Schlesinger's *Sunday, Bloody Sunday* (1971), another piercing view of contemporary British mores, as seen through the experiences of three emotionally entangled people.

With his first American-made film, *Midnight Cowboy* (1969), Schlesinger penetrated an environment as far removed from London as Earth from Mars. Working with Waldo Salt's adroit screenplay (from James Leo Herlihy's novel), Schlesinger depicted in sharply revealing detail the curious friendship that forms between two homeless drifters in New York City: a self-styled Texas cowboy named Joe Buck (Jon Voight) and Dustin Hoffman's ailing, streetwise Ratso. Their relationship as they prowl the tawdry Times Square area became the focal

point of the film's vision of hell on earth. The film, Schlesinger, and Waldo Salt all won Oscars.

Schlesinger's films over the past decade do not include a major commercial success, but some of them deserve wider recognition and closer analysis. In particular, *The Day of the Locust* (1975), adapted from Nathanael

OPPOSITE   Planet of the Apes: FRANKLIN J. SCHAFFNER *(Fox, 1968)*. *Trapped in a society where apes are the sovereign creatures, Taylor (Charlton Heston) is hosed down by his captors. An ingenious, amusing adventure-fantasy, the movie offered an antiwar message in its closing moments.*

ABOVE   Iceman: FRED SCHEPISI *(Universal, 1984)*. *Timothy Hutton (left) played Dr. Stanley Shephard and John Lone was the Iceman, returned to life after forty thousand deep-frozen years. Under Schepisi's direction, Lone gave an astonishing and moving performance.*

RIGHT   Midnight Cowboy: JOHN SCHLESINGER *(United Artists, 1969)*. *Joe Buck (Jon Voight) tries to help an ailing Ratso Rizzo (Dustin Hoffman) in a scene from Schlesinger's pungent film. The story trapped the two protagonists in New York City's shabby, dangerous nighttime world.*

PRECEDING PAGES   The Day of the Locust: JOHN SCHLESINGER *(Paramount, 1975)*. *On a Hollywood set, the Battle of Waterloo is filmed for a historical epic; later, the set will collapse in ruins. Schlesinger offered a feverish, apocalyptic vision of the decline of the West as exemplified by Hollywood in the late thirties.*

West's novel, was an audacious and compelling, if somewhat incoherent, look at Hollywood in the thirties as the cosmos of a declining civilization. West's gallery of grotesques vividly came to life in the film, which resembled Robert Altman's *Nashville* in its panoramic overview of an America toppling into madness. Schlesinger offered a far more comic view of rampant American lunacy in his underrated 1981 farce *Honky Tonk Freeway.* He also brought a reasonably firm and incisive style to *The Falcon and the Snowman* (1985), based on the true story of two young men from different backgrounds who stole government secrets and were caught and imprisoned.

In these and other films, John Schlesinger has proved to be an intelligent director and a consummate craftsman, with the ability to elicit strong performances from his actors. The heady combination of critical and popular approval that greeted *Midnight Cowboy* has continued to elude him—*Marathon Man* (1976), a contemporary thriller with some singularly unpleasant sequences, attracted audiences while alienating many reviewers, and *Yanks* (1979), a nostalgic wartime romance, pleased many critics but found a shortage of viewers. Yet the skill that Schlesinger brings to filmmaking is not elusive, and it should continue to serve him well in the years ahead.

★

MARTIN SCORSESE (born 1942)   One of the most interesting and controversial of the young directors who won recognition in the seventies, Martin Scorsese creates a world of his own in his films, one that seems to exist on the dark side of the moon. Urban, hostile, and often violent, and photographed with an endlessly nervous camera, it is inhabited mainly by desperate losers cursing a world that threatens them at every turn. With his brooding face and coiled intensity, Robert De Niro enbodies these characters in many Scorsese films: as the doomed small-time hood in *Mean Streets* (1973), as the obsessed, ultimately murderous Travis Bickle in *Taxi Driver* (1976), as the chip-on-his-shoulder musician in *New York, New York* (1977), and as the self-destructive boxer Jake La Motta (his Oscar-winning performance) in *Raging Bull* (1980). Scorsese's tone turned positively acrid and scathing in *The King of Comedy* (1983), in which De Niro played an unconsciously repulsive loser and would-be comedian named Rupert Pupkin who ultimately achieves television fame by kidnapping his idol (Jerry Lewis). Scorsese's only conventionally commercial movie, *Alice Doesn't Live Here Anymore* (1974), was an unexpected success, winning an Oscar for Ellen Burstyn as a striving

waitress. His rock-concert documentary *The Last Waltz* (1978) also received strong reviews. In 1985, Scorsese directed *After Hours,* a black, offbeat comedy about a young man's nightmare experiences in New York City's Soho. His most recent film, *The Color of Money* (1986), stars Paul Newman and Tom Cruise in a sequel to Robert Rossen's *The Hustler* (1961).

★

GEORGE SEATON (1911–1979)   George Seaton turned to directing in the mid-forties after some years as a screenwriter, with credits that extended all the way in style from *A Day at the Races* (1937) to *The Song of Bernadette* (1943). While many of his films as a director succeeded at the box office, few were distinguished. Seaton wrote most of his own screenplays, in which the self-absorbed male leading character, so full of himself and his own needs and problems that he has no room for anything—or anyone—else, often appears. This applies to Bing Crosby's alcoholic actor in *The Country Girl* (1954), William Holden's arrogant major in *The Proud and the Profane* (1956), Clark Gable's cocky newspaper editor in *Teacher's Pet* (1958), and Fred Astaire's hedonistic father in *The Pleasure of His Company* (1961). Seaton's two most popular movies are separated by twenty-three years: *Miracle on 34th Street* (1947), a cheerful Christmas fable that had Kris Kringle (Edmund Gwenn) appearing in

person at Macy's Department Store, and *Airport* (1970), one of the first multistar "disaster" movies that attracted moviegoers in the seventies.

★

MACK SENNETT (1880–1960)   One of the greatest and certainly most influential masters of silent screen comedy, Mack Sennett perfected the sort of freewheeling, primitive slapstick that taught many future directors about the timing and staging of elaborate physical gags. Over the years, working with his own Keystone Company and other studios, his early crude, vulgar, improvisational style gave way to much more polished efforts, but the rambunctious spirit remained intact, with lunatic cops, mustachioed villains, and coy bathing beauties all converging in a merry mélange of physical humor. Out of Sennett's company of players came many of the gifted comedians of the silent era, including Charlie Chaplin, Fatty Arbuckle, Chester Conklin, Ford Sterling, and Mabel Normand.

Sennett came to films in 1908, after performing in burlesque and musical comedy. For several years at Biograph Studios, mainly between 1908 and 1911, he acted in many short films directed by D. W. Griffith, then moved to directing after studying the film techniques that were virtually being invented every day. In 1912, joining with two associates, he formed the Keystone Company to turn out his one- and two-reel slapstick comedies, brash knockabout farces that poked fun at the social and theatrical conventions of the day. Sennett's practice was to gather his actors at any location—such as a park or a beach—where they would work together to improvise comic situations on the spot. His goal was to keep the actors in perpetual motion; soon his frenzied car chases became a staple attraction of early moviegoing.

In 1915 Sennett joined with Griffith and Thomas Ince to form the Triangle Corporation, which absorbed Keystone. There he supervised the direction of many uninhibited farces that took advantage of the increased budgets and improved production facilities available to him before he organized his own company, Mack Sen-

nett Comedies, in 1917 to produce two-reelers and some feature-length films. A number of them starred the talented Mabel Normand, whose impeccable timing and sense of fun brightened all her films. Later in the twenties, Sennett launched the baby-faced, childlike comedian Harry Langdon in his first films.

Sennett's brand of humor did not wear well with sound, but he continued to work diligently, if much less rewardingly, at producing and again directing (after a long hiatus) many comedy shorts for Educational Films and Paramount. However, he simply was no longer in demand, and he retired from filmmaking in the midthirties, virtually penniless. He returned only to act as technical adviser on *Hollywood Cavalcade* (1939) at Fox, where he was given the token title of associate producer. At the Oscar ceremonies of 1937, he was honored with a special Academy Award that acclaimed him as "the master of fun, a discoverer of stars, and a sympathetic, kindly, understanding comedy genius."

★

VINCENT SHERMAN (born 1906)   A feature director since 1939, after some years as an actor and writer, Vincent Sherman spent most of the forties at Warners, where he specialized in suffering ladies—and oh, how they suffered (usually from man trouble)—in films that would make today's feminists shudder. He was skilled

ABOVE   Teddy at the Throttle: MACK SENNETT (*Sennett Productions, 1917*). *Gloria Swanson and Wallace Beery, actually married at the time, in one of Mack Sennett's many short films.*
OPPOSITE   Miracle on 34th Street: GEORGE SEATON (*Fox, 1947*). *At a Christmas party, Kris Kringle (Edmund Gwenn) admires the tree with his new friends, John Payne, Maureen O'Hara, and Natalie Wood. Seaton's engaging comedy became a holiday staple for years, even earning a musicalized version for the stage and a television remake.*

at putting such actresses as Ida Lupino (*The Hard Way*, 1942), Ann Sheridan (*Nora Prentiss* and *The Unfaithful*, 1947), and Joan Crawford (*The Damned Don't Cry*, 1950) through the emotional wringer, then usually leaving them to dry their tears of remorse on the hero's shoulder.

Sherman's adaptation of John Van Druten's *Old Acquaintance* (1943), with Bette Davis and Miriam Hopkins, was not nearly as slick or as well-appointed as George Cukor's updated version, *Rich and Famous* (1981), but it was vastly more entertaining, and his version of John Patrick's play *The Hasty Heart* (1949) earned honest tears with its moving story of a dying Scottish soldier. Bette Davis starred in one of Sherman's most popular forties films, *Mr. Skeffington* (1945), playing a vain society beauty who, late in life, learns the true meaning of love and sacrifice from her long-devoted, blinded husband (Claude Rains). In the fifties, with "women's" films out of fashion, Sherman turned to more aggressive heroines who gave as good as they got (Rita Hayworth in *Affair in Trinidad*, 1952; Juliette Greco in *The Naked Earth*, 1959), as well as out-and-out melodrama, as in *The Garment Jungle*

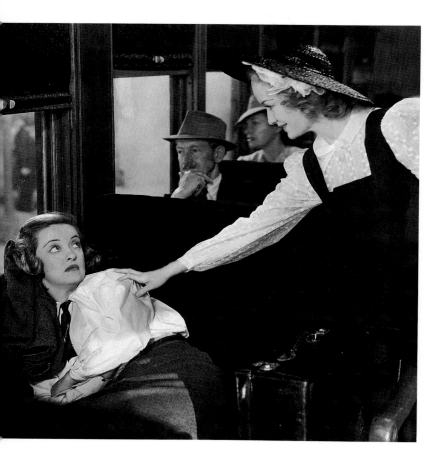

(1957) or *A Fever in the Blood* (1961). He held on to his franchise on slick soap opera with *The Young Philadelphians* (1959).

★

GEORGE SIDNEY (born 1916)   The son of show people, George Sidney rose from the ranks at MGM, moving up from messenger boy to sound technician, to film editor, to assistant director, and, finally—while still barely twenty—to director of the studio's screen tests. He was finally given his first feature film in 1941—a modest comedy called *Free and Easy*. With his first musical, *Thousands Cheer* (1943), he had clearly found his most compatible niche. The movie set the mode for his later MGM musicals: cheerful, tuneful, and uncommonly entertaining. He directed Esther Williams in her first starring film, *Bathing Beauty* (1944), working with the crew to create equipment that could photograph her underwater ballet, and his loose, improvisational style did wonders for the lively, still warmly remembered musical *Anchors Aweigh* (1945), which featured Gene Kelly's delightful dance with the animated Jerry the Mouse. Many of Sidney's musicals contain beguiling sequences, such as the Oscar-winning "On the Atchison, Topeka and the Santa Fe" number in *The Harvey Girls* (1946), the spectacular finale of *Annie Get Your Gun* (1950), and Ann Miller's dance with her three suitors in *Kiss Me Kate* (1953). He directed a version of *Show Boat* (1951) in which the colorful production and glorious music did much to override the deficiencies. His MGM credits also include two lavish, fast-paced adventure films, *The Three Musketeers* (1948) and *Scaramouche* (1952).

In the late fifties, Sidney became an independent producer and director, releasing his films mainly through Columbia. Highlights of this period include *The Eddy Duchin Story* (1956), which offset a lugubrious story with lovely music and stunningly beautiful New York photography, and *Pal Joey* (1957), which removed much of

LEFT   Old Acquaintance: VINCENT SHERMAN (*Warner Bros.*, 1943). *Bette Davis and Miriam Hopkins share a friendship that follows a rocky course over many years. Sherman adapted John Van Druten's play into an entertaining drama that gave excellent acting opportunities to the competing stars.*
OPPOSITE, ABOVE   Visions of Eight: YURI OZEROV, MAI ZETTERLING, ARTHUR PENN, MICHAEL PHLEGHAR, KON ICHIKAWA, MILOS FORMAN, CLAUDE LELOUCH, JOHN SCHLESINGER (*Cinema 5, 1973*). *John Schlesinger (center) directs the final portion of this eight-part documentary film about the 1972 Olympics.*
OPPOSITE, BELOW   After Hours: MARTIN SCORSESE (*Warner Bros.*, 1985). *In New York's threatening nighttime world of Soho, Griffin Dunne (at right) talks with bartender John Heard. In the course of the film, Dunne finds himself caught up in events that are both funny and terrifying.*

the bite of the original stage musical but retained some of the lilting Rodgers and Hart score. Sidney also made good use of Ann-Margret's unabashed sexiness in *Bye Bye Birdie* (1963), *Viva Las Vegas* (1964), and *The Swinger* (1966). He retired from filmmaking after directing *Half a Sixpence* in 1968.

★

DON SIEGEL (born 1912)   One of the most durable and admired directors of strong action films, Don Siegel offers a dark vision of American life: the American dream turned into an urban nightmare. Siegel's cities are wastelands where human vermin breed, to be destroyed by cynical loners like Dirty Harry. His cheerless small-town streets and claustrophobic prison cells are wastelands of another kind, but no less deadly or violent. Even Siegel's many Western vistas contain no reassurance—no pioneer affirmation lightens the gloomy aura of *Death of a Gunfighter* (1969, completed by Siegel after Robert Totten left), *The Beguiled*, or *The Shootist*. If all this sounds pessimistic, it can also be exciting. At his best— and critics in the late sixties began to understand how good he can be—Siegel is an able craftsman who offers tightly constructed narratives and well-staged action scenes.

In films from 1933, Siegel worked his way up the Warners ladder, finally creating and developing the montage department that kept him busier than many feature directors. After directing two Oscar-winning short films, he received his first feature assignment, a low-budget Victorian melodrama called *The Verdict* (1946), with Sydney Greenstreet and Peter Lorre. Two years later, he left Warners to direct films for RKO and (on loan) for Universal and Columbia. *The Big Steal* (1949), a complicated, fast-paced, and scenic crime drama starring Robert Mitchum, stood out from the others.

By 1954 Siegel had moved to Allied Artists, where he was to do some of his best early work. His prison film *Riot in Cell Block 11* (1954) won respectful and even enthusiastic notices for its unflinching depiction of life behind bars. However, a modestly budgeted science-fiction thriller attracted the most attention. *Invasion of the Body Snatchers* (1956) succeeded on more than one level: as a genuinely chilling tale of a small California town taken over by aliens who resemble its inhabitants, and

Annie Get Your Gun: GEORGE SIDNEY *(MGM, 1950). Howard Keel and Betty Hutton appear at the center of the film's spectacular finale. Sidney's direction captured all the gusto and brash, uninhibited good cheer of the musical play.*

as a political allegory warning of the dangers of nonconformity in the age of Senator Joe McCarthy. Whatever the interpretation, the movie excelled in sequences that conveyed the numbing horror of being stalked by neighbors.

No major box-office hits followed *Body Snatchers*, but some of Siegel's Westerns and crime films displayed his brisk, efficient style as well as his essentially gloomy point of view. In a violent or hostile world, Mickey Rooney's psychotic gangster *Baby Face Nelson* (1957), Elvis Presley's embittered Indian in *Flaming Star* (1960), and Steve McQueen's dangerously antisocial soldier in *Hell Is for Heroes* (1962) could not hope to survive. By the mid sixties, Siegel was working heavily in television, and one feature, a remake of Robert Siodmak's *The Killers* (1964), was released to theaters. It starred Ronald Reagan (as a villain) in his last film role.

By 1968, Siegel was back to directing features. He launched his most successful period with a police drama called *Madigan*. Within a few years he had developed his special relationship with Clint Eastwood, directing him in a series of crime films and Westerns that altered the actor's image from the stalwart Western policeman of *Coogan's Bluff* (1968) to the sullen, avenging, self-styled New York cop of *Dirty Harry* (1972). In between these films Eastwood starred for Siegel in several Westerns, none stranger (or more misogynistic) than *The Beguiled* (1971), in which Eastwood appeared as a wounded Civil War soldier who becomes the catalyst for expressions of jealousy and sexuality in a ladies' seminary.

Siegel's seventies films present a mixed bag, including *Charley Varrick* (1973), an enjoyable, cleverly wrought crime film about an ingenious bank robber (Walter Matthau); a British-made spy film called *The Black Windmill* (1974), starring Michael Caine; and *The Shootist* (1976), John Wayne's last film, which was both a worthy entry in the passing-of-the-West subgenre and an implied tribute to all the sturdy heroes Wayne had ever

played. The actor performed with mellow assurance under Siegel's efficient direction. One last reunion with Clint Eastwood yielded *Escape from Alcatraz* (1979), something of a departure from Eastwood's usual fare and a fairly gritty if familiar prison melodrama based on a true story. Siegel's last film to date, appropriately called *Jinxed* (1982), was a feeble, trouble-plagued attempt at black comedy starring Bette Midler. It was a regrettable ending to an exceptionally interesting career.

★

ROBERT SIODMAK (1900–1973)   Robert Siodmak evokes the night world of *film noir*: Alan Curtis stalking the streets and bars in search of the mysterious *Phantom Lady*; Burt Lancaster in the deep shadows of his room, stoically awaiting the arrival of *The Killers*; mute Dorothy McGuire, watched in the darkness by a maniac bent on murder in *The Spiral Staircase*. For a period of time in the forties, mostly at Universal, Robert Siodmak directed these and other tense thrillers with forthright assurance.

Born in Tennessee but raised in Germany from infancy, Siodmak worked in the German film industry of the twenties as a title writer and editor before turning to directing in 1929 with the semidocumentary *People on Sunday*. (Fellow employees on this film included his brother Curt, later a screenwriter and occasional director, as well as Billy Wilder and Fred Zinnemann.) Being Jewish,

---

OPPOSITE, ABOVE   Kiss Me Kate: GEORGE SIDNEY *(MGM, 1953). Ann Miller offers a sizzling rendition of ''Too Darn Hot'' in Sidney's entertaining film version of the long-running Broadway musical. Howard Keel and Kathryn Grayson costarred as the theatrical couple, once married, who battle their way through a musicalized production of* The Taming of the Shrew.

OPPOSITE, BELOW   The Shootist: DON SIEGEL *(Paramount, 1976). In his final role, John Wayne played J. B. Books, a dying legendary gunfighter who decides to leave the scene in a carefully arranged shoot-out. Wayne's shrewdly observed if idealized characterization gave this Western an added measure of strength and believability.*

ABOVE   Dirty Harry: DON SIEGEL *(Warner Bros., 1971). Policeman ''Dirty Harry'' Callahan (Clint Eastwood) ''makes his day'' by shooting an enemy of society in Siegel's rapid-fire, controversial crime melodrama. Note the marquee advertising Eastwood's film* Play Misty for Me, *released that same year.*

mak, uncharacteristic) spoof of pirate movies, starring Burt Lancaster in an athletic role light-years removed from his debut as the doomed Swede in *The Killers*. In 1953 Siodmak returned to France and then to Germany, continuing to make films overseas.

★

DOUGLAS SIRK (born 1900)   Douglas Sirk went through several careers (and names) before emerging in Hollywood as the director of a number of visually striking— and now greatly admired—films of the forties and fifties. Born Claus Detlev Sierk in Denmark, he became a successful stage director and producer in Germany under the name of Detlef Hans Sierck, switched to films as the Nazis rose to power, and finally immigrated to America in 1937. In Hollywood he changed his name again, to Douglas Sirk, and worked as a director, almost exclusively at Universal Pictures. After making many light comedies and a few thrillers, Sirk specialized in glossy soap opera in which glamorous actresses such as Lana Turner and Jane Wyman suffered romantic tribulations while remaining well-dressed. Among his emotional orgies were *Magnificent Obsession* (1954), *All That Heaven Allows* (1956), *Interlude* (1957), and his last film, *Imitation of Life* (1959). One of his most popular (and to many, best) movies was *Written on the Wind* (1956), a feverish melodrama of sex among the Texas rich. In recent years, Sirk's films have been intensely reevaluated; he is now

Siodmak fled from Germany after the Nazi takeover in 1933 and ultimately came to Hollywood in 1940. By the mid-forties, after several routine films, he was able to apply the brooding Germanic style of his early years to his studio assignments. In his black-and-white thrillers he excelled at moving characters with ambiguous motives through webs of treachery and violence.

The Killers (1946), a well-wrought extension of the Hemingway story (which was reproduced almost intact in the opening scene), was Siodmak's best work. (The screenplay was actually written by—but uncredited to— John Huston, working with Anthony Veiller.) Siodmak proved adept at suggesting the workings of a disordered mind in such melodramas as *The Suspect* (1945), *Uncle Harry* (1945), and, especially, *The Spiral Staircase* (1945), which built up a mood of psychological terror as a killer on the loose stalks the physically afflicted.

Siodmak's early fifties films did not measure up to his earlier work, although his last American-made film, *The Crimson Pirate* (1952), was an entertaining (and for Siod-

regarded by some critics and scholars as a superior director whose best films, for all their glossy veneer, reveal dark and cynical undercurrents in American society.

★

VICTOR SJÖSTRÖM (SEASTROM) (1879–1960) One of the great pioneers of Swedish filmmaking, Victor Sjöström was already a well-known stage actor and director when he began directing movies in 1912. By 1920 he had made forty films, in addition to writing and acting in many of them. Along with Mauritz Stiller, Sjöström created an impressive Swedish cinema—mature, imaginative, and amazingly advanced in its techniques.

In 1923, Sjöström came to Hollywood, where his name was Americanized to Seastrom. He directed the first MGM production, a sensitive adaptation of Leonid Andreyev's circus drama *He Who Gets Slapped* (1924), with Lon Chaney and Norma Shearer. Unfortunately, most of Sjöström's early silent films have been lost, as has his 1928 Garbo vehicle, *The Divine Woman*, a fictionalized biography of Sarah Bernhardt. Of the films that have survived, the two greatest are unquestionably *The Scarlet Letter* (1926) and *The Wind* (1928), austere dramas in which the forbidding landscapes reflect the inner lives of the characters. *The Wind*, in particular, is a stunning film in which Lillian Gish gives a compelling performance as a woman driven to the brink of madness in the lonely windswept desert of Texas. Sjöström directed only a few more films and eventually returned to Sweden, where he resumed his acting career, notably as the troubled old professor in Ingmar Bergman's *Wild Strawberries* (1957).

★

I sort of know what works. STEVEN SPIELBERG, "Dialogue on Film," *American Film*, September 1978.

STEVEN SPIELBERG (born 1947) Steven Spielberg remembers. A lifelong film enthusiast, he remembers what made us go to the movies in the first place: the sense of magic and wonder, the exhilaration of being moved, frightened, or simply entertained, the pleasure at seeing distant worlds re-created or watching gifted people giving generously of their talents. Combined with an astonishing technical virtuosity for one so relatively young and an instinctive understanding of the current film market, this deeply rooted love of movies has translated into a phenomenally successful career.

A dedicated and doggedly ambitious filmmaker from the start, Spielberg won his first contest at age thirteen with a forty-minute war film. Later, he worked for a year

to complete his first feature, a science-fiction adventure called *Firelight*. With *Amblin'* (1964), a 35-millimeter short about hitchhikers, he succeeded in drawing attention to his developing skill; it led to a contract, at age twenty-one, with Universal. He directed a number of television plays, including *Duel* (1971), an acclaimed and later theatrically released thriller about a California businessman (Dennis Weaver) who finds himself mysteri-

ABOVE The Wind: VICTOR SJÖSTRÖM *(MGM, 1928). Lillian Gish's artistry gave stature to this melodramatic tale revolving around the tribulations of a Texas farm wife. Sjöström made effective use of the forbidding landscape of the Mojave Desert, where the movie was filmed.*

OPPOSITE, ABOVE The Spiral Staircase: ROBERT SIODMAK *(RKO, 1945). Deaf-mute Helen Capel (Dorothy McGuire) tries desperately to escape a psychotic killer who preys on handicapped girls. Siodmak used shadowed photography and darkly ominous sets to generate a sense of lurking terror.*

OPPOSITE, BELOW All That Heaven Allows: DOUGLAS SIRK *(Universal-International, 1956). Widow Jane Wyman (center) precipitates a scandal by falling in love with a younger man (Rock Hudson). Agnes Moorehead played Wyman's friend. Typically, Sirk's film lavished expensive production values on its soap-operatic plot.*

ously being pursued by a Diesel truck with an unseen driver.

Spielberg made his feature debut with *The Sugarland Express* (1974), a lively comedy-drama concerning a young Texas couple who become fugitives (and media celebrities) when they refuse to give up their child for adoption. The movie won some good reviews, but it was Spielberg's next film, *Jaws* (1975), that put him on the map. A blockbuster of awesome proportions, it was a superbly crafted melodrama about the terrorizing of a New England resort town by a carniverous white shark. The movie drew on the familiar conventions of the horror genre (the ominous music, the stalking monster, the shock effects), including sketchy characterizations, but the sudden jolts were cleverly spaced, black humor lightened the mood agreeably, and Spielberg staged the whole enterprise with professional aplomb, despite staggering production problems. (The movie was nominated for an Oscar; it won in the categories of editing, sound, and musical score.) For his next project, Spielberg gave himself an even more daunting assignment: an epic-sized new version of the sort of science-fiction movie he had loved in the fifties, such as *The Day the Earth Stood Still*. The film, *Close Encounters of the Third Kind* (1977), proved an impressive spectacle focusing on the ultimate meeting of humans and alien creatures. The climactic sequence—the face-to-face ''encounter of the third kind''—was one of the most moving and beautiful ever conceived for the science-fiction genre. Spielberg received his first Oscar nomination.

After a misfire with *1941* (1979), a massive, exhausting comedy about an imagined invasion of California after Pearl Harbor, Spielberg resumed his amazing track record with *Raiders of the Lost Ark* (1981), a funny and spectacular throwback to the old adventure films of the thirties and forties, stamped once again with Spielberg's uncannily right cinematic sense and his appreciation of past moviegoing pleasures. (He was helped immensely by coproducer George Lucas, who also contributed the story line with Philip Kaufman, and by Lawrence Kas-

dan's adroit, more than slightly tongue-in-cheek screenplay.) Several years later, Spielberg directed an equally successful sequel, *Indiana Jones and the Temple of Doom* (1984).

Unquestionably, Spielberg's greatest achievement to date has been *E.T.: The Extra-Terrestrial* (1982). Currently the largest-grossing film of all time, this enchanting modern-day fable concerned an appealing alien creature, lost on Earth, who becomes friends with a young boy (Henry Thomas) and is ultimately returned to his own planet. The film's sense of fun and magic, its exhilarating pace and warmly winning characters, and its splendid special effects endeared it to viewers of all ages. Like many mythic films, *E.T.* lay itself open to various interpretations (was it an eighties version of *The Wizard of Oz* or possibly a religious parable?); however, most people were content to enjoy it and cherish the visitor from outer space.

In the past few years, Spielberg has served as producer and close supervisor of films like *Poltergeist* (1982) and *Gremlins* (1984), which combine humor and horror, with a somewhat disturbing emphasis on the horror and explicit violence. Popular with audiences, they lack the charm, finesse, and virtuosity of Spielberg's own movies. He was on much sturdier ground with his engaging and enormously successful production of *Back to the Future* (1985), directed by Robert Zemeckis. Spielberg himself directed one episode of *Twilight Zone—The Movie* (1983), a heavily whimsical tale of elderly folk who become children on one magical night.

Most recently, Spielberg moved into a more ''adult'' area with his adaptation of Alice Walker's prize-winning novel, *The Color Purple* (1985). At first glance, this thirty-year chronicle of the ordeal, resilience, and ultimate triumph of a black Southern woman named Celie (Whoopi Goldberg) seems worlds removed from Spielberg's previous films, but a closer look reveals a strong family resemblance. In its way, *The Color Purple* is as much of a fable as any of Spielberg's other efforts: a Dickensian tale complete with wrenching separations, joyful reunions, and a pitifully abused heroine who, improbably, comes into her own, with every plot complication tidily resolved. Spielberg won the Directors Guild Award for his direction.

Now that the ''boy wonder'' is no longer a boy, where does he go from here? One hopes that he will continue to remember the feelings that propelled him into filmmaking from an early age, not for the sake of repeating successful formulas but to continually refreshen and revitalize his perspective. Whether he chooses to produce

---

OPPOSITE, ABOVE   E.T.: The Extra-Terrestrial: STEVEN SPIELBERG *(Universal, 1982). Elliott (Henry Thomas), with E.T. concealed in his bicycle basket, flees from the government men searching for the alien. Spielberg's magical fantasy pleased audiences with its fable-like story of an endearing outer-space visitor and the young friends he makes on Earth.*

OPPOSITE, BELOW   The Color Purple: STEVEN SPIELBERG *(Warner Bros., 1985). Spielberg rehearses a scene with Whoopi Goldberg, who played the sorely put-upon Celie in this over-the-years tale based on Alice Walker's novel. Although Spielberg softened the book in many ways, he gave the film the benefit of his story-telling ability and craftsmanship.*

or direct, the result will probably please legions of moviegoers.

★

JOHN M. STAHL (1886–1950)   After directing many silent films from 1914 on (including such provocative titles as *The Child Thou Gavest Me*, 1921, and *Why Men Leave Home*, 1924), John Stahl moved into the sound era with a well-developed visual style and the ability to make even the most outrageous corn palatable. In the thirties, he was best known for directing the sort of woman-oriented tear-jerker (*Back Street*, 1932; *Imitation of Life*, 1934; *Magnificent Obsession*, 1935) that director Douglas Sirk and others would remake on a more grandiose scale in the sixties. Stahl's versions seem more honestly concerned with the emotional upheavals of his put-upon heroines than the remakes, which lavished more attention on decorating the sets and the leading ladies. Stahl's single MGM film, *Parnell* (1937), about the Irish leader, qualifies as Clark Gable's most disastrous flop. Viewers refused to digest this mulligan stew of politics and romance.

At Fox in the forties, Stahl directed decent but tame adaptations of popular novels (*The Keys of the Kingdom*, 1944; *Leave Her to Heaven*, 1945); the studio's contract players—Gregory Peck, Gene Tierney, Linda Darnell, among others—lacked color and charisma, and the results were lukewarm. Stahl's best film at Fox was one of his first—an amiable period comedy called *Holy Matrimony* (1943), based on Arnold Bennett's novel *Buried Alive* about a reclusive artist who assumes the identity of his dead butler.

★

I attempt to make my work completely homogeneous. Image, sound, abstraction, and the effect of these on the beholder are interlaced and must follow an inner rhythm and an orchestration which, though it vanishes with the film, remains as a **Nachlang.** *It is this after-timbre, this ghost-resonance, this lasting vibration that I seek—though I may not achieve it.*   JOSEF VON STERNBERG, in a letter to Rafael Bosch, 3 October 1960, cited in Herman G. Weinberg, *Josef von Sternberg: A Critical Study* (New York: E. P. Dutton, 1967), p. 138.

JOSEF VON STERNBERG (1894–1969)   Josef von Sternberg ranks high among the great film directors, and if style were all, he might rank even higher. One of the supreme visual stylists of the screen, Sternberg was primarily concerned with the pictorial composition of his films, using light and shadow rather than plot or dialogue to develop

his exotic characters and their motivations. At the center of his unique cinematic vision was Marlene Dietrich, beautiful and enigmatic, swathed in costumes decorated with sequins, ruffles, and feathers, photographed through scrims and veils or sheets of rain or billows of fog and smoke. If Sternberg had a painter's concept of motion pictures, using the camera as a brush, then Dietrich, starring in his best-remembered films, was his eternal model.

Sternberg's movies, while masterly, have inevitably been called superficial, remote, and cold. Many of his films bear the imprint of the talented people who worked with him—scenarist Jules Furthman, art director Hans Dreier, designer Travis Banton, cinematographer Lee Garmes, and others—but all their efforts were filtered through the autocratic Sternberg, whose touch could indeed be chilly. His films contain any number of passionate encounters and liaisons, but they generate little heat; we are not especially moved by Amy Jolly's

Imitation of Life: JOHN M. STAHL (*Universal, 1934*). *With her doggedly loyal housekeeper, Aunt Delilah (Louise Beavers), Bea Pullman (Claudette Colbert) builds her life and her business. One of the most popular tear-jerkers of the thirties, the film touched on usually avoided racial matters.*

decision to follow her lover into the desert, or by Shanghai Lily's rekindled affair with her officer. Emotion is replaced by effect, and actors such as Dietrich, Clive Brook, Brian Aherne, and Herbert Marshall (whose acting always suffered from frostbite) become no more important—or animated—than the settings and costumes.

Born Josef Sternberg in Vienna (the "von" was added later by a producer who thought it sounded classier), the director came to America at a very early age, returned to Vienna to finish school, and finally settled in Hollywood in 1924. Only a year after he entered filmmaking, working at all of its aspects, he directed his first feature film, a waterfront drama called *The Salvation Hunters* (1925). His original, although unformed, style attracted attention and brought him more projects—which ended disastrously for Sternberg. Two films he directed for MGM were remade by another director, and a third film, made for Charlie Chaplin, was never released.

Sternberg's fortunes changed in 1926 when he joined Paramount as an assistant director. He had a success with his first feature film for the studio, *Underworld* (1927), a pioneer gangster film replete with striking pictorial touches that turned a conventional story of an arrogant hood's rise and fall into a doom-laden exercise in shadowed evil. His next few films, especially *The Docks of New York* (1928), also displayed impressive visual qualities. In 1930, after completing his first talkie, Sternberg traveled to Germany to direct *The Blue Angel*. Searching for a woman to play the leading role of the coldhearted temptress Lola-Lola, he found a minor German actress named Marlene Dietrich. She appeared opposite the eminent Emil Jannings in the harsh psychological drama about a respected professor who is destroyed by his lust for a sluttish cabaret singer. Sternberg molded Dietrich into an international film star, a figure of mysterious glamour and beauty.

Sternberg's six Paramount films with Dietrich marked the peak of his career. Totally in control of every component—he was notorious for his imperious manner and overbearing arrogance (he even dressed for the role, wearing boots and an occasional turban)—he created exotic vehicles that would display his star to best advantage. In his first, *Morocco* (1930), Dietrich played a world-weary cabaret singer named Amy Jolly, who becomes the center of a triangle involving Legionnaire Gary Cooper, whom she loves, and wealthy Adolphe Menjou, who understands her all too well. All the Sternbergian characteristics converged in this film: Dietrich's odd, sometimes ambiguous sexuality, a sense of muted depravity, feelings and attitudes expressed in glances, gestures, and camera angles.

These characteristics were intensified in Sternberg's third and best film with Dietrich, *Shanghai Express* (1932). Around Shanghai Lily's romance with Captain Harvey, Sternberg wove a mesmerizing melodramatic tale of the colorful passengers aboard the train, complete with steamy assignations, political intrigue, and noble sacrifice. Although the dialogue (by Jules Furthman) was wittier than usual, it did not distract Sternberg from his primary interest—he photographed his star, by way of Lee Garmes, with infinite care and dazzling variety, including the famous shot of her hands praying for her imperiled lover. Among the other films Sternberg made with Dietrich, his last, *The Devil Is a Woman* (1935), gave the star one of her most erotic roles as a wicked temptress, but the one that came the closest to matching *Shanghai Express* was *The Scarlet Empress* (1934), an ambitious and ornate drama about Russia's Catherine the Great. Studded with beautiful as well as grotesque and

Shanghai Express: JOSEF VON STERNBERG (*Paramount, 1932*). *The enigmatic Shanghai Lily (Marlene Dietrich) rekindles her love affair with Captain Donald Harvey (Clive Brook). Sternbergian touches, especially gauzy photography of the leading lady, permeate this exotic romantic melodrama.*

perverse moments, it epitomized Sternberg's unique virtues and deficiencies: uncommon stylistic brilliance in the service of an uninvolving story and overstuffed production.

Sternberg's subsequent career suffered the consequences of his intractable personality and the studios' unsympathetic attitude toward his kind of personal filmmaking. After directing two films for Columbia—a sometimes effective, low-budget version of *Crime and Punishment* (1935), with Peter Lorre as Raskolnikov, and an airy Grace Moore musical, *The King Steps Out* (1936)—Sternberg went to England, where he became involved with an aborted production of *I, Claudius*, referred to in the documentary about it as "The Epic That Never Was." He reached a low point in his career with *The Shanghai Gesture* (1941), an exotic melodrama of almost sublime silliness. After years of inactivity or indifferent projects, he directed one of his most interesting films: *Anatahan*, also known as *The Saga of Anatahan* (1953), related the true story of a group of Japanese marines who refused to believe that the war was over—and lost.

One of the screen's true originals and *auteurs*, Josef von Sternberg spun his own hypnotic web of images, using the movement of the camera to "emotionalize empty space." "The greatest art in motion picture photography," he wrote, "is to be able to give life to the dead space that exists between the lens and the subject before it." Often the subject was no more than rain slashing against a window, steam from a departing

train, or smoke from a cigarette, used to generate a mood or a feeling. Most gloriously, it was the face of Dietrich, almost imperceptibly expressing the weary disillusion of a lifetime. In his films, Sternberg created a total vision unlike any other, and if it remains aloof to some, to many others it is the unique achievement of a major film director.

★

GEORGE STEVENS (1904–1975) Can a director's reputation survive the barbed arrows of leading film critics? Indeed it can, and George Stevens is one of the best examples. In the sixties, Stevens received harsh treatment from Richard Schickel ("one of the overrated") and Stanley Kauffmann ("one of the most overrated craftsmen in American film history"); they and others interpreted his methodical, fastidious attention to every production detail—once considered a principal virtue—as the lumbering movement of an elephant determined to tap-dance. The pendulum has swung back, and today George Stevens rates as one of Hollywood's most dependable, most technically assured directors, with a well-developed visual style and an enviable record that includes not only some of the blithest genre films of the thirties (*Swing Time*, *Gunga Din*) but also such durable achievements as *Shane* and *A Place in the Sun*. (An excellent 1984 documentary, *George Stevens: A Filmmaker's Journey*, helped to set things right.) If a number of his films betray a certain heaviness or a lack of sparkle (*Woman of the Year*, for example, is much less effervescent than George Cukor's *Adam's Rib* or *Pat and Mike*), Stevens's accomplishments remain very real.

Stevens started in films in 1921 as an assistant cameraman, and by 1927 he had joined the Hal Roach comedy unit, working with Roach, Leo McCarey, and others in turning out many of the hilarious Laurel and Hardy short films. By the early thirties he was directing his own comedy shorts and graduated to feature films for Universal. At RKO, he finally came into his own, directing a group of films that offered the kind of polished, well-crafted entertainment thirties audiences could often expect. His first major success was *Alice Adams* (1935), a keenly observed slice of Americana that gave Katharine Hepburn one of her most appealing early roles. The following year he directed the magical team of Fred Astaire and Ginger Rogers in one of their most captivating musi-

The Scarlet Empress: JOSEF VON STERNBERG *(Paramount, 1934). The empress Catherine the Great (Marlene Dietrich) lingers in the palace, surrounded by grotesque statuary. Sternberg exercised complete control over the film, even insisting on conducting the orchestra that played the musical score.*

cals, *Swing Time* (1936). Like Mark Sandrich and other directors, Stevens could do little to relieve the foolishness of the plot, but he managed to frame the musical numbers with an extra sheen and elegance. He also directed *Gunga Din* (1939), one of the screen's most rousing adventure films, which glided over its racist overtones with cheeky humor and aplomb.

In the early forties, joining Columbia as a producer-director, he brought his professional and unhurried style to *Penny Serenade* (1941), an unabashedly tear-jerking drama about a tragedy-plagued couple (Irene Dunne

Gunga Din: GEORGE STEVENS *(RKO, 1939). British soldiers Cary Grant, Victor McLaglen, and Douglas Fairbanks, Jr., face combat with their customary bravado. Hidden among the natives (second from the left) is heroic little Gunga Din (Sam Jaffe).*

and Cary Grant), and *The Talk of the Town* (1942), a comedy that inserted some reflections on the nature of justice and the law into its triangular romance involving Grant, Jean Arthur, and Ronald Colman. He also directed Arthur in *The More the Merrier* (1943), a comedy about the Washington wartime housing shortage and possibly the best example of Stevens's leisurely, charming approach to romantic comedy. Then, in a one-picture loan-out to MGM, Stevens entered the annals of film history by directing Katharine Hepburn and Spencer Tracy in their first film together, *Woman of the Year* (1942), at Hepburn's request. Except for a few slack and overly sentimental sections, he meshed the disparate personalities into a winning team.

Following World War II and a brief return to RKO to

direct Irene Dunne in a long, episodic, but pleasing adaptation of the stage hit *I Remember Mama* (1948), Stevens moved on to more ambitious projects. In the fifties, he directed the three films for which he is best remembered. His adaptation of Theodore Dreiser's *An American Tragedy* into *A Place in the Sun* (1951) removed most of the sociological underpinnings of Dreiser's novel, substituting a softer psychological approach to the story of an ambitious young man (Montgomery Clift) who moves inexorably to his doom by way of a fatal combination of circumstances. Stevens created a mesmerizing *mise en scène*—his work won an Oscar—and drew first-rate performances from his actors (including a shimmeringly lovely Elizabeth Taylor as Clift's inamorata and Shelley Winters as his pathetic victim). Stevens created a classic Western—perhaps a shade self-consciously—in *Shane* (1953), a stunningly staged and even majestic re-creation of every myth about the American frontier. The long-established rituals involving the West's gunfighters, ranchers, and homesteaders took on an archetypal meaning under Stevens's confident direction. Stevens's version of Edna Ferber's novel *Giant* (1956), a long, sprawling epic about three generations of Texans, won him a second Academy Award. Now it is largely remembered as the last film of the legendary James Dean, who, as the surly, malignant ranch hand who becomes an oil baron, gives an Actors Studio performance totally at odds with the glossy Hollywood acting of the rest of the cast.

Following *Giant*, Stevens directed only a few new

films, giving each project months and sometimes years of painstaking preparation, shooting, and postproduction. He faithfully translated the moving memoir and play *The Diary of Anne Frank* (1959) to the screen, although it did not achieve the expected impact, due in part to the weak casting of Millie Perkins as Anne. (William Mellor's striking black-and-white photography contributed immensely to the mood.) Critics savaged Stevens's long and expensive Biblical epic, *The Greatest Story Ever Told* (1965), as a ponderous film with a star-filled cast (John Wayne, Charlton Heston, et al.) and a greeting-card approach that divested the story of Jesus, played by Max von Sydow, of all plausibility.

On the whole, George Stevens has succeeded in surviving the critical slings and arrows to take an honored place among the great film directors. It may be true that his status declined as his budgets increased, or that his well-known conscientiousness as a director did not always transmute into cinematic art. But his craftsmanship was undeniable—he used the entire lexicon of

ABOVE   The Greatest Story Ever Told: GEORGE STEVENS (*United Artists, 1965*). *George Stevens (at the right) directs the Last Supper, with Max von Sydow as Jesus. Stevens's Biblical epic contained some splendidly staged sequences, but the excessive length, heavy-footed pace, and distracting cameo star appearances detracted from the overall effect.*

LEFT   The Diary of Anne Frank: GEORGE STEVENS (*Fox, 1959*). *A poignant final moment as the Franks and their friends await the arrival of the Gestapo. Left to right: Richard Beymer, Diane Baker, Lou Jacobi, Gusti Huber, Millie Perkins, Joseph Schildkraut, and Shelley Winters.*

filmmaking with skill and confidence—as well as his ability to draw able performances from his actors. Many of those who worked with him would not hesitate to call him a giant.

★

ROBERT STEVENSON (1905–1986) Robert Stevenson's career as a director extended over many years; inevitably, it had its shares of highs and lows. Most of the high points came after he joined the Walt Disney organization in 1956, where he directed many cheerful, undemanding entertainments such as *The Absent-Minded Professor* (1961), *That Darn Cat* (1965), and *The Love Bug* (1969). His Disney career peaked with his direction of the delightful musical fantasy *Mary Poppins* (1964), which won high praise for its charming screenplay, lilting score, and well-executed special effects, plus an Oscar for Julie Andrews as the magical nanny. It must have helped that Stevenson was born in London. Earlier, in the forties, Stevenson directed respectable versions of familiar stories, including that perennial tear-jerker *Back Street* (1941), highlighted by Margaret Sullavan's glowing performance as the somewhat masochistic mistress of Charles Boyer, and Charlotte Brontë's *Jane Eyre* (1944),

featuring a suitably flamboyant performance by Orson Welles as Mr. Rochester.

★

... it was like seeing a corpse in a graveyard. I found it in its narrow casket among plenty of dust and a terrible stink. I found a thin part of the backbone and a little bone of the shoulder. And, naturally, I became sick, it made me very sick because I had worked on this film for two years of my life, without any salary. ERICH VON STROHEIM, on seeing the truncated version of *Greed* for the first time, in Andrew Sarris, ed., *Interviews with Film Directors* (New York: The Bobbs-Merrill Company, 1967), p. 434.

ERICH VON STROHEIM (1885–1957) The face on the screen is that of a Prussian officer, thin-lipped, hard, cruel, and vindictive, with one monocled eye gazing contemptuously upon a corruptible world. This was the

© Walt Disney Productions

ABOVE The Merry Widow: ERICH VON STROHEIM *(MGM, 1925). John Gilbert engages "merry widow" Mae Murray in a steamy dance. Stroheim transformed the popular musical comedy into a bizarre film drenched in decadence.*
LEFT Mary Poppins: ROBERT STEVENSON *(Buena Vista, 1964). Julie Andrews starred as P. L. Travers's sensible, magical nanny in Walt Disney's enchanting fantasy. Dick Van Dyke played her chimney sweep friend Bert, and Karen Dotrice and Matthew Garber were her winsome charges.*

face of the actor that American audiences in World War I came to know as "The Man You Love to Hate." But there were other faces that Erich von Stroheim showed to or hid from the world, and they were all part of this fascinating and enigmatic figure. There was the illusionary Stroheim, who chose to invent a history for himself. There was the private Stroheim, who married three times, twice briefly and disastrously. There was the profligate Stroheim, who enraged and antagonized studio heads by spending staggering sums on his films and whose efforts were seldom released without severe cuts. There was the actor Stroheim, who could suggest subtle, often disturbing nuances within the limitations of his persona. But above all, there was the director Stroheim, the reckless, supremely talented, and deeply influential man who looms large in film history.

Early in his career, Stroheim had created the myth that he was a member of a distinguished Prussian royal family and that he had served with distinction as an officer in the cavalry. In truth, he was the son of a Jewish hatter who had settled in Vienna, where Stroheim was born. And although he had served briefly in the Austro-Hungarian army, he had never been a cavalry officer. Everyone agrees, however, that he immigrated to America somewhere between 1906 and 1909 and arrived in Hollywood in 1914. There he became a regular member of

D. W. Griffith's company, working at various jobs before taking on, in 1917, the kind of film role with which he became identified: the sneering, sardonic Prussian officer. Audiences readily took to hissing at this monocled madman.

When the war ended, rendering obsolete Stroheim's kind of role (no more Huns required), he turned to directing. His first film, *Blind Husbands* (1919), immediately set the mold for his future efforts. Acting not only as director but also as scenarist, set designer, and leading player, he created a film that was remarkably subtle and sophisticated for its time, as well as rich in the sort of intricate detail in settings and costumes that would become associated with his films. A triangle drama about a Prussian officer (Stroheim) who makes advances to an American doctor's wife, it did not shrink from suggesting the wife's sexual frustration. Strong sexual overtones also figured in Stroheim's next two films, *The Devil's Pass Key* (1919) and *Foolish Wives* (1921), which continued to deal with the romantic dalliances of neglected wives.

Foolish Wives was Stroheim's first major film, as well as the first to suffer from the director's wild and unchecked extravagance. Among many outrageous demands, he insisted that the studio build a life-size replica of Monte Carlo, and the rumor persists that he wanted the sol-

diers to wear the correct underwear under their uniforms. The studio subjected this film—and all of his subsequent films—to heavy editing. Although it was hugely successful and influential (it inspired Jean Renoir to become a filmmaker), Stroheim was fired for overspending by Irving Thalberg, Universal's young production head, midway through the filming of his next movie, *Merry-Go-Round*. Thalberg genuinely admired Stroheim's talent but deplored his excesses and tantrums.

Ironically, Stroheim found himself working for Thalberg again on his next production, *Greed* (1924), when the Goldwyn Studios, where he had worked on the film for some time, merged with the Metro Company and named Thalberg as its production chief. The complex story of what happened to Stroheim's legendary masterwork has been told many times, and with many variations and discrepancies. The one clear fact is that it was reduced from forty-two reels to ten, and this version is all that remains. However, even in its mutilated form it is a work of awesome power, a corrosive study of lives destroyed by unbridled greed. Stroheim depicted the sordid lives of a group of lower-middle-class Americans with unblinking honesty, and he portrayed sexual desire in a blunt fashion that could only have outraged the moralists of the day. He also drew from ZaSu Pitts, later wasted as a fluttery comedienne, an astonishing performance as the protagonist's money-obsessed and doomed young wife.

While the raging controversy over *Greed* weakened Stroheim's position with producers, he managed to make one more film for MGM. *The Merry Widow* (1925), to the studio's dismay, turned out to be a dark-hued comedy with intimations of perversion and debauchery. (The critic for the *New York Times* remarked that the film was "not a production to which one ought to take those who have finer sensibilities.") Stroheim followed *The Merry Widow* with *The Wedding March* (1928), another tale of decadent life in old Vienna during the declining Hapsburg empire. Later that year, his proclivities resulted in an aborted venture called *Queen Kelly* (1928). Angered by Stroheim's excessive style and spending habits, Gloria Swanson, who was both producer and star, fired him in the middle of production.

Greed: ERICH VON STROHEIM (*Goldwyn, 1924*). McTeague (Gibson Gowland) beats his wife Trina (ZaSu Pitts) when she refuses to turn over her money. Stroheim's masterwork fell prey to the cutter's shears, yet even in its truncated version, it remains a powerfully corrosive film, astonishing in its naturalistic detail.

At the beginning of the sound era, Stroheim completed one talking film, *Walking Down Broadway*, in 1933, but it was shelved and later entirely reshot by Alfred Werker as *Hello Sister!* Forced to abandon directing, he returned to acting, appearing in a number of European and American productions, most notably in Jean Renoir's magnificent *Grand Illusion* (1938). His portrayal of the aristocratic German officer von Rauffenstein was a subtle variation on all the Prussians he had ever played. (Stroheim suggested to Renoir that he wear an iron corset and chin brace.) Stroheim was also memorable as Max, the reserved and enigmatic butler (as well as ex-husband and ex-director) to has-been movie queen Norma Desmond (Gloria Swanson) in Billy Wilder's diamond-hard *Sunset Boulevard* (1950). In his final years, plagued by illness and personal anxieties, he continued to take occasional film or stage roles, hoping in vain for one more director's assignment.

Whether one regards him as a martyred genius or an autocratic director without a shred of practicality or self-control, there is no doubt that Erich von Stroheim, perhaps more than any other director, edged motion pictures into the real world, using naturalistic detail to expose the dark underside of society at its highest—and lowest—levels. He strode through the film industry like (take your pick) a colossus or a blunderbuss, leaving behind footprints that many other directors have tried to fill.

★

JOHN STURGES (born 1911)   A director of many sturdy action films, John Sturges edited and directed documentaries and training films before turning to feature films in 1946. Many of his movies involve characters in jeopardy, trapped in a hostile environment from which they can escape only through violent confrontation. Thus we have Ethel Barrymore a desperate prisoner in her own home in *Kind Lady* (1951), or Barbara Stanwyck frantically trying to keep her husband from drowning while dealing with a hunted killer in *Jeopardy* (1953), or one-armed Spencer Tracy facing Robert Ryan and his hoodlums in the desert in Sturges's best-known film, *Bad Day at Black Rock* (1955). The latter film, essentially a Western in a contemporary setting, made interesting use of the wide CinemaScope screen. Sturges's vigorous Westerns, which probably contain his best work, have also ended with explosive showdowns, as the isolated but intrepid hero and his cohorts take on Indians (*Escape from Fort Bravo*, 1953), a murderous family (*Gunfight at the O.K. Corral*, 1957), or marauding bandits (*The Magnificent*

Seven, 1960). Interestingly, Sturges returned to the Wyatt Earp–Doc Holliday story of *Gunfight at the O.K. Corral* a decade later in *Hour of the Gun* (1967). In keeping with the revisionist attitude of the sixties, the later version focused on the demythification rather than the creation of a legend.

Sturges did best with scenes played at a fast, suspenseful clip; *The Great Escape* (1963), for example, is an exciting adventure film despite its length. When he had to slow down to a more measured pace he foundered, as with the heavy-handed *By Love Possessed* (1961) and his adaptation of Ernest Hemingway's *The Old Man and the Sea* (1958), in which Spencer Tracy tried gamely to inject some life into a static, one-note situation.

★

When the last dime is gone, I'll sit on the curb outside with a pencil and a ten cent notebook, and start the whole thing over again. PRESTON STURGES, in *The Book of Hollywood Quotes*, compiled by Gary Herman (London: Omnibus Press, 1979), p. 53.

PRESTON STURGES (1898–1959) Could anyone have guessed that the inventor of the first nonsmear, kissproof lipstick would become the screen's foremost satirist? Hardly. But then nothing in the life of Preston Sturges, from his unusual childhood and young manhood to his precipitous decline, could be said to have followed a straight or standard line. His life, like his movie world of charlatans, blowhards, and stammering victims, was filled with surprising turns of events. One thing is clear: at the peak of his fame, he was a unique figure in motion pictures, a writer-director (one of the first of an increasing number) who poked outrageous fun at the country's most cherished ideals and lofty pretensions.

Born in Chicago, Sturges was the son of Mary Desti, a close friend of Isadora Duncan, who was determined to make her son an "artist" as well as a success in business. At sixteen, as manager of one of the branches of his mother's cosmetics business, he invented the nonsmear lipstick. However, none of his other inventions worked, and by age thirty he considered himself an abject failure. Abruptly, Sturges decided to reverse his fortune by becoming a successful playwright. With his second play, a lively comedy called *Strictly Dishonorable* (1929), he scored a major success on Broadway. When his next three plays failed, he turned to screenwriting. With the same single-minded determination, he managed to become the author of a number of highly regarded sce-

narios, including *The Power and the Glory* (1933), a fascinating forerunner of *Citizen Kane*, and *Easy Living* (1937), a breezy Cinderella comedy with Jean Arthur.

After turning out the screenplay for a likable comedy-drama called *Remember the Night* (1940), Sturges wrote the script for *The Great McGinty*, a rowdy satirical comedy about political chicanery in the early years of the century. In another abrupt career decision, Sturges offered to sell Paramount the script for ten dollars—if the studio would let him direct it. The studio agreed, and *The Great McGinty* (1940) became a critical hit and a modest commercial success, winning an Oscar (Sturges's only one) for his funny and astringent screenplay. The story of how a hungry tramp named Dan McGinty (Brian Donlevy) rose to become a leading politician, only to end up as a bartender in a banana republic, was peppered with Sturges's sharp-edged, sardonic humor.

Sturges's next film as writer-director, *Christmas in July* (1940), told a mildly amusing story about an ambitious young man (Dick Powell) who erroneously believes he has won a radio contest. The movie took some genial

---

Bad Day at Black Rock: JOHN STURGES *(MGM, 1955). A one-armed stranger in a dusty Western town, Spencer Tracy ultimately comes into violent confrontation with coldly vicious Robert Ryan. The wide CinemaScope screen emphasized the isolation of the characters in a forbidding environment.*

jabs at America's mania for contests and its fondness for creating "instant" celebrities, but it succeeded more as an introduction to members of Sturges's stock company of players. Raymond Walburn, Franklin Pangborn, and William Demarest (who had appeared in *McGinty*) admirably embodied the unique Sturges combination of knavery, bombast, and humbug. Sturges followed this modest effort with *The Lady Eve* (1941), a romantic comedy about a beautiful cardsharp (Barbara Stanwyck) who captivates, deceives, and ultimately marries a naive young millionaire (Henry Fonda). The movie had a good number of increasingly familiar Sturgesian components, including some well-executed slapstick and a cluster of eccentric participants, such as Stanwyck's disreputable cardsharp father, "Handsome" Harry (Charles Coburn).

Sturges moved into full gear with his next film, the first to take aim at contemporary American concerns and values. One of the few Sturges comedies to blend serious and even grim ingredients with the usual amount of buffoonery, *Sullivan's Travels* (1941) championed the need—and even the importance—of comedy in an increasingly tragic world. This black-edged farce concerned a film director of fluffy comedies (Joel McCrea) who embarks on a cross-country journey disguised as a tramp to gather research for a serious film that would create "a canvas of suffering humanity." He learns—the hard and painful way—that making people laugh is as noble an endeavor as making them cry. ("It isn't much but it's better than nothing in this cockeyed caravan!") A curious mixture of solemnity and prankishness, the movie had many enthusiastic admirers.

Sturges followed this with *The Palm Beach Story* (1942), an intermittently funny romantic comedy memorable for the presence of the Ale and Quail Club, a group of rowdy millionaires who accompany the heroine (Claudette Colbert) on a train to Miami Beach. By early 1944 Sturges had returned to full-bodied satire with one of his best-remembered films, *The Miracle of Morgan's Creek*. A hectic and outrageous farce, the movie had the audacity, at a time when America was fighting a war to uphold its democratic principles, to puncture holes in some of the country's most revered institutions, including motherhood and marriage. Betty Hutton starred as a scatterbrained small-town girl who becomes pregnant by an anonymous soldier during one wild evening. (She cannot remember marrying him.) In desperate trouble, she turns to her most ardent admirer, a certified idiot named Norval (Eddie Bracken). Sturges's nose-thumbing irreverence struck a refreshingly iconoclastic note at the time.

Chinless and in a perpetual dither, Eddie Bracken also starred in Sturges's next, and in many ways best, film, *Hail the Conquering Hero* (1944). More sustained in its wit

ABOVE Hail the Conquering Hero: PRESTON STURGES (*Paramount, 1944*). *Phony "hero" Woodrow Truesmith (Eddie Bracken) is welcomed home by the townspeople, accompanied by mother Georgia Caine and girlfriend Ella Raines. Sturges's sharp-edged screenplay and direction demolished some sacred cows, especially America's unquestioning worship of its war heroes.*
LEFT Sullivan's Travels: PRESTON STURGES (*Paramount, 1941*). *Film director John L. Sullivan (Joel McCrea) begins a pilgrimage that will ultimately teach him something about life, laughter, and movie-making. Sturges wrote and directed this sly, satirical comedy-drama.*

and point of view than any other of his films, it not only took a few swipes at motherhood but also aimed at an even more sacrosanct target: America's adulation of its wartime heroes. Bracken played Woodrow Lafayette Pershing Truesmith, a 4-F misfit who is cajoled into returning home as a fake war hero. He is welcomed enthusiastically, and even put up for mayor, when events and a troubled conscience lead him to reveal the truth. Ironically, his candor only endears him further to the addled townsfolk. This ending fittingly capped a movie flavored throughout with Sturges's edge of malice and cynicism.

Hail the Conquering Hero marked Sturges's pinnacle; his subsequent films missed the corrosive wit and embracing ebullience of his early work. *The Great Moment* (1944) was a curiosity: it combined a straightforward account of the work of Dr. William Morton (Joel McCrea), the dentist who first used ether as an anesthetic, with sections of slapstick performed by Sturges's familiar cast of rowdies. In what turned out to be a one-film arrangement with Howard Hughes, Sturges wrote and directed *The Sin of Harold Diddlebock* (1947, later reedited and rereleased in 1950 as *Mad Wednesday*), one final, unsuccessful attempt by Harold Lloyd to make a successful sound film. Sturges fared much better with *Unfaithfully Yours* (1948), a clever, uneven comedy about a fiercely jealous orchestra conductor (Rex Harrison) who conjures up (in frequently funny dream sequences) various ways of disposing of his presumedly wayward—but actually innocent—wife (Linda Darnell).

Sturges's final decade was a sad one, marked by periods of inactivity and a number of potentially interesting but aborted projects. In a last film for Fox, which had produced *Unfaithfully Yours*, he made *The Beautiful Blonde from Bashful Bend* (1949), an energetic but clumsy little Technicolor farce starring Betty Grable as a sharp-shooting frontier girl who, through a series of mishaps, is forced to pose as a prim schoolmarm. His final film, *The French They Are a Funny Race* (1957), based on a French book called *The Notebooks of Major Thompson*, was a poorly received satirical comedy about the marriage of a very British major (Jack Buchanan) to a very French girl (Martine Carol).

On the whole, Preston Sturges's reputation continues to rest on the comedies he made at Paramount during his period of highest creativity—*Sullivan's Travels*, *The Miracle of Morgan's Creek*, and, especially, *Hail the Conquering Hero*. Whatever his faults—a penchant for misplaced slapstick, an inconsistency in tone, and a childish fondness for "comic" names (Hackensacker, Kocken-

locker, Swampdumper)—these films reveal Sturges as a genuine American original, a man who pointed the way for many writer-directors (Billy Wilder, John Huston, and others), and whose mocking wit and jaundiced view of our foibles in this "cockeyed caravan" mark him as the Jonathan Swift of his day, or, as Andrew Sarris aptly put it, "the Breughel of American comedy directors."

★

FRANK TASHLIN (1913–1972)   It should come as no surprise to viewers of Frank Tashlin's frenetic farces that he began his career as an animator and comic-strip artist— his movies set in motion the kinetic action and knockabout humor of a cartoon, and many of his characters display the single-stroke simplicity of the animator's pen. He turned from animation to screenwriting in the mid-forties (*The Paleface*, *The Good Humor Man*), then to direction in the early fifties. His best-known films (and best-liked by French critics, who made Tashlin a cult figure for a while) star Jerry Lewis: *Rock-a-Bye Baby* (1958), *The Geisha Boy* (1958), *Cinderfella* (1960), and others are mainly strings of comedy routines for Lewis, ranging from heavy-handed to funny, all with their share of in-

ABOVE   The Girl Can't Help It: FRANK TASHLIN (*Fox, 1956*). *Tom Ewell hands the telephone to blonde sex symbol Jayne Mansfield. Tashlin's movies, to say the least, lacked subtlety; occasionally, however, their unabashed vulgarity generated some laughs.*
OPPOSITE   The Beautiful Blonde from Bashful Bend: PRESTON STURGES (*Fox, 1949*). *Preston Sturges (left) talks over a scene with star Betty Grable. Sturges's knockabout Western farce was more frantic than funny, garnering a few laughs in the parody shoot-out at the end.*

ventive gags and flashes of parody. Some admire Tashlin's brash, vulgar farces for Fox—*The Girl Can't Help It* (1956) and *Will Success Spoil Rock Hunter?* (1957)—although their leering yet satirical approach to Jayne Mansfield would probably send some of today's more humorless feminists into either a rage or cardiac arrest. Toward the end of his career, Tashlin directed two Doris Day comedies (*The Glass Bottom Boat*, 1966; *Caprice*, 1967), leading one to conclude that his brand of slapstick may require the uninhibited antics of Jerry Lewis or the comic finesse of Tom Ewell and Tony Randall.

★

NORMAN TAUROG (1899–1981) One has to admire a director who could work with Mario Lanza, Jerry Lewis, and Elvis Presley and manage to retain his sanity or at least his equilibrium. But then, starting as a child actor with Thomas Ince must have taught Norman Taurog resilience at an early age. For four decades, Taurog was the ideal studio director, turning out scores of enjoyable, usually successful movies, whatever the studio. At Paramount in the thirties, he won an Oscar for guiding little Jackie Cooper through his first feature-length movie, *Skippy* (1931), and skimmed his way through assorted Bing Crosby and Maurice Chevalier musicals. Before joining MGM late in the decade, he directed two films for other studios: *The Adventures of Tom Sawyer* (Selznick, 1938), an appealing Technicolor version of Mark Twain's

Girl Crazy: NORMAN TAUROG (*MGM, 1943*). *Judy Garland and Mickey Rooney lead the cowboys and cowgirls in the film's rousing finale, staged by Busby Berkeley to the Gershwin song "I Got Rhythm." Taurog kept the movie lively, taking advantage of the supercharged energy of his leading players.*

story, and *Mad about Music* (Universal, 1938), one of the most pleasing of the Deanna Durbin vehicles. At MGM, brash, multitalented Mickey Rooney seemed to be Taurog's special charge; he directed the actor in five films over the years, starting with the enormously popular *Boys Town* (1938) and ending, unfortunately, with *Words and Music* (1948), in which Rooney gave a dismal performance as Lorenz Hart. Taurog also directed Judy Garland in three films, notably *Girl Crazy* (1943), with Rooney.

Toward the end of the forties, MGM launched big-voiced Mario Lanza as his generation's successor to Enrico Caruso, and it was Taurog's unenviable task to direct the wildly temperamental Lanza in his first two films, *That Midnight Kiss* (1949) and *The Toast of New Orleans* (1950). In the fifties, he returned to Paramount to direct Dean Martin and Jerry Lewis in many of their knockabout comedies, then went on to guide swivel-hipped Elvis Presley through some of his musicals. A director like Taurog is seldom honored by his peers, but he succeeded in entertaining audiences with the ease and efficiency of a genuine craftsman.

★

RICHARD THORPE (born 1896)   The amazingly productive, indefatigable Richard Thorpe had already directed many low-budget films when he joined MGM in the mid-thirties. At that "studio of the stars" for over thirty years, he honed his craft, working in all genres with enthusiasm and technical proficiency. His films tended to vary greatly in quality, the best including the artful thriller *Night Must Fall* (1937) and the sprightly musical *Three Little Words* (1950). In the thirties and forties, he mixed amiable light comedies like *Double Wedding* (1937) and *What Next, Corporal Hargrove?* (1945) with such pleasantly foolish musicals as *Two Girls and a Sailor* (1944) and *A Date with Judy* (1948). During these decades, in a steady barrage of filmmaking, he coped with the jungle bellowing of Tarzan and his animal friends, the unrelieved hamminess of Wallace Beery, and the canine capers of Lassie.

In the fifties, with larger budgets behind him, Thorpe grappled with the large-scale logistics of a series of handsome but fairly cumbersome adventure films, including *The Prisoner of Zenda* (1952), *Ivanhoe* (1952), and *Knights of the Round Table* (1954). He directed Mario Lanza in the singer's long-hoped-for dream role of *The Great Caruso* (1951); luckily, the soaring music overshadowed the inane screenplay, which bore little resemblance to the facts. In the years before his retirement in 1967, Thorpe traded mostly in youth-oriented froth such as *Fun in Acapulco* (1963), with Elvis Presley, and *The Truth about Spring* (1965), with Hayley Mills.

★

JACQUES TOURNEUR (1904–1977)   Son of the famous silent-film director Maurice Tourneur, Jacques Tourneur began directing American feature-length films in 1939, after years of working as a script clerk and editor on his father's films, as a director of French films, and as a second-unit director at MGM. (Together with Val Lewton, he directed the storming of the Bastille in *A Tale of Two Cities*, 1935.) In the early forties, he joined Lewton's horror film unit (playfully known as "The Snake Pit"), where he directed his two best-remembered films, *Cat People* (1942) and *I Walked with a Zombie* (1943). Low-keyed and chilling, these modestly produced films achieved their shock effects through implication. (People today still recall, with a delicious *frisson*, the swimming pool sequence in *Cat People*, or Frances Dee walking through the sugar-cane fields with her catatonic patient in *Zombie*.)

Tourneur's subsequent films were uneven, but there were highlights: the terrifying opening scene in *The Leop-*

Night Must Fall: RICHARD THORPE (MGM, 1937). *Crochety old Mrs. Bransom (Dame May Whitty) will later become a victim of Robert Montgomery's deceptively charming, homicidal Danny. Mrs. Bransom's frustrated niece Olivia (Rosalind Russell) already harbors her suspicions. Richard Thorpe's adaptation of Emlyn Williams's play neatly generated the requisite chills.*

as well as three others. And, on a lesser note, he directed the first major MGM Tarzan movie, *Tarzan the Ape Man* (1932). He coproduced and directed *San Francisco* (1936), one of the screen's great spectacles. Slapstick comedies, emotional dramas, historical spectacles, and lighthearted mysteries poured forth under his aegis.

Van Dyke also had an interesting early career. He was one of D. W. Griffith's assistants on *Intolerance* and began directing feature films as far back as 1917. In the late twenties, he attracted attention when he took over the direction of *White Shadows of the South Seas* from Robert J. Flaherty. The film, one of the first to combine a fictional story with documentary footage, was followed by two Van Dyke films of the same kind: the crude but still exciting *Trader Horn* (1931) and *Eskimo* (1933). His major credits all lay ahead, however, and they were to be an enjoyable lot.

★

CHARLES VIDOR (1900–1959)   A proficient but uninspired director, Budapest-born Charles Vidor is perhaps best remembered as the director of Rita Hayworth's two most representative films, *Cover Girl* (1944) and *Gilda* (1946). *Cover Girl* owes much more to Hayworth's sheer spectacular presence and Gene Kelly's inventive dancing than to Vidor's tepid run-through of the plot, and we remember Hayworth's sexy "Put the Blame on Mame" number in *Gilda* long after the delirious erotic melodrama guided by Vidor has faded from memory. Still, Vidor chalked up some respectable credits over his thirty years of directing, including several small-scale but tidy thrillers (*Blind Alley*, 1939; *Ladies in Retirement*, 1941); two well-managed biographical films (*Love Me or Leave Me*, 1955, on singer Ruth Etting, and *The Joker Is Wild*, 1957, on comedian Joe E. Lewis); and a placid but attractively mounted version of Ferenc Molnár's *The Swan* (1956), with Grace Kelly.

Essentially, Vidor was a plodding director, even when he had good material at his disposal. His musical *Hans Christian Andersen* (1952), despite an attractive production and Frank Loesser's appealing score, seemed oddly enervated (unfortunately, Danny Kaye contributed to the ennui with a listless performance as the Danish author of fairy tales). His version of *A Farewell to Arms* for David O. Selznick (1957) was bloated and heavy, and Vi-

Gilda: CHARLES VIDOR *(Columbia, 1946). Lushly beautiful Gilda (Rita Hayworth) ignites the screen with her striptease to "Put the Blame on Mame." Although Vidor's moody melodrama had its share of absurdity, Hayworth was never sexier.*

dor failed to draw convincing performances out of Jennifer Jones and Rock Hudson as Hemingway's war-ravaged lovers.

★

The highest goal of a filmmaker is to entertain, to stun, to move, to enthrall—and only in a secondary sense are we here to instruct. We need not apologize for our caprices with material, our so-called "formulas," our "excesses," our unsophistication—as long as our base responsibility and motive is to make palatable and exciting entertainment for our audience.   KING VIDOR, "Me—and My Spectacle," *Films and Filming*, October 1959, p. 6.

KING VIDOR (1894–1982)   In 1915 a penniless young Texan named King Vidor arrived in California with his wife Florence to make his way in the film business. By the twenties Florence was a major star appearing in a number of successful films, and King was rising in the ranks as a promising director. (They were separated in 1923 and later divorced.) With the release of *The Big Parade* in 1925, Vidor was firmly established as one of the screen's major directors, a position he retained for nearly four decades. In projects that ranged from purely commercial to deeply personal, in films that made innovative use of cinematic techniques, he forged a distinguished career that has yet to be properly evaluated. There are qualifications that inevitably come to mind. His greatest achievements, in fact, were confined to the silent and early sound eras; some of his later films (*The Fountainhead, Ruby Gentry, Beyond the Forest*) are so deliriously intense that they teeter precariously on the edge of parody. Yet few directors could match the originality, the daring, or the innate understanding of the possibilities of film that he displayed during his peak period.

After managing his own small studio for a while, Vidor joined Metro and then Goldwyn, becoming part of the merged company of MGM in 1924. By the following year, he was ready for an important assignment, and luckily it turned out to be *The Big Parade*. One of the durable war films, it used a conventional but touching love story between an American soldier (John Gilbert) and a French peasant girl (Renee Adoree) as its center. Around their romance, Vidor constructed an epic vision of combat, using the camera expressively to capture the terror and disorientation of battle. Images of war—men falling or caught in the light of the flares—had never been so vivid or intense. Nor could filmgoers forget the agonized parting of the soldier and his beloved Melisande, probably one of the most anthologized of movie scenes.

The Big Parade catapulted Vidor into the front rank of directors, and he confirmed this status with The Crowd, released over two years later in 1928. An unusually bleak and uncompromising film, it related the plight of a young office worker (James Murray) and his wife (Eleanor Boardman) in a faceless, pitiless city where personal tragedy is treated with indifference. The Crowd achieved astonishing effects with its use of the camera to suggest the hero's coglike anonymity, his inability to make anyone aware of his pain and suffering. Vidor received his first Oscar nomination for The Crowd.

With the arrival of talking films, Vidor was anxious to experiment in exciting new ways with the juxtaposition of sound and image. The opportunity came with Hallelu-jah! (1929), the first all-black sound feature film and a dramatic musical that extended the possibilities of the new technology. Filming largely on location in Tennessee, Vidor intensified his story of murder and redemption in the Deep South by making the soundtrack (the natural noises of the swamp, the singing voices of the poor blacks) work closely with the camera's eye view of the action. Hallelujah! was a critical success—Vidor won a second Oscar nomination—although a very few noted that, despite Vidor's sincere intentions, the story had unmistakable racist overtones, showing the blacks as sexually obsessed, childlike, and fearful.

Throughout the thirties, Vidor had few opportunities to exercise his penchant for experimentation. In 1934, he

directed one of his most personal projects, a film about the plight of the American farmer entitled *Our Daily Bread*. A plea for action against the nation's agrarian ills, the movie was clearly influenced by the Soviet cinema (especially in its famous irrigation sequence) and by other filmmakers such as D.W. Griffith and F. W. Murnau. In his adaptation of Elmer Rice's play *Street Scene* (1931), Vidor used a restless mobile camera to probe every corner of the slum setting. Later in the decade, he transformed James Hilton's popular best seller *The Citadel* (1938) into a commendable film about a doctor (Robert Donat, in an excellent performance) who must recover his lost ideals. However, most of Vidor's films of the decade were smoothly rendered pulp, such as *The Champ* (1931, his third Oscar nomination), *The Wedding Night* (1935), and *Stella Dallas* (1937).

For the balance of his career in the forties and fifties, Vidor seemed to have lost much of his footing. Back at MGM in the early forties, he directed a rousing Technicolor adventure film, *Northwest Passage* (1940). He failed to make much of *Comrade X* (1940), a feeble echo of Ernst Lubitsch's *Ninotchka*; *H. M. Pulham, Esq.* (1941), a pallid version of J. P. Marquand's novel; or *An American Romance* (1944), a well-intentioned but rambling tale of an immigrant's rise to power. His most prestigious assignment came from David O. Selznick, to direct Selznick's ambitious epic Western *Duel in the Sun* (1947). Its story involved, among other things, a fierce range war, family squabbling, and, above all, a love-hate relationship so passionate and all-consuming that it ended with both parties shooting each other in a bloody encounter and dying in each other's arms. Both lurid and undeniably gripping, the movie showed Vidor's mastery of scenes of sweeping action.

Vidor's apparent fascination with steamy love affairs continued to surface in his films. However, devoid of the Western splendors of *Duel in the Sun*, all the sexual gasping and heaving revealed itself as less than compelling in such films as *Beyond the Forest* (1949), with Bette Davis as a bored, promiscuous housewife; *The Fountainhead* (1949), derived from Ayn Rand's novel, with architect Gary Cooper clutching rich girl Patricia Neal at

regular intervals; and *Ruby Gentry* (1952), in which sultry swamp girl Jennifer Jones harbors an obsessive passion for wealthy Charlton Heston.

Vidor's last few films returned him to the epic size, but not the setting, of *Duel in the Sun*. His elaborate production of *War and Peace* (1956) attempted to re-create the sweep and power of Tolstoy's novel. In some sequences, especially Napoleon's retreat from Moscow, it succeeded admirably. But the principal characters in the teeming story, played with no excess of passion by such estimable stars as Audrey Hepburn and Henry Fonda, did not come alive, their conflicts and tribulations dwarfed by the spectacle surrounding them. (The movie, however, won Vidor one last Oscar nomination.) Several years later, after directing *Solomon and Sheba* (1959), Vidor retired from filmmaking.

At the Oscar ceremonies in 1979, King Vidor received an honorary award for "his incomparable achievement as a cinematic creator and innovator." No doubt there were many in the audience who applauded with enthusiasm, recognizing that in the days when the movies were learning to find their voice, this director had dared to extend the boundaries of film and had worked to turn the new technology in the direction of a developing art. Along with other pioneers, King Vidor had helped to show them the way. The honor, and the recognition, were long overdue.

OPPOSITE   The Big Parade: KING VIDOR (MGM, 1925). *In a climactic scene from Vidor's classic war film, John Gilbert (left) curses the war that has mortally wounded his friend Karl Dane. Tom O'Brien supports the dying Dane. Vidor's battle scenes succeeded brilliantly in expressing the awesome sweep of battle.*

RIGHT   Stella Dallas: KING VIDOR (United Artists, 1937). *After watching her daughter's wedding ceremony from behind the gate, hapless Stella Dallas (Barbara Stanwyck) is asked to move along by the police. Vidor's direction gave a professional gloss to this perennially popular tear-jerker.*

every good Walsh film. And there is Walsh himself, getting the job done, and getting it right, without pretensions or illusions. Gregory Peck called Walsh "a literate, colorful roughneck," and James Cagney referred to him as "my scamp friend." He was, above all, a Hollywood original whose films, he would be glad to know, are still fun to watch.

★

CHARLES WALTERS (1911–1982)   The fact that Charles Walters's nearly two dozen musicals for MGM lack greatness should not obscure their virtues. He kept *Easter Parade* (1948) reasonably buoyant during the intervals in which Fred Astaire and Judy Garland were not diverting us with Irving Berlin's songs; he guided Leslie Caron through one of her best roles after her triumph in *An American in Paris,* as the enchanting waif *Lili* (1953), and there are those who believe that *Billy Rose's Jumbo* (1962), with its lovely Rodgers and Hart score and fetching performance by Doris Day, was somewhat better than its reviews indicated. From his first musical (*Good News,* 1947) to his last (*The Unsinkable Molly Brown,* 1964), he offered sprightly entertainment.

Unfortunately, Walters, despite his years as an actor,

dancer, and choreographer—he choreographed a number of MGM musicals in the early forties—never developed a distinctive style, nor did he have the advantage of witty books by Betty Comden and Adolph Green. (The team wrote only one screenplay for a Walters musical—*The Barkleys of Broadway,* 1949, which reunited the team of Fred Astaire and Ginger Rogers one last time—but it rivaled the RKO musicals in silliness.) On some occasions, Walters had to cope with grievous miscast-

ABOVE   Too Wise Wives: LOIS WEBER *(Paramount, 1921). Claire Windsor and Louis Calhern in a scene from Lois Weber's film. Many of Weber's films were, in a sense, early feminist tracts dealing with the role of women in society.*
LEFT   Lili: CHARLES WALTERS *(MGM, 1953). Lili (Leslie Caron), a wistful French orphan, joins a carnival where her only friends are the puppets. Walters's beguiling little musical featured the song "Hi-Lili, Hi-Lo."*
OPPOSITE   The Year of Living Dangerously: PETER WEIR *(MGM/UA, 1983). Director Peter Weir goes over a scene with his star Mel Gibson (left) during the filming of this romantic adventure.*

ing, especially in the case of *High Society* (1956), which tried to palm off Bing Crosby as an upper-crust man about town and Frank Sinatra as a chip-on-his-shoulder magazine writer. Walters's comedy films were unmemorable; the most palatable boasted actors who could rise above the material, as witness the civilized playing of Celeste Holm and David Wayne in *The Tender Trap* (1955). Curiously, three of his comedy titles sound like warning signs for city streets or parks: *Don't Go Near the Water* (1957), *Please Don't Eat the Daisies* (1960), and *Walk, Don't Run* (1966), his last film.

★

LOIS WEBER (1882–1939)   Starting as an actress in the early years of film, Lois Weber went into direction in 1912, becoming the highest-paid woman director in the world and one of the most widely respected. (At the height of her career, she was given her own studio by Universal.) Her principal goal was to dramatize moral and spiritual values in an entertaining way; she also took on controversial subjects in her films. Her most sensational movie, *Where Are My Children?* (1916), codirected with her husband, actor Phillips Smalley, dared to deal frankly with the problems of women in a changing world. This concern is reflected in many of her titles, including *To Please One Woman* (1920), *Too Wise Wives* (1921), and *What Do Men Want?* (1921). She wrote most of the films she directed.

★

PETER WEIR (born 1944)   One of the most interesting figures in the new wave of Australian directors, Peter Weir followed his first film, a black comedy called *The Cars That Ate Paris* (1974), with a movie that won international attention. *Picnic at Hanging Rock* (1975) baffled and mesmerized audiences with its moody, enigmatic tale of the disappearance of three schoolgirls and their teacher in 1900. Another fairly cryptic film, *The Last Wave* (1978), was less well received. The more straightforward—and more successful—*Gallipoli* (1981) powerfully dramatized war's waste and folly in its story of a futile World War I battle. (The final image—a freeze frame of the young soldier at the exact moment a bullet kills him—was unforgettable.) Weir moved into more commercial areas with *The Year of Living Dangerously* (1983). A melodrama set in Indonesia during the fall of the Sukarno regime, it impressed with its atmospheric view of an unstable society in turmoil but foundered somewhat in its romantic story. *Witness* (1985), his first American film, won enthusiastic notices and an Oscar nomination for its first-rate combination of suspenseful thriller and appealing love story. Harrison Ford (in a charismatic, Oscar-nominated performance) starred as a Philadelphia policeman fleeing from his corrupt and murderous colleagues into Amish country. Ford also played the leading role in Weir's 1986 adventure film *Mosquito Coast.*

263

stylized, studio-bound production and preachy ending were decidedly untypical. The underrated *Yellow Sky* (1948), a gritty little Western about a group of mismatched people at violent odds in an Arizona ghost town, was more in Wellman's style.

Most of Wellman's fifties movies were unexceptional, although a few attracted audiences (*The High and the Mighty*, 1954, in particular). Wellman tried to duplicate the cold, hard, uncompromising atmosphere of *The Ox-Bow Incident* with *Track of the Cat* (1954), a tale of a wrangling California ranch family, from another novel by Walter Van Tilburg Clark, but he was defeated by a cryptic, lumbering script that sounded too often like a parody of Eugene O'Neill. *Blood Alley* (1955) and *Darby's Rangers* (1958) were merely routine action films, as was Wellman's last film, *Lafayette Escadrille* (1958), which concerned the renowned World War I flying group. (Wellman dispelled the myth that he had flown with the Escadrille, affirming that he actually flew with a group that admired and emulated the Escadrille.)

Richard Schickel has called Wellman "an American original," and indeed he was. Originals are not required to be perfect, only different, and Wellman had his share of failed enterprises. However, his best films can still stand alone in their portrayals of men under stress— only Howard Hawks surpasses him in this regard—and in their clear-eyed if cranky view of mankind at its best and worst.

★

JAMES WHALE (1896–1957) The fact that James Whale drowned in a pool at his home under mysterious circumstances makes a strangely appropriate footnote to a career best known for films of mystery and horror. English-born Whale came to America after years of stage work as an actor, set designer, and director. After his first film—a screen version of *Journey's End* (1930), the war play he had staged in London and New York—he turned to what would become his specialty, with memorable results. *Frankenstein* (1931), *The Old Dark House* (1932), *The Invisible Man* (1933), and *The Bride of Frankenstein* (1935) are classics of the horror genre, all characterized by expressionistic touches and black humor. *The Bride of Frankenstein* is best, simultaneously funny and terrifying (and yes, occasionally touching), with an inimitable Dr. Praetorius in Ernest Thesiger.

Whale's nonhorror films (*Waterloo Bridge*, 1931; *One More River*, 1934; and others) often had the same elegance, restraint, and excellent camerawork that the hor-

independent spirit from studio to studio (MGM, more than any other); wherever he landed, his skill with actors and his ability to tell a crackling, often sardonically flavored story seldom deserted him. His penchant for dealing with groups of men under stress took him inevitably into the war and Western modes. His two World War II dramas—*The Story of G.I. Joe* (1945) and *Battleground* (1949)—can be numbered among the best in the genre. The former film, based on the reportage of journalist Ernie Pyle, paid homage to the American infantryman with a rare emotional honesty and directness. Among Wellman's Westerns of the period (*The Great Man's Lady*, 1942; *Buffalo Bill*, 1944), there was one undeniable curiosity: *The Ox-Bow Incident* (1943), from a novel by Walter Van Tilburg Clark. This was not a conventional horse opera but a chilling study of lynch-mob mentality. Its rugged, unadorned acting and its concern with a social issue were typical of Wellman, but its oddly

ABOVE The Ox-Bow Incident: WILLIAM A. WELLMAN (*Fox, 1943*). *The pathetic innocent victims (Dana Andrews, Anthony Quinn, and Francis Ford, huddled at the left) await their fate at the hands of a revenge-minded lynch mob. (Frank Conroy, right, played one of the leaders.) Wellman's bleak Western drama found little favor with the studio or with audiences.*
OPPOSITE Blood Alley: WILLIAM A. WELLMAN (*Warner Bros., 1955*). *Wellman (behind camera) directs a scene for this adventure film concerning a ship's captain (John Wayne) who leads several hundred Chinese to freedom from Communist domination. Wellman worked best with films that focused on characters much like himself: rough-hewn men of action.*

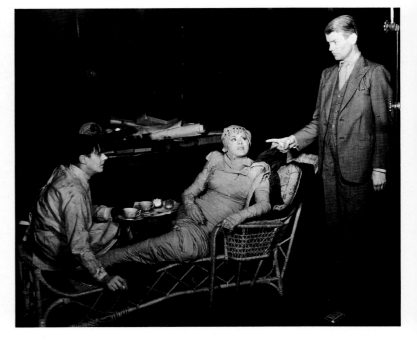

ror films displayed, the most durable being his 1936 version of *Show Boat*. Much superior to the other two versions, this *Show Boat* captured most of the sentiment, charm, and musical splendor of the classic Jerome Kern –Oscar Hammerstein musical, with a superlative cast headed by Irene Dunne, Allan Jones, Helen Morgan, and Paul Robeson. In the early forties, Whale retired from films in order to paint.

★

Listen, every career has its ups and downs. It's just that in our business it goes a little faster. One year you're on the* New York Times *Ten Best Pictures List and the next year you're one of the Hundred Neediest Cases. BILLY WILDER, interview with Jon Bradshaw in *New York,* cited in *Action,* January–February 1976, p. 32.

BILLY WILDER (born 1906)   Since his American debut as a director in 1942, Billy Wilder has been variously characterized as witty, caustic, cynical, and outrageous, a man who delights in exposing the dark side of the American dream or skewering the nation's foibles and prejudices, usually with laughter. In Wilder's world, an

LEFT   The Invisible Man: JAMES WHALE *(Universal, 1933). The innkeeper Mrs. Hall (Una O'Connor) shrieks at the sight of Jack Griffin (Claude Rains), who is trying to hide his invisible status from the world. In his curious film debut, Rains was seen only briefly, at the end of the film.*
RIGHT   The Bride of Frankenstein: JAMES WHALE *(Universal, 1935). Director Whale (right) relaxes on the set with his stars Colin Clive and Elsa Lanchester, who is appropriately garbed as the Bride. Whale's mixture of humor and horror made this sequel to his original* Frankenstein *a uniquely satisfying example of the genre.*

insurance salesman will deal in murder, a Hollywood writer will gladly prostitute himself for the Big Chance, and a newspaper reporter will risk the life of a helpless man to get the Big Story. Even the comic characters in Wilder's movies often behave in venal, corrupt, and self-serving ways.

Whatever the perceptions of Billy Wilder that have accumulated for well over forty years, he can safely be regarded as one of the screen's finest and most original directors. And yet the critical consensus on his work has often been less than favorable. Andrew Sarris has written that "all of Wilder's films decline in retrospect because of visual and structural deficiencies" (*The American Cinema,* p. 166). Back in 1951, Penelope Houston commented that Wilder "seems to lack the powers of analysis which his cold, observant style demands" (*Sight & Sound,* June 1951). Throughout the fifties and sixties, review after review deplored his ruthless cynicism, profound misanthropy, or sheer tastelessness. Wilder himself has not been unaffected by these attacks, and not even the effusions of a gala celebration of his achievements by the Film Society of Lincoln Center in 1982 could diminish his wry understanding of his status. ("People say, 'It wasn't your year.' Well, it hasn't been my decade.") Still, not even the most jaundiced of critics could be immune to the durable brilliance of Billy Wilder's greatest films.

Born in Sucha, Austria (now part of Poland), Wilder studied briefly at the University of Vienna before becoming a newspaper reporter known for his dogged persistence in getting interviews. He moved to Berlin, where he established an even greater reputation as an aggressive crime reporter and a popular man about town. Attracted by the movies, he began writing silent film scenarios, finally scoring a success with *People on Sunday* (*Menschen am Sonntag*, 1929), which boasted a stellar number of future filmmakers among its credits. Wilder wrote the screenplay with Curt Siodmak, the film was codirected by Robert Siodmak and Edgar Ulmer, and it was photographed by Fred Zinnemann and Eugen Schüfftan (later Eugene Shuftan). With Hitler's rise to power, Wilder, who is Jewish, fled to Paris, where he coscripted and codirected a film called *Mauvaise Graine* in 1933.

Wilder finally reached Hollywood, his ultimate destination, in 1934. After a few impecunious years, he succeeded in acquiring a writer's contract at Paramount. Here, after working for a while on his own, he teamed up with the suave, courtly Charles Brackett, an unlikely but fruitful collaboration that resulted in some of the best screenplays of the late thirties and early forties, including the sparkling screwball comedy *Midnight* (1939), the classic comedy *Ninotchka* (1939), and the romantic drama *Hold Back the Dawn* (1941). When Wilder turned to directing, ostensibly to "protect" his screenplays from being badly mutilated by such directors as Mitchell Leisen (they shared a mutual dislike), Brackett became his producer, and the team continued to write together. Their first film, *The Major and the Minor* (1942), was a cheerful if none too credible comedy about a young woman (Ginger Rogers) who disguises herself as a twelve-year-old. Major Ray Milland's bewildered attraction to "little" Miss Rogers gave an early example of Wilder's penchant for touching on potentially dangerous areas of humor.

A hit at the box office, *The Major and the Minor* launched Wilder in his director's career, but it in no way foreshadowed the kind of film he would make throughout the forties. Little humor, except of the harsh and mordant kind, graced his *film noir* masterpiece *Double Indemnity* (1944), which Wilder wrote with Raymond Chandler. Adapted from James M. Cain's novel, the film is a model of its kind, a hard-edged melodrama of sleazy passion and cold-blooded murder, played to perfection

by Barbara Stanwyck as the definitive *femme fatale* and Fred MacMurray, brilliantly cast against type, as her willing accomplice and ultimate victim. Wilder had an even greater success the following year with *The Lost Weekend* (1945), a bold (for its time) drama on the torments of an alcoholic writer (Ray Milland), derived from Charles Jackson's novel. Graphic and unsparing, the film made Paramount's executives uneasy, but it was released to great acclaim, winning the Oscar as Best Picture. Milland also won, as did Wilder (as director and cowriter with Brackett).

ABOVE Double Indemnity: BILLY WILDER (*Paramount, 1944*). *Barbara Stanwyck lures unwitting insurance agent Fred MacMurray into her spider's web. The ultimate film noir, Wilder's adaptation of James M. Cain's novel chilled audiences with its unvarnished tale of treachery and murder.*
RIGHT The Lost Weekend: BILLY WILDER (*Paramount, 1945*). *Ray Milland finds himself compelled to take one more drink. Wilder directed and coauthored (with Charles Brackett) this grim drama of an alcoholic writer, startling audiences with the unsparing realism of its details.*

Wilder was riding high, and after *A Foreign Affair* (1948), a comedy that provoked some hostility with its cynical view of the American postwar presence in Berlin, he reached a career peak with the 1950 release of his scathing and masterly *Sunset Boulevard.* The storm of protest and controversy that often broke over a Wilder film rose to a peak of intensity over this Hollywood story steeped in acid, about a once-great, now-deranged film star and her young, opportunistic lover. The abrasive, satirical Wilder-Brackett script gave no quarter to the Hollywood dream factory, and the performances of Gloria Swanson and William Holden as the distinctly odd couple (also Erich von Stroheim as the star's loyal butler and ex-husband) stunned with their unsparing honesty. The movie received eleven Oscar nominations, winning only for its art direction and its story and screenplay. It was Wilder's last collaboration with Brackett.

The harshness of *Sunset Boulevard* looked mild, however, compared with *Ace in the Hole* (also known as *The Big Carnival,* 1951), Wilder's vitriolic view of opportunistic journalism, in which reporter Kirk Douglas deliberately exploits the plight of a man trapped in a cave-in. The film's unrelieved nastiness proved too much for audiences, who gave Wilder his first major failure. Through the balance of the fifties, Wilder worked in a much lighter vein, turning out comedies that ranged from blithe (*Sabrina,* 1954, a modern-day fairy tale marred by the miscasting of the male leads) and sophisticated (*Love in the Afternoon,* 1957, with Gary Cooper and Audrey Hepburn) to the other end of the spectrum (*The Seven Year Itch,* 1955, a version of the Broadway hit that was spoiled by the censorship strictures of the day). Wilder also presented smoothly professional entertainments such as *Stalag 17* (1953), a popular prisoner-of-war comedy-drama that won an Oscar for William Holden, and Agatha Christie's devilishly clever courtroom thriller *Witness for the Prosecution* (1958), which had audiences reeling with its triple-surprise ending.

These were, for the most part, agreeable films, but they gave little scope to the masterly Wilder, who only resurfaced at the close of the fifties with his classic comedy, *Some Like It Hot* (1959). A howlingly funny movie set in the twenties, it concerned two band musicians (Tony Curtis and Jack Lemmon) who, disguised as women, join an all-girl band to escape execution by the mob. (Marilyn Monroe was its luscious, tippling singer.) Behind the copious laughter (and the jokes and comic situations never let up), Wilder once again flirted with dangerous areas for a comedy, including transvestism, sexual impotence, and gangland mass murder. Any unsavory implications, however, were submerged in the general hilarity, much of it contributed by Lemmon's marvelously manic performance and by veteran Joe E. Brown as a lecherous old millionaire. Wilder followed *Some Like It Hot* with another major success. A comedy with a distinctly sour aftertaste, *The Apartment* (1960) attempted to make a hero of an office worker (Jack Lemmon) who seeks advancement in business by lending his apartment to company executives for sexual assignations. The adroit screenplay by Wilder and I. A. L. Diamond (Wilder's talented collaborator since 1957) and engaging performances by Lemmon and Shirley MacLaine did much to conceal the basically distasteful nature of the enterprise. The movie and Wilder received Academy Awards, and Wilder shared a writing Oscar with Diamond.

For all their considerable merit, none of Wilder's subsequent films matched his earlier efforts in critical or popular appeal, although several (such as *The Private Life of Sherlock Holmes,* 1970) warrant greater attention. Earli-

---

OPPOSITE Some Like It Hot: BILLY WILDER *(United Artists, 1959). Billy Wilder (in white cap and glasses) directs Tony Curtis and Marilyn Monroe in a scene from the movie. One of the funniest comedies ever made, the film hurtled through its gags, double entendres, and farcical situations with gleeful abandon under Wilder's skilled direction.*

RIGHT The Apartment: BILLY WILDER *(United Artists, 1960). Jack Lemmon and Shirley MacLaine in a scene from Billy Wilder's acerbic, award-winning comedy. Lemmon's weak, opportunistic hero finds reformation in love, yet the change comes somewhat too late to make him entirely sympathetic.*

er themes and interests cropped up again: in such comedies as *One, Two, Three* (1961) and *Avanti!* (1972), Wilder further explored his fascination with the clash of American and European cultures that he initially revealed in *A Foreign Affair*. He continued to attack the crassness and greedy opportunism of human behavior in such films as *Kiss Me, Stupid* (1964), a comedy with very few champions that brought down the wrath of a "Condemned" rating from the Catholic Church's Legion of Decency, and *The Fortune Cookie* (1966), which won a supporting Oscar for Walter Matthau as Jack Lemmon's scheming brother-in-law, who involves him in a fraudulent lawsuit. In recent years, Wilder teamed these two actors in perfunctory and surprisingly routine films (*The Front Page*, 1974; *Buddy Buddy*, 1981).

The disparaging critical remarks notwithstanding (he has been called "a curdled Lubitsch, romanticism gone sour"), Billy Wilder ranks high in the echelon of film directors. (The American Film Institute confirmed this assessment by awarding Wilder its Life Achievement Award in 1986.) Few writer-directors have proved as capable of matching the wit of their screenplays with the dexterity of their directing style. Few filmmakers have succeeded in creating such a memorable gallery of grasping, greedy cheats, fools, and swindlers. And if Wilder's sentiment sometimes tastes like Viennese whipped cream turned slightly rancid, it can also be said that, on occasion, he has been able to keep the romanticism pure and simple, as witness Audrey Hepburn's starry-eyed heroines of *Sabrina* and *Love in the Afternoon*.

Billy Wilder once remarked, "To be a good director, one has to know the script, and then, to be like a general under fire. The screenplay is the battle plan. The filming is when the bullets are flying" (in Zolotow, *Billy Wilder in Hollywood*, p. 131). On the whole, he has survived the Hollywood wars with distinction.

★

ROBERT WISE (born 1914) Take three directors. The first was responsible for *The Body Snatcher*, a small masterwork of horror, modest in scope but rich in evocative detail. The second directed the finest boxing film ever made, a compact little drama called *The Set-Up*. The third codirected what is arguably the greatest film musical of the sixties, the towering adaptation of the Leonard Bernstein–Stephen Sondheim stage success, *West Side Story*. These are impressive credits for three directors—and triply impressive for one. The man behind the camera in all three films was, of course, Robert Wise.

A consummate craftsman who has worked in a variety of styles and dimensions, Wise started in films as an assistant cutter at RKO, finally becoming one of the studio's most accomplished editors. As an editor of Orson Welles's two classics, *Citizen Kane* (1941) and *The Magnificent Ambersons* (1942), he played a crucial role in carrying out Welles's innovative concepts. He honed his skill further with such films as William Dieterle's *All That Money Can Buy* (1941), a budget-conscious but striking adaptation of "The Devil and Daniel Webster," and Richard Wallace's *The Fallen Sparrow* (1947). His first assignment as a director came when he replaced Gunther von Fritsch on an intriguing thriller about the fantasy world of children, foolishly titled *The Curse of the Cat People* (1944) to cash in on Jacques Tourneur's earlier success, *Cat People*. As a new member of Val Lewton's horror film unit, Wise also directed *The Body Snatcher* (1945), a macabre tale of a nineteenth-century Edinburgh doctor (Henry Daniell) in thrall to an odious, blackmailing grave robber (Boris Karloff).

Wise directed other good films at RKO, including a surprisingly nasty *film noir* entitled *Born to Kill* (1947). His best film before leaving the studio was his last. A trim drama about one crucial evening in the life of a broken-down fighter (Robert Ryan), *The Set-Up* (1949) exposed the brutal side of the boxing game without resorting to histrionics. It featured grittily real boxing footage and a strong performance by Robert Ryan as Stoker Thompson.

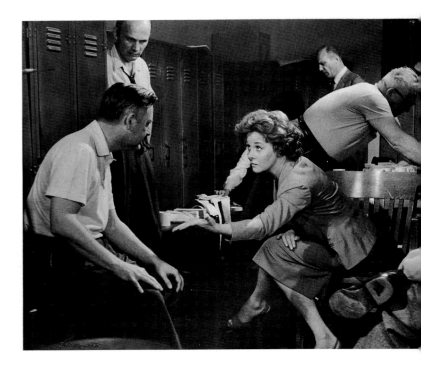

At Fox, MGM, and other studios in the fifties, Wise directed a number of solidly entertaining films that included the perennial science-fiction favorite *The Day the Earth Stood Still* (1951); the multistar business drama *Executive Suite* (1954); and *Somebody Up There Likes Me* (1956), with Paul Newman as boxer Rocky Graziano. The last film, while glossier and more expansive than *The Set-Up*, lacked the condensed power of the earlier movie. Toward the end of the decade, Wise directed Susan Hayward in a fierce, harrowing (and Oscar-winning) performance as condemned murderess Barbara Graham in *I Want to Live!* (1958). Hayward's bravura acting enhanced Wise's effective handling of the explosive subject matter.

By the sixties, Wise had traveled a vast distance from his days at RKO with their restricted budgets. His first production of the decade, codirected with Jerome Robbins, was *West Side Story* (1961): a brilliantly conceived and elaborately staged musical drama, it used *Romeo and Juliet* as the springboard for its story of two warring New York street gangs. From its justly famous opening sequence, in which the camera swooped down from an aerial view of the city to zoom in on gang members dancing down a slum street, to its somber climax, *West Side Story* electrified the screen. Leonard Bernstein's soaring

music, Jerome Robbins's exciting dances, and an exemplary cast headed by Natalie Wood and Rita Moreno all came together under Wise's able guidance. The film won that year's Oscar, as did Wise and Robbins.

Undoubtedly Wise's finest achievement in the sixties, *West Side Story* could never hope to match the popularity of the film he directed four years later. *The Sound of Music* (1965) was a phenomenon—a widely loved and extraordinarily successful film version of the Rodgers and Hammerstein stage musical that had delighted audiences for years. Filmgoers responded with enthusiasm, tolerating the treacly, synthetic story of the Austrian Trapp Family Singers and the young novitiate Maria who becomes their guiding star and concentrating on the melodious score, the lovely scenery, and Julie Andrews's captivating, wisely sensible performance as Maria that muted some of the heavy sentiment and coyness. Although

ABOVE The Sound of Music: ROBERT WISE *(Fox, 1965). Julie Andrews as the mischievous Maria sings the title song in the justifiably famous opening of this immensely popular musical. The lilting score by Rodgers and Hammerstein did much to offset the movie's treacly story and dialogue.*
OPPOSITE I Want to Live!: ROBERT WISE *(United Artists, 1958). Susan Hayward gets instruction from director Robert Wise (seated at left). Wise guided Hayward to an Academy Award in this harrowing true drama of a woman condemned to the gas chamber.*

Wise would have no greater box-office hit in the sixties (or in any other decade, for that matter), he made several other notable films during that period. *The Haunting* (1963), a bizarre tale of the supernatural, proved that the director had not fully surrendered his franchise on the low-key, small-scale horror film. *The Sand Pebbles* (1966), an ambitious but only intermittently successful film about America's involvement in China in the mid-twenties, offered an excellent performance by Steve McQueen as a sailor; unfortunately, the movie was overlong and diffuse. *Star!* (1968), a rambling account of the life of actress Gertrude Lawrence, played by Julie Andrews, turned out to be a disappointment. The lavish musical numbers made up in part for the weak narrative.

Wise appeared to run out of steam in the seventies. *The Hindenburg* (1975), his elaborate dramatization of the 1934 air disaster, won little favor with either the critics or the public; the widely touted *Star Trek—The Motion Picture* (1979), while welcomed by "trekkies," was judged too slow and cumbersome for general audiences, despite the well-managed special effects. On a much smaller scale, the scenic *Two People* (1973), a romantic drama about a fashion model (Lindsay Wagner) and a Vietnam deserter (Peter Fonda), had little substance behind its story; *Audrey Rose* (1977), which concerned a young girl who may or may not be possessed by the spirit of a dead child, failed to repeat Wise's previous success with tales of lurking terror.

Despite these lapses, Robert Wise can surely be numbered among the distinguished film directors who brought skill and creativity to projects large and small.

★

SAM WOOD (1883–1949) Sam Wood qualifies as a Neglected Director. It may be that his many craftsmanlike, entertaining films for MGM and other studios do not call for detailed critical comment, or it may be that his extreme right-wing politics alienated those who might choose to write about him. Yet he warrants closer attention if only for such movies as *A Night at the Opera* (1935), one of the Marx Brothers' best, *Goodbye, Mr. Chips* (1939), a gentle exercise in Anglophile sentiment, which

won Robert Donat a well-deserved Oscar, *Our Town* (1940), and *Kings Row* (1942). The fact that he ably handled such disparate views of small-town life as *Our Town* (bittersweet nostalgia, coated with cosmic meaning) and *Kings Row* (where the local activities include incest and sadism) attests to the skill he honed as a director since the twenties.

Wood gave his considerable best to virtually every kind of film: unbridled farce (*A Day at the Races*, 1937), equally unbridled sentimental drama (*Stablemates*, 1938), comedy (*The Devil and Miss Jones*, 1941), and war movie (*Command Decision*, 1949). Occasionally he directed films that epitomized the personae of their leading players: Ginger Rogers's wry, common-sense attitude (which always brought Fred Astaire down to earth) was particularly apt for Christopher Morley's working-class heroine *Kitty Foyle* (1940; she won an Oscar), and Gary Cooper solidified his brave, humble American stance as doomed ballplayer Lou Gehrig in *The Pride of the Yankees* (1942). Cooper fared less well under Wood's direction in such films as the ambitious but muddled Hemingway drama *For Whom the Bell Tolls* (1943) and the overfancy *Saratoga Trunk* (made in 1943, released in 1946), both with a ravishing Ingrid Bergman. Wood's well-honed professionalism and his ability to evoke honest sentiment is evident throughout his next-to-last film, *The Stratton Story* (1949), concerning the ordeal of baseball player Monty Stratton (James Stewart), who lost his leg in an accident.

RIGHT A Night at the Opera: SAM WOOD *(MGM, 1935). The Marx Brothers (Groucho, Chico, and Harpo) assemble with the police and the imperious Margaret Dumont at the climax of this wild-and-woolly farce. No director dared to tame the lunatic brothers, and Wood was no exception.*
OPPOSITE The Pride of the Yankees: SAM WOOD *(RKO, 1942). A fatally ill Lou Gehrig (Gary Cooper) prepares to address the adoring crowd with his poignant final words. Cooper's stoic, reticent acting style meshed well with Wood's unobtrusive craftsmanship.*

★

I have a theory: It is not to bore the audience. That's a good theory. It sometimes seems that all pictures are too long, mine included, but this is always what I try to avoid. That's why we have previews. If we see the film getting slow or somebody falling asleep or walking out, then you try to correct something to keep the interest up. WILLIAM WYLER, "Dialogue on Film," *American Film*, April 1976, p. 52.

WILLIAM WYLER (1902–1981) The legend of William Wyler as director has two facets. One is the personal Wyler, the demanding, unrelenting, whip-cracking director who insisted on countless takes and who was the scourge of actors. The other facet (and it is, of course, much more important) is that of the Wyler whose fuming and fussing, as well as dauntless perfectionism, produced a remarkable number of durable films. One of the screen's most distinguished, most thoroughly professional directors, William Wyler was a meticulous craftsman who, in movie after movie, deftly melded every aspect of film into memorable images.

Wyler did it all: family dramas, Westerns, romantic comedies, costume spectacles, edge-of-the-seat thrillers, and one elaborate musical. He transformed classic novels and popular plays into films that took on their own vibrant life away from the printed page or the prosceni-

um arch. Whatever the genre or whatever the source, Wyler revealed an uncommon understanding of the human condition and of the dreams and disappointments woven into the fabric of existence. While he was born in Alsace (then part of Germany) to Swiss-German-Jewish parents, Wyler absorbed the American dream, and he invested the characters who move through such films as *Dodsworth, The Best Years of Our Lives,* and *Friendly Persuasion* with a convincing native shrewdness, honesty, and integrity.

Wyler was brought to New York in 1920 by his mother's cousin Carl Laemmle, then head of Universal Pictures. Within a year he came to Hollywood to learn the craft of filmmaking from the bottom up. By 1925 he had risen to become an assistant director with substantial credits, and not long afterward he began directing two-reel Westerns, most notably a third version of Peter B. Kyne's story "The Three Godfathers," this one called *Hell's Heroes* (1929), as well as more prestigious sound films. In his first important credit, *Counsellor-at-Law* (1933), an adaptation of Elmer Rice's play about a troubled New York lawyer (John Barrymore), Wyler demonstrated his continually developing grasp of the medium by moving the camera in and out of an expanded stage set rather than "opening up" the story in the usual—and usually ineffective—fashion. Also for Universal, Wyler directed a charming romantic comedy, *The Good Fairy* (1935), written by Preston Sturges; it starred Margaret Sullavan, who became Wyler's first wife.

That year, Wyler left Universal to direct his first film for Samuel Goldwyn, who had seen and admired Wyler's last Universal movie, *The Gay Deception* (1935). *These Three* (1936), adapted from Lillian Hellman's stage drama *The Children's Hour,* avoided the censor's scissors by changing the well-known central theme of lesbianism (a malicious student accuses two women teachers of having an affair) to a conventional romantic triangle. The spirit of the play remained intact, and the film worked beautifully, due not only to Wyler's adroit direction but also to Gregg Toland's subtle photography and superb performances by Merle Oberon and Miriam Hopkins as the teachers and little Bonita Granville as their tormenter.

These Three marked the beginning of a long and often bristling relationship with Samuel Goldwyn: an inevitable clash of two strong-willed men who insisted on controlling all aspects of their productions. Creatively, the collaboration was fruitful, producing a series of outstanding motion pictures that set a hallmark for smooth craftsmanship and solid professionalism for years to come. These films had several elements in common: a superior screenplay, a rich and fastidiously detailed production, and top-drawer performances—all skillfully blended by Wyler. *Dodsworth* (1936) turned Sinclair Lewis's novel and Sidney Howard's stage adaptation (Howard himself wrote the screenplay) into an incisive, intelligent drama of a deteriorating marriage, with Wyler drawing peerless performances from Walter Huston, Ruth Chatterton, and Mary Astor. *Dead End* (1937) boasted an astonishing New York set by Richard Day and a fine ensemble performance by a cast (Joel McCrea, Sylvia Sidney, Humphrey Bogart) that fully realized Sidney Kingsley's social drama of slum life. Wyler climaxed this productive decade with a film version of Emily Brontë's *Wuthering Heights* (1939) that is usually numbered among Hollywood's great films. A hauntingly lovely and moving romantic drama, it captured much of the novel's feverish intensity under Wyler's expert direction. As the ferocious Heathcliff, young Laurence Olivier demonstrated a riveting power and appeal. (He claimed for many years that Wyler made him realize his potential as a film actor.)

During this period, Wyler enjoyed (or perhaps endured) a special relationship with Bette Davis. As with Wyler and Goldwyn, it was a clash of strong wills, but the results usually warranted the conflict. Wyler first directed her in *Jezebel* (1938), a floridly romantic drama of the Old South that gave the actress one of her best roles as the willful belle Julie (very much like Scarlett O'Hara)

and her second Academy Award. She reached the top of her form as the lying adulteress who meets her fate in the Malayan moonlight in *The Letter* (1940). Wyler made this powerful drama of murder and deception based on Somerset Maugham's story and play into a masterly study of muted passion exploding into violence. The Wyler-Davis collaboration climaxed with the film version of Lillian Hellman's play *The Little Foxes* (1941). Wyler directed Hellman's corrosive examination of a vicious Southern family with a dexterity and a precision that still impress, and Gregg Toland's deep-focus photography captured every nuance, every revealing detail. Once again, the acting was perfection, with Patricia Collinge leading all the other cast members as the cowed, alcoholic Birdie.

Before he left for service in World War II (as head of an air force combat camera crew), Wyler directed one last film, which became his most popular effort to date. Hollywood's tribute to the indomitability of the British in wartime, *Mrs. Miniver* (1942) moved American audiences to admiration and tears (the British themselves found it painfully unreal and patronizing). The film received the Academy Award, as did Wyler, Greer Garson (as the stalwart Kay Miniver), and Teresa Wright (as her ill-fated daughter-in-law). Wyler returned from the service, where he had made several well-regarded documentaries, to direct one last film for Sam Goldwyn—*The Best Years of Our Lives* (1946), generally acknowledged to be Wyler's finest. Derived from Mackinlay Kantor's novel *Glory for Me*, the film was an observant and deeply felt study of the problems faced by three returning veterans (Fredric March, Dana Andrews, and Harold Russell, who had actually lost his hands in the war). Sensitively written and played, with only a few lapses into sentimentality, it became virtually an emblem of its time and place. It won a number of Oscars, including a second one for Wyler.

Wyler continued to turn out solid and impressive films, mostly for Paramount, that benefited from his incisive direction. He demonstrated his skill with actresses by directing one veteran and one fledgling actress in Os-

LEFT   Wuthering Heights: WILLIAM WYLER *(United Artists, 1939). Cathy (Merle Oberon) expires, to the despair of her lover Heathcliff (Laurence Olivier). Looking on are David Niven, Donald Crisp, and Flora Robson. Although the Ben Hecht–Charles MacArthur screenplay used only part of the Brontë novel, the film had a romantic intensity, due in part to Olivier's magnetic performance as the tormented Heathcliff.*

OPPOSITE   Jezebel: WILLIAM WYLER *(Warner Bros., 1938). William Wyler instructs Bette Davis in a scene for this popular romantic melodrama. Davis, who wanted to play Scarlett O'Hara in* Gone with the Wind, *got her chance to portray another tempestuous Southern belle, and she won an Academy Award under Wyler's astute direction.*

car-winning performances. Olivia de Havilland conveyed all the vulnerability, desperation, and, ultimately, steely resilience of Henry James's spinster heroine of *Washington Square* in *The Heiress* (1949), while young Audrey Hepburn glowed as a runaway princess in her first American film, *Roman Holiday* (1953). Wyler also dealt expertly with the pungent melodrama of *Detective Story* (1951) and *The Desperate Hours* (1955) and with the sprawling Western adventure of *The Big Country* (1958).

Wyler had a special success with *Friendly Persuasion* (1956), his first film in color and a richly detailed, compassionate drama of a Quaker family's involvement in the Civil War. To close out the decade, he directed a lavish remake of *Ben-Hur* (1959)—over thirty years earlier he had been an assistant on the silent version—giving full rein to the inevitable spectacle while attempting somewhat deeper characterization than is usual in such films. Even so, the exceptionally intelligent screenplay (by Karl Tunberg and other hands, especially Christopher Fry) was submerged by the expected giant sequences, such as the breathtaking chariot race staged by Andrew Marton and Yakima Canutt. *Ben-Hur* received a record number of Oscars (eleven), including one for Wyler and the film.

If Wyler's films in the sixties lacked some of the finesse of his earlier work, they still offered rewards. He could not resist remaking *The Children's Hour* (1962) using the original lesbian theme; the result, however, did not justify the experiment. He found a much more fascinating, if somewhat stifling, subject in *The Collector*

(1965), based on John Fowles's novel about a psychotic young Englishman (Terence Stamp) who keeps a young girl (Samantha Eggar) prisoner in his cellar. Directing Barbra Streisand (a formidable task) in her film debut in *Funny Girl* (1968), he gave her the leeway to repeat her bravura stage performance as Fanny Brice. Streisand emerged as a giant star, winning the year's Academy Award in a tie with Katharine Hepburn; Wyler probably emerged with a giant headache, although he denied quarreling with her. He retired a few years later, after directing one last film, *The Liberation of L. B. Jones* (1970), a drama of racial tensions in the South.

Wyler was greatly honored in his lifetime, winning three Academy Awards and nine nominations and receiving the Irving G. Thalberg Memorial Award in 1965. In 1976 he was presented with the American Film Institute's prestigious Life Achievement Award. He has been enthusiastically praised by his peers and generally ad-

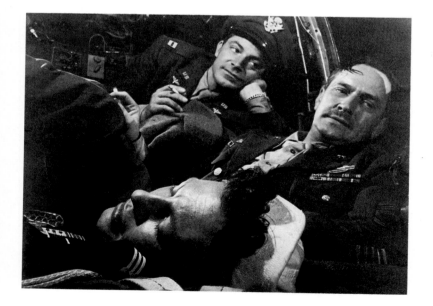

ABOVE   *The Heiress*: WILLIAM WYLER *(Paramount, 1949). Shy spinster Catherine Sloper (Olivia de Havilland) enjoys the amorous attention of her suitor Morris Townsend (Montgomery Clift). Wyler's skillful direction brought a warmth and intimacy to this adaptation of Henry James's novel* Washington Square *and its stage dramatization.*

LEFT   *The Best Years of Our Lives*: WILLIAM WYLER *(RKO, 1946). Returning home after the war, Dana Andrews, Fredric March, and Harold Russell talk about their plans and misgivings. Wyler's polished production spoke eloquently for a new generation of postwar servicemen.*

mired by critics and scholars. It is true that a dissident strain insists that Wyler is merely an expert craftsman with no personal vision and a cool emotional detachment. However, we should remember that the former charge is leveled frequently at directors who work proficiently and successfully in various styles and genres without baring their private inclinations and demons. As for emotional detachment, space cannot allow the citing of scenes and sequences in Wyler films that express deeply held feelings, played with taste and discretion. We need only recall the moment in *The Best Years of Our Lives* when Fredric March returns home, and wife Myrna Loy reacts to his presence before she sees him. It is one privileged—and emotionally satisfying—moment among many others in the films of a great director.

★

PETER YATES (born 1929) Hollywood imported English-born Peter Yates when he revealed an ability to handle fast action with the 1967 melodrama *Robbery*. Yates quickly showed his mettle with *Bullitt* (1968), a riveting crime drama starring Steve McQueen, which featured one of the most exciting car chases ever filmed. (Frank Keller's editing of the film won an Oscar.) Two other crime films, *The Hot Rock* (1972) and *The Friends of Eddie Coyle* (1973), also kept audiences attentive, although the latter ultimately turned off many viewers with its grim story of a doomed ex-convict. Yates did not fare as well when he switched genres: he was unable to

subdue Barbra Streisand's assertive (to some, abrasive) personality in the labored farce *For Pete's Sake* (1974), and the slapdash adventure film *The Deep* (1977), although audiences enjoyed it, had little to recommend it besides fine underwater photography. However, Yates scored his greatest success since *Bullitt* with *Breaking Away* (1979), an engaging and spirited movie about college-age friends in Indiana. (Steve Tesich's screenplay received an Academy Award.) In recent years, Yates's credits have been variable: he returned to the crime thriller with the twisty and gripping *Eyewitness* (1981) and drew bravura performances from Albert Finney and Tom Courtenay in *The Dresser* (1983), based on Ronald Harwood's play. On the other hand, *Krull* (1983) failed as an epic fantasy, and many reviewers judged *Eleni* (1985), based on Nicholas Gage's account of his mother's death at the hands of Communist guerrillas in Greece, too disjointed to give the intended emotional impact.

★

BUD YORKIN (born 1926) Bud Yorkin was a highly successful producer-director in television when he entered films in the sixties. After directing two fairly excruciating comedies (*Come Blow Your Horn*, 1963, and *Never Too Late*, 1965), he redeemed himself amply with *Divorce American Style* (1967), a funny, surprisingly biting com-

ABOVE Divorce American Style: BUD YORKIN (Columbia, 1967). *Dick Van Dyke and Debbie Reynolds play soon-to-be-divorced sparring partners in Yorkin's sharply amusing comedy. The movie never surpassed its opening sequence, in which a divorce lawyer standing on a hill "conducts" the nasty marital arguments raging in the houses down below.*

LEFT The Dresser: PETER YATES (Columbia, 1983). *Albert Finney prepares for a performance as King Lear with the assistance of his doggedly loyal dresser, Tom Courtenay. Both actors delivered commanding performances in this film version of Ronald Harwood's play.*

edy about a couple (Debbie Reynolds and Dick Van Dyke) heading for Splitsville. His next few films were much less amusing, although *Start the Revolution Without Me* (1970), a lunatic farce that aimed its barbs at Hollywood's costume epics, hit the target more often than one would expect. Gene Wilder and Donald Sutherland co-starred as two sets of mismatched twins who meet at the time of the French Revolution. Yorkin's most recent movie, *Twice in a Lifetime* (1985), brought him back to *Divorce American Style,* this time the dark side of divorce. In this wrenching drama, a middle-aged steelworker (Gene Hackman) leaves his dull but decent wife (Ellen Burstyn) for a barmaid (Ann-Margret). Hackman and Burstyn worked diligently at creating believable characters, but the movie confirmed—and pandered to—the audience's conventional expectations. Burstyn acquires a new life (and a new hairdo) while Hackman is deserted by his family (serves him right) after his daughter's wedding.

★

FRED ZINNEMANN (born 1907)   Over the years Fred Zinnemann has not been treated kindly by most critics. Although he is acknowledged as a hard-working and meticulous craftsman who has mastered the technical skills, he is often accused of being dull, humorless, and, especially, emotionally distant. Then one recalls, among other scenes, Jarmila Novotna rushing to embrace her little lost son in *The Search,* or Audrey Hepburn's face glowing with religious fervor in *The Nun's Story,* or Jane Fonda and Vanessa Redgrave's last surreptitious meeting in the café in *Julia* ("My beloved friend, leave!"), and the accusation seems unjustified. Fred Zinnemann may have a tendency to academic dryness (*A Man for All Seasons,* while visually striking, is a rather arid film of a rather arid play), but he deserves high marks for a lifetime of outstanding achievement.

Born in Vienna, Zinnemann deserted the legal profession for the movies after viewing the films of Erich von Stroheim and King Vidor. He became a cameraman, working on such films as the famous semidocumentary *People on Sunday* (*Menschen am Sonntag,* 1929), before immigrating to America. In Hollywood he worked as assistant to Berthold Viertel, among others, and learned about filmmaking from Robert Flaherty, who influenced him enormously. He also appeared as an extra in Lewis Milestone's *All Quiet on the Western Front.* By 1937 he was directing shorts for MGM, one of which won him an Oscar (*That Mothers Might Live,* 1938), and by 1941 he gained assignments to feature films.

Zinnemann's first major film, *The Seventh Cross* (1944), contained some dramatically effective scenes in its story of an anti-Nazi German (Spencer Tracy) desperately try-

LEFT   The Search: FRED ZINNEMANN (*MGM, 1948*). *Fred Zinnemann (seated) directs a scene for this wrenching drama of a Czech mother's search for her young son. Zinnemann drew a remarkable performance from little Ivan Jandl as the displaced boy.*
OPPOSITE, ABOVE LEFT   Breaking Away: PETER YATES (*Fox, 1979*). *Dennis Christopher starred as the young bicyclist from Indiana who triumphs in the climactic race. Yates's engaging movie was an unexpected success, winning praise for its screenplay, its performances, and Yates's sturdy direction.*
OPPOSITE, ABOVE RIGHT   A Man for All Seasons: FRED ZINNEMANN (*Columbia, 1966*). *Zinnemann discusses a scene with Robert Shaw, who played King Henry VIII. The film, the star (Paul Scofield as Sir Thomas More), Zinnemann, and Robert Bolt (who adapted his play for the screen) all won Academy Awards, and Zinnemann also received the Directors Guild Award.*
OPPOSITE, BELOW   Julia: FRED ZINNEMANN (*Fox, 1977*). *In a Berlin café, Julia (Vanessa Redgrave) and her dear friend Lillian Hellman (Jane Fonda) meet for the last time. Part of the film concerned Hellman's search for Julia's whereabouts in the early years of the Nazi onslaught and, later, her search for Julia's child.*

ing to flee the country. However, Zinnemann did not win international acclaim until *The Search* (1948), a poignant and stirring drama of a Czech mother's tireless search for her young son (Ivan Jandl). (Montgomery Clift made his screen debut as a soldier who "adopts" the boy.) He consolidated his reputation with *Act of Violence* (1949), an uncommonly vivid melodrama, and *The Men* (1950), a sensitive film about paraplegics that introduced Marlon Brando to the movies.

Zinnemann reached a peak of success in the early fifties with two films, *High Noon* (1952) and *From Here to Eternity* (1953). Ostensibly a Western about a beleaguered marshal (Gary Cooper) who must face his enemies alone, *High Noon* also carried in its screenplay (by Carl Foreman) an implicit cry of protest against the indifference to the prevailing onslaught of Senator Joseph McCarthy. Most viewers, however, accepted it as a taut action film, attracted by its driving title song, Cooper's solid performance, and a classic showdown scene. (It won four Oscars, although the director's award went to

John Ford for *The Quiet Man*.) In *From Here to Eternity*, he adapted James Jones's best-selling novel into a scorching and cynical view of the military just before Pearl Harbor. The film won five Oscars, including Zinnemann's first.

For the balance of the decade, Zinnemann had his share of hits and misses. Although Carson McCullers's lovely but fragile play *The Member of the Wedding* (1953) all but collapsed under the camera's close scrutiny, Michael Gazzo's play *A Hatful of Rain* (1957), concerning a drug addict and his wife, worked quite well on the screen, managing to build emotional intensity with a subject relatively new to films. Zinnemann's adaptation of Rodgers and Hammerstein's *Oklahoma!* (1955), filmed in the Todd-AO process, dwarfed this essentially small, sweet folk musical. He closed out the fifties, however, with one of his finest films, *The Nun's Story* (1959), a stunning drama that tapped rare sources of feeling in its evocation of the religious life.

From the sixties on, Zinnemann's credits were sparse and variable, ranging from the warmth and robust hu-

286

mor of *The Sundowners* (1960) to the turgidity of *Behold a Pale Horse* (1964) and climaxing with the panoplied splendor of *A Man for All Seasons* (1966), which earned him a third Oscar. He returned to top form with *Julia* (1977), which concerned the long friendship of playwright Lillian Hellman (Jane Fonda) and the free-spirited, dedicated Julia (Vanessa Redgrave, in one of her

---

ABOVE   A Man for All Seasons: FRED ZINNEMANN *(Columbia, 1966). Sir Thomas More (Paul Scofield) steadfastly defends his position of conscience in this resplendent if somewhat pedantic version of Robert Bolt's play.*
OPPOSITE   The Member of the Wedding: FRED ZINNEMANN *(Columbia, 1953). Zinnemann's screen version of Carson McCullers's lovely, evocative play stubbornly refused to come to life, despite the best efforts of (left to right) Julie Harris, Ethel Waters, and Brandon de Wilde.*
OVERLEAF   A Chorus Line: RICHARD ATTENBOROUGH *(Embassy, 1985).*

most luminous performances). Zinnemann succeeded in keeping the elements of the story—nostalgic reminiscence, wartime suspense, and mystery detection—in complete balance, and, aided by Alvin Sargent's astute screenplay and Douglas Slocombe's evocative photography, he scored a triumph.

After scanning Zinnemann's credits, it is difficult to agree with Andrew Sarris's assertion that "his true vocation remains the making of antimovies for antimoviegoers" (*The American Cinema*, p. 169). When we look at Sgt. Prewitt in *From Here to Eternity*, at Sir Thomas More in *A Man for All Seasons*, and at Julia in *Julia*, we can see that Fred Zinnemann has given us many glowing films that examine, with quiet eloquence, the role of the person of integrity in a society without conscience.

APPENDIXES

Winners of the Directors Guild of America Award for Theatrical Direction

---

Each year since 1948, the members of the Directors Guild of America have bestowed an award on the film director whose theatrical feature has been judged as the most distinguished of that year. In the following listing, both winners and nominees are cited, with this exception: from 1948 to 1952, quarterly as well as annual winners were announced; for these years only, the nominees in each quarter are not included. Annual winners are indicated with an asterisk*.

1948–1949
FRED ZINNEMANN, *The Search* (winner, first quarter)
HOWARD HAWKS, *Red River* (winner, second quarter)
ANATOLE LITVAK, *The Snake Pit* (winner, third quarter)
*JOSEPH L. MANKIEWICZ, *A Letter to Three Wives* (winner, fourth quarter)

1949–1950
MARK ROBSON, *Champion* (winner, first quarter)
ALFRED WERKER, *Lost Boundaries* (winner, second quarter)
*ROBERT ROSSEN, *All the King's Men* (winner, third quarter)
CAROL REED, *The Third Man* (winner, fourth quarter)

1950–1951
JOHN HUSTON, *The Asphalt Jungle* (winner, first quarter)
BILLY WILDER, *Sunset Boulevard* (winner, second quarter)
*JOSEPH L. MANKIEWICZ, *All about Eve* (winner, third quarter)
VINCENTE MINNELLI, *Father's Little Dividend* (winner, fourth quarter)

1951
ALFRED HITCHCOCK, *Strangers on a Train* (winner, first quarter)
*GEORGE STEVENS, *A Place in the Sun* (winner, second quarter)
VINCENTE MINNELLI, *An American in Paris* (winner, third quarter)

Because of a change in the presentation date, 1951 had only three quarterly winners.

1952
CHARLES CRICHTON, *The Lavender Hill Mob* (winner, first quarter)
JOSEPH L. MANKIEWICZ, *Five Fingers* (winner, second quarter)
FRED ZINNEMANN, *High Noon* (winner, third quarter)
*JOHN FORD, *The Quiet Man* (winner, fourth quarter)

1953
*FRED ZINNEMANN, *From Here to Eternity*
CHARLES WALTERS, *Lili*
WILLIAM WYLER, *Roman Holiday*

GEORGE STEVENS, *Shane*
BILLY WILDER, *Stalag 17*

1954
WILLIAM WELLMAN, *The High and the Mighty*
ALFRED HITCHCOCK, *Rear Window*
*ELIA KAZAN, *On the Waterfront*
BILLY WILDER, *Sabrina*
GEORGE SEATON, *The Country Girl*

1955
JOHN STURGES, *Bad Day at Black Rock*
ELIA KAZAN, *East of Eden*
JOHN FORD, *Mister Roberts*
*DELBERT MANN, *Marty*
JOSHUA LOGAN, *Picnic*

1956
ROBERT ROSSEN, *Alexander the Great*
HENRY KING, *Carousel*
GEORGE SIDNEY, *The Eddy Duchin Story*
*GEORGE STEVENS, *Giant*
WALTER LANG, *The King and I*
NUNNALLY JOHNSON, *The Man in the Gray Flannel Suit*
ALFRED HITCHCOCK, *The Man Who Knew Too Much*
ROY ROWLAND, *Meet Me in Las Vegas*
JOHN FORD, *The Searchers*
CAROL REED, *Trapeze*
ALFRED HITCHCOCK, *The Trouble with Harry*

1957
MARK ROBSON, *Peyton Place*
JOSHUA LOGAN, *Sayonara*
SIDNEY LUMET, *12 Angry Men*
BILLY WILDER, *Witness for the Prosecution*
*DAVID LEAN, *The Bridge on the River Kwai*

1958
RICHARD BROOKS, *The Brothers Karamazov*
STANLEY KRAMER, *The Defiant Ones*
MARK ROBSON, *The Inn of the Sixth Happiness*
ROBERT WISE, *I Want to Live!*
*VINCENTE MINNELLI, *Gigi*

1959
GEORGE STEVENS, *The Diary of Anne Frank*
FRED ZINNEMANN, *The Nun's Story*
BILLY WILDER, *Some Like It Hot*
OTTO PREMINGER, *Anatomy of a Murder*
*WILLIAM WYLER, *Ben-Hur*

1960
*BILLY WILDER, *The Apartment*
RICHARD BROOKS, *Elmer Gantry*
ALFRED HITCHCOCK, *Psycho*
JACK CARDIFF, *Sons and Lovers*
FRED ZINNEMANN, *The Sundowners*

1961
BLAKE EDWARDS, *Breakfast at Tiffany's*
J. LEE THOMPSON, *The Guns of Navarone*
ROBERT ROSSEN, *The Hustler*
STANLEY KRAMER, *Judgment at Nuremberg*

*ROBERT WISE AND JEROME ROBBINS, *West Side Story*

1962
PETER USTINOV, *Billy Budd*
JOHN FRANKENHEIMER, *The Manchurian Candidate*
PIETRO GERMI, *Divorce—Italian Style*
JOHN HUSTON, *Freud*
*DAVID LEAN, *Lawrence of Arabia*
STANLEY KUBRICK, *Lolita*
SIDNEY LUMET, *Long Day's Journey into Night*
KEN ANNAKIN, ANDREW MARTON, AND BERNHARD WICKI, *The Longest Day*

1963
FEDERICO FELLINI, *8½*
ELIA KAZAN, *America America*
RALPH NELSON, *Lilies of the Field*
*TONY RICHARDSON, *Tom Jones*
MARTIN RITT, *Hud*

1964
*GEORGE CUKOR, *My Fair Lady*
PETER GLENVILLE, *Becket*
JOHN HUSTON, *The Night of the Iguana*
STANLEY KUBRICK, *Dr. Strangelove*
ROBERT STEVENSON, *Mary Poppins*

1965
SIDNEY FURIE, *The Ipcress File*
SIDNEY LUMET, *The Pawnbroker*
JOHN SCHLESINGER, *Darling*
ELLIOT SILVERSTEIN, *Cat Ballou*
*ROBERT WISE, *The Sound of Music*

1966
RICHARD BROOKS, *The Professionals*
JOHN FRANKENHEIMER, *Grand Prix*
LEWIS GILBERT, *Alfie*
JAMES HILL, *Born Free*
NORMAN JEWISON, *The Russians Are Coming the Russians Are Coming*
CLAUDE LELOUCH, *A Man and a Woman*
SILVIO NARIZZANO, *Georgy Girl*
MIKE NICHOLS, *Who's Afraid of Virginia Woolf?*
*FRED ZINNEMANN, *A Man for All Seasons*

1967
RICHARD BROOKS, *In Cold Blood*
NORMAN JEWISON, *In the Heat of the Night*
STANLEY KRAMER, *Guess Who's Coming to Dinner*
*MIKE NICHOLS, *The Graduate*
ARTHUR PENN, *Bonnie and Clyde*

1968
*ANTHONY HARVEY, *The Lion in Winter*
STANLEY KUBRICK, *2001: A Space Odyssey*
PAUL NEWMAN, *Rachel, Rachel*
CAROL REED, *Oliver!*
WILLIAM WYLER, *Funny Girl*

1969
COSTA-GAVRAS, *Z*
GEORGE ROY HILL, *Butch Cassidy and the Sundance Kid*
DENNIS HOPPER, *Easy Rider*

SYDNEY POLLACK, *They Shoot Horses, Don't They?*
*JOHN SCHLESINGER, *Midnight Cowboy*

1970
ROBERT ALTMAN, *M*A*S*H*
ARTHUR HILLER, *Love Story*
DAVID LEAN, *Ryan's Daughter*
BOB RAFELSON, *Five Easy Pieces*
*FRANKLIN J. SCHAFFNER, *Patton*

1971
PETER BOGDANOVICH, *The Last Picture Show*
*WILLIAM FRIEDKIN, *The French Connection*
STANLEY KUBRICK, *A Clockwork Orange*
ROBERT MULLIGAN, *Summer of '42*
JOHN SCHLESINGER, *Sunday, Bloody Sunday*

1972
JOHN BOORMAN, *Deliverance*
*FRANCIS FORD COPPOLA, *The Godfather*
BOB FOSSE, *Cabaret*
GEORGE ROY HILL, *Slaughterhouse Five*
MARTIN RITT, *Sounder*

1973
BERNARDO BERTOLUCCI, *Last Tango in Paris*
WILLIAM FRIEDKIN, *The Exorcist*
*GEORGE ROY HILL, *The Sting*
SIDNEY LUMET, *Serpico*
GEORGE LUCAS, *American Graffiti*

1974
FRANCIS FORD COPPOLA, *The Conversation*
*FRANCIS FORD COPPOLA, *The Godfather: Part II*
BOB FOSSE, *Lenny*
SIDNEY LUMET, *Murder on the Orient Express*
ROMAN POLANSKI, *Chinatown*

1975
ROBERT ALTMAN, *Nashville*
*MILOS FORMAN, *One Flew over the Cuckoo's Nest*
STANLEY KUBRICK, *Barry Lyndon*
SIDNEY LUMET, *Dog Day Afternoon*
STEVEN SPIELBERG, *Jaws*

1976
*JOHN AVILDSEN, *Rocky*
SIDNEY LUMET, *Network*
ALAN J. PAKULA, *All the President's Men*
MARTIN SCORSESE, *Taxi Driver*
LINA WERTMULLER, *Seven Beauties*

1977
*WOODY ALLEN, *Annie Hall*
GEORGE LUCAS, *Star Wars*
HERBERT ROSS, *The Turning Point*
FRED ZINNEMANN, *Julia*
STEVEN SPIELBERG, *Close Encounters of the Third Kind*

1978
HAL ASHBY, *Coming Home*
*MICHAEL CIMINO, *The Deer Hunter*
WARREN BEATTY and BUCK HENRY, *Heaven Can Wait*

ALAN PARKER, *Midnight Express*
PAUL MAZURSKY, *An Unmarried Woman*

1979
FRANCIS FORD COPPOLA, *Apocalypse Now*
PETER YATES, *Breaking Away*
*ROBERT BENTON, *Kramer vs. Kramer*
WOODY ALLEN, *Manhattan*
JAMES BRIDGES, *The China Syndrome*

1980
DAVID LYNCH, *The Elephant Man*
*ROBERT REDFORD, *Ordinary People*

RICHARD RUSH, *The Stunt Man*
MICHAEL APTED, *Coal Miner's Daughter*
MARTIN SCORSESE, *Raging Bull*

1981
*WARREN BEATTY, *Reds*
HUGH HUDSON, *Chariots of Fire*
LOUIS MALLE, *Atlantic City*
MARK RYDELL, *On Golden Pond*
STEVEN SPIELBERG, *Raiders of the Lost Ark*

1982
*RICHARD ATTENBOROUGH, *Gandhi*

TAYLOR HACKFORD, *An Officer and a Gentleman*
WOLFGANG PETERSEN, *Das Boot*
SYDNEY POLLACK, *Tootsie*
STEVEN SPIELBERG, *E.T.: The Extra-Terrestrial*

1983
BRUCE BERESFORD, *Tender Mercies*
INGMAR BERGMAN, *Fanny and Alexander*
*JAMES L. BROOKS, *Terms of Endearment*
LAWRENCE KASDAN, *The Big Chill*
PHILIP KAUFMAN, *The Right Stuff*

1984
ROBERT BENTON, *Places in the Heart*
*MILOS FORMAN, *Amadeus*
NORMAN JEWISON, *A Soldier's Story*
ROLAND JOFFE, *The Killing Fields*
DAVID LEAN, *A Passage to India*

1985
RON HOWARD, *Cocoon*
JOHN HUSTON, *Prizzi's Honor*
SYDNEY POLLACK, *Out of Africa*
*STEVEN SPIELBERG, *The Color Purple*
PETER WEIR, *Witness*

Recipients of the D. W. Griffith Award

The D. W. Griffith Award is given by the Directors Guild of America as its highest honor for lifetime achievement.

1953: CECIL B. DeMILLE	1970: FRED ZINNEMANN
1954: JOHN FORD	1972: WILLIAM A. WELLMAN
1956: HENRY KING	1973: DAVID LEAN
1957: KING VIDOR	1980: GEORGE CUKOR
1959: FRANK CAPRA	1982: ROUBEN MAMOULIAN
1960: GEORGE STEVENS	1983: JOHN HUSTON
1961: FRANK BORZAGE	1984: ORSON WELLES
1965: WILLIAM WYLER	1985: BILLY WILDER
1968: ALFRED HITCHCOCK	1986: JOSEPH L. MANKIEWICZ

Honorary Life Members of the Directors Guild of America

1938: D. W. GRIFFITH	1957: DONALD CRISP
1940: MARSHALL NEILAN	1959: GEORGE SIDNEY
1941: FRANK CAPRA	1973: DAVID LEAN
1945: MAURICE TOURNEUR	1974: CHARLES CHAPLIN
1948: TOD BROWNING	1977: H. C. POTTER
1949: REX INGRAM	1978: DAVID BUTLER
1951: J. P. McGOWAN	1981: JOSEPH L. MANKIEWICZ

1983: ELIA KAZAN AND ROBERT WISE

Nondirector life members: Mabel Walker Willebrandt, Louis B. Mayer, Walt Disney, Y. Frank Freeman, Hobe Morrison, Joseph C. Youngerman, Jack L. Warner, Darryl F. Zanuck, Lew Wasserman.

SELECTED BIBLIOGRAPHY

Bare, Richard. *The Film Director*. New York: Collier Books, 1971.

Bayer, William. *The Great Movies*. New York: Grosset & Dunlap, 1973.

Bogdanovich, Peter. *Fritz Lang in America*. New York: Praeger Publishers, 1967.

Brownlow, Kevin. *The Parade's Gone By...*. New York: Alfred A. Knopf, 1968.

Canham, Kingsley. *Michael Curtiz/Raoul Walsh/Henry Hathaway*. The Hollywood Professionals, vol. 1. New York: A. S. Barnes & Co.; London: The Tantivy Press, 1973.

Capra, Frank. *The Name above the Title*. New York: The Macmillan Company, 1971.

Chierichetti, David. *Hollywood Director*. New York: Curtis Books, 1973.

Coursodon, Jean-Pierre, with Pierre Sauvage. *American Directors*. New York: McGraw-Hill Book Company, 1983.

Crist, Judith. *Take 22: Moviemakers on Moviemaking*. New York: The Viking Press, 1984.

Dmytryk, Edward. *On Screen Directing*. Boston and London: Focal Press, 1964.

Feineman, Neil. *Persistence of Vision: The Films of Robert Altman*. New York: Arno Press, 1978.

Finler, Joel W. *The Movie Directors Story*. New York: Crescent Books, 1985.

Freeman, David. *The Last Days of Alfred Hitchcock*. Woodstock, N.Y.: The Overlook Press, 1984.

Gottesman, Ronald, ed. *Focus on Orson Welles*. Englewood Cliffs, N.J.: Prentice-Hall, 1976.

Hochman, Stanley, ed. *American Film Directors*. New York: Frederick Ungar Publishing Co., 1974.

Huston, John. *An Open Book*. New York: Alfred A. Knopf, 1980.

Kael, Pauline; Mankiewicz, Herman J.; and Welles, Orson. *The Citizen Kane Book*. Boston: Little, Brown and Company, 1971.

Kass, Judith M. (Siegel) and Rosenthal, Stuart (Browning). *Tod Browning/Don Siegel*. The Hollywood Professionals, vol. 4. New York: A. S. Barnes & Co.; London: The Tantivy Press, 1975.

Katz, Ephraim. *The Film Encyclopedia*. New York: Thomas Y. Crowell, 1979.

Kerr, Walter. *The Silent Clowns*. New York: Alfred A. Knopf, 1975.

Koszarski, Richard. *Hollywood Directors, 1914–1940*. New York: Oxford University Press, 1976.

Leyda, Jay, ed. *Voices of Film Experience: 1894 to the Present*. New York: Macmillan Publishing Co., 1977.

Lloyd, Ronald. *American Film Directors*. New York and London: Franklin Watts, 1976.

Lyon, Christopher. *The International Dictionary of Films and Filmmakers*. Vol. 2. Chicago: St. James Press, 1984.

McBride, Joseph. *Orson Welles*. New York: Pyramid Publications, 1977.

McBride, Joseph, and Wilmington, Michael. *John Ford*. New York: Da Capo Press, 1975.

McCaffrey, Donald W. *Focus on Chaplin*. Englewood Cliffs, N.J.: Prentice-Hall, 1971.

Macdonald, Dwight. *Dwight Macdonald on Movies*. Englewood Cliffs, N.J.: Prentice-Hall, 1969.

Masden, Axel. *William Wyler: An Authorized Biography*. New York: Thomas Y. Crowell Company, 1973.

Meyer, William R. *Warner Brothers Directors: The Hard-Boiled, the Comic, and the Weepers*. New Rochelle, N.Y.: Arlington House, 1978.

Milne, Tom. *Mamoulian*. Bloomington, Ind.: Indiana University Press, 1969.

Minnelli, Vincente, with Hector Arce. *I Remember It Well*. Garden City, N.Y.: Doubleday & Company, 1974.

Moss, Robert F. *Charlie Chaplin*. New York: Pyramid Publications, 1975.

Pratley, Gerald. *The Cinema of John Huston*. South Brunswick, N.J., and New York: A. S. Barnes & Co., 1977.

Preminger, Otto. *Preminger: An Autobiography*. Garden City, N.Y.: Doubleday & Company, 1977.

Robinson, David. *Chaplin: His Life and Art*. New York: McGraw-Hill Book Company, 1985.

Roud, Richard, ed. *Cinema: A Critical Dictionary—The Major Film-Makers*. 2 vols. New York: The Viking Press, 1980.

Sarris, Andrew. *The American Cinema: Directors and Directions, 1929–1968*. New York: Frederick Ungar Publishing Co., 1968.

———, ed. *Interviews with Film Directors*. New York: The Bobbs-Merrill Company, 1967.

Schickel, Richard. *D. W. Griffith: An American Life*. New York: Simon and Schuster, 1984.

Sennett, Ted. *Great Hollywood Movies*. New York: Harry N. Abrams, 1983.

———. *Hollywood Musicals*. New York: Harry N. Abrams, 1981.

Spoto, Donald. *The Dark Side of Genius: The Life of Alfred Hitchcock*. Boston: Little, Brown and Company, 1983.

Truffaut, François, with Helen G. Scott. *Hitchcock*. New York: Simon and Schuster, 1967.

Walsh, Raoul. *Each Man in His Time: The Life Story of a Director*. New York: Farrar, Straus and Giroux, 1974.

Weinberg, Herman G. *Josef von Sternberg*. New York: E. P. Dutton & Co., 1967.

———. *The Lubitsch Touch*. New York: E. P. Dutton & Co., 1968.

Wellman, William A. *A Short Time for Insanity: An Autobiography*. New York: Hawthorn Books, 1974.

Zolotow, Maurice. *Billy Wilder in Hollywood*. New York: G. P. Putnam's Sons, 1977.

FILMOGRAPHIES

Each entry lists all the feature films, including feature documentaries, credited to the director. (No short films are cited by title.) The date given is the release date, and the studio or releasing company is also cited for each sound film. However, studios are not given for the silent films, since these are often obscure or difficult to ascertain.

If a film is known by more than one title, the second will follow the first in parentheses. If a film was co-directed, the codirector is noted in parentheses after the film title.

Foreign films are cited by title when the films were an integral or significant part of the director's career. Otherwise the number of foreign films is merely noted.

Key to abbreviations used:

Doc: Feature documentary
AA: Allied Artists
AFD: Associated Film Distribution Corp.
AI: American-International
Associated British: Associated British Film
  Distributors
Atlantic: Atlantic Releasing Corp.
BIP: British International Pictures
BV: Buena Vista
Cinerama: Cinerama Releasing Corp.
Col: Columbia
FN: First National
Fox: 20th Century-Fox
Ladd: The Ladd Co.
Lopert: Lopert Films, Inc.
MGM: Metro-Goldwyn-Mayer
Mon: Monogram
NG: National General
Par: Paramount
Rep: Republic
Selznick: Selznick Releasing
UA: United Artists
Univ: Universal
WB: Warner Bros.

ROBERT ALDRICH (1918–1983) 1953: *The Big Leaguer* (MGM). 1954: *World for Ransom* (AA); *Apache* (UA); *Vera Cruz* (UA). 1955: *Kiss Me Deadly* (UA); *The Big Knife* (UA). 1956: *Autumn Leaves* (Col); *Attack!* (UA). 1959: *The Angry Hills* (MGM); *Ten Seconds to Hell* (UA). 1961: *The Last Sunset* (Univ-International). 1962: *What Ever Happened to Baby Jane* (WB); *Sodom and Gomorrah* (*Sodoma e Gomorra*) (Italy, U.S.; Fox, 1963). 1963: *4 for Texas* (WB). 1965: *Hush . . . Hush, Sweet Charlotte* (Fox). 1966: *The Flight of the Phoenix* (Fox). 1967: *The Dirty Dozen* (MGM). 1968: *The Legend of Lylah Clare* (MGM); *The Killing of Sister George* (Cinerama). 1970: *Too Late the Hero* (Cinerama). 1971: *The Grissom Gang* (Cinerama). 1972: *Ulzana's Raid* (Univ). 1973: *Emperor of the North Pole* (*Emperor of the North*) (Fox). 1974: *The Longest Yard* (Par). 1975: *Hustle* (Par). 1977: *Twilight's Last Gleaming* (AA); *The Choirboys* (Univ/MCA). 1979: *The Frisco Kid* (WB). 1981: *. . . All the Marbles* (MGM/UA).
Uncredited: 1957: *The Garment Jungle* (with Vincent Sherman; Col). Uncompleted: 1969: *The Greatest Mother of Them All*.

WOODY ALLEN (born 1935) 1969: *Take the Money and Run* (Cinerama). 1971: *Bananas* (UA). 1972: *Everything You Always Wanted to Know about Sex** (**But Were Afraid to Ask*) (UA). 1973: *Sleeper* (UA). 1975: *Love and Death* (UA). 1977: *Annie Hall* (UA). 1978: *Interiors* (UA). 1979: *Manhattan* (UA). 1980: *Stardust Memories* (UA). 1982: *A Midsummer Night's Sex Comedy* (Orion/WB). 1983: *Zelig* (Orion/WB). 1984: *Broadway Danny Rose* (Orion). 1985: *The Purple Rose of Cairo* (Orion). 1986: *Hannah and Her Sisters* (Orion).

ROBERT ALTMAN (born 1925) 1957: *The Delinquents* (UA); *The James Dean Story* (Doc; with George W. George; WB). 1968: *Countdown* (WB). 1969: *That Cold Day in the Park* (Canada, U.S.; Commonwealth United). 1970: *M*A*S*H* (Fox); *Brewster McCloud* (MGM). 1971: *McCabe and Mrs. Miller* (WB). 1972: *Images* (Ireland; Col). 1973: *The Long Goodbye* (UA). 1974: *Thieves Like Us* (UA); *California Split* (Col). 1975: *Nashville* (Par). 1976: *Buffalo Bill and the Indians or Sitting Bull's History Lesson* (UA). 1977: *3 Women* (Fox). 1978: *A Wedding* (Fox). 1979: *A Perfect Couple* (Fox); *Quintet* (Fox). 1980: *Health* (Fox); *Popeye* (Par). 1982: *Come Back to the Five and Dime, Jimmy Dean, Jimmy Dean* (Cinecom International). 1983: *Streamers* (UA Classics). 1984: *Secret Honor* (Sandcastle 5). 1985: *O. C. and Stiggs* (MGM/UA); *Fool for Love* (Cannon).

MICHAEL APTED (born 1941) 1973: *The Triple Echo* (Great Britain; Altura). 1975: *Stardust* (Great Britain; Col). 1977: *The Squeeze* (Great Britain; WB). 1979: *Agatha* (Great Britain; WB). 1980: *Coal Miner's Daughter* (Univ). 1981: *Continental Divide* (Univ). 1983: *Kipperbang* (MGM/UA Classics); *Gorky Park* (Orion). 1984: *Firstborn* (Par). 1985: *Bring On the Night* (Doc; A & M Films). 1986: *Critical Condition* (Par).

DOROTHY ARZNER (1900–1979) 1927: *Fashions for Women; Get Your Man; 10 Modern Commandments*. 1928: *Manhattan Cocktail*. 1929: *The Wild Party* (Par). 1930: *Sarah and Son* (Par); *Paramount on Parade* ("The Gallows Song—Nichavo" sequence; Par); *Anybody's Woman* (Par). 1931: *Honor among Lovers* (Par); *Working Girls* (Par). 1932: *Merrily We Go to Hell* (Par). 1933: *Christopher Strong* (RKO). 1934: *Nana* (*Lady of the Boulevard*) (UA). 1936: *Craig's Wife* (Col). 1937: *The Bride Wore Red* (UA). 1940: *Dance, Girl, Dance* (RKO). 1943: *First Comes Courage* (Col).
Uncredited: 1930: *Charming Sinners* (with Robert Milton; Par). 1937: *The Last of Mrs. Cheyney* (with Richard Boleslawski; MGM).

HAL ASHBY (born 1936) 1970: *The Landlord* (UA). 1971: *Harold and Maude* (Par). 1973: *The Last Detail* (Col). 1975: *Shampoo* (Col). 1976: *Bound for Glory* (UA). 1978: *Coming Home* (UA). 1979: *Being There* (UA). 1981: *Second Hand Hearts* (Par). 1982: *Lookin' to Get Out* (Par). 1983: *Let's Spend the Night Together* (Doc; Embassy). 1985: *The Slugger's Wife* (Col). 1986: *8 Million Ways to Die* (PSO).

RICHARD ATTENBOROUGH (born 1923) 1969: *Oh! What a Lovely War!* (Great Britain; Par). 1972: *Young Winston* (Great Britain; Col). 1977: *A Bridge Too Far* (Great Britain; UA). 1978: *Magic* (Fox). 1982: *Gandhi* (Great Britain, India; Col). 1985: *A Chorus Line* (Embassy).

JOHN G. AVILDSEN (born 1937) 1969: *Turn On to Love* (Haven International). 1970: *Guess What We Learned in School Today?* (Cannon); *Joe* (Cannon). 1971: *Cry Uncle!* (Cambist); *Okay Bill* (Four Star Excelsior). 1972: *The Stoolie* (Jama). 1973: *Save the Tiger* (Par). 1975: *Fore Play* (with Bruce Malmuth and Robert McCarty; Cinema National); *W. W. and the Dixie Dancekings* (Fox). 1976: *Rocky* (UA). 1978: *Slow Dancing in the Big City* (UA). 1980: *The Formula* (MGM/UA). 1982: *Neighbors* (Col).

1983: *A Night in Heaven* (Fox). 1984: *The Karate Kid* (Col).

LLOYD BACON (1890–1955) 1926: *Broken Hearts of Hollywood; Private Izzy Murphy*. 1927: *Finger Prints; White Flannels; The Heart of Maryland; A Sailor's Sweetheart; Brass Knuckles*. 1928: *Pay as You Enter; The Lion and the Mouse; Women They Talk About; The Singing Fool* (WB). 1929: *Stark Mad; No Defense; Honky Tonk; Say It with Songs* (WB); *So Long Letty* (WB). 1930: *The Other Tomorrow* (FN); *She Couldn't Say No* (WB); *A Notorious Affair* (FN); *Moby Dick* (WB); *The Office Wife* (WB). 1931: *Sit Tight* (WB); *Kept Husbands* (RKO); *Fifty Million Frenchmen* (WB); *Gold Dust Gertie* (WB); *Honor of the Family* (FN). 1932: *Manhattan Parade* (WB); *Fireman Save My Child* (FN); *Alias the Doctor* (FN); *The Famous Ferguson Case* (FN); *Miss Pinkerton* (FN); *Crooner* (FN); *You Said a Mouthful* (FN). 1933: *42nd Street* (WB); *Picture Snatcher* (WB); *Mary Stevens, M.D.* (WB); *Footlight Parade* (WB); *Son of a Sailor* (FN). 1934: *Wonder Bar* (FN); *A Very Honorable Guy* (FN); *He Was Her Man* (WB); *Here Comes the Navy* (WB); *6-Day Bike Rider* (WB). 1935: *Devil Dogs of the Air* (WB); *In Caliente* (FN); *Broadway Gondolier* (WB); *The Irish in Us* (WB); *Frisco Kid* (WB). 1936: *Sons o' Guns* (WB); *Cain and Mabel* (WB); *Gold Diggers of 1937* (FN). 1937: *Marked Woman* (WB); *Ever Since Eve* (WB); *San Quentin* (FN); *Submarine D-1* (WB). 1938: *A Slight Case of Murder* (WB); *Cowboy from Brooklyn* (WB); *Racket Busters* (WB); *Boy Meets Girl* (WB). 1939: *Wings of the Navy* (WB); *The Oklahoma Kid* (WB); *Indianapolis Speedway* (WB); *Espionage Agent* (WB). 1940: *A Child Is Born* (WB); *Invisible Stripes* (WB); *Three Cheers for the Irish* (WB); *Brother Orchid* (WB); *Knute Rockne—All American* (WB). 1941: *Honeymoon for Three* (WB); *Footsteps in the Dark* (WB); *Affectionately Yours* (WB); *Navy Blues* (WB). 1942: *Larceny, Inc.* (WB); *Wings for the Eagle* (WB); *Silver Queen* (UA). 1943: *Action in the North Atlantic* (WB). 1944: *Sunday Dinner for a Soldier* (WB). 1945: *Captain Eddie* (Fox). 1946: *Home Sweet Homicide* (Fox); *Wake Up and Dream* (Fox). 1947: *I Wonder Who's Kissing Her Now* (Fox). 1948: *You Were Meant for Me* (Fox); *Give My Regards to Broadway* (Fox); *Don't Trust Your Husband* (*An Innocent Affair*) (UA). 1949: *Mother Is a Freshman* (Fox); *It Happens Every Spring* (Fox); *Miss Grant Takes Richmond* (Col). 1950: *Kill the Umpire* (Col); *The Good Humor Man* (Col); *The Fuller Brush Girl* (Col). 1951: *Call Me Mister* (Fox); *The Frogmen* (Fox); *Golden Girl* (Fox). 1953: *The I Don't Care Girl* (Fox); *The Great Sioux Uprising* (Univ); *Walking My Baby Back Home* (Univ). 1954: *The French Line* (RKO); *She Couldn't Say No* (RKO).

JOHN BADHAM (born 1939) 1976: *The Bingo Long Traveling All-Star and Motor Kings* (Univ). 1977: *Saturday Night Fever* (Par). 1979: *Dracula* (Univ). 1981: *Whose Life Is It, Anyway?* (MGM/UA). 1983: *Blue Thunder* (Col); *WarGames* (MGM/UA). 1985: *American Flyer* (WB). 1986: *Short Circuit* (Tri-Star).

WARREN BEATTY (born 1937) 1978: *Heaven Can Wait* (with Buck Henry; Par). 1981: *Reds* (Par).

ROBERT BENTON (born 1932) 1972: *Bad Company* (Par). 1977: *The Late Show* (WB). 1979: *Kramer vs. Kramer* (Col). 1982: *Still of the Night* (MGM/UA). 1984: *Places in the Heart* (Tri-Star).

BRUCE BERESFORD (born 1940) 1972: *The Adventures of Barry McKenzie* (Australia; Double Head Productions). 1974: *Barry McKenzie Holds His Own* (Australia; Satori). 1976: *Don's Party* (Australia; Satori). 1977: *The Getting of Wisdom* (Australia; Atlantic). 1978: *Money

Movers (Australia; South Australian Film Corp). 1980: *Breaker Morant* (Australia; New World/Quartet). 1981: *The Club* (Australia; South Australian Film Corp); *Puberty Blues* (Australia; Universal Classics). 1983: *Tender Mercies* (Univ/AFD). 1985: *King David* (U.S., Great Britain; Par). 1986: *Crimes of the Heart* (MGM).

BUSBY BERKELEY (1895–1976) 1933: *She Had to Say Yes* (with George Amy; FN). 1935: *Gold Diggers of 1935* (FN); *Bright Lights* (FN); *I Live for Love* (WB). 1936: *Stage Struck* (FN). 1937: *The Go Getter* (WB); *Hollywood Hotel* (WB). 1938: *Men Are Such Fools* (WB); *Garden of the Moon* (WB); *Comet over Broadway* (WB). 1939: *They Made Me a Criminal* (WB); *Babes in Arms* (MGM); *Fast and Furious* (MGM). 1940: *Forty Little Mothers* (MGM); *Strike Up the Band* (MGM). 1941: *Blonde Inspiration* (MGM); *Babes on Broadway* (MGM). 1942: *For Me and My Gal* (MGM). 1943: *The Gang's All Here* (Fox). 1946: *Cinderella Jones* (WB). 1949: *Take Me Out to the Ball Game* (MGM).

CURTIS (KURT) BERNHARDT (1899–1981) 1926–33: 12 German films; 1934–39: 4 French films. 1940: *My Love Came Back* (WB); *The Lady with Red Hair* (WB). 1941: *Million Dollar Baby* (WB). 1942: *Juke Girl* (WB). 1943: *Happy Go Lucky* (Par). 1945: *Conflict* (WB). 1946: *Devotion* (WB); *My Reputation* (WB); *A Stolen Life* (WB). 1947: *Possessed* (WB). 1949: *High Wall* (MGM); *The Doctor and the Girl* (MGM). 1951: *Payment on Demand* (RKO); *Sirocco* (Col); *The Blue Veil* (RKO). 1952: *The Merry Widow* (MGM). 1953: *Miss Sadie Thompson* (Col). 1954: *Beau Brummell* (MGM). 1955: *Interrupted Melody* (MGM). 1956: *Gaby* (MGM). 1961: *Damon and Pythias* (MGM). 1963: *Stefanie in Rio* (Casino). 1964: *Kisses for My President* (WB).

BUDD BOETTICHER (born 1916) 1944: *One Mysterious Night* (Col); *The Missing Juror* (Col). 1945: *A Guy, a Gal and a Pal* (Col); *Escape in the Fog* (Col); *Youth on Trial* (Col). 1946: *The Fleet That Came to Stay* (Par). 1948: *Assigned to Danger* (Eagle-Lion); *Behind Locked Doors* (Eagle-Lion). 1949: *The Wolf Hunters* (Mon); *Black Midnight* (Mon). 1950: *Killer Shark* (Mon). 1951: *The Bullfighter and the Lady* (Rep); *The Sword of D'Artagnan* (Univ); *The Cimarron Kid* (Univ). 1952: *Red Ball Express* (Univ); *Bronco Buster* (Univ); *Horizons West* (Univ). 1953: *City Beneath the Sea* (Univ); *Seminole* (Univ); *The Man from the Alamo* (Univ); *East of Sumatra* (Univ); *Wings of the Hawk* (Univ). 1955: *The Magnificent Matador* (Fox). 1956: *The Killer Is Loose* (UA); *Seven Men from Now* (WB). 1957: *The Tall T* (Col); *Decision at Sundown* (Col). 1958: *Buchanan Rides Alone* (Col). 1959: *Ride Lonesome* (Col); *Westbound* (WB). 1960: *Comanche Station* (Col); *The Rise and Fall of Legs Diamond* (WB). 1971: *A Time for Dying* (Etoile). 1972: *Arruza* (Doc; Avco Embassy). 1985: *Lusitano* (Doc; Boetticher Productions).

PETER BOGDANOVICH (born 1939) 1968: *Targets* (Par). 1971: *Directed by John Ford* (Doc; American Film Institute); *The Last Picture Show* (Col). 1972: *What's Up, Doc?* (WB). 1973: *Paper Moon* (Par). 1974: *Daisy Miller* (Par). 1975: *At Long Last Love* (Fox). 1976: *Nickelodeon* (Col). 1979: *Saint Jack* (New World). 1982: *They All Laughed* (UA Classics). 1985: *Mask* (Univ).

JOHN BOORMAN (born 1933) 1965: *Having a Wild Weekend* (Great Britain; WB). 1967: *Point Blank* (MGM). 1968: *Hell in the Pacific* (Cinerama). 1970: *Leo the Last* (Great Britain; UA). 1972: *Deliverance* (WB). 1974: *Zardoz* (Great Britain; Fox). 1977: *Exorcist II: The Heretic* (WB). 1981: *Excalibur* (Great Britain, Ireland; Orion/WB). 1985: *The Emerald Forest* (Great Britain; Embassy).

FRANK BORZAGE (1893–1962) 1916: *The Land of Lizards; Silent Shelby; Immediate Lee.* 1917: *Flying Colors; Until They Get Me.* 1918: *The Gun Woman; The Shoes That Danced; Innocent's Progress; Society for Sale; An Honest Man; Who Is to Blame?; The Ghost Flower; The Curse of Iku.* 1919: *Toton; Prudence of Broadway; Whom the Gods Destroy.* 1920: *Humoresque.* 1921: *The Duke of Chimney Butte; Get-Rich-Quick Wallingford.* 1922: *Back Pay; Billy Jim; The Good Provider; The Valley of Silent Men; The Pride of Palomar.* 1923: *Children of the Dust; The Nth Commandment; The Age of Desire.* 1924: *Secrets.* 1925: *The Lady; Daddy's Gone a'Hunting; The Circle; Lazybones; Wages for Wives.* 1926: *The First Year; The Dixie Merchant; Early to Wed; Marriage License?.* 1927: *Seventh Heaven.* 1928: *Street Angel* (Fox). 1929: *The River* (Fox); *Lucky Star* (Fox); *They Had to See Paris* (Fox). 1930: *Song o' My Heart* (Fox); *Liliom* (Fox). 1931: *Doctors' Wives* (Fox); *Bad Girl* (Fox); *Young as You Feel* (Fox). 1932: *After Tomorrow* (Fox); *Young America* (Fox); *A Farewell to Arms* (Par). 1933: *Man's Castle* (Col); *Secrets* (UA). 1934: *No Greater Glory* (Col); *Little Man What Now?* (Univ); *Flirtation Walk* (FN). 1935: *Living on Velvet* (FN); *Stranded* (WB); *Shipmates Forever* (FN). 1936: *Desire* (Par); *Hearts Divided* (FN). 1937: *Green Light* (WB); *History Is Made at Night* (UA); *The Big City* (MGM); *Mannequin* (MGM). 1938: *Three Comrades* (MGM); *The Shining Hour* (MGM). 1939: *Disputed Passage* (Par). 1940: *The Mortal Storm* (MGM); *Strange Cargo* (MGM); *Flight Command* (MGM). 1941: *Smilin' Through* (MGM); *The Vanishing Virginian* (MGM). 1942: *Seven Sweethearts* (MGM). 1943: *Stage Door Canteen* (UA); *His Butler's Sister* (Univ). 1944: *'Til We Meet Again* (Par). 1945: *The Spanish Main* (RKO). 1946: *I've Always Loved You* (Rep); *The Magnificent Doll* (Univ). 1947: *That's My Man* (Rep). 1949: *Moonrise* (Rep). 1958: *China Doll* (UA). 1959: *The Big Fisherman* (BV).

JOHN BRAHM (1893–1982) 1936: *Broken Blossoms* (Great Britain; Twickenham). 1937: *Counsel for Crime* (Col). 1938: *Penitentiary* (Col); *Girls' School* (Col). 1939: *Let Us Live* (Col); *Rio* (Univ). 1940: *Escape to Glory* (Col). 1941: *Wild Geese Calling* (Fox). 1942: *The Undying Monster* (Fox). 1943: *Tonight We Raid Calais* (Fox); *Wintertime* (Fox). 1944: *The Lodger* (Univ); *Guest in the House* (UA). 1945: *Hangover Square* (Fox); *Three Little Girls in Blue* (replaced by H. Bruce Humberstone; Fox). 1946: *The Locket* (RKO). 1947: *The Brasher Doubloon* (Fox); *Singapore* (Univ). 1951: *Il Ladro di Venezia* (Fox). 1952: *The Miracle of Our Lady of Fatima* (WB); *Face to Face* (with Bretaigne Windust; RKO). 1953: *The Diamond Queen* (WB). 1954: *The Mad Magician* (Col); *Die Goldene Pest* (Germany). 1955: *Von Himmel Gefallen (Special Delivery)* (Germany, United States); *Bengazi* (RKO). 1967: *Hot Rods to Hell* (MGM).

HERBERT BRENON (1880–1958) 1912: *All for Her; The Clown's Triumph; Leah the Forsaken.* 1913: *Kathleen Mavourneen; The Angel of Death; Ivanhoe; The Anarchist.* 1914: *Absinthe; Across the Atlantic; Neptune's Daughter* (with Otis Turner). 1915: *The Kreutzer Sonata; The Clemenceau Case; The Two Orphans; Sin; The Soul of Broadway.* 1916: *Whom the Gods Destroy; A Daughter of the Gods; War Brides; Marble Heart; The Ruling Passion.* 1917: *The Eternal Sin; The Lone Wolf; The Fall of the Romanoffs; Empty Pockets.* 1918: *Victory and Peace; The Passing of the Third Floor Back.* 1919: *Principessa Misteriosa; Twelve-Ten; A Sinless Sinner.* 1920: *Chains of Evidence.* 1921: *The Passion Flower; The Sign on the Door; The Wonderful Thing.* 1922: *Any Wife; A Stage Romance; Shackles of Gold; Moonshine Valley.* 1923: *The Custard Cup; The Rustle of Silk; Sister Against Sister; The Woman with Four Faces; The Spanish Dancer.* 1924: *Shadows of Paris; The Breaking Point; The Side Show of Life; The Alaskan; Peter Pan.* 1925: *The Little French Girl; The Street of Forgotten Men.* 1926: *The Song and Dance Man; Dancing Mothers; Beau Geste; The Great Gatsby; God Gave Me Twenty Cents; A Kiss for Cinderella.* 1927: *The Telephone Girl; Sorrell and Son.* 1928: *Laugh, Clown, Laugh.* 1929: *The Rescue* (Samuel Goldwyn). 1930: *Lummox* (UA); *The Case of Sergeant Grischa* (RKO). 1931: *Beau Ideal* (RKO); *Transgression* (RKO). 1932: *Girl of the Rio* (RKO). 1933: *Wine, Women and Song* (Chadwick). 1935: *Royal Cavalcade* (Doc; episode; Great Britain; BIP); *Honors Easy* (Great Britain; BIP). 1936: *Living Dangerously* (Great Britain; BIP); *Someone at the Door* (Great Britain; BIP). 1937: *The Dominant Sex* (Great Britain; BIP); *Spring Handicap* (Great Britain; Associated British Picture Corp). 1938: *Housemaster* (Great Britain; Associated British Picture Corp); *Yellow Sands* (Great Britain; Associated British Picture Corp). 1939: *Black Eyes* (Great Britain; Associated British Picture Corp). 1940: *The Flying Squad* (Associated British Picture Corp).

JAMES BRIDGES (born 1936) 1970: *The Baby Maker* (NG). 1973: *The Paper Chase* (Fox). 1977: *9/30/55 (September 30, 1955)* (Univ). 1979: *The China Syndrome* (Col). 1980: *Urban Cowboy* (Par). 1984: *Mike's Murder* (Ladd/WB). 1985: *Perfect* (Col).

JAMES L. BROOKS (born 1940) 1983: *Terms of Endearment* (Par).

MEL BROOKS (born 1926) 1968: *The Producers* (Avco Embassy). 1970: *The Twelve Chairs* (UMC). 1973: *Blazing Saddles* (WB). 1974: *Young Frankenstein* (Fox). 1976: *Silent Movie* (Fox). 1977: *High Anxiety* (Fox). 1981: *History of the World, Part I* (Fox).

RICHARD BROOKS (born 1912) 1950: *Crisis* (MGM). 1951: *The Light Touch* (MGM); *Deadline U.S.A.* (Fox). 1953: *Battle Circus* (MGM); *Take the High Ground* (MGM). 1954: *Flame and the Flesh* (MGM); *The Last Time I Saw Paris* (MGM). 1955: *The Blackboard Jungle* (MGM). 1956: *The Last Hunt* (MGM); *The Catered Affair* (MGM). 1957: *Something of Value* (MGM). 1958: *Cat on a Hot Tin Roof* (MGM); *The Brothers Karamazov* (MGM). 1960: *Elmer Gantry* (UA). 1962: *Sweet Bird of Youth* (MGM). 1965: *Lord Jim* (Col). 1966: *The Professionals* (Col). 1967: *In Cold Blood* (Col). 1969: *The Happy Ending* (UA). 1971: *$ (Dollars)* (Col). 1975: *Bite the Bullet* (Col). 1977: *Looking for Mr. Goodbar* (Par). 1982: *Wrong Is Right* (Col). 1985: *Fever Pitch* (MGM/UA).

CLARENCE BROWN (born 1890) 1920: *The Great Redeemer* (with Maurice Tourneur); *The Last of the Mohicans* (with Maurice Tourneur). 1921: *The Foolish Matrons* (with Maurice Tourneur). 1922: *The Light in the Dark.* 1923: *Don't Marry for Money; The Acquittal.* 1924: *The Signal Tower; Butterfly; Smouldering Fires.* 1925: *The Goose Woman; The Eagle.* 1926: *Kiki.* 1927: *Flesh and the Devil.* 1928: *Trail of '98; A Woman of Affairs.* 1929: *Wonder of Women* (MGM). 1930: *Navy Blues* (MGM); *Anna Christie* (MGM); *Romance* (MGM). 1931: *Inspiration* (MGM); *A Free Soul* (MGM); *Possessed* (MGM). 1932: *Emma* (MGM); *Letty Lynton* (MGM); *The Son-Daughter* (MGM). 1933: *Looking Forward* (MGM); *Night Flight* (MGM). 1934: *Sadie McKee* (MGM); *Chained* (MGM). 1935: *Anna Karenina* (MGM); *Ah, Wilderness!* (MGM). 1936: *Wife vs. Secretary* (MGM); *The Gorgeous Hussy* (MGM). 1937: *Conquest* (MGM). 1938: *Of Human Hearts* (MGM). 1939: *Idiot's Delight* (MGM); *The Rains Came* (Fox). 1940: *Edison the Man* (MGM). 1941: *Come Live with Me* (MGM); *They Met in Bombay* (MGM). 1943: *The Human Comedy* (MGM). 1944: *The White Cliffs of Dover* (MGM); *National Velvet* (MGM). 1946: *The Yearling* (MGM). 1947: *Song of Love* (MGM). 1949: *Intruder in the Dust* (MGM). 1950: *To Please a Lady* (MGM). 1951: *It's a Big Country* (episode; MGM); *Angels in the Outfield* (MGM). 1952: *When in Rome* (MGM); *Plymouth Adventure* (MGM).

Uncredited: 1923: *Robin Hood, Jr.* (with Clarence Bricker).

TOD BROWNING (1882–1962) 1917: *Jim Bludso* (with Wilfred Lucas); *A Love Sublime* (with Wilfred Lucas); *Hands Up!* (with Wilfred Lucas); *Peggy, the Will-o'-the-Wisp; The Jury of Fate.* 1918: *The Eyes of Mystery; The Brazen Beauty; The Legion of Death; Revenge; Which Woman?; The Deciding Kiss; Set Free.* 1919: *The Wicked Darling; The Exquisite Thief; The Unpainted Woman; The Petal on the Current; Bonnie, Bonnie Lassie.* 1920: *The Virgin of Stamboul.* 1921: *Outside the Law; No Woman Knows.* 1922: *The Wise Kid; The Man Under Cover; Under Two Flags.* 1923: *Drifting; White Tiger; The Day of Faith.* 1924: *The Dangerous Flirt; Silk Stocking Sal.* 1925: *The Unholy Three; Dollar Down; The Mystic.* 1926: *The Black Bird; The Road to Mandalay.* 1927: *The Show; The Unknown; London after Midnight.* 1928: *The Big City; West of Zanzibar.* 1929: *Where East Is East; The Thirteenth Chair* (MGM). 1930: *Outside the Law* (Univ). 1931: *Dracula* (Univ); *The Iron Man* (Univ). 1932: *Freaks* (MGM). 1933: *Fast Workers* (MGM). 1935: *Mark of the Vampire*

(MGM). 1936: *The Devil Doll* (MGM). 1939: *Miracles for Sale* (MGM).

DAVID BUTLER (1894–1979) 1927: *High School Hero; Win That Girl*. 1928: *The News Parade; Prep and Pep*. 1929: *Masked Emotions; Fox Movietone Follies of 1929* (Fox); *Chasing Through Europe* (with Alfred Werker; Fox); *Sunny Side Up* (Fox). 1930: *Just Imagine* (Fox); *High Society Blues* (Fox). 1931: *Delicious* (Fox); *A Connecticut Yankee* (Fox); *Business and Pleasure* (Fox). 1932: *Down to Earth* (Fox); *Handle with Care* (Fox). 1933: *Hold Me Tight* (Fox); *My Weakness* (Fox). 1934: *Bottoms Up* (Fox); *Handy Andy* (Fox); *Have a Heart* (MGM); *Bright Eyes* (Fox). 1935: *The Little Colonel* (Fox); *The Littlest Rebel* (Fox); *Doubting Thomas* (Fox). 1936: *Captain January* (Fox); *White Fang* (Fox); *Pigskin Parade* (Fox). 1937: *You're a Sweetheart* (Univ); *Ali Baba Goes to Town* (Fox). 1938: *Kentucky* (Fox); *Kentucky Moonshine* (Fox); *Straight, Place and Show* (Fox). 1939: *East Side of Heaven* (Univ); *That's Right—You're Wrong* (RKO). 1940: *If I Had My Way* (Univ); *You'll Find Out* (RKO). 1941: *Caught in the Draft* (Par); *Playmates* (RKO). 1942: *Road to Morocco* (Par); *They Got Me Covered* (RKO). 1943: *Thank Your Lucky Stars* (WB). 1944: *Shine On, Harvest Moon* (WB); *The Princess and the Pirate* (RKO). 1945: *San Antonio* (WB). 1946: *The Time, the Place and the Girl* (WB); *Two Guys from Milwaukee* (WB). 1947: *My Wild Irish Rose* (WB). 1948: *Two Guys from Texas* (WB). 1949: *Look for the Silver Lining* (WB); *It's a Great Feeling* (WB); *John Loves Mary* (WB); *The Story of Seabiscuit* (WB). 1950: *Tea for Two* (WB); *The Daughter of Rosie O'Grady* (WB). 1951: *Painting the Clouds with Sunshine* (WB); *Lullaby of Broadway* (WB). 1952: *Where's Charley?* (WB); *April in Paris* (WB). 1953: *By the Light of the Silvery Moon* (WB); *Calamity Jane* (WB). 1954: *The Command* (WB); *King Richard and the Crusaders* (WB). 1955: *Jump into Hell* (WB); *Glory* (RKO). 1956: *The Girl He Left Behind* (WB). 1961: *The Right Approach* (Fox). 1967: *C'mon Let's Live a Little* (Par).

FRANK CAPRA (born 1897) 1926: *The Strong Man*. 1927: *Long Pants; For the Love of Mike*. 1928: *That Certain Thing; So This Is Love; The Matinee Idol; The Way of the Strong; Say It with Sables; Submarine; The Power of the Press*. 1929: *The Younger Generation* (Col); *The Donovan Affair* (Col); *Flight* (Col). 1930: *Ladies of Leisure* (Col); *Rain or Shine* (Col). 1931: *Dirigible* (Col); *The Miracle Woman* (Col); *Platinum Blonde* (Col). 1932: *Forbidden* (Col); *American Madness* (Col); *The Bitter Tea of General Yen* (Col). 1933: *Lady for a Day* (Col). 1934: *It Happened One Night* (Col); *Broadway Bill* (Col). 1936: *Mr. Deeds Goes to Town* (Col). 1937: *Lost Horizon* (Col). 1938: *You Can't Take It with You* (Col). 1939: *Mr. Smith Goes to Washington* (Col). 1941: *Meet John Doe* (WB). 1942: *Prelude to War* (U.S. Govt); *The Nazis Strike* (with Anatole Litvak; U.S. Govt); *Divide and Conquer* (with Anatole Litvak; U.S. Govt). 1944: *The Battle of China* (with Anatole Litvak; U.S. Govt); *Arsenic and Old Lace* (WB). 1946: *It's a Wonderful Life* (RKO). 1948: *State of the Union* (MGM). 1950: *Riding High* (Par). 1951: *Here Comes the Groom* (Par). 1959: *A Hole in the Head* (UA). 1961: *Pocketful of Miracles* (UA).

JOHN CARPENTER (born 1948) 1974: *Dark Star* (Jack H. Harris Enterprises). 1976: *Assault on Precinct 13* (Turtle Releasing Co). 1978: *Halloween* (Compass International). 1980: *The Fog* (Avco Embassy). 1981: *Escape from New York* (Avco Embassy). 1982: *The Thing* (Univ). 1983: *Christine* (Col). 1984: *Starman* (Col).

JOHN CASSAVETES (born 1929) 1961: *Shadows* (Lion International). 1962: *Too Late Blues* (Par). 1963: *A Child Is Waiting* (UA). 1968: *Faces* (Continental). 1970: *Husbands* (Col). 1971: *Minnie and Moskowitz* (Univ). 1974: *A Woman under the Influence* (Faces International). 1976: *The Killing of a Chinese Bookie* (Faces International). 1979: *Opening Night* (Faces International). 1980: *Gloria* (Col). 1984: *Love Streams* (Cannon). 1985: *Big Trouble* (Col).

GILBERT CATES (born 1934) 1967: *Rings Around the World* (Col). 1970: *I Never Sang for My Father* (Col).

1973: *Summer Wishes, Winter Dreams* (Col). 1976: *One Summer Love (Dragonfly)* (AI). 1979: *The Promise* (Univ). 1980: *The Last Married Couple in America* (Univ); *Oh, God! Book II* (WB).

CHARLES CHAPLIN (1889–1977) 1914: *Caught in a Cabaret* (with Mabel Normand); *Caught in the Rain; A Busy Day; The Fatal Mallet; Her Friend the Bandit* (with Mabel Normand); *Mabel's Busy Day* (with Mabel Normand); *Mabel's Married Life* (with Mabel Normand); *Laughing Gas; The Property Man; The Face on the Barroom Floor; Recreation; The Masquerader; His New Profession; The Rounders; The New Janitor; Those Love Pangs; Dough and Dynamite; Gentlemen of Nerve; His Musical Career; His Trysting Place; Getting Acquainted; His Prehistoric Past*. 1915: *His New Job; A Night Out; The Champion; In the Park; The Jitney Elopement; The Tramp; By the Sea; Work; A Woman; The Bank; Shanghaied; A Night at the Show; Carmen; Triple Trouble*. 1916: *The Floorwalker; The Fireman; The Vagabond; One A.M.; The Count; The Pawnshop; Behind the Screen; The Rink*. 1917: *Easy Street; The Cure; The Immigrant; The Adventurer*. 1918: *A Dog's Life; The Bond; Shoulder Arms*. 1919: *Sunnyside; A Day's Pleasure*. 1921: *The Kid; The Idle Class*. 1922: *Pay Day*. 1923: *The Pilgrim; A Woman of Paris*. 1925: *The Gold Rush*. 1928: *The Circus*. 1931: *City Lights* (UA). 1936: *Modern Times* (UA). 1940: *The Great Dictator* (UA). 1947: *Monsieur Verdoux* (UA). 1952: *Limelight* (UA). 1957: *A King in New York* (Archway). 1967: *A Countess from Hong Kong* (Univ).

MICHAEL CIMINO (born 1943) 1974: *Thunderbolt and Lightfoot* (UA). 1978: *The Deer Hunter* (Univ). 1980: *Heaven's Gate* (UA). 1985: *Year of the Dragon* (MGM/UA).

JACK CONWAY (1887–1952) 1915: *The Penitents*. 1916: *The Beckoning Trail; The Social Buccaneers; The Silent Battle; The Measure of a Man; Judgment of the Guilty; The Mainspring; Bitter Sweet*. 1917: *A Jewel in the Pawn; Polly Redhead; Her Soul's Inspiration; The Little Orphan; Come Through; The Charmer; The Bond of Fear; Because of a Woman*. 1918: *Her Decision; You Can't Believe Everything; Little Red Decides; Desert Law; Restless Souls*. 1919: *A Diplomatic Mission; Lombardi Ltd*. 1920: *The Servant in the House; Riders of the Dawn (Desert of Wheat); The Dwelling Place of Light; The Money Changers; The U.P. Trail*. 1921: *A Daughter of the Law; The Kiss; The Millionaire; The Rage of Paris; The Spenders*. 1922: *Across the Deadline; Another Man's Shoes; Don't Shoot; The Long Chance; Step On It!*. 1923: *Lucretia Lombard; The Prisoner; Quicksands; Sawdust; Trimmed in Scarlet; What Wives Want*. 1924: *The Trouble Shooter; The Heart Buster; The Roughneck*. 1925: *The Hunted Woman; The Only Thing*. 1926: *Brown of Harvard; Soul Mates*. 1927: *The Understanding Heart; Twelve Miles Out*. 1928: *The Smart Set; Bringing Up Father; While the City Sleeps; Alias Jimmy Valentine* (MGM). 1929: *Our Modern Maidens*. 1930: *Untamed* (MGM); *They Learned about Women* (with Sam Wood; MGM); *The Unholy Three* (MGM); *New Moon* (MGM). 1931: *The Easiest Way* (MGM); *Just a Gigolo* (MGM). 1932: *Arsene Lupin* (MGM); *But the Flesh Is Weak* (MGM); *Red-Headed Woman* (MGM). 1933: *Hell Below* (MGM); *The Nuisance* (MGM); *Solitaire Man* (MGM). 1934: *Viva Villa!* (MGM); *The Girl from Missouri* (MGM); *The Gay Bride* (MGM). 1935: *One New York Night* (MGM); *A Tale of Two Cities* (MGM). 1936: *Libeled Lady* (MGM). 1937: *Saratoga* (MGM). 1938: *A Yank at Oxford* (MGM); *Too Hot to Handle* (MGM). 1939: *Let Freedom Ring* (MGM); *Lady of the Tropics* (MGM). 1940: *Boom Town* (MGM). 1941: *Love Crazy* (MGM); *Honky Tonk* (MGM). 1942: *Crossroads* (MGM). 1943: *Assignment in Brittany* (MGM). 1944: *Dragon Seed* (with Harold S. Bucquet; MGM). 1947: *High Barbaree* (MGM); *The Hucksters* (MGM). 1948: *Julia Misbehaves* (MGM).

FRANCIS COPPOLA (born 1939) 1961: *Tonight for Sure* (Premier Pictures). 1963: *Dementia 13* (AI). 1967: *You're a Big Boy Now* (7 Arts). 1968: *Finian's Rainbow* (WB). 1969: *The Rain People* (WB). 1972: *The Godfather* (Par). 1974: *The Conversation* (Par); *The Godfather: Part II* (Par).

1979: *Apocalypse Now* (UA). 1981: *One from the Heart* (Col). 1983: *The Outsiders* (WB); *Rumble Fish* (Univ). 1984: *The Cotton Club* (Orion). 1986: *Peggy Sue Got Married* (Tri-Star).

ROGER CORMAN (born 1926) 1955: *Five Guns West* (AI); *The Apache Woman* (AI). 1956: *The Day the World Ended* (AI); *Swamp Woman* (Woolner Bros); *The Oklahoma Woman* (AI); *The Gunslinger* (American Releasing Corp); *It Conquered the World* (AI). 1957: *Not of This Earth* (AI); *The Undead* (AI); *Naked Paradise* (AI); *Attack of the Crab Monsters* (AA); *Rock All Night* (AI); *Teenage Doll* (AA); *Carnival Rock* (Howco); *Sorority Girl* (AI); *The Viking Woman and the Sea Serpent* (AI). 1958: *War of the Satellites* (AA); *The She Gods of Shark Reef* (AI); *Machine Gun Kelly* (AI); *Teenage Caveman* (AI). 1959: *I, Mobster* (Fox); *A Bucket of Blood* (AI); *The Wasp Woman* (AI). 1960: *Ski Troop Attack* (Filmgroup); *The House of Usher* (AI); *The Little Shop of Horrors* (Filmgroup); *The Last Woman on Earth* (Filmgroup). 1961: *Creature from the Haunted Sea* (Filmgroup); *Atlas* (Filmgroup); *The Pit and the Pendulum* (AI). 1962: *The Intruder (I Hate Your Guts)* (Pathe-America); *The Premature Burial* (AI); *Tales of Terror* (AI); *Tower of London* (AI). 1963: *The Raven* (AI); *The Terror* (AI); *''X''—The Man with the X-Ray Eyes* (AI); *The Haunted Palace* (AI); *The Young Racers* (AI). 1964: *The Secret Invasion* (UA); *The Masque of the Red Death* (Great Britain, U.S.; AI). 1965: *The Tomb of Ligeia* (AI). 1966: *The Wild Angels* (AI). 1967: *The St. Valentine's Day Massacre* (Fox); *The Trip* (AI). 1968: *Target: Harry* (under the name of Harry Neill; ABC Pictures Int). 1970: *Bloody Mama* (AI); *Gas-s-s-s! . . . Or It Became Necessary to Destroy the World in Order to Save It!* (AI). 1971: *Von Richtofen and Brown* (UA).

COSTA-GAVRAS (born 1933) 1966: *The Sleeping Car Murders* (France; 7 Arts). 1968: *Shock Troops (Un Homme de Trop)* (France, Italy; UA). 1969: *Z* (France, Algeria; Cinema 5). 1970: *The Confession* (France; Par). 1972: *State of Siege* (France; Cinema 5). 1975: *Special Section* (France, Italy, West Germany; Univ). 1979: *Clair de Femme* (France, Italy, West Germany; Atlantic). 1982: *Missing* (Univ). 1983: *Hanna K.* (France; Universal Classics).

JOHN CROMWELL (1888–1979) 1929: *Close Harmony* (with Edward Sutherland; Par); *The Dance of Life* (with Edward Sutherland; Par). 1930: *The Mighty* (Par); *Street of Chance* (Par); *Tom Sawyer* (Par); *The Texan* (Par); *For the Defense* (Par). 1931: *Scandal Sheet* (Par); *Rich Man's Folly* (Par); *The Vice Squad* (Par); *Unfaithful* (Par). 1932: *The World and the Flesh* (Par). 1933: *Sweepings* (RKO); *The Silver Cord* (RKO); *Double Harness* (RKO); *Ann Vickers* (RKO). 1934: *Spitfire* (RKO); *This Man Is Mine* (RKO); *Of Human Bondage* (RKO); *The Fountain* (RKO). 1935: *Jalna* (RKO); *Village Tale* (RKO); *I Dream Too Much* (RKO). 1936: *Little Lord Fauntleroy* (UA); *To Mary—with Love* (Fox); *Banjo on My Knee* (Fox). 1937: *The Prisoner of Zenda* (UA). 1938: *Algiers* (UA). 1939: *Made for Each Other* (UA); *In Name Only* (RKO). 1940: *Abe Lincoln·in Illinois* (RKO); *Victory* (Par). 1941: *So Ends Our Night* (UA). 1942: *Son of Fury* (Fox). 1944: *Since You Went Away* (UA). 1945: *The Enchanted Cottage* (RKO). 1946: *Anna and the King of Siam* (Fox). 1947: *Dead Reckoning* (Col); *Night Song* (RKO). 1950: *Caged* (WB); *The Company She Keeps* (RKO). 1951: *The Racket* (RKO). 1958: *The Goddess* (Col). 1959: *The Scavengers* (Par). 1960: *A Matter of Morals* (UA).

ALAN CROSLAND (1894–1936) 1917: *The Light in Darkness; The Apple-Tree Girl; Kidnapped*. 1918: *The Whirlpool; The Unbeliever*. 1919: *The Country Cousin*. 1920: *Broadway and Home; The Flapper; Youthful Folly; Greater Than Fame; Point of View*. 1921: *Worlds Apart; Is Life Worth Living?; Room and Board*. 1922: *Why Announce Your Marriage?; Shadows of the Sea; The Prophet's Paradise; Slim Shoulders; The Snitching Hour; A Face in the Fog*. 1923: *Enemies of Women*. 1924: *Under the Red Robe; Three Weeks; Miami; Sinners in Heaven; Unguarded Women*. 1925: *Bobbed Hair; Contraband; Compromise*. 1926: *Don Juan*. 1927: *When a Man Loves; The Beloved Rogue; Old San Francisco; The Jazz Singer*. 1928: *Glorious Betsy;*

The Scarlet Lady. 1929: *On with the Show* (WB); *General Crack* (WB). 1930: *Big Boy* (WB); *The Furies* (FN); *Song of the Flame* (FN); *Viennese Nights* (WB). 1931: *Captain Thunder* (WB); *Children of Dreams* (WB). 1932: *The Silver Lining* (UA); *Week Ends Only* (Fox). 1934: *Massacre* (FN); *Midnight Alibi* (FN); *The Personality Kid* (WB); *The Case of the Howling Dog* (WB). 1935: *The White Cockatoo* (WB); *It Happened in New York* (Univ); *Mister Dynamite* (Univ); *Lady Tubbs* (Univ); *King Solomon of Broadway* (Univ); *The Great Impersonation* (Univ).

JAMES CRUZE (1884–1942) 1918: *Too Many Millions*. 1919: *The Dub; The Roaring Roads; Alias Mike Moran; You're Fired; The Love Burglar; The Lottery Man; Hawthorne of the U.S.A.; An Adventure in Hearts*. 1920: *Terror Island; Mrs. Temple's Telegram; A Full House; Always Audacious; What Happened to Jones; Food for Scandal; The Sins of St. Anthony*. 1921: *Charm School; The Dollar a Year Man; Crazy to Marry; Gasoline Gus*. 1922: *One Glorious Day; Is Matrimony a Failure?; The Dictator; The Old Homestead; Thirty Days*. 1923: *The Covered Wagon; Hollywood; Ruggles of Red Gap; To the Ladies*. 1924: *The Garden of Weeds; The Fighting Coward; The City That Never Sleeps; The Enemy Sex; Merton of the Movies*. 1925: *The Goose Hangs High; Beggar on Horseback; Waking Up the Town; Welcome Home; Marry Me; The Pony Express*. 1926: *Mannequin; Old Ironsides*. 1927: *We're All Gamblers; The City Gone Wild*. 1928: *On to Reno; Red Mark; Excess Baggage; The Mating Call*. 1929: *The Duke Steps Out; A Man's Man; The Great Gabbo* (World Wide). 1930: *Once a Gentleman* (World Wide); *She Got What She Wanted* (Tiffany). 1931: *Salvation Nell* (Tiffany). 1932: *Washington Merry-Go-Round* (Col); *If I Had a Million* (Par). 1933: *Sailor Be Good* (RKO); *Racetrack* (World Wide); *I Cover the Waterfront* (UA); *Mr. Skitch* (Fox). 1934: *David Harum* (Fox); *Their Big Moment* (RKO). 1935: *Helldorado* (Fox); *Two-Fisted* (Par). 1936: *Sutter's Gold* (Univ). 1937: *The Wrong Road* (Rep). 1938: *Prison Nurse* (Rep); *The Gangs of New York* (Rep); *Come on Leathernecks* (Rep).

Unreleased: 1921: *Leap Year* (Par); *Fast Freight* (Par).

GEORGE CUKOR (1899–1983) 1930: *Grumpy* (with Cyril Gardner; Par); *The Virtuous Sin* (with Louis Gasnier; Par); *The Royal Family of Broadway* (with Cyril Gardner; Par). 1931: *Tarnished Lady* (Par); *Girls about Town* (Par). 1932: *One Hour with You* (with Ernst Lubitsch; Par); *What Price Hollywood* (RKO); *A Bill of Divorcement* (RKO); *Rockabye* (RKO). 1933: *Our Betters* (RKO); *Dinner at Eight* (MGM); *Little Women* (RKO). 1934: *David Copperfield* (MGM). 1935: *Sylvia Scarlett* (RKO). 1936: *Romeo and Juliet* (MGM). 1937: *Camille* (MGM). 1938: *Holiday* (Col). 1939: *Zaza* (Par); *The Women* (MGM). 1940: *The Philadelphia Story* (MGM); *Susan and God* (MGM). 1941: *A Woman's Face* (MGM); *Two-Faced Woman* (MGM). 1942: *Her Cardboard Lover* (MGM). 1943: *Keeper of the Flame* (MGM). 1944: *Gaslight* (MGM); *Winged Victory* (Fox). 1947: *A Double Life* (Univ); *Desire Me* (with Mervyn LeRoy; MGM). 1949: *Edward, My Son* (MGM); *Adam's Rib* (MGM). 1950: *A Life of Her Own* (MGM); *Born Yesterday* (Col). 1951: *The Model and the Marriage Broker* (Fox). 1952: *The Marrying Kind* (Col); *Pat and Mike* (MGM). 1953: *The Actress* (MGM). 1954: *A Star Is Born* (WB); *It Should Happen to You* (Col). 1956: *Bhowani Junction* (MGM). 1957: *Les Girls* (MGM); *Wild Is the Wind* (Par). 1960: *Heller in Pink Tights* (Par); *Let's Make Love* (Fox); *Song Without End* (with Charles Vidor; Col). 1962: *The Chapman Report* (WB). 1964: *My Fair Lady* (WB). 1969: *Justine* (replaced Joseph Strick; Fox). 1972: *Travels with My Aunt* (MGM). 1976: *The Blue Bird* (Fox). 1981: *Rich and Famous* (MGM/UA).

Uncredited: 1939: *Gone with the Wind* (with credited Victor Fleming and uncredited Sam Wood; MGM). Uncompleted: 1962: *Something's Got to Give* (Fox).

MICHAEL CURTIZ (1888–1962) 1912–19: 43 Hungarian films; 1919: 2 Swedish films; 1919–24: 20 Austrian films; 1925–26: 3 German-Austrian films (all silent). 1926: *The Third Degree*. 1927: *A Million Bid; The Desired Woman; Good Time Charley*. 1928: *Tenderloin* (WB); *Noah's Ark* (WB). 1929: *Hearts in Exile* (WB); *The Glad Rag Doll* (WB); *Madonna of Avenue A* (WB); *The Gamblers* (WB). 1930: *Mammy* (WB); *Under a Texas Moon* (WB); *The Matrimonial Bed* (WB); *Bright Lights* (FN); *A Soldier's Plaything* (WB); *River's End* (WB). 1931: *God's Gift to Women* (WB); *The Mad Genius* (WB). 1932: *The Woman from Monte Carlo* (FN); *Alias the Doctor* (FN); *The Strange Love of Molly Louvain* (FN); *Doctor X* (FN); *Cabin in the Cotton* (FN). 1933: *20,000 Years in Sing Sing* (FN); *The Mystery of the Wax Museum* (FN); *The Keyhole* (WB); *Private Detective 62* (WB); *Goodbye Again* (FN); *The Kennel Murder Case* (WB); *Female* (FN). 1934: *Mandalay* (FN); *British Agent* (FN); *Jimmy the Gent* (WB); *The Key* (WB). 1935: *Black Fury* (WB); *The Case of the Curious Bride* (WB); *Front Page Woman* (WB); *Little Big Shot* (WB); *Captain Blood* (WB). 1936: *The Walking Dead* (WB); *The Charge of the Light Brigade* (WB). 1937: *Mountain Justice* (WB); *Stolen Holiday* (WB); *Kid Galahad* (WB); *The Perfect Specimen* (WB). 1938: *Gold Is Where You Find It* (WB); *The Adventures of Robin Hood* (with William Keighley; WB); *Four Daughters* (WB); *Four's a Crowd* (WB); *Angels with Dirty Faces* (WB). 1939: *Dodge City* (WB); *Daughters Courageous* (WB); *Four Wives* (WB); *The Private Lives of Elizabeth and Essex* (WB). 1940: *Virginia City* (WB); *The Sea Hawk* (WB); *Santa Fe Trail* (WB). 1941: *The Sea Wolf* (WB); *Dive Bomber* (WB); *Captains of the Clouds* (WB). 1942: *Yankee Doodle Dandy* (WB); *Casablanca* (WB). 1943: *Mission to Moscow* (WB); *This Is the Army* (WB). 1944: *Passage to Marseille* (WB); *Janie* (WB). 1945: *Roughly Speaking* (WB); *Mildred Pierce* (WB). 1946: *Night and Day* (WB). 1947: *Life with Father* (WB); *The Unsuspected* (WB). 1948: *Romance on the High Seas* (WB). 1949: *My Dream Is Yours* (WB); *Flamingo Road* (WB); *The Lady Takes a Sailor* (WB). 1950: *Young Man with a Horn* (WB); *Bright Leaf* (WB); *The Breaking Point* (WB). 1951: *Jim Thorpe—All American* (WB); *Force of Arms* (WB). 1952: *I'll See You in My Dreams* (WB); *The Story of Will Rogers* (WB). 1953: *The Jazz Singer* (WB); *Trouble along the Way* (WB). 1954: *The Boy from Oklahoma* (WB); *The Egyptian* (Fox); *White Christmas* (Par). 1955: *We're No Angels* (Par). 1956: *The Scarlet Hour* (Par); *The Vagabond King* (Par); *The Best Things in Life Are Free* (Fox). 1957: *The Helen Morgan Story* (WB). 1958: *The Proud Rebel* (BV); *King Creole* (Par). 1959: *The Hangman* (Par); *The Man in the Net* (UA). 1960: *The Adventures of Huckleberry Finn* (MGM); *A Breath of Scandal* (Par). 1961: *Francis of Assisi* (Fox); *The Comancheros* (Fox).

JULES DASSIN (born 1911) 1942: *Nazi Agent* (MGM); *The Affairs of Martha* (MGM); *Reunion in France* (MGM). 1943: *Young Ideas* (1943). 1944: *The Canterville Ghost* (MGM). 1945: *A Letter for Evie* (MGM); *Two Smart People* (MGM). 1947: *Brute Force* (Univ). 1948: *The Naked City* (Univ). 1949: *Thieves' Highway* (Fox). 1950: *Night and the City* (Fox). 1955: *Rififi (Du Rififi Chez les Hommes)* (France; Pathe). 1958: *He Who Must Die (Celui Qui Doit Mourir)* (France; Kassler Films Inc). 1960: *Where the Hot Wind Blows (La Loi)* (France; MGM); *Never on Sunday* (Greece; Lopert). 1962: *Phaedra* (U.S., France, Greece; Lopert). 1964: *Topkapi* (UA). 1966: *10:30 P.M. Summer* (U.S., Spain; Lopert). 1968: *Survival '67* (U.S., Israel; United); *Up Tight* (Par). 1970: *Promise at Dawn* (Avco Embassy). 1978: *A Dream of Passion* (U.S., Greece; Avco Embassy). 1981: *Circle of Two* (World Northal).

DELMER DAVES (1904–1977) 1943: *Destination Tokyo* (WB). 1944: *The Very Thought of You* (WB); *Hollywood Canteen* (WB). 1945: *Pride of the Marines* (WB). 1947: *The Red House* (UA); *Dark Passage* (WB). 1948: *To the Victor* (WB). 1949: *A Kiss in the Dark* (WB); *Task Force* (WB). 1950: *Broken Arrow* (Fox). 1951: *Bird of Paradise* (Fox). 1952: *Return of the Texan* (Fox). 1953: *Treasure of the Golden Condor* (Fox); *Never Let Me Go* (MGM). 1954: *Demetrius and the Gladiators* (Fox); *Drum Beat* (WB). 1956: *Jubal* (Col); *The Last Wagon* (Fox). 1957: *3:10 to Yuma* (Col). 1958: *Cowboy* (Col); *Kings Go Forth* (UA); *The Badlanders* (MGM). 1959: *The Hanging Tree* (WB); *A Summer Place* (WB). 1961: *Parrish* (WB); *Susan Slade* (WB). 1962: *Rome Adventure* (WB). 1963: *Spencer's Mountain* (WB). 1964: *Youngblood Hawke* (WB). 1965: *The Battle of the Villa Fiorita* (WB).

ROY DEL RUTH (1895–1961) 1925: *Eve's Lover; Hogan's Alley*. 1926: *Three Weeks in Paris; The Man Upstairs; The Little Irish Girl; Footloose Widows; Across the Pacific*. 1927: *Wolf's Clothing; The First Auto; Ham and Eggs at the Front*. 1928: *If I Were Single; Five and Ten Cent Annie; Powder My Back; The Terror* (WB). 1929: *Beware of Bachelors* (WB); *Conquest* (WB); *The Desert Song* (WB); *The Hottentot* (WB); *Gold Diggers of Broadway* (WB); *The Aviator* (WB). 1930: *Hold Everything* (WB); *The Second Floor Mystery* (WB); *Three Faces East* (WB); *The Life of the Party* (WB). 1931: *My Past* (WB); *Divorce among Friends* (WB); *The Maltese Falcon* (WB); *Larceny Lane* (WB); *Side Show* (WB); *Blonde Crazy* (WB). 1932: *Taxi* (WB); *Beauty and the Boss* (WB); *Winner Take All* (WB); *Blessed Event* (WB). 1933: *Employees' Entrance* (FN); *The Mind Reader* (FN); *The Little Giant* (FN); *Bureau of Missing Persons* (FN); *Captured* (WB); *Lady Killer* (WB). 1934: *Bulldog Drummond Strikes Back* (UA); *Upper World* (WB); *Kid Millions* (UA). 1935: *Folies Bergere* (UA); *Broadway Melody of 1936* (MGM); *Thanks a Million* (Fox). 1936: *It Had to Happen* (Fox); *Private Number* (Fox); *Born to Dance* (MGM). 1937: *On the Avenue* (Fox); *Broadway Melody of 1938* (MGM). 1938: *Happy Landing* (Fox); *My Lucky Star* (Fox). 1939: *Tail Spin* (Fox); *The Star Maker* (Par); *Here I Am a Stranger* (Fox). 1940: *He Married His Wife* (Fox). 1941: *Topper Returns* (UA); *The Chocolate Soldier* (MGM). 1942: *Maisie Gets Her Man* (MGM). 1943: *Du Barry Was a Lady* (MGM). 1944: *Broadway Rhythm* (MGM); *Barbary Coast Gent* (MGM). 1947: *It Happened on Fifth Avenue* (AA). 1948: *The Babe Ruth Story* (AA). 1949: *Red Light* (UA); *Always Leave Them Laughing* (WB). 1950: *The West Point Story* (WB). 1951: *On Moonlight Bay* (WB); *Starlift* (WB); *About Face* (WB). 1952: *Stop, You're Killing Me* (WB). 1953: *Three Sailors and a Girl* (WB). 1954: *Phantom of the Rue Morgue* (WB). 1959: *The Alligator People* (Fox). 1960: *Why Must I Die?* (AI).

CECIL B. DEMILLE (1881–1959) 1914: *The Squaw Man* (with Oscar Apfel); *The Call of the North; The Virginian; What's His Name; The Man from Home; Rose of the Rancho*. 1915: *The Girl of the Golden West; The Warrens of Virginia; The Unafraid; The Captive; The Wild Goose Chase; The Arab; Chimmie Fadden; Kindling; Carmen; Chimmie Fadden Out West; The Cheat; The Golden Chance*. 1916: *Temptation; The Trail of the Lonesome Pine; The Heart of Nora Flynn; Maria Rosa; The Dream Girl*. 1917: *Joan the Woman; Romance of the Redwoods; The Little American; The Woman God Forgot; The Devil Stone*. 1918: *The Whispering Chorus; Old Wives for New; We Can't Have Everything; Till I Come Back to You; The Squaw Man*. 1919: *Don't Change Your Husband; For Better, for Worse; Male and Female*. 1920: *Why Change Your Wife?; Something to Think About*. 1921: *Forbidden Fruit; The Affairs of Anatol; Fool's Paradise*. 1922: *Saturday Night; Manslaughter*. 1923: *Adam's Rib; The Ten Commandments*. 1924: *Triumph; Feet of Clay*. 1925: *The Golden Bed; The Road to Yesterday*. 1926: *The Volga Boatman*. 1927: *The King of Kings*. 1929: *The Godless Girl* (Pathe); *Dynamite* (MGM). 1930: *Madam Satan* (MGM). 1931: *The Squaw Man* (MGM). 1932: *The Sign of the Cross* (Par). 1933: *This Day and Age* (Par). 1934: *Four Frightened People* (Par); *Cleopatra* (Par). 1935: *The Crusades* (Par). 1937: *The Plainsman* (Par). 1938: *The Buccaneer* (Par). 1939: *Union Pacific* (Par). 1940: *North West Mounted Police* (Par). 1942: *Reap the Wild Wind* (Par). 1944: *The Story of Dr. Wassell* (Par). 1947: *Unconquered* (Par). 1949: *Samson and Delilah* (Par). 1952: *The Greatest Show on Earth* (Par). 1956: *The Ten Commandments* (Par).

WILLIAM DE MILLE (1878–1955) 1916: *Anton, the Terrible; The Black List; The Heir to the Hoorah; The Ragamuffin; The Sowers; The Soul of Kura San*. 1917: *Hashimura Togo; The Ghost House; The Secret Game; Yellow Tickets*. 1918: *The Widow's Might; One More American; The Honor of His House; Mirandy Smiles; The Mystery Girl*. 1920: *The Tree of Knowledge; Jack Straw; The Prince Chap; Conrad in Quest of His Youth; Midsummer Madness*. 1921: *What Every Woman Knows; After the Show; The Lost Romance; Miss Lulu Bett*. 1922: *Bought and Paid For; Nice People; Clarence*. 1923: *The World's Applause; Grumpy; Only 38; The Marriage Maker*. 1924: *Don't Call It Love;*

Icebound; The Bedroom Window; The Fast Set. 1925: *Locked Doors; Men and Women; Lost—a Wife; New Brooms.* 1926: *The Splendid Crime; The Runaway; For Alimony Only.* 1927: *The Little Adventuress* (PDC). 1928: *Craig's Wife; Tenth Avenue.* 1929: *The Doctor's Secret* (Pathe); *The Idle Rich* (MGM). 1930: *This Mad World* (MGM); *Passion Flower* (MGM). 1932: *Two Kinds of Women* (Par). 1933: *His Double Life* (with Arthur Hopkins; Par).

Unreleased: 1919: *Peg o' My Heart* (Par).

JONATHAN DEMME (born 1944) 1974: *Caged Heat* (New World). 1975: *Crazy Mama* (New World). 1976: *Fighting Mad* (Fox). 1977: *Handle with Care (Citizens Band)* (Par). 1979: *Last Embrace* (UA). 1980: *Melvin and Howard* (Univ). 1983: *Swing Shift* (WB). 1984: *Stop Making Sense* (Doc; Cinecom International/Island Alive). 1986: *Something Wild* (Orion).

BRIAN DE PALMA (born 1940) 1968: *Murder a la Mod* (Aries); *Greetings* (Sigma III). 1969: *The Wedding Party* (with Wilford Leach and Cynthia Munroe; Powell Prod. Plus/Ondine). 1970: *Dionysus in '69* (with Robert Fiore and Bruce Rubin; Sigma III); *Hi, Mom!* (Sigma III). 1972: *Get to Know Your Rabbit* (WB). 1973: *Sisters* (AI). 1974: *Phantom of the Paradise* (Fox). 1976: *Obsession* (Col); *Carrie* (UA). 1978: *The Fury* (Fox). 1980: *Home Movies* (UA Classics); *Dressed to Kill* (Filmways). 1981: *Blow Out* (Filmways). 1983: *Scarface* (Univ). 1984: *Body Double* (Col). 1986: *Wise Guys* (MGM).

ANDRE DE TOTH (born 1910) 1939: 5 Hungarian films. 1943: *Passport to Suez* (Col). 1944: *None Shall Escape* (Col); *Dark Waters* (UA). 1947: *Ramrod* (UA); *The Other Love* (UA). 1948: *Pitfall* (UA). 1949: *Slattery's Hurricane* (Fox). 1951: *Man in the Saddle* (Col). 1952: *Carson City* (WB); *Springfield Rifle* (WB); *Last of the Comanches* (Col). 1953: *House of Wax* (WB); *The Stranger Wore a Gun* (Col); *Thunder over the Plains* (WB). 1954: *Riding Shotgun* (WB); *The City Is Dark (Crime Wave)* (WB); *The Bounty Hunter* (WB); *Tanganyika* (Univ). 1955: *The Indian Fighter* (UA). 1957: *Monkey on My Back* (UA); *Hidden Fear* (UA). 1959: *The Two-Headed Spy* (Col); *Day of the Outlaw* (UA). 1960: *Man on a String* (Col); *Morgan the Pirate* (MGM); *The Mongols (I Mongoli)* (with Leopoldo Savona; France, Italy; Royal Film/France Cinema Productions). 1963: *Gold for the Caesars* (France, Italy; MGM, 1964). 1968: *Play Dirty* (UA).

Uncredited: 1944: *Since You Went Away* (with John Cromwell; UA); *Guest in the House* (with John Brahm; UA).

WILLIAM DIETERLE (1893–1972) 1923–30: 11 German silent and sound films. 1931: *The Last Flight* (FN); *Her Majesty Love* (FN). 1932: *Man Wanted* (WB); *Jewel Robbery* (WB); *The Crash* (FN); *Scarlet Dawn* (WB); *Six Hours to Live* (Fox); *Lawyer Man* (WB). 1933: *Grand Slam* (WB); *Adorable* (Fox); *The Devil's in Love* (Fox); *From Headquarters* (WB). 1934: *Fashions of 1934* (WB); *Fog over Frisco* (FN); *Madame Du Barry* (WB); *The Firebird* (WB); *The Secret Bride* (WB). 1935: *Dr. Socrates* (WB); *A Midsummer Night's Dream* (with Max Reinhardt; WB). 1936: *The Story of Louis Pasteur* (WB); *The White Angel* (WB); *Satan Met a Lady* (WB). 1937: *The Great O'Malley* (WB); *Another Dawn* (WB); *The Life of Emile Zola* (WB). 1938: *Blockade* (UA). 1939: *Juarez* (WB); *The Hunchback of Notre Dame* (RKO). 1940: *Dr. Ehrlich's Magic Bullet* (MGM); *A Dispatch from Reuters* (WB). 1941: *All That Money Can Buy (The Devil and Daniel Webster)* (RKO). 1942: *Syncopation* (RKO); *Tennessee Johnson* (MGM). 1944: *Kismet* (MGM); *I'll Be Seeing You* (UA). 1945: *Love Letters* (Par); *This Love of Ours* (Univ). 1946: *The Searching Wind* (Par). 1949: *Portrait of Jennie* (Selznick); *The Accused* (Par); *Volcano* (UA); *Rope of Sand* (Par). 1950: *Paid in Full* (Par); *Dark City* (Par). 1951: *September Affair* (Par); *Peking Express* (Par). 1952: *Boots Malone* (Col); *Red Mountain* (Par); *The Turning Point* (Par). 1953: *Salome* (Col). 1954: *Elephant Walk* (Par). 1956: *Magic Fire* (Rep). 1957: *Omar Khayyam* (Par). 1959–60: 3 European films. 1965: *The Confession* (Golden Eagle).

Uncredited: 1946: *Duel in the Sun* (with credited King Vidor and uncredited Josef von Sternberg; Selznick).

EDWARD DMYTRYK (born 1908) 1935: *The Hawk* (Herman Wohl). 1939: *Television Spy* (Par). 1940: *Emergency Squad* (Par); *Mystery Sea Raider* (Par); *Golden Gloves* (Par); *Her First Romance* (Mon). 1941: *The Devil Commands* (Col); *Under Age* (Col); *Sweetheart of the Campus* (Col); *The Blonde from Singapore* (Col); *Confessions of Boston Blackie* (Col); *Secrets of the Lone Wolf* (Col). 1942: *Counter Espionage* (Col); *Seven Miles from Alcatraz* (RKO). 1943: *The Falcon Strikes Back* (RKO); *Hitler's Children* (RKO); *Captive Wild Woman* (Univ); *Behind the Rising Sun* (RKO); *Tender Comrade* (RKO). 1945: *Murder My Sweet* (RKO); *Back to Bataan* (RKO); *Cornered* (RKO); *Till the End of Time* (RKO). 1947: *Crossfire* (RKO); *So Well Remembered* (RKO). 1949: *Give Us This Day* (Eagle-Lion); *Obsession (The Hidden Room)* (British Lion). 1952: *Mutiny* (Univ); *The Sniper* (Col); *Eight Iron Men* (Col). 1953: *The Juggler* (Col). 1954: *Broken Lance* (Fox); *The Caine Mutiny* (Col); *The End of the Affair* (Col). 1955: *Soldier of Fortune* (Fox); *The Left Hand of God* (Fox). 1956: *The Mountain* (Par). 1957: *Raintree County* (MGM). 1958: *The Young Lions* (Fox). 1959: *Warlock* (Fox); *The Blue Angel* (Fox). 1962: *Walk on the Wild Side* (Col); *The Reluctant Saint* (Davis Royal). 1964: *The Carpetbaggers* (Par); *Where Love Has Gone* (Par). 1965: *Mirage* (Univ). 1966: *Alvarez Kelly* (Col). 1968: *Anzio* (Col); *Shalako* (Cinerama). 1972: *Bluebeard* (Cinerama). 1975: *The Human Factor* (Brynaston). 1976: *He Is My Brother* (Atlantic).

Uncredited: 1939: *Million Dollar Legs* (with Nick Grinde; Par).

STANLEY DONEN (born 1924) 1949: *On the Town* (with Gene Kelly; MGM). 1951: *Royal Wedding* (MGM). 1952: *Love Is Better Than Ever* (MGM); *Singin' in the Rain* (with Gene Kelly; MGM); *Fearless Fagan* (MGM). 1953: *Give a Girl a Break* (MGM). 1954: *Seven Brides for Seven Brothers* (MGM); *Deep in My Heart* (MGM). 1955: *It's Always Fair Weather* (with Gene Kelly; MGM). 1957: *Funny Face* (Par); *The Pajama Game* (with George Abbott; WB); *Kiss Them for Me* (Fox). 1958: *Indiscreet* (WB); *Damn Yankees* (with George Abbott; WB). 1960: *Once More, with Feeling* (Col); *Surprise Package* (Col); *The Grass Is Greener* (Univ). 1963: *Charade* (Univ). 1966: *Arabesque* (Univ). 1967: *Two for the Road* (Fox); *Bedazzled* (Fox). 1969: *Staircase* (Fox). 1974: *The Little Prince* (Great Britain; Par). 1975: *Lucky Lady* (Fox). 1978: *Movie Movie* (WB). 1979: *Saturn 3* (AFD). 1983: *Blame It on Rio* (Fox).

GORDON DOUGLAS (born 1909) 1936: *General Spanky* (with Fred Newmeyer; MGM). 1939: *Zenobia* (UA). 1940: *Saps at Sea* (UA). 1941: *Road Show* (with Hal Roach and Hal Roach, Jr.; UA); *Broadway Limited* (UA); *Niagara Falls* (UA). 1942: *The Devil with Hitler* (RKO); *The Great Gildersleeve* (RKO). 1943: *Gildersleeve's Bad Day* (RKO); *Gildersleeve on Broadway* (RKO). 1944: *Gildersleeve's Ghost* (RKO); *A Night of Adventure* (RKO); *Girl Rush* (RKO); *The Falcon in Hollywood* (RKO). 1945: *Zombies on Broadway* (RKO); *First Yank into Tokyo* (RKO). 1946: *Dick Tracy vs. Cueball* (RKO); *San Quentin* (RKO). 1948: *If You Knew Susie* (RKO); *The Black Arrow* (Col); *Walk a Crooked Mile* (Col). 1949: *Mr. Soft Touch* (with Henry Levin; Col); *The Doolins of Oklahoma* (Col). 1950: *The Nevadan* (Col); *Fortunes of Captain Blood* (Col); *Rogues of Sherwood Forest* (Col); *Kiss Tomorrow Goodbye* (WB); *Between Midnight and Dawn* (Col). 1951: *The Great Missouri Raid* (Par); *Only the Valiant* (WB); *I Was a Communist for the F.B.I.* (WB); *Come Fill the Cup* (WB). 1952: *Mara Maru* (WB); *The Iron Mistress* (WB). 1953: *She's Back on Broadway* (WB); *The Charge at Feather River* (WB); *So This Is Love* (WB). 1954: *Them* (WB); *Young at Heart* (WB). 1955: *The McConnell Story* (WB); *Sincerely Yours* (WB). 1956: *Santiago* (WB). 1957: *The Big Land* (WB); *Bombers B-52* (WB). 1958: *Fort Dobbs* (WB); *The Fiend Who Walked the West* (Fox). 1959: *Up Periscope* (WB); *Yellowstone Kelly* (WB). 1961: *Gold of the Seven Saints* (WB); *The Sins of Rachel Cade* (WB); *Claudelle English* (WB). 1962: *Follow That Dream* (UA). 1963: *Call Me Bwana* (UA). 1964: *Robin and the Seven Hoods* (WB); *Rio Conchos* (Fox). 1965: *Sylvia* (Par); *Harlow* (Par). 1966: *Stagecoach* (Fox); *Way . . . Way Out* (Fox). 1967: *In Like Flint* (Fox); *Chuka* (Par); *Tony Rome* (Fox). 1968: *The Detective* (Fox); *Lady in Cement* (Fox). 1970: *Skullduggery* (Univ); *Barquero* (UA); *They Call Me Mister Tibbs!* (UA). 1973: *Slaughter's Big Rip-Off* (AI). 1978: *Viva Knievel!* (WB).

ALLAN DWAN (1885–1981) 1914: *Richelieu; Wildflower; The County Chairman; The Straight Road; The Conspiracy; The Unwelcome.* 1915: *The Foundling* (film destroyed, redirected by John B. O'Brien in 1916); *The Dancing Girl; David Harum; The Love Route; The Commanding Officer; The Pretty Sister of Jose; A Girl of Yesterday; May Blossom; Jordan Is a Hard Road.* 1916: *Betty of Greystone; The Habit of Happiness; The Good Bad Man: An Innocent Magdalene; The Half-Breed; Manhattan Madness; Fifty-Fifty.* 1917: *Panthea; The Fighting Odds; A Modern Musketeer.* 1918: *Mr. Fix-It; Bound in Morocco; He Comes Up Smiling; Cheating Cheaters.* 1919: *Getting Mary Married; The Dark Star; Soldiers of Fortune.* 1920: *The Luck of the Irish; The Forbidden Thing; The Scoffer.* 1921: *A Perfect Crime; A Broken Doll; The Sin of Martha Queed; In the Heart of a Fool.* 1922: *The Hidden Woman; Superstition; Robin Hood.* 1923: *The Glimpses of the Moon; Lawful Larceny; Zaza; Big Brother.* 1924: *A Society Scandal; Manhandled; Her Love Story; Wages of Virtue; Argentine Love.* 1925: *Night Life in New York; Coast of Folly; Stage Struck.* 1926: *Sea Horses; Padlocked; Tin Gods; Summer Bachelors.* 1927: *The Music Master; The Joy Girl; East Side, West Side; French Dressing.* 1928: *The Big Noise.* 1929: *The Iron Mask; Tide of the Empire* (MGM); *The Far Call* (Fox); *Frozen Justice* (Fox); *South Sea Rose* (Fox). 1930: *What a Widow!* (UA); *Man to Man* (FN). 1931: *Chances* (FN); *Wicked* (Fox). 1932: *While Paris Sleeps* (Fox). 1933: *Her First Affair* (Associated British); *Counsel's Opinion* (London Films/Par). 1934: *The Morning After (I Spy)* (Wardour/Majestic). 1935: *Black Sheep* (Fox); *Navy Wife* (Fox). 1936: *The Song and Dance Man* (Fox); *Human Cargo* (Fox); *High Tension* (Fox); *15 Maiden Lane* (Fox). 1937: *Woman-Wise* (Fox); *That I May Live* (Fox); *One Mile from Heaven* (Fox); *Heidi* (Fox). 1938: *Rebecca of Sunnybrook Farm* (Fox); *Josette* (Fox); *Suez* (Fox). 1939: *The Three Musketeers* (Fox); *The Gorilla* (Fox); *Frontier Marshal* (Fox). 1940: *Sailor's Lady* (Fox); *Young People* (Fox); *Trail of the Vigilantes* (Univ). 1941: *Look Who's Laughing* (RKO); *Rise and Shine* (Fox). 1942: *Friendly Enemies* (UA); *Here We Go Again* (RKO). 1943: *Around the World* (RKO). 1944: *Up in Mabel's Room* (UA); *Abroad with Two Yanks* (UA). 1945: *Brewster's Millions* (UA). 1946: *Getting Gertie's Garter* (UA); *Rendezvous with Annie* (Rep). 1947: *Calendar Girl* (Rep); *Northwest Outpost* (Rep); *Driftwood* (Rep). 1948: *The Inside Story* (Rep); *Angel in Exile* (with Philip Ford; Rep). 1949: *Sands of Iwo Jima* (Rep). 1950: *Surrender* (Rep). 1951: *Belle Le Grand* (Rep); *The Wild Blue Yonder* (Rep). 1952: *I Dream of Jeanie* (Rep); *Montana Belle* (RKO). 1953: *The Woman They Almost Lynched* (Rep); *Sweethearts on Parade* (Rep). 1954: *Flight Nurse* (Rep); *Silver Lode* (RKO); *Passion* (RKO); *Cattle Queen of Montana* (RKO). 1955: *Escape to Burma* (RKO); *Pearl of the South Pacific* (RKO); *Tennessee's Partner* (RKO). 1956: *Slightly Scarlet* (RKO); *Hold Back the Night* (AA). 1957: *The River's Edge* (Fox); *The Restless Breed* (Fox). 1958: *Enchanted Island* (WB). 1961: *The Most Dangerous Man Alive* (Col).

Uncredited: 1934: *Hollywood Party* (with Richard Boleslawski and Roy Rowland, all uncredited; MGM).

BLAKE EDWARDS (born 1922) 1955: *Bring Your Smile Along* (Col). 1956: *He Laughed Last* (Col). 1957: *Mister Cory* (MGM). 1958: *This Happy Feeling* (Univ). 1959: *The Perfect Furlough* (Univ); *Operation Petticoat* (Univ). 1960: *High Time* (Fox). 1961: *Breakfast at Tiffany's* (Par). 1962: *Experiment in Terror* (WB); *Days of Wine and Roses* (WB). 1964: *The Pink Panther* (UA); *A Shot in the Dark* (UA). 1965: *The Great Race* (WB). 1966: *What Did You Do in the War, Daddy?* (UA). 1967: *Gunn* (WB). 1968: *The Party* (UA). 1970: *Darling Lili* (Par). 1971: *Wild Rovers* (MGM). 1972: *The Carey Treatment* (MGM). 1974: *The Tamarind Seed* (Avco Embassy). 1975: *Return of the Pink Panther* (Great Britain; UA). 1976: *The Pink Panther Strikes Again* (Great Britain; UA). 1978: *Revenge of the*

Pink Panther (Great Britain; UA). 1979: *10* (Orion/WB). 1981: *S.O.B.* (Par). 1982: *Victor/Victoria* (MGM/UA); *Trail of the Pink Panther* (MGM/UA). 1983: *Curse of the Pink Panther* (MGM/UA); *The Man Who Loved Women* (Col). 1984: *Micki and Maude* (Col). 1986: *A Fine Mess* (Col).

George Fitzmaurice (1885–1940) 1914: *The Quest of the Sacred Gem; The Bomb Boy.* 1915: *Stop Thief!; Via Wireless; Who's Who in Society; The Money Master; The Commuters; At Bay.* 1916: *The Test; Big Jim Garrity; Arms and the Woman; New York; The Romantic Journey.* 1917: *Blind Man's Luck; The Iron Heart; The Mark of Cain; The Recoil; The On-the-Square Girl; The Hunting of the Hawk; Sylvia of the Secret Service.* 1918: *Innocence; The Naulahka; The Hillcrest Mystery; The Narrow Path; The Japanese Nightingale.* 1919: *The Cry of the Weak; Our Better Selves; Common Clay; The Witness for the Defense; The Avalanche; Profiteer; A Society Exile; Counterfeit.* 1920: *On with the Dance; The Right to Love; Idols of Clay.* 1921: *Paying the Piper; Experience; Forever.* 1922: *Three Live Ghosts; To Have and to Hold; The Man from Home; Kick In.* 1923: *Bella Donna; The Cheat; The Eternal City.* 1924: *Cytherea; Tarnish.* 1925: *A Thief in Paradise; The Dark Angel; His Supreme Moment.* 1926: *The Son of the Sheik* (UA). 1927: *The Night of Love* (UA); *The Tender Hour* (FN); *Rose of the Golden West* (FN); *The Love Mart* (FN). 1928: *Lilac Time; The Barker.* 1929: *His Captive Woman; The Man and the Moment; The Locked Door* (UA); *Tiger Rose* (WB). 1930: *The Devil to Pay* (UA); *One Heavenly Night* (UA); *The Bad One* (UA); *Raffles* (with Harry D'Abbadie D'Arrast; UA). 1931: *Strangers May Kiss* (MGM); *The Unholy Garden* (UA). 1932: *Mata Hari* (MGM); *As You Desire Me* (MGM). 1934: *All Men Are Enemies* (Fox). 1936: *Petticoat Fever* (MGM); *Suzy* (MGM). 1937: *The Emperor's Candlesticks* (MGM); *Live, Love and Learn* (MGM). 1938: *Arsene Lupin Returns* (MGM); *Vacation from Love* (MGM). 1940: *Adventure in Diamonds* (Par).

Robert J. Flaherty (1884–1951) 1922: *Nanook of the North* (Doc). 1926: *Moana: A Romance of the Golden Age* (Doc). 1928: *White Shadows of the South Seas* (with W. S. Van Dyke). 1931: *Tabu* (with F. W. Murnau; Par). 1934: *Man of Aran* (Doc; Gaumont-British). 1937: *Elephant Boy* (with Zoltan Korda; UA). 1948: *Louisiana Story* (Doc; Lopert).

Victor Fleming (1883–1949) 1920: *When the Clouds Roll By* (with Ted Reed); *The Mollycoddle.* 1921: *Mama's Affair; Woman's Place.* 1922: *Anna Ascends; Red Hot Romance; The Lane That Had No Turning.* 1923: *Dark Secrets; The Law of the Lawless; To the Last Man; The Call of the Canyon.* 1924: *Empty Hands; Code of the Sea.* 1925: *Adventure; The Devil's Cargo; A Son of His Father; Lord Jim.* 1926: *Blind Goddess; Mantrap.* 1927: *The Rough Riders; The Way of All Flesh; Hula.* 1928: *The Awakening.* 1929: *Abie's Irish Rose; Wolf Song; The Virginian* (Par). 1930: *Common Clay* (Fox); *Renegades* (Fox). 1931: *Around the World in 80 Minutes* (with Douglas Fairbanks; UA). 1932: *The Wet Parade* (MGM); *Red Dust* (MGM). 1933: *The White Sister* (MGM); *Bombshell* (MGM). 1934: *Treasure Island* (MGM). 1935: *Reckless* (MGM); *The Farmer Takes a Wife* (Fox). 1937: *Captains Courageous* (MGM). 1938: *Test Pilot* (MGM). 1939: *The Wizard of Oz* (MGM); *Gone with the Wind* (MGM). 1941: *Dr. Jekyll and Mr. Hyde* (MGM). 1942: *Tortilla Flat* (MGM). 1944: *A Guy Named Joe* (MGM). 1945: *Adventure* (MGM). 1948: *Joan of Arc* (RKO).

Uncredited: 1937: *The Good Earth* (with credited Sidney Franklin and uncredited George Hill and Gustav Machaty; MGM). Unfinished: 1941: *The Yearling* (abandoned, reshot in 1946 by Clarence Brown; MGM).

John Ford (1895–1973) 1917: *Straight Shooting; The Secret Man; A Marked Man; Bucking Broadway.* 1918: *The Phantom Riders; Wild Women; Thieves' Gold; The Scarlet Drop; Hell Bent; A Woman's Fool; Three Mounted Men.* 1919: *Roped; A Fight for Love; Bare Fists; Riders of Vengeance; The Outcasts of Poker Flat; The Ace of the Saddle; The Rider of the Law; A Gun Fightin' Gentleman; Marked Men.* 1920: *The Prince of Avenue A; The Girl in No. 29; Hitchin' Posts; Under Sentence; Just Pals.* 1921: *The Big Punch; The Freeze-Out; The Wallop; Desperate Trails; Action; Sure Fire; Jackie.* 1922: *Little Miss Smiles; Silver Wings* (with Edwin Carewe); *The Village Blacksmith.* 1923: *The Face on the Barroom Floor; Three Jumps Ahead; Cameo Kirby; North of Hudson Bay; Hoodman Blind.* 1924: *The Iron Horse; Hearts of Oak.* 1925: *Lightnin'; Kentucky Pride; The Fighting Heart; Thank You.* 1926: *The Shamrock Handicap; Three Bad Men; The Blue Eagle.* 1927: *Upstream.* 1928: *Mother Machree; Four Sons; Hangman's House; Riley the Cop.* 1929: *Strong Boy; The Black Watch* (Fox); *Salute* (Fox); *Men Without Women* (Fox). 1930: *Born Reckless* (Fox); *Up the River* (Fox). 1931: *Seas Beneath* (Fox); *The Brat* (Fox); *Arrowsmith* (UA). 1932: *Air Mail* (Univ); *Flesh* (MGM). 1933: *Pilgrimage* (Fox); *Dr. Bull* (Fox). 1934: *The Lost Patrol* (RKO); *The World Moves On* (Fox); *Judge Priest* (Fox). 1935: *The Whole Town's Talking* (Col); *The Informer* (RKO); *Steamboat 'Round the Bend* (Fox). 1936: *The Prisoner of Shark Island* (Fox); *The Last Outlaw* (RKO); *Mary of Scotland* (RKO); *The Plough and the Stars* (RKO). 1937: *Wee Willie Winkie* (Fox); *The Hurricane* (UA). 1938: *Four Men and a Prayer* (Fox); *Submarine Patrol* (Fox). 1939: *Stagecoach* (UA); *Young Mr. Lincoln* (Fox); *Drums along the Mohawk* (Fox). 1940: *The Grapes of Wrath* (Fox); *The Long Voyage Home* (UA). 1941: *Tobacco Road* (Fox); *How Green Was My Valley* (Fox). 1945: *They Were Expendable* (MGM). 1946: *My Darling Clementine* (Fox). 1947: *The Fugitive* (RKO). 1948: *Fort Apache* (RKO); *Three Godfathers* (MGM). 1949: *She Wore a Yellow Ribbon* (RKO). 1950: *When Willie Comes Marching Home* (Fox); *Wagonmaster* (RKO); *Rio Grande* (Rep). 1951: *This Is Korea!* (Rep/U.S. Navy). 1952: *What Price Glory* (Fox); *The Quiet Man* (Rep). 1953: *The Sun Shines Bright* (Rep); *Mogambo* (MGM). 1955: *The Long Gray Line* (Col); *Mister Roberts* (with Mervyn LeRoy; WB). 1956: *The Searchers* (WB). 1957: *The Wings of Eagles* (MGM); *The Rising of the Moon* (WB). 1958: *The Last Hurrah* (Col). 1959: *Gideon of Scotland Yard* (Col); *The Horse Soldiers* (UA). 1960: *Sergeant Rutledge* (WB). 1961: *Two Rode Together* (Col). 1962: *The Man Who Shot Liberty Valance* (Par). 1963: *How the West Was Won* ("The Civil War" episode; MGM); *Donovan's Reef* (Par). 1964: *Cheyenne Autumn* (WB). 1965: *Young Cassidy* (with Jack Cardiff; MGM). 1966: *Seven Women* (MGM).

Uncredited: 1938: *The Adventures of Marco Polo* (with Archie Mayo; UA). 1949: *Pinky* (with Elia Kazan; Fox).

Milos Forman (born 1932) 1963: *Competition* (Czechoslovakia; Brandon). 1964: *Black Peter* (Czechoslovakia; Billings). 1966: *Loves of a Blonde* (Czechoslovakia; Prominent). 1968: *The Fireman's Ball* (Czechoslovakia; Cinema 5). 1971: *Taking Off* (Univ). 1973: *Visions of Eight* (Doc; episode; Cinema 5). 1975: *One Flew over the Cuckoo's Nest* (UA). 1979: *Hair* (UA). 1981: *Ragtime* (Par). 1984: *Amadeus* (Orion).

Bob Fosse (born 1927) 1969: *Sweet Charity* (Univ). 1972: *Cabaret* (AA). 1974: *Lenny* (UA). 1979: *All That Jazz* (Fox). 1983: *Star 80* (WB/Ladd).

John Frankenheimer (born 1930) 1957: *The Young Stranger* (Univ). 1961: *The Young Savages* (UA). 1962: *All Fall Down* (MGM); *Birdman of Alcatraz* (UA); *The Manchurian Candidate* (UA). 1964: *Seven Days in May* (Par). 1965: *The Train* (U.S., France, Italy; UA). 1966: *Seconds* (Par); *Grand Prix* (MGM). 1968: *The Fixer* (Great Britain; MGM). 1969: *The Gypsy Moths* (MGM); *The Extraordinary Seaman* (MGM). 1970: *I Walk the Line* (Col). 1971: *The Horsemen* (Col). 1973: *The Iceman Cometh* (American Film Theatre); *Impossible Object* (France, Italy; Valoria). 1974: *99 and 44/100% Dead* (Fox). 1975: *The French Connection II* (Fox). 1976: *Black Sunday* (Par). 1979: *Prophecy* (Par). 1982: *The Challenge* (Embassy). 1985: *The Holcroft Covenant* (Thorn EMI/ Landau Productions). 1986: *52 Pick-Up* (Cannon).

Sidney Franklin (1893–1972) 1915: *Let Katy Do It* (with Chester Franklin); *Martha's Vindication* (with Chester Franklin). 1916: *The Children in the House* (with Chester Franklin); *Going Straight* (with Chester Franklin); *The Little Schoolma'am* (with Chester Franklin); *Gretchen the Greenhorn* (with Chester Franklin); *A Sister of Six* (with Chester Franklin). 1917: *Jack and the Beanstalk* (with Chester Franklin); *Aladdin and the Wonderful Lamp* (with Chester Franklin); *Babes in the Wood.* 1918: *Ali Baba and the Forty Thieves* (with Chester Franklin); *Six Shooter Andy; Confession; The Bride of Fear; The Safety Curtain; Treasure Island* (with Chester Franklin); *Her Only Way; Fan-Fan* (with Chester Franklin); *The Heart of Wetona; The Forbidden City.* 1919: *Probation Wife; Heart o' the Hills; The Hoodlum.* 1920: *Two Weeks; Unseen Forces.* 1921: *Not Guilty; Courage.* 1922: *Smilin' Through; The Primitive Lover; East Is West.* 1923: *Brass; Dulcy; Tiger Rose.* 1924: *Her Night of Romance.* 1925: *Her Sister from Paris; Learning to Love.* 1926: *The Duchess of Buffalo; Beverly of Graustark.* 1927: *Quality Street.* 1928: *The Actress.* 1929: *Wild Orchids; The Last of Mrs. Cheyney; Devil May Care* (MGM). 1930: *The Lady of Scandal* (MGM); *A Lady's Morals* (MGM). 1931: *The Guardsman* (MGM); *Private Lives* (MGM). 1932: *Smilin' Through* (MGM). 1933: *Reunion in Vienna* (MGM). 1934: *The Barretts of Wimpole Street* (MGM). 1935: *The Dark Angel* (UA). 1937: *The Good Earth* (MGM). 1957: *The Barretts of Wimpole Street* (MGM).

William Friedkin (born 1939) 1967: *Good Times* (Col). 1968: *The Birthday Party* (Great Britain; Continental); *The Night They Raided Minsky's* (UA). 1970: *The Boys in the Band* (NG). 1971: *The French Connection* (Fox). 1973: *The Exorcist* (WB). 1977: *Sorcerer* (Univ/ Par). 1978: *The Brink's Job* (Univ). 1980: *Cruising* (UA). 1983: *Deal of the Century* (WB). 1985: *To Live and Die in L.A.* (SLM Prod).

Samuel Fuller (born 1911) 1949: *I Shot Jesse James* (Screen Guild). 1950: *The Baron of Arizona* (Lippert). 1951: *The Steel Helmet* (Lippert); *Fixed Bayonets* (Fox). 1952: *Park Row* (UA). 1953: *Pickup on South Street* (Fox). 1954: *Hell and High Water* (Fox). 1955: *House of Bamboo* (Fox). 1957: *Run of the Arrow* (Fox); *Forty Guns* (Fox); *China Gate* (Fox). 1958: *Verboten!* (Col). 1959: *The Crimson Kimono* (Col). 1961: *Underworld U.S.A.* (Col). 1962: *Merrill's Marauders* (WB). 1963: *Shock Corridor* (AA). 1964: *The Naked Kiss* (AA). 1970: *Shark!* (U.S., Mexico; Heritage). 1972: *Dead Pigeon on Beethoven Street* (West Germany; Emerson). 1980: *The Big Red One* (UA). 1983: *Thieves after Dark* (France; Parafrance).

Unreleased: 1982: *White Dog* (Par).

Tay Garnett (1894–1977) 1928: *Celebrity.* 1929: *The Spieler* (Pathe); *The Flying Fool* (Pathe); *Oh, Yeah!* (Pathe). 1930: *Her Man* (Pathe); *Officer O'Brien* (Pathe). 1931: *Bad Company* (Pathe). 1932: *Prestige* (RKO); *One Way Passage* (WB); *Okay America* (Univ); *Destination Unknown* (Univ). 1933: *S.O.S. Iceberg* (Univ). 1935: *China Seas* (MGM); *She Couldn't Take It* (Col). 1936: *Professional Soldier* (Fox). 1937: *Slave Ship* (Fox); *Love Is News* (Fox); *Stand-In* (WB). 1938: *The Joy of Living* (RKO). 1939: *Trade Winds* (UA); *Eternally Yours* (UA). 1940: *Slightly Honorable* (UA); *Seven Sinners* (Univ). 1941: *Cheers for Miss Bishop* (UA). 1942: *My Favorite Spy* (RKO). 1943: *Bataan* (MGM); *The Cross of Lorraine* (MGM). 1944: *Mrs. Parkington* (MGM). 1945: *The Valley of Decision* (MGM). 1946: *The Postman Always Rings Twice* (MGM). 1947: *Wild Harvest* (Par). 1949: *A Connecticut Yankee in King Arthur's Court* (Par). 1950: *Fireball* (Fox). 1951: *Cause for Alarm* (MGM); *Soldiers Three* (MGM). 1952: *One Minute to Zero* (RKO). 1953: *Main Street to Broadway* (MGM). 1954: *The Black Knight* (Col). 1956: *Seven Wonders of the World* (Doc; episode; Cinerama). 1960: *The Night Fighters* (UA). 1963: *Cattle King* (MGM). 1970: *The Delta Factor* (Continental). 1972: *The Mad Trapper* (Alaska Pictures). 1973: *Timber Tramp* (Alaska Pictures).

Michael Gordon (born 1909) 1942: *Boston Blackie Goes Hollywood* (Col); *Underground Agent* (Col). 1943: *One Dangerous Night* (Col); *Crime Doctor* (Col). 1947: *The Web* (Univ). 1948: *Another Part of the Forest* (Univ); *An Act of Murder* (Univ). 1949: *The Lady Gambles* (Univ). 1950: *Woman in Hiding* (Univ); *Cyrano de Bergerac* (UA). 1951: *I Can Get It for You Wholesale* (Fox);

The Secret of Convict Lake (Fox). 1953: *Wherever She Goes* (Australia; Mayer-Kingsley). 1959: *Pillow Talk* (Univ). 1960: *Portrait in Black* (Univ). 1962: *Boys' Night Out* (MGM). 1963: *For Love or Money* (Univ); *Move Over, Darling* (Fox). 1965: *A Very Special Favor* (Univ). 1966: *Texas Across the River* (Univ). 1968: *The Impossible Years* (MGM). 1970: *How Do I Love Thee?* (Cinerama).

EDMUND GOULDING (1891–1959)   1925: *Sun Up; Sally, Irene and Mary*. 1926: *Paris*. 1927: *Women Love Diamonds*. 1928: *Love*. 1929: *The Trespasser* (UA). 1930: *The Devil's Holiday* (Par); *Paramount on Parade* (episode; Par). 1931: *Reaching for the Moon* (UA); *The Night Angel* (Par). 1932: *Blondie of the Follies* (MGM); *Grand Hotel* (MGM). 1934: *Riptide* (MGM). 1935: *The Flame Within* (MGM). 1937: *That Certain Woman* (WB). 1938: *The Dawn Patrol* (WB); *White Banners* (WB). 1939: *Dark Victory* (WB); *The Old Maid* (WB); *We Are Not Alone* (WB). 1940: *'Til We Meet Again* (WB). 1941: *The Great Lie* (WB). 1943: *The Constant Nymph* (WB); *Claudia* (Fox); *Forever and a Day* (episode; RKO). 1946: *The Razor's Edge* (Fox); *Of Human Bondage* (WB). 1947: *Nightmare Alley* (Fox). 1949: *Everybody Does It* (Fox). 1950: *Mister 880* (Fox). 1952: *We're Not Married* (Fox); *Down among the Sheltering Palms* (Fox). 1956: *Teenage Rebel* (Fox). 1958: *Mardi Gras* (Fox).

ALFRED E. GREEN (1889–1960)   1917: *The Lad and the Lion; The Princess of Patches; Lost and Found; Little Lost Sister*. 1919: *The Web of Chance*. 1920: *A Double-Dyed Deceiver; Silk Husbands and Calico Wives*. 1921: *Just Out of College; The Man Who Had Everything; Through the Back Door* (with Jack Pickford); *Little Lord Fauntleroy* (with Jack Pickford). 1922: *The Ghost Breaker; The Bachelor Daddy; Come on Over; Our Leading Citizen; The Man Who Saw Tomorrow; Back Home and Broke*. 1923: *The Ne'er-Do-Well; Woman-Proof*. 1924: *Pied Piper Malone; In Hollywood with Potash and Perlmutter; Inez from Hollywood*. 1925: *Sally; The Man Who Found Himself; The Talker*. 1926: *The Girl from Montmartre; Irene; Ella Cinders; It Must Be Love; Ladies at Play*. 1927: *The Auctioneer; Is Zat So?; Two Girls Wanted; Come to My House*. 1928: *Honor Bound*. 1929: *Making the Grade; Disraeli* (WB). 1930: *The Green Goddess* (WB); *The Man from Blankley's* (WB); *Old English* (WB); *Sweet Kitty Bellairs* (WB). 1931: *Smart Money* (WB); *Men of the Sky* (FN); *The Road to Singapore* (WB). 1932: *Union Depot* (FN); *It's Tough to Be Famous* (FN); *The Rich Are Always with Us* (FN); *The Dark Horse* (FN); *Silver Dollar* (FN). 1933: *Parachute Jumper* (WB); *The Narrow Corner* (WB); *Baby Face* (WB); *I Loved a Woman* (FN). 1934: *As the Earth Turns* (WB); *Dark Hazard* (FN); *Side Streets* (FN); *Housewife* (WB); *The Merry Frinks* (FN); *Gentlemen Are Born* (FN). 1935: *A Lost Lady* (FN); *Sweet Music* (WB); *The Girl from 10th Avenue* (FN); *Here's to Romance* (Fox); *The Goose and the Gander* (WB); *Dangerous* (WB). 1936: *Colleen* (WB); *The Golden Arrow* (FN); *They Met in a Taxi* (Col); *Two in a Crowd* (Univ); *More Than a Secretary* (Col). 1937: *Let's Get Married* (Col); *The League of Frightened Men* (Col); *Mr. Dodd Takes the Air* (WB); *Thoroughbreds Don't Cry* (MGM). 1938: *The Duke of West Point* (UA); *Ride a Crooked Mile* (Par). 1939: *King of the Turf* (UA); *The Gracie Allen Murder Case* (Par); *20,000 Men a Year* (Fox). 1940: *Shooting High* (Fox); *Flowing Gold* (WB); *East of the River* (WB). 1941: *Adventure in Washington* (Col); *Badlands of Dakota* (Univ). 1942: *The Mayor of 44th Street* (RKO); *Meet the Stewarts* (Col). 1943: *Appointment in Berlin* (Col); *There's Something about a Soldier* (Col). 1944: *Mr. Winkle Goes to War* (Col); *Strange Affair* (Col). 1945: *A Thousand and One Nights* (Col). 1946: *The Jolson Story* (Col); *Tars and Spars* (Col). 1947: *Copacabana* (UA); *The Fabulous Dorseys* (UA). 1948: *Four Faces West* (UA); *The Girl from Manhattan* (UA). 1949: *Cover-Up* (UA). 1950: *Sierra* (Univ). 1951: *The Jackie Robinson Story* (Eagle-Lion); *Two Gals and a Guy* (UA). 1952: *Invasion U.S.A.* (Col). 1953: *The Eddie Cantor Story* (WB); *Paris Model* (Col). 1954: *Top Banana* (UA).

D. W. GRIFFITH (1875–1948)   1908–13: over 450 short films. 1914: *Judith of Bethulia; The Battle of the Sexes; The Escape; Home, Sweet Home; The Avenging Conscience*. 1915: *The Birth of a Nation*. 1916: *Intolerance*. 1918:

Hearts of the World; The Great Love; The Greatest Thing in Life. 1919: *A Romance of Happy Valley; The Girl Who Stayed at Home; Broken Blossoms; True Heart Susie; Scarlet Days; The Greatest Question*. 1920: *The Idol Dancer; The Love Flower; Way Down East*. 1921: *Dream Street*. 1922: *Orphans of the Storm; One Exciting Night*. 1923: *The White Rose*. 1924: *America; Isn't Life Wonderful*. 1925: *Sally of the Sawdust*. 1926: *That Royale Girl; The Sorrows of Satan*. 1928: *Drums of Love; The Battle of the Sexes*. 1929: *Lady of the Pavements*. 1930: *Abraham Lincoln*. 1931: *The Struggle* (UA).

Uncredited: 1940: *One Million B.C.* (with Hal Roach and Hal Roach, Jr.; UA).

TAYLOR HACKFORD (born 1945)   1980: *The Idolmaker* (UA). 1982: *An Officer and a Gentleman* (Par). 1984: *Against All Odds* (Col). 1985: *White Nights* (Col).

ANTHONY HARVEY (born 1931)   1966: *Dutchman* (Great Britain; Continental). 1968: *The Lion in Winter* (Great Britain; Avco Embassy). 1971: *They Might Be Giants* (Univ). 1974: *The Abdication* (Great Britain; WB). 1979: *Players* (Par). 1980: *Eagle's Wing* (Great Britain; International Picture Show). 1981: *Richard's Things* (Great Britain; New World). 1984: *Grace Quigley (The Ultimate Solution of Grace Quigley)* (Cannon).

HENRY HATHAWAY (1898–1985)   1932: *Heritage of the Desert* (Par); *Wild Horse Mesa* (Par). 1933: *Under the Tonto Rim* (Par); *Sunset Pass* (Par); *Man of the Forest* (Par); *To the Last Man* (Par); *The Thundering Herd* (Par). 1934: *The Last Round-Up* (Par); *Come on Marines!* (Par); *The Witching Hour* (Par); *Now and Forever* (Par). 1935: *The Lives of a Bengal Lancer* (Par); *Peter Ibbetson* (Par). 1936: *The Trail of the Lonesome Pine* (Par); *Go West, Young Man* (Par). 1937: *Souls at Sea* (Par). 1938: *Spawn of the North* (Par). 1939: *The Real Glory* (UA). 1940: *Johnny Apollo* (Fox); *Brigham Young, Frontiersman* (Fox). 1941: *The Shepherd of the Hills* (Par); *Sundown* (UA). 1942: *Ten Gentlemen from West Point* (Fox); *China Girl* (Fox). 1944: *Home in Indiana* (Fox); *Wing and a Prayer* (Fox). 1945: *Nob Hill* (Fox); *The House on 92nd Street* (Fox). 1946: *The Dark Corner* (Fox). 1947: *13 Rue Madeleine* (Fox); *Kiss of Death* (Fox). 1948: *Call Northside 777* (Fox). 1949: *Down to the Sea in Ships* (Fox). 1950: *The Black Rose* (Fox). 1951: *You're in the Navy Now* (Fox); *Fourteen Hours* (Fox); *Rawhide* (Fox); *The Desert Fox* (Fox). 1952: *Diplomatic Courier* (Fox); *O. Henry's Full House* ("The Clarion Call" episode; Fox). 1953: *Niagara* (Fox); *White Witch Doctor* (Fox). 1954: *Prince Valiant* (Fox); *Garden of Evil* (Fox). 1955: *The Racers* (Fox). 1956: *The Bottom of the Bottle* (Fox); *23 Paces to Baker Street* (U.S., Great Britain; Fox). 1957: *Legend of the Lost* (UA). 1958: *From Hell to Texas* (Fox). 1959: *Woman Obsessed* (Fox). 1960: *Seven Thieves* (Fox); *North to Alaska* (Fox). 1963: *How the West Was Won* ("The Rivers," "The Plains," and "The Outlaws" episodes; MGM). 1964: *Circus World* (Par). 1965: *The Sons of Katie Elder* (Par). 1966: *Nevada Smith* (Par). 1967: *The Last Safari* (Great Britain; Par). 1968: *5 Card Stud* (Par). 1969: *True Grit* (Par). 1971: *Raid on Rommel* (Univ); *Shootout* (Univ). 1974: *Hangup (Super Dude)* (Univ).

Uncredited: 1970: *Airport* (with George Seaton; Univ).

HOWARD HAWKS (1896–1977)   1926: *The Road to Glory; Fig Leaves*. 1927: *The Cradle Snatchers; Paid to Love*. 1928: *A Girl in Every Port; Fazil; The Air Circus* (with Lewis Seiler; Fox). 1929: *Trent's Last Case*. 1930: *The Dawn Patrol* (FN). 1931: *The Criminal Code* (Col). 1932: *The Crowd Roars* (WB); *Scarface: The Shame of a Nation* (UA); *Tiger Shark* (FN). 1933: *Today We Live* (MGM). 1934: *Twentieth Century* (Col). 1935: *Barbary Coast* (UA); *Ceiling Zero* (FN). 1936: *The Road to Glory* (Fox); *Come and Get It* (with William Wyler; UA). 1938: *Bringing Up Baby* (RKO). 1939: *Only Angels Have Wings* (Col). 1940: *His Girl Friday* (Col). 1941: *Sergeant York* (WB); *Ball of Fire* (RKO). 1943: *Air Force* (WB). 1944: *To Have and Have Not* (WB). 1946: *The Big Sleep* (WB). 1948: *Red River* (UA); *A Song Is Born* (RKO). 1949: *I Was a Male War Bride* (Fox). 1952: *The Big Sky* (RKO); *O. Henry's Full House* ("The Ransom of Red Chief" epi-

sode; Fox); *Monkey Business* (Fox). 1953: *Gentlemen Prefer Blondes* (Fox). 1955: *Land of the Pharaohs* (WB). 1959: *Rio Bravo* (WB). 1962: *Hatari!* (Par). 1964: *Man's Favorite Sport?* (Univ). 1965: *Red Line 7000* (Par). 1967: *El Dorado* (Par). 1970: *Rio Lobo* (NG).

Uncredited: 1917: *The Little Princess* (with Marshall Neilan). 1933: *The Prizefighter and the Lady* (with W. S. Van Dyke; MGM). 1934: *Viva Villa!* (with Jack Conway; MGM). 1943: *The Outlaw* (with Howard Hughes, 1940; RKO). 1951: *The Thing* (with Christian Nyby; RKO).

GEORGE ROY HILL (born 1922)   1962: *Period of Adjustment* (MGM). 1963: *Toys in the Attic* (UA). 1964: *The World of Henry Orient* (UA). 1966: *Hawaii* (UA). 1967: *Thoroughly Modern Millie* (Univ). 1969: *Butch Cassidy and the Sundance Kid* (Fox). 1972: *Slaughterhouse Five* (Univ). 1973: *The Sting* (Univ). 1975: *The Great Waldo Pepper* (Univ). 1977: *Slap Shot* (Univ). 1979: *A Little Romance* (U.S., France; Orion/WB). 1982: *The World According to Garp* (WB). 1984: *The Little Drummer Girl* (WB).

WALTER HILL (born 1942)   1975: *Hard Times* (Col). 1978: *The Driver* (Fox). 1979: *The Warriors* (Par). 1980: *The Long Riders* (UA). 1981: *Southern Comfort* (Fox). 1982: *48 Hrs.* (Par). 1984: *Streets of Fire* (Univ). 1985: *Brewster's Millions* (Univ). 1986: *Extreme Prejudice* (Carolco).

ARTHUR HILLER (born 1923)   1957: *The Careless Years* (UA). 1963: *The Miracle of the White Stallions* (BV); *The Wheeler Dealers* (MGM). 1964: *The Americanization of Emily* (MGM). 1966: *Promise Her Anything* (Par); *Penelope* (MGM). 1967: *Tobruk* (Univ); *The Tiger Makes Out* (Col). 1969: *Popi* (UA). 1970: *The Out-of-Towners* (Par); *Love Story* (Par). 1971: *Plaza Suite* (Par); *The Hospital* (UA). 1972: *Man of La Mancha* (Italy, U.S.; UA). 1974: *The Crazy World of Julius Vrooder* (Fox). 1975: *The Man in the Glass Booth* (American Film Theatre). 1976: *W. C. Fields and Me* (Univ); *Silver Streak* (Fox). 1979: *The In-Laws* (Col); *Nightwing* (Col). 1981: *Making Love* (Fox). 1982: *Author! Author!* (Fox). 1983: *Romantic Comedy* (MGM/UA). 1984: *The Lonely Guy* (Univ); *Teachers* (MGM/UA). 1986: *Outrageous Fortune* (Touchstone/Interscope Communications).

ALFRED HITCHCOCK (1899–1980)   1925: *The Pleasure Garden* (Great Britain). 1926: *The Mountain Eagle* (Great Britain); *The Lodger* (Great Britain). 1927: *Downhill* (Great Britain); *Easy Virtue* (Great Britain); *The Ring* (Great Britain). 1928: *The Farmer's Wife* (Great Britain); *Champagne* (Great Britain). 1929: *The Manxman* (Great Britain); *Blackmail* (Great Britain; BIP). 1930: *Elstree Calling* (with Adrian Brunel; Great Britain; BIP); *Juno and the Paycock* (Great Britain; BIP); *Murder* (Great Britain; BIP). 1931: *The Skin Game* (Great Britain; BIP). 1932: *Rich and Strange* (Great Britain; BIP); *Number Seventeen* (Great Britain; BIP). 1933: *Waltzes from Vienna* (Great Britain; Gaumont-British). 1934: *The Man Who Knew Too Much* (Great Britain; Gaumont-British). 1935: *The Thirty-Nine Steps* (Great Britain; Gaumont-British). 1936: *The Secret Agent* (Great Britain; Gaumont-British); *Sabotage* (Great Britain; Gaumont-British). 1937: *Young and Innocent* (Great Britain; Gaumont-British). 1938: *The Lady Vanishes* (Great Britain; Gainsborough). 1939: *Jamaica Inn* (Great Britain; Mayflower). 1940: *Rebecca* (UA); *Foreign Correspondent* (UA). 1941: *Mr. and Mrs. Smith* (RKO); *Suspicion* (RKO). 1942: *Saboteur* (Univ). 1943: *Shadow of a Doubt* (Univ). 1944: *Lifeboat* (Fox); *Bon Voyage* (Great Britain; Associated British); *Aventure Malgache* (Great Britain; Associated British). 1945: *Spellbound* (UA). 1946: *Notorious* (RKO). 1947: *The Paradine Case* (Selznick). 1948: *Rope* (Transatlantic). 1949: *Under Capricorn* (Transatlantic). 1950: *Stage Fright* (WB). 1951: *Strangers on a Train* (WB). 1952: *I Confess* (WB). 1954: *Dial M for Murder* (WB); *Rear Window* (Par). 1955: *To Catch a Thief* (Par). 1956: *The Trouble with Harry* (Par); *The Man Who Knew Too Much* (Par). 1957: *The Wrong Man* (WB). 1958: *Vertigo* (Par). 1959: *North by Northwest* (MGM). 1960: *Psycho* (Par). 1963: *The Birds* (Univ). 1964: *Marnie*

(Univ). 1966: *Torn Curtain* (Univ). 1969: *Topaz* (Univ). 1972: *Frenzy* (Univ). 1976: *Family Plot* (Univ).
Unfinished: 1922: *Number Thirteen; Always Tell Your Wife* (with Seymour Hicks).

Ron Howard (born 1954) 1978: *Grand Theft Auto* (New World). 1982: *Night Shift* (Ladd/WB). 1984: *Splash* (BV). 1985: *Cocoon* (Fox). 1986: *Gung Ho* (Par).

William K. Howard (1899–1954) 1921: *Get Your Man* (with George Hill); *Play Square; What Love Will Do.* 1922: *Extra! Extra!; Deserted at the Altar; Captain Fly-By-Night; Lucky Dan.* 1923: *The Fourth Musketeer; Danger Ahead; Let's Go.* 1924: *The Border Legion; East of Broadway.* 1925: *The Thundering Herd; Code of the West; The Light of Western Stars.* 1926: *Red Dice; Bachelor Brides; Volcano; Gigolo.* 1927: *White Gold; The Main Event.* 1928: *A Ship Comes In; The River Pirate.* 1929: *Christina; The Valiant* (Fox); *Love, Live and Laugh* (Fox). 1930: *Good Intentions* (Fox); *Scotland Yard* (Fox). 1931: *Don't Bet on Women* (Fox); *Transatlantic* (Fox); *Surrender* (Fox). 1932: *The Trial of Vivienne Ware* (Fox); *The First Year* (Fox); *Sherlock Holmes* (Fox). 1933: *The Power and the Glory* (Fox). 1934: *This Side of Heaven* (MGM); *The Cat and the Fiddle* (MGM); *Evelyn Prentice* (MGM). 1935: *Vanessa, Her Love Story* (MGM); *Rendezvous* (MGM); *Mary Burns, Fugitive* (Par). 1936: *The Princess Comes Across* (Par). 1937: *Fire over England* (UA); *Murder on Diamond Row (The Squeaker)* (UA). 1939: *Back Door to Heaven* (Par). 1940: *Money and the Woman* (WB). 1941: *Bullets for O'Hara* (WB). 1942: *Klondike Fury* (Mon). 1943: *Johnny Come Lately* (UA). 1944: *When the Lights Go On Again* (PRC). 1945: *A Guy Could Change* (Rep).

Hugh Hudson (born 1936) 1981: *Chariots of Fire* (Great Britain; Ladd/WB). 1984: *Greystoke: The Legend of Tarzan, Lord of the Apes* (Great Britain, U.S.; WB). 1985: *Revolution* (WB).

John Huston (born 1906) 1941: *The Maltese Falcon* (WB). 1942: *In This Our Life* (WB); *Across the Pacific* (WB). 1948: *The Treasure of the Sierra Madre* (WB); *Key Largo* (WB). 1949: *We Were Strangers* (Col). 1950: *The Asphalt Jungle* (MGM). 1951: *The Red Badge of Courage* (MGM). 1952: *The African Queen* (UA); *Moulin Rouge* (Great Britain; UA). 1954: *Beat the Devil* (Great Britain; UA). 1956: *Moby Dick* (Great Britain; WB). 1957: *Heaven Knows, Mr. Allison* (Fox). 1958: *The Barbarian and the Geisha* (Fox); *The Roots of Heaven* (Fox). 1960: *The Unforgiven* (UA). 1961: *The Misfits* (UA). 1962: *Freud* (Univ). 1963: *The List of Adrian Messenger* (Univ). 1964: *The Night of the Iguana* (MGM). 1966: *The Bible* (Italy; Fox). 1967: *Reflections in a Golden Eye* (WB); *Casino Royale* (with Val Guest, Ken Hughes, Joseph McGrath, and Robert Parrish; Great Britain; Col). 1969: *A Walk with Love and Death* (Great Britain; Fox); *Sinful Davey* (Great Britain; UA). 1970: *The Kremlin Letter* (Fox). 1972: *Fat City* (Col). 1973: *The Life and Times of Judge Roy Bean* (NG); *The Mackintosh Man* (U.S., Great Britain; WB). 1975: *The Man Who Would Be King* (Great Britain; AA). 1979: *Wise Blood* (New Line Cinema). 1981: *Phobia* (Canadian; Par); *Victory* (Par). 1982: *Annie* (Col). 1984: *Under the Volcano* (Universal Classics). 1985: *Prizzi's Honor* (Fox).

Rex Ingram (1892–1950) 1916: *The Great Problem; Broken Fetters; The Chalice of Sorrows.* 1917: *Black Orchids; The Reward of the Faithless; The Pulse of Life; The Flower of Doom; The Little Terror.* 1918: *His Robe of Honor; Humdrum Brown.* 1919: *The Day She Paid.* 1920: *Under Crimson Skies; Shore Acres; Hearts Are Trumps.* 1921: *The Four Horsemen of the Apocalypse; The Conquering Power.* 1922: *Turn to the Right; The Prisoner of Zenda; Trifling Women.* 1923: *Where the Pavement Ends; Scaramouche.* 1924: *The Arab.* 1926: *Mare Nostrum; The Magician.* 1927: *The Garden of Allah.* 1929: *The Three Passions* (UA). 1933: *Love in Morocco (Baroud)* (Ideal).

Norman Jewison (born 1926) 1962: *40 Pounds of Trouble* (Univ). 1963: *The Thrill of It All* (Univ). 1964: *Send Me No Flowers* (Univ). 1965: *The Art of Love* (Univ); *The Cincinnati Kid* (MGM). 1966: *The Russians Are Coming the Russians Are Coming* (UA). 1967: *In the Heat of the Night* (UA). 1968: *The Thomas Crown Affair* (UA). 1969: *Gaily, Gaily* (UA). 1971: *Fiddler on the Roof* (UA). 1973: *Jesus Christ, Superstar* (Univ). 1975: *Rollerball* (UA). 1978: *F.I.S.T.* (UA). 1979: *. . . And Justice for All* (Col). 1982: *Best Friends* (WB). 1984: *A Soldier's Story* (Col). 1985: *Agnes of God* (Col).

Garson Kanin (born 1912) 1938: *A Man to Remember* (RKO); *Next Time I Marry* (RKO). 1939: *The Great Man Votes* (RKO); *Bachelor Mother* (RKO). 1940: *My Favorite Wife* (RKO); *They Knew What They Wanted* (RKO). 1941: *Tom, Dick and Harry* (RKO). 1945: *The True Glory* (with Carol Reed; Col). 1969: *Where It's At* (UA); *Some Kind of Nut* (UA).

Phil Karlson (1908–1985) 1944: *A Wave, a Wac and a Marine* (Mon). 1945: *There Goes Kelly* (Mon).; *G.I. Honeymoon* (Mon); *The Shanghai Cobra* (Mon). 1946: *Dark Alibi* (Mon); *Live Wires* (Mon); *The Missing Lady* (Mon); *Swing Parade of 1946* (Mon); *Bowery Bombshell* (Mon); *Wife Wanted* (Mon). 1947: *Black Gold* (AA); *Kilroy Was Here* (Mon); *Louisiana* (Mon). 1948: *Adventures in Silverado* (Col); *Rocky* (Mon); *Thunderhoof* (Col); *Ladies of the Chorus* (Col). 1949: *Down Memory Lane* (Eagle-Lion); *The Big Cat* (Eagle-Lion). 1950: *The Iroquois Trail* (UA); *Lorna Doone* (Col). 1951: *The Texas Rangers* (Col); *Mask of the Avenger* (Col); *Scandal Sheet* (Col). 1952: *Kansas City Confidential* (UA); *The Brigand* (Col). 1953: *99 River Street* (UA). 1954: *They Rode West* (Col). 1955: *Hell's Island* (Par); *Tight Spot* (Col); *Five Against the House* (Col); *The Phenix City Story* (AA). 1957: *The Brothers Rico* (Col). 1958: *Gunman's Walk* (Col). 1960: *Hell to Eternity* (AA); *Key Witness* (MGM). 1961: *The Secret Ways* (Univ). 1962: *The Scarface Mob* (UA); *Kid Galahad* (UA). 1963: *Rampage* (WB). 1966: *The Silencers* (Col). 1967: *A Time for Killing* (Col). 1969: *The Wrecking Crew* (Col). 1970: *Hornets' Nest* (UA). 1972: *Ben* (Cinerama). 1973: *Walking Tall* (Cinerama). 1974: *Framed* (Par).

Lawrence Kasdan (born 1949) 1981: *Body Heat* (Ladd/WB). 1983: *The Big Chill* (Col). 1985: *Silverado* (Col).

Philip Kaufman (born 1936) 1965: *Goldstein* (with Benjamin Manaster; Altura). 1969: *Fearless Frank* (AI). 1972: *The Great Northfield, Minnesota Raid* (Univ). 1974: *The White Dawn* (Par). 1978: *Invasion of the Body Snatchers* (UA). 1979: *The Wanderers* (Orion/WB). 1983: *The Right Stuff* (Ladd/WB).

Elia Kazan (born 1909) 1945: *A Tree Grows in Brooklyn* (Fox). 1947: *Sea of Grass* (Fox); *Boomerang!* (Fox); *Gentleman's Agreement* (Fox). 1949: *Pinky* (Fox). 1950: *Panic in the Streets* (Fox). 1951: *A Streetcar Named Desire* (WB). 1952: *Viva Zapata!* (Fox). 1953: *Man on a Tightrope* (Fox). 1954: *On the Waterfront* (Col). 1955: *East of Eden* (WB). 1956: *Baby Doll* (WB). 1957: *A Face in the Crowd* (WB). 1960: *Wild River* (Fox). 1961: *Splendor in the Grass* (WB). 1963: *America America* (WB). 1969: *The Arrangement* (WB). 1972: *The Visitors* (UA). 1975: *The Last Tycoon* (Par).

Buster Keaton (1895–1966) 1923: *The Three Ages* (with Edward Cline); *Our Hospitality* (with Jack Blystone). 1924: *Sherlock Jr.; The Navigator* (with Donald Crisp). 1925: *Seven Chances; Go West.* 1927: *Battling Butler; The General* (with Clyde Bruckman).

William Keighley (1889–1984) 1932: *The Match King* (with Howard Bretherton; FN). 1933: *Ladies They Talk About* (with Howard Bretherton; WB). 1934: *Easy to Love* (WB); *Journal of a Crime* (FN); *Dr. Monica* (WB); *Big-Hearted Herbert* (WB); *Kansas City Princess* (WB); *Babbitt* (FN). 1935: *The Right to Live* (WB); *G-Men* (WB); *Mary Jane's Pa* (FN); *Special Agent* (WB); *Stars over Broadway* (with Busby Berkeley; WB). 1936: *The Singing Kid* (FN); *The Green Pastures* (with Marc Connelly; WB); *Bullets or Ballots* (FN); *God's Country and the Woman* (WB). 1937: *The Prince and the Pauper* (WB); *Varsity Show* (WB). 1938: *The Adventures of Robin Hood* (with Michael Curtiz; WB); *Valley of the Giants* (WB); *Secrets of an Actress* (WB); *Brother Rat* (WB). 1939: *Yes, My Darling Daughter* (WB); *Each Dawn I Die* (WB). 1940: *The Fighting 69th* (WB); *Torrid Zone* (WB); *No Time for Comedy* (WB). 1941: *Four Mothers* (WB); *The Bride Came C.O.D.* (WB); *The Man Who Came to Dinner* (WB). 1942: *George Washington Slept Here* (WB). 1947: *Honeymoon* (RKO). 1948: *The Street with No Name* (Fox). 1950: *Rocky Mountain* (WB). 1951: *Close to My Heart* (WB). 1953: *The Master of Ballantrae* (WB).

Gene Kelly (born 1912) 1949: *On the Town* (with Stanley Donen; MGM). 1952: *Singin' in the Rain* (with Stanley Donen; MGM). 1955: *It's Always Fair Weather* (with Stanley Donen; MGM). 1956: *Invitation to the Dance* (MGM). 1957: *The Happy Road* (MGM). 1958: *The Tunnel of Love* (MGM). 1962: *Gigot* (Fox). 1967: *A Guide for the Married Man* (Fox). 1969: *Hello, Dolly!* (Fox). 1970: *The Cheyenne Social Club* (NG). 1976: *That's Entertainment, Part 2* (new sequences; MGM/UA).

Irvin Kershner (born 1923) 1958: *Stakeout on Dope Street* (WB). 1959: *The Young Captives* (Par). 1961: *The Hoodlum Priest* (UA). 1963: *A Face in the Rain* (Embassy). 1964: *The Luck of Ginger Coffey* (Canada; Continental). 1966: *A Fine Madness* (WB). 1967: *The Flim Flam Man* (Fox). 1970: *Loving* (Col). 1972: *Up the Sandbox* (NG). 1974: *S*P*Y*S* (U.S., Great Britain; Fox). 1976: *The Return of a Man Called Horse* (UA). 1978: *Eyes of Laura Mars* (Col). 1980: *The Empire Strikes Back* (Fox). 1983: *Never Say Never Again* (WB).

Henry King (1886–1982) 1915: *Who Pays?* 1916: *Pay Dirt; The Stained Pearl; Little Mary Sunshine; Once upon a Time; Joy and the Dragon; Shadows and Sunshine.* 1917: *Twin Kiddies; Told at Twilight; Sunshine and Gold; The Bride's Silence; Sands of Sacrifice; The Spectre of Suspicion; Souls in Pawn; The Mainspring; Southern Pride; A Game of Wits; The Mate of the Sally Ann.* 1918: *Beauty and the Rogue; Powers That Prey; Hearts or Diamonds?; The Locked Heart; When a Man Rides Alone; Hobbs in a Hurry; Cupid by Proxy; All the World to Nothing.* 1919: *The Child of M'sieu; Where the West Begins; Some Liar; Brass Buttons; A Sporting Chance; This Hero Stuff; Six Feet Four; A Fugitive from Matrimony; 23½ Hours Leave.* 1920: *Haunting Shadows; The White Dove; Uncharted Channels; One Hour Before Dawn; Dice of Destiny; Help Wanted—Male.* 1921: *When We Were 21; Mistress of Shenstone; Salvage; The Sting of the Lash; Tol'able David.* 1922: *Seventh Day; Sonny; Bond Boy.* 1923: *Fury; The White Sister.* 1924: *Romola.* 1925: *Any Woman; Sackcloth and Scarlet; Stella Dallas.* 1926: *Partners Again; The Winning of Barbara Worth.* 1927: *The Magic Flame.* 1928: *The Woman Disputed* (with Sam Taylor). 1929: *She Goes to War* (UA). 1930: *Hell Harbor* (UA); *Lightnin'* (Fox); *The Eyes of the World* (Fox). 1931: *Merely Mary Ann* (Fox); *Over the Hill* (Fox). 1932: *The Woman in Room 13* (Fox). 1933: *State Fair* (Fox); *I Loved You Wednesday* (with William Cameron Menzies; Fox). 1934: *Carolina* (Fox); *Marie Galante* (Fox). 1935: *One More Spring* (Fox); *Way Down East* (Fox). 1936: *The Country Doctor* (Fox); *Lloyds of London* (Fox); *Ramona* (Fox). 1937: *Seventh Heaven* (Fox). 1938: *In Old Chicago* (Fox); *Alexander's Ragtime Band* (Fox). 1939: *Jesse James* (Fox); *Stanley and Livingstone* (Fox). 1940: *Little Old New York* (Fox); *Maryland* (Fox); *Chad Hanna* (Fox). 1941: *A Yank in the RAF* (Fox); *Remember the Day* (Fox). 1942: *The Black Swan* (Fox). 1943: *The Song of Bernadette* (Fox). 1944: *Wilson* (Fox). 1945: *A Bell for Adano* (Fox). 1946: *Margie* (Fox). 1947: *Captain from Castile* (Fox). 1948: *Deep Waters* (Fox). 1949: *Twelve O'Clock High* (Fox); *Prince of Foxes* (Fox). 1950: *The Gunfighter* (Fox). 1951: *I'd Climb the Highest Mountain* (Fox); *David and Bathsheba* (Fox). 1952: *Wait Till the Sun Shines, Nellie* (Fox); *O. Henry's Full House* ("Gift of the Magi" episode; Fox); *The Snows of Kilimanjaro* (Fox). 1953: *King of the Khyber Rifles* (Fox). 1955: *Untamed* (Fox); *Love Is a Many-Splendored Thing* (Fox). 1956: *Carousel* (Fox). 1957: *The Sun Also Rises* (Fox). 1958: *The Bravados* (Fox). 1959: *This Earth Is Mine* (Univ); *Beloved Infidel* (Fox). 1962: *Tender Is the Night* (Fox).
Uncredited: 1958: *The Old Man and the Sea* (with John Sturges; WB).

Henry Koster (born 1905) 1932–35: 7 films: 2 German, 2 Hungarian-Austrian, 1 Austrian-Italian, 1 Italian, 1 Austrian. 1936: *Three Smart Girls* (Univ). 1937: *100 Men and a Girl* (Univ). 1938: *The Rage of Paris* (Univ). 1939: *First Love* (Univ); *Three Smart Girls Grow Up* (Univ). 1940: *Spring Parade* (Univ). 1941: *It Started with Eve* (Univ). 1942: *Between Us Girls* (Univ). 1944: *Music for Millions* (MGM). 1946: *Two Sisters from Boston* (MGM). 1947: *The Unfinished Dance* (MGM); *The Bishop's Wife* (RKO). 1948: *The Luck of the Irish* (Fox). 1949: *Come to the Stable* (Fox); *The Inspector General* (WB). 1950: *Wabash Avenue* (Fox); *My Blue Heaven* (Fox); *Harvey* (Univ). 1951: *Mr. Belvedere Rings the Bell* (Fox); *No Highway in the Sky* (Fox); *Elopement* (Fox). 1952: *O. Henry's Full House* ("The Cop and the Anthem" episode; Fox); *Stars and Stripes Forever* (Fox); *My Cousin Rachel* (Fox). 1953: *The Robe* (Fox). 1954: *Desiree* (Fox). 1955: *A Man Called Peter* (Fox); *The Virgin Queen* (Fox); *Good Morning, Miss Dove* (Fox). 1956: *D-Day the Sixth of June* (Fox); *The Power and the Prize* (MGM). 1957: *My Man Godfrey* (Univ). 1958: *Fraulein* (Fox). 1959: *The Naked Maja* (UA). 1960: *The Story of Ruth* (Fox). 1961: *Flower Drum Song* (Univ). 1962: *Mr. Hobbs Takes a Vacation* (Fox). 1963: *Take Her, She's Mine* (Fox). 1965: *Dear Brigitte* (Fox); *The Singing Nun* (MGM).

Stanley Kramer (born 1913) 1955: *Not as a Stranger* (UA). 1957: *The Pride and the Passion* (UA). 1958: *The Defiant Ones* (UA). 1959: *On the Beach* (UA). 1960: *Inherit the Wind* (UA). 1961: *Judgment at Nuremberg* (UA). 1963: *It's a Mad Mad Mad Mad World* (UA). 1965: *Ship of Fools* (Col). 1967: *Guess Who's Coming to Dinner* (Col); *The Secret of Santa Vittoria* (UA). 1970: *R.P.M.* (Col). 1971: *Bless the Beasts & Children* (Col). 1973: *Oklahoma Crude* (Col). 1977: *The Domino Principle* (Avco Embassy). 1979: *The Runner Stumbles* (Fox).

Stanley Kubrick (born 1928) 1953: *Fear and Desire* (Joseph Burstyn, Inc). 1955: *Killer's Kiss* (UA). 1956: *The Killing* (UA). 1957: *Paths of Glory* (UA). 1960: *Spartacus* (Univ). 1962: *Lolita* (Great Britain; MGM). 1964: *Dr. Strangelove or: How I Learned to Stop Worrying and Love the Bomb* (Great Britain; Col). 1968: *2001: A Space Odyssey* (Great Britain; MGM). 1971: *A Clockwork Orange* (Great Britain; WB). 1975: *Barry Lyndon* (Great Britain; WB). 1980: *The Shining* (Great Britain; WB). 1986: *Full Metal Jacket* (WB).

Gregory La Cava (1892–1952) 1921: *His Nibs*. 1924: *Restless Wives; The New School Teacher*. 1925: *Womanhandled*. 1926: *So's Your Old Man; Let's Get Married; Say It Again*. 1927: *The Gay Defender; Paradise for Two; Running Wild; Tell It to Sweeney*. 1928: *Feel My Pulse; Half a Bride*. 1929: *Saturday's Children* (FN); *Big News* (Pathe). 1930: *His First Command* (Pathe). 1931: *Laugh and Get Rich* (RKO); *Smart Woman* (RKO). 1932: *Symphony of Six Million* (RKO); *The Age of Consent* (RKO); *The Half-Naked Truth* (RKO). 1933: *Gabriel over the White House* (MGM); *Bed of Roses* (RKO); *Gallant Lady* (UA). 1934: *The Affairs of Cellini* (UA); *What Every Woman Knows* (MGM). 1935: *Private Worlds* (Par); *She Married Her Boss* (Col). 1936: *My Man Godfrey* (Univ). 1937: *Stage Door* (RKO). 1939: *Fifth Avenue Girl* (RKO). 1940: *Primrose Path* (RKO). 1941: *Unfinished Business* (Univ). 1942: *Lady in a Jam* (Univ). 1947: *Living in a Big Way* (MGM).

Fritz Lang (1890–1976) 1919–34: 12 silent and 3 sound German films, including *Dr. Mabuse, the Gambler* (1921); *Metropolis* (1927); and *M* (1931). 1936: *Fury* (MGM). 1937: *You Only Live Once* (UA). 1938: *You and Me* (Par). 1940: *The Return of Frank James* (Fox). 1941: *Western Union* (Fox); *Man Hunt* (Fox). 1943: *Hangmen Also Die* (UA). 1944: *Ministry of Fear* (Par); *The Woman in the Window* (RKO). 1945: *Scarlet Street* (Univ). 1946: *Cloak and Dagger* (WB). 1948: *Secret Beyond the Door* (Univ). 1950: *House by the River* (Rep); *American Guerrilla in the Philippines* (Fox). 1952: *Rancho Notorious* (RKO); *Clash by Night* (RKO). 1953: *The Blue Gardenia* (WB); *The Big Heat* (Col). 1954: *Human Desire* (Col). 1955: *Moonfleet* (MGM). 1956: *While the City Sleeps* (RKO); *Beyond a Reasonable Doubt* (RKO). 1958–60: 2 German films.

Uncredited: 1941: *Confirm or Deny* (with Archie Mayo; Fox).

Walter Lang (1898–1972) 1925: *Red Kimono*. 1926: *The Carnival Girl; The Earth Woman; The Golden Web; Money to Burn*. 1927: *By Whose Hand?; The College Hero; The Ladybird; Sally in Our Alley; The Satin Woman*. 1928: *The Desert Bride; The Night Flyer*. 1929: *The Spirit of Youth*. 1930: *The Big Fight* (World Wide); *Brothers* (Col); *Cock o' the Walk* (with Roy William Neill; World Wide); *The Costello Case* (World Wide); *Hello Sister* (World Wide). 1931: *Command Performance* (Tiffany); *Hell Bound* (Tiffany); *Women Go On Forever* (Tiffany). 1932: *No More Orchids* (Col). 1933: *The Warrior's Husband* (Fox); *Meet the Baron* (MGM). 1934: *The Party's Over* (Col); *The Mighty Barnum* (UA); *Whom the Gods Destroy* (Col). 1935: *Carnival* (Col). 1936: *Love Before Breakfast* (Univ). 1937: *Wife, Doctor and Nurse* (Fox); *Second Honeymoon* (Fox). 1938: *The Baroness and the Butler* (Fox); *I'll Give a Million* (Fox). 1939: *The Little Princess* (Fox). 1940: *The Blue Bird* (Fox); *Star Dust* (Fox); *The Great Profile* (Fox); *Tin Pan Alley* (Fox). 1941: *Moon over Miami* (Fox); *Week-end in Havana* (Fox). 1942: *Song of the Islands* (Fox); *The Magnificent Dope* (Fox). 1943: *Coney Island* (Fox). 1944: *Greenwich Village* (Fox). 1945: *State Fair* (Fox). 1946: *Sentimental Journey* (Fox); *Claudia and David* (Fox). 1947: *Mother Wore Tights* (Fox). 1948: *Sitting Pretty* (Fox); *When My Baby Smiles at Me* (Fox). 1949: *You're My Everything* (Fox). 1950: *Cheaper by the Dozen* (Fox); *The Jackpot* (Fox). 1951: *On the Riviera* (Fox). 1952: *With a Song in My Heart* (Fox). 1953: *Call Me Madam* (Fox). 1954: *There's No Business Like Show Business* (Fox). 1956: *The King and I* (Fox). 1957: *Desk Set* (Fox). 1959: *But Not for Me* (Fox). 1960: *Can-Can* (Fox); *The Marriage-Go-Round* (Fox). 1961: *Snow White and the Three Stooges* (Fox).

David Lean (born 1908) 1942: *In Which We Serve* (with Noel Coward; Great Britain; Univ). 1944: *This Happy Breed* (Great Britain; Univ). 1945: *Blithe Spirit* (Great Britain; UA). 1946: *Brief Encounter* (Great Britain; Univ). 1947: *Great Expectations* (Great Britain; Univ). 1948: *Oliver Twist* (Great Britain; UA). 1949: *One Woman's Story (The Passionate Friends)* (Great Britain; Univ). 1950: *Madeleine* (Great Britain; Univ). 1952: *Breaking Through the Sound Barrier (The Sound Barrier)* (Great Britain; UA). 1954: *Hobson's Choice* (Great Britain; UA). 1955: *Summertime (Summer Madness)* (Great Britain; UA). 1957: *The Bridge on the River Kwai* (Great Britain; Col). 1962: *Lawrence of Arabia* (Great Britain; Col). 1965: *Doctor Zhivago* (Great Britain; MGM). 1970: *Ryan's Daughter* (Great Britain; MGM). 1984: *A Passage to India* (Great Britain; Col).

Mitchell Leisen (1898–1972) 1933: *Cradle Song* (Par). 1934: *Death Takes a Holiday* (Par); *Murder at the Vanities* (Par). 1935: *Behold My Wife* (Par); *Four Hours to Kill* (Par); *Hands Across the Table* (Par); *13 Hours by Air* (Par). 1936: *The Big Broadcast of 1937* (Par). 1937: *Swing High, Swing Low* (Par); *Easy Living* (Par). 1938: *The Big Broadcast of 1938* (Par); *Artists and Models Abroad* (Par). 1939: *Midnight* (Par). 1940: *Remember the Night* (Par); *Arise My Love* (Par). 1941: *I Wanted Wings* (Par); *Hold Back the Dawn* (Par). 1942: *The Lady Is Willing* (Par); *Take a Letter, Darling* (Par). 1943: *No Time for Love* (Par). 1944: *Lady in the Dark* (Par); *Frenchman's Creek* (Par); *Practically Yours* (Par). 1945: *Kitty* (Par); *Masquerade in Mexico* (Par). 1946: *To Each His Own* (Par). 1947: *Suddenly It's Spring* (Par); *Golden Earrings* (Par). 1948: *Dream Girl* (Par). 1949: *Song of Surrender* (Par); *Bride of Vengeance* (Par). 1950: *Captain Carey U.S.A.* (Par); *No Man of Her Own* (Par). 1951: *The Mating Season* (Par); *Darling, How Could You!* (Par). 1952: *Young Man with Ideas* (MGM). 1953: *Tonight We Sing* (Fox). 1955: *Bedevilled* (MGM). 1957: *The Girl Most Likely* (Univ). 1967: *Spree* (Doc; with Walon Green; Trans American).

Robert Z. Leonard (1889–1968) 1914: *The Master Key*. 1915: *The Silent Command; Heritage; Judge Not, or the Woman of Mona Diggings*. 1916: *The Crippled Hand* (with David Kirkland); *The Plow Girl; The Love Girl; The Eagle's Wings; Little Eve Edgarton; Secret Love*. 1917: *The Little Orphan; At First Sight; The Primrose Ring; A Mormon Maid; Princess Virtue*. 1918: *Face Value; The Bride's Awakening; Her Body in Bond; Danger—Go Slow; Modern Love*. 1919: *The Delicious Little Devil; The Big Little Person; What Am I Bid?; The Scarlet Shadow; The Way of a Woman; Miracle of Love*. 1920: *April Folly; The Restless Sex*. 1921: *The Gilded Lily; Heedless Moths; Peacock Alley*. 1922: *Fascination; Broadway Rose*. 1923: *Jazzmania; The French Doll; Fashion Row*. 1924: *Circe, the Enchantress; Mademoiselle Midnight; Love's Wilderness*. 1925: *Cheaper to Marry; Bright Lights; Time, the Comedian*. 1926: *Dance Madness; The Waning Sex; Mademoiselle Modiste*. 1927: *The Demi-Bride; A Little Journey; Adam and Evil; Tea for Three*. 1928: *Baby Mine; The Cardboard Lover; A Lady of Chance*. 1929: *Marianne* (MGM). 1930: *In Gay Madrid* (MGM); *The Divorcee* (MGM); *Let Us Be Gay* (MGM). 1931: *The Bachelor Father* (MGM); *It's a Wise Child* (MGM); *Five and Ten* (MGM); *Susan Lenox—Her Fall and Rise* (MGM). 1932: *Lovers Courageous* (MGM); *Strange Interlude* (MGM). 1933: *Peg o' My Heart* (MGM); *Dancing Lady* (MGM). 1934: *Outcast Lady* (MGM). 1935: *After Office Hours* (MGM); *Escapade* (MGM). 1936: *The Great Ziegfeld* (MGM); *Piccadilly Jim* (MGM). 1937: *Maytime* (MGM); *The Firefly* (MGM). 1938: *The Girl of the Golden West* (MGM). 1939: *Broadway Serenade* (MGM). 1940: *New Moon* (MGM); *Pride and Prejudice* (MGM); *Third Finger, Left Hand* (MGM). 1941: *Ziegfeld Girl* (MGM); *When Ladies Meet* (MGM). 1942: *We Were Dancing* (MGM); *Stand By for Action* (MGM). 1943: *The Man from Down Under* (MGM). 1944: *Marriage Is a Private Affair* (MGM). 1945: *Week-End at the Waldorf* (MGM). 1946: *The Secret Heart* (MGM). 1947: *Cynthia* (MGM). 1948: *B. F.'s Daughter* (MGM). 1949: *The Bribe* (MGM); *In the Good Old Summertime* (MGM). 1950: *Nancy Goes to Rio* (MGM); *Duchess of Idaho* (MGM); *Grounds for Marriage* (MGM). 1951: *Too Young to Kiss* (MGM). 1952: *Everything I Have Is Yours* (MGM). 1953: *The Clown* (MGM); *The Great Diamond Robbery* (MGM). 1954: *Her Twelve Men* (MGM). 1955: *The King's Thief* (MGM); *Beautiful But Dangerous (La Donna Più Bella del Mondo)* (Italy; Fox). 1956: *Kelly and Me* (Univ).

Mervyn LeRoy (born 1900) 1927: *No Place to Go*. 1928: *Harold Teen; Flying Romeos; Oh Kay!* 1929: *Naughty Baby* (FN); *Hot Stuff* (FN); *Little Johnny Jones* (FN); *Broadway Babies* (FN). 1930: *Playing Around* (FN); *Numbered Men* (FN); *Little Caesar* (FN); *Showgirl in Hollywood* (FN); *Top Speed* (FN). 1931: *Gentleman's Fate* (FN); *Too Young to Marry* (WB); *Broad-Minded* (FN); *Local Boy Makes Good* (FN); *Five Star Final* (FN); *Tonight or Never* (UA). 1932: *High Pressure* (WB); *Two Seconds* (FN); *The Heart of New York* (WB); *Big City Blues* (WB); *Three on a Match* (FN); *I Am a Fugitive from a Chain Gang* (WB). 1933: *Gold Diggers of 1933* (WB); *Tugboat Annie* (MGM); *Hard to Handle* (WB); *Elmer the Great* (FN); *The World Changes* (FN). 1934: *Hi! Nellie!* (WB); *Heat Lightning* (WB); *Happiness Ahead* (FN). 1935: *Sweet Adeline* (WB); *Oil for the Lamps of China* (WB); *Page Miss Glory* (WB); *I Found Stella Parish* (FN). 1936: *Anthony Adverse* (WB); *Three Men on a Horse* (FN). 1937: *The King and the Chorus Girl* (WB); *They Won't Forget* (WB). 1938: *Fools for Scandal* (WB). 1940: *Waterloo Bridge* (MGM); *Escape* (MGM). 1941: *Blossoms in the Dust* (MGM); *Johnny Eager* (MGM); *Unholy Partners* (MGM). 1942: *Random Harvest* (MGM). 1943: *Madame Curie* (MGM). 1944: *Thirty Seconds over Tokyo* (MGM). 1946: *Without Reservations* (RKO). 1947: *Desire Me* (with George Cukor; MGM). 1948: *Homecoming* (MGM). 1949: *Little Women* (MGM); *Any Number Can Play* (MGM); *East Side, West Side* (MGM). 1951: *Quo Vadis* (MGM). 1952: *Lovely to Look At* (MGM); *Million Dollar Mermaid* (MGM); *Latin Lovers* (MGM). 1954: *Rose Marie* (MGM). 1955: *Mister Roberts* (with John Ford; WB); *Strange Lady in Town* (WB). 1956: *The Bad Seed* (WB); *Toward the Unknown* (WB). 1958: *No Time for Sergeants* (WB); *Home Before Dark* (WB). 1959: *The FBI Story* (WB). 1960: *Wake Me When It's Over* (Fox). 1961: *The Devil at 4 O'Clock* (Col). 1962: *A Majority of One* (WB); *Gypsy* (WB). 1963: *Mary, Mary* (WB). 1965: *Moment to Moment* (MGM).

Uncredited: 1968: *The Green Berets* (with credited John Wayne and Ray Kellogg; WB/7 Arts).

RICHARD LESTER (born 1932) 1962: *Ring-a-Ding Rhythm (It's Trad, Dad)* (Great Britain; Col). 1963: *The Mouse on the Moon* (Great Britain; UA). 1964: *A Hard Day's Night* (Great Britain; UA). 1965: *The Knack . . . and How to Get It* (Great Britain; Lopert); *Help!* (Great Britain; UA). 1966: *A Funny Thing Happened on the Way to the Forum* (Great Britain; UA). 1967: *Teenage Rebellion (Mondo Teeno)* (with Norman Herbert; Great Britain, U.S.; Trans American); *How I Won the War* (Great Britain; UA). 1968: *Petulia* (U.S., Great Britain; WB). 1969: *The Bed Sitting Room* (Great Britain; UA). 1974: *The Three Musketeers (The Queen's Diamonds)* (Great Britain; Fox); *Juggernaut* (Great Britain; UA). 1975: *The Four Musketeers (Milady's Revenge)* (Great Britain; Fox). 1976: *Royal Flash* (Great Britain; Fox); *Robin and Marian* (Great Britain; Col); *The Ritz* (WB). 1979: *Butch and Sundance: The Early Days* (Fox); *Cuba* (UA). 1981: *Superman II* (U.S., Great Britain; WB). 1983: *Superman III* (U.S., Great Britain; WB). 1984: *Finders Keepers* (WB).

ALBERT LEWIN (1894–1968) 1942: *The Moon and Sixpence* (UA). 1945: *The Picture of Dorian Gray* (MGM). 1947: *The Private Affairs of Bel Ami* (UA). 1951: *Pandora and the Flying Dutchman* (MGM). 1953: *Saadia* (MGM). 1957: *The Living Idol* (MGM).

ANATOLE LITVAK (1902–1974) 1930–32: 6 German films. 1933: *Sleeping Car* (Great Britain; Gaumont-British). 1933–37: 4 French films. 1937: *The Woman I Love* (RKO); *Tovarich* (WB). 1938: *The Amazing Dr. Clitterhouse* (WB); *The Sisters* (WB). 1939: *Confessions of a Nazi Spy* (WB). 1940: *Castle on the Hudson* (WB); *City for Conquest* (WB); *All This and Heaven Too* (WB). 1941: *Out of the Fog* (WB); *Blues in the Night* (WB). 1942: *This Above All* (Fox); *The Nazis Strike* (with Frank Capra; U.S. Govt); *Divide and Conquer* (with Frank Capra; U.S. Govt). 1943: *The Battle of Russia* (Fox). 1944: *The Battle of China* (with Frank Capra; U.S. Govt). 1945: *War Comes to America* (RKO). 1947: *The Long Night* (RKO). 1948: *Sorry, Wrong Number* (Par); *The Snake Pit* (Fox). 1951: *Decision Before Dawn* (Fox). 1953: *Act of Love* (UA). 1955: *The Deep Blue Sea* (Fox). 1956: *Anastasia* (Fox). 1959: *The Journey* (MGM). 1961: *Goodbye Again* (UA). 1963: *Five Miles to Midnight* (UA). 1967: *The Night of the Generals* (Col). 1971: *The Lady in the Car with Glasses and a Gun* (Col).

FRANK LLOYD (1888–1960) 1915: *For His Superior's Honor; Billie's Baby; Eleven in One; Fate's Alibi; From the Shadows; The Bay of Seven Islands; Dr. Mason's Temptation; A Double Deal in Pork; An Arrangement with Fate; Little Mr. Fixer; In the Grasp of the Law; His Last Trick; The Little Girl of the Attic; The Pinch; The Prophet of the Hills; Martin Lowe—Fixer; Paternal Love; Their Golden Wedding; $10,000 Dollars; The Toll of Youth; Trickery; To Redeem an Oath; The Source of Happiness; To Redeem a Value; The Gentleman from Indiana.* 1916: *The Call of the Cumberlands; The Tongues of Men; Madame President; An International Marriage; The Code of Marcia Gray; The Intrigue; The Making of Maddalena; Sins of Her Parents; The Stronger Love; David Garrick.* 1917: *The Price of Silence; The Heart of a Lion; American Methods; A Tale of Two Cities; When a Man Sees Red.* 1919: *The Kingdom of Love; Les Miserables; The Blindness of Divorce; True Blue; For Freedom; The Rainbow Trail; The Riders of the Purple Sage; The Man Hunter; Pitfalls of a Big City; The World and Its Women.* 1920: *The Loves of Letty; The Silver Horde; The Woman in Room 13; Madame X; The Great Lover.* 1921: *A Tale of Two Worlds; Roads to Destiny; A Voice in the Dark; The Invisible Power; The Man from Lost River; The Sin Flood.* 1922: *The Grim Comedian; The Eternal Flame; Oliver Twist.* 1923: *The Voice from the Minaret; Within the Law; Ashes of Vengeance.* 1924: *Black Oxen; The Silent Watcher; The Sea Hawk.* 1925: *Winds of Chance; Her Husband's Secret; The Splendid Road.* 1926: *The Wise Guy; The Eagle of the Sea.* 1927: *Children of Divorce.* 1928: *Adoration.* 1929: *The Divine Lady; Weary River; Drag* (FN); *Dark Streets* (FN); *Young Nowheres* (FN). 1930: *Son of the Gods* (FN); *The Way of All Men* (FN); *The Lash* (FN). 1931: *The Right of Way* (FN); *The Age for Love* (UA); *East Lynne* (Fox). 1932: *A Passport to Hell* (Fox). 1933: *Cavalcade* (Fox); *Berkeley Square* (Fox); *Hoopla* (Fox). 1934:

Servant's Entrance (Fox). 1935: *Mutiny on the Bounty* (MGM). 1936: *Under Two Flags* (Fox). 1937: *Maid of Salem* (Par); *Wells Fargo* (Par). 1938: *If I Were King* (Par). 1939: *Rulers of the Sea* (Par). 1940: *The Howards of Virginia* (Col). 1941: *The Lady from Cheyenne* (Col); *This Woman Is Mine* (Univ). 1943: *Forever and a Day* (episode; RKO). 1945: *Blood on the Sun* (UA). 1954: *The Shanghai Story* (Rep). 1955: *The Last Command* (Rep).

JOSHUA LOGAN (born 1908) 1938: *I Met My Love Again* (with Arthur Ripley; UA). 1955: *Picnic* (Col). 1956: *Bus Stop* (Fox). 1957: *Sayonara* (WB). 1958: *South Pacific* (Fox). 1960: *Tall Story* (WB). 1961: *Fanny* (WB). 1964: *Ensign Pulver* (WB). 1967: *Camelot* (WB-7 Arts). 1969: *Paint Your Wagon* (Par).

JOSEPH LOSEY (1909–1984) 1948: *The Boy with Green Hair* (RKO). 1950: *The Lawless* (Par). 1951: *The Prowler* (UA); *M* (Col); *The Big Night* (UA). 1952: *Stranger on the Prowl* (under the name of Andrea Forzano; Italy; UA). 1954: *The Sleeping Tiger* (under the name of Victory Hanbury; Great Britain; Anglo-Amalgamated). 1955: *Finger of Guilt (The Intimate Stranger)* (under the name of Joseph Walton; Great Britain; Anglo-Amalgamated). 1956: *Time Without Pity* (Great Britain; Eras). 1958: *The Gypsy and the Gentleman* (Great Britain; Rank). 1959: *Blind Date (Chance Meeting)* (Great Britain; Par). 1960: *The Concrete Jungle (The Criminal)* (Great Britain; Fanfare). 1961: *The Damned (These Are the Damned)* (Great Britain; Col). 1962: *Eva* (France, Italy; Times Film Corporation). 1963: *The Servant* (Great Britain; Landau). 1964: *King and Country* (Great Britain; AA). 1966: *Modesty Blaise* (Great Britain; Fox). 1967: *Accident* (Great Britain; Cinema 5). 1968: *Boom!* (Great Britain, U.S.; Univ); *Secret Ceremony* (Great Britain, U.S.; Univ). 1970: *Figures in a Landscape* (Great Britain; NG). 1971: *The Go-Between* (Great Britain; Col). 1972: *The Assassination of Trotsky* (France, Italy, Great Britain; Cinerama). 1973: *A Doll's House* (Great Britain, France; Tomorrow Entertainment). 1974: *Galileo* (Great Britain, Canada; American Film Theatre). 1975: *The Romantic Englishwoman* (Great Britain; New World). 1977: *Mr. Klein* (France, Italy; Quartet). 1978: *The Roads to the South (Les Routes du Sud)* (France; Parafrance). 1979: *Don Giovanni* (France; New Yorker). 1983: *The Trout (La Truite)* (France; Triumph/Col). 1984: *Steaming* (Great Britain; World Film Services, Ltd).

ERNST LUBITSCH (1892–1947) 1914–22: 38 German silent films. 1923: *Rosita.* 1924: *The Marriage Circle; Three Women; Forbidden Paradise.* 1925: *Kiss Me Again; Lady Windermere's Fan.* 1926: *So This Is Paris?.* 1927: *The Student Prince.* 1928: *The Patriot.* 1929: *Eternal Love; The Love Parade* (Par). 1930: *Paramount on Parade* (three episodes with Maurice Chevalier; Par); *Monte Carlo* (Par). 1931: *The Smiling Lieutenant* (Par). 1932: *The Man I Killed (Broken Lullaby)* (Par); *One Hour with You* (with George Cukor; Par); *Trouble in Paradise* (Par); *If I Had a Million* ("The Clerk" episode; Par). 1933: *Design for Living* (Par). 1934: *The Merry Widow* (MGM). 1937: *Angel* (Par). 1938: *Bluebeard's Eighth Wife* (Par). 1939: *Ninotchka* (MGM). 1940: *The Shop Around the Corner* (MGM). 1941: *That Uncertain Feeling* (UA). 1942: *To Be or Not to Be* (UA). 1943: *Heaven Can Wait* (Fox). 1946: *Cluny Brown* (Fox). 1948: *That Lady in Ermine* (completed by uncredited Otto Preminger; Fox).

GEORGE LUCAS (born 1944) 1971: *THX 1138* (WB). 1973: *American Graffiti* (Univ). 1977: *Star Wars* (Fox).

SIDNEY LUMET (born 1924) 1957: *12 Angry Men* (UA). 1958: *Stage Struck* (RKO). 1959: *That Kind of Woman* (Par). 1960: *The Fugitive Kind* (UA). 1962: *A View from the Bridge* (France, Italy; AA); *Long Day's Journey into Night* (Embassy). 1964: *Fail Safe* (Col). 1965: *The Pawnbroker* (Landau Productions/AA); *The Hill* (Great Britain; MGM). 1966: *The Group* (UA). 1967: *The Deadly Affair* (Great Britain; Col). 1968: *Bye Bye Braverman* (WB); *The Sea Gull* (Great Britain; WB). 1969: *The Appointment* (MGM). 1970: *Last of the Mobile Hot-Shots* (WB); *King: A Filmed Record...Montgomery to Memphis*

(Doc; with Joseph L. Mankiewicz; Maron Films Ltd). 1971: *The Anderson Tapes* (Col). 1972: *Child's Play* (Par). 1973: *The Offense* (Great Britain; UA); *Serpico* (Par). 1974: *Lovin' Molly* (Col); *Murder on the Orient Express* (Great Britain; Par). 1975: *Dog Day Afternoon* (WB). 1976: *Network* (MGM/UA). 1977: *Equus* (Great Britain; UA). 1978: *The Wiz* (Univ). 1980: *Just Tell Me What You Want* (Col). 1981: *Prince of the City* (Orion/WB). 1982: *Deathtrap* (WB); *The Verdict* (Fox). 1983: *Daniel* (Par). 1984: *Garbo Talks* (MGM/UA). 1986: *Power* (Fox); *The Morning After* (Lorimar).

LEO McCAREY (1898–1969) 1921: *Society Secrets.* 1929: *Red Hot Rhythm* (Pathe); *The Sophomore* (Pathe). 1920: *Let's Go Native* (Par); *Wild Company* (Fox); *Part Time Wife* (Fox). 1931: *Indiscreet* (UA). 1932: *The Kid from Spain* (UA); *Duck Soup* (Par). 1934: *Six of a Kind* (Par); *Belle of the Nineties* (Par). 1935: *Ruggles of Red Gap* (Par). 1936: *The Milky Way* (Par). 1937: *Make Way for Tomorrow* (Par); *The Awful Truth* (Col). 1939: *Love Affair* (RKO). 1942: *Once upon a Honeymoon* (RKO). 1944: *Going My Way* (Par). 1945: *The Bells of St. Mary's* (RKO). 1948: *Good Sam* (RKO). 1952: *My Son John* (Par). 1957: *An Affair to Remember* (Fox). 1958: *Rally Round the Flag, Boys!* (Fox). 1961: *Satan Never Sleeps* (Fox).

NORMAN Z. McLEOD (1898–1964) 1928: *Taking a Chance.* 1930: *Along Came Youth* (with Lloyd Corrigan; Par). 1931: *Monkey Business* (Par); *Finn and Hattie* (with Norman Taurog; Par); *Touchdown* (Par). 1932: *The Miracle Man* (Par); *Horse Feathers* (Par); *If I Had a Million* ("The Forger" episode; Par). 1933: *Mama Loves Papa* (Par); *Alice in Wonderland* (Par); *A Lady's Profession* (Par). 1934: *Many Happy Returns* (Par); *Melody in Spring* (Par). 1935: *Here Comes Cookie* (Par); *Redheads on Parade* (Fox). 1936: *Pennies from Heaven* (Col); *Early to Bed* (Par); *Mind Your Own Business* (Par). 1937: *Topper* (MGM). 1938: *Merrily We Live* (MGM); *There Goes My Heart* (UA). 1939: *Topper Takes a Trip* (UA); *Remember?* (MGM). 1940: *Little Men* (RKO); *The Trial of Mary Dugan* (MGM). 1941: *Lady Be Good* (MGM); *Jackass Mail* (MGM). 1942: *Panama Hattie* (MGM); *The Powers Girl* (UA). 1943: *Swing Shift Maisie* (MGM). 1946: *The Kid from Brooklyn* (RKO). 1947: *The Secret Life of Walter Mitty* (RKO); *Road to Rio* (Par). 1948: *The Paleface* (Par); *Isn't It Romantic?* (Par). 1950: *Let's Dance* (Par). 1951: *My Favorite Spy* (Par). 1952: *Never Wave at a Wac* (RKO). 1954: *Casanova's Big Night* (Par). 1957: *Public Pigeon No. 1* (Univ). 1959: *Alias Jesse James* (UA).

ROUBEN MAMOULIAN (born 1898) 1929: *Applause* (Par). 1931: *City Streets* (Par). 1932: *Dr. Jekyll and Mr. Hyde* (Par); *Love Me Tonight* (Par). 1933: *The Song of Songs* (Par); *Queen Christina* (MGM). 1934: *We Live Again* (UA). 1935: *Becky Sharp* (replaced Lowell Sherman; RKO). 1936: *The Gay Desperado* (UA). 1937: *High, Wide and Handsome* (Par). 1939: *Golden Boy* (Col). 1940: *The Mark of Zorro* (Fox). 1941: *Blood and Sand* (Fox). 1942: *Rings on Her Fingers* (Fox). 1944: *Laura* (replaced by Otto Preminger; Fox). 1948: *Summer Holiday* (MGM). 1957: *Silk Stockings* (MGM).

Uncredited: 1950: *The Wild Heart* (with credited Michael Powell and Emeric Pressburger; Great Britain; Fox, 1952).

JOSEPH L. MANKIEWICZ (born 1909) 1946: *Dragonwyck* (Fox); *Somewhere in the Night* (Fox). 1947: *The Late George Apley* (Fox); *The Ghost and Mrs. Muir* (Fox). 1948: *Escape* (Fox). 1949: *A Letter to Three Wives* (Fox); *House of Strangers* (Fox). 1950: *No Way Out* (Fox); *All about Eve* (Fox). 1951: *People Will Talk* (Fox). 1952: *Five Fingers* (Fox). 1953: *Julius Caesar* (MGM). 1954: *The Barefoot Contessa* (U.S., Italy; UA). 1955: *Guys and Dolls* (MGM). 1958: *The Quiet American* (UA). 1959: *Suddenly, Last Summer* (Col). 1963: *Cleopatra* (Fox). 1967: *The Honey Pot* (Great Britain, U.S., Italy; UA). 1970: *There Was a Crooked Man...* (WB); *King: A Filmed Record... Montgomery to Memphis* (Doc; with Sidney Lumet; Maron Films Ltd). 1972: *Sleuth* (Great Britain; Fox).

ANTHONY MANN (1906–1967) 1942: *Dr. Broadway* (Par); *Moonlight in Havana* (Univ). 1943: *Nobody's Dar-*

ling (Rep). 1944: *My Best Gal* (Rep); *Strangers in the Night* (Rep). 1945: *The Great Flamarion* (Rep); *Two O'Clock Courage* (RKO); *Sing Your Way Home* (RKO). 1946: *Strange Impersonation* (Rep); *The Bamboo Blonde* (RKO). 1947: *Desperate* (RKO); *Railroaded* (Eagle-Lion). 1948: *T-Men* (Eagle-Lion); *Raw Deal* (Eagle-Lion). 1949: *Reign of Terror* (Eagle-Lion); *Border Incident* (MGM); *Side Street* (MGM). 1950: *Devil's Doorway* (MGM); *The Furies* (Par); *Winchester 73* (Univ). 1951: *The Tall Target* (MGM). 1952: *Bend of the River* (Univ). 1953: *The Naked Spur* (MGM); *Thunder Bay* (Univ). 1954: *The Glenn Miller Story* (Univ). 1955: *The Far Country* (Univ); *Strategic Air Command* (Par); *The Man from Laramie* (Col); *The Last Frontier* (Col). 1956: *Serenade* (WB). 1957: *Men in War* (UA); *The Tin Star* (Par). 1958: *God's Little Acre* (UA); *Man of the West* (UA). 1960: *Cimarron* (completed by Charles Walters; MGM). 1961: *El Cid* (AA). 1964: *The Fall of the Roman Empire* (Par). 1965: *The Heroes of Telemark* (Col). 1968: *A Dandy in Aspic* (completed by uncredited Laurence Harvey).

Uncredited: 1948: *He Walked By Night* (with Alfred Werker; Eagle-Lion). 1949: *Follow Me Quietly* (with Richard Fleischer; RKO). 1951: *Quo Vadis* (with Mervyn LeRoy; MGM). 1957: *Night Passage* (with James Neilson; Univ). 1960: *Spartacus* (with Stanley Kubrick; Univ).

DANIEL MANN (born 1912) 1952: *Come Back, Little Sheba* (Par). 1954: *About Mrs. Leslie* (Par). 1955: *The Rose Tattoo* (Par); *I'll Cry Tomorrow*. 1956: *Teahouse of the August Moon* (MGM). 1958: *Hot Spell* (Par). 1959: *The Last Angry Man* (Col). 1960: *The Mountain Road* (Col); *Butterfield 8* (MGM). 1961: *Ada* (MGM). 1962: *Five Finger Exercise* (Col); *Who's Got the Action?* (Par). 1963: *Who's Been Sleeping in My Bed?* (Par). 1965: *Judith* (Par). 1966: *Our Man Flint* (Fox). 1968: *For Love of Ivy* (Cinerama). 1969: *A Dream of Kings* (NG). 1971: *Willard* (Cinerama). 1972: *The Revengers* (NG). 1973: *Interval* (Avco Embassy); *Maurie (Big Mo)* (NG). 1974: *Lost in the Stars* (American Film Theatre). 1976: *Journey into Fear* (Stirling Gold). 1978: *Matilda* (AI).

DELBERT MANN (born 1920) 1955: *Marty* (UA). 1957: *The Bachelor Party* (UA). 1958: *Desire under the Elms* (Par); *Separate Tables* (UA). 1959: *Middle of the Night* (Col). 1960: *The Dark at the Top of the Stairs* (WB). 1961: *The Outsider* (Univ). 1962: *Lover Come Back* (Univ); *That Touch of Mink* (Univ). 1963: *A Gathering of Eagles* (Univ). 1964: *Dear Heart* (WB). 1965: *Quick Before It Melts* (MGM). 1966: *Mister Buddwing* (MGM). 1967: *Fitzwilly* (UA). 1968: *The Pink Jungle* (Univ). 1971: *Kidnapped* (Great Britain; AI). 1976: *Birch Interval* (Gamma III). 1982: *Night Crossing* (BV).

GEORGE MARSHALL (1891–1975) 1916: *Love's Lariat*. 1917: *The Man from Montana*. 1918: *The Embarrassment of Riches*. 1919: *The Adventures of Ruth*. 1920: *Ruth of the Rockies; Prairie Trails*. 1921: *After Your Own Heart; Hands Off; The Jolt; A Ridin' Romeo; Why Trust Your Husband?*. 1922: *The Lady from Longacre; Smiles Are Trumps*. 1923: *Haunted Valley; Don Quickshot of the Rio Grande; Men in the Raw; Where Is This West?*. 1926: *A Trip to Chinatown*. 1927: *The Gay Retreat*. 1932: *Pack Up Your Troubles* (with Raymond McCarey; MGM). 1934: *Ever Since Eve* (Fox); *Wild Gold* (Fox); *She Learned about Sailors* (Fox); *365 Nights in Hollywood* (Fox). 1935: *Life Begins at Forty* (Fox); *$10 Raise* (Fox); *In Old Kentucky* (Fox); *Show Them No Mercy* (Fox); *Music Is Magic* (Fox). 1936: *A Message to Garcia* (Fox). 1937: *The Crime of Dr. Forbes* (Fox); *Can This Be Dixie?* (Fox); *Nancy Steele Is Missing* (Fox); *Love under Fire* (Fox). 1938: *The Goldwyn Follies* (UA); *Battle of Broadway* (Fox); *Hold That Coed* (Fox). 1939: *You Can't Cheat an Honest Man* (Univ); *Destry Rides Again* (Univ). 1940: *The Ghost Breakers* (Par); *When the Daltons Rode* (Univ). 1941: *Pot o' Gold* (UA); *Texas* (Col). 1942: *Valley of the Sun* (RKO); *The Forest Rangers* (Par); *Star Spangled Rhythm* (Par). 1943: *True to Life* (Par); *Riding High* (Par). 1944: *And the Angels Sing* (with Claude Binyon; Par). 1945: *Murder, He Says* (Par); *Incendiary Blonde* (Par). 1946: *The Blue Dahlia* (Par); *Monsieur Beaucaire* (Par). 1947: *The Perils of Pauline* (Par); *Variety Girl* (Par). 1948: *Hazard* (Par); *Tap Roots* (Par). 1949: *My Friend Irma* (Par). 1950: *Fancy Pants* (Par); *Never a Dull Moment* (RKO). 1951: *A Millionaire for Christy* (Fox). 1952: *The Savage* (Par). 1953: *Off Limits* (Par); *Scared Stiff* (Par); *Houdini* (Par); *Money from Home* (Par). 1954: *Red Garters* (Par); *Duel in the Jungle* (WB); *Destry* (Univ). 1955: *The Second Greatest Sex* (Univ). 1956: *Pillars of the Sky* (Univ). 1957: *The Guns of Fort Petticoat* (Col); *Beyond Mombasa* (Col); *The Sad Sack* (Par). 1958: *The Sheepman* (MGM); *Imitation General* (MGM). 1959: *It Started with a Kiss* (MGM); *The Mating Game* (MGM); *The Gazebo* (MGM). 1961: *Cry for Happy* (Col). 1962: *The Happy Thieves* (UA); *How the West Was Won* ("The Railroad" episode; MGM). 1963: *Papa's Delicate Condition* (Par). 1964: *Dark Purpose (L'Intrigo)* (Italy, France, U.S.; Univ); *Advance to the Rear* (MGM). 1966: *Boy, Did I Get a Wrong Number!* (UA). 1967: *Eight on the Lam* (UA). 1968: *The Wicked Dreams of Paula Schultz* (UA). 1969: *Hook, Line and Sinker* (Col).

ARCHIE MAYO (1891–1968) 1926: *Money Talks; Unknown Treasures; Christine of the Big Tops*. 1927: *Johnny Get Your Hair Cut* (with B. Reeves Eason); *Quarantined Rivals; Dearie; Slightly Used; The College Widow*. 1928: *Beware of Married Men; Crimson City; State Street Sadie; On Trial* (WB); *My Man*. 1929: *Sonny Boy; The Sap; Is Everybody Happy?* (WB); *The Sacred Flame* (WB). 1930: *Vengeance* (Col); *Wide Open* (WB); *Courage* (WB); *Oh! Sailor Beware!* (WB); *The Doorway to Hell* (WB). 1931: *Illicit* (WB); *Svengali* (WB); *Bought* (WB). 1932: *Under 18* (WB); *The Expert* (WB); *Two Against the World* (WB); *Night after Night* (Par). 1933: *The Life of Jimmy Dolan* (WB); *The Mayor of Hell* (WB); *Ever in My Heart* (WB); *Convention City* (WB). 1934: *Gambling Lady* (WB); *Desirable* (WB); *The Man with Two Faces* (WB). 1935: *Go into Your Dance* (WB); *Bordertown* (WB); *The Case of the Lucky Legs* (WB). 1936: *The Petrified Forest* (WB); *I Married a Doctor* (FN); *Give Me Your Heart* (WB). 1937: *Black Legion* (WB); *Call It a Day* (WB); *It's Love I'm After* (WB). 1938: *The Adventures of Marco Polo* (UA); *Youth Takes a Fling* (Univ). 1939: *They Shall Have Music* (UA). 1940: *The House Across the Bay* (UA); *Four Sons* (Fox). 1941: *The Great American Broadcast* (Fox); *Charley's Aunt* (Fox); *Confirm or Deny* (replaced uncredited Fritz Lang; Fox). 1942: *Moontide* (replaced uncredited Fritz Lang; Fox); *Orchestra Wives* (Fox). 1943: *Crash Dive* (Fox). 1944: *Sweet and Low Down* (Fox). 1946: *A Night in Casablanca* (UA); *Angel on My Shoulder* (UA).

PAUL MAZURSKY (born 1930) 1969: *Bob & Carol & Ted & Alice* (Col). 1970: *Alex in Wonderland* (MGM). 1973: *Blume in Love* (WB). 1974: *Harry and Tonto* (Fox). 1976: *Next Stop, Greenwich Village* (Fox). 1978: *An Unmarried Woman* (Fox). 1980: *Willie and Phil* (Fox). 1982: *Tempest* (Col). 1984: *Moscow on the Hudson* (Col). 1986: *Down and Out in Beverly Hills* (BV).

LEWIS MILESTONE (1895–1980) 1925: *Seven Sinners*. 1926: *The Cave Man; The New Klondike*. 1927: *Two Arabian Knights*. 1928: *The Garden of Eden; The Racket*. 1929: *Betrayal; New York Nights* (UA). 1930: *All Quiet on the Western Front* (Univ). 1931: *The Front Page* (UA). 1932: *Rain* (WA). 1933: *Hallelujah, I'm a Bum* (UA). 1934: *The Captain Hates the Sea* (Col). 1935: *Paris in Spring* (Par). 1936: *Anything Goes* (Par); *The General Died at Dawn* (Par). 1940: *Of Mice and Men* (UA); *The Night of Nights* (American Releasing); *Lucky Partners* (RKO). 1941: *My Life with Caroline* (RKO). 1943: *Edge of Darkness* (WB); *The North Star* (RKO). 1944: *The Purple Heart* (Fox). 1945: *A Walk in the Sun* (Fox). 1946: *The Strange Love of Martha Ivers* (Par). 1948: *The Arch of Triumph* (UA); *No Minor Vices* (MGM). 1949: *The Red Pony* (Rep). 1951: *Halls of Montezuma* (Fox). 1952: *Kangaroo* (Fox); *Les Miserables* (Fox). 1953: *Melba* (UA). 1954: *They Who Dare* (Associated Artists); *La Vedova (The Widow)* (Italy; Distributors Corporation, 1955). 1959: *Pork Chop Hill* (UA). 1960: *Ocean's 11* (WB). 1962: *Mutiny on the Bounty* (MGM).

Uncredited: 1963: *PT-109* (with Leslie H. Martinson; WB). 1966: *The Dirty Game* (replaced credited Terence Young; AI).

JOHN MILIUS (born 1944) 1973: *Dillinger* (AI). 1975: *The Wind and the Lion* (MGM/UA). 1978: *Big Wednesday* (WB). 1982: *Conan the Barbarian* (Univ). 1984: *Red Dawn* (MGM/UA).

VINCENTE MINNELLI (born 1910) 1943: *Cabin in the Sky* (MGM); *I Dood It* (MGM). 1944: *Meet Me in St. Louis* (MGM). 1945: *Yolanda and the Thief* (MGM); *The Clock* (MGM). 1946: *Ziegfeld Follies* (MGM); *Undercurrent* (MGM). 1948: *The Pirate* (MGM). 1949: *Madame Bovary* (MGM). 1950: *Father of the Bride* (MGM). 1951: *An American in Paris* (MGM); *Father's Little Dividend* (MGM). 1952: *The Bad and the Beautiful* (MGM); *The Story of Three Loves* (MGM). 1953: *The Band Wagon* (MGM). 1954: *The Long, Long Trailer* (MGM); *Brigadoon* (MGM). 1955: *Kismet* (MGM); *The Cobweb* (MGM). 1956: *Lust for Life* (MGM); *Tea and Sympathy* (MGM). 1957: *Designing Woman* (MGM). 1958: *Gigi* (MGM); *The Reluctant Debutante* (MGM). 1959: *Some Came Running* (MGM). 1960: *Home from the Hill* (MGM); *Bells Are Ringing* (MGM). 1962: *The Four Horsemen of the Apocalypse* (MGM); *Two Weeks in Another Town* (MGM). 1963: *The Courtship of Eddie's Father* (MGM). 1964: *Goodbye Charlie* (Fox). 1965: *The Sandpiper* (MGM). 1970: *On a Clear Day You Can See Forever* (Par). 1976: *A Matter of Time* (U.S., Italy; AI).

Uncredited: 1946: *Till the Clouds Roll By* (with Richard Whorf; MGM).

ROBERT MULLIGAN (born 1925) 1957: *Fear Strikes Out* (Par). 1960: *The Rat Race* (Par). 1961: *The Great Imposter* (Univ); *Come September* (Univ). 1962: *The Spiral Road* (Univ); *To Kill a Mockingbird* (Univ). 1963: *Love with the Proper Stranger* (Par). 1965: *Baby, the Rain Must Fall* (Col). 1966: *Inside Daisy Clover* (WB). 1967: *Up the Down Staircase* (WB). 1969: *The Stalking Moon* (NG). 1971: *The Pursuit of Happiness* (Col); *Summer of '42* (WB). 1972: *The Other* (Fox). 1975: *The Nickel Ride* (Fox). 1979: *Bloodbrothers* (WB); *Same Time, Next Year* (Univ). 1982: *Kiss Me Goodbye* (Fox).

F. W. MURNAU (1888–1931) 1919–26: 17 German silent films, including *Nosferatu* (1922); *Der Letze Mann (The Last Laugh)* (1924); and *Faust* (1926). 1927: *Sunrise*. 1928: *Four Devils*. 1931: *Tabu* (with Robert J. Flaherty; Par).

JEAN NEGULESCO (1900–1984) 1941: *Singapore Woman* (WB). 1944: *The Mask of Dimitrios* (WB); *The Conspirators* (WB). 1946: *Three Strangers* (WB); *Nobody Lives Forever* (WB). 1947: *Humoresque* (WB); *Deep Valley* (WB). 1948: *Johnny Belinda* (WB); *Road House* (Fox). 1949: *The Forbidden Street (Britannia Mews)* (Fox). 1950: *Under My Skin* (Fox); *Three Came Home* (Fox); *The Mudlark* (Fox). 1951: *Take Care of My Little Girl* (Fox). 1952: *Phone Call from a Stranger* (Fox); *Lydia Bailey* (Fox); *Lure of the Wilderness* (Fox); *O. Henry's Full House* ("The Last Leaf" episode; Fox). 1953: *Titanic* (Fox); *How to Marry a Millionaire* (Fox); *Scandal at Scourie* (MGM). 1954: *Three Coins in the Fountain* (Fox); *Woman's World* (Fox). 1955: *Daddy Long Legs* (Fox); *The Rains of Ranchipur* (Fox). 1957: *Boy on a Dolphin* (Fox). 1958: *The Gift of Love* (Fox); *A Certain Smile* (Fox). 1959: *Count Your Blessings* (MGM); *The Best of Everything* (Fox). 1962: *Jessica* (U.S., Italy, France; UA). 1964: *The Pleasure Seekers* (Fox). 1970: *Hello-Goodbye* (Fox); *The Invincible Six* (U.S., Iran; Continental).

MARSHALL (MICKEY) NEILAN (1891–1958) 1915: *The Chronicles of Bloom Center* (series of two-reelers). 1916: *The Cycle of Fate; The Prince Chap; The Country That God Forgot*. 1917: *Those Without Sin; The Bottle Imp; The Tides of Barnegat; The Girl at Home; The Silent Partner; Freckles; The Jaguar's Claws; Rebecca of Sunnybrook Farm; The Little Princess*. 1918: *Stella Maris; Amarilly of Clothes Line Alley; M'Liss; Hit-the-Trail Holliday; The Heart of the Wilds; Out of a Clear Sky*. 1919: *Three Men and a Girl; Daddy Long Legs; The Unpardonable Sin*. 1920: *Her Kingdom of Dreams; In Old Kentucky; The River's End; Don't Ever Marry* (with Victor Heerman); *Go and Get It* (with Henry Symonds). 1921: *Dinty* (with John W. MacDermott); *Bob Hampton of Placer; Bits of Life*. 1922: *The Lotus Eater; Fools First; Minnie* (with Frank Urson); *Penrod;*

The Stranger's Banquet. 1923: *The Eternal Three* (with Frank Urson); *The Rendezvous*. 1924: *Dorothy Vernon of Haddon Hall; Tess of the D'Urbervilles*. 1925: *The Sporting Venus; The Great Love*. 1926: *Mike; The Skyrocket; Wild Oats Lane; Diplomacy; Everybody's Acting*. 1927: *Venus of Venice; Her Wild Oat*. 1928: *Three-Ring Marriage; Take Me Home; Taxi 13; His Last Haul*. 1929: *The Awful Truth* (Pathe); *Tanned Legs* (RKO); *The Vagabond Lover* (RKO). 1930: *Sweethearts on Parade* (Col). 1934: *Chloe* (Pinnacle); *Social Register* (Col); *The Lemon Drop Kid* (Par). 1935: *This Is the Life* (Fox). 1937: *Sing While You're Able* (Ambassador); *Swing It, Professor* (Ambassador).

Ralph Nelson (born 1916) 1962: *Requiem for a Heavyweight* (Col). 1963: *Lilies of the Field* (UA); *Soldier in the Rain* (AA). 1964: *Fate Is the Hunter* (Fox); *Father Goose* (Univ). 1965: *Once a Thief* (MGM). 1966: *Duel at Diablo* (UA). 1968: *Counterpoint* (Univ); *Charly* (Cinerama). 1970: *. . . tick . . . tick . . . tick . . .* (MGM); *Soldier Blue* (Avco Embassy). 1971: *Flight of the Doves* (Great Britain; Col). 1972: *The Wrath of God* (MGM). 1975: *The Wilby Conspiracy* (Great Britain; UA). 1976: *Embryo* (Cine Artists). 1977: *A Hero Ain't Nothin' but a Sandwich* (New World).

Fred Niblo (1874–1948) 1918: *A Desert Wooing; The Marriage Ring; When Do We Eat?; Fuss and Feathers*. 1919: *Happy Though Married; The Haunted Bedroom; The Law of Men; Partners Three; The Virtuous Thief; Stepping Out; What Every Woman Learns*. 1920: *The Woman in the Suitcase; Dangerous Hours; Sex; The False Road; Hairpins; Her Husband's Friend; The Mark of Zorro*. 1921: *Silk Hosiery; Mother o' Mine; Greater Than Love; The Three Musketeers*. 1922: *The Woman He Married; Rose o' the Sea; Blood and Sand*. 1923: *The Famous Mrs. Fair; Strangers of the Night*. 1924: *Thy Name Is Woman; The Red Lily*. 1926: *Ben-Hur; The Temptress*. 1927: *Camille; The Devil Dancer*. 1928: *The Enemy; Two Lovers; The Mysterious Lady; Dream of Love*. 1930: *Redemption* (MGM); *Way Out West* (MGM). 1931: *Young Donovan's Kid* (MGM); *The Big Gamble* (Pathe).

Mike Nichols (born 1931) 1966: *Who's Afraid of Virginia Woolf?* (WB). 1967: *The Graduate* (Avco Embassy). 1970: *Catch-22* (Par). 1971: *Carnal Knowledge* (Avco Embassy). 1973: *The Day of the Dolphin* (Avco Embassy). 1975: *The Fortune* (Col). 1980: *Gilda Live* (Doc; WB). 1983: *Silkwood* (Fox). 1986: *Heartburn* (Par).

Max Ophuls (Opuls) (1902–1957) 1930–33: 6 German films; 1933–40: 10 films, 8 French, 1 Italian, 1 Dutch. 1947: *The Exile* (Univ). 1948: *Letter from an Unknown Woman* (Univ). 1949: *Caught* (MGM); *The Reckless Moment* (Col). 1950: *La Ronde* (France; Hakim). 1952: *Le Plaisir* (France; Mayer-Kingsley). 1953: *The Earrings of Madame de . . .* (France; Arian). 1955: *Lola Montès* (France; Gamma/Oska).

Uncredited: 1950: *Vendetta* (with credited Mel Ferrer and uncredited Stuart Heisler, Howard Hughes, and Preston Sturges; RKO).

Alan J. Pakula (born 1928) 1969: *The Sterile Cuckoo* (Par). 1971: *Klute* (WB). 1973: *Love and Pain and the Whole Damned Thing* (Great Britain, U.S.; Col). 1974: *The Parallax View* (Par). 1976: *All the President's Men* (WB). 1978: *Comes a Horseman* (UA). 1979: *Starting Over* (Par). 1981: *Rollover* (Orion/WB). 1982: *Sophie's Choice* (Univ/AFD). 1985: *Dream Lover* (MGM/UA).

Alan Parker (born 1944) 1976: *Bugsy Malone* (Great Britain; Par). 1978: *Midnight Express* (Great Britain; Col). 1980: *Fame* (MGM/UA). 1982: *Shoot the Moon* (MGM/UA); *Pink Floyd—The Wall* (Great Britain; MGM/UA). 1985: *Birdy* (Tri-Star). 1986: *Angel Heart* (Tri-Star).

Sam Peckinpah (1925–1984) 1961: *The Deadly Companions* (Pathe-America). 1962: *Ride the High Country* (MGM). 1965: *Major Dundee* (Col). 1969: *The Wild Bunch* (WB-7 Arts). 1970: *The Ballad of Cable Hogue* (WB). 1971: *Straw Dogs* (Great Britain; Cinerama). 1972: *The Getaway* (NG); *Junior Bonner* (Cinerama). 1973: *Pat Garrett and Billy the Kid* (MGM). 1974: *Bring Me the Head of Alfredo Garcia* (UA). 1975: *The Killer Elite* (UA). 1977: *Cross of Iron* (Great Britain, West Germany; Avco Embassy). 1978: *Convoy* (UA). 1983: *The Osterman Weekend* (Fox).

Arthur Penn (born 1922) 1958: *The Left-Handed Gun* (WB). 1962: *The Miracle Worker* (UA). 1965: *Mickey One* (Col). 1966: *The Chase* (Col). 1967: *Bonnie and Clyde* (WB). 1969: *Alice's Restaurant* (UA). 1970: *Little Big Man* (NG). 1973: *Visions of Eight* (Doc; episode; Cinema 5). 1975: *Night Moves* (WB). 1976: *The Missouri Breaks* (UA). 1981: *Four Friends* (Filmways). 1985: *Target* (WB). 1986: *Dead of Winter* (Bloomgarden Prods).

Frank Perry (born 1930) 1962: *David and Lisa* (Continental). 1963: *Ladybug Ladybug* (UA). 1968: *The Swimmer* (Col). 1969: *Last Summer* (AA); *Trilogy* (AA). 1970: *Diary of a Mad Housewife* (Univ). 1971: *Doc* (UA). 1972: *Play It as It Lays* (Univ). 1974: *Man on a Swing* (Par). 1975: *Rancho Deluxe* (UA). 1981: *Mommie Dearest* (Par). 1982: *Monsignor* (Fox). 1985: *Compromising Positions* (United Film Distribution).

Sidney Poitier (born 1924) 1972: *Buck and the Preacher* (Col). 1973: *A Warm December* (NG). 1974: *Uptown Saturday Night* (WB). 1975: *Let's Do It Again* (WB). 1977: *A Piece of the Action* (WB). 1980: *Stir Crazy* (Col). 1982: *Hanky Panky* (Col). 1985: *Fast Forward* (Col).

Roman Polanski (born 1933) 1963: *Knife in the Water* (Poland; Kanawha). 1964: *The Beautiful Swindlers (Les Plus Belles Escroqueries Du Monde)* (with Ugo Grigoretti, Claude Chabrol, and Hiromichi Horikawa; France, Italy, Japan, Holland; Jack Ellis Films). 1965: *Repulsion* (Great Britain; Royal Films International). 1966: *Cul de Sac* (Great Britain; Sigma III). 1967: *The Fearless Vampire Killers or Pardon Me But Your Teeth Are in My Neck (Dance of the Vampires)* (Great Britain; MGM). 1968: *Rosemary's Baby* (Par). 1971: *Macbeth* (Great Britain; Col). 1973: *What?* (Italy, France, West Germany; Avco Embassy). 1974: *Chinatown* (Par). 1976: *The Tenant* (France, U.S.; Par). 1980: *Tess* (France, Great Britain; Col). 1986: *Pirates* (MGM/UA).

Sydney Pollack (born 1934) 1965: *The Slender Thread* (Par). 1966: *This Property Is Condemned* (Par). 1968: *The Scalphunters* (UA). 1969: *Castle Keep* (Col); *They Shoot Horses, Don't They?* (Cinerama). 1972: *Jeremiah Johnson* (WB). 1973: *The Way We Were* (Col). 1975: *The Yakuza* (WB); *Three Days of the Condor* (Par). 1977: *Bobby Deerfield* (Col). 1979: *The Electric Horseman* (Col). 1981: *Absence of Malice* (Col). 1982: *Tootsie* (Col). 1985: *Out of Africa* (Univ).

Otto Preminger (1906–1986) 1931: *Die Grosse Liebe* (Austria, Germany). 1936: *Under Your Spell* (Fox). 1937: *Danger—Love at Work* (Fox). 1943: *Margin for Error* (Fox). 1944: *In the Meantime, Darling* (Fox); *Laura* (Fox). 1945: *A Royal Scandal* (Fox); *Fallen Angel* (Fox). 1946: *Centennial Summer* (Fox). 1947: *Forever Amber* (Fox); *Daisy Kenyon* (Fox). 1949: *The Fan* (Fox). 1950: *Whirlpool* (Fox); *Where the Sidewalk Ends* (Fox). 1951: *The 13th Letter* (Fox). 1953: *The Moon Is Blue* (UA); *Angel Face* (RKO). 1954: *River of No Return* (Fox); *Carmen Jones* (Fox). 1955: *The Man with the Golden Arm* (UA); *The Court-Martial of Billy Mitchell* (WB). 1957: *Saint Joan* (UA). 1958: *Bonjour Tristesse* (Col). 1959: *Anatomy of a Murder* (Col); *Porgy and Bess* (Col). 1960: *Exodus* (UA). 1962: *Advise and Consent* (Col). 1963: *The Cardinal* (Col). 1965: *In Harm's Way* (Par); *Bunny Lake Is Missing* (Great Britain; Col). 1967: *Hurry Sundown* (Par). 1968: *Skidoo* (Par). 1970: *Tell Me That You Love Me, Junie Moon* (Par). 1971: *Such Good Friends* (Par). 1975: *Rosebud* (UA). 1979: *The Human Factor* (Great Britain; UA).

Bob Rafelson (born 1934) 1968: *Head* (Col). 1970: *Five Easy Pieces* (Col). 1972: *The King of Marvin Gardens* (Col). 1976: *Stay Hungry* (UA). 1981: *The Postman Always Rings Twice* (Par).

Irving Rapper (born 1898) 1941: *Shining Victory* (WB); *One Foot in Heaven* (replaced Anatole Litvak; WB). 1942: *The Gay Sisters* (WB); *Now, Voyager* (WB). 1944: *The Adventures of Mark Twain* (WB). 1945: *Rhapsody in Blue* (WB); *The Corn Is Green* (WB). 1946: *Deception* (WB). 1947: *The Voice of the Turtle* (WB). 1949: *Anna Lucasta* (Col). 1950: *The Glass Menagerie* (WB). 1952: *Another Man's Poison* (UA). 1954: *Forever Female* (Par); *Bad for Each Other* (Col). 1956: *Strange Intruder* (AA); *The Brave One* (RKO). 1958: *Marjorie Morningstar* (WB). 1959: *The Miracle* (WB). 1960–61: 2 Italian films. 1970: *The Christine Jorgensen Story* (UA). 1978: *Born Again* (Avco Embassy).

Nicholas Ray (1911–1979) 1948: *They Live by Night* (RKO). 1949: *A Woman's Secret* (RKO); *Knock on Any Door* (Col). 1950: *In a Lonely Place* (Col); *Born to Be Bad* (RKO). 1951: *On Dangerous Ground* (RKO); *Flying Leathernecks* (RKO). 1952: *The Lusty Men* (RKO). 1954: *Johnny Guitar* (Rep). 1955: *Run for Cover* (Par); *Rebel Without a Cause* (WB). 1956: *Hot Blood* (Col); *Bigger Than Life* (Fox). 1957: *The True Story of Jesse James* (Fox). 1958: *Bitter Victory* (Col); *Wind Across the Everglades* (WB); *Party Girl* (MGM). 1960: *The Savage Innocents* (Par). 1961: *King of Kings* (MGM). 1963: *55 Days at Peking* (AA).

Uncredited: 1952: *Macao* (with Josef von Sternberg; RKO).

Robert Redford (born 1937) 1980: *Ordinary People* (Par).

Karel Reisz (born 1926) 1959: *We Are the Lambeth Boys* (Great Britain; Rank). 1961: *Saturday Night and Sunday Morning* (Great Britain; Continental). 1964: *Night Must Fall* (Great Britain; Embassy). 1966: *Morgan! (Morgan: A Suitable Case for Treatment)* (Great Britain; Cinema 5). 1969: *Isadora (The Loves of Isadora)* (Great Britain; Univ). 1974: *The Gambler* (Par). 1978: *Who'll Stop the Rain?* (UA). 1981: *The French Lieutenant's Woman* (Great Britain; UA). 1985: *Sweet Dreams* (Tri-Star).

Tony Richardson (born 1928) 1959: *Look Back in Anger* (Great Britain; WB). 1960: *The Entertainer* (Great Britain; Continental). 1961: *Sanctuary* (Fox). 1962: *The Loneliness of the Long Distance Runner* (Great Britain; Continental); *A Taste of Honey* (Great Britain; Continental). 1963: *Tom Jones* (Great Britain; Lopert). 1965: *The Loved One* (MGM). 1966: *Mademoiselle* (France, Great Britain; Lopert). 1967: *The Sailor from Gibraltar* (Great Britain; Lopert). 1968: *The Charge of the Light Brigade* (Great Britain; UA). 1969: *Laughter in the Dark* (Great Britain, France; Lopert); *Hamlet* (Great Britain; Col). 1970: *Ned Kelly* (Great Britain; UA). 1973: *A Delicate Balance* (American Film Theatre); *Dead Cert* (Great Britain; UA). 1977: *Joseph Andrews* (Great Britain; Par). 1982: *The Border* (Univ). 1984: *The Hotel New Hampshire* (Orion).

Michael Ritchie (born 1938) 1969: *Downhill Racer* (Par). 1972: *Prime Cut* (NG); *The Candidate* (WB). 1975: *Smile* (UA). 1976: *The Bad News Bears* (Par). 1978: *Semi-Tough* (UA). 1979: *An Almost Perfect Affair* (Par). 1980: *The Island* (Univ). 1983: *The Survivors* (Col). 1986: *Wildcats* (WB); *The Golden Child* (Par).

Martin Ritt (born 1920) 1957: *Edge of the City* (MGM); *No Down Payment* (Fox). 1958: *The Long, Hot Summer* (MGM). 1959: *The Black Orchid* (Par); *The Sound and the Fury* (Fox). 1960: *Five Branded Women* (Yugoslavia, Italy, U.S.; Par). 1961: *Paris Blues* (UA). 1962: *Hemingway's Adventures of a Young Man* (Fox). 1963: *Hud* (Par). 1964: *The Outrage* (MGM). 1965: *The Spy Who Came in from the Cold* (Great Britain; Par). 1967: *Hombre* (Fox). 1968: *The Brotherhood* (Par). 1970: *The Molly Maguires* (Par); *The Great White Hope* (Fox). 1972: *Sounder* (Fox); *Pete 'n' Tillie* (Univ). 1974: *Conrack* (Fox). 1976: *The Front* (Col). 1978: *Casey's Shadow* (Col). 1979: *Norma Rae* (Fox). 1981: *Back Roads* (WB). 1983: *Cross Creek* (Univ/AFD). 1986: *Murphy's Romance* (Col).

Jerome Robbins (born 1918) 1961: *West Side Story* (with Robert Wise; UA).

MARK ROBSON (1913–1978)   1943: *The Seventh Victim* (RKO); *The Ghost Ship* (RKO); *Youth Runs Wild* (RKO). 1945: *Isle of the Dead* (RKO). 1946: *Bedlam* (RKO). 1949: *Champion* (UA); *Home of the Brave* (UA); *Roughshod* (RKO); *My Foolish Heart* (RKO). 1950: *Edge of Doom* (RKO). 1951: *Bright Victory* (Univ); *I Want You* (RKO). 1953: *Return to Paradise* (UA). 1954: *Hell Below Zero* (Col); *Phffft* (Col). 1955: *The Bridges at Toko-Ri* (Par); *A Prize of Gold* (Col); *Trial* (MGM). 1956: *The Harder They Fall* (Col). 1957: *The Little Hut* (MGM); *Peyton Place* (Fox). 1958: *The Inn of the Sixth Happiness* (Fox). 1960: *From the Terrace* (Fox). 1963: *Nine Hours to Rama* (Fox); *The Prize* (MGM). 1964: *Von Ryan's Express* (Fox). 1966: *Lost Command* (Col). 1967: *Valley of the Dolls* (Fox). 1969: *Daddy's Gone a-Hunting* (NG). 1971: *Happy Birthday, Wanda June* (Col). 1973: *Limbo* (Univ). 1974: *Earthquake* (Univ). 1979: *Avalanche Express* (Fox).

HERBERT ROSS (born 1927)   1969: *Goodbye, Mr. Chips* (Great Britain; MGM). 1970: *The Owl and the Pussycat* (Col). 1971: *T. R. Baskin* (Par). 1972: *Play It Again, Sam* (Par). 1973: *The Last of Sheila* (WB). 1975: *Funny Lady* (Col); *The Sunshine Boys* (MGM/UA). 1976: *The Seven-Per-Cent Solution* (Great Britain; Univ). 1977: *The Turning Point* (Fox); *The Goodbye Girl* (WB). 1978: *California Suite* (Col). 1980: *Nijinsky* (Par). 1981: *Pennies from Heaven* (MGM/UA). 1982: *I Ought to Be in Pictures* (Fox). 1983: *Max Dugan Returns* (Fox). 1984: *Footloose* (Par). 1985: *Protocol* (WB).

ROBERT ROSSEN (1908–1966)   1947: *Johnny O'Clock* (Col); *Body and Soul* (UA). 1949: *All the King's Men* (Col). 1951: *The Brave Bulls* (Col). 1955: *Mambo* (Par). 1956: *Alexander the Great* (UA). 1957: *Island in the Sun* (Fox). 1959: *They Came to Cordura* (Col). 1961: *The Hustler* (Fox). 1964: *Lilith* (Col).

WESLEY RUGGLES (1889–1972)   1917: *For France*. 1918: *The Blind Adventure*. 1919: *The Winchester Woman*. 1920: *Piccadilly Jim*; *The Desperate Hero*; *The Leopard Woman*; *Love*. 1921: *The Greater Claim*; *Uncharted Seas*; *Over the Wire*. 1922: *Wild Honey*; *If I Were Queen*. 1923: *Slippery Magee*; *Mr. Billings Spends His Dime*; *The Remittance Woman*; *The Heart Raider*. 1924: *The Age of Innocence*. 1925: *The Plastic Age*; *Broadway Lady*. 1926: *The Kick-Off*; *A Man of Quality*. 1927: *Beware of Widows*; *Silk Stockings*. 1928: *Fourflusher*; *Finders Keepers*. 1929: *Street Girl* (RKO); *Scandal* (Univ); *Girl Overboard* (Univ); *Condemned* (UA); *The Haunted Lady* (Univ). 1930: *Honey* (Par); *The Sea Bat* (MGM). 1931: *Cimarron* (RKO); *Are These Our Children?* (RKO). 1932: *No Man of Her Own* (Par); *Roar of the Dragon* (RKO). 1933: *The Monkey's Paw* (RKO); *College Humor* (Par); *I'm No Angel* (Par). 1934: *Bolero* (Par); *Shoot the Works* (Par). 1935: *The Gilded Lily* (Par); *Accent on Youth* (Par); *The Bride Comes Home* (Par). 1936: *Valiant Is the Word for Carrie* (Par). 1937: *True Confession* (Par); *I Met Him in Paris* (Par). 1938: *Sing, You Sinners* (Par). 1939: *Invitation to Happiness* (Par). 1940: *Too Many Husbands* (Col); *Arizona* (Col). 1941: *You Belong to Me* (Col). 1942: *Somewhere I'll Find You* (MGM). 1943: *Slightly Dangerous* (MGM). 1944: *See Here, Private Hargrove* (MGM). 1946: *London Town* (Great Britain; Rank).

MARK RYDELL (born 1934)   1968: *The Fox* (Claridge). 1969: *The Reivers* (NG). 1972: *The Cowboys* (WB). 1974: *Cinderella Liberty* (Fox). 1976: *Harry and Walter Go to New York* (Col). 1979: *The Rose* (Fox). 1981: *On Golden Pond* (Univ/AFD). 1984: *The River* (Univ).

MARK SANDRICH (1900–1945)   1928: *Runaway Girls*. 1930: *The Talk of Hollywood* (World Wide). 1933: *Melody Cruise* (RKO); *Aggie Appleby, Maker of Men* (RKO). 1934: *Hips, Hips, Hooray* (RKO); *Cockeyed Cavaliers* (RKO); *The Gay Divorcee* (RKO). 1935: *Top Hat* (RKO). 1936: *Follow the Fleet* (RKO); *A Woman Rebels* (RKO). 1937: *Shall We Dance* (RKO). 1938: *Carefree* (RKO). 1939: *Man About Town* (Par). 1940: *Buck Benny Rides Again* (Par); *Love Thy Neighbor* (Par). 1941: *Skylark* (Par). 1942: *Holiday Inn* (Par). 1943: *So Proudly We Hail* (Par). 1944: *Here Come the Waves* (Par); *I Love a Soldier* (Par).

FRANKLIN J. SCHAFFNER (born 1920)   1963: *The Stripper* (Fox). 1964: *The Best Man* (UA). 1965: *The War Lord* (Univ). 1968: *The Double Man* (Great Britain; WB); *Planet of the Apes* (Fox). 1970: *Patton* (Fox). 1971: *Nicholas and Alexandra* (Great Britain; Col). 1973: *Papillon* (AA). 1977: *Islands in the Stream* (Par). 1978: *The Boys from Brazil* (Fox). 1981: *Sphinx* (Orion/WB). 1982: *Yes, Giorgio* (MGM/UA).

FRED SCHEPISI (born 1939)   1973: *Libido* (with John B. Murray, Tim Burstall, and David Baker; Producers and Directors Guild of Australia). 1976: *The Devil's Playground* (Australia; Entertainment Marketing). 1978: *The Chant of Jimmie Blacksmith* (Australia; New Yorker). 1982: *Barbarosa* (Univ/AFD). 1984: *Iceman* (Univ). 1985: *Plenty* (Great Britain; Fox).

JOHN SCHLESINGER (born 1926)   1962: *A Kind of Loving* (Great Britain; Continental). 1963: *Billy Liar* (Great Britain; Continental). 1965: *Darling* (Great Britain; Embassy). 1967: *Far from the Madding Crowd* (Great Britain; MGM). 1969: *Midnight Cowboy* (UA). 1971: *Sunday, Bloody Sunday* (Great Britain; UA). 1973: *Visions of Eight* (Doc; episode; Cinema 5). 1975: *The Day of the Locust* (Par). 1976: *Marathon Man* (Par). 1979: *Yanks* (Great Britain; Univ). 1981: *Honky Tonk Freeway* (Univ/AFD). 1985: *The Falcon and the Snowman* (Orion).

MARTIN SCORSESE (born 1942)   1968: *Who's That Knocking at My Door?* (Joseph Brenner Associates). 1972: *Boxcar Bertha* (AI). 1973: *Mean Streets* (WB). 1974: *Alice Doesn't Live Here Anymore* (WB). 1976: *Taxi Driver* (Col). 1977: *New York, New York* (UA). 1978: *The Last Waltz* (Doc; UA). 1980: *Raging Bull* (UA). 1983: *The King of Comedy* (Fox). 1985: *After Hours* (WB). 1986: *The Color of Money* (Touchstone).

GEORGE SEATON (1911–1979)   1945: *Billy Rose's Diamond Horseshoe* (Fox); *Junior Miss* (Fox). 1946: *The Shocking Miss Pilgrim* (Fox). 1947: *Miracle on 34th Street* (Fox). 1948: *Apartment for Peggy* (Fox). 1949: *Chicken Every Sunday* (Fox). 1950: *The Big Lift* (Fox); *For Heaven's Sake* (Fox). 1952: *Anything Can Happen* (Par). 1953: *Little Boy Lost* (Par). 1954: *The Country Girl* (Par). 1956: *The Proud and the Profane* (Par). 1958: *Teacher's Pet* (Par). 1961: *The Pleasure of His Company* (Par); *The Counterfeit Traitor* (Par). 1963: *The Hook* (MGM). 1964: *36 Hours* (MGM). 1968: *What's So Bad About Feeling Good?* (Univ). 1970: *Airport* (Univ). 1973: *Showdown* (Univ).

MACK SENNETT (1880–1960)   1910–15: hundreds of short films; 1929–35: 30 short films. 1914: *Tillie's Punctured Romance*. 1921: *Home Talent* (with James E. Abbe). 1922: *Oh Mabel Behave* (with Ford Sterling). 1928: *The Good-Bye Kiss*. 1930: *Midnight Daddies* (World Wide). 1933: *Hypnotized* (M.H.S. Productions).

VINCENT SHERMAN (born 1906)   1939: *The Return of Doctor X* (WB). 1940: *Saturday's Children* (WB); *The Man Who Talked Too Much* (WB). 1941: *Flight from Destiny* (WB); *Underground* (WB). 1942: *All Through the Night* (WB); *The Hard Way* (WB). 1943: *Old Acquaintance* (WB). 1944: *In Our Time* (WB). 1945: *Mr. Skeffington* (WB); *Pillow to Post* (WB); *Janie Gets Married* (WB). 1947: *Nora Prentiss* (WB); *The Unfaithful* (WB). 1949: *The Adventures of Don Juan* (WB); *The Hasty Heart* (WB). 1950: *Backfire* (WB); *The Damned Don't Cry* (WB); *Harriet Craig* (Col). 1951: *Goodbye, My Fancy* (WB). 1952: *Lone Star* (MGM); *Affair in Trinidad* (Col). 1956: *Difendo il Mio Amore* (Italy). 1957: *The Garment Jungle* (Col). 1959: *The Naked Earth* (Fox); *The Young Philadelphians* (WB). 1960: *Ice Palace* (WB). 1961: *The Second Time Around* (Fox); *A Fever in the Blood* (WB). 1968: *The Young Rebel (Cervantes)* (Italy, Spain, France; AI).

GEORGE SIDNEY (born 1916)   1941: *Free and Easy* (MGM). 1942: *Pacific Rendezvous* (MGM). 1943: *Pilot No. 5* (MGM); *Thousands Cheer* (MGM). 1944: *Bathing Beauty* (MGM). 1945: *Anchors Aweigh* (MGM). 1946: *The Harvey Girls* (MGM); *Holiday in Mexico* (MGM). 1947: *Cass Timberlane* (MGM). 1948: *The Three Muske-*

teers (MGM). 1949: *The Red Danube* (MGM). 1950: *Annie Get Your Gun* (MGM); *Key to the City* (MGM). 1951: *Show Boat* (MGM). 1952: *Scaramouche* (MGM). 1953: *Young Bess* (MGM); *Kiss Me Kate* (MGM). 1955: *Jupiter's Darling* (MGM). 1956: *The Eddy Duchin Story* (Col). 1957: *Jeanne Eagels* (Col); *Pal Joey* (Col). 1960: *Who Was That Lady?* (Col); *Pepe* (Col). 1963: *Bye Bye Birdie* (Col); *A Ticklish Affair* (MGM). 1964: *Viva Las Vegas* (MGM). 1966: *The Swinger* (Par). 1968: *Half a Sixpence* (Great Britain; Par).

DON SIEGEL (born 1912)   1946: *The Verdict* (WB). 1949: *Night unto Night* (WB); *The Big Steal* (RKO). 1952: *Duel at Silver Creek* (Univ); *No Time for Flowers* (RKO). 1953: *Count the Hours* (RKO); *China Venture* (Col). 1954: *Riot in Cell Block 11* (AA); *Private Hell 36* (Filmmakers). 1955: *An Annapolis Story* (AA). 1956: *Invasion of the Body Snatchers* (AA); *Crime in the Streets* (AA). 1957: *Baby Face Nelson* (AA). 1958: *Spanish Affair* (Spain; Par); *The Lineup* (Col); *The Gun Runners* (UA). 1959: *Hound Dog Man* (Fox); *Edge of Eternity* (Col). 1960: *Flaming Star* (Fox). 1962: *Hell Is for Heroes* (Par). 1964: *The Killers* (Univ). 1968: *Madigan* (Univ); *Coogan's Bluff* (Univ). 1969: *Death of a Gunfighter* (with Robert Totten, both under name of Allen Smithee; Univ). 1970: *Two Mules for Sister Sara* (U.S., Mexico; Univ). 1971: *The Beguiled* (Univ). 1972: *Dirty Harry* (WB). 1973: *Charley Varrick* (Univ). 1974: *The Black Windmill* (Great Britain; Univ). 1976: *The Shootist* (Par). 1977: *Telefon* (MGM/UA). 1979: *Escape from Alcatraz* (Par). 1980: *Rough Cut* (Par). 1982: *Jinxed* (MGM/UA).

ROBERT SIODMAK (1900–1973)   1929–33: 7 silent and sound German films; 1936–39: 8 French films. 1941: *West Point Widow* (Par). 1942: *Fly by Night* (Par); *The Night Before the Divorce* (Fox); *My Heart Belongs to Daddy* (Par). 1943: *Someone to Remember* (Rep); *Son of Dracula* (Univ). 1944: *Cobra Woman* (Univ); *Phantom Lady* (Univ); *Christmas Holiday* (Univ). 1945: *The Suspect* (Univ); *Conflict* (WB); *Uncle Harry (The Strange Affair of Uncle Harry)* (Univ); *The Spiral Staircase* (RKO). 1946: *The Killers* (Univ); *The Dark Mirror* (Univ). 1947: *Time Out of Mind* (Univ). 1948: *Cry of the City* (Fox). 1949: *The Great Sinner* (MGM); *Criss Cross* (Univ). 1950: *Thelma Jordon (The File on Thelma Jordon)* (Par); *Deported* (Univ). 1951: *The Whistle at Eaton Falls* (Col). 1952: *The Crimson Pirate* (WB). 1954–69: 11 German, French, and Italian films. 1959: *The Rough and the Smooth (Portrait of a Sinner)* (Renown). 1967: *Custer of the West* (Cinerama).

DOUGLAS SIRK (born 1900)   1935–37: 9 German films. 1943: *Hitler's Madman* (MGM). 1944: *Summer Storm* (UA). 1946: *A Scandal in Paris* (UA). 1947: *Lured* (UA). 1948: *Sleep, My Love* (UA). 1949: *Shockproof* (Col); *Slightly French* (Col). 1950: *Mystery Submarine* (Univ). 1951: *The First Legion* (UA); *Thunder on the Hill* (Univ); *The Lady Pays Off* (Univ); *Weekend with Father* (Univ). 1952: *No Room for the Groom* (Univ); *Has Anybody Seen My Gal?* (Univ); *Meet Me at the Fair* (Univ). 1953: *Take Me to Town* (Univ); *All I Desire* (Univ). 1954: *Taza, Son of Cochise* (Univ); *Magnificent Obsession* (Univ); *Sign of the Pagan* (Univ). 1955: *Captain Lightfoot* (Univ). 1956: *All That Heaven Allows* (Univ-International); *There's Always Tomorrow* (Univ); *Written on the Wind* (Univ). 1957: *Battle Hymn* (Univ); *Interlude* (Univ); *The Tarnished Angels* (Univ). 1958: *A Time to Love and a Time to Die* (Univ). 1959: *Imitation of Life* (Univ).

Uncredited: 1948: *Siren of Atlantis* (with Gregg Tallas; UA). 1956: *Never Say Goodbye* (with Jerry Hopper; Univ).

VICTOR SJÖSTRÖM (SEASTROM) (1879–1960)   1912–23: 40 silent Swedish films. 1924: *He Who Gets Slapped*; *Name the Man*. 1925: *Confessions of a Queen*; *Tower of Lies*. 1926: *The Scarlet Letter*. 1928: *The Wind*; *The Divine Woman*; *Masks of the Devil*. 1930: *A Lady to Love* (MGM); *Markurells I Wadkoping* (Sweden; also in German-language version). 1937: *Under the Red Robe* (Fox).

STEVEN SPIELBERG (born 1947)   1974: *The Sugarland Express* (Univ). 1975: *Jaws* (Univ). 1977: *Close Encoun-*

ters of the Third Kind (Col). 1979: *1941* (Univ/Col). 1981: *Raiders of the Lost Ark* (Par). 1982: *E.T.: The Extra-Terrestrial* (Univ). 1983: *Twilight Zone—The Movie* (episode; WB). 1984: *Indiana Jones and the Temple of Doom* (Par). 1985: *The Color Purple* (WB).

John M. Stahl (1886–1950) 1918: *Wives of Men; Suspicion.* 1919: *Her Code of Honor; A Woman under Oath; Greater Than Love.* 1920: *Women Men Forget; The Woman in His House.* 1921: *Sowing the Wind; The Child Thou Gavest Me.* 1922: *The Song of Life; One Clear Call; Suspicious Wives.* 1923: *The Wanters; The Dangerous Age.* 1924: *Why Men Leave Home; Husbands and Lovers.* 1925: *Fine Clothes.* 1926: *Memory Lane; The Gay Deceiver.* 1927: *Lovers?; In Old Kentucky.* 1930: *A Lady Surrenders* (Univ). 1931: *Seed* (Univ); *Strictly Dishonorable* (Univ). 1932: *Back Street* (Univ). 1933: *Only Yesterday* (Univ). 1934: *Imitation of Life* (Univ). 1935: *Magnificent Obsession* (Univ). 1937: *Parnell* (MGM). 1938: *Letter of Introduction* (Univ). 1939: *When Tomorrow Comes* (Univ). 1941: *Our Wife* (Col). 1942: *Immortal Sergeant* (Fox). 1943: *Holy Matrimony* (Fox). 1944: *The Eve of St. Mark* (Fox); *The Keys of the Kingdom* (Fox). 1945: *Leave Her to Heaven* (Fox). 1947: *The Foxes of Harrow* (Fox). 1948: *The Walls of Jericho* (Fox). 1949: *Father Was a Fullback* (Fox); *Oh, You Beautiful Doll* (Fox).

Josef Von Sternberg (1894–1969) 1925: *The Salvation Hunters.* 1926: *The Exquisite Sinner.* 1927: *Underworld.* 1928: *The Last Command; The Dragnet; The Docks of New York.* 1929: *The Case of Lena Smith; Thunderbolt* (Par). 1930: *Der Blaue Engel (The Blue Angel)* (Germany; UFA); *Morocco* (Par). 1931: *Dishonored* (Par); *An American Tragedy* (Par). 1932: *Shanghai Express* (Par); *Blonde Venus* (Par). 1934: *The Scarlet Empress* (Par). 1935: *The Devil Is a Woman* (Par); *Crime and Punishment* (Col). 1936: *The King Steps Out* (Col). 1939: *Sergeant Madden* (MGM). 1941: *The Shanghai Gesture* (UA). 1952: *Macao* (with uncredited Nicholas Ray; RKO). 1953: *Anatahan (The Saga of Anatahan)* (Japan; Arias Films). 1957: *Jet Pilot* (with uncredited Howard Hughes; Univ).

Uncredited: 1925: *The Masked Bride* (with Christy Cabanne). 1927: *Children of Divorce* (with Frank Lloyd; Par). 1946: *Duel in the Sun* (with credited King Vidor and uncredited William Dieterle; Selznick). Uncompleted: 1937: *I, Claudius.* Unreleased: 1926: *The Sea Gull (Woman of the Sea)* (Charles Chaplin Films).

George Stevens (1904–1975) 1933: *The Cohens and Kellys in Trouble* (Univ). 1934: *Bachelor Bait* (RKO); *Kentucky Kernels* (RKO). 1935: *Laddie* (RKO); *The Nitwits* (RKO); *Alice Adams* (RKO); *Annie Oakley* (RKO). 1936: *Swing Time* (RKO). 1937: *Quality Street* (RKO); *A Damsel in Distress* (RKO). 1938: *Vivacious Lady* (RKO). 1939: *Gunga Din* (RKO). 1940: *Vigil in the Night* (RKO). 1941: *Penny Serenade* (Col). 1942: *Woman of the Year* (MGM); *The Talk of the Town* (Col). 1943: *The More the Merrier* (Col). 1948: *I Remember Mama* (RKO). 1951: *A Place in the Sun* (Par). 1952: *Something to Live For* (Par). 1953: *Shane* (Par). 1956: *Giant* (WB). 1959: *The Diary of Anne Frank* (Fox). 1965: *The Greatest Story Ever Told* (UA). 1970: *The Only Game in Town* (Fox).

Robert Stevenson (1905–1986) 1932: *Happily Ever After* (Great Britain; Gaumont-British). 1933: *Falling for You* (Great Britain; Woolf & Freedman). 1936: *Jack of All Trades* (Great Britain; Gaumont-British); *Nine Days a Queen (Tudor Rose)* (Great Britain; Gaumont-British); *The Man Who Lived Again (The Man Who Changed His Mind)* (Great Britain; Gaumont-British). 1937: *King Solomon's Mines* (Great Britain; Gaumont-British); *Non-Stop New York* (Great Britain; General Film Distributors). 1938: *To the Victor (Owd Bob)* (Great Britain; Gaumont-British). 1939: *The Ware Case* (Great Britain; Associated British); *A Young Man's Fancy* (Great Britain; Associated British); *Return to Yesterday* (Great Britain; Associated British). 1940: *Tom Brown's Schooldays* (RKO). 1941: *Back Street* (Univ). 1942: *Joan of Paris* (RKO). 1943: *Forever and a Day* (episode; RKO). 1944: *Jane Eyre* (RKO). 1947: *Dishonored Lady* (UA). 1948: *To the Ends of the Earth* (RKO). 1949: *The Woman on Pier 13 (I Married a Communist)* (RKO). 1950: *Walk Softly, Stranger* (RKO). 1951: *My Forbidden Past* (RKO). 1952: *The Las Vegas Story* (RKO). 1957: *Johnny Tremain* (BV); *Old Yeller* (BV). 1959: *Darby O'Gill and the Little People* (BV). 1960: *Kidnapped* (Great Britain, U.S.; BV). 1961: *The Absent-Minded Professor* (BV). 1962: *In Search of the Castaways* (Great Britain, U.S.; BV). 1963: *Son of Flubber* (BV). 1964: *Mary Poppins* (BV); *The Misadventures of Merlin Jones* (BV). 1965: *The Monkey's Uncle* (BV); *That Darn Cat* (BV). 1967: *The Gnome-Mobile* (BV). 1968: *Blackbeard's Ghost* (BV). 1969: *The Love Bug* (BV). 1971: *Bedknobs and Broomsticks* (BV). 1974: *Herbie Rides Again* (BV); *The Island at the Top of the World* (BV). 1975: *One of Our Dinosaurs Is Missing* (Great Britain, U.S.; BV). 1976: *The Shaggy D.A.* (BV).

Erich von Stroheim (1885–1957) 1919: *Blind Husbands.* 1920: *The Devil's Pass Key.* 1921: *Foolish Wives.* 1923: *Merry-Go-Round* (replaced by Rupert Julian). 1924: *Greed.* 1925: *The Merry Widow.* 1928: *The Wedding March* (Part II released as *The Honeymoon*); *Queen Kelly* (revised version supervised by Gloria Swanson, Edmund Goulding). 1933: *Walking Down Broadway* (with uncredited Raoul Walsh; revised by Alfred Werker for release as *Hello Sister!;* Fox).

John Sturges (born 1911) 1946: *The Man Who Dared* (Col); *Shadowed* (Col); *Alias Mr. Twilight* (Col). 1947: *For the Love of Rusty* (Col); *Keeper of the Bees* (Col). 1948: *Best Man Wins* (Col); *The Sign of the Ram* (Col). 1949: *The Walking Hills* (Col). 1950: *The Capture* (RKO); *Mystery Street* (MGM); *Right Cross* (MGM); *The Magnificent Yankee* (MGM). 1951: *Kind Lady* (MGM); *The People Against O'Hara* (MGM); *It's a Big Country* (episode; MGM). 1952: *The Girl in White* (MGM). 1953: *Jeopardy* (MGM); *Fast Company* (MGM); *Escape from Fort Bravo* (MGM). 1955: *Bad Day at Black Rock* (MGM); *Underwater!* (RKO); *The Scarlet Coat* (MGM). 1956: *Backlash* (MGM). 1957: *Gunfight at the O.K. Corral* (Par). 1958: *The Law and Jake Wade* (MGM); *The Old Man and the Sea* (WB). 1959: *Last Train from Gun Hill* (Par); *Never So Few* (MGM). 1960: *The Magnificent Seven* (UA). 1961: *By Love Possessed* (UA). 1962: *Sergeants 3* (UA). 1963: *A Girl Named Tamiko* (Par); *The Great Escape* (UA). 1965: *The Satan Bug* (UA); *The Hallelujah Trail* (UA). 1967: *Hour of the Gun* (UA). 1968: *Ice Station Zebra* (MGM). 1969: *Marooned* (Col). 1972: *Joe Kidd* (Univ). 1973: *Chino (The Valdez Horses)* (Italy, Spain, France; Intercontinental). 1974: *McQ* (WB). 1977: *The Eagle Has Landed* (Great Britain; Col).

Preston Sturges (1898–1959) 1940: *The Great McGinty* (Par); *Christmas in July* (Par). 1941: *The Lady Eve* (Par); *Sullivan's Travels* (Par). 1942: *The Palm Beach Story* (Par). 1944: *The Miracle of Morgan's Creek* (Par); *Hail the Conquering Hero* (Par); *The Great Moment* (Par). 1947: *The Sin of Harold Diddlebock* (re-released in 1950 as *Mad Wednesday;* UA). 1948: *Unfaithfully Yours* (Fox). 1949: *The Beautiful Blonde from Bashful Bend* (Fox). 1957: *The French They Are a Funny Race* (Continental Distributing).

Uncredited: 1950: *Vendetta* (with credited Mel Ferrer and uncredited Stuart Heisler, Howard Hughes, and Max Ophuls; RKO).

Frank Tashlin (1913–1972) 1952: *The First Time* (Col); *Son of Paleface* (Par). 1953: *Marry Me Again* (RKO). 1954: *Susan Slept Here* (RKO). 1955: *Artists and Models* (Par); *The Lieutenant Wore Skirts* (Fox). 1956: *Hollywood or Bust* (Par); *The Girl Can't Help It* (Fox). 1957: *Will Success Spoil Rock Hunter?* (Fox). 1958: *Rock-a-Bye Baby* (Par); *The Geisha Boy* (Par). 1959: *Say One for Me* (Fox). 1960: *Cinderfella* (Par). 1961: *Bachelor Flat* (Fox). 1962: *It's Only Money* (Par). 1963: *The Man from the Diner's Club* (Par); *Who's Minding the Store?* (Par). 1964: *The Disorderly Orderly* (Par). 1966: *The Alphabet Murders* (MGM); *The Glass Bottom Boat* (MGM). 1967: *Caprice* (Fox). 1968: *The Private Navy of Sgt. O'Farrell* (UA).

Uncredited: 1951: *The Lemon Drop Kid* (with Sidney Lanfield; Par).

Norman Taurog (1899–1981) 1928: *The Farmer's Daughter.* 1929: *Lucky Boy* (with Charles C. Wilson). 1930: *Sunny Skies* (Tiffany); *Hot Curves* (Tiffany); *Troopers Three* (with B. Reeves Eason; Tiffany); *Follow the Leader* (Par). 1931: *Finn and Hattie* (with Norman Z. McLeod; Par); *Skippy* (Par); *Newly Rich* (Par); *Huckleberry Finn* (Par); *Sooky* (Par). 1932: *Hold 'em Jail* (RKO); *The Phantom President* (Par); *If I Had a Million* ("The Auto" episode; Par). 1933: *A Bedtime Story* (Par); *The Way to Love* (Par). 1934: *We're Not Dressing* (Par); *Mrs. Wiggs of the Cabbage Patch* (Par); *College Rhythm* (Par). 1935: *The Big Broadcast of 1936* (Par). 1936: *Strike Me Pink* (Par); *Reunion* (Fox); *Rhythm on the Range* (Par). 1937: *You Can't Have Everything* (Fox); *Fifty Roads to Town* (Fox). 1938: *Mad about Music* (Univ); *The Adventures of Tom Sawyer* (UA); *Boys Town* (MGM). 1939: *The Girl Downstairs* (MGM); *Lucky Night* (MGM). 1940: *Broadway Melody of 1940* (MGM); *Young Tom Edison* (MGM); *Little Nellie Kelly* (MGM). 1941: *Men of Boys Town* (MGM); *Design for Scandal* (MGM). 1942: *Are Husbands Necessary?* (Par); *A Yank at Eton* (MGM). 1943: *Presenting Lily Mars* (MGM); *Girl Crazy* (MGM). 1946: *The Hoodlum Saint* (MGM). 1947: *The Beginning or the End* (MGM). 1948: *The Bride Goes Wild* (MGM); *Big City* (MGM); *Words and Music* (MGM). 1949: *That Midnight Kiss* (MGM). 1950: *Please Believe Me* (MGM); *The Toast of New Orleans* (MGM); *Mrs. O'Malley and Mr. Malone* (MGM). 1951: *Rich, Young and Pretty* (MGM). 1952: *Room for One More* (WB); *Jumping Jacks* (Par); *The Stooge* (Par). 1953: *The Stars Are Singing* (Par); *The Caddy* (Par). 1954: *Living It Up* (Par). 1955: *You're Never Too Young* (Par). 1956: *The Birds and the Bees* (Par); *Pardners* (Par); *Bundle of Joy* (RKO). 1957: *The Fuzzy Pink Nightgown* (UA). 1958: *Onionhead* (WB). 1959: *Don't Give Up the Ship* (Par). 1960: *Visit to a Small Planet* (Par); *G.I. Blues* (Par). 1961: *Blue Hawaii* (Par); *All Hands on Deck* (Fox). 1962: *Girls! Girls! Girls!* (Par). 1963: *It Happened at the World's Fair* (Par); *Palm Springs Weekend* (WB). 1965: *Tickle Me* (AA); *Sergeant Deadhead* (AI); *Dr. Goldfoot and the Bikini Machine* (AI). 1966: *Spinout* (MGM). 1967: *Double Trouble* (MGM). 1968: *Speedway* (MGM); *Live a Little, Love a Little* (MGM).

Richard Thorpe (born 1896) 1924: *Battling Buddy; Bringing Home the Bacon; Fast and Fearless; Hard Hittin' Hamilton; Rarin' to Go; Rip Roarin' Roberts; Rough Ridin'; Thundering Romance; Walloping Wallace.* 1925: *The Desert Demon; Double Action Daniels; Fast Fightin'; Full Speed; Galloping On; Gold and Grit; On the Go; Quicker 'n Lightnin'; Saddle Cyclone; A Streak of Luck; Tearin' Loose.* 1926: *Twin Triggers; Double Dealing; The Bandit Buster; The Bonanza Buckaroo; College Days; Coming an' Going; The Dangerous Dub; Deuce High; Easy Going; The Fighting Cheat; Josselyn's Wife; Rawhide; Riding Rivals; Roaring Rider; Speedy Spurs; Trumpin' Trouble; Twisted Triggers.* 1927: *Between Dangers; The Cyclone Cowboy; The Desert of the Lost; The First Night; The Galloping Gobs; The Interferin' Gent; The Meddlin' Stranger; The Obligin' Buckaroo; Pals in Peril; Ride 'em High; The Ridin' Rowdy; Roarin' Broncs; Skedaddle Gold; Soda Water Cowboy; Tearin' into Trouble; White Pebbles.* 1928: *The Ballyhoo Buster; The Cowboy Cavalier; Desperate Courage; The Flying Buckaroo; Saddle Mates; The Valley of Hunted Men; The Vanishing West; Vultures of the Sea.* 1929: *The Bachelor Girl; King of the Kongo; The Fatal Warning.* 1930: *Border Romance* (Tiffany); *The Dude Wrangler* (World Wide); *The Thoroughbred* (Tiffany); *Under Montana Skies* (Tiffany); *The Utah Kid* (Tiffany); *Wings of Adventure* (Tiffany); *The Lone Defender* (Mascot). 1931: *The Lawless Woman* (Chesterfield); *King of the Wild* (Mascot); *Lady from Nowhere* (Chesterfield); *Wild Horses* (with Sidney Algier; M.H. Hoffman); *Sky Spider* (Action); *Grief Street* (Chesterfield); *Neck and Neck* (World Wide); *The Devil Plays* (Chesterfield). 1932: *Cross Examination* (Artclass); *Murder at Dawn* (Big Four); *Forgotten Women* (Mon); *Probation* (Chesterfield); *Midnight Lady* (Chesterfield); *Escapade* (Invincible); *Forbidden Company* (Invincible); *Beauty Parlor* (Chesterfield); *The King Murder* (Chesterfield); *The Thrill of Youth* (Invincible); *Slightly Married* (Chesterfield). 1933: *Women Won't Tell* (Chesterfield); *Secrets of Wu Sin* (Chesterfield); *Love Is Dangerous* (Chesterfield); *Forgotten* (Invincible); *Strange People* (Chesterfield); *I Have Lived* (Chesterfield); *Noto-*

rious but Nice (Chesterfield); *A Man of Sentiment* (Chesterfield); *Rainbow over Broadway* (Chesterfield). 1934: *Murder on the Campus* (Chesterfield); *The Quitter* (Chesterfield); *City Park* (Chesterfield); *Stolen Sweets* (Chesterfield); *Green Eyes* (Chesterfield); *Cheating Cheaters* (Univ); *Secret of the Chateau* (Univ). 1935: *Strange Wives* (Univ); *Last of the Pagans* (MGM). 1936: *The Voice of Bugle Ann* (MGM); *Tarzan Escapes* (MGM). 1937: *Dangerous Number* (MGM); *Night Must Fall* (MGM); *Double Wedding* (MGM). 1938: *Love Is a Headache* (MGM); *Man-Proof* (MGM); *The First Hundred Years* (MGM); *The Toy Wife* (MGM); *The Crowd Roars* (MGM); *Three Loves Had Nancy* (MGM). 1939: *The Adventures of Huckleberry Finn* (MGM); *Tarzan Finds a Son* (MGM). 1940: *The Earl of Chicago* (MGM); *20 Mule Team* (MGM); *Wyoming* (MGM). 1941: *The Bad Man* (MGM); *Barnacle Bill* (MGM); *Tarzan's Secret Treasure* (MGM). 1942: *Joe Smith, American* (MGM); *White Cargo* (MGM); *Tarzan's New York Adventure* (MGM); *Apache Trail* (MGM). 1943: *Three Hearts for Julia* (MGM); *Above Suspicion* (MGM). 1944: *Cry Havoc* (MGM); *Two Girls and a Sailor* (MGM); *The Thin Man Goes Home* (MGM). 1945: *Thrill of a Romance* (MGM); *Her Highness and the Bellboy* (MGM); *What Next, Corporal Hargrove?* (MGM). 1947: *Fiesta* (MGM); *This Time for Keeps* (MGM). 1948: *A Date with Judy* (MGM); *On an Island with You* (MGM); *The Sun Comes Up* (MGM). 1949: *Big Jack* (MGM); *Challenge to Lassie* (MGM); *Malaya* (MGM). 1950: *Black Hand* (MGM); *Three Little Words* (MGM). 1951: *Vengeance Valley* (MGM); *The Great Caruso* (MGM); *The Unknown Man* (MGM); *It's a Big Country* (episode; MGM). 1952: *Carbine Williams* (MGM); *Ivanhoe* (MGM); *The Prisoner of Zenda* (MGM). 1953: *The Girl Who Had Everything* (MGM); *All the Brothers Were Valiant* (MGM). 1954: *Knights of the Round Table* (MGM); *The Student Prince* (MGM); *Athena* (MGM). 1955: *The Prodigal* (MGM); *Quentin Durward* (MGM). 1957: *Ten Thousand Bedrooms* (MGM); *Tip on a Dead Jockey* (MGM); *Jailhouse Rock* (MGM). 1959: *The House of the Seven Hawks* (MGM). 1960: *Killers of Kilimanjaro* (MGM); *The Tartars (I Tartari)* (Italy; MGM). 1961: *The Honeymoon Machine* (MGM). 1962: *The Horizontal Lieutenant* (MGM). 1963: *Follow the Boys* (MGM); *Fun in Acapulco* (Par). 1965: *The Golden Head* (Hungary, U.S.; Cinerama); *The Truth about Spring* (Univ); *That Funny Feeling* (Univ). 1967: *The Last Challenge* (MGM).

JACQUES TOURNEUR (1904–1977) 1931–34: 4 French films. 1939: *They All Came Out* (MGM); *Nick Carter, Master Detective* (MGM). 1940: *Phantom Raiders* (MGM). 1941: *Doctors Don't Tell* (Rep). 1942: *Cat People* (RKO). 1943: *I Walked with a Zombie* (RKO); *The Leopard Man* (RKO). 1944: *Experiment Perilous* (RKO); *Days of Glory* (RKO). 1946: *Canyon Passage* (Univ). 1947: *Out of the Past* (RKO). 1948: *Berlin Express* (RKO). 1949: *Easy Living* (RKO). 1950: *Stars in My Crown* (MGM); *The Flame and the Arrow* (WB). 1951: *Circle of Danger* (Eagle-Lion); *Anne of the Indies* (Fox). 1952: *Way of a Gaucho* (Fox). 1953: *Appointment in Honduras* (RKO). 1955: *Stranger on Horseback* (AA); *Wichita* (AA). 1956: *Great Day in the Morning* (RKO); *Nightfall* (Col). 1958: *Curse of the Demon* (Col); *The Fearmakers* (UA). 1959: *Timbuktu* (UA). 1960: *The Giant of Marathon (La Battaglia di Maratona)* (Italy; MGM). 1965: *A Comedy of Terrors* (AI); *War Gods of the Deep* (AI).

MAURICE TOURNEUR (1876–1961) 1912–13: 14 French silent films. 1914: *The Man of the Hour; Mother; The Wishing Ring; The Pit.* 1915: *The Ivory Snuff Box; The Cub; Trilby; The Irish Snuff Box; A Butterfly on the Wheel; Alias Jimmy Valentine.* 1916: *The Closed Road; The Pawn of Fate; The Hand of Peril; The Rail Rider.* 1917: *The Velvet Paw; A Girl's Folly; The Poor Little Rich Girl; The Pride of the Clan; The Whip; Barbary Sheep; A Doll's House; The Undying Flame; The Law of the Land; Exile; The Rise of Jennie Cushing.* 1918: *The Rose of the World; The Blue Bird; Sporting Life; Woman.* 1919: *Prunella; Victory; The Broken Butterfly; The White Heather; The Life Line.* 1920: *The County Fair; The Great Redeemer* (with Clarence Brown); *Treasure Island; The White Circle; The Lady's Garter; The Last of the Mohicans* (with Clarence Brown); *Deep Waters.* 1921: *The Bait; The Foolish Matrons* (with Clarence Brown). 1922: *Lorna Doone.* 1923: *The Christian; The Brass Bottle; Jealous Husbands; The Isle of Lost Ships; While Paris Sleeps.* 1924: *The White Moth; Torment.* 1925: *Sporting Life; Never the Twain Shall Meet; Clothes Make the Pirate.* 1926: *Aloma of the South Seas; Old Loves and New.* 1927: *L'Equipage* (France). 1929–48: 24 films, 23 French, 1 German.

Uncredited: 1929: *The Mysterious Island* (with credited Lucien Hubbard; MGM).

W. S. VAN DYKE (1889–1943) 1917: *The Land of Long Shadows; The Range Boss; Open Places; Men of the Desert; Gift o' Gab.* 1918: *The Lady of the Dugout.* 1920: *The Hawk's Trail; Daredevil Jack.* 1921: *Double Adventure; The Avenging Arrow* (with William J. Bowman). 1922: *White Eagle* (with Fred Jackson); *According to Hoyle; The Boss of Camp 4; Forget-Me-Not.* 1923: *The Little Girl Next Door; The Destroying Angel; The Miracle Makers; You Are in Danger.* 1924: *Loving Lies; The Beautiful Sinner; Half-a-Dollar Bill; Winner Take All; The Battling Fool.* 1925: *Barriers Burned Away; Gold Heels; Hearts and Spurs; The Trail Rider; The Ranger of the Big Pines; The Timber Wolf; The Desert's Price.* 1926: *The Gentle Cyclone; War Paint.* 1927: *Winners of the Wilderness; California; The Heart of the Yukon; Eyes of the Totem; Spoilers of the West.* 1928: *Foreign Devils; Wyoming; Under the Black Eagle; White Shadows of the South Seas* (with Robert J. Flaherty). 1929: *The Pagan.* 1931: *Trader Horn* (MGM); *Never the Twain Shall Meet* (MGM); *Guilty Hands* (MGM); *The Cuban Love Song* (MGM). 1932: *Tarzan, the Ape Man* (MGM); *Night Court* (MGM). 1933: *Penthouse* (MGM); *The Prizefighter and the Lady* (MGM); *Eskimo* (MGM). 1934: *Manhattan Melodrama* (MGM); *The Thin Man* (MGM); *Forsaking All Others* (MGM); *Laughing Boy* (MGM); *Hide-Out* (MGM). 1935: *Naughty Marietta* (MGM); *I Live My Life* (MGM). 1936: *Rose Marie* (MGM); *His Brother's Wife* (MGM); *San Francisco* (MGM); *The Devil Is a Sissy* (MGM); *Love on the Run* (MGM); *After the Thin Man* (MGM). 1937: *Personal Property* (MGM); *They Gave Him a Gun* (MGM); *Rosalie* (MGM). 1938: *Marie Antoinette* (MGM); *Sweethearts* (MGM). 1939: *Stand Up and Fight* (MGM); *It's a Wonderful World* (MGM); *Andy Hardy Gets Spring Fever* (MGM); *Another Thin Man* (MGM). 1940: *I Take This Woman* (new version of film begun by Josef von Sternberg and taken over by Frank Borzage; MGM). 1941: *Rage in Heaven* (MGM); *The Feminine Touch* (MGM); *Shadow of the Thin Man* (MGM); *Dr. Kildare's Victory* (MGM). 1942: *I Married an Angel* (MGM); *Cairo* (MGM); *Journey for Margaret* (MGM).

Uncredited: 1923: *Ruth of the Range* (with Ernest Warde).

CHARLES VIDOR (1900–1959) 1934: *Sensation Hunters* (Mon); *Double Door* (Par). 1935: *Strangers All* (RKO); *The Arizonian* (RKO); *His Family Tree* (RKO). 1936: *Muss 'em Up* (RKO). 1937: *A Doctor's Diary* (Par); *The Great Gambini* (Par); *She's No Lady* (Par). 1939: *Blind Alley* (Col); *Romance of the Redwoods* (Col); *Those High Grey Walls* (Col). 1940: *My Son, My Son* (Col); *The Lady in Question* (Col). 1941: *New York Town* (Par); *Ladies in Retirement* (Col). 1942: *The Tuttles of Tahiti* (RKO). 1943: *The Desperadoes* (Col). 1944: *Cover Girl* (Col); *Together Again* (Col). 1945: *A Song to Remember* (Col); *Over 21* (Col). 1946: *Gilda* (Col). 1947: *The Guilt of Janet Ames* (Col). 1948: *The Loves of Carmen* (Col). 1951: *It's a Big Country* (episode; MGM). 1952: *Hans Christian Andersen* (RKO). 1953: *Thunder in the East* (Par). 1954: *Rhapsody* (MGM). 1955: *Love Me or Leave Me* (MGM). 1956: *The Swan* (MGM). 1957: *The Joker Is Wild* (Par); *A Farewell to Arms* (replaced John Huston; Fox). 1960: *Song Without End* (with George Cukor; Col).

Uncredited: 1932: *The Mask of Fu Manchu* (with Charles J. Brabin; MGM).

KING VIDOR (1894–1982) 1919: *The Turn in the Road; Better Times; The Other Half; Poor Relations; The Jack-Knife Man.* 1920: *The Family Honor.* 1921: *Love Never Dies; The Sky Pilot.* 1922: *Woman, Wake Up; The Real Adventure; Dusk to Dawn; Wild Oranges.* 1923: *Conquering the Woman; Peg o' My Heart; The Woman of Bronze; Three Wise Fools; Happiness.* 1924: *His Hour; Wine of Youth; Wife of the Centaur.* 1925: *Proud Flesh; The Big Parade.* 1926: *La Boheme; Bardelys the Magnificent.* 1928: *The Crowd; Show People; The Patsy.* 1929: *Hallelujah!* (MGM). 1930: *Not So Dumb* (MGM); *Billy the Kid* (MGM). 1931: *Street Scene* (UA); *The Champ* (MGM). 1932: *Bird of Paradise* (RKO); *Cynara* (UA). 1933: *The Stranger's Return* (MGM). 1934: *Our Daily Bread* (UA). 1935: *The Wedding Night* (Par); *So Red the Rose* (Par). 1936: *The Texas Rangers* (Par). 1937: *Stella Dallas* (UA). 1938: *The Citadel* (MGM). 1940: *Northwest Passage* (MGM); *Comrade X* (MGM). 1941: *H. M. Pulham, Esq.* (MGM). 1944: *An American Romance* (MGM). 1947: *Duel in the Sun* (Selznick). 1948: *A Miracle Can Happen (On Our Merry Way)* (with Leslie Fenton; UA). 1949: *The Fountainhead* (WB); *Beyond the Forest* (WB). 1951: *Lightning Strikes Twice* (WB). 1952: *Japanese War Bride* (Fox); *Ruby Gentry* (Fox). 1955: *Man Without a Star* (Univ). 1956: *War and Peace* (Par). 1959: *Solomon and Sheba* (UA).

RAOUL WALSH (1887–1980) 1915: *The Regeneration; Carmen.* 1916: *The Honor System; Blue Blood and Red; The Serpent.* 1917: *The Conqueror; Betrayed; This Is the Life; The Pride of New York; The Silent Lie; The Innocent Sinner.* 1918: *The Woman and the Law; The Prussian Cur; On the Jump; Every Mother's Son; I'll Say So.* 1919: *Evangeline; The Strongest; Should a Husband Forgive?.* 1920: *From Now On; The Deep Purple.* 1921: *The Oath; Serenade.* 1922: *Kindred of the Dust.* 1923: *Lost and Found on a South Sea Island.* 1924: *The Thief of Bagdad.* 1925: *East of Suez; The Spaniard; The Wanderer.* 1926: *The Lucky Lady; The Lady of the Harem; What Price Glory.* 1927: *The Monkey Talks; The Loves of Carmen.* 1928: *Sadie Thompson; The Red Dance; Me, Gangster.* 1929: *Hot for Paris* (Fox); *In Old Arizona* (with Irving Cummings; Fox); *The Cock-Eyed World* (Fox). 1930: *The Big Trail* (Fox). 1931: *The Man Who Came Back* (Fox); *Women of All Nations* (Fox); *The Yellow Ticket* (Fox). 1932: *Wild Girl* (Fox); *Me and My Gal* (Fox). 1933: *Sailor's Luck* (Fox); *The Bowery* (UA); *Going Hollywood* (MGM). 1935: *Under Pressure* (Fox); *Baby-Face Harrington* (MGM); *Every Night at Eight* (Par). 1936: *Klondike Annie* (Par); *Big Brown Eyes* (Par); *Spendthrift* (Par). 1937: *You're in the Army Now (O.H.M.S.)* (Great Britain; Gaumont-British); *When Thief Meets Thief (Jump for Glory)* (Great Britain; Criterion); *Artists and Models* (Par); *Hitting a New High* (RKO). 1938: *College Swing* (Par). 1939: *St. Louis Blues* (Par); *The Roaring Twenties* (WB). 1940: *Dark Command* (Rep); *They Drive by Night* (WB). 1941: *High Sierra* (WB); *The Strawberry Blonde* (WB); *Manpower* (WB); *They Died with Their Boots On* (WB). 1942: *Desperate Journey* (WB); *Gentleman Jim* (WB). 1943: *Background to Danger* (WB); *Northern Pursuit* (WB). 1944: *Uncertain Glory* (WB). 1945: *Objective Burma* (WB); *Salty O'Rourke* (Par); *The Horn Blows at Midnight* (WB). 1946: *The Man I Love* (WB). 1947: *Pursued* (WB); *Cheyenne* (WB). 1948: *Silver River* (WB); *Fighter Squadron* (WB); *One Sunday Afternoon* (WB). 1949: *Colorado Territory* (WB); *White Heat* (WB). 1951: *Along the Great Divide* (WB); *Captain Horatio Hornblower* (WB); *Distant Drums* (WB). 1952: *Glory Alley* (MGM); *The World in His Arms* (Univ); *The Lawless Breed* (Univ); *Blackbeard the Pirate* (RKO). 1953: *She Devils* (RKO); *A Lion Is in the Streets* (WB); *Gun Fury* (Col). 1954: *Saskatchewan* (Univ). 1955: *Battle Cry* (WB); *The Tall Men* (Fox). 1956: *The Revolt of Mamie Stover* (Fox); *The King and Four Queens* (UA). 1957: *Band of Angels* (WB). 1958: *The Naked and the Dead* (WB); *The Sheriff of Fractured Jaw* (Fox). 1959: *A Private's Affair* (Fox). 1960: *Esther and the King* (Fox). 1961: *Marines, Let's Go* (Fox). 1964: *A Distant Trumpet* (WB).

Uncredited: 1933: *Walking Down Broadway* (with uncredited Erich von Stroheim; revised by Alfred Werker for release as *Hello Sister!*; Fox). 1946: *San Antonio* (with David Butler; WB). 1947: *Stallion Road* (with James V. Kern; WB). 1950: *Montana* (with Ray Enright; WB). 1951: *The Enforcer* (with Bretaigne Windust; WB).

CHARLES WALTERS (1911–1982) 1947: *Good News* (MGM). 1948: *Easter Parade* (MGM). 1949: *The Barkleys of Broadway* (MGM). 1950: *Summer Stock* (MGM). 1951: *Three Guys Named Mike* (MGM); *Texas Carnival* (MGM).

1952: *The Belle of New York* (MGM). 1953: *Lili* (MGM); *Dangerous When Wet* (MGM); *Torch Song* (MGM); *Easy to Love* (MGM). 1955: *The Glass Slipper* (MGM); *The Tender Trap* (MGM). 1956: *High Society* (MGM). 1957: *Don't Go Near the Water* (MGM). 1959: *Ask Any Girl* (MGM). 1960: *Please Don't Eat the Daisies* (MGM). 1961: *Two Loves* (MGM). 1962: *Billy Rose's Jumbo* (MGM). 1964: *The Unsinkable Molly Brown* (MGM). 1966: *Walk, Don't Run* (Col).

Lois Weber (1882–1939) 1914: *The Fool and His Money; The Merchant of Venice* (with Phillips Smalley); *False Colors*. 1915: *Hop, the Devil's Brew* (with Phillips Smalley); *Sunshine Molly; A Cigarette, That's All; Scandal; Hypocrites* (with Phillips Smalley); *It's No Laughing Matter*. 1916: *The Dumb Girl of Portici* (with Phillips Smalley); *Saving the Family Name; The People vs. John Doe; Idle Wives; Where Are My Children?* (with Phillips Smalley); *The Flirt* (with Phillips Smalley). 1917: *The Price of a Good Time; Even You and I; The Hand That Rocks the Cradle; The Mysterious Mrs. Musselwhite*. 1918: *For Husbands Only; The Doctor and the Woman; Borrowed Clothes*. 1919: *Mary Regan; A Midnight Romance; When a Girl Loves; Home; Forbidden*. 1920: *To Please One Woman*. 1921: *Too Wise Wives; What's Worth While?; The Blot; What Do Men Want?*. 1923: *A Chapter in Her Life*. 1926: *The Marriage Clause*. 1927: *Sensation Seekers; The Angel of Broadway*. 1934: *White Heat* (Pinnacle).

Peter Weir (born 1944) 1971: *Three to Go* (episode; Australia; Commonwealth Film Unit Production). 1974: *The Cars That Ate Paris (The Cars That Eat People)* (Australia; New Line Cinema). 1975: *Picnic at Hanging Rock* (Australia; Atlantic). 1978: *The Plumber* (Australia; Barbary Coast); *The Last Wave* (Australia; World Northal). 1981: *Gallipoli* (Australia; Par). 1983: *The Year of Living Dangerously* (Australia; MGM/UA). 1985: *Witness* (Par). 1986: *Mosquito Coast* (Saul Zaentz Productions).

Orson Welles (1915–1985) 1941: *Citizen Kane* (RKO). 1942: *The Magnificent Ambersons* (RKO). 1946: *The Stranger* (RKO). 1948: *The Lady from Shanghai* (Col); *Macbeth* (Rep). 1952: *Othello* (U.S., Italy; UA). 1955: *Mr. Arkadin* (Spain, Switzerland; WB). 1958: *Touch of Evil* (Univ). 1962: *The Trial* (France, Italy, West Germany; Astor). 1967: *Chimes at Midnight (Falstaff)* (Spain, Switzerland; Peppercorn/Wormser). 1969: *The Immortal Story* (France; Altura). 1977: *F for Fake* (France, Italy, West Germany; Specialty).
Unfinished: 1972: *The Other Side of the Wind*.

William A. Wellman (1896–1975) 1923: *The Man Who Won; Second Hand Love; Big Dan; Cupid's Fireman*. 1924: *The Vagabond Trail; Not a Drum Was Heard; The Circus Cowboy*. 1925: *When Husbands Flirt*. 1926: *The Boob; The Cat's Pajamas; You Never Know Women*. 1927: *Wings*. 1928: *The Legion of the Condemned; Ladies of the Mob; Beggars of Life* (Par). 1929: *Chinatown Nights* (Par); *The Man I Love* (Par); *Woman Trap* (Par). 1930: *Dangerous Paradise* (Par); *Young Eagles* (Par); *Maybe It's Love* (WB). 1931: *Other Men's Women* (WB); *The Public Enemy* (WB); *The Star Witness* (WB); *Night Nurse* (WB); *Safe in Hell* (FN). 1932: *The Hatchet Man* (FN); *Love Is a Racket* (FN); *So Big* (WB); *The Purchase Price* (WB); *The Conquerors* (RKO). 1933: *Frisco Jenny* (FN); *Central Airport* (FN); *Lilly Turner* (FN); *Wild Boys of the Road* (FN); *Heroes for Sale* (FN); *Midnight Mary* (MGM); *College Coach* (WB). 1934: *Looking for Trouble* (UA); *Stingaree* (RKO); *The President Vanishes* (Par). 1935: *Call of the Wild* (UA). 1936: *The Robin Hood of El Dorado* (MGM); *Small Town Girl* (MGM). 1937: *A Star Is Born* (UA); *Nothing Sacred* (UA). 1938: *Men with Wings* (Par). 1939: *Beau Geste* (Par); *The Light That Failed* (Par). 1941: *Reaching for the Sun* (Par). 1942: *Roxie Hart* (Fox); *The Great Man's Lady* (Par); *Thunder Birds* (Fox). 1943: *Lady of Burlesque* (UA); *The Ox-Bow Incident* (Fox). 1944: *Buffalo Bill* (Fox). 1945: *This Man's Navy* (MGM); *The Story of G.I. Joe* (Fox). 1946: *Gallant Journey* (Col). 1947: *Magic Town* (RKO). 1948: *The Iron Curtain* (Fox); *Yellow Sky* (Fox). 1949: *Battleground* (MGM). 1950: *The Next Voice You Hear* (MGM); *The Happy Years* (MGM). 1951: *It's a Big Country* (episode; MGM); *Across the Wide Missouri* (MGM); *Westward the Women* (MGM). 1952: *My Man and I* (MGM). 1953: *Island in the Sky* (WB). 1954: *The High and the Mighty* (WB); *Track of the Cat* (WB). 1955: *Blood Alley* (WB). 1956: *Goodbye, My Lady* (WB). 1958: *Darby's Rangers* (WB); *Lafayette Escadrille* (WB).

James Whale (1896–1957) 1930: *Journey's End* (Tiffany). 1931: *Waterloo Bridge* (Univ); *Frankenstein* (Univ). 1932: *The Old Dark House* (Univ); *The Impatient Maiden* (Univ). 1933: *The Invisible Man* (Univ); *The Kiss Before the Mirror* (Univ); *By Candlelight* (Univ). 1934: *One More River* (Univ). 1935: *The Bride of Frankenstein* (Univ); *Remember Last Night?* (Univ). 1936: *Show Boat* (Univ). 1937: *The Road Back* (Univ); *The Great Garrick* (WB). 1938: *Sinners in Paradise* (Univ); *Port of Seven Seas* (MGM); *Wives Under Suspicion* (Univ). 1939: *The Man in the Iron Mask* (Univ); *Green Hell* (Univ). 1941: *They Dare Not Love* (Col).
Unfinished: 1949: *Hello Out There*.

Billy Wilder (born 1906) 1933: *Mauvaise Graine* (with Alexander Esway; Germany). 1942: *The Major and the Minor* (Par). 1943: *Five Graves to Cairo* (Par). 1944: *Double Indemnity* (Par). 1945: *The Lost Weekend* (Par). 1948: *The Emperor Waltz* (Par); *A Foreign Affair* (Par). 1950: *Sunset Boulevard* (Par). 1951: *Ace in the Hole (The Big Carnival)* (Par). 1953: *Stalag 17* (Par). 1954: *Sabrina* (Par). 1955: *The Seven Year Itch* (Fox). 1957: *The Spirit of St. Louis* (WB); *Love in the Afternoon* (AA). 1958: *Witness for the Prosecution* (UA). 1959: *Some Like It Hot* (UA). 1960: *The Apartment* (UA). 1961: *One, Two, Three* (UA). 1963: *Irma La Douce* (UA). 1964: *Kiss Me, Stupid* (Lopert). 1966: *The Fortune Cookie* (UA). 1970: *The Private Life of Sherlock Holmes* (U.S., Great Britain; UA). 1972: *Avanti!* (U.S., Italy; UA). 1974: *The Front Page* (Univ). 1979: *Fedora* (West Germany, France; UA). 1981: *Buddy Buddy* (MGM/UA).

Robert Wise (born 1914) 1944: *The Curse of the Cat People* (with Gunther von Fritsch; RKO); *Mademoiselle Fifi* (RKO). 1945: *The Body Snatcher* (RKO); *A Game of Death* (RKO). 1946: *Criminal Court* (RKO). 1947: *Born to Kill* (RKO). 1948: *Mystery in Mexico* (RKO); *Blood on the Moon* (RKO). 1949: *The Set-Up* (RKO). 1950: *Two Flags West* (Fox); *Three Secrets* (WB). 1951: *The House on Telegraph Hill* (Fox); *The Day the Earth Stood Still* (Fox). 1952: *The Captive City* (UA); *Something for the Birds* (MGM). 1953: *The Desert Rats* (Fox); *Destination Gobi* (Fox); *So Big* (WB). 1954: *Executive Suite* (MGM). 1955: *Helen of Troy* (Italy, France; WB). 1956: *Tribute to a Bad Man* (MGM); *Somebody Up There Likes Me* (MGM). 1957: *This Could Be the Night* (MGM); *Until They Sail* (MGM). 1958: *Run Silent, Run Deep* (UA); *I Want to Live!* (UA). 1959: *Odds Against Tomorrow* (UA). 1961: *West Side Story* (with Jerome Robbins; UA). 1962: *Two for the Seesaw* (UA). 1963: *The Haunting* (Great Britain, U.S.; MGM). 1965: *The Sound of Music* (Fox). 1966: *The Sand Pebbles* (Fox). 1968: *Star! (Those Were the Happy Times)* (Fox). 1971: *The Andromeda Strain* (Univ). 1973: *Two People* (Univ). 1975: *The Hindenburg* (Univ). 1977: *Audrey Rose* (UA). 1979: *Star Trek—The Motion Picture* (Par).

Sam Wood (1883–1949) 1920: *Double Speed; Excuse My Dust; The Dancin' Fool; Sick Abed; What's Your Hurry?; City Sparrow*. 1921: *Her Beloved Villain; Peck's Bad Boy; Her First Elopement; The Snob; The Great Moment; Under the Lash; Don't Tell Everything*. 1922: *Her Husband's Trademark; Her Gilded Cage; The Impossible Mrs. Bellew; Beyond the Rocks*. 1923: *My American Wife; Prodigal Daughters; Bluebeard's Eighth Wife; His Children's Children*. 1924: *The Female; The Next Corner; Bluff; The Mine with the Iron Door*. 1925: *The Re-Creation of Brian Kent*. 1926: *Fascinating Youth; One Minute to Play*. 1927: *Rookies; A Racing Romeo; The Fair Co-ed*. 1928: *The Latest from Paris; Telling the World*. 1929: *It's a Great Life* (MGM); *So This Is College* (MGM). 1930: *The Girl Said No* (MGM); *The Richest Man in the World* (MGM); *They Learned about Women* (with Jack Conway; MGM); *Sins of the Children* (MGM); *Way for a Sailor* (MGM); *Paid* (MGM). 1931: *A Tailor-Made Man* (MGM); *The Man in Possession* (MGM); *Get-Rich-Quick Wallingford* (MGM). 1932: *Huddle* (MGM); *Prosperity* (MGM). 1933: *The Barbarian* (MGM); *Hold Your Man* (MGM); *Christopher Bean* (MGM). 1934: *Stamboul Quest* (MGM). 1935: *A Night at the Opera* (MGM); *Let 'em Have It* (UA). 1936: *Whipsaw* (MGM); *The Unguarded Hour* (MGM). 1937: *A Day at the Races* (MGM); *Madame X* (MGM); *Navy, Blue and Gold* (MGM). 1938: *Lord Jeff* (MGM); *Stablemates* (MGM). 1939: *Goodbye, Mr. Chips* (MGM). 1940: *Our Town* (UA); *Raffles* (UA); *Rangers of Fortune* (Par); *Kitty Foyle* (RKO). 1941: *The Devil and Miss Jones* (RKO). 1942: *Kings Row* (WB); *The Pride of the Yankees* (RKO). 1943: *For Whom the Bell Tolls* (Par). 1944: *Casanova Brown* (RKO). 1945: *Guest Wife* (RKO). 1946: *Saratoga Trunk* (Par); *Heartbeat* (RKO). 1947: *Ivy* (Univ). 1949: *The Stratton Story* (MGM); *Command Decision* (MGM); *Ambush* (MGM).
Uncredited: 1939: *Gone with the Wind* (with credited Victor Fleming and uncredited George Cukor; MGM).

William Wyler (1902–1981) 1926: *Lazy Lightning; The Stolen Ranch*. 1927: *Blazing Days; Hard Fists; Desert Dust; Straight Shootin'; Shooting Straight; The Border Cavalier*. 1928: *Thunder Riders; Anybody Here Seen Kelly?* 1929: *The Shakedown* (Univ); *The Love Trap* (Univ); *Hell's Heroes* (Univ). 1930: *The Storm* (Univ). 1932: *A House Divided* (Univ); *Tom Brown of Culver* (Univ). 1933: *Her First Mate* (Univ); *Counsellor-at-Law* (Univ). 1934: *Glamour* (Univ). 1935: *The Good Fairy* (Univ); *The Gay Deception* (Col). 1936: *These Three* (UA); *Come and Get It* (with Howard Hawks; UA); *Dodsworth* (UA). 1937: *Dead End* (UA). 1938: *Jezebel* (WB). 1939: *Wuthering Heights* (UA). 1940: *The Westerner* (UA); *The Letter* (WB). 1941: *The Little Foxes* (RKO). 1942: *Mrs. Miniver* (MGM). 1944: *The Memphis Belle* (Par); *The Fighting Lady* (Fox). 1946: *The Best Years of Our Lives* (RKO). 1949: *The Heiress* (Par). 1951: *Detective Story* (Par). 1952: *Carrie* (Par). 1953: *Roman Holiday* (Par). 1955: *The Desperate Hours* (Par). 1956: *Friendly Persuasion* (AA). 1958: *The Big Country* (UA). 1959: *Ben-Hur* (MGM). 1962: *The Children's Hour* (UA). 1965: *The Collector* (Col). 1966: *How to Steal a Million* (Fox). 1968: *Funny Girl* (Col). 1970: *The Liberation of L. B. Jones* (Col).
Uncredited: 1932: *The Old Dark House* (with James Whale; Univ).

Peter Yates (born 1929) 1963: *Summer Holiday* (Great Britain; AI). 1964: *One Way Pendulum* (Great Britain; Lopert). 1967: *Robbery* (Great Britain; Avco Embassy). 1968: *Bullitt* (WB). 1969: *John and Mary* (Fox). 1971: *Murphy's War* (Great Britain; Par). 1972: *The Hot Rock* (Fox). 1973: *The Friends of Eddie Coyle* (Par). 1974: *For Pete's Sake* (Col). 1976: *Mother, Jugs and Speed* (Fox). 1977: *The Deep* (Col). 1979: *Breaking Away* (Fox). 1981: *Eyewitness* (Fox). 1983: *Krull* (U.S., Great Britain; Col); *The Dresser* (Great Britain; Col). 1985: *Eleni* (WB).

Bud Yorkin (born 1926) 1963: *Come Blow Your Horn* (Par). 1965: *Never Too Late* (WB). 1967: *Divorce American Style* (Col). 1968: *Inspector Clouseau* (Great Britain; UA). 1970: *Start the Revolution Without Me* (Great Britain; WB). 1972: *The Thief Who Came to Dinner* (WB). 1985: *Twice in a Lifetime* (The Yorkin Co). 1986: *Public Enemy* (Cannon).

Fred Zinnemann (born 1907) 1935: *The Wave* (Doc; with Emilio Gomez Muriel; Mexico; Strand). 1942: *Kid Glove Killer* (MGM); *Eyes in the Night* (MGM). 1944: *The Seventh Cross* (MGM). 1946: *Little Mr. Jim* (MGM). 1947: *My Brother Talks to Horses* (MGM). 1948: *The Search* (U.S., Switzerland; MGM). 1949: *Act of Violence* (MGM). 1950: *The Men* (Col). 1951: *Teresa* (MGM). 1952: *High Noon* (UA). 1953: *The Member of the Wedding* (Col); *From Here to Eternity* (Col). 1955: *Oklahoma!* (Magna). 1957: *A Hatful of Rain* (Fox). 1959: *The Nun's Story* (WB). 1960: *The Sundowners* (WB). 1964: *Behold a Pale Horse* (Col). 1966: *A Man for All Seasons* (Col). 1973: *The Day of the Jackal* (Univ). 1977: *Julia* (Fox). 1982: *Five Days One Summer* (Ladd/WB).

INDEX

Page numbers in *italics* indicate illustrations.

307

CREDITS

PHOTOCREDITS

Eugene Cook: 111; Louis Goldman: 6–7, 81 right, 92, 119, 208; The Kobal Collection: 4–5, 8, 8–9, 10, 20, 24 above left and below, 47, 81 left, 93 above, 101 above, 109, 204, 229 above, 248, 258–59, 285; © Marvin Lichtner/Lee Gross Associates: 49, 57 right; Jerry Ohlinger's Movie Material Store: 18, 24 above right, 28 below, 32 below, 89 above and below, 90 below, 91, 101 below, 156, 201, 205, 211 above, 259 right; © Allan Pappe/Lee Gross Associates: 90 above, 288; Phototeque: 104, 222–23; George Sidney: 63, 230, 231; © Phil Stern/Hollywood Photographers Archives: 2–3, 139, 271; © Bob Willoughby/Lee Gross Associates: 78–79, 100, 179 right; © Bob Willoughby/Hollywood Photographers Archives: 185 above.

FILM COPYRIGHTS

Page 1: *All That Jazz*, © 1979 Columbia Pictures Industries, Inc. 4–5: *Camille*, 1937, © 1936 Metro-Goldwyn-Mayer Corporation. Renewed 1963 Metro-Goldwyn-Mayer Inc. 6–7:

Exodus, Copyright © 1960 Carlyle-Alpina, S.A. 8–9: *Singin' in the Rain*, © 1952 Loew's Incorporated. Renewed 1979 Metro-Goldwyn-Mayer Inc. 12: *Moby Dick*, Copyright © 1956 Warner Bros. Pictures, Inc. 17: *Mata Hari*, ©1932 Metro-Goldwyn-Mayer Distributing Corporation. Renewed 1959 Loew's Incorporated 20: *Sleeper*, Copyright © 1973 Jack Rollins and Charles H. Joffe Productions 21: *What Ever Happened to Baby Jane*, © 1962 Associates and Aldrich Company, Inc. 22: *Hannah and Her Sisters*, 1986, © 1985 Orion Pictures 23: *Manhattan*, Copyright © 1979 United Artists Corporation 24 above right: *McCabe and Mrs. Miller*, © 1971 Warner Bros. Inc. 24 below left: *Coal Miner's Daughter*, 1980, Copyright © by Universal Pictures, a Division of Universal City Studios, Inc. All Rights Reserved. Courtesy of MCA Publishing Rights, a Division of MCA, Inc. 24 below right: *Coming Home*, Copyright © 1978 United Artists Corporation 26: *Manhattan Cocktail*, © 1928, Renewed 1955 Paramount Famous Lasky Corp. 27: *Craig's Wife*, © 1936, renewed 1964 Columbia Pictures Corp. 28 above: *Gandhi*, © 1982 Carolina Bank Ltd. and National Film Development Corporation Ltd. 28 below: *Reds*, © 1981 Paramount Pictures Corporation. All rights reserved. Courtesy of Paramount Pictures Corporation. 29: *Rocky*, Copyright ©

1976 United Artists Corporation 30: *Footlight Parade*, Copyright © 1933 Warner Bros. Pictures, Inc. Renewed 1961 United Artists Associated, Inc. 31 left and right: *Kramer vs. Kramer*, © 1979 Columbia Pictures Industries, Inc. 32 above: *Places in the Heart*, © 1984 Tri-Star Pictures 32 below: *The Emerald Forest*, © 1985 Embassy Films Associates 33 above: *Tender Mercies*, 1983, Copyright © by Universal Pictures, a Division of Universal City Studios, Inc. All Rights Reserved. Courtesy of MCA Publishing Rights, a Division of MCA, Inc. 33 below: *Gold Diggers of 1935*, Copyright © 1935 First National Pictures, Inc. Renewed 1962 United Artists Associated, Inc. 34: *Possessed*, Copyright © 1947 Warner Bros. Pictures, Inc. Renewed 1974 United Artists Television, Inc. 35: *The Last Picture Show*, © 1971 Last Picture Show Productions, Inc. 36: *A Farewell to Arms*, 1932, Copyright © by Universal Pictures, a Division of Universal City Studios, Inc. All Rights Reserved. Courtesy of MCA Publishing Rights, a Division of MCA, Inc. 37: *The Mortal Storm*, © 1940 Loew's Incorporated. Renewed 1967 Metro-Goldwyn-Mayer Inc. 38: *Hangover Square*, © 1945, renewed 1972 Twentieth Century Fox Film Corporation 39 above: *Terms of Endearment*, © 1983 Paramount Pictures Corporation. All rights reserved. Courtesy of Paramount Pictures Corpora-